Keep this book — need it and use your career.

About the American Hotel & Lodging Association (AH&LA)

Founded in 1910, AH&LA is the trade association representing the lodging industry in the United States. AH&LA is a federation of state lodging associations throughout the United States with 11,000 lodging properties worldwide as members. The association offers its members assistance with governmental affairs representation, communications, marketing, hospitality operations, training and education, technology issues, and more. For information, call 202-289-3100.

LODGING, the management magazine of AH&LA, is a "living textbook" for hospitality students that provides timely features, industry news, and vital lodging information.

About the American Hotel & Lodging Educational Institute (EI)

An affiliate of AH&LA, the Educational Institute is the world's largest source of quality training and educational materials for the lodging industry. EI develops textbooks and courses that are used in more than 1,200 colleges and universities worldwide, and also offers courses to individuals through its Distance Learning program. Hotels worldwide rely on EI for training resources that focus on every aspect of lodging operations. Industry-tested videos, CD-ROMs, seminars, and skills guides prepare employees at every skill level. EI also offers professional certification for the industry's top performers. For information about EI's products and services, call 800-349-0299 or 407-999-8100.

About the American Hotel & Lodging Educational Foundation (AH&LEF)

An affiliate of AH&LA, the American Hotel & Lodging Educational Foundation provides financial support that enhances the stability, prosperity, and growth of the lodging industry through educational and research programs. AH&LEF has awarded millions of dollars in scholarship funds for students pursuing higher education in hospitality management. AH&LEF has also funded research projects on topics important to the industry, including occupational safety and health, turnover and diversity, and best practices in the U.S. lodging industry. For information, go to www.ahlef.org.

INTERNATIONAL HOTELS
Development and Management

Educational Institute Books

UNIFORM SYSTEM OF ACCOUNTS FOR THE LODGING INDUSTRY
Tenth Revised Edition

RESORT DEVELOPMENT AND MANAGEMENT
Second Edition
Chuck Y. Gee

PLANNING AND CONTROL FOR FOOD AND BEVERAGE OPERATIONS
Sixth Edition
Jack D. Ninemeier

UNDERSTANDING HOSPITALITY LAW
Fourth Edition
Jack P. Jefferies/Banks Brown

SUPERVISION IN THE HOSPITALITY INDUSTRY
Fourth Edition
Raphael R. Kavanaugh/Jack D. Ninemeier

MANAGEMENT OF FOOD AND BEVERAGE OPERATIONS
Fourth Edition
Jack D. Ninemeier

MANAGING FRONT OFFICE OPERATIONS
Seventh Edition
Michael L. Kasavana/Richard M. Brooks

MANAGING SERVICE IN FOOD AND BEVERAGE OPERATIONS
Third Edition
Ronald F. Cichy/Philip J. Hickey, Jr.

THE LODGING AND FOOD SERVICE INDUSTRY
Sixth Edition
Gerald W. Lattin

SECURITY AND LOSS PREVENTION MANAGEMENT
Second Edition
Raymond C. Ellis, Jr./David M. Stipanuk

HOSPITALITY INDUSTRY MANAGERIAL ACCOUNTING
Sixth Edition
Raymond S. Schmidgall

PURCHASING FOR FOOD SERVICE OPERATIONS
Ronald F. Cichy/Jeffery D Elsworth

MANAGING TECHNOLOGY IN THE HOSPITALITY INDUSTRY
Fifth Edition
Michael L. Kasavana/John J. Cahill

BASIC HOTEL AND RESTAURANT ACCOUNTING
Sixth Edition
Raymond Cote

ACCOUNTING FOR HOSPITALITY MANAGERS
Fifth Edition
Raymond Cote

CONVENTION MANAGEMENT AND SERVICE
Seventh Edition
Milton T. Astroff/James R. Abbey

HOSPITALITY SALES AND MARKETING
Fifth Edition
James R. Abbey

MANAGING HOUSEKEEPING OPERATIONS
Third Edition
Margaret M. Kappa/Aleta Nitschke/Patricia B. Schappert

DIMENSIONS OF TOURISM
Joseph D. Fridgen

HOSPITALITY TODAY: AN INTRODUCTION
Sixth Edition
Rocco M. Angelo/Andrew N. Vladimir

MANAGING BAR AND BEVERAGE OPERATIONS
Lendal H. Kotschevar/Mary L. Tanke

ETHICS IN HOSPITALITY MANAGEMENT: A BOOK OF READINGS
Edited by Stephen S. J. Hall

HOSPITALITY FACILITIES MANAGEMENT AND DESIGN
Third Edition
David M. Stipanuk

MANAGING HOSPITALITY HUMAN RESOURCES
Fourth Edition
Robert H. Woods

RETAIL MANAGEMENT FOR SPAS

HOSPITALITY INDUSTRY FINANCIAL ACCOUNTING
Third Edition
Raymond S. Schmidgall/James W. Damitio

INTERNATIONAL HOTELS: DEVELOPMENT AND MANAGEMENT
Second Edition
Chuck Yim Gee

QUALITY SANITATION MANAGEMENT
Ronald F. Cichy

HOTEL INVESTMENTS: ISSUES & PERSPECTIVES
Fourth Edition
Edited by Lori E. Raleigh and Rachel J. Roginsky

LEADERSHIP AND MANAGEMENT IN THE HOSPITALITY INDUSTRY
Second Edition
Robert H. Woods/Judy Z. King

MARKETING IN THE HOSPITALITY INDUSTRY
Fourth Edition
Ronald A. Nykiel

CONTEMPORARY HOSPITALITY MARKETING
William Lazer/Roger Layton

UNIFORM SYSTEM OF ACCOUNTS FOR THE HEALTH, RACQUET AND SPORTSCLUB INDUSTRY

CONTEMPORARY CLUB MANAGEMENT
Second Edition
Edited by Joe Perdue for the Club Managers Association of America

RESORT CONDOMINIUM AND VACATION OWNERSHIP MANAGEMENT: A HOSPITALITY PERSPECTIVE
Robert A. Gentry/Pedro Mandoki/Jack Rush

ACCOUNTING FOR CLUB OPERATIONS
Raymond S. Schmidgall/James W. Damitio

TRAINING AND DEVELOPMENT FOR THE HOSPITALITY INDUSTRY
Debra F. Cannon/Catherine M. Gustafson

UNIFORM SYSTEM OF FINANCIAL REPORTING FOR CLUBS
Sixth Revised Edition

HOTEL ASSET MANAGEMENT: PRINCIPLES & PRACTICES
Edited by Paul Beals and Greg Denton

MANAGING BEVERAGE SERVICE
Lendal H. Kotschevar/Ronald F. Cichy

FOOD SAFETY: MANAGING WITH THE HACCP SYSTEM
Second Edition
Ronald F. Cichy

UNIFORM SYSTEM OF FINANCIAL REPORTING FOR SPAS

FUNDAMENTALS OF DESTINATION MANAGEMENT AND MARKETING
Edited by Rich Harrill

ETHICS IN THE HOSPITALITY AND TOURISM INDUSTRY
Second Edition
Karen Lieberman/Bruce Nissen

HOSPITALITY AND TOURISM MARKETING
William Lazer/Melissa Dallas/Carl Riegel

INTERNATIONAL HOTELS

Development and Management

Second Edition

Chuck Yim Gee
Contributing Author: A. J. Singh

American
Hotel & Lodging
Educational Institute

Disclaimer

This publication is designed to provide accurate and authoritative information in regard to the subject matter covered. It is sold with the understanding that the publisher is not engaged in rendering legal, accounting, or other professional service. If legal advice or other expert assistance is required, the services of a competent professional person should be sought.
—*From the Declaration of Principles jointly adopted by the American Bar Association and a Committee of Publishers and Associations.*

The author, Chuck Yim Gee, and contributing author, A. J. Singh, are solely responsible for the contents of this publication. All views expressed herein are solely those of the author and the contributing author and do not necessarily reflect the views of the American Hotel & Lodging Educational Institute (the Institute) or the American Hotel & Lodging Association (AH&LA).

Nothing contained in this publication shall constitute a standard, an endorsement, or a recommendation of the Institute or AH&LA. The Institute and AH&LA disclaim any liability with respect to the use of any information, procedure, or product, or reliance thereon by any member of the hospitality industry.

©2008
By the AMERICAN HOTEL & LODGING
EDUCATIONAL INSTITUTE
2113 N. High Street
Lansing, Michigan 48906-4221

The American Hotel & Lodging
Educational Institute is a nonprofit
educational foundation.

All rights reserved. No part of this
publication may be reproduced, stored in
a retrieval system, or transmitted, in any
form or by any means—electronic,
mechanical, photocopying, recording, or
otherwise—without prior permission of the
publisher.

Printed in the United States of America
1 2 3 4 5 6 7 8 9 10 15 14 13 12 11 10 09 08

ISBN 978-0-86612-329-7

Editors: Timothy J. Eaton
Jim Purvis
Bridgette Redman
M. Carrie Pickett

Cover photo: Mandarin Oriental, Kuala Lumpur, and the Petronas Towers, Kuala Lumpur, Malaysia. Used by permission of Mandarin Oriental Hotel Group and Mandarin Oriental, Kuala Lumpur.

Contents

Preface	xv
About the Author and Contributing Author	xvii

Part I Overview and Historical Perspective 1

1 Globalization, Tourism, and the Lodging Sector 3

Globalization and the Business World 3

The Dissolution of Borders • Tourism in the Global Environment • Defining the Transnational Hotel Company

The Tourism Industry 6

The Economic Impact of Travel and Tourism • The Geographic Distribution of Tourism • Travel Demand Determinants

The International Lodging Industry 13

Global Distribution and Structure • Global Hotel Performance • Types of Hotel Products • Hotel Guests

Challenges of the Globalized Lodging Industry 19
Summary 20

2 The Emergence of International Hotels 25

Historical Aspects 25

The Development of Chains • Development Abroad

American Hotel Chains 34

Separation of Ownership from Management • Segmentation and Foreign Expansion

Profiles of Selected International Chains That Began in America ... 35

Hilton • InterContinental • Sheraton • Holiday Inn • Hyatt • Choice Hotels International

European Chains 40

Club Méditerranée • Accor • Le Méridien • Sol Meliá

Indian Chains 45

The Taj Group • Oberoi

Asia-Pacific Chains 47

    New Otani • Nikko • Mandarin Oriental • Peninsula • Dusit International

An African Chain 50

The Airline Connection 51

    Advantages of Linkage • Disadvantages of Linkage • Major Linkages

Mergers and Acquisitions 54

    Consolidation • Strategic Alliances

Summary 56

3 Political Aspects of the International Travel, Tourism, and Lodging Industry 61

Barriers to Travel, Tourism Investment, and Business 62

    Barriers Affecting Travelers • Lodging Investment Barriers • Lodging Operational Barriers

Government Hotel Regulations 69

    Price Control Measures • Labor Regulations • Room Taxes • Other Regulations • The Competitiveness Index

International Organizations Dealing with Barriers 72

    World Tourism Organization • Organization for Economic Cooperation and Development • General Agreement on Tariffs and Trade • International Monetary Fund • International Hotel & Restaurant Association • World Travel & Tourism Council

The Need for Government Support 77

    Foreign Investment Incentives • Bureaucratic Red Tape • Tourism Policy

National Tourism Organizations 80

International Lodging Chains and Developing Countries 81

    Identifying Advantages and Disadvantages • Maximizing Returns from Tourism • Lodging Chains and Host Governments — Inevitable Conflict

Political Stability 84

    Impact on Investment Decisions • Impact on Travelers

Travel Advisories 88

    Political Motivations

Political Risk 92

Difficulty of Assessing Political Risk • Reducing Vulnerability in Risky Situations • Management Control in an Unstable Environment

Crisis Management.. 97

The Written Crisis Management Plan

Summary.. 98
Appendix: Excerpt from a Hotel Crisis Management Plan 102

Part II International Hotel Investment, Development, and Agreements 121

4 Financing International Hotels.. 123

Financial Structuring for Hotel Development 124

Equity Financing • Debt Considerations • Criteria for Loans • Interest Rates • Public and Private Sector Funding

Current Sources of Capital: A Global Perspective 131

Foreign Financing

Hotel Financing in Developing Countries 134

Development Banks • Other Lending Sources

Government Investment Incentives 137

Abatement of Capital Outlay • Abatement of Operating Expenses • Securing the Investment • Selective Incentives • Excessive Bureaucracy

Publicly Listed and Privately Owned Lodging Companies............ 142

Equity Investments in the United States • Equity Investments in Europe • Equity Investments in Asia

Accounting Conventions 151

Reconciliation • Tax Rules • Uniform Systems of Accounts

Summary... 155

5 The Decision to Go Global 161

Balancing Global and Local Perspectives... 161

Glocalization

Transnational, Global, and Multinational Organizations 163

The Case for International Expansion • Target Regions • Potential Problems and Considerations

viii Contents

Geographic Distribution 168
   Distribution Patterns • Variations by Hotel Type

Foreign Hotel Chains in the United States... 169
Industry Structure... 170
Ownership and Types of Affiliations... 170
   Management Agreements • Equity Participation • Affiliation Considerations

Operating in a Multinational Environment 175
   The Environment • Centralization and Decentralization • Operation Planning and Control

Summary 178

6 Developing an International Hotel Project 183

The Development Team 184
   The Developer • The Hotel Operator and Other Consultants

The Five Phases of Hotel Development.. 185
Where to Develop 186
   Business Environment Analysis • Market Potential • Forecasting Sales • Profitability Versus Risk

Infrastructure Requirements 189
   Water • Power • Communication • Sewage and Drainage • Transportation • Health–Care Provisions • Labor Force • Security

Working with an Established Development Plan 194
Identifying a Specific Site 194
   Land Availability • Zoning

The Preliminary Site and Building Analysis....................................... 199
Market Feasibility Study... 200
   Information Gathering

The Approval Process 203
   Environmental Impact Statements • Impact Fee Assessments • Working with Local Interests

Design Considerations 204
   Architectural Themes • Design Trends • Physical Surroundings • Urban Design • Older Structures

Design and Construction in a Cross–Cultural Environment 208
   Understanding Foreign Business Practices

Contents ix

      Building Requirements 208

          Regulatory Control • Fire Safety • Security • Hygiene • Electricity and Gas

      Global Initiatives for Sustainable Development................................. 211
      Summary 213

7 International Hotel Contracts and Agreements 219

      Selecting the Hotel Company 219
      Management Contracts 220

          Management Contract Services • Management Fee Structures • Contract Length and Renewal Options • Contract Termination • Control of Operations • Budgeting and Spending Limits • Insurance • Governing or Applicable Law • Staffing • Restrictive Covenants • Arbitration • Global Trends and Issues

      The Joint Venture 230
      Franchise Agreements 231

          Advantages and Disadvantages • Agreement Contents • Franchise Fees • Agreement Length and Termination • Hotel Name

      Summary 233

Part III Human Resources and Cultural Diversity 237

8 Understanding Cultural Diversity 239

      Working with Foreign Colleagues... 239

          The U.S. Workforce • The Effects of Cultural Diversity • The Foreign–Based Hotel Company

      Cultural Perceptions 244

          Time • Cultural Thought Patterns • Communication • Personal Space and Touch • Material Possessions • Family Roles and Relationships • Religion • Personal Achievement • Competitiveness and Individuality

      Business Protocol 249

          Greetings • Gift–Giving • Business Cards • Names and Titles • Dining Concerns

      Cultural Considerations in Negotiations 252

          Cultural Negotiating Styles • Improving the Negotiating Process

      Cultural Perspectives of Management.. 257

          View of the Job • Managers as Paternalistic Leaders • Management and Power Perceptions • Power Distance and Individualism

      Summary 260

x Contents

9 Selection and Preparation of International Hotel Executives ... 267

Hotel Openings for Expatriates 267
Local Versus Expatriate Hiring 268

> Selecting Managers for the Hotel Abroad • Skills Transfer • Work Visa and Immigration Restrictions • Expatriates in Asia • The Cost of Expatriate Employment • Hiring the Local National • Regional Hospitality Education and Training

Expatriate Manager Selection 277

> The High Cost of Personnel Mistakes • The Many Hats of an Expatriate Manager • Evaluating Candidates for Foreign Assignments • Expatriate Acculturation

The Expatriate Manager's Contract 281
Pre-Departure Training 282

> Designing Pre-Departure Training Programs • Pre-Departure Training Options

Health Considerations 289
Other Pre-Departure Activities 290
Culture Shock 290
Excessive Acculturation 291
Repatriation 291

> Reverse Culture Shock and Readjustment • Minimizing Repatriation Difficulties

Summary 293

10 International Human Resource Management 299

The Field of IHRM 299
Employee Acquisition 302

> Employment Ratios • Labor Supply • Possible Solutions for Labor Shortages

Recruitment 305

> Imported Labor/Immigrants • Job Perceptions Affecting Recruitment • Family or Educational Status • Impacts of Hotel Class • Hiring for Joint Ventures • Factors Affecting the Hiring Decision

Orientation 308

> Cultural Attitudes toward Service • Universality of Hospitality

Training in a Multicultural Environment 310
Supervision 311

> Motivation and Productivity • Decision–Making • Communication

Contents   **xi**

Compensation and Benefits	317
Trade Unions and Unionism	318
Contrasting Examples of Unionism	
Human Resource Development	320
Performance Appraisals • Corrective Actions	
Discharge	322
Summary	323

Part IV International Hotel Operations 327

11 Special Considerations in Managing International Hotel Operations 329

Hotel Activities and the Management Process	329
Organizing the International Hotel	333
Managing Corporate Culture in the International Hotel	334
Exporting Corporate Culture • Corporate Culture Impacts • Cultural Perspectives at the Top	
Managing Communication in the International Hotel	337
Communicating with the Host Community • Language Differences	
Managing Guest Service	340
Provisions for the International Guest • Observing Protocol • The International Business Traveler	
Managing International Hotel Operations	347
Accounting for International Hotels • Purchasing • Utilities • Equipment Maintenance • Security	
Legal Issues	356
Innkeepers' Liability • IH&RA's Hotel Regulations • UNIDROIT Efforts • Environmental Regulations and Voluntary Guidelines	
Summary	359
Appendix A: International Symbols for the Hospitality Industry	363
Appendix B: International Hotel Regulations	365

12 International Hotel Classifications and Standards 369

Historic Perspectives	369
Fundamentals of Classification Systems	370
Criteria • Use of Symbols • Classification Authority • Objective Assessments	

Contents

Problems and Issues of International Hotel Classification............... 374

Subjectivity • Quality and Quantity of Service and Facilities • "Let the Market Rule" • Obstacles to International Agreement • Cost • Industry Objections • Government Perspective • Cultural Influence on Standards and Service • Variations in Facilities • Harmony Versus Homogeny • Advantages and Positive Attributes

Selected Classification Systems in Practice... 380

Guide Michelin • Mobil Travel Guide • American Automobile Association • Britain's Harmonized Classification System • Ireland's Classification System • Spain's Regional Approach • Other Classification Systems

Toward Worldwide Standards.. 388
World-Class Service Standards.. 389
Summary.. 390

13 International Hotel Sales and Marketing............................... 395

Internationalizing the Hotel... 395
Market Research... 396

Guest Analysis • Competition Analysis • Forecasting Demand • Research Sources

Developing an International Marketing Strategy............................... 398

Corporate Marketing and Sales Efforts • Accounting for Cultural Differences • Marketing U.S. Hotels to Foreign Visitors

Understanding Various Travel Distribution Systems........................ 401

Automated Global Distribution Systems • Travel Agents and the Hotel Booking Process • Working with Travel Agents • Common Hotel–Travel Agency Relationship Problems • Resolving Relationship Problems • Tour Operators • Hotel Representation Companies and Consortia

Segmentation.. 412

Ways to Segment • Branding

Product Positioning... 416
Promotional Tools and Techniques... 417

Advertising • Collateral Materials and Sales Promotions • Cooperative Marketing • Public Relations • Frequent-Guest Programs • Property Website • Effectiveness of Tools/Techniques

Personal Selling.. 426

Travel Trade Shows • Travel Missions • Familiarization Tours

Summary.. 432

Contents xiii

Part V		**Looking Ahead**	**437**
14		**Global Competition and the Future**	**439**
		Long-Term Tourism Growth Trends	439

Factors Influencing Future Growth • Demographic, Economic, and Social Trends • Competition from Other Sources

Deregulation and Free Trade		444
The European Union's Impact on Travel and Tourism		444

European Union Tourism Policy • Transportation • Tour Operators • Travel Agents • The Hotel Industry • Standardized Currency • Travel Costs • Specific Countries

Tourism Growth by Region 450

Europe • North America • Asia and the Pacific • South and Central America • Africa • Middle East

Privatization 456

Airline Privatization

Transportation Developments 457

Aircraft Technology • Space Travel • Train Technology • Deregulation • Transportation Infrastructure

Technology and Automation	460
Global Distribution Systems	461
Development Issues	462
Tourism and the Environment	464

Hotels and the Environment • The Environment's Importance to Tourism

Alternative Tourism	468
Human Resource Issues	471
Hotel Company Diversification and Growth	473

Mergers, Acquisitions, and Cooperative Arrangements

	Conclusion	475
	Index	**477**

Preface

DURING THE CLOSING YEARS of the twentieth century, even the most casual observer of history could hardly fail to notice the rapid pace of changes taking place around the world with respect to the restructuring of political, social, and economic systems. With the ending of the Cold War, the contest over military superiority has given way to a new contest emphasizing economic prosperity at home and competitiveness in trade abroad. The leaders of major socialist countries, including the former USSR and China, have been quick to shift from centralized state-planned economies to competitive market-driven models. Today's economic paradigm is clearly one of international trade and globalism to serve the twin aims of peace and prosperity in a new world order.

The new world order of the twenty-first century is imposing broader instructional demands on many professional disciplines in higher education, including the hospitality and tourism field, which by every measure is already the world's largest economic activity. Students preparing for leadership roles in tomorrow's worldwide lodging industry will need a fuller understanding and deeper appreciation of management and marketing applications within a globalized context rather than a purely domestic one. This is not to say that all graduates will become international hotel managers. But because competition and hotel standards are becoming more international, hospitality schools will have the responsibility to prepare students for a work environment that promises not only to be more global in scope, but increasingly culturally diverse at home.

This text is the product and culmination of considerable research and many years of observing, talking with international hotel CEOs and general managers, and working with hotels in international settings. While there are numerous publications available on hotel management or specific subjects within the broader subject of hospitality management, relatively little comprehensive writing exists on the international or cross-cultural aspects of the lodging industry. Indeed, only recently have the general business disciplines recognized the importance of international perspectives. Foreign languages, once elective subjects in the business curricula, are quickly becoming basic requirements to enhance cultural understanding in management. A growing number of business schools throughout the United States and elsewhere are adding internationally focused courses to the curricula and adopting a more global approach toward such traditional subjects as management, marketing, and finance. Likewise, business-related research and publications are increasingly slanted toward international concerns.

Thanks to the explosive growth of travel and tourism over the past three decades, the hotel industry has always tended to be more internationally oriented than many other businesses. Since the mid-eighties, moreover, the trend toward globalization in the hotel industry has been particularly marked. A significant increase in U.S. chains operating abroad has been evidenced and, at the same time, growing numbers of other transnational lodging firms now have operations in the United States and elsewhere.

This text is intended to assist hospitality educators who are interested in teaching hotel management from an international perspective by providing a text that treats various aspects of hotel development and management in international terms. Throughout the text, there has been an attempt to integrate personal observations, academic perspectives, and research with actual examples from hotels around the world, so that professionals working in the field, as well as students of hospitality management, may find information of substantive value.

Chuck Y. Gee
Honolulu, Hawaii

About the Author and Contributing Author

Until his retirement in 2000, author **Chuck Yim Gee** was dean of the University of Hawaii School of Travel Industry Management dating from 1976, and later interim dean of the University of Hawaii College of Business Administration as well. Under his leadership, the school gained prominence in the Pacific-Asia region as the original model for tourism, hospitality, and transportation education under the inclusive umbrella of Travel Industry Management. Previously, he held appointments on the faculties of the University of Denver (where he was concurrently Director of University Food Services/Summer Housing), Oregon State University, and the former Technology and Development Institute of the East West Center. Since 1978, he has been a tourism advisor in four provinces of China, holding honorary professorships at six universities, among them Nankai University, the Beijing University of International Studies, and Shanghai Normal University. Over his long career, he has undertaken tourism projects in countries outside of Asia and the Pacific, including Canada, Latin America, South America, and parts of Europe and Africa. His experience in the global lodging industry included service on the founding board of directors of the Regent International Hotels chain based in Hong Kong, which until its sale in the mid-1990s operated some 18 luxury properties on four continents.

Gee has authored, co-authored, or edited numerous other publications, including *Resort Development and Management, The Travel Industry, Professional Travel Agency Management, International Tourism: A Global Perspective,* and *The Story of the Pacific Asia Travel Association.*

Now in his post-retirement career, Gee serves as advisor and consultant to various institutions, small business enterprises, international hotels, and tourism organizations. He remains active in the Pacific Asia Travel Association (PATA), where he is a life member, and the Academic Advisory Council of voluntary travel and non-travel-related associations—which includes, among others, the Institute of Certified Travel Agents, the Pacific Rim Foundation, the Board of Trustees of Kuakini Health System, the Kuakini Medical Center board, and the China-Hawaii Chamber of Commerce (of which he is a founding director).

His service to the State of Hawaii under three governors included chairmanship of the statewide Tourism Policy Council (Department of Business, Economic Development & Tourism); chairmanship of the Council on Tourism Education and Training (Department of Labor & Industrial Relations); and membership on the board of directors, Hawaii Visitor & Convention Bureau.

Gee was thrice appointed to the 15-member Travel and Tourism Advisory Board of the United States Department of Commerce under three administrations. In his capacity as appointed U.S. delegate to the World Tourism Organization, he was recognized for his assistance in drafting the landmark Manila Declaration on World Tourism in 1980 (pertaining to the universal human rights to travel and tourism), the drafting of the Male Declaration on Sustainable Tourism and the Environment for Asia-Pacific Tourism Ministers in 1997, and the Macao Resolution on Tourism Human Resource Development in 1999. On behalf of the first Bush Administration and USAID, he undertook an assignment to develop a national tourism plan for Ecuador. In 1995, he was appointed as a Hawaii delegate to the first White House Conference on Travel and Tourism to consider the proposal for establishing national travel and tourism policies.

An active board member of many tourism and service related organizations, he received the 1992 "Award of Excellence for Tourism Education" given by the National Tourism Administration of the People's Republic of China, PATA's 1991 Grand Award for Individual Educational Accomplishment, PATA's Life Member Award, PATA's Presidential Award in 1986, the 1987 NOAH Award given by the Academy of Tourism Organizations, and the 1988 Travel Industry Hall of Leaders Award presented by the Travel Industry Association of America. He is an honorary Fellow of the International Academy for the Study of Tourism. To recognize his contributions to the travel and tourism field worldwide, the University of Denver conferred on him the Honorary Doctorate of Public Service in 1991. The State of Hawaii honored him as "State Manager of the Year" in 1995. At the advent of the new millennium, the Honolulu Star-Bulletin named Dean Emeritus Chuck Yim Gee on the list of 100 individuals who "made a difference" for the State of Hawaii during the Twentieth Century.

Contributing author and associate professor **A. J. Singh** is the Professor of International Lodging, Finance and Real Estate Finance in *The* School of Hospitality Business at Michigan State University. In 1998, after working closely with 38 industry leaders representing the lodging, real estate, and financial services industries, Singh completed a two-year research project that made a major contribution to the literature by predicting the structure of the U.S. lodging industry and its future sources of financing. In partnership with industry and other faculty colleagues, Singh's goal is to establish *The* School of Hospitality Business as the leading solution provider for issues and problems related to International Lodging and Hospitality Real Estate. Dr. Singh was jointly responsible for the establishment of The Hospitality Business Real Estate and Development Specialization at Michigan State University. He currently teaches the Hospitality Business Real Estate, International Lodging Development and Management, and Financial Management courses at *The* School.

Dr. Singh earned his undergraduate from the University of Delhi in India, his M.S. from Purdue University in Hotel Restaurant and Institutional Management, and his Ph.D. in Park, Recreation, and Tourism from Michigan State University. He is an active member of HAMA (Hospitality Asset Managers Association), CHRIE (Council of Hotel, Restaurant & Institutional Education), AHFME (Association of Hospitality Financial Management Educators), ISHC (International Society of

Hospitality Consultants), and ULI (Urban Land Institute). He was recently invited to join the International Society of Hospitality Consultants, an industry advisory group consisting of hospitality investment and operations advisors. Dr. Singh works closely with the Center for International Business Education and Research at Michigan State University in his role as the Director of Study Abroad for the College of Business. He is also a member of the Global Hoteliers Club, an association of international hotel general managers.

Dr. Singh has more than 15 years of hospitality business experience in various management positions in the United States and India. He has worked for Oberoi Hotels, Stouffer Hotels, and Hyatt Hotels. In 1999, he taught financial management at Centre International de Glion, a prestigious hotel management school in Switzerland. He has also conducted many real estate market and feasibility studies while working as a consultant for Laventhol & Horwath. Other accomplishments include working with the American Hotel & Lodging Educational Institute to develop training materials and case studies for their books and certification programs. In 1999, he worked closely with Executive Education at MSU to assist in the implementation of an alternative officing arrangement for General Motors using hotel management service concepts. The National Institute of Standards and Technology appointed him to the 2006 Board of Examiners for the Malcolm Baldrige National Quality Award. He received the Richard Lewis Award for Quality and Innovation in 2006. He currently conducts two study abroad programs to India, Dubai, Thailand, Hong Kong, Macau, and Southern China.

Part I

Overview and Historical Perspective

Chapter 1 Outline

Globalization and the Business World
    The Dissolution of Borders
    Tourism in the Global Environment
    Defining the Transnational Hotel Company
The Tourism Industry
    The Economic Impact of Travel and Tourism
    The Geographic Distribution of Tourism
    Travel Demand Determinants
The International Lodging Industry
    Global Distribution and Structure
    Global Hotel Performance
    Types of Hotel Products
    Hotel Guests
Challenges of the Globalized Lodging Industry

Competencies

1. Summarize the factors that have contributed to globalization and a global economy, define the term *transnational* as applied to a hotel company, and cite competitive advantages of transnational hotels. (pp. 3–6)

2. Describe the tourism industry, including tourism's economic impact and geographic distribution, and discuss travel demand determinants. (pp. 6–13)

3. Describe the international lodging industry, explain its global distribution and structure, and summarize global hotel performance. (pp. 13–16)

4. Identify types of hotel products, discuss types of hotel guests, and summarize some of the challenges faced by the global lodging industry. (pp. 17–20)

1

Globalization, Tourism, and the Lodging Sector

As we move into the twenty-first century, a new world order is creating an increasingly interdependent global economic system. Declining trade and investment barriers, advances in transportation and telecommunications, and a globally dispersed and integrated production and marketing supply chain for goods and services will have a significant impact on the travel, tourism, and hospitality industry. The fall of communism and the subsequent shift to market-based economic systems in the former Soviet Union and Eastern Europe have had a ripple effect through the world. Most notably, countries such as India, which launched its economic reforms in 1991, and China, which is moving progressively toward free market reforms, have entered the world stage as major economic forces and leading players in the world trade for goods and services. The same trend is taking hold in Latin America, where dictators are being replaced with democratic systems, free market reforms, and movement to privatization. However, the rosy global outlook is tempered with a countervailing view that the modernization and westernization that has accompanied the economic reforms has also resulted in the rise of fundamentalism and its extreme manifestation: global terrorism. The new century that awaits travel, tourism, and hospitality enterprises presents a landscape of both opportunities and risks.

Globalization and the Business World

As recently as 45 years ago, the international enterprise was a relatively rare phenomenon, and the term **multinational** was seldom heard. Today, many companies have transcended the multinational phase and operate as **transnational** or global companies. These labels reflect a major shift in the structure of the world market for goods and services—a shift to a competitive framework that has far-reaching impacts for almost all industries.

    Foreign investment and ownership have been particularly evident since many countries liberalized their foreign investment policies and aggressively courted foreign investments with generous fiscal incentives. As a result of these policies, the volume of world trade has grown much faster than the volume of world output. From 1950 to 2000, world trade grew 20 times, with an average growth rate of 6.7 percent in the 1990s.[1] Complementing the growth in world trade, the flow of foreign direct investment grew from a meager $25 million in 1975 to $1.3 trillion in 2006.[2] There have been increased inflows across all three groups of economies:

developed countries, developing countries, and the transition economies of Europe and the Commonwealth of Independent States (CIS). While the United States maintained its leadership role in attracting foreign direct investment, the largest inflows among developing countries occurred in China, Hong Kong, and Singapore. For transition economies, the Russian Federation was the lead host country. Various surveys point to continued growth of foreign direct investment led by strategic investments from well-capitalized global firms seeking new markets, lower production costs, greater outsourcing, reduced regulatory barriers, and the benefits of increased liberalization policies in many countries across the globe. Moreover, a global debate on trade in services is under way.

The internationalization of business ownership and management in industry after industry has had a major impact on the travel, tourism, and hospitality industry. Changes in communication technologies and transportation, among others, have catapulted tourism into political, economic, financial, and cultural prominence as one of the world's most powerful agents in global economic development.

From a more practical standpoint, these trends have resulted in intensified demand and competition for airline seats and hotel accommodations in various parts of the world. Sophisticated marketing and reservations technologies have put large international travel-service-related companies such as hotels in the best position to profit from global market access. Unquestionably, **globalization**—along with technological developments in telecommunications and transportation—has contributed to the rise of hotel mega-chains that possess not only transferable management and marketing expertise, but also the financial backing for geographic expansion.

The Dissolution of Borders

The existence of a global economy indicates that consumers are becoming less concerned with the country of origin of a particular product or service and more concerned with its quality, price, design, value, and appeal. In the information technologies world, for example, the market for IBM mainframes or Dell laptops is no longer defined by geographical borders but by the products' appeal to users, regardless of who owns the company or where plants and factories are located. Geopolitical boundaries have largely disappeared on a competitive map that shows the true flows of financial and industrial activity. Indeed, foreign exchange, stock markets, and other trading facilities have already made money a legitimate global commodity that can change hands quickly around the world. Hospitality and tourism have long been recognized as industries that not only transcend international boundaries, but bridge cultural gaps as well.

Perhaps the most influential force in the dissolution of national borders is the increasing flow of communication. Today, people everywhere are increasingly able to obtain information directly from all corners of the world with fewer government interventions. Thanks to the worldwide revolution in information technologies and telecommunications, people around the globe have instantaneous access to social, political, economic, and cultural news and events through many channels in various formats (including multi-media). Combined with the rapid advances in transportation technologies, the world is indeed shrinking.

International travel has also contributed to global awareness. It has often been noted that travel is the ultimate form of interpersonal communication. Through travel, there is more personal awareness of real world conditions—both good and bad—and other environments—both beautiful and ugly. There might also be a greater appreciation for other cultures and for diversity. Travel may be the ultimate educator in teaching the importance of knowing which actions and words have different interpretations from one country to the next.

When information flows with relative freedom, old geographic barriers become almost irrelevant, and global needs lead to the development of global products. For business leaders and managers, this flow of information results in fiercer competition and puts a high premium on strategies and organizational designs to meet the requirements of a borderless world. A borderless world, however, does not suggest that there will be a homogenization of taste and preferences, nor does it imply that global products can ignore local considerations. Companies have increasingly recognized the need to tailor products, services, and marketing strategies for each market. In creating a global product, companies must be able to understand and respond to specific or segmented customer needs as well as local business system requirements.

Successful global corporations today are fundamentally different from the colonial-style multinationals of the 1960s and 1970s. Today's companies do not try to push their domestically developed products on foreign markets; rather, they aim to serve customers in all key markets with equal dedication. Their value systems are typically more universal, not strictly dominated by home-country dogma. Ideally, in a global corporation, home-country identity eventually gives way to corporate identity, or global branding. And regardless of the country of origin, company workers should be able to communicate fully and confidently with their colleagues or customers anywhere in the world. In practice, few companies have learned to operate entirely in such a fashion, but the signs of movement in this direction are unmistakable.

Tourism in the Global Environment

Although most travel worldwide is still domestically oriented, the growing prosperity of emerging economies and a relaxation of travel restrictions are creating a new class of international outbound travelers seeking travel experiences in countries within their region and in other parts of the world. Both domestic and international travel are influenced by the rising importance of international trade, interdependent economies, and the development of global trading blocks, such as the European Union and North America under the North American Free Trade Agreement. Hotels operating in this international environment clearly need to have a more global perspective in all aspects of hotel development, financing, marketing, and management. Foreign hotel investments originating from Asia, for instance, require knowledge of Asian business perspectives, protocol, cultural behavior, and value systems. On the other hand, domestic hotel operators competing with foreign hotels that have penetrated their markets must understand global hotel operating standards or risk losing market share to these transnational competitors.

Defining the Transnational Hotel Company

A transnational corporation is essentially a multiplant firm with operations that transcend national boundaries; it has been defined as "an enterprise which owns and controls income-generating assets in more than one country."[3] In a United Nations report entitled *Transnational Corporations in International Tourism*, this definition was expanded to include "not only foreign firms with direct investments in a particular host country, but those firms having all major forms of contractual arrangements and enterprises in host countries," thereby dropping the need for foreign direct investment that is frequently absent from hotel transnational activity. Despite considerable growth in the area of international services (particularly in hotel development), there continue to be problems in defining, classifying, measuring, comparing, and explaining service transnationals.

For the past 45 years, tourism has been at the forefront of international trade in services. Much of the tourism-related expansion across boundaries has been driven by the expansion of international trade, the emergence of new business centers throughout the world, and the enlarging multinational infrastructure offering "service networks" (for example, computerized reservation systems) to travelers.

The competitive advantages of transnational hotel companies include their ability to establish global marketing and purchasing networks and their expertise in satisfying the demands of present and potential customers, specifically with regard to product quality, price, and consistent service delivery. Quality is the most important variable determining competitiveness in the international lodging industry. Transnational hotel companies that have been able to establish and sustain a strong brand image and quality control consistently outperform their competition. The emergence of international or transnational hotel companies and the increased competition that has accompanied this emergence have, in turn, helped contribute to more effective hotel operations, more efficient use of resources, and the growing globalization of the economy.

As international trade and the interdependence of the world's economies accelerate, there is likely to be continued pressure for transnational hotel development to keep pace with travel trends and demands. Moreover, the transnational hotel company of tomorrow will not only be larger in size and turnover volume, but may be of any nationality if recent history is any indicator.

The Tourism Industry

The tourism industry is a collection of diverse products and services sold by highly fragmented industry sectors through a complex distribution chain. Besides lodging operations, tourism is generally said to include transportation services (airlines, rail, motor buses, car rental firms, recreational vehicles); eating and drinking places; sightseeing, amusement, gaming, and recreation services; and some aspects of retailing and financial services.

Tourism is part of the "services revolution" that is dramatically changing local, national, and regional economies as well as the global economy. It has been one of the world's most consistent growth industries over the past 50 years, and prospects for the continued growth of international tourism appear promising. Furthermore, governments in many countries are encouraging the growth of both domestic and international tourism as a means of job creation, economic diversification, and income redistribution within national borders. International tourism is also a source of foreign exchange.

Tourism's contributions to the world are more than financial, however. Travel advances educational and recreational values and, in general, enhances the quality of life in much of the world. Former United Nations Secretary General Javier Pérez de Cuéllar once made the point that "Tourism leads to strengthening mutual understanding among individuals, a vital element for the safeguard of peace, as well as providing greater knowledge of the world and hence, broader tolerance of different ways of thinking and life styles."[4]

Despite several setbacks to world tourism—the fuel crisis in the early 1970s, the world recessions in the early 1980s and early 1990s, terrorism, continued political conflicts in certain parts of the world, earthquakes, hurricanes, global health epidemics, wars—the desire to travel has proved quite resilient. The populations of the main travel-generating countries now regard holidays as a near-essential part of consumer expenditure. Many individuals are willing to protect their holidays by forgoing other forms of consumption. Even in bad times, people do not stop traveling, but simply adjust their travel behavior in various ways in order to have their vacation trips. Furthermore, the globalization of companies provides additional impetus to international travel for business meetings and conventions.

The Economic Impact of Travel and Tourism

In a departure from the traditional measure of tourism, which relied primarily on visitor arrivals and receipts, the World Travel and Tourism Council (WTTC) adopted the standardized United Nation's measurement of travel and tourism economic impact on an economy's personal consumption, business spending, capital investment, government expenditures, **gross domestic product**, and employment. Known as Travel and Tourism Satellite Accounting, it is perhaps the most significant recent development that provides an accurate assessment of the contribution of travel and tourism to the national and global economy. According to a 2008 WTTC report, global travel and tourism in 2008 is expected to post $7.9 trillion of economic activity; the total is expected to grow to $14.8 trillion by 2018.[5]

Domestic travel significantly exceeds international travel in developed countries with large populations that have access to diverse destinations and attractions within their own borders. In the United States, for instance, domestic travel accounts for around 90 percent of total travel volume in movements—mostly by private automobile—and revenues. For that reason, the U.S. lodging industry has focused mainly on the domestic market, with motels playing a bigger role than in any other country. In smaller countries, especially those sharing a common border with a larger neighbor, international travel dominates for opposite reasons: fewer, if any, attractions to keep people home and the ease of outbound day trips.

As recorded by the World Tourism Organization (WTO), international tourist arrivals have shown a steady increase. Just from 1995 to 2006, international tourist arrivals grew from under 500 million to nearly 850 million, an average annual growth rate of nearly 5 percent. The WTO is forecasting that international tourism arrivals will reach 1.6 billion in 2020.

Exhibit 1   International Tourist Arrivals by Region, 1990–2006

	\multicolumn{5}{c	}{International Tourist Arrivals (millions)}	Market share (%)	\multicolumn{2}{c	}{Change (%)}	Average annual growth (%)
	1990	1995	2000	2005	2006	2006	05/04	06/05	'00–'06
World	436	536	684	803	846	100	5.5	5.4	3.6
Europe	262.3	310.8	392.5	438.7	460.8	54.4	4.3	5.0	2.7
Northern Europe	28.3	35.8	42.6	51.0	54.9	6.5	7.8	7.6	4.3
Western Europe	108.6	112.2	139.7	142.6	149.8	17.7	2.6	5.0	1.2
Central/Eastern Europe	31.5	60.0	69.4	87.8	91.2	10.8	2.2	3.9	4.7
Southern/Mediter. Europe	93.9	102.7	140.8	157.3	164.9	19.5	5.9	4.8	2.7
Asia and the Pacific	56.2	82.5	110.6	155.3	167.2	19.8	7.8	7.7	7.1
North-East Asia	26.4	41.3	58.3	87.5	94.0	11.1	10.3	7.4	8.3
South-East Asia	21.5	28.8	36.9	49.3	53.9	6.4	4.9	9.3	6.5
Oceania	5.2	8.1	9.2	10.5	10.5	1.2	3.7	0.4	2.2
South Asia	3.2	4.2	6.1	8.0	8.8	1.0	4.7	11.0	6.4
Americas	92.8	109.0	128.2	133.2	135.9	16.1	5.9	2.0	1.0
North America	71.7	80.7	91.5	89.9	90.7	10.7	4.7	0.9	-0.2
Caribbean	11.4	14.0	17.1	18.8	19.4	2.3	3.7	3.5	2.2
Central America	1.9	2.6	4.3	6.3	7.0	0.8	13.2	10.8	8.2
South America	7.7	11.7	15.3	18.2	18.8	2.2	11.9	3.0	3.5
Africa	15.2	20.1	27.9	37.3	40.7	4.8	8.8	9.2	6.5
North Africa	8.4	7.3	10.2	13.9	14.9	1.8	8.9	7.4	6.5
Subsaharan Africa	6.8	12.8	17.7	23.3	25.8	3.0	8.8	10.4	6.5
Middle East	9.6	13.7	24.5	38.3	41.8	4.9	5.9	8.9	9.3

Source: World Tourism Organization (2007).

The Geographic Distribution of Tourism

As shown in Exhibit 1, Europe is the destination of approximately 54.4 percent of the world's international travelers, while North America represents about 10.7 percent. About half of all international tourism expenditures take place in Europe. Europe's position as the world's major regional destination has remained unchanged since the 1950s, but in terms of growth, the Asia-Pacific region and the Middle East have exhibited the highest rates of growth for the past ten years. The Asia-Pacific region, led primarily by China, now represents approximately 20 percent of the world market share of international tourists.

It was not until the 1970s that developing countries began to tap into the international tourism market. During the 1980s, the Asia-Pacific region moved from being a minor player in the international tourism scene to becoming the fastest-growing and most talked about region of the world. Between 1980 and 1992, arrivals in the region's primary countries increased nearly threefold, from 21 to 58 million, at an average annual growth rate of 8.9 percent—more than double the world average. The fastest-growing markets were Australia, China, Hong Kong, South Korea, and Thailand.[6] Despite several setbacks, such as health epidemics (SARS and the bird flu) and the appreciation of the Japanese yen and the Australian and New Zealand dollars, the region has for the past 15 years recorded average annual growth rates of approximately 7 percent, a rate twice the world average.

Exhibit 2   International Tourist Departures by Region, 1990–2006

	International Tourist Departures (millions)					Change (%)		Market share (%)	Average annual growth (%)
	1990	1995	2000	2005	2006	05/04	06/05	2006	'00–'06
World	436	536	684	803	846	5.5	5.4	100	3.6
From:									
Europe	252.3	310.9	398.3	452.3	473.7	4.3	4.7	56.3	2.9
Asia and the Pacific	59.2	86.8	114.8	154.7	166.5	6.8	7.7	19.3	6.4
Americas	99.8	108.5	131.0	137.1	142.2	5.8	3.7	17.1	1.4
Middle East	8.2	9.6	13.8	22.8	24.8	11.5	8.9	2.8	10.3
Africa	9.9	12.8	16.3	21.8	24.5	7.0	12.1	2.7	7.1
Origin not specified[1]	6.6	7.5	9.4	14.1	14.7	16.0	4.3	1.8	7.7
Same region	349.9	431.4	541.0	638.0	668.9	4.8	4.9	79.5	3.6
Other regions	79.5	97.2	133.1	150.7	162.7	7.5	7.9	18.8	3.4

1 Countries that could not be allocated to a specific region of origin. As information is derived from inbound tourism data this occurs when data on the country of origin is missing or when a category such as 'other countries of the world' is used grouping countries together that are not separately specified.

Source: World Tourism Organization (2007).

Factors influencing travel growth in this region included the opening of new air routes, massive investments in new international-class hotels, the provision of cheaper travel and accommodations packages, increased marketing and promotional activities, new recreational products and tourism destinations, and the relaxation of government travel barriers. Perhaps the greatest stimulus to travel growth in the region has been the extraordinary economic development and growth of such countries or areas as Japan, Hong Kong, South Korea, Singapore, Taiwan, and, most of all, China. In the second wave of economic development, Thailand, Malaysia, Indonesia, and India are fostering the growth of interregional travel and tourism.

For the past few years, an emerging tourism destination beginning to get noticed is in the Middle East. The United Arab Emirates, led by Dubai's commitment to diversify its economy and reduce its reliance on its dwindling oil reserves, has been recording double-digit growth in international tourism arrivals since 1995. By creating tourism products on a mega size and scale, Dubai is positioning itself as the tourism destination of choice in the Middle East and an economic hub for the region.

Outbound Tourism. Even though about 80 percent of international travel takes place within the same region, travel between different regions has been growing faster than intraregional travel for the past few years. The outbound travel market (see Exhibit 2) is dominated by Europe, which represents over 56 percent of all outbound tourism, followed by Asia and the Pacific (19.3 percent) and the Americas (17.1 percent). However, rising levels of disposable income coupled with lowered travel restrictions in the emerging countries of Northeast Asia, Southeast Asia, Central and Eastern Europe, the Middle East, and South Africa are producing rapid growth in outbound travel from these regions. In 2006, international tourism expenditures were $733 billion, of which about half were generated by the top 10 nations: Germany, United States, United Kingdom, France, Japan, China, Italy, Canada, Russian Federation, and Republic of Korea.[7]

Travel Demand Determinants

Many countries have natural advantages such as climate or geography that attract visitors. But travel demand is also based on several primary economic determinants, as well as other categories of determinants, including leisure and the quality of life and demographic changes, which we discuss in this section. Other factors include transportation and information access, convenience, the perceived safety of the destination, and trendiness of the destination (for some markets). Variations in these factors clearly influence international travel flows.

Primary Economic Determinants. The primary economic determinants of international travel demand are:

- The level of economic development and economic conditions in both the sending and receiving countries.
- The cost of travel within destination countries.
- Exchange rates.
- Changes in real consumer income.
- The comparative average cost of trips abroad relative to trips at home.

On a macro level, economic growth in a country generally leads to an increase in disposable income and changes in social policies such as leave entitlements. Increases in trade and commerce derived from economic growth similarly fuel demand for business travel. Conversely, the main depressants of business travel are a poor economy and high unemployment levels.

Demand for hotel accommodations is obviously linked with demand for travel, which is sensitive to the economic cycles in both sending and receiving countries and in the international economy as a whole. One of the major factors influencing overseas travel patterns is the exchange rate. There is a significant inverse relationship between the exchange rate and the number of foreign visitors to a country. International tourism is an export industry: when rates go down, people consume more of it; when rates go up, they consume less of it or they may trade down. Mexico's devaluation of the peso in the late 1980s, for instance, had the immediate effect of encouraging its neighbors from the north to visit Mexico, where the dollar could buy first-class services and products relatively cheaply—for example, a four-star hotel room for $30 and steak dinner with wine for two for $15, compared with $75 for a similar room and $60 for a similar meal in the United States during the same time period. Just as a weak peso has attracted U.S. visitors to Mexico, so the persistent strengthening of the yen over the dollar was a major factor in encouraging Japanese tourists to visit the United States in the 1990s.

However, it is important to temper this relationship with other factors that affect travel. For example, despite the weakening of the U.S. dollar in recent years, the number of international visitors to the United States has shown an overall negative rate of growth from 2000 to 2006, with individual source markets displaying different travel behavior. Such traditionally strong overseas source markets as the United Kingdom, Japan, Germany, and France have shown negative growth rates during this period. On the other hand, travelers from Canada, Mexico, South Korea, and Australia maintained an overall positive rate of growth. Travel from China, India, and Ireland posted the highest rates of growth during this period, ranging from 28 to 43 percent.[8] Factors that may explain these anomalies in the travel pattern include restrictive entry requirements following the September 11 terrorist attacks in 2001, competition from other destinations and marketing and promotion issues, improved business relationships between countries, required travel to visit friends and family, and the proximity of international travel.

Providers of tourism services (transportation and attractions, as well as hotels) also exercise a significant influence on the volume of tourism to a particular destination through the availability, quality, price, and promotion of their services. Adequate public investment in transportation and attractions infrastructure and private investment (or public-private co-investments) in hotels, restaurants, transport equipment, recreation, and entertainment are essential to both the qualitative and quantitative aspects of destination development.

Leisure and the Quality of Life. At its first general assembly in Manila in 1980, the World Tourism Organization, which then comprised 107 nations, unanimously adopted the Manila Declaration on World Tourism. Among other things, the declaration stressed leisure and tourism as human entitlements. Article 4 reads:

> The right to use of leisure, and in particular the right to access to holidays and to freedom of travel and tourism, a natural consequence of the right to work, is recognized as an aspect of the fulfillment of the human being by the Universal Declaration of Human Rights as well as by the legislation of many states. It entails for society the duty of providing for its citizens the best practical, effective and non-discriminatory access to this type of activity. Such an effort must be in harmony with the priority, institution and tradition of each individual country.[9]

The tourism and hospitality industry has been the primary benefactor of these changed attitudes and trends in a large part of the world.

Evidence that attitudes have changed can be noted in the gradual shortening of the American workweek over the past 160 years. In 1850, the average workweek spanned 70 hours. Forty years later, the average had shrunk to 53 hours; by 1920, to 50; and today the average person spends under 40 hours per week at work.

The strength of unions worldwide and the growth of progressive management have also had an impact on the length of the workweek, as have new attitudes toward health, physical and mental stress, and the importance of rest and relaxation.

Paid vacations—an important influence on travel since the 1930s—have become standard custom in most countries of the world, and leisure is considered one of the more meaningful entitlements in one's work life. Vacation entitlements vary greatly by country. The trend toward longer holiday entitlements in most countries is likely to result in more frequent trips—particularly short trips—as has been the West European experience. Increasingly, global events requiring years of planning—the Olympic Games, the World's Fair, and regional or national conventions and congresses—are viewed not only as significant attractions but as major economic activities in their own right.

Demographic Changes. At more than 6.6 billion people, the world's population continues to grow.[10] More people hold jobs (and better-paying jobs) than ever before, populations are better educated, and the means of communication and air travel are improving rapidly. In a world of increasing prosperity and tempered inflation, real disposable income continues to increase in most areas, making possible an increase in spending for discretionary travel, both short- and long-term.

Besides natural population growth, most industrialized countries are also undergoing other significant demographic changes, including the aging of their populations, a growth in two-income households, later marriages (especially in Japan, where couples marry at the oldest average age in the world—28.5 for men and 25.8 for women), the increase of young families, and the emergence of the nontraditional family. All of these examples point to changing consumer behavior, since different groups have different needs, interests, and consumption patterns. For the lodging industry, some of the more relevant demographic changes may be the following:

- In many industrialized countries, there will be a higher proportion of senior citizens with healthy retirement savings and ample disposable incomes for leisure travel. (For example, in January of 2006, the first of America's 78 million Baby Boomers—those born during the so-called "baby boom" lasting from 1946 to 1964—began turning 60 years old.) This segment is physically healthier, better educated, and more mobile than earlier cohorts. With both time and income available, senior citizens are more inclined to travel than ever before and, although they will patronize hotels in all categories from budget to luxury, they have a tendency toward using better-class accommodations.

- Young professionals constitute a major travel market in developed countries where the two-income household is a fact of life. In the United States, the so-called Generation X and Generation Y jointly constitute a market of over 121 million and are now reaching positions of power and affluence. Worldwide, the 25 to 44 age group tends to be better educated and more widely traveled than previous generations and places a high priority on travel as a means of broadening personal experience. These individuals often postpone marriage and childbearing and have fewer financial or family burdens that hamper travel. Their time constraints often shorten trip duration, but they travel more frequently. This category of traveler is generally affluent, status-conscious, and brand-loyal.

- The family vacation represents an important travel trend, especially during the peak summer months, despite attempts by many destinations to reduce seasonality by promoting family packages at other times of the year. With so many households where both parents work, vacation time together is viewed as a means of reuniting family members, often across generational lines. Families on vacation tend to favor resorts or destinations that offer something for every member, especially children. However, as developed countries amend their school times toward longer school years, the nature of this market may change.

- More women than ever before are in the global workforce. For two-income households at the higher end, disposable income may encourage foreign travel and resort holidays. On the other hand, the single female traveler—whether traveling for pleasure or business—is an emerging travel segment in her own right. Hotels all over the world are becoming more sensitive in catering to women's needs on the road, including the provision of daycare/learning center facilities, alternative menus with lighter meals, fitness/wellness centers, security-designed facilities, and improved lighting in bathrooms.

The foregoing demographic and social trends will affect the way that the industry creates and delivers products and services. Travel and tourism businesses need to understand and develop strategies to address the multi-generational needs, wants, and desires. Hoteliers, for instance, must offer designs and amenities that cater to the special needs of the senior market as well as the younger market that has a different concept of design, style, and technology. In an age of "mass customization," the ability of businesses to match and exceed the guest expectations for a unique experience will separate the winners from the losers.

The International Lodging Industry

The lodging industry is by nature an international one. As international trade and business expand, the international linkage will become even more important for the industry.

Defining the international lodging industry is not an easy task. Broadly, it can be defined as an industry that exports hospitality services and generates export income. In a sense, the lodging industry has always been international, because most hotels have received foreign guests at one time or another.

As the industry has evolved over the years, its structure has grown more complex with respect to scope, ownership, management, and affiliation. There are many models one may observe, including the following:

- Independently owned and operated properties
- Properties that are independently owned but chain-operated or chain-affiliated and operated under management contracts
- Chain-owned and -operated properties
- Franchised properties
- Referral group properties
- Others

Independently owned and operated properties outnumber chain-affiliated properties worldwide, but in terms of number of rooms, chain hotels are the dominant sector. Independently owned and operated properties tend to be smaller; they may be owned by individuals, families, partnerships, syndicates, or corporations. Large chain-affiliated hotels may be owned by one or more individuals or a group (for example, a pension fund, a government, a development bank, a large conglomerate). Some owners play a passive role in property management, some an active role.

With respect to hotel chains, there are companies that own and operate hotels; management companies that operate hotels through the use of management agreements with little or no ownership involvement; and companies that simply franchise their hotel name without providing any management or operating expertise aside from marketing. There are also hotel management companies that manage franchised or non-franchised hotels for their owners and hotel referral organizations that provide reservation services and limited marketing services for their members.

In practice, many different combinations of the foregoing exist, and the line distinguishing one type of arrangement from another is often fuzzy. Furthermore, the industry's structure tends to be influenced by geographical orientation. Whereas North American hotel firms are more inclined to expand using contractual agreements (either management contracts or franchising), Asian companies typically seek equity investments. European companies typically prefer at least some equity involvement in conjunction with management contracts.

Historically, airline-affiliated hotels helped to internationalize the lodging industry. However, these ventures generally proved to be unsuccessful and resulted in the divestment of the entities. For example, in 1980, Pan American sold its chain of InterContinental Hotels to Grand Metropolitan and TWA transferred its interests to its holding company, Trans World Corporation. More recently, Air France sold its Meridien hotel chain to Forte and Aer Lingus was divested from its Copthorne Hotel Group. Replacing these merger and ownership interests has been a series of reciprocal marketing alliances. For instance, hotel companies such as Marriott, Hilton, and Mandarin Oriental have an alliance with British Airways that allows passengers and hotel guests to earn mileage points when booking reservations within the network of partners.[11]

Some hotel chains and management companies are part of a larger enterprise or group of enterprises. For example, the Prince Hotel Group is part of the Seibu Group—a Japanese conglomerate including railways, a baseball team, hotels, and other businesses. Large tour operators, particularly in Europe, have also been known to own or manage hotels.

Properties may be affiliated with a number of hotel companies, either through ownership, management, franchise, or referral group arrangements, and the matter may be further complicated when two or more chains are involved in the operation of a hotel. Such is the case of some Oberoi Trident properties in New Delhi that are part of the Oberoi group of hotels but nevertheless have a marketing franchise agreement with Hilton.

Management contracts and franchise affiliations are the primary method by which some of the major hotel companies (primarily from the United States) grow internationally. Typically in these cases, a local investor, government entity, or investment entity that owns the physical assets of the hotel and real estate will sign a contractual agreement with a chain to manage and/or market the hotel.

In the three major regions of the world where the hotel trade is most developed—North America, Europe, and the Asia-Pacific region—the structure of the industry varies considerably. In North America, the industry is characterized by management contracts, franchised chains, referral systems, and a marketing approach that emphasizes name brands. Although many properties are independently owned and run, operators often attempt to position or "brand" their hotels against well-known brands in targeting particular market segments. Branding clearly serves an important market function in at least two principal ways: (1) it promotes standards and standardization of products associated with the brand name, and (2) it helps buyers and sellers function, since branded products are generally more reliable than unbranded.

In Europe, there is an important overlay of chains and branded products interspersed with lesser-known independent hotels. Trends indicate that the branded or chain segment of the market will continue to grow and to some extent may follow the North American model in terms of development. Still, the majority of Europe's hotel stock remains in the hands of small family businesses. These privately owned small hotels represent an important section of European accommodations, although it is a section that will find the challenges of new technology and new ways of marketing increasingly difficult to handle. More of these hotels understandably have joined major referral systems and have become brand-name affiliated, but many have not. The diversity and individuality of small properties are often held up as selling points to a smaller market of sophisticated travelers.

In the Asia-Pacific region, the travel industry generates large volumes of business and group tours, and is centered on the more organized and formal distribution channels of the travel trade. Both the city center hotels whose business is based on the business traveler and the coastal resort hotels aimed primarily at the pleasure traveler tend to be large facilities affiliated with regional or international chains. Except in Japan, there is no great tradition of family-run enterprises. The region's hotel stock is, for the most part, internationally promoted, marketed, and managed through the most advanced systems and techniques.

Global Distribution and Structure

According to a WTO estimate, the global lodging industry had approximately 19.4 million hotel rooms in 2005. Europe and the Americas held about 69 percent of the global room inventory, an amount down from the 83 percent those regions held in 1975. The total market share of Europe and the Americas has been falling because the growth rates in hotel rooms available in other regions have been much higher than the European and American growth rates. Between 1975 and 2005, the average annual global growth rate in rooms was 2.8 percent. Europe's growth rate during that period was only 1.6 percent, while the Americas grew at a rate of 2.9 percent. At the same time, however, booming economies pushed the average annual growth rates in Africa, the Asia-Pacific region, and the Middle East to 4.3 percent, 4.6 percent, and 6.2 percent, respectively. Between 1975 and 2005, the number of rooms in the Asia-Pacific region quadrupled from 1.2 million to 4.8 million, while the number of rooms in Africa and the Middle East nearly quadrupled as well, going from 300,000 to 1.1 million rooms.[12]

The rapid growth of transnational hotel companies in developing and developed countries reflects a number of factors: the worldwide growth of travel and tourism since 1960; the emergence of new business centers in all parts of the world;

changing social and economic trends; and the significant advantages that international hotel corporations have over domestic corporations. These advantages are associated with economies of scale of operation or distribution in such areas as advertising, central reservation systems, global promotions, bulk purchasing, specialized knowledge of design and construction, and operational standardization. Although most international hotel chains are organized and controlled by a relatively small corporate head office, it is generally understood that these chains can ensure a flow of guests to their properties because of worldwide brand-name recognition and reservations access. International hotel companies are also able to offer professional staffing, management expertise, technical advice and consultation, first-rate training programs, and operating standards and systems—all of which are important in running a capital-intensive service enterprise dependent on sound internal operations for cash flow and asset growth.

From the hotel companies' perspective, there are important reasons for looking outward:

- To find new markets as a prime route to corporate growth
- To enhance profit lines from new areas that promise high revenues
- To spread risk by capitalizing on differences in the business cycle in different areas of the world

International development, above all, allows hotel companies to boost the global coverage of their brands and to gain prestige and the benefits of global brand marketing.

During the 1980s, large-scale foreign investment and hotel mergers and acquisitions created an industry that has changed the face of commercial centers and resort areas around the world. Even in the United States—where the concept of transnational hotel operations was born—many foreign hotel companies now have a strong presence in major gateway cities, wooing the American domestic traveler with "international style" ambience and service standards, superb cuisine, and luxury amenities, much to the chagrin of U.S. hotel operators who previously had no foreign competition. French chains provide exceptional foods and beverages, with a decor that emphasizes their French heritage and flavor. The Japanese sell the grace and serenity associated with Japan, and the British promote a history of traditional service and understated elegance. Americans excel in providing the marketplace with a variety of options matched to the needs and pocketbooks of the guests.

Global Hotel Performance

As reflected in Exhibit 3, the highest RevPAR (revenue per available room) globally during the 2006–2007 period occurred in the Middle East and Africa, followed by Europe. Operating profit margins as measured by income before fixed charges were highest in the Middle East/Africa at 49 percent, with other regions earning in the mid-30s. Based on the growth trajectory of the economies, it is expected that the highest rates of hotel performance will include specific countries in Asia and the Middle East.

Exhibit 3   Global Hotel Performance by Region, 2006–2007

	Middle East and Africa	Asia-Pacific	Europe	North America
Occupancy %	66.5–69.7%	70.6–69.7%	68.9–69.1%	63.3–63.3%
ADR	$144.5–$168.26	$115.58–$129.33	$137.74–$161.25	$98.44–$104.46
RevPAR US	$96.11–$117.28	$81.55–$89.98	$94.90–$111.45	$62.35–$66.09
Income before fixed charges (2005)	49%	36%	36%	33%

Source: www.hotelbenchmark.com.

Types of Hotel Products

For the past 30 years, the hotel industry has developed new products and niches to cater to the changing needs and lifestyles of the guests. These differentiated hotel products, primarily the creation of the branded hotel companies in the United States, have since then been "exported" throughout the world. Concepts such as airport hotels, convention hotels, extended-stay or serviced apartments, conference centers, budget hotels, condo hotels, timeshare products, casino hotels, integrated resorts, and senior living centers were all developed to cater to a particular unfilled segment of the market.

While the branded products described primarily dominate the North American market, these brands, which are part of large multinational hotel corporations, are penetrating larger parts of the Asian, Middle Eastern, and European markets. Some regions have been particularly resistant to the influence of branded hotel product and have relied primarily on the traditional forms of hospitality. These traditional forms may even dominate the industry in a given country or region.

It is important to understand these alternative forms of lodging in the context of the international lodging industry. For example, while 45 percent of visitors to Portugal stay in hotels, about the same proportion stay in **pensions**, or guesthouses, and the others stay in hotel apartments, motels, and state-operated inns locally known as **posadas**. Most tourists in Spain do not stay in commercial hotels, but prefer to choose from a wide range of apartments, traditional inns, guesthouses, farms, and self-service establishments. Spain's world-renowned **paradors**—historic buildings such as castles, palaces, convents, and monasteries converted into hotels and operated by the state—also offer visitors a unique alternative to contemporary hotels.

The Swiss lodging industry is still dominated by small family-owned/operated establishments. The Swiss offer a large selection of alternative accommodations, such as health spas, youth hostels, and camping sites, in addition to international-class hotels. In Germany, hotels account for only about 46 percent of total beds available, while guesthouses and bed-and-breakfast establishments each account for about 20 percent. Health resorts and spas also constitute an important lodging segment in Germany.

The accommodations industry in Asian cities tends to be characterized by large international-class or luxury hotels. In Japan, accommodations fall broadly into two categories—the conventional hotel accommodation of various grades and standards and the traditional Japanese **ryokan** with *tatami* mat floors and Japanese landscaped gardens. In Malaysia, accommodations include government rest houses, youth hostels, and private home or village stays (experiencing everyday life in an area by staying with a family, in a dormitory, or in another facility). In India, the heritage hotel movement has taken strong hold and provides the guest with the unique experience of staying in ancient forts, villas, and palaces of the former royalty and rulers in India. A majority of them are operated by families who reside in or near the premises and serve as interpreters (and some might say curators) of these hotels, which are interactive museums, each with its own distinctive history.

Hotel Guests

The international travel market is broadly classified in two groups: those who travel for business or governmental affairs and those who travel for pleasure, sometimes referred to as discretionary travelers. At times, it is difficult to draw the distinction between these categories, because many trips have more than one purpose. Travelers to conventions, for instance, often combine business with a holiday, bringing their spouses and other family members along for the entire trip. Depending on which hat the traveler is wearing—business or leisure—he or she may behave differently in planning the trip and choosing accommodations.

The distinction between business and pleasure travelers has important implications for hotels. Business travelers, on the average worldwide, are much more likely to stay in hotels. Not surprisingly, business demand tends to be relatively upscale, more stable, and generally not as price-sensitive as non-business travel. For the pleasure traveler, value is a greater consideration in selecting accommodations; ambience and recreational facilities are also important.

Business Travelers. Trips for pleasure or pure tourism outnumber business trips, but business travelers are the largest users of hotel accommodations and services worldwide. Business travelers—over 70 percent of whom are white-collar employees whose expenses are usually company-paid—rate convenience, transportation schedules, and the comfort level of accommodations as their primary travel considerations. The following features are generally more important than cost to most traveling executives:

- Appropriate class of property
- Convenient location
- Comfortable surroundings
- Corporate and recreational facilities
- High service standards
- Inviting atmosphere
- Impressive lobby decor and room furnishings

In addition to travel for the purpose of conducting business or government transactions, business travel includes meetings, conferences, conventions, corporate gatherings, and educational activities. A more recent category is incentive travel, whereby a company uses travel as a motivator and reward for salespeople, dealers, distributors, and employees who meet or exceed sales quotas or other performance measures. Incentive travel is becoming an important segment of business travel.

Pleasure Travelers. About 40 percent of the worldwide demand for hotel accommodations is leisure-oriented. Pleasure travelers, whose expenses are usually out of pocket, are more likely than other travelers to share rooms or avoid hotels altogether, opting instead to stay with friends or relatives or use alternative types of lodging. They represent the most price-sensitive segment of the travel market. Discretionary travelers are quick to react not only to political situations, but also to economic conditions, price hikes, discount incentives, and so on. For this reason, airlines and hotels find that value packaging, loyalty awards, and other incentives will typically have greater effect with pleasure travelers than with business travelers.

Guest Origins. At a broad level, travelers may be classified as domestic or foreign. Each of these categories accounts for about half of the hotel business worldwide; however, there are wide variations by region. In North America, the domestic market has historically provided around 77 percent of hotel business, with foreign travelers accounting for 23 percent. In Africa and the Middle East, the situation is more balanced. Foreign travelers account for 55 percent of hotel occupancy. Similarly, the European lodging market, as a whole, usually attracts a balanced mix of approximately 43 percent foreign travelers to 57 percent domestic visitors. But in some European tourism destinations such as Austria and Portugal, foreign stays are known to exceed 70 percent on the average.

Sources of Reservations. Sources of hotel reservations vary among the different regions of the world. On a worldwide basis in 2003, 34 percent of hotel reservations were made directly by the hotel guest; travel agents and tour operators accounted for 29 percent, and reservations systems for 17 percent.[13] Travel agents and tour operators play a more important role in Asia, Oceania, and Latin America than in any other region of the world, whereas North Americans have a greater tendency to book directly or through the Internet.

Challenges of the Globalized Lodging Industry

The globalization of the lodging industry has implications for both hotel companies and individual hoteliers. Certainly, flexibility and the ability to adjust one's style or corporate philosophy to circumstances and the environment are fundamental to success and acceptability. This requires that a number of differences be addressed.

One of the greatest challenges of international expansion is understanding and coming to terms with the cultural, political, social, and religious makeup of the host country. It is critical for one to become knowledgeable in these areas before building a hotel or undertaking a transnational obligation. There are as many different ways of conducting business as there are places to conduct business. Both the international hotel company and the prospective manager need to be aware of standard or prevailing business practices covering negotiating styles, government and business protocol, managerial prerogatives, and marketing approaches.

In many countries, community and internal organizational relationships, as well as business ties, need to be slowly and carefully cultivated to ensure a smooth functioning operation without undue business disruptions. Hotel operators must have a thorough knowledge of the financial, political, labor, and marketing climates of the countries in which they do business. Vast differences exist among countries in terms of customs, values, languages, and general work or social behaviors. Despite the already international nature of the lodging industry, hotel managers are often ill equipped to manage this diversity or to meet the varying needs of different nationalities as guests or workers.

Hotel managers operating in the new global environment must have a cosmopolitan outlook, as opposed to the more nationalistic view of the past. Tomorrow's international hotel managers may be perceived virtually as corporate citizens of the world. Their responsibilities may encompass working with owners from one country, imported workers from another, a diverse domestic or host-country workforce, and expatriate specialists and managers who have transferred from other properties—not to mention providing service to guests from many nations. Additionally, these international hotel managers must maintain satisfactory relationships with the hotel's corporate offices and the various interest groups in their host community. They are concerned not only with the well-being of their hotels, but with assisting sister hotels in the network and promoting the progress of their host countries and the evolving world economy.

Summary

In this chapter, we have looked at a number of changing environmental forces shaping the rise of transnational hotel companies in an increasingly globalized economy. Among the more significant changes affecting the worldwide lodging industry are such factors as the extraordinary political shifts of the latter twentieth and early twenty-first centuries; the dismantling of trade barriers by numerous governments to encourage foreign investments and to facilitate international business; the continuous growth of world travel and tourism over the past four decades; increased visitor flows within and beyond national borders; and the restructuring of the lodging industry with respect to scope, ownership, management, affiliation, and consumption behavior.

As the world moves into the new millennium, it is clear that future hotel managers and their staffs must be better prepared to work in an environment that will be undoubtedly different from the past. The climate of tomorrow's lodging industry promises to be more cosmopolitan in every sense of the word, one where people in this profession must know how to deal with cultural diversity in terms of transnational ownership and management, organizational structure, and global marketplace needs as the established order of the day.

Endnotes

1. World Trade Organization, *International Trade Trends and Statistics, 2002* (Geneva: WTO, 2002) and WTO press release, "Trade Recovered in 2002 but Uncertainty Continues," April 22, 2003.

2. United Nations, *World Investment Report, 2007* (New York and Geneva: United Nations, 2007).

3. Frank Go and J. R. Brent Ritchie, "Tourism and Transnationalism," *Tourism Management*, December 1990, p. 287.

4. Somerset Waters, *The Big Picture: Travel Industry World Yearbook,* 1990, p. 9.

5. World Travel & Tourism Council, *Progress and Priorities: 2008/09,* p. 5.

6. *Tourism Trends Worldwide and in East Asia and the Pacific 1980–1992,* World Tourism Organization, p. 12.

7. World Tourism Organization, *Tourism Highlights, 2007.*

8. Global Insight, Office of Travel and Tourism Industries to International Trade Administration, Department of Commerce.

9. David Edgell Jr., *International Tourism Policy* (New York: Van Nostrand Reinhold, 1990), p. 164.

10. http://www.census.gov/ipc/www/popclockworld.html.

11. Pat Hanlon, *Global Airlines: Competition in Transnational Industry,* Third Ed. (Oxford: Elsevier, 2007), pp. 308–309.

12. All figures in this paragraph are taken from a presentation given by John G. C. Kester of the World Tourism Organization at the International Hotel & Restaurant Association Annual Statutory Meetings held in Nice, France, on October 27, 2006.

13. Horwath International, *Worldwide Hotel Industry Study 2003.*

Key Terms

globalization—The move toward a world economy and market.

gross domestic product—Income from production within a nation; this term excludes a country's earnings from another country; the term *gross net product* includes earnings from other countries.

multinational—A company having headquarters, as well as operations, in more than one country.

paradors—In Spain, historic buildings such as castles, palaces, convents, and monasteries converted into hotels and operated by the government.

pensions—European guesthouses or boarding houses.

posadas—State-operated inns in Spain and Portugal; also called pousadas.

ryokan—Traditional Japanese lodging accommodations with *tatami* mat floors and Japanese landscaped gardens.

transnational—A company having headquarters in one country and operations in several countries.

travel demand determinants—Factors instrumental in influencing travel.

Review Questions

1. What factors have contributed to globalization and a global economy?
2. What are transnational hotel companies?
3. What types of businesses does the tourism industry comprise?
4. What are tourism's major contributions to the world?
5. How does the volume of domestic travel compare with the volume of international travel in large, developed countries? in smaller countries sharing a common border with a larger country?
6. What factors have influenced travel growth in the Asia-Pacific region?
7. International travel is affected by what economic determinants? other determinants?
8. What demographic changes are likely to have a significant effect on the international lodging industry?

Chapter 2 Outline

Historical Aspects
    The Development of Chains
    Development Abroad
American Hotel Chains
    Separation of Ownership from Management
    Segmentation and Foreign Expansion
Profiles of Selected International Chains That Began in America
    Hilton
    InterContinental
    Sheraton
    Holiday Inn
    Hyatt
    Choice Hotels International
European Chains
    Club Méditerranée
    Accor
    Le Méridien
    Sol Meliá
Indian Chains
    The Taj Group
    Oberoi
Asia-Pacific Chains
    New Otani
    Nikko
    Mandarin Oriental
    Peninsula
    Dusit Thani
An African Chain
The Airline Connection
    Advantages of Linkage
    Disadvantages of Linkage
    Major Linkages
Mergers and Acquisitions
    Consolidation
    Strategic Alliances

Competencies

1. List the innovations introduced by American hotels in the early twentieth century, trace the development of U.S. hotel chains from 1901 to World War II, and identify some of the risks that deterred American hotels from expanding internationally. (pp. 25–28)

2. Summarize the post-World War II developments that led to international hotel expansion. (pp. 28–29)

3. Outline the factors affecting international hotel expansion into European, North American, Middle Eastern, and Asia-Pacific markets. (pp. 29–34)

4. Describe the separation of hotel ownership from management and explain its significance, and summarize the two-pronged growth strategies of hotel chains. (pp. 34–35)

5. Identify six international hotel chains that began in the United States, and describe the innovations they introduced. (pp. 35–40)

6. Identify four European, two Indian, one African, and five Asia-Pacific hotel chains, and describe their distinguishing characteristics. (pp. 40–51)

7. Summarize the development of airline-hotel relationships and cite the chief advantages and disadvantages of hotel-airline alliances. (pp. 51–53)

8. Describe the effects of mergers and acquisitions, consolidation, and strategic alliances on the international lodging industry. (pp. 54–56)

2

The Emergence of International Hotels

THROUGHOUT ITS HISTORY, the lodging industry has been in a constant state of evolution as it has tried to better meet the needs and expectations of the traveling public. Hotel products themselves reflect changing trends, lifestyles, and economics, as well as transportation and technological advancements and shifting politics. Over the past century, the industry has introduced many innovations, ranging from indoor plumbing to sophisticated telecommunications systems, computerized energy systems, international reservations networks, and information technology—based in-room amenities and services.

Recessions, political conflicts, energy crises, inflation, skilled labor shortages, low productivity, severe overbuilding, competition, foreign exchange fluctuations, debt and cash flow crunches, and numerous ownership changes have all had an impact on hotel occupancy rates and profitability at some time. Adversity, however, has never impeded the progress of the lodging industry; if anything, environmental changes have generally served to improve the variety and quality of hotel products, putting affordable hotel services within the reach of the public in a large part of the world. The new global marketplace promises to make the hotel business of the future infinitely more challenging and, at the same time, to present new opportunities for growth.

Historical Aspects

The hospitality industry has come a long way from the primitive inns of centuries past where transient lodgings often consisted of little more than a crudely furnished room with a pallet for a bed.

Innkeeping first flourished under the Roman empire. At its peak, the empire had 51,000 miles of roads with inns placed at every 30-mile mark. Each of the main cities had a fair-sized hotel, usually owned and managed by the municipal government. Largely because of the protection provided by the empire, there was more travel during this period than there had been at any previous time. With the decline of the Roman empire, long-distance travel diminished and was once again undertaken only when absolutely necessary. Religious pilgrimage became the primary travel motivation, and hospitality on the road fell largely to charitable organizations and religious orders.[1]

Commercial ventures in hospitality reappeared with the emergence of strong cities and nation states, mostly in Europe. In England, for example, inns gained a reputable standing around the fifteenth century, often being named after the powerful families on whose land holdings they were established. Like their Roman predecessors, these inns were primarily alehouses that sometimes provided rough overnight accommodations. With the development and extension of the first public transport system—the intercity stagecoach network—the volume of travelers grew rapidly, as did the number of inns to serve them. The advent of the railroad in the early nineteenth century encouraged the establishment of new and larger hotels near train stations, heralding a new era for the lodging industry. Locations near the wharfs of maritime cities were also popular sites for hotels.

In the 1800s, the U.S. lodging industry achieved international recognition with the opening of the Tremont House in Boston in 1829. The Tremont's architect, Isaiah Rogers, became famous for his hotel designs, which were imitated in Europe and elsewhere.

In the early twentieth century, sleeping rooms, even in luxury hotels, were still generally small and uncomfortable, and guests spent most of their time relaxing or socializing in spacious lobbies, libraries, or similar public rooms. America's E. M. Statler was one of the first to recognize that not all guests wanted to socialize and that many would prefer the privacy of their rooms. His hotels were among the first to offer private baths, larger guestrooms, room service, in-room radios, and hotel-to-hotel reservation services.[2] Many of the basic amenities and operating controls that are among today's industry standards—running water, telephones, and light switches by the door—were Statler innovations.

Other technological advances introduced by U.S. hotels—indoor plumbing, sewage disposal systems, central heating, air conditioning, the passenger elevator, electric lighting, and the application of modern communication systems to the hospitality industry—were quickly adopted by hotels internationally. In the late twentieth century, hotels continued to adapt their amenities, designs, and services to customize their products to the changing lifestyles and needs of their guests. The introduction of hotel spas, business centers, self check-in kiosks, design-based boutique hotels, non-smoking hotels, and innovative bathroom and bedroom fixtures (such as the heavenly bath and heavenly bed introduced by Starwood Hotels) are examples of recent market-induced innovations that continue to be adopted by hotels internationally.

The Development of Chains

For centuries, the hotel business could at best be described as a cottage industry, each hotel being a privately owned, independent enterprise. Occasionally, a well-known hotel would successfully spin off a few namesakes under the same management but such examples were few and far between. The first notable exception was the César Ritz group. Ritz was usually paid a retainer to appoint and oversee the managers of separately owned hotels. That arrangement, a precursor of the hotel management contract of later years, also allowed the hotel to advertise itself as a Ritz hotel. The Ritz chain peaked near the end of the nineteenth century with luxury hotels established in many major European cities and beyond, including Cairo, Johannesburg, and New York.[3] Today, the Ritz name remains synonymous with luxury and first-class service.

E. M. Statler, in addition to his many other contributions to innkeeping, developed one of the first modern chains. Starting with one hotel in 1901, the Statler enterprise expanded eventually to a chain of ten major hotels. Statler was the first to point out the economic and financial advantages of operating several large hotels under a single management. By centralizing purchasing, cost control, and marketing, he was able to improve operating profits. Most of his hotels were similar in name, style, and size. Despite Statler's success, the chain concept was slow to catch on in the period between the two world wars, and independent owners of some of America's then best known hotels generally looked down on chain operators.[4]

Conrad Hilton, Ernest Henderson, and Robert Moore were other early hotel pioneers who played significant roles in the development of the chain concept and were among the first to operate internationally. Conrad Hilton, in particular, is credited as the originator of the hotel management contract that fostered the growth of the hotel management company. Kemmons Wilson and Wallace Johnson, founders of Holiday Inn, fully capitalized on the chain concept during the 1950s and 1960s by franchising the Holiday Inn name and establishing a national reservations network. Franchising permitted more rapid chain expansion than was possible solely by managing and/or owning hotels. This course has since become a standard practice of many hotel and motel companies, especially in the budget category.

Pre–World War II Orientation. Although American hotel architecture and other technological and managerial innovations were being copied by hotels overseas, U.S. hotel companies did not venture outside the continental United States until after World War II. The British and the Swiss were the only national groups who went abroad to manage hotels in any number, but their foreign hotels were few. Although Ritz hotels in various countries relied for advice on the Ritz Management Company, they were not actually controlled by the company.

Hotel investment outside one's home country incurs high risks. For one, it is more difficult for a hotelier to discern the best locations in a foreign city or suburb. Financing, depending on the source, is usually more complicated and difficult to obtain—especially in the case of developing countries where construction, staffing, local customs, business methods, and so on can be radically different. Often, several sources of funding may be required when no one bank is willing to assume the risk of underwriting the total loan. Also, the risk of nationalization or a drastic reduction in hotel guests during times of political upheaval is ever present. Like any other international business, hotels operating abroad have their problems with currency fluctuations and restrictions on the **repatriation** of profits. Additionally, foreign hotel chains often face competition from domestic hotels, sometimes from hotels that are government-owned and -subsidized.

Before World War II, these and other problems were sufficient to deter American hoteliers from investing money in hotels abroad. Besides, the industry's economic focus was essentially domestic and there were enough changes in the American market to keep life interesting at home. This situation changed with World War II. News reports and the newsreels in theaters all over America provided coverage of U.S., Allied, and Axis forces in far-off lands as the war progressed. American soldiers, their families, and the average citizen became more familiar with exotic names of places around the globe. With the return of peace and prosperity, there was a natural desire for Americans to travel to places made familiar by war and the media.

Post–World War II Developments. Early international expansion efforts were initiated to some degree by the American imperative for economic development of lesser-developed countries. U.S. President Franklin D. Roosevelt, as part of his "good neighbor" policy toward Latin America, encouraged several U.S. corporations to build hotels in that region. Roosevelt saw this as a means of improving the economic performance of Latin American and Caribbean nations through increased tourism and foreign-exchange earnings from the United States, and as one of the ways to achieve his goal of "hemisphere solidarity."

Pan American Airways (Pan Am), then America's preeminent international carrier, responded quickly to the call for international hotel development. However, Pan Am's efforts to build a hotel abroad did not get under way until 1946, when it formed InterContinental Hotels Corporation (IHC) as a wholly owned subsidiary. IHC had a dual role: to serve international travelers, especially Pan Am passengers, and to house airline crews. The first InterContinental hotel, located in Belem, Brazil, was acquired in 1949. By 1982, when Pan Am sold its hotel subsidiary to Grand Metropolitan, InterContinental had expanded to 109 hotels worldwide.[5] Hilton's first project in Puerto Rico in 1948 was also to some extent an answer to the call to assist the region.

The post-war role of the U.S. lodging industry in the economic development of Latin America and the Caribbean had a parallel in Europe. The urgent task of reconstructing the war-torn economies of the Continent became a prime concern of U.S. foreign policy after the war, and American hotel companies were encouraged to assist. Additionally, European study groups were organized to visit the United States for the purpose of learning about and adopting advances in American hotelkeeping in order to better serve the particular hospitality needs of the American tourist. All of this helped to promote the internationalization of the lodging industry.

Air Transportation Links. Just as earlier forms of sea and land transport had influenced the development of inns, hotels, motels, and resorts along major seaports, transit routes, and terminal points, air transportation had an impact on hotel development by extending the industry's geographic reach. Besides the pioneering efforts of InterContinental and Hilton in international hotel operations in Latin America and the Caribbean, the Paris-based Club Méditerranée was also active in building holiday resorts during the early 1950s, initially in the Mediterranean countries, then in the Caribbean.

During the late 1950s, the air charter industry made new Mediterranean destinations available to Europeans. In Western Europe, this signaled the beginning of mass demand for tour packages and the construction of hotels in new resort destinations. The Boeing 707 was placed into regularly scheduled transatlantic service in 1959, reducing travel time across the Atlantic from weeks by steamship (or about 13 hours by propeller-driven aircraft) to about eight hours and putting an end to the era of transatlantic luxury steamship travel. As jet transportation became faster, cheaper, and more widely available, travel for business and pleasure accelerated, giving rise to the development of large, modern inner-city hotels in such places as London, Paris, Rome, Athens, and Amsterdam. Gradually, long-distance travel that was previously available only to the relatively affluent became accessible to the middle class, and mass travel and hotel development soared.

Development Abroad

As the world gradually converged toward a global marketplace, lodging chains, management companies, and developers all began looking for opportunities to serve an ever-increasing international clientele. Large hotel companies also realized that a strong overseas presence helped domestic properties gain a share of the foreign travel market. The economics of comparative advantages played a role in foreign hotel development, especially in developing countries where the costs of land and labor, if not always material and capital, are substantially less than in developed countries.

Circumstances at home often affect hotel development abroad. Domestic hotel companies in the United States, for instance, have at times been encouraged to go abroad because of overcapacity or saturation in their home markets. Moreover, many companies, having simply run out of viable locations for their particular niche products, look abroad for new opportunities to expand.

Until the 1960s, the developed areas of the world attracted most of the attention of the international hotel companies. The earliest efforts focused on developments in large gateway cities and world capitals, since these properties would pose the lowest financial risks and attract the most investors. The general strategy was to get the brand name established in large cities and then move into secondary markets and resort areas. With the widespread use of jet aircraft for mass travel, international hotel companies began to increase their presence in the developing parts of the world.

Expansion in Europe. The first international hotel chains to expand into Europe were American chains that followed American transnational manufacturing companies during the period of reconstruction after World War II. In 1946, the Interdepartmental Foreign Travel Committee of the U.S. government began to consider the role of travel and tourism in the new international order and the contribution this sector could make to the expansion of trade, the creation of financial stability, and the promotion of economic understanding. It was determined that the potential foreign-exchange earnings for Europe from U.S. tourism flows would eliminate the problems of the "dollar gap" and should be made an integral part of the Marshall Plan to help Europe help itself. As a result, U.S. hotels were encouraged to expand on the Continent.[6]

While European hotel chains were also developing during this period—for instance, Charles Forte purchased Trust Houses to create Trusthouse Forte and Joseph Maxwell formed the Grand Metropolitan chain in the United Kingdom—they generally remained within their national boundaries.

It was primarily in the well-established international gateway cities such as London, Paris, and Rome that the chains established themselves. Cities in Ireland, Spain, and Scandinavia did not attract much interest at this point, partly because they were developing their own domestic hotel chains, and also because few U.S. manufacturers moved into these areas during the period of post-war reconstruction.[7]

As intra-European air traffic grew, European hotel chains began to expand across the Continent. Like their American counterparts, the European chains had as their largest market domestic travelers seeking familiar hotel accommodations. The energy crisis of 1973 and the recession that followed virtually halted European hotel construction, and interest in Europe by international hotel chains waned. With the emergence of new capital markets fostered by growing oil wealth and export trade, attention was diverted to the Middle East and, gradually, the Pacific Basin.

It was not until the latter part of the 1980s that a second wave of international hotel chains began to develop an interest in Europe, spurred by the European Economic Community's decision to move toward a single European market by removing trade barriers among its member nations. International hotel chains such as Ramada, Marriott, Nikko, Oberoi, and Taj International all looked to establish themselves in European cities.

Since most of the prime locations in Europe were taken during the first round of development in the 1960s and 1970s, it has been more difficult to secure suitable sites in well-established cities; consequently, international hotel operators have had to consider the purchase of existing properties for expansion or redevelopment. Chains have been aggressively seeking locations in cities that are growing as a result of having attracted new technology-based industries or having become major financial centers. Such cities as Vienna and Brussels, which play an important role in international affairs, have attracted considerable interest from international chains, as have the burgeoning cities and sunbelt destinations in the newly industrialized countries of Spain and Portugal. The Scandinavian countries, on the other hand, have received relatively little attention. Scandinavian cities are small, have well-established domestic hotel companies, and as a result offer few suitable sites for new international hotels.[8]

Not only is the cost of site purchase and construction in European cities generally much higher than in other regions, but planning restrictions and high labor costs impose further barriers to entry. Non-European chains have found this market more difficult to break into than Middle Eastern or Asian markets, since in Europe they have had to compete with established domestic hotel chains.

Europe currently has close to 38 percent of the world's hotel rooms, although many hotels located outside the big cities are privately owned and run, and small family-run properties are common. The degree of hotel chain penetration in Europe varies by country. Generally speaking, countries that are home to large nationally-based hotel groups such as France, Spain, Germany, and the UK have the highest amount of chain penetration, which ranges from 25 percent to 35 percent of the total number of rooms.[9] Because of the volume of travel to this region, and with the opening of Eastern Europe to western tourism and development, Europe as a whole remains an important market for major international hotel chains and investors.

Expansion and growth in Europe in recent years has been, and in the future will be, driven by a combination of new capital sources such as private equity funds, high net worth individuals from the Middle East seeking trophy properties, the use of real estate investment trusts (REITs) as an equity investment form, and the increasing opportunities emanating from Eastern and Central European countries as they are absorbed into an expanding European Union.[10]

Expansion in North America. Except for the presence of a few Canadian-based chains, the lodging industry of North America was virtually the exclusive province of U.S. chains and independent operators until fairly recently. Today, the situation has changed to become a two-way street, with offshore hotel companies expanding into North America as North American hotel companies continue their expansion abroad. The latter part of the 1980s marked a turning point when foreign hotel corporations began to entrench themselves into the U.S. market, attracted by such factors as the stability of the U.S economy and lower construction and operating costs than in many of the newly industrialized countries. Perhaps the single most important factor was the availability of comparatively cheap real estate in the United States due to the decline in value of the dollar and the vulnerability of financially weak hotels.

The acquisition of Hilton International by Ladbroke PLC, Travelodge and Viscount by Forte PLC, Westin Hotels by Aoki Corporation, and InterContinental Hotels by Seibu Saison, Omni by Wharf Holdings, the Aircoa Group by Regal and the merger of Holiday Corporation with the hotel division of Bass PLC were all products of the changing business environment of the 1980s. Deregulation and loose credit policies led to overexpansion in the United States and resulted in an over-supply of hotel products in the early 1990s. This over-supply, coupled with recession, a liquidity crisis, the first Gulf War, the bursting of the Japanese bubble economy, uncertainty over the effects of the European Union, and a financial crisis in the Eastern bloc, halted the expansion of the lodging industry until the mid-1990s.

The U.S. lodging industry entered a recovery mode and expanded from the mid-1990s to 2000 as a result of new capital sources, increased demand, an information technology—fueled economy, and operating efficiencies as a result of a wave of mergers and acquisitions resulting in a more consolidated industry.

Despite the slowdown immediately following the 2001 terrorist attacks and subsequent war in Iraq, the period from 2003 to the present has seen very strong performance in the U.S. lodging industry. A flood of inexpensive debt and the rise of private equity funds have fueled industry expansion. The weakness of the U.S. dollar and the ability to invest in hotel companies either through private equity or public companies has resulted in the growth of foreign investments into North American hotel sector.

Foreign investment has also entered the Canadian lodging industry—a market in which major U.S., British, French, and Asian companies have all sought to strengthen their influence.

Expansion in the Middle East. Hotel developers and operators were attracted to the Middle East in the early 1970s by the region's newfound economic prosperity. The enormous increase in wealth of Middle East oil-producing countries following OPEC's price rises in the early 1970s triggered a round of hotel construction. Oil-rich royal families built large and ultra-luxurious properties for themselves and their business associates. The high-risk factors associated with economic and political instability and the complex problems of hotel development were counteracted with the promise of high room rates and high occupancies. Several hotel chains went ahead with ambitious expansion plans operating under the philosophy that the risks were worth taking in the new burgeoning market.

As the price of oil slumped in the 1980s, however, so too did room occupancies and hotel profits. The region's failure to broaden its economic base sufficiently to weather the slump also proved a detriment to tourism growth. Continuing political difficulties in Iran, Iraq, Kuwait, Israel, and other areas exacerbated the situation. During one of the upheavals in Iran, for example, all three of the Hyatt properties were taken over by the government. The first Persian Gulf War itself brought the lodging industry to a virtual standstill. Consequently, hotel development interest in most parts of the Middle East waned significantly until the mid-1990s.

Since then, the Middle East has become the fastest growing region in terms of tourism arrivals, with a compound annual growth rate of 10.2 percent from 1995 to 2006 based on WTO statistics. High oil prices and the resulting affluence in the region have resulted in a high amount of intraregional tourism. Led by regional superstars such as the UAE and Dubai in particular, who have made tourism development the centerpiece of their economic diversification strategy, the Middle East is seeing an all-time high in foreign direct investment in the hotel sector. In addition, the major international brands have an increasing presence in the region. Hospitality Valuation Services, an international investment advisory firm, estimates that the region will have approximately 82,000 new hotel rooms in the next four years, of which 50 percent are expected to be developed in the UAE.[11]

Expansion in the Asia-Pacific Region. During the past three decades, many international hotel chains have concentrated their development activities in Asia, particularly in the Pacific Rim countries. The new properties have typically been large luxury hotels affiliated with major international brands. Mass travel came late to the region and demand for accommodations has been supported by the high growth rate of tourism. Small hotels do not fit well with the huge volume of organized travel that the Asia-Pacific region hosts. Initially, brand-name international class hotels were established and operated by such U.S. hotel chains as Hilton International, InterContinental, Hyatt International, Sheraton, Holiday Inns, and a few others. By the 1980s, European, Japanese, and Asian brand-name hotels began to appear in many of the primary and sometimes secondary cities of Asia and the Pacific.

Asia-Pacific development was fueled in the 1970s by numerous reports predicting that the Pacific Rim would be the fastest growing economic area in the world as it entered the twenty-first century. Exotic locales, shopping opportunities, and beautiful beaches in many areas, in addition to the region's flourishing commercial centers and expanding markets, made it a natural for visitors from all over the world. Nearly every hotel chain of stature pursued development in the area.

For example, when China opened to the West in 1978, its hotel stock expanded dramatically. Between 1984 and 1988 alone, hotel rooms in China increased 200 percent. In some cities, the result was a severe overcapacity. In other areas too, including Singapore and parts of Malaysia, Indonesia, Thailand, New Zealand, and Australia, hotel developers either overestimated the demand or underestimated the increase in supply of other new hotels being planned. China, however, received particular attention from international hotel developers and operators who assumed that the previously non-existent tourist industry and the opening of trade ties with other countries would result in high occupancies and large hotel profits. The country was already facing a severe room glut in most cities when the Tiananmen Square incident of 1989 put a large jolt into that country's tourist industry, cutting hotel occupancies to 20 to 30 percent levels virtually overnight.[12]

China still faces structural reform limitations, such as state ownership, inefficient management, and unprofitable domestic operations. However, a confluence of many factors in the last few years has led to a torrid pace of hotel real estate development and associated international hotel chain presence in China. These factors include the double digit growth of its economy, an increasing demand fueled by a rising middle class, the growth of its economic centers, its use of special economic zones, and the popularity of its tourism and recreational hubs, including Hong Kong and Macau. The Chinese government's emphasis on investing in modern transportation and the associated infrastructure of roads and airports, its inclusion of tourism as a priority sector in its five-year plan, and the growing desire and ability of the domestic Chinese tourist to travel within the country bodes well for all segments of the hotel industry, in particular the budget segment.

As a whole, international hotel companies have experienced mixed results in the Asia-Pacific region. Although early pioneers profited, latecomers found themselves competing in saturated markets facing overcapacity even as hotel development in the region continued. Sharp population increases in the area, together with rising levels of economic activity and standards of living in the newly industrialized countries and the proximity of emerging travel destinations, have unfolded great opportunities for travel to and from the region. Developers contend that the hotel developments anticipate future growth in tourism and business travel or real estate investments in which equity growth of the property is the real objective. Moreover, the higher gross operating margins (although they are not as high as they once were) make the operation of four- and five-star luxury hotels much more feasible in the Asia-Pacific region than in Europe or the United States.

Although overdevelopment exists in some cities, new resort destinations and business centers in countries such as China (Macau included), India, Vietnam, Thailand, and Singapore are receiving increased development attention. Several factors underpin this development and investment interest:

- Positive macro-economic indicators
- Strong hotel performance
- Liquidity provided by opportunity funds
- Asian REITs
- Improved connectivity provided by a surge in low cost carriers
- Regional and domestic investors buoyed by the profitable performance of their core (non-hospitality) businesses
- Intense competition among international hotel brands that each have focused Asia strategies in their growth plans

The convergence of these factors has resulted in the growth of new and unique hotel products and the development of entirely new tourism destinations. Macau and Singapore, with their casinos, MICE (meetings, incentives, conferences and conventions, events and exhibitions), entertainment, hotel- and retail-driven integrated resort products, are examples of these growing mega destination development projects.

American Hotel Chains

Although the early traditions of hostelry were established in Europe, it was clearly the Americans who facilitated globalization of the lodging industry. American chains are responsible for the separation of property ownership from hotel management, the segmentation of hotel products, the standardization of operations, the development of standards in hotel construction, chain marketing affiliation, franchising, and centralized computer reservation systems. This section deals with the separation of ownership from management and the segmentation of hotel products.

Separation of Ownership from Management

A characteristic of the early hotel pioneers was that they were real estate oriented. Entrepreneurs owned the property and buildings they operated. They thought and dealt in terms of fundamental real estate values rather than hotel management. Managing a hotel was incidental to the goal of increasing the market value of a property over its book value, then selling the property and using the profits for other hotels.[13]

Hyatt was one of the first chains to recognize the advantages of separating a hotel's basic real estate from its operation. Hyatt separated the two aspects—business versus property—by setting up one company to operate the properties and another to own the real estate, a model many international hotel chains follow today. Eventually, most U.S. chains expanded by selling much of their capital-intensive real estate, while retaining management rights. Through the redeployment of assets, the process enabled chains to grow more rapidly, with emphasis on the acquisition of superior properties.

During the 1970s and 1980s, chains worked with owners and developers to open the newest, largest, and most upscale hotels, as the role of independent hotels became significantly reduced. The combined effect of **economies of scale** and the sheer size of the major chains has tended to put the independent operator at an increasing disadvantage. The ultimate boost to chains was given by lenders, who were generally more willing to advance funds for new properties when they were operated by a reputable chain.

Segmentation and Foreign Expansion

Facing an increasingly competitive marketing environment and needing to perpetuate their established growth patterns, chains began following a two-pronged approach: (1) developing segmented hotel products and (2) rapidly expanding in foreign markets. Because the trend toward chain affiliation was newer abroad, the chains had a greater opportunity for gaining new market shares. For U.S. chains with prominent brand names, expansion in foreign markets became an important factor in their overall growth strategies.

In the early years of tourism development, foreign governments assumed the financial risk for hotel projects by providing guarantees or equity participation, while the hotel company provided name recognition in addition to operational and marketing expertise. A brand name and expertise were essentially what countries wanted to buy. Indeed, the first American hotel in an overseas country usually ended up serving as that country's hotel school for training local people for hospitality employment elsewhere in the country.

The early American chains on foreign shores, such as Hilton and InterContinental, were able to negotiate attractive contracts with little more at stake than the provision of plans, personnel, and sometimes soft loans or deferred fees. The market has since become more competitive; some form of equity participation is often required and management contracts are not as favorable to hotel companies as they once were. The days when hotel operators could demand and get a healthy percentage of gross operating profit, and therefore a guaranteed low-risk profit, are over. In many cases now, international management contracts require the operator to provide certain performance guarantees to the owner. In many Chinese hotel management contracts, the presence and role of an owner's representative is a standard clause in the agreement. American chains now face a barrage of European and Asian hotel chains that can match them in service standards and outbid them with equity from cash-rich investors.

The international lodging industry is still dominated by American companies, however. Of the top 50 hotel chains in the world, 25 have their headquarters in the United States. But European and Asian companies are rapidly progressing, through acquisitions, mergers, and physical expansion.

Profiles of Selected International Chains That Began in America

Hilton

In 1919, Conrad Hilton traveled to Cisco, Texas, to buy a bank and cash in on the profits of the oil boom then under way. As it turned out, the bank wanted too much money, but Hilton noted that the local rooming houses were prospering from the large population of oil workers. Hilton convinced his partners to buy the Mobley Hotel instead. His assessment of the hotel's financial promise was correct and Hilton was on his way to becoming one of world's most renowned hoteliers. By 1930, Hilton owned or controlled eight properties. During the Great Depression, Hilton defaulted on many of his loans and several hotels were repossessed. Acknowledged for his management expertise, however, he was asked to operate many of the foreclosed hotels and, by 1939, he had managed to reassume control or ownership of most. Hilton was again ready to expand and did so by acquiring some of the grandest hotels of the day—The Plaza, the Palmer House, the Stevens (which later became the Conrad Hilton), and eventually the Waldorf-Astoria. Hilton also managed to acquire the Statler Hotel chain in what was, at the time, the largest private real estate transaction in history.

After World War II, a number of factors laid the groundwork for Hilton's international expansion: a strong U.S. dollar, pent-up travel demand, greatly improved commercial air travel, and the Marshall Plan. In 1947, Hilton became the first hotel company to be listed on the New York Stock Exchange. In 1949, Hilton International was formed as a wholly owned subsidiary of Hilton Hotels to manage properties outside the United States. Hilton had no interest in owning foreign real estate. His strategy was to provide technical design assistance, his name, and management expertise to local governments or investors. Thus was born the modern hotel management contract.

Hilton actually had secured his first management contract in 1948 to operate the first major hotel built by the Commonwealth of Puerto Rico under its "Operation Bootstrap" program for rapid economic growth. The success of the Caribe Hilton was the forerunner of a tourism boom for the island, as well as for many other Caribbean countries and for Hilton International. It was followed by similar arrangements in Madrid, Istanbul, and Mexico City. By 1964, Hilton International operated 29 hotels in 22 countries.

In 1964, Hilton International was spun off from Hilton Hotels Corporation and became a public company. Hilton Hotels retained the exclusive right to the Hilton name in the United States and Hilton International retained the exclusive right to the Hilton name outside the United States. The only remaining connection between the two companies would be the jointly owned Hilton Reservation Service. With the increasing globalization of travel, Hilton International established Vista International in 1979 in order to expand hotel operations in the United States. Likewise, in 1983 Hilton Hotel Corporation created a subsidiary, Conrad International, to develop hotels outside the United States.

Hilton International was bought by TWA in 1967, sold to the Allegis Corporation in 1987, and later that year sold again to Ladbroke Group PLC, when Allegis disbanded. Since that time, the most extensive development program in the company's history has been implemented. In 2006, Hilton Hotels Corporation acquired the lodging assets of Hilton International, which made Hilton Hotels a seamless global company with nearly 3,000 hotels in 78 countries. In its most recent transaction in 2007, Hilton Hotels Corporation was privatized as it merged with The Blackstone Group, a private equity firm.

InterContinental

InterContinental, or InterContinental Hotels Corporation (IHC), was formed in 1946 as a wholly owned subsidiary of Pan Am. As earlier noted, Pan Am had been urged by President Roosevelt to form a subsidiary hotel company to help promote tourism and trade, and to strengthen diplomatic relations with South America. The first hotel opened in Belem, Brazil, and IHC hotels were soon spread throughout Latin America and the Caribbean.

During the early 1960s, InterContinental opened hotels to serve the growing number of airline passengers on both business and pleasure trips in Europe, Asia, Africa, and the Pacific. In Asia, IHC was the first company—long before others—to open on the exotic island of Bali in Indonesia. So high was the demand for space that in order to secure room reservations, travelers also had to book their flights on

Pan Am. Also in the early 1960s, the first InterContinental hotel in the Middle East opened in Lebanon and quickly established its leading position in the region. By 1964, the chain had also made inroads into Eastern Europe and in the 1980s IHC was the leading international hotel group represented in that region. The 1970s saw a period of rapid growth; despite being located in many of the world's trouble spots, InterContinental continued acquiring new properties. The company eventually became a two-tier operator by re-designating lesser properties as Forum Hotels and reserving the InterContinental name for classic and newer properties.

IHC is known for its unique hotel architecture, which is typically designed to reflect the local environment. The chain is also noted for its restoration of hotels. Palaces, government buildings, and coach houses are among the structures Inter-Continental has chosen for its restorations. There is probably no finer example of the company's commitment to the cultural environment than IHC's restoration and transformation of the former treasury building in Sydney, Australia, into an outstanding hotel.

InterContinental was sold to Grand Metropolitan PLC, one of the largest diversified companies in the United Kingdom in 1981 for $500 million. The chain was purchased in 1988 by Saison Overseas Holdings B.V., which was owned by the Saison Group of Japan and by SAS International Hotels. In 1991, SAS sold its stake to the Saison Group.

InterContinental was then acquired by Bass hotel holdings in 1998, when the British brewing company made several strategic cross border hotel acquisitions. After Bass Brewers was sold (along with the name "Bass"), the hotels group became Six Continents in 2000. Three years later, InterContinental Group was formed by separation into two operating companies with all the hotels and soft drinks going to InterContinental Hotels Group PLC. Currently, IHG is the largest hotel company in the world with over 3,800 hotels under seven distinct brands in over 100 countries. The company in recent years moved back to its franchising and management contract roots by divesting most of its real estate and focusing on an "asset light" strategy, deriving most of its revenue from franchise fees and management contracts.

Sheraton

In the depth of America's Great Depression, two Boston entrepreneurs, Ernest Henderson and Robert Lowell Moore, found themselves in possession—through mortgage defaults and small cash payments—of several run-down New England hotels. Although neither had any experience in lodging, the partners soon had ambitions for a budding hotel chain. Since one of their new acquisitions bore an expensive electric roof sign with the name "Sheraton," which would cost too much to remove, the name was adopted for all other units. After World War II, the founders acquired additional distressed properties and, through judicious upgrading, enhanced their value. In 1949, Sheraton acquired two Canadian hotel chains, thus becoming an international chain. The 1961 opening of the Tel Aviv Sheraton marked the company's first inter-continental linkage.

Innovation and expansion have been the hallmarks of Sheraton's success. "Reservatron," launched in 1958, became the industry's first automated electronic reservations system, and made Sheraton the first chain to centralize and computerize the reservations function. Sheraton was also the first consumer company to develop a toll-free telephone system for direct consumer access.

Sheraton's growth accelerated after 1968 when it became a wholly owned subsidiary of ITT, and a global perspective has been the basis for Sheraton's development philosophy ever since. Opportunities in places like China, Africa, and the Eastern Bloc were aggressively pursued and welcomed into the Sheraton network. Sheraton currently operates in 61 countries, with a network of owned, leased, managed, and franchised hotels, inns, resorts, and all-suite properties.

In 1985, Sheraton became the first international hotel company to open a hotel in China bearing its own name—The Great Wall Sheraton Hotel Beijing. Sheraton was also the first Western hotel company to sign a joint venture with the Soviet Union to develop hotels in Moscow.

Sheraton became a part of Starwood Lodging (now Starwood Hotels & Resorts) in 1998 when it acquired ITT Sheraton Corporation for $14.8 billion. It is the largest brand in Starwood's portfolio of almost 900 properties and 265,000 hotel rooms in 95 countries. The Sheraton brand (including its select service brand, 4 Points by Sheraton) consists of 522 hotels (58 percent of Starwood) and 148,000 rooms. As with InterContinental Hotels, Starwood's growth strategy centers on franchising and management contracts, with selective investments in hotel real estate.

Holiday Inn

Dissatisfaction with motels during a family trip in 1951 persuaded Kemmons Wilson to start his own company offering standardized motels across the United States. Wilson built the first four Holiday Inns himself and then took on a partner, Wallace Johnson, to help him build additional units. Limited amenities, clean rooms, low rates, and attention to detail were the guiding principles for the first Holiday Inns. Neither partner had hotel experience, but they developed a team of enthusiastic young professionals, instituted modern financial and management techniques, and became the largest hotel chain in the United States. In 1960, Holiday Inn operated its first property outside the United States, in Montreal. The chain entered the European market in 1968, the Asian market in 1973, and the South American market in 1974.

Wilson and Johnson were the first to fully capitalize on the chain concept during the 1950s and 1960s by franchising the Holiday Inn name and establishing a national reservations network. They realized that, with very little capital investment (since the responsibility for capital funding of the hotel project was passed on to the franchisee), the returns to the franchisor could be extremely high. Design, construction, and purchasing costs could be kept low and marketing costs and overhead could be spread over a wider base. Travelers became familiar with the brand name and would call the national reservations center, knowing there would likely be a Holiday Inn in their intended destination. Holiday Inn's franchising concept was soon copied by most other major hotel companies.

Originally known for its motor inns along highways in the United States, the chain eventually took the name Holiday Corporation, moved into more urban areas, expanded internationally, and diversified with new lodging concepts. In 1989, the Holiday Inn brand was sold to Bass PLC. For many years the largest hotel company, Holiday Inn is now part of InterContinental Hotels Group and has a global room inventory of 416,000 rooms and 3,125 hotels, making it the largest brand in the IHG system, with 82 percent of its hotels.

Hyatt

Hyatt Hotels Corporation, founded by the Pritzker family of Chicago, was a late starter in the field of major upscale urban hotels, but was quick to catch up. In 1957, while on a business trip to Los Angeles, Jay Pritzker bought a small hotel near the soon-to-burgeon international airport and expanded rapidly afterwards. In 1967, the chain's premium upscale concept was born with the opening of the Hyatt Regency in Atlanta, featuring a dramatic lobby atrium that was to set the standard for many years. In these luxury properties, emphasis was placed on a "total experience" theme for upscale travelers, with deluxe amenities such as concierge services and fresh flowers and bathrobes in each room. Hyatt was one of the first major U.S. chains to place emphasis on unique in-hotel dining facilities, again stressing the total experience. The goal was not only to attract hotel guests to tables, but customers from the surrounding market as well.[14] Hyatt International was formed in 1969. The first hotel under Hyatt International management was the Hyatt Regency Hong Kong, followed by the Hyatt Regency Manila and the Hyatt Regency Acapulco. In 1989, Camp Hyatt, the industry's first chain-wide children's program, was introduced.

As mentioned earlier, Hyatt was one of the first chains to perceive the advantages of separating a hotel's basic real estate from the hotel's operating functions. The Pritzkers divided the operation by setting up one company to operate the properties and another to own the real estate.

In 2004, the Pritzker family consolidated its holdings by combining domestic and international hotels operations under the umbrella of Global Hyatt. Global Hyatt Corporation creates luxury and upscale hotels and has more than 700 hotels and resorts (and more than 136,000 rooms) in 44 countries. The company's affiliates own, operate, manage, and franchise Hyatt-branded hotels and resorts under the Park Hyatt, Grand Hyatt, Hyatt Regency, Hyatt Resorts, Hyatt, Hyatt Place, and Hyatt Summerfield Suites brands. In April 2007, Hyatt launched its newest global brand, Andaz. Global Hyatt Corporation is also the owner of Hyatt Vacation Ownership, Inc., and operator of the Hyatt Vacation Club and fractional residential properties and U.S. Franchise Systems, Inc, which franchises Hawthorn Suites and Microtel Inns and Suites.

Choice Hotels International

Established more than 50 years ago by seven southern hoteliers, Choice Hotels International, formerly known as Quality International, is today one of the largest franchise hotel systems in the world, with more than 3,000 hotels, inns, suites, and resorts comprising more than 271,000 guestrooms in 30 countries. These include hotels marketed under the Comfort, Quality, Clarion, Sleep, Rodeway, Econo Lodge, and Friendship names, and all-suite hotels in three market segments.

Choice Hotels' history since 1981 has been one of innovation and firsts in a number of areas. The original Quality Courts chain was the first such referral network in the industry. It was the first chain to implement a systemwide no-smoking rooms program, the first to introduce midpriced all-suites, and the first to pay travel agent commissions in every major foreign currency. Its most important contribution, however, was the introduction of the concept of brand segmentation within the hotel industry, establishing a three-tiered hotel system consisting of limited-service budget hotels; full-service midpriced hotels; and full-service luxury hotels.

The company's aggressive international expansion began in 1985 with the opening of two new reservations centers in Phoenix, Arizona, and London, England. Within a year, Choice had locations in Switzerland, Germany, and the United Kingdom. In 1986, the company added its first hotels in Italy and France and began development efforts in Ireland and India.

In 1989, the company stepped up its international development efforts, targeting Japan, Turkey, South America, and the Caribbean for future growth. Other areas of expansion include Canada, the United Kingdom, continental Europe, and Australia. In 1990, Quality International was renamed Choice Hotels International. In 1993, Choice continued its rapid international growth, entering into agreements with Journey's End in Canada and Premivere and Saphir Hotels in France. In 1996, Choice Hotels split from Manor Care, and the next year spun off its U.S. company-owned hotels as Sunburst Hospitality. It also sold its European holdings to former hotel brand Friendly Hotels to operate under Choice Hotels' brand names.

The company began a reimaging campaign in 2001 that included new logos for the Comfort Suites, Quality, and Sleep Inn brands. It also announced the creation of a centralized franchise-services department. In 2002, the company agreed to buy 55 percent of franchise partner Flag Choice Hotel, which franchises 400 properties in Australia and New Zealand. Embarking upon a major expansion campaign, the company added more than 15,000 rooms to its portfolio during 2004 to reach a total of about 400,000 rooms. The following year, Choice Hotels opened its 5,000th location. It also launched a new chain of select-service hotels, Cambria Suites, targeting primarily business travelers, and entered the extended-stay market by acquiring the Suburban Extended Stay Hotel brand from Suburban Franchise Systems. Its first Cambria Suites hotel opened in Boise, Idaho, in 2007.

Choice Hotels International follows an exclusive franchise model of business operations with more than 5,300 locations in the United States and about 40 other countries. Its flagship brands include Comfort Inn, one of the largest limited-service chains with more than 2,400 properties, and Quality Inn, which serves the midscale hotel segment through more than 1,100 locations. Its Econo Lodge chain offers lodging primarily for budget-minded travelers. Other brands include the full-service Clarion chain, Rodeway Inn budget hotels, and Sleep Inn. Approximately 22 percent of Choice's franchise agreements are international, with major concentrations in Canada, France, Australia, the United Kingdom, and Scandinavia.

European Chains

While the American chains were the first to venture abroad, European hotel chains eventually followed suit. At first the movement toward internationalization was slow, but it accelerated in the late 1980s when home markets stagnated. European chains adopted many U.S. hotel management techniques, often adding a European flavor, and then re-exporting the concept to the United States and elsewhere. European operators made extensive use of the management contract, but they were also willing to participate in equity to gain a presence in major markets.

Club Méditeranée

Club Méditeranée (Club Med) was founded as a sports association in France in 1950 by Gerard Blitz, a former member of the Belgian Olympic Team, along with a group of his friends. The initial Club Med venture was a "vacation village" in Majorca, Spain, which opened to a membership of 2,500. This first venture consisted of a tent village in which members slept in sleeping bags and took turns cooking meals and washing dishes.

Club Med's unique approach to vacationing stemmed from a belief that what urban people needed on vacation was a society and environment radically different from their daily lives—a society in which there were no barriers, rules, or restraints. All facilities were to be easily and freely available and dress was to be always casual. Club Med also had a policy of not having many modern-day "distractions" such as televisions, radios, newspapers, clocks, or phones, in keeping with its vacation escape philosophy. Each vacation village took on an architectural look reflective of the host country or region. A typical village featured bungalow-style units in small clusters.

By 1977, the Club operated 77 villages with 54,000 beds in 24 countries. The villages were located throughout the Mediterranean countries, the Caribbean, the Middle East, Africa, Mexico, and the South Pacific. With an active pay-for-stay membership (not a dues-paying membership) of over one million, Club Med was the largest vacation organization of its kind. Members were primarily from France, other Western European countries, and North and Central America.[15]

Since its inception, Club Med has attempted to anticipate societal and travel trends and respond with the right products. During the 1980s, the Club Med concept encountered some serious problems, one of the more important being demographic obsolescence. The Club had developed a reputation as a haven for swinging singles, but its prime market was maturing and was no longer satisfied with the Club Med experience. Married people with children made up a large portion of the market.

Club Med altered its services and facilities accordingly. Many villages were changed to provide a broader, wholesome family appeal, and the company's ads and brochures began to feature children. Several villages offered separate baby clubs for members with infants and mini-clubs for those with older children. Many properties were changed from the traditional "village" model to more closely resemble conventional resort hotels.

Club Med also noted the growing interest of corporations in using resorts for meetings and incentive travel trips and moved to take advantage of it. Under the banner "Rent-a-Village," it began renting entire club villages to corporations. Noting the trend toward weekend and mini-vacations, the Club in 1988 changed its policy of offering packages only in one-week units.[16] By the early 1990s, Club Med had added Club Jr. (for younger guests), Club Renaissance (for older guests), and "Les Villas" a chain of small upscale hotels designed to serve guests visiting nearby tourist attractions.

Club Med continues to be the leader in its field, and now operates in more than 30 countries. Based on the company's 2006 Annual Report, Club Med's growth strategy is to focus increasingly on the up-market customer base, which it estimates at 60 million worldwide. Furthermore, Club Med is expanding its service offerings to include special services for families and specifically infants and teenagers. Its current customer market base is still Europe, at about 68 percent; however, it expects future growth to occur in the Asian markets. Their present inventory of villages, boats, and villas is 86, with a total of 56,055 beds. About 58 percent of the inventory is leased, 35 percent owned and only about 7 percent under management contract.

Accor

Paul Dubrale and Gerard Pelisson built their first American-style motel on a French roadside in 1967. From that modest beginning, rooms, sales, and profits rose steadily as the company expanded. By 1992, Accor operated hotels in more countries than any other hotel chain.

The Mercure hotel chain was acquired by Dubrale and Pelisson in 1975 and the Sofitel chain in 1980. Originally known as Novotel, the Accor name was taken with the merger of Novotel and Jacques Borel International in 1983. Formule 1 was created in 1985, Motel 6 was acquired in 1990, and a merger with Pullman was completed in 1992.

The hotel company first entered the U.S. market in 1979 with the upscale Sofitel. Part of Accor's international expansion strategy, particularly with the upscale Sofitel hotels, has been to promote a strong food and beverage operation in order to attract local patrons and to compensate for the lack of name recognition in the United States. In some hotels, food and beverage sales generated as much as half of gross revenues.

One of the first hotel companies to recognize the value of segmentation, Accor operates numerous brands and lodging products, ranging from the four-star Sofitel and Pullman, three-star Novotel and Mercure, and two-star Ibis/Urbis to the one-star Formule 1 and Motel 6. It has another brand name, Hotelia, oriented toward older hotel guests. Well-known in Europe, Accor includes as its strengths its clearly defined products and its targeted audiences. Most hotels are affiliated through management contracts or franchise agreements.

In 1990, when Accor agreed to pay $2.3 billion for the U.S.-based budget chain Motel 6, many analysts considered the price an overpayment. Accor believed the brand name to be worth the price, particularly as Motel 6 operated under the same principle as Formule 1, offering a clean, comfortable room for the lowest price in the market. The Formule 1 concept is an innovative one. Guestrooms in France measure 97 square feet and have a double bed, bunk bed, wash basin, storage, worktable, wardrobe, and TV. A shower with an automatic self-cleaning system is placed between groups of four rooms. A manager is on duty several hours in the morning and evening; at other times, an automated teller machine takes over and guests obtain keys by inserting a credit card in a machine. Formule 1 is being cloned across Europe, and there are plans to apply similar cost-saving techniques to Motel 6.

Expanding largely through acquisition, Accor is the largest hotel company (with respect to the number of rooms managed) on the European continent and fifth largest in the world. It is continuing to grow internationally, stressing continued European expansion, but also looking to Asia and North America. The company currently has more than 4,000 hotels in 90 countries, of which 21 percent are company-owned, 40 percent are leased, 20 percent are operated under management contract, and 19 percent are franchised. More than 68 percent of its revenues are derived from operations in Europe, but it has aggressive growth plans in Asia, China in particular. It plans to lead this growth in Asia with the upper economy brand Ibis, which it plans to make the global market leader. Accor's growth strategy is based on a long-term business plan known as the Accor Model, the key elements of which are a well-balanced approach of geographical and brand distribution, a cautious approach to assess country and financial risks, and a well supported approach in which the growth is supported with network of resources such as a multi brand sales force, database driven revenue management, global reservation system, and strong brands.[17]

Accor holds a 28.9 percent stake in Club Med. As a result, both Accor and Club Med have entered into several customer-focused synergistic programs. Examples include joint purchasing agreements, cross selling links via websites, inclusion of Club Med in Accor's loyalty programs, and creation of a Club Med—generated fitness product for Sofitel and Novotel brands.

Le Méridien

Méridien was created in 1972 by Air France through the merger of company-owned hotels with other acquisitions to meet the airline's growing need to house passengers and to address the rooms shortage in Paris at that time. Méridien's initial name was Hotel France International. Soon after its establishment, however, the young chain merged with the privately owned French hotel company Les Relais Aeriens to form Societe des Hotels Méridien. The company initially managed hotels in France, then rapidly expanded its operations to the Middle East. Within 20 years, Méridien built a chain of 54 hotels in 50 cities worldwide, halfway to its goal of operating in 100 cities around the globe. Expansion has followed the pattern of Air France's routes. In 1976, Méridien began making its way into North America.

Air France's development of the Méridien chain was pursued, in part, because of the airline's desire to expand the French national culture. President Henri Marescot stated in 1977:

> We carry the flag for France in different places. All our food and beverage managers and chefs are French; we have French discotheques, French-oriented stores and cinema clubs that show French films every night. Things French have an attraction in faraway places and practically all the large hotels in the world today are controlled by American interests. Thus, the Méridien chain acts as a cultural projection of France.[18]

Méridien's policy is to run elegant hotels in which people feel comfortable. Most hotels are of medium size. In keeping with its cultural philosophy, Méridien's advertising continues to stress "French tradition" and "superlative French cuisine." Fashion being quintessentially French, uniforms worn by Méridien staff are created by French fashion designers. The company's strong commitment to cuisine is evidenced by its agreements with world-renowned French chefs to act as consultants to Méridien hotels outside France.

After a series of sales starting in 1996, Le Méridien was finally acquired by Starwood Hotels & Resorts in 2005 as a strategic acquisition to help Starwood enter markets where Le Méridien had a strong presence, namely Europe and Asia. In addition, the brand's European flair and passion for food, art, and style filled gaps in Starwood's portfolio of brands. There are currently 143 Le Méridiens globally. The brand is mainly concentrated in the Middle East, Africa, and Asia, where 66 percent of the hotels are located. Only about 6 percent of its hotels are located in the Americas.

Sol Meliá

Gabriel Escarrer Julia, founder and president of Grupo Sol, began working on the island of Majorca at the age of 15 as a Thomas Cook tour operator. In 1953, at age 18, he rented and operated the 35-room El Paso Hotel in Palma, Majorca's chief city. With the money made from this project, he went on to rent a second hotel. In 1956, Escarrer formed an independent hotel company, Hoteles Mallorquines. Throughout the 1950s and 1960s he continued to acquire hotels on Majorca and in 1974 he expanded the operation to the Canary Islands. The Sol Hotels brand name was adopted in 1976 to reflect expansion to the Costa del Sol region.

Escarrer acquired the Hotasa chain and its presence in Spain's major cities in 1984. An international division of Sol was established in 1985, and the first property outside of Spain was built in Bali, Indonesia. Cadena Meliá, a prestigious chain with hotels in Spain, Venezuela, Colombia, and Iraq was acquired in 1987 and Grupo Sol was formed as the parent company to oversee both the Sol and Meliá chains. Sol Hotels are three- and four-star resort properties, primarily oceanfront. Meliá is a five-star brand encompassing large resorts and urban business hotels.[19]

Grupo Sol, renamed Sol Meliá in 1996, is still based where it began on Majorca. It is strong in city and resort properties and is taking the acquisition route to grow both domestically and internationally. Sol Meliá is now Spain's largest, Europe's third largest, and the world's twelfth largest hotel firm. As of 2006, it operated 406 hotels, a majority of which are five-star properties, with 80,830 rooms in 35 countries. About 46 percent of its hotels are located in Spain, 22 percent in other parts of Europe, 3 percent in Asia, and 29 percent in Latin America and the Caribbean

On June 2, 1996, Sol Meliá became the first hotel management company in Europe to be floated on the stock exchange. Just prior to the flotation, the company had been split into two: Inmotel Inversions that owned the hotels and the new Sol Meliá S.A., a hotel management company and target of the flotation. The company was reintegrated with the property ownership company in 1999, which provided a strong spur for the company's growth.

In its overseas locations, Sol Meliá has attempted to deliver European-style service and ambiance. Most managers and supervisors at overseas properties come from Sol Meliá's own training school where they are indoctrinated in the company's philosophy and service standards. Each property offers a restaurant featuring Spanish cuisine. Though each of the Sol Meliá hotels has a unique structure appropriate to its setting, Spanish architects and designers are engaged. Its first U.S. property, near Disney World, was designed as a Spanish village with townhouse villas surrounded by gardens and lakes.

Indian Chains

Although India receives relatively few international visitors (4.6 million in 2006) and historically has given tourism low priority in national development, it is the home of several reputable international hotel chains.[20] The Oberoi and the Taj groups may not be as familiar to travelers as other hotel brands, but they are recognized in the industry for exceptional standards of quality and service. Well established in their native country, both hotel groups have slowly developed a network of properties outside India and in recent years have been aggressively seeking global expansion opportunities. Following the economic reforms in India after 1991, Indian hotel chains have recorded impressive performance results.

India's plentiful supply of labor and the friendliness of the Indian people provide the ingredients for a first-rate hotel industry. Training has also played an important role, with all the leading hotel groups having their own schools and in-house training programs. The emphasis on quality training is confirmed by the export of Indian hotel management expertise and the large number of Indians recruited to work at all levels in the hotel business abroad. Besides providing the training function, Indian hotel groups have also pursued other forms of vertical integration. Each group has its own travel agency/inbound tour operation, as well as catering and transport companies, engineering, architectural, and other consultancy services, hotel computer software development firms, retail shops, and so on.

The Taj Group

The Taj Group, a subsidiary of the Indian Hotels Company, which is part of the Tata group of companies, is generally considered the oldest hotel chain in India. Its flagship, the Taj Mahal Hotel in Bombay, opened in 1903. The establishment of this legendary hotel resulted from the needs of the steel industry. At the turn of the century, the development of an industrial base, including the construction of steel factories, was a national priority. To entice good engineers and architects to work at the plants, however, decent accommodations had to be found. The construction of the Taj Mahal Hotel satisfied this need. It was a single hotel enterprise until about 1970. Today, the Taj Group has grown to 82 hotels, including 16 international properties. The company remains based in Mumbai (formerly Bombay) and operates the company hotel assets under a varied ownership and operating structure. Some properties are directly owned by The Indian Hotels Company, others are partnerships and joint ventures with associate companies and subsidiaries, while another category is based on management contract arrangements with third-party owners.

The Taj Group is represented in all the major metropolitan cities and tourist towns in India. It is organized into three operating divisions: Taj Luxury Hotels, Taj Business Hotels, and Taj Leisure Hotels.

The Taj Group's international expansion started much later than Oberoi's, but it is now the leading Indian hotel group in terms of number of properties and rooms abroad. It is also the largest Asian-based hotel chain outside the Orient. Taj's expansion abroad has taken in all types and standards of properties, catering to every sector of the business and tourism markets. Many of the hotels do not carry the Taj name. The group has adopted a strategy of buying older hotels that have slipped in prestige in key international markets. Taj renovates the hotels in elegant fashion, then operates them under the company's high standards of service and comfort. The Taj Group's aggressive expansion plans include geographical growth, identification of emerging lifestyle niches, and marketing alliances. Besides growing domestically, its international expansion plans include the United States, the Middle East, Africa, and South Asia. Tapping into the growing economy segment of the domestic hotel industry, it recently launched Ginger to cater to the budget-conscious traveler seeking affordable and clean accommodations. Building on the Indian philosophy of healing and wellness, the Group has made a major commitment to the development and operation of spas. Also, in response to the growing need of some business travelers needing extended-stay accommodations due to client site assignments and to the rise of multinational company executives traveling and relocating to India, the company is seriously considering investments into the serviced apartment concept in India.

Oberoi

Oberoi Hotels, a subsidiary of East India Hotels, is the product of India's best-known hotel pioneer, Mohan Singh Oberoi. Oberoi started in the business as a front desk clerk in 1922 in Simla, then the summer capital of British India. He acquired his first hotel, the Clarkes Hotel in Simla, in 1934 by mortgaging all his assets and his wife's jewelry. The hotel industry in India was in its infancy at that time, and Oberoi became the first Indian national to enter the hotel field. Previously, Indian hotels were owned by British and Swiss families, and they primarily served British residents. Oberoi expanded his group of hotels and in 1965 introduced the first five-star deluxe hotel in India—the Oberoi InterContinental in New Delhi, managed by InterContinental for Oberoi.

Oberoi concentrates mainly on the deluxe end of the market, serving the domestic and international affluent traveler. Its five-star hotels stress personalized service to such an extent that the hotels employ an average of three persons per room.

Oberoi's expansion in India has been less significant than Taj's, though most of its 32 managed hotels are owned by the group and it often generates higher profits. Oberoi was the first Indian chain to look outside the country for expansion and has a presence in five countries outside India. International expansion was begun in the 1960s with the Soaltee Oberoi in Kathmandu and the historic Mena House Oberoi in Cairo. International expansion plans have slowed due to a change in development strategy: instead of aiming for growth in turnover and number of properties at the expense of profitability, the focus is on profitability and quality

The Mena House Oberoi, Cairo, Egypt. (Courtesy of Oberoi)

assurance so that all properties conform to the same deluxe standards. Oberoi has restricted its international expansion to the Middle East, North Africa, and Southeast Asia, partly through choice and partly because the right properties have not been available in other markets.

Asia-Pacific Chains

The rapid increase of international visitors to the Asia-Pacific region over the past 40 years has not only attracted the interest of Western hotel chains, it has also spawned the development of several Asian-based chains, primarily from Japan and Hong Kong. Cheap labor and available land were once major factors in the region's development strategies, but the impetus today is the region's strong economic growth. Many chains, firmly established in their own markets with sterling reputations, have now set aggressive overseas expansion plans. For example, Asia's three major Hong Kong–based hotels—Mandarin Oriental, Peninsula, and Shangri-La—which consistently appear on the list of the world's best hotels, continue to expand within the region, but also venture outside the region. The pioneering Tokyu Group in Japan continues to develop its Pan Pacific chain, and Japan's two airline-backed hotel chains, Nikko and ANA Hotels, are also expanding aggressively. The rapidly growing China-based Jin Jiang Hotels is currently ranked seventeenth in the world based on number of rooms.

Japanese hotel companies have expanded internationally primarily to meet the needs of Japanese travelers going abroad, while Hong Kong hoteliers have attempted to export and transplant their renowned and revered service quality standards. Even though labor is often more expensive outside of Hong Kong, these operators are counting on service to provide their competitive edge. Most of the Hong Kong hotels are owned and managed by people with hotel backgrounds, but another tier of Hong Kong hotel companies has recently emerged that is decidedly Chinese in origin and outlook. These companies are owned by Hong Kong Chinese families who have grown wealthy in real estate and are using their financial strength to enter the global hotel market, acquiring not only five-star hotels but also hotel management companies. They have made rapid progress in the past few years. The companies include New World Development Company (which currently has 15 hotels in Hong Kong, China, and Southeast Asia), Harbour Plaza Hotels & Resorts, the Hongkong and Shanghai Hotels, Ltd., and Regal Hotels.

A discussion covering a few of the more prominent Asian hotel chains follows.

New Otani

The original New Otani Hotel in Tokyo was completed just before the Olympic games in 1964—a time when the lodging industry was still a relatively foreign concept to most Japanese. Considered by many to be an innovative hotel, the New Otani was the tallest building in Japan and, with 1,000 rooms, the largest hotel in the country. It was the personal project of Yonetaro Otani, a self-made man, former sumo wrestler, and owner of a successful steel company. Yonetaro was asked by the governor of Tokyo to develop a hotel for the upcoming Olympic games and, although he had no former hotel experience, he accepted the challenge. Ten years after the original structure was built, an additional 40-story tower was added, and the 400-year-old ten-acre Japanese garden that surrounded the hotel was restored.

The New Otani group's first overseas operation was the New Otani Kaimana Beach in Hawaii in 1976, which joined the nine Japanese hotels operated by the group at that time. The New Otani Hotel and Garden, Los Angeles, opened in 1977, complete with a half-acre Japanese "Garden in the Sky" constructed on the fourth floor. A walkway takes guests through approximately 100 species of exotic vegetation as well as waterfalls and the unusual red Sado stones that came from Yonetaro Otani's personal collection. The Los Angeles hotel is designed to combine Western convenience and comfort with the traditions and gracious service of Japan. Authentic Japanese-style suites are accommodation options.

New Otani was once described as the best Japanese-style hotel company in the United States. Its success has required striking a balance between Japanese and American hospitality concepts and management styles.[21] New Otani now operates 34 hotels in four countries.

Nikko

JAL Hotels was established as a subsidiary of Japan Air Lines in 1970. The name was changed to Nikko Hotels International in 1984. Initially the chain was established to serve the domestic Japanese travel market, but within a few years it became Japan's largest international hotel chain. Nikko's initial international expansion strategy was to serve Japanese travelers going abroad in large numbers for the first time, thanks to the new jumbo jets and easing of outbound travel restrictions. The company's first hotels outside Japan and Southeast Asia were in France and Germany. After acquiring international experience in these markets, Nikko entered the North American market with the purchase of the Essex House in New York in 1985. Nikko's goal is to have a hotel in each of JAL's more than 50 gateway cities worldwide. As of 2006, it had 53 hotels, most of which are in Japan. Unlike other hotel chains, Nikko has built almost all of its owned hotels in accordance with its own specifications. Besides company-owned hotels, Nikko also operates properties under management contracts and enters into reservations agreements.

From its early days, Nikko has changed its marketing strategy, seeking a broader mix of international clientele. Its objective now is to attract international business travelers from all markets, not just Japanese travelers.

Nikko hotels are largely Western in architecture and design, but they incorporate Japanese touches—landscaped Japanese gardens, specially designed *tatami* rooms, Japanese-style flower arrangements, Japanese tea service, and a discipline and spirit of service emphasizing meticulous attention to guest comfort. Nikko's management teams are a mixture of Asian, American, and European talent. In Japan, the chain includes a collection of *ryokan* throughout the archipelago.

Mandarin Oriental

Hong Kong–based Mandarin Oriental traces its history from 1926 when its first owner, Hong Kong Land, acquired the Gloucester Hotel in Hong Kong. In 1974, the group expressed its intention to expand into the rest of Asia with hotels that reflected the Hong Kong Mandarin Oriental's standards. The group went through various corporate changes. Eventually part of the equity was sold to the public and the company was listed on the Hong Kong stock exchange. The hotel group at first adopted Mandarin International Hotels as its brand name, but this was changed to Mandarin Oriental in 1986, partly to avoid confusion with the unrelated Singapore Mandarin group and partly to identify the company more closely with its other famous hotel in Bangkok, the Oriental. In the mid-1980s, the company decided to extend its hotels beyond the Asian region, largely through equity purchases.

Mandarin Oriental's corporate statement simply says it aims "to be the best." It does not have many hotels, and its preference would be to have five good hotels in five years rather than twenty inconsistent hotels in as many years. Mandarin Oriental's operational savvy has established a strong reputation for the name, some considering it to be the best hotel operator in the world. Mandarin Oriental currently operates 39 hotels in 23 countries. The aim of the company is to be recognized as the best luxury hotel group in the world and expand into the major business centers and key leisure destinations around the world.

Peninsula

The Peninsula Group is actually the marketing and operations name for Hongkong and Shanghai Hotels, which is publicly listed, though largely controlled by one family. It has roots that go back to the 1860s; the flagship Peninsula Hotel in Hong Kong was opened in 1928. Despite its widespread reputation, Peninsula

The world-famous Peninsula Hotel in Hong Kong. (Courtesy of Peninsula)

operates only a few unique hotels in select locations such as Hong Kong, New York, Bangkok, Chicago, Beijing, Manila, and Tokyo.

Dusit International

Dusit International was founded as Dusit Thani in 1949 with the Princess Hotel in Bangkok. It was Thailand's first lodging chain and remains its largest. Since its beginnings, the hotel group has specialized in deluxe hotels built on the hospitality tradition of the Thai culture. Dusit's brand promise as noted in its company profile is *the delivery of an experience that enlivens the individual spirit no matter what the journey*. The group has 19 hotels (under three brands—Dusit Thani, Dusit D2, and Dusit Princess) and two serviced apartments. Most are in Thailand, but Dusit has grown to include hotels in Japan, the Philippines, the United States, and Dubai.

An African Chain

The Southern Sun Hotel Corporation was founded in 1969 when Southern African Breweries and Sol Kerzner joined hands to create The Southern Sun hotel group. In 1983, South African Breweries split its hotel interests to form Southern Sun and Sun International. The latter is headed by Sol Kerzner and retains all the casino hotels with Southern Sun as a 20 percent stakeholder. Southern Sun is the largest owner and operator of hotels on the African continent. In 2006, it ranked fifty-fifth in the world in terms of the number of rooms available. The group has grown to 79 hotels providing more than 13,000 rooms. In 1979, Southern Sun Hotel Holdings became a publicly listed corporation on the Johannesburg Stock Exchange in the beverages and hotel sector. It delisted in 1990.

The company is owned by Tsogo Sun Holdings, the country's largest black empowerment hotel and gaming company, whose shareholding is split between Tsogo Investment Holding Company (51 percent) and SABMiller (49 percent). Its portfolio of hotels ranges from deluxe to budget and has master franchise agreements with InterContinental brands. The company operations were restructured in 2005 when it moved from managing to owning the hotels.

Although Southern Sun is not a transnational corporation at this time, most of its properties and operations fully meet international standards in terms of hotels, market outreach, and services.

The Airline Connection

The airlines have cultivated the centuries-old lodging-transportation relationship to a greater extent than any of the other transportation modes—stagecoach, steamship, railroad, or automobile. The two industries have been closely linked since 1946, when InterContinental Hotels Corporation was created as a subsidiary of Pan American Airways. As air travel demand grew, the ability of the airlines to expand was constrained by the limited supply of hotel accommodations in many of the international gateway cities or resort destinations served by its carriers. As a result, many airlines would in due course develop or acquire their own hotels as a way of ensuring that their passengers and their flight crews had somewhere to sleep.

In addition to ensuring rooms for passengers, the airlines in time found that alliances with hotels could help:

- Protect existing business and develop future travel business
- Expand the airlines' revenue base with additional profit centers
- Stimulate tourism development in destinations served by the carriers
- Expand national culture[22]

For U.S. airlines falling under the jurisdiction of the former Civil Aeronautics Board, having affiliated hotels in strategic locations was an important determinant in being awarded certain air routes. For European airlines, increasing pressures for air liberalization on the Continent and the resultant potential threat to revenues and profits helped to promote the airline-hotel connection as a means of staying competitive through diversification.

As airlines' involvement with hotels grew, the nature of the relationship changed from a single pattern of ownership and merger to a complex mixture of partial ownership and working agreements.

In an attempt to keep pace with Pan Am and InterContinental, TWA acquired Hilton International in 1967, and United Airlines merged with Western International (now Westin) Hotels in 1970. In the early 1970s, Air France launched what would later become the Méridien hotel chain, and Japan Air Lines (JAL) founded what would become its Nikko hotel chain. Although these alliances may appear similar, in actuality the financial and management structures were quite different. Pan Am invested in and appointed managers for some of its InterContinental hotels; but others in which Pan Am had no investment were operated strictly under management contracts or franchise agreements. Following the pattern established by Conrad Hilton, TWA's Hilton International hotels operated exclusively with management contracts and no equity participation. United Airlines owned or held management contracts for its Westin Hotels.

Before long the monogamous hotel-airline links were augmented by multiple affiliations. For example, InterContinental became associated with some of the flag carriers of countries in which its hotel properties were located. The new multiple links in many respects mirrored the airline industry's complicated reciprocal relationships with other carriers for ticketing, baggage handling, and other activities. The formation of the European Hotel Corporation, a multinational consortium of hotels formed by five airlines in 1968, was indicative of the new relationships.

If a hotel firm could affiliate with several airlines, an airline could certainly associate with several hotel companies. KLM did this by taking a minority position in more than a dozen hotels located in existing or former Dutch territories. Golden Tulip, formed in 1961 as a reservations group of independent hotels, eventually became a wholly owned subsidiary of KLM with approximately 350 first-class and deluxe hotels operating on five continents. Although Lufthansa already held interest in the international Penta chain of three-star hotels and the InterContinental franchise in West Germany, it bought a 10 percent stake in the prestigious Kempinski Hotels in 1986.

By 1977, more than 60 airlines were connected with hotel operations encompassing some 200,000 rooms. And although the initial objective of the airlines' entry into the hotel business was to serve the carriers' principal interest in filling seats on their respectively assigned routes, this philosophy changed as airlines came to regard hotels as profit centers in their own right. Aer Lingus, for one, approached hotel ownership as a counterbalance for its airline business. Instead of developing hotels within its flight system, Aer Lingus purchased the small U.S. chain of Dunfey Hotels in 1976 for the stated purpose of being in locations that had no connection with the airline, thereby smoothing the carrier's earnings stream through countercyclical hotel operations.

Advantages of Linkage

There are synergistic benefits to be gained from an airline-hotel partnership. The natural advantages include having common "ownership" of customers and the potential for joint marketing and promotion efforts. With the increasing sophistication of computerized reservation systems and the possibility for tie-ins and bookings, the potential for increasing market share and squeezing out smaller, less well-connected competitors is great. At its base level, association with hotels is part of an airline's battle for improved market share. In some markets, the sale of an airplane seat is predicated on the availability of a hotel room; this was certainly the situation in heavily trafficked commercial centers in Asia during the late 1980s when there were serious room shortages at peak seasons for business or holiday travel. Even if airlines do not own hotels outright, most want to affiliate through various other business arrangements—minority investments, leaseholds, management contracts, franchises, joint ventures, special-representation arrangements, frequent flier program tie-ins, and reservation systems linkage.

Disadvantages of Linkage

Hotel affiliations have not always given airlines the advantages they hoped for, and some airlines have stayed clear of hotel involvement altogether. Some partnerships have proved productive while others have not. In many cases, operating economies and other synergistic results have been quite incidental and often these gains have been more than offset by diseconomies. Most airlines have found far fewer joint-marketing benefits or cross-traffic referrals from the alliance than originally anticipated.

American Airlines, among others, learned an important lesson during its brief experiment with the hotel business—namely, that hotel managers should run hotels and airline executives should run airlines. Since American generally developed its own hotels rather than acquiring them, it often lacked seasoned hotel management and the hotel chain did poorly, costing the airline tens of millions of dollars before it was sold. One analyst of airline diversification noted that success in the airline-hotel relationship depended on whether the hotel business was acquired or developed internally. The former scenario, which included seasoned managers and effective competitive strategies as part of the acquisition, almost always outperformed the latter situation where hotels were too closely tied to the operation of airlines.[23]

Major Linkages

During the late 1980s, some carriers divested themselves of their hotel interests—some recognizing that hotels often follow the same boom and bust patterns typical of the airlines themselves, thus offering no real diversification in holdings. Some airline-owned hotel chains were sold simply because the carriers needed cash, as was the case when the now defunct Pan Am sold InterContinental and when TWA sold Hilton International. Air France sold their Le Méridien hotel chain, Aer Lingus divested itself from The Copthorne Hotel Group, and KLM sold its interest in Golden Tulip, as did Lufthansa with its Kempenski hotel group. The SAS Group recently sold its interest in The Rezidor Hotel Group, which is the master franchisee for the Carlson hotel's Radisson brands. Some Asian airline companies remain connected to the hotels, as Nikko hotels are part of Japan Airlines, Cathay Pacific's major shareholder, the Swire Group, has a property development unit with investments in select hotels in the USA, China, and Papua, New Guinea. ANA recently signed a hotel operating joint venture with InterContinental Hotel Group and formed the newly created IHG ANA Hotels Group. The new group will merge the existing ANA and IHG hotels in Japan into the newly formed company and create a broader ownership and hotel operating platform in Japan.[24]

European and Asian airlines have continued to invest in hotels, but their interest is no longer a sustained one. Based on the trend of demergers and divestments between airline and hotel companies in the last several years, it would seem that in the foreseeable future, the relationship between these two related industry sectors will be more in the form of strategic alliances, joint venture deals, and cross marketing arrangements than vertical integration.

Mergers and Acquisitions

Never before has a single period of time brought about such dramatic and sweeping changes to the fundamental structures of the lodging industry as the 1980s. Mergers and acquisitions were the name of the game, as the lodging industry expanded globally and key brand names became the target of hoteliers and investors on the move. The spate of hotel company mergers, acquisitions, and buyouts pushed the international lodging industry into the financial limelight, making it among the most leveraged and competitive businesses in the world.

Major chains from all areas have looked increasingly to Europe, North America, and the Asia-Pacific region to expand their chains for new avenues to profits and growth. Economies of scale, globalization, the need to have representation in key markets and access to new markets, and saturation in home markets have all played a part in the movement toward expansion through mergers and acquisitions.

Starting with the takeover of InterContinental by Grand Metropolitan in 1981, international mergers and acquisitions increased in frequency and magnitude. The trend accelerated in 1987 when operators like Holiday Corporation began selling off their international divisions to European concerns, forever altering the list of major players worldwide and changing the balance of power within the industry.

Mergers and acquisitions are likely to continue, although the environment for making deals is getting tougher and investors are moving more cautiously as they evaluate investment opportunities at home and abroad. The major theme of international mergers and acquisitions since 2005 has been the role of private equity firms in purchasing public companies in major public-to-private deals. These transactions have included hotel real estate portfolio acquisitions from public hotel companies wanting to monetize their real estate and acquisitions of whole companies and underperforming single assets. Some of the notable acquisitions during this period include the following:

- Since March 2004, The Blackstone Group has acquired MeriStar Hospitality Corp. for $2.6 billion, Extended Stay America for $3.1 billion, Prime Hospitality Corp. for $800 million, Wyndham International for $3.2 billion, LaQuinta for $3.4 billion, and most recently Hilton for $26 billion.
- Acquisition for $1.9 billion of IHG's UK portfolio of 73 hotels by Lehman Brothers and the government of Singapore.
- Blackstone's $790 million purchase in June 2006 of Hospitality Europe, an owner of about 3,200 branded rooms.
- Colony Capital made a strategic investment in Accor in 2005.
- In 2006, the Canadian luxury hotel operator Fairmont Hotels & Resorts was purchased by a joint venture between Prince Alwaleed bin Talal's Kingdom Hotels International and Colony Capital, which acquired all of Fairmont's outstanding common shares for a total price of $3.9 billion in an all-cash transaction.
- Also in 2006, Four Seasons was taken private through a consortium of three investors: Isadore Sharp (CEO of Four Seasons), Prince Alwaleed bin Talal, and Bill Gates's investment vehicle Cascade Investments.

Exhibit 1   Companies in the Most Countries

Company	Number of Countries
InterContinental Hotels Group (IHG)	100
Starwood Hotels & Resorts Worldwide	95
Accor	90
Hilton Hotels Corp.	78
Best Western International	78
Carlson Hospitality Worldwide	70
Marriott International	68
Wyndham Hotel Group	55
Golden Tulip Hospitality/THL	49
The Rezidor Hotel Group	49
Global Hyatt Corp.	44
Choice Hotels International	40
Club Méditerranée	40
Four Seasons Hotels & Resorts	31
TUI AG/TUI Hotels and Resorts	29

Source: *Hotels* Giants Survey 2007.

Consolidation

Consolidation in the lodging industry is often viewed as a "survival of the fittest" syndrome. Because of product oversupply and the lodging chains' voracious appetite for growth, firms have been acquiring each other in a feeding frenzy. In the end, the predominance of a few large national and international corporations or mega-chains is likely to prevail. An increase in the percentage of rooms affiliated with major chains, and the growing concentration of rooms and marketing expertise in the hands of a few solid organizations such as IHG, Starwood, Accor, Hilton, Marriott, and Wyndham—whose international multi-site operations have the capability of attracting a broad customer base—seem to be pointing in the direction of consolidation. Exhibit 1 lists hotel companies by the number of countries in which they operate as of 2007.

Many analysts predict that the multinational mega-chains will grow at the expense of some of the smaller, and perhaps newer, chains as the cost of sustaining a small or start-up lodging company becomes prohibitive. Created through a combination of mergers, acquisitions, buyouts, and joint ventures, these mega-chains are likely to have several different brands of lodging differentiated by price and product. The adoption of shared corporate structures, overhead, technology, and reservation systems to run multiple brands will make it increasingly difficult for smaller competitors to operate at the same profit margins.

Some major hotel players, on the other hand, have considered the enormous investment and commitment required to operate hotels on an international scale and have decided to withdraw.

And although mega-chains are becoming more prominent, some smaller regional hotel companies have combined to create marketing treaties or joint marketing and reservation companies in order to compete. Smaller chains under effective management, such as Mandarin Oriental, Nikko, Taj, and Kempinski, are also proving they can survive with careful niche marketing and strong product quality control.

During the past 25 years, the hospitality industry has witnessed the real effects of Asian predominance in world economic power. In addition to the rapid growth of travel both into and out of Asia, the new economic predominance has resulted in Asian companies—many of which are newcomers to the hotel trade—becoming major players in international hotel acquisitions. Until Japan's "bubble economy" burst at the beginning of the 1990s, the Japanese were the primary Asian players in hotel acquisitions, but cash-rich Hong Kong investors have been following the same path. In recent times, North American properties or chains were the chief targets of both groups of investors.

Strategic Alliances

The current bent on the merger theme is that partnerships are in, purchase is out. With few funds available for development today, hotels are entering into alliances on a marketing basis. Often, a smaller hotel chain will want to be affiliated with one of the larger chains in order to tap into their global reservation systems, as is the case in the recent ANA-IHG joint venture. The trend reflects the need of small independents and regional chains to form partnerships with the world's largest global hotel companies if they want to survive the competitive global tourism market.

Summary

In this chapter, we have examined international lodging from a historical as well as a developmental context. We have seen how the lodging industry has successfully adapted itself to suit the times—from the Roman Empire's roadside inns to today's international hotel chains located in virtually every country. Most of the lodging industry's changes were necessitated by changes in transportation systems, which facilitated mass travel and hence the demand for different forms of lodging.

The lodging climate after World War II was marked by the foreign expansion of American hotels such as Hilton International and Pan Am's InterContinental. With the advent of the jet plane in the late 1950s, rapid development of American chains in Europe and Latin America paralleled the growing demands of mass travel, often in partnership with or as subsidiaries of air carriers. Today, hotels continue their ties with all sectors of the transportation and travel network—especially with the airline industry, providing rooms for affiliated carriers' passengers and flight crews while gaining access to the airlines' computer reservations systems.

During the 1980s, emerging transnational hotel chains based in Europe, Canada, Asia, and elsewhere quickly caught up with American chains, generally specializing in niche markets in five-star or four-star properties, and in recent times in budget properties as well. The late 1980s began a period marked by mergers and acquisitions because of volatile global economies, saturated markets, and leveraging by financially strong companies. Consolidation of hotels into mega-chains became more prominent, while smaller chains joined marketing consortiums or partnerships in order to survive shifting marketplace changes. International hotels that have survived the consolidation are now positioned to confront the new global challenges that will have an even greater impact on their operations.

Endnotes

1. Albert J. Gomes, *Hospitality in Transition* (New York: American Hotel & Motel Association, 1985), p. 3.
2. Daniel Lee, *Lodging*, 1984, p. 20.
3. Ibid., p. 23.
4. Saul Leonard, "Hotel Chains in the USA: Review of an Industry in Transition," *Travel and Tourism Analyst*, October 1987, p. 44.
5. Gomes, p. 10.
6. Albert Gomes, "American Hotel Influence, Innovations Extend Overseas," *Hotel and Motel Management*, October 12, 1987, p. 42.
7. Mike McVey, "International Hotel Chains in Europe," *Travel and Tourism Analyst*, September 1986, p. 6.
8. Ibid., p. 21.
9. *International Hotel Industry Travel and Tourism Intelligence*, October 2003, p. 97.
10. Jones Lang LaSalle Hotels, *Hotel Investment Highlight Europe*, July 2006.
11. *Middle East Hotel Survey—Outlook Market Trends and Opportunities: 2007 Edition.* Hospitality Valuation Services.
12. McVey, p. 4.
13. Leonard, p. 45.
14. Ibid.
15. "Club Méditerranée (A)," *Harvard Case Studies*, Harvard Business School, 1978, p. 1.
16. Alastair Morrison, *Hospitality and Travel Marketing* (New York: Delmar, 1989), p. 250.
17. *The International Hotel Industry, Travel and Tourism Intelligence*, October 2003, p. 164.
18. Harold Lane, "Marriages of Necessity: Airline-Hotel Liaisons," *Cornell Hotel and Restaurant Administration Quarterly*, May 1986, p. 74.
19. Lincoln Avery, "New Venues for the Old World Touch," *Hotel and Resort Industry*, July 1990, p. 21.
20. Nancy Cockrell, "India's Hotel Sector & International Expansion," *Travel and Tourism Analyst*, No. 2, 1991, p. 26.
21. Daryl Wyckoff and James Hill, "The New Otani," *Harvard Case Studies*, Harvard Business School, 1983, p. 1.

22. Lane, p. 74.
23. Ibid., p. 79.
24. "IHG Targets Japan with ANA Deal," *Hotels,* December 2006, p. 12.

Key Terms

consolidation—The combination of two or more corporations to form a new corporation.

economies of scale—Cost savings resulting from centralized, pooled, or otherwise shared production or resources.

repatriation—Bringing an expatriate worker back from a foreign assignment to his or her home country; the return of money or other resources to the country of origin.

Review Questions

1. What were some of the innovations introduced by American hoteliers in the early twentieth century?
2. What situations and events influenced international hotel expansion efforts after World War II?
3. When and why did foreign hotel operations begin establishing themselves in the United States?
4. What factors influenced hotel expansion in the Middle East? in the Asia-Pacific region?
5. What is meant by the separation of ownership from management? What have been its effects with regard to the international hotel industry?
6. What major international hotel chains began in the United States?
7. What are some significant characteristics of European hotel chains? Indian hotel chains? Asia-Pacific hotel chains?
8. What are the chief advantages and disadvantages of airline-hotel alliances?
9. What are some of the major airline-hotel linkages?
10. What effect did the mergers and acquisitions begun in the 1980s have on the lodging industry?

Chapter 3 Outline

Barriers to Travel, Tourism Investment, and Business
    Barriers Affecting Travelers
    Lodging Investment Barriers
    Lodging Operational Barriers
Government Hotel Regulations
    Price Control Measures
    Labor Regulations
    Room Taxes
    Other Regulations
    The Competitiveness Index
International Organizations Dealing with Barriers
    World Tourism Organization
    Organization for Economic Cooperation and Development
    General Agreement on Tariffs and Trade
    International Monetary Fund
    International Hotel & Restaurant Association
    World Travel & Tourism Council
The Need for Government Support
    Foreign Investment Incentives
    Bureaucratic Red Tape
    Tourism Policy
National Tourism Organizations
International Lodging Chains and Developing Countries
    Identifying Advantages and Disadvantages
    Maximizing Returns from Tourism
    Lodging Chains and Host Governments—Inevitable Conflict
Political Stability
    Impact on Investment Decisions
    Impact on Travelers
Travel Advisories
    Political Motivations
Political Risk
    Difficulty of Assessing Political Risk
    Reducing Vulnerability in Risky Situations
    Management Control in an Unstable Environment
Crisis Management
    The Written Crisis Management Plan

Competencies

1. Identify and describe various barriers to travel, including both those affecting travelers and those affecting businesses dealing with travelers, and list typical governmental hotel regulations. (pp. 61–71)

2. Identify and describe several international organizations that deal with barriers to travel and tourism. (pp. 72–77)

3. Explain why government support of tourism is critical to the success of the industry, outline the different types of support governments typically offer, and describe the role and common tasks of national tourism organizations. (pp. 77–81)

4. State the advantages and disadvantages of international hotel chain involvement in developing countries and identify typical areas of potential conflict between chains and host governments. (pp. 81–84)

5. Describe several ways in which political instability reduces travel and tourism, including historical examples, and describe the uses of travel advisories. (pp. 84–92)

6. Identify several types of political risk and approaches to risk assessment, as well as measures that can be taken to reduce risk. (pp. 92–97)

7. Explain the importance of crisis management and state the typical contents of a written crisis management plan. (pp. 97–98)

3

Political Aspects of the International Travel, Tourism, and Lodging Industry

THE POLITICAL STABILITY of nations and political actions of governments and organizations affect the international travel, tourism, and lodging industry in profound ways. First, governments at various levels legislate policies for the conduct of commerce, trade, and business; establish immigration policies and work visas; enact and enforce labor legislation; regulate construction, zoning, and land use; grant or approve operating licenses and permits; provide investment incentives or disincentives; impose an array of taxes; and much more. All of these actions affect the ability of the private sector to do business and compete on a level playing field. Depending on how a firm's interest is affected, laws, regulations, and policies may be fair or unfair, favorable or unfavorable, strict or flexible. Many countries intentionally erect political barriers that circumvent foreign competition in order to protect their domestic enterprises. Although these barriers are gradually being dismantled in the new global environment, many still remain in place and not all countries are eager to cooperate.

Second, a government may have a favorable or unfavorable tourism policy. One such policy deals with facilitation—the ease with which people may enter or leave a country. By imposing strict requirements or high fees for passports or visas, a government may discourage residents from leaving or visitors from entering. A government may also discourage its nationals from visiting another country by issuing travel advisories for various reasons.

Third, government can support the private sector by promoting travel, tourism, national and international events, and tourism and hospitality education and training. The private sector has always participated to some extent in these activities. However, it has neither the resources nor the political clout to completely support these activities, which are central to the development and perpetuation of a successful visitor industry.

In this chapter, we will examine some of the ways in which the travel industry, and hotels in particular, are affected by the political actions of governments and other international agencies. We will also examine the topics of political stability, risk-taking, political risk insurance, and crisis management. It should become apparent that political issues are of great consequence in operating a hotel outside (and sometimes within) one's home country. It should also be evident that the topic of international or transnational hotels cannot be separated from a discussion of travel and tourism, which provides both perspective and context.

Barriers to Travel, Tourism Investment, and Business

Travel barriers that impede the movement of people across national boundaries have a significant impact on travel flow, volume, and revenues. Because many governments have begun to recognize the benefits of inbound tourism, they have focused more attention on the promotion of inbound tourism and on developmental activities. Not enough has been done to reduce or remove restrictions to outbound travel or to promote two-way travel on a worldwide basis. However, changes are occurring even in countries known for their restrictive tourism policies. Recent tourism statistics show an accelerating upward trend in inter-regional and long-haul outbound travel from Asia, which reflects the relaxation of travel policies in China and other Asian countries. For example, China's policy of creating bilateral agreements with specific destinations led to the granting of "Approved Destination Status" to 132 countries in 2007, resulting in an increase of Chinese group (leisure) travel to these countries.[1]

Often, governments impose barriers as perceived solutions to such national problems as trade deficits, illegal immigration, and foreign competition. Governments seldom assess the impact of their laws and regulations on tourism. Unfortunately, government policies concerning international relations—whether political, economic, financial, or social—often conflict with and override tourism interests. Because the tourism industry is so fragmented, tourism-related enterprises have generally not had the effective voice in government that other constituencies enjoy. In order to measure the full economic impact of the travel and tourism industry, the World Travel & Tourism Council (WTTC) created the Tourism Satellite Accounting (TSA) system in 1999. Using sophisticated research methodology, the WTTC for the first time was able to establish objective measures of the industry's global economic impact. Since then, TSA measures have been used in several countries to influence government policies in favor of the tourism industry.

Many other factors over which governments have some control adversely affect international travel. These include inconveniences arising from differences in language and culture, the need for multilingual signage in public places, currency restrictions, visa restrictions, urban congestion, airport capacity limits, airport obsolescence, adequate hotel and meeting facilities, and so on. Many of these obstacles result directly from government actions, inactions, or regulations. Impediments fall under two general categories: those affecting travelers, and those affecting the businesses dealing with travelers. Exhibit 1 outlines several possible obstacles that governments can create. Many of these government actions can be viewed as forms of protectionism. Obstacles to travelers will be discussed in the next section. We will then look at barriers specifically affecting lodging companies.

Exhibit 1 Potential Government-Based Impediments to Travel

Obstacles Affecting Travelers

Imposed by home country:
- Currency restrictions imposed on residents
- Conditions and procedures for issue of travel documents
- Customs allowances and procedures for returning residents
- Restrictions on overseas travel
- High exit visa tax for residents

Imposed by host country:
- Currency restrictions imposed on visitors
- Entry visas, identity documents, limitations on duration of stay
- Formalities concerning entry of motor vehicles, pleasure boats, or other craft
- Formalities concerning applicability of drivers licenses, car insurance, and so forth
- Restrictions on acquisition of property by non-nationals (for example, condos)
- Taxes on foreign visitors

Obstacles Affecting Transnational Lodging Companies

Investment/establishment obstacles:
- Limitations on foreign investment or equity participation
- Requirement for equity participation of foreign hotel companies
- Restrictions on import of special equipment, building materials
- Requirements for placing of contracts (for example, for site development) with local enterprises
- Discriminatory taxes on foreign hotel enterprises
- Land tenure or ownership restrictions
- Financial incentives for domestic hotel development
- Lack of information on investing
- Requirement for excessive government approvals

Operating obstacles:
- Restrictions on transfer of funds into and out of the country
- Restrictions on expatriate personnel (resident aliens with work visas)
- Requirements for non-national employees (for example, visas, work permits)
- Training and promotion requirements for local workers
- Restriction or excessive taxation of imported goods
- Limitations on access to reservation systems
- Subsidies for domestic hotels
- Currency exchange restrictions and delays

Barriers Affecting Travelers

Documentation. Documentation obstacles can be imposed either by the home country or the host country. Passports and exit visas for outbound travelers are generally issued freely with proof of citizenship, a recent photograph, and a fee. In some cases, however, a government may restrict travel unless it is to a country whose culture, religion, or political system is friendly with its own. A government may also make the exit visa procedure cumbersome or expensive to discourage outbound travel. Developing countries tend to have more burdensome exit procedures.

Entry visas are used for health, safety, and immigration reasons. The host country usually issues them freely to qualified visitors to encourage inbound travel for restricted periods of time. Procedures for acquiring visas, however, vary widely from country to country and even embassy to embassy, and certain entry visas can be difficult to obtain. The visa waiver program established by the United States in 1986 with the objective of eliminating unnecessary barriers to travel, stimulating the U.S. tourism industry, and permitting the Department of State to focus consular resources in other areas, remains in effect for 27 participating countries. However, after the terrorist attacks on the World Trade Center and the Pentagon in 2001, procedures for acquiring a visa for visiting the United States have become stricter and process times have become longer. The Department of State now has a website, "Destination USA: Secure Borders, Open Doors," to communicate these new procedures to prospective visa applicants who wish to travel to the United States.

In some cases, the procedural difficulty of obtaining entry visas seems to be related to the host country's experience of nationals of specific countries illegally overstaying their allowed visitation period. Sometimes visa restrictions are politically motivated. For example, most Middle Eastern countries deny or make difficult entry to anyone whose passport indicates visits to Israel.

While documentation is clearly important for security and social reasons, documentation requirements can act as impediments to travel when documents are disapproved arbitrarily, when document procedures are overly burdensome or delayed, or when excessive fees are charged. To the extent that international travel is discouraged, documentation requirements create market access problems for hotels.

Exchange Controls. Many countries throughout the world impose currency restrictions or tax their residents' foreign travel. These measures are intended to discourage outbound travel in favor of domestic travel, to conserve foreign exchange, and/or to defend the country's balance of payments position. In general, exchange controls and currency restrictions are lessening globally, but they still remain in various forms. For example, in Australia there are no limitations on the amount of money that can be brought in, but any cash amount over AU$5,000 needs to be declared. In the Czech Republic, the import/export of amounts over 200,000 CZK must be registered with customs. Fiscal charges when departing a country are also in effect in various countries.

Currency restrictions or **travel allowances** limit the amount of exchange residents of a country may purchase from banks to cover travel expenses incurred abroad. If the limitations are severe, outbound travel will decrease dramatically.

In 1983, France adopted temporary restrictions on the amount of money French citizens could take abroad. Although the restrictions were imposed for balance of payments reasons and were later rescinded, they had a detrimental impact on the tourism earnings of other countries. In most countries imposing currency restrictions, business travelers have a higher allowance than leisure travelers. Another control is to limit or prohibit residents' use of credit cards abroad.

Travel allowances are probably the most common form of trade barrier confronting the international tourism industry and the barrier that most distorts the balance of trade in the travel account. Once an allowance has been spent, all spending—in practical terms, the trip itself—essentially must end. On the other hand, in order to attract inbound travel, countries have also been known to give visitors preferential exchange rates that enable them to purchase travel-related goods and services more cheaply—sometimes at prices below fair market value.

Some countries require their residents to purchase travel insurance or to deposit a prescribed amount—equivalent either to the amount of foreign exchange they buy or to a fixed percentage of the estimated total trip costs—in a non-interest-bearing account. Some countries impose exit taxes. The Israeli government levies a travel tax on all citizens when they leave the country. While this tax encourages Israelis to travel domestically rather than abroad, it also discourages Israelis living abroad from visiting home.

Customs Regulations. A country will generally impose duties (taxes imposed on imports to restrict purchase or earn revenues) on at least some of the goods its nationals purchase abroad when those nationals bring these goods home with them after their travels. Duty-free allowances for returning travelers vary widely among countries. High duties and small duty-free allowances serve to limit expenditures by travelers in foreign countries. Burdensome declaration forms and time-consuming customs inspections also discourage purchases abroad.

Lodging Investment Barriers

Lodging companies can face many government-imposed obstacles that limit market access and establishment.

Equity Requirements. Although it is never easy for outside investors to find compatible local partners, some countries specify a minimum required equity from local nationals or place limitations on foreign investments in the establishment of hotels. These requirements are intended to promote domestic economic development and to encourage local involvement or to reduce outside speculation. They may, however, impede foreign lodging companies or developers who do not want to lose control of operations that bear their name or whose low profit margins may not justify the sharing of profits with a local partner.

Governments of developing countries often recognize the need for foreign investment capital to assist tourism development. Such governments may adjust the external equity requirements according to the size of the project. For example, a government might permit 75-percent foreign equity participation in large-scale projects, but only minority foreign equity participation in smaller-scale projects. Such measures provide opportunities for local investors with limited finances to participate in the hotel business without discouraging foreign investors for the larger projects.

In many instances, equity investment rules are based on a particular sector being given priority by the host government for development and investment. For example, as part of the current liberalization policies and economic reforms in India, removal of equity restrictions on foreign-direct-investment holdings and an opening up of more sectors to foreign investors has resulted in several sectors attracting international investment. The real estate sector (hotels included) is currently at the forefront of the Indian government's agenda, given its potential to propel economic growth. As such, foreign direct investment up to 100 percent of the investment is permitted, albeit with some restrictions.

Some governments require equity participation from an international company as a condition for that company's obtaining a management contract. This can be a problem for international management companies that prefer to avoid equity positions.

Policies Favoring National Enterprises. Foreign hotel companies are at an obvious disadvantage when investment policies are biased in favor of domestic hotel owners. Provisions favorable to domestic owners may include less-stringent administrative regulations for domestic operators, financial and fiscal incentives, or subsidies enabling domestic hotels to compete with artificially low rates. Laws requiring government approval of the duration of management contracts and fee structures may also impede foreign hotel companies. Although sometimes justified as protecting nationals from burdensome contractual terms, these laws often intrude in areas regarded by many to be the exclusive province of the parties to the agreement.

Finally, outsiders often find it difficult to get good information, which is the lifeblood of investment decisions. Although **transparency** (that is, the lack of hidden conditions or clauses) is critical to effective decision-making, governments may make little or no effort to provide foreign companies with information about investment conditions, climate, or rules. Jones Lang LaSalle Hotels, a global investment services firm, tracks the real estate transparency score for 56 countries as an important measure of assessing investment risk (see Exhibit 2).

Lodging Operational Barriers

Governments may have restrictions that affect lodging operations and transactions which sometimes result in treatment that is perceived as unfair and discriminatory.

Foreign Remittances. Lodging companies may be discouraged from investing in a foreign country because of the difficulty of transferring and remitting funds. In countries with strict currency exchange controls, operators may not be able to obtain sufficient foreign exchange to cover their management fees, franchise fees, licensing fees, overseas service fees, earnings, or even operating costs incurred in currencies other than that of the host country. Delays in currency conversion, particularly for credit card companies, act as a major obstacle to the necessary commerce of travel. In some cases, hotels have been unable to operate profitably

Exhibit 2   Real Estate Transparency Worldwide

Tier 1 Countries			Tier 2 Countries		
1	Australia	1.15	11	Finland	1.63
2	United States	1.15	12	Germany	1.67
3	New Zealand	1.20	13	South Africa	1.77
4	Canada	1.21	14	Denmark	1.84
5	United Kingdom	1.25	15	Austria	1.85
6	Hong Kong	1.30	16	Ireland	1.85
7	Netherlands	1.37	17	Belgium	1.88
8	Sweden	1.38	18	Spain	1.91
9	France	1.40	19	Switzerland	1.94
10	Singapore	1.44	20	Norway	1.96
			21	Italy	2.14
			22	Malaysia	2.21
			23	Japan	2.40
			24	Portugal	2.44

Tier 3 Countries			Tier 4 Countries		
25	Mexico	2.51	42	P. R. China	3.50
26	Czech Republic	2.69	43	Macau	3.65
27	Hungary	2.76	44	United Arab Emirates	3.77
28	Poland	2.76	45	Costa Rica	3.83
29	Israel	2.85	46	Indonesia	3.90
30	Taiwan	2.85	47	Turkey	4.04
31	South Korea	2.88	48	Peru	4.08
32	Slovakia	2.99	49	Romania	4.08
33	Chile	3.11	50	Colombia	4.10
34	Greece	3.13	51	Uruguay	4.13
35	Russia	3.22	52	Saudi Arabia	4.14
36	Philippines	3.30	53	Panama	4.18
37	Brazil	3.31			
38	Slovenia	3.35	**Tier 5 Countries**		
39	Thailand	3.40	54	Egypt	4.30
40	Argentina	3.41	55	Venezuela	4.43
41	India	3.46	56	Vietnam	4.69

Tier 1 = High transparency; Tier 2 = Transparent; Tier 3 = Semi-Transparent; Tier 4 = Low Transparency; Tier 5 = Opaque

Source: Adapted from *Hotel Investment Outlook 2007*, Jones Lang LaSalle Hotels.

because they were prohibited from converting their receipts into foreign currencies for remittance.

Many countries have limits on the repatriation of profits and other monies that impede the establishment of foreign-owned companies.

Import Restrictions. Governments commonly establish import restrictions and/or place high taxes on imports to discourage the consumption of foreign products or services. In many countries, foreign hotel operators are often subjected to extreme delays or denials of import authorization for needed equipment, furnishings, or supplies. These limitations not only hamper operating efficiencies, but also have a negative impact on the hotel's quality or image in serving an international clientele.

Another import-related problem is restrictions on the use of foreign-made promotional and advertising materials, or the imposition of taxes on the entry of such material. Such "domestic content laws" can prevent hotels from making the most efficient use of resources.

Governments often place high tariffs on the importation of specific products. China, for one, imposes high taxes on such imported foods as beef, veal, and seafood. Another major concern for hoteliers is that, while original equipment and furnishings required to build and equip the hotel may come duty free, parts and replacements are frequently heavily taxed. Such tax policies can play havoc with hotel operations. Take the case of the Philippines. During the early 1980s, in an effort to improve a failing economy and reduce reliance on imports, the government ordered various bans and restrictions on imported meat, liquor, and equipment. For restricted imports, letters of credit (necessary for customs) were difficult to obtain, even when the amount of the desired import was within the new restrictions' guidelines. As a result, most hotels were unable to get their import shipments for about 11 months. The effect of these bans and restrictions was to push up local prices as suppliers cashed in on a sellers' market. Hotel operating costs soared. Food and beverage managers complained that prices rose as much as 300 to 400 percent for some products.[2]

Governments may also institute temporary restrictions on imported goods if they represent a safety or health hazard. Recent cases include import restrictions by the European Union and other countries after the foot-and-mouth disease outbreak that infected cattle in the United Kingdom, and import restrictions by many countries on birds and bird products after the global outbreak of the bird flu.

Domestic Personnel Requirements. Domestic personnel requirements and restrictions on foreign hires affect one of the major functions of hotel management—maintaining a pool of qualified and talented personnel at the executive and specialized-skill levels. Most countries strictly control the entrance of immigrants and enforce laws against illegal entrants. However, inflexibility in granting of work permits to foreign nationals can create difficulties for the hotel operator.

When there are restrictions on the remittance of income to the home country or regulations against payment of wages in foreign currency, it may also be difficult to attract needed personnel. To avoid the impact of these remittance regulations, the lodging company often must provide for optional payment methods.

As part of its agreement with the host government, a foreign lodging company may be required to provide specified types of training for the local workforce. It may also be required to promote local personnel into responsible positions, often long before their experience qualifies them.

Access to Data. Another concern for hotel operators considering investments in developing countries may be the lack of an efficient telecommunications system to facilitate transborder data flows. This could affect such matters as information on flight and hotel availabilities, bookings, billings, and so forth. The inability to link up with major computer reservations systems can have a devastating effect on the marketing of international hotels.

Other Barriers. Some atypical problems facing hotels operating outside the home country may include the following: prohibitions on insurance coverage by non-national companies (resulting in more expensive coverage under more restrictive conditions); lack of equal access to local credit sources; lack of adequate legal protection for trademarks, trade names, and copyrights; and discriminatory taxation. Additionally, some governments impose strict regulations that limit the operating freedom of hotel managers. We discuss this topic in the next section.

Government Hotel Regulations

Although hotel regulations have existed since the end of the nineteenth century to cover such concerns as fire precautions, sanitation, hygienic food handling, and so on, most regulations are of recent origin. In many countries today, hotels are heavily regulated or licensed not only to protect consumers (by ensuring minimum quality and safety standards), but also to promote financial responsibility and avoid potential local conflicts.

Although regulations can serve important and useful functions, governments sometimes abuse their regulatory power to exert unwarranted control over the industry. For example, when business licenses and permits are denied or delayed without valid reasons, competition is unfairly limited and the marketplace is disrupted. Inspections and classifications may be encouraging and positive when they are intended to improve the overall quality of hotel products and services (assuming the public inspection system is competent). However, as instruments of arbitrary government control, they can pose a serious threat to the industry.

Price Control Measures

Some governments regulate or fix hotel rates. Price control measures include government approval of room rates, government-established rate ceilings or ranges, subsidies for certain types of accommodations, and regulations on the display of prices—all of which restrict management decisions. The Italian government, for instance, establishes a minimum publishable tariff for each hotel category, limiting an operator's ability to adjust rates in response to market conditions. For a time, the Philippine government also instituted a policy of controlled rates, preventing operators from setting their own tariffs. The purpose was to reduce price wars among hotels during a downturn in tourism.

Labor Regulations

Government regulations unquestionably affect the labor market for hotels. Working conditions such as the number of hours worked, time off, salary, and social benefits can all be legislated. Restrictions or excessive red tape involved with hiring expatriates or third-country nationals, obtaining work visas, and so forth also have an impact on hotel operations.

The Singapore government, for one, closely monitors the labor requirements of hotels. At one point during a severe labor shortage, government officials from the labor ministry urged hotels to reduce their employee-to-room ratio. They also took actions that in essence allocated labor according to hotel classification standards. In 1988, Singapore raised its levy on workers in the hotel industry from $140 to $170; in 1990, the levy was increased to $280. The government's intent was to ensure that the hotel industry would not siphon off much-needed labor from other business sectors. At the same time, it did not want to encourage the industry to import more foreign workers. In the early 1980s, the Philippine government issued six different wage orders over a short time to protect workers from rampant inflation. The result for some hotels was a doubling of payroll costs.

Strong labor unions in some countries also affect the cost of hotel operations. In Australia, restrictive union work rules, frequent strikes, vacations, and overtime pay for holiday and weekend work have curtailed full service in some hotels on weekends and holidays. During labor-management disputes regarding work, an Australian union may practice "work-to-rule" tactics, which means following rules to the letter; this results in low work output and higher operational costs.

Room Taxes

An occupancy or room tax, sometimes called a bed tax, is a state or local use tax assessed as a percentage of the room tariff. It is typically passed on from the hotel to users. The room tax is considered progressive, since it falls more heavily on high-end users than on low-end users. Because the room tax is applied equally to all hotels, the competitive advantage or disadvantage for any particular property within the destination is relatively small. However, a high occupancy tax tends to place the destination itself in an unfavorable position with competing destinations that do not have such a tax. An excessive bed tax encourages tour packagers and wholesalers to consider alternative but similar destinations without such taxes, if the sellers are operating under tight profit margins.

Of course, the lodging industry opposes the imposition of a room tax. For governments facing financial difficulties, however, it is a lesser evil than raising taxes on residents. Visitors, after all, have no vote or voice at local polls. Furthermore, frequent travelers have grown used to such taxes and there is little likelihood of active resistance. Governmental rationale for the bed tax is that it helps to recoup some of the cost of public infrastructural investment and to pay for the service requirements of visitors. Room tax rates today can run anywhere from 3 to 25 percent. The United States has some of the lowest rates; Europe has some of the highest. The government's administrative costs of collecting the tax are minimal, as most of this burden is shifted to hotel operators.

Other Regulations

Other government regulations that affect hotels include safety and hygiene standards covering sanitary facilities and water treatment. Fire safety legislation varies considerably from country to country and even from city to city. Some governments have established general guidelines that have no legal force. Others have model codes, but do not compel local authorities to adopt them. Still others have stringently enforced fire safety regulations. Where water scarcity is a problem, the government may require hotel operators to use sea or "gray" water for toilet flush or grounds use, and to provide their own water supply for drinking, cooking, and guest needs.

Building code regulations also affect the development and management of hotels. Some island destinations promoting low density hotel development, for example, stipulate that no building can rise higher than a coconut tree. Other regulations are concerned with the use of locally available building materials, specified beach or frontage setbacks, or conformance to indigenous architectural designs. Bali, for instance, requires all resort hotels to follow the Balinese temple form and landscape in design and layout.

The Competitiveness Index

The most comprehensive effort to measure the impact of government hotel regulations and other factors on a country's attractiveness as a tourism destination, both for travelers and from a development perspective, is the Travel and Tourism Competitiveness Index. The index was developed by the World Economic Forum in 2005 and 2006 in partnership with global multilateral tourism organizations such as the World Travel & Tourism Council, World Tourism Organization, and International Air Transport Association, as well as global industry partners.

The index captures the competitiveness profile of 124 economies based on three broad categories of variables that facilitate or drive travel and tourism competitiveness. These categories are summarized into three sub-indexes of the Index:

1. Regulatory framework

2. Business environment and infrastructure

3. Human, cultural, and natural resources

Within these three sub-indexes are 13 "pillars" of travel and tourism competitiveness (see Exhibit 3). These pillars are in turn made up of a number of individual variables. For example, the "policy rules and regulations" pillar consists of variables that make it conducive to develop tourism industries in those countries. The individual variables measured within this pillar include foreign ownership restrictions, property rights, rules governing foreign direct investment, visa requirements, and openness of bilateral air service agreements.

Countries with high Travel and Tourism Competitiveness Index scores show higher levels of tourism arrivals and receipts than other countries.

Exhibit 3 Travel and Tourism Competitiveness Index

```
                    Travel and Tourism Competitiveness Index

    Subindex A:                  Subindex B:                 Subindex C:
  T&T regulatory          T&T business enviroment       T&T human, cultural, and
    framework               and infrastructure            natural resources

Policy rules and          Air transport infrastructure    Human resources
regulations

Environmental regulation  Ground transport infrastructure National tourism perception

Safety and security       Tourism infrastructure          Natural and cultural
                                                          resources

Health and hygiene        ICT infrastructure

Prioritization of         Price competitiveness in
Travel & Tourism          the T&T industry
```

Source: World Economic Forum, *Travel and Tourism Competitiveness Report 2007.*

International Organizations Dealing with Barriers

In most instances, lodging chains deal directly with governments to alleviate problems encountered in investing in and operating foreign properties. However, this case-by-case approach is usually less than ideal. A number of international organizations work to facilitate international trade in tourism, but most of these organizations also treat travel-related problems in a piecemeal fashion. Consequently, progress in removing tourism trade barriers has been slow and sporadic. Although there is increasing coordination among international organizations on tourism matters, greater cooperation, interaction, and government support are needed to improve each organization's effectiveness and reduce the adverse effects of the rules and regulations of governments and international conventions.

World Tourism Organization

The World Tourism Organization (UNWTO) is a specialized agency of the United Nations and the leading international organization for tourism. It serves as a forum for tourism policy issues and is a valuable source of tourism knowledge at the global level. Of the several international organizations involved with some aspect of travel, only the UNWTO, with its 150 member states and 302 affiliate industry members, is devoted exclusively to tourism at the global level. The UNWTO has five priority functions: tourism marketing and promotion, education and training, research and statistics, environment and health, and facilitation. It is the responsibility of the Facilitation Committee to report on existing governmental requirements or practices that impede international travel, to propose measures to simplify entry and exit formalities, and to develop a set of standards and recommended practices to be presented to member states for adoption.

Organization for Economic Cooperation and Development

The Organization for Economic Cooperation and Development (OECD) is concerned with broad economic, trade, and investment issues. It has taken a leadership role in identifying and working toward the reduction of travel barriers. The OECD Tourism Committee developed a general set of non-binding codes or guidelines for tourism; it has also reviewed and assessed tourism obstacles and made recommendations for action within the OECD. In 1985, the OECD approved a new "Instrument on International Tourism Policy" in an effort to reduce impediments to travel. Based on a comprehensive inventory of obstacles to international tourism, the instrument reaffirmed the importance of tourism to the political, social, and economic well-being of the member countries. It also set up formal procedures for identifying specific travel impediments and taking cooperative steps to eliminate them.

Although OECD countries account for most of the world's tourism, the OECD has only 30 members. Many developing countries are neither represented in the organization nor directly affected by its decisions and recommendations.

General Agreement on Tariffs and Trade

The objectives of the **General Agreement on Tariffs and Trade (GATT)** are to liberalize world trade and to place it on a secure basis, thereby contributing to global economic growth and development. GATT (which is both an agreement and an organization with a secretariat and a working staff) is considered the central institutional basis of the present international trading system. It covers the world's major industrialized and developing countries. GATT agreements provide a framework within which international trade negotiations are conducted and trade disputes resolved.

Although the rules and procedures for GATT apply mainly to merchandise trade, the organization is well suited to deal with trade in services, including tourism. For example, the dispute settlement procedures of GATT could be used when hotels have difficulty importing needed equipment, materials, and other goods. On the basis of resolutions negotiated by the signatories, the organization has developed an internationally recognized set of rules and procedures for consultation, negotiation, and dispute settlement. GATT has been a major influence in gradually reducing world tariffs to their lowest level in history.

Trade in services, previously excluded, has now been included in the GATT framework. Since the 1970s, the service economy has soared in developed countries to become a key factor in world trade development. As noted in Exhibit 4, the world trade in commercial services stood at $2,755 billion in 2006, with travel bringing in $745 billion, which represents 27 percent of the trade in commercial services globally. The GATT Uruguay Agreement provided, for the first time ever,

Exhibit 4 World Trade in Commercial Services by Category, 2006

	Value ($billion)	Share				
	2006	2000	2003	2004	2005	2006
Exports						
All commercial services	2755	100.0	100.0	100.0	100.0	100.0
Transportation services	630	23.3	22.2	23.1	23.4	22.9
Travel	745	32.1	29.2	28.8	27.9	27.1
Other commercial services	1380	44.6	48.5	48.2	48.7	50.0
Imports						
All commercial services	2650	100.0	100.0	100.0	100.0	100.0
Transportation services	750	28.2	26.6	27.7	28.4	28.4
Travel	695	30.0	28.4	27.9	27.1	26.2
Other commercial services	1205	41.8	45.1	44.4	44.5	45.4

Source: World Trade Organization.

a section on "Negotiations on Trade in Services" under the **General Agreement on Trade in Services (GATS).** The goal of GATS is to free up international trade policies through the reduction or elimination of monetary barriers (for example, license fees), non-monetary barriers (for example, quota limits), and other barriers that hamper true international competition.

International Monetary Fund

The **International Monetary Fund (IMF)** influences exchange controls and financial policy on a global scale. It monitors members' compliance with a convention designed to ensure orderly exchange arrangements by promoting exchange rate stability and avoiding trade and payment restrictions that would harm international economic interests. The IMF conducts annual consultations with member countries, then reports on laws and regulations concerning import and export payments, foreign investment, and exchange control requirements on capital receipts or payments for residents or non-residents. These reports exert some pressure on countries to liberalize their restrictions. Topics of concern include measures and practices that affect the individual intending to travel, and formalities that affect payment for services performed by non-residents—for example, remittances of royalties, consultancy fees, and expatriate earnings.

International Hotel & Restaurant Association

The International Hotel & Restaurant Association (IH&RA) was founded in Paris in 1946. Now located in Geneva, IH&RA has long been involved with public policies dealing with international hotel regulations, education and training, and other issues. From its founding until about 1980, IH&RA membership comprised mainly independent hoteliers—the largest constituency representing Europe—and it was a fairly exclusive organization. Because of the wealth and position of most independent hotel owners, IH&RA members succeeded in keeping international hotel and restaurant chains out of the organization until the 1990s, when the organization began to soften its stance. Today, hotel and restaurant chains that are IH&RA members are prominently listed on the association's website.

Structure of the IH&RA. The changing structure of the worldwide hotel industry over the past few decades and the large increase in the market share of chain-affiliated properties gained at the expense of independently owned properties led IH&RA to gradually open its membership to international chains. IH&RA recognized that its traditional membership was declining and it was poorly represented in some key parts of the world, notably Asia and the Pacific, which detracted from its lobbying power as a world body. Today, national hotel associations, hotel chains, restaurant chains, and affiliate members such as hotel schools and suppliers hold memberships in IH&RA. With the changes in membership structure, IH&RA's power base has shifted from individual members to a network of national associations and hotel chains.

Program of Work. IH&RA works as a liaison with national associations and other international organizations. In recent years, it has been actively involved in professional training and human resource development in conjunction with the International Labor Organization (ILO) and the UNWTO. It has staged conferences and seminars on a wide range of international hotel industry concerns. IH&RA has a Management Information Systems (MIS) Working Group that addresses automation issues, including CRS development. The association has also begun to address environmental issues.

IH&RA has long been involved with legislative and fiscal matters affecting the industry. One of the more important issues taken up by IH&RA concerns the uniform international hotelkeeper's contract advocated by the International Institute for the Unification of Private Law (UNIDROIT), whose goal is to harmonize or coordinate the laws of different countries affecting the private sector. For a number of years, UNIDROIT has attempted to establish a draft model of an international hotelkeeper's contract that IH&RA opposes both in principle and content.

In an effort to settle some of the longstanding problems between hotels and travel agents dealing with such matters as contracts, reservations, payments, and cancellations, IH&RA was once party to a convention with the Universal Federation of Travel Agents Associations (UFTAA) that governed negotiations between hotels and travel agents. Because of U.S. anti-trust laws, however, U.S. hotels could not be party to such discussions or arrangements. IH&RA eventually disbanded the convention unilaterally. A non-binding "code of practice" is viewed as an alternative way of promoting harmonious relations between hotels and travel agents and of providing practical guidance to both parties. When misunderstandings and disagreements arise, the IH&RA and UFTAA Arbitration Service is available to either party for dispute settlement. IH&RA has also worked with UFTAA and the International Air Transport Association (IATA) to develop a universal voucher, confirmation, and central payment system for hotels and travel agents (comparable to the airline system); however, this too has run into conflict with U.S. anti-trust laws.

With respect to future objectives, IH&RA membership has directed its association to focus efforts on representing the hotel industry's interests and acting as a spokesorganization and lobbyist before governments, global industry partners, and other international associations. One of its major general mandates is to improve the current image of the lodging industry and increase governments' appreciation of the industry's economic contributions. Hoteliers everywhere have become increasingly aware of the growing importance of international legislation, covering such important matters as airline deregulation, automation and global central reservation systems, health and safety regulations, internal security, and so forth. Other general priorities include continuously collecting and disseminating information on behalf of the international hospitality industry and providing a forum for airing and resolving common industry problems.

In its role to continuously monitor regulatory and industry issues and to advocate legislation and policies supporting the international hospitality industry, IH&RA works through a number of councils, such as the National Association of Chief Executives Council. These councils identify issues, set priorities, and propose initiatives for IH&RA. Examples of the types of issues and concerns that IH&RA addresses include the following:

- *International standards*—IH&RA opposes the ISO move to establish international standards for hotel and restaurant services without industry support.
- *Check-in/check-out*—IH&RA opposes a consumer movement for an international standard ensuring total flexibility in check-in/check-out times.
- *International hotel classification scheme*—IH&RA opposes global requests for a single international hotel classification scheme.
- *Internet trademark infringement on the Internet*—this includes the use and/or purchase of hotel trade names by e-distribution intermediaries.
- *Worker migration*—the inability of good workers to get to available temporary jobs.
- *Skills and worker shortages*—the shortage of approximately 5 million workers in the next five years
- *Pandemics and the Avian flu*—the need for responsible communications and accurate travel advisories.
- *Terrorism guidelines*—action/reaction strategies in the event of a terrorism incident.
- *Corporate social responsibility*—are we truly credited with the work we do? Are there opportunities for improvement?
- *Food safety*—is the hotel and restaurant industry responsible from "farm to fork"? Where does our responsibility start and end?
- *Obesity*—is the food service industry responsible? What about consumers?
- *Disaster avoidance*—creation of operating guidelines for communities to prepare for disasters.
- *Diversity at the management level*—the need for management to more accurately reflect the employee mix.

- *The environment and sustainable tourism*—the promotion and recognition of innovative operating and development practices designed to make the industry more sustainable.[3]

Under its new organizational direction and membership structure, IH&RA today is in a stronger position to implement a strategic plan that will better represent the hotel industry's interests on a global scale.

World Travel & Tourism Council

The World Travel & Tourism Council (WTTC) was established in 1990 to address the need to (1) give the fragmented travel and tourism industry recognition as the world's biggest industry and provider of jobs, and (2) provide a single voice to convey this reality to elected officials and policy makers worldwide. The three main goals that came out of WTTC's early meetings were:

1. Promote recognition of the travel and tourism industry's economic contribution.
2. Expand markets in harmony with the environment.
3. Reduce barriers to growth.

To help achieve these goals, WTTC created a way to measure the global economic impact of travel and tourism known as the Tourism Satellite Accounting (TSA) system. Working with research partner Oxford Economic Forecasting, WTTC now produces annual global impact studies and forecasts for 176 countries, in addition to various other research studies. TSA data and other WTTC research are used by WTTC members to influence tourism policies in their respective industry sectors and countries.

Today the WTTC has a membership base of 100 members representing the largest and most influential travel and tourism organizations in the world. The membership list reads like a veritable who's who of global travel and tourism leaders. In keeping with the vision of WTTC's original founders, the organization still holds the same core values and mission: governments recognizing travel and tourism as a top priority; business balancing economics with people, culture, and the environment; and a shared pursuit of long-term growth and prosperity.

Recent initiatives by the council include the development of a crisis forecasting model and regional initiatives in China and the European Union designed to identify and eliminate barriers to growth. Highlighting the importance of understanding and discussing barriers to travel and tourism, the major theme for WTTC's 2007 Global Summit was "Breaking Barriers and Managing Growth." The consensus from the conference discussions was that some governments have shown an understanding of how travel and tourism can turn challenges into opportunities and optimize the synergies between the public and private sectors, but such governments are still very much in the minority.

The Need for Government Support

The need for government involvement and support of the tourism industry at national, regional, and local levels is critical. First, tourism does not exist in isolation from the rest of the economy. It requires infrastructural support, including airports, roads, transport, telecommunications, and other public services that in many cases government can best provide. Second, if the major benefits of tourism are to be realized, the local workforce must be educated and trained to provide quality tourism products and services. This requires government incentives to provide privately funded training or the establishment of government-supported training programs. Third, to promote tourism interest abroad, government support is needed to establish national tourism promotion offices in other countries. Fourth, only governments can provide for the issuance of visas for visitors and others through overseas consulates and embassies. And fifth, international events important to tourism (such as the International Olympics; the World's Fair and Exhibition; the World Cup; and world or regional conferences, conventions, trade fairs and the like) all require government sponsorship or support to secure a bid for one's country.

To win government support, the industry must have political support. Unfortunately, more often than not, residents and therefore governments view tourism with a degree of skepticism or disdain as an industry. It is therefore important for hotel operators (as well as others in the tourism industry) not only to understand the vital role that both government and politics play, but also to become active players themselves. Holding memberships in the local hotel association and the local chamber of commerce is usually the beginning of involvement with local politics and public issues.

Foreign Investment Incentives

Many governments encourage foreign hotel investments by offering financial incentives as part of their tourism development strategy. This approach is used particularly when national capital resources cannot be mobilized, when local entrepreneurs are not interested, or when it is believed that the managerial and marketing know-how of foreign hotels would best serve the country's developmental goals.

Interest in non-domestic hotel projects depends largely on the potential investors' evaluation of the political and economic climate of the host country and their investment criteria. Government incentives to stimulate foreign hotel investment, therefore, must be related to investment criteria such as cash flow and financial return. Most incentives are designed either to reduce the required investment outlay or to lower comparative operating costs. Specific financial incentives include duty concessions and tax holidays; other forms of government support that may also be used to facilitate and encourage outside investment include:

- Making information and advice available to prospective investors
- Helping prospective investors obtain necessary approvals
- Providing government guarantees
- Passing legislation favorable to foreign investment
- Providing for fair arbitration to settle disputes and conflicts that may require third-party intervention

- Providing adequate infrastructure
- Making available training for hotel workers or training incentives and allowances
- Sponsoring promotion of the visitor industry

By selectively using incentives, governments can direct hotel development in accordance with national tourism policies by favoring specific property types, sizes, and locations.

Bureaucratic Red Tape

Government supports the lodging industry whenever it minimizes bureaucratic red tape and hastens the approval process required for foreign hotel projects. For example, China and other emerging tourism destinations such as India and the UAE have established "special economic zones," "trade clusters," or "free zones" that reduce red tape and provide financial, infrastructure, and other incentives to attract international businesses. Especially in China and Dubai, the implementation of these special zones has resulted in an increase of foreign direct investments to these countries.

Tourism Policy

From a social standpoint, tourism has been all but ignored by most governments at every level. More and more countries and local governments, however, are beginning to think of tourism when considering economic development policies. They are looking for ways to minimize social problems while promoting optimal economic benefits in terms of employment, tax revenues, and foreign investments. There is increased recognition that tourism development needs to be planned for and managed in an organized, sustained, and appropriate way not only to optimize economic returns, but also to achieve social goals.

Policy Options. Many countries have developed explicit tourism policies covering the type, volume, and level of tourism to be fostered and developed. These policies have a significant impact on hotel investments and development. In some countries, governments have even assumed the role of developer in the absence of adequate private sector response. These governments have built hotels and other capital-intensive structures to promote tourism in underdeveloped or priority target areas. It is not unusual for a government of a developing country to designate a site for a hotel or resort project, outline the nature and scale of development, arrange a source of finance, and then look for an operator or a commercial developer to take over or buy a stake in the project.

Other issues that affect the hotel investor or operator may include government decisions or policies on pursuing domestic versus international tourism; "class" versus "mass" tourism; centralization versus decentralization of tourism decision-making among national, provincial, and county authorities; and integrated versus enclave tourism (that is, the degree of interaction between residents and visitors in resort destinations). These tourism issues often overlap, leading to umbrella policies covering diverse interests—public and private, domestic and international. Government responses to tourism and hospitality industry development choices have varied greatly. These variations depend as much upon political, cultural, social, environmental, and geographical considerations as upon economic factors.

Understanding the visitor's impact in social and environmental terms as well as economic terms is important in tourism planning. In many areas, attention is being given to the quality of the visit, the length of stay, and repeat visitors. With respect to hotel development, many destinations have policies that encourage so-called class tourism—the development of full-service luxury hotels that attract higher-yield visitors and maximize the turnover (or revenue) from tourism investments—while shying away from mass tourism, which requires budget and economy accommodations. Mass tourism requires infrastructure (water, roads, sewers, power, airport runways for jumbo jet landings, etc.) that many destinations do not have. It also tends to cause more damage to the environment. Many destinations (for example, Bermuda) see steady, controlled growth as critical for success in the long run. Other government policies may encourage the development of indigenously oriented small-scale hotels, as these may lessen the need for imported materials and skilled labor for construction and operations. They may also provide greater opportunities at higher levels of management for the local workforce.

For many years, the Organization for Economic Cooperation and Development has regularly reviewed national policies on tourism in order to deepen mutual understanding of current tourism policy issues; identify gaps, shortcomings, and successes in national tourism policies; and evaluate the economic, social, and environmental impacts of those policies. Other international organizations discussed earlier in the chapter also debate and discuss tourism policies in their conferences, summits, and forums on a regular basis.

National Tourism Organizations

National tourism organizations (NTOs) are usually charged with carrying out the tourism policies of a country. While marketing/promoting the country as a visitor destination is the common function of NTOs, their jurisdiction and level of power to determine and implement policies vary widely among countries. Some NTOs are located at the cabinet or ministry level and have considerable influence. Others function at a departmental or subcabinet level, while still others operate as quasi-government, quasi-industry corporations with lesser degrees of influence.

A survey conducted by the UNWTO reveals that NTOs around the world are involved in the following activities and issues (in descending order of frequency):

1. Official tourism representation at the national and international levels
2. Research, studies, surveys, and statistics
3. Tourism promotion abroad (that is, field representation in other countries)
4. Tourism planning and development
5. International tourism promotion (that is, centralized general marketing of all programs above the field-office level)

6. Regulation and supervision of tourist enterprises
7. Facilitation
8. Tourist reception and information
9. Tourism vocational training
10. Preservation, protection, and use of historical, cultural, and handicraft resources
11. Ecology and the environment[4]

Most of these activities and issues have a direct or indirect impact on the viability of the lodging industry.

International Lodging Chains and Developing Countries

The role of international lodging chains in national development has been an important one. In many cases, such chains have been the catalyst needed to energize a developing country's plan for tourism growth. Lodging chains can provide technological, operational, and marketing know-how and other forms of support. Although this assistance is very helpful in the initial stages of tourism development, it is important from a government's perspective that the role of these chains complement the country's goals and tourism aspirations. A key goal is the transference of technology and expertise in hotel administration.

Identifying Advantages and Disadvantages

The UNWTO and other groups have conducted studies of government opinions concerning the benefits and drawbacks of lodging chain involvement in developing countries. In a 1985 survey examining the experience of developing countries in dealing with tourism transnational corporations (TNCs), the UNWTO found somewhat mixed results (see Exhibit 5). The benefits of lodging TNCs to developing countries were perceived to include largely technical services that are related to market feasibility studies, planning, construction, technology, marketing and promotion, transfer of technical skills, and management expertise. Speeding up the pace of tourism development has been identified as the most significant benefit of international hotel company involvement. The international hotel companies' experience, ready production techniques, and trouble-shooting abilities enable them to accomplish the initial stages of development more rapidly and efficiently than their domestic counterparts in most instances.

On the negative side, TNCs are not always attuned to the local culture or to the stage of development of the country. They often seem reluctant to hire locally to fill senior positions. International lodging companies frequently employ expatriate personnel at higher salaries, which are usually paid in foreign currency and eventually "leaked" out of the local economy to the expatriates' home countries. Training of the local labor force is not always emphasized as much as governments believe it should be, and the training offered is not always appropriate for the needs of the country. Developing countries often require foreign hotel operators to

82 Chapter 3

Exhibit 5   Experience of Developing Countries in Dealing with Transnational Tourism Corporations

Question	True %	Partly true %	Untrue %
1. Transnational corporations (TNCs) have to some extent influenced the *type of tourism activity* attracted to developing countries	36	55	9
2. *Lack of bargaining power* is the main problem of developing countries in dealing with TNCs	50	41	9
3. Developing countries are *insufficiently informed* about the various transnational corporations and forms of their involvement in tourism development	50	27	23
4. TNCs appear at times *reluctant to employ local managers* and senior staff	59	32	9
5. The most significant benefit of TNC involvement is in *speeding up the pace of tourism development*	45	32	23
6. The most significant lasting contribution made by TNCs to the developing countries is the *transfer of skills,* product knowledge, technology and product techniques	27	64	9
7. The working methods and training schemes of TNCs are *not always adapted* to the stage of development of the receiving country	45	45	9
8. Often, *TNCs give less emphasis to training local personnel* than to meeting production targets and deadlines	59	32	9

Note: Tourism transnational corporations (TNCs) have been defined by the WTO as foreign enterprises providing services for movements of persons with direct investments or other major forms of contractual arrangement in one or more receiving countries.

Source: *The Role of Transnational Tourism Enterprises in the Development of Tourism,* World Tourism Organization, 1985.

agree to provide appropriate training to locals before they will sanction management contracts.

Maximizing Returns from Tourism

The 1985 UNWTO survey cited earlier also addressed the principal strategies adopted by developing countries to maximize benefits of TNC involvement. As

Exhibit 6 Strategies to Maximize Benefits of TNC Involvement

Strategies	% of application	% Rate of success
• *Adopting legislation or regulations* to ensure that TNCs do not exploit their monopoly power or act in such a way as to conflict with national economic development goals	73	75
• *Taking fiscal or other measures* to ensure that an equitable share of the economic benefits of tourism development are retained in the receiving country	73	75
• *Seeking greater self-reliance in training and in technology* transfer in order to reduce dependence on external sources	68	87
• *Making use of impartial and expert advice* during contract negotiations with TNCs	55	75
• Dealing with *several TNCs based in different countries* to encourage competition between them	55	75
• In recognition of the variety of motivations both obligatory and non-obligatory governing the movements of persons, *seeking to develop new and alternative markets* for which relatively simple products can be offered that do not require the substantial involvement of TNCs	55	83
• *Encouraging competition between TNCs and domestic tourism enterprises*	45	70
• *Strengthening bargaining power* of individual countries through multilateral action (such as consultation) taken by groups of receiving countries	41	44

Source: *The Role of Transnational Tourism Enterprises in the Development of Tourism*, World Tourism Organization, 1985.

shown in Exhibit 6, the majority of developing countries use legislation and fiscal measures to obtain an equitable share of the economic benefits and to ensure that hotels do not act in conflict with national development goals. Many countries also seek greater reliance on training and technology transfer to reduce dependence on external sources. Still other countries have applied strategies to develop alternative markets not requiring substantial involvement of international lodging companies. All of these strategies have proven successful. Over half the respondent countries make use of impartial and expert advice during contract negotiations, or deal with several TNCs at once to foster competition. TNCs based in other countries may compete with other TNCs and/or with domestic firms.[5]

Lodging Chains and Host Governments—Inevitable Conflict

The governments of most developing countries prefer to encourage locally developed hotel projects. However, they also realize that internationally recognized chains provide marketability for an area's tourism industry and may contribute significantly to its growth. Despite the attendant problems, therefore, such chains also represent opportunities.

For many years, lodging companies were essentially able to write their own tickets when entering developing countries. Governments simply lacked sufficient knowledge of alternatives and bargaining power. This situation is rapidly changing in a world of instant information access. Developing countries' governments have gained sophistication and understanding about the way foreign companies conduct their business and about how they affect the host country's economy and social life. These governments have begun to reevaluate questions of ownership, capital, price structure, and employment.

The differing perceptions and priorities of governments and hotel companies have led to inevitable conflicts and have sometimes bred misunderstandings and suspicions. As profit-making enterprises, hotels are obligated to stockholders or owners to maximize profits. However, this priority often runs counter to the priorities of the host government, which is responsible for the welfare of all its citizens and for equalizing opportunity and access to basic goods and services. Governments are primarily concerned with issues of employment, foreign exchange, taxation, and the increased circulation of national currency. This gap in perceptions and values and the parties' inability to understand and accept each other's motives often prevent them from achieving mutually satisfactory solutions.

To many local residents, foreign companies represent an alien power and outside control. To the extent that there has been no real effort to train and promote host country nationals to positions of responsibility, the conflict is accentuated.

Expatriate managers in developing countries need to be aware of the potential for conflict that is built into their relationship with public officials. They need to be prepared and trained to manage situations created by this conflict. International hotel operators should equip their managers to understand priority differences and how to reconcile opposing interests. A critical cross-cultural skill for general managers is the ability to reach and maintain a satisfactory understanding with their hosts.

For the foreseeable future, TNCs will continue to play an important role in developing countries, given their technology and global market outreach. Nonetheless, the relationship is best defined as an evolving one, as governments look to maximize the benefits of association and minimize the negative aspects of dependency. The best relationship is a realistic one based on mutual respect and an understanding of the host country's aspirations and policies for economic and social development. This type of approach will increase the hotel company's chances for enjoying the benefits of a stable and amicable long-term collaboration.

Political Stability

Political stability is one of the cornerstones of tourism development. The lodging industry is affected by political problems in at least two ways. First, political instability discourages hotel investment. Second, political crises significantly deter travel to affected areas.

Impact on Investment Decisions

Domestic investment decisions tend to focus on the financial or economic variables of a project. Potential investors in a foreign venture will also look at the stability of the host country. Indeed, the absence of sociopolitical stability in a country is likely to make any investment unacceptably risky, even when extraordinary incentives are offered. Thus, while return on investment may be perceived as the driving force in the foreign investment decision, political instability may be perceived as a restraining force.

Impact on Travelers

Good news may be interesting, but bad news sells newspapers. Attacks on travelers or the places they visit will almost certainly receive wide media coverage, which is an attractive proposition for those seeking publicity. Indeed, over the past several decades, the tourist industry has been used as a kind of indicator of the severity of a political crisis, a means of quantifying the impact.

Major acts or threats of violence such as hijackings, bombings, and other terrorist acts in airplanes, sea vessels, transportation terminals, and other public areas have had profound effects on international travel. Fear of terrorism is known to discourage people from going to affected destinations and even from traveling altogether. Terrorist acts or threats appear to be a given fact of modern travel. The relationship between tourism and terrorism gained international notoriety in 1972, when Palestinian terrorists attacked Israeli athletes during the Olympic Games and the drama was viewed by millions around the world. Acts of terrorism on tourists continued sporadically in the years following. However, since the terrorist attacks on the World Trade Center and the Pentagon on September 11, 2001, the world has witnessed an escalation of terrorism acts. Because hotels and other elements of the travel and tourism infrastructure such as buses and subways are viewed as "soft targets," we have seen bombing incidents involving these elements in such locations as London, Madrid, India, Bali (Indonesia), and Egypt. Tourists are often targeted, as they represent capitalism and conspicuous consumption, values associated with the West and abhorred by many fundamentalist terrorist groups. In other instances, where tourism is state-sponsored, attacks on tourists may represent an attack on their government.

Political problems tend to affect business travel less than pleasure travel. In this respect, hotels catering predominantly to a business clientele have an edge over properties that cater mostly to holiday travelers. But in high-risk destinations, even the staunchest of business travelers will seek alternative ways of transacting business.

Traveler reaction to political problems also differs among nationalities. On the whole, Europeans appear less concerned about internal civil unrest or terrorism than Americans, Australians, and Japanese. Germans, Swiss, and Dutch are considered among the traveling stalwarts who will go almost anywhere. Europeans tend to see themselves as being politically neutral and therefore less likely to be targets of political victimization.

Notable cases documenting the adverse impact of political disturbances on travel, tourism, and hotels are presented in the following sections. These examples pulled from the history of the past few decades make it clear just how much of an impact political instability can have on travel and tourism.

The Mediterranean. The attacks at the Rome, Vienna, and Athens airports in 1985–86, combined with the TWA 847 hijacking and the Achille Lauro shipjacking in 1985, provoked broad travel consumer reaction, most notably trip cancelations. For example, immediately after the TWA hijacking, 1.4 *million* U.S. travelers canceled reservations for travel abroad. The European/Arab/Mediterranean travel market lost an estimated $1 billion in tourism revenues to terrorism in 1985. American group tours to Europe and the Middle East dropped by 50 to 60 percent in 1986. Hotel occupancy in some areas dropped by as much as 40 points.

Philippines. Hotels in the Philippines have been suffering the ill effects of political instability for decades. Martial law under the Marcos regime, the assassination of Benigno Aquino in 1983, and communist insurgencies are all political circumstances that have played havoc with tourist arrivals and occupancy rates. Several hotels throughout this period had to cease operations. The Development Bank of the Philippines, which originally financed many of these projects, took over several hotels. Ferdinand Marcos was forced into exile in 1986 and the country has undertaken many democratic reforms in the years since, but attempted military coups, attacks by Muslim separatists, and political scandals continue to plague the country and hamper its travel and tourism industry.

China. During the Tiananmen Square incident in the spring of 1989, in which the government of the People's Republic of China forcefully put down student demonstrations, the first consideration of hotel management was to evacuate guests and expatriate personnel safely. Public emotions ran high and huge numbers of cancelations were initiated by both tour operators and potential travelers. Most countries flew special airline charters to evacuate their citizens.

The continued negative publicity and travel advisories from a number of countries virtually eliminated tourism and hotel demand in China. Short-term and longer-term tour cancelations came as bad news for hoteliers already confronted with room gluts in major cities. Some hotels reported occupancies as low as 10 percent despite the fact that rates had been slashed as much as 80 percent.[6] Staples such as milk, oil, and cooking gas were hard to get and hotels were ordered to disconnect satellite dishes so that foreign news accounts of the incident could not be heard. As a result of this political crisis, many hotel developers tried to renegotiate contract terms and loan repayment schedules for existing projects. Several joint venture hotel projects that were in the development phase lost their funding and most expansion plans for Chinese hotels were permanently shelved.

Africa. Political unrest, which is a constant fact of life in Africa, has played a central role in limiting the expansion of the tourism and hotel industries on this continent. A cloud of civil unrest overshadows many countries, and incessant hostilities have prevented a viable tourism industry from developing in many parts of

Africa. While there is a great deal of potential for tourism development in Africa and some hotel projects have been quite successful, foreign investment interest has been low due to economic and political instability, inadequate infrastructure, strict currency exchange controls, and other problems.

Central and South America. Similar to Africa, the countries of Central and South America have continuously struggled to overcome economic woes, political unrest, and civil wars. The history of constant tensions has created a negative image with respect to tourism that has been difficult to modify. This has proved to be a major deterrent in developing a viable tourism or hotel industry. In some Latin countries, however, the situation is beginning to change, led by vigorous government reforms to strengthen democratic elections, reduce runaway inflation, and move toward market economies. Consequently, major hotel chains are renewing their interest in these countries.

Persian Gulf War. On January 16, 1991, as Allied bombings began on Baghdad, the world's tourism industry was plunged into one of its bleakest periods in modern times. Countries issued advisories one after the other to warn their citizens about potential hazards of traveling to affected areas, especially as terrorist threats intensified. In Japan, authorities issued a general statement advising Japanese to avoid unnecessary travel, and politicians urged Japanese citizens not to travel while people were dying on battlefields. The negative effects of the Gulf War were felt immediately by surrounding countries. Hotels in Israel were so empty that some were used to shelter immigrants. Egypt, Jordan, Turkey, and other Middle Eastern destinations also lost a high proportion of their usual visitors. In fact, hotel cancelations poured in all over the world. Bangkok, Thailand, was particularly hard hit because of constant rumors in the media that it had become the center of an Iraqi terrorist network. Some Bangkok hotels accustomed to 80 to 90 percent occupancies reported occupancy dropping as much as 60 points. Hotels in almost every destination in the world experienced occupancy drops of 20 to 30 percent.

The war also triggered an oil scare that resulted in higher air transport costs. The price of jet fuel soared, which affected the airline industry and led to substantial fare increases. The increased cost of travel, together with fears of terrorist acts, dampened travel demand to all destinations (although those destinations perceived as safe lost less than those seen as unsafe).

Iraq War. More recently, the ongoing conflict in Iraq—variously referred to as the Iraq War, Gulf War II, or Second Persian Gulf War—has had many negative global consequences for tourism since the fighting began in March 2003. First, international tourism arrivals from Western countries to the Middle East have fallen because of the perception of risk. Second, travel to the United States has fallen, due to a combination of more restrictive visa policies and an anti-American sentiment as a result of the war. Third, tourism development projects in the region have been put on hold or cancelled. Of course, the most severe consequences have been felt in Iraq itself. Much of its tourism infrastructure is damaged or obsolete. Tourists fear to enter the country. Important historical, religious, and cultural sites that could someday be a draw for tourists are being destroyed, damaged, or looted.[7] A return to the tourism Iraq enjoyed in the 1970s, when the country drew millions of travelers from around the world, seems far off.

The Yaounde Hilton, Cameroon. (Courtesy of the Yaounde Hilton)

Spillover Impact of Political Events. Political instability has an unfortunate spillover effect from one area to the next. Turmoil in China, for example, has an impact on all of Asia; terrorist flare-ups in Israel have a dampening affect on tourism not only to Israel but to other Middle Eastern countries as well. On the other hand, political problems in one area of the world may benefit competing destinations deemed to be safer. The terrorist events in Europe in the mid 1980s, for instance, had a devastating effect on European tourism and hotel bookings, but helped the tourism industries of both the Caribbean and Hawaii.

Travel Advisories

One of the consequences of political instability is the issuance of **travel advisories** by governments warning citizens to avoid travel to the area in question. Such warnings, also issued during outbreaks of contagious diseases, can be devastating for travel-related businesses, especially hotels, airlines, and tour operators. It is understandable, therefore, that the tourism bureau of an affected destination will respond quickly to travel advisories in an attempt to stem the damage to the industry.

Travel advisories are typically issued by a country's state department or its equivalent. The information usually originates with the embassies or consulates in the affected country.

The U.S. State Department offers advice to travelers. This advice may come in the form of a "Travel Warning," which is a recommendation to Americans to avoid visiting certain countries because of safety or security concerns; details of the potential threats are provided for each country. The State Department also

The Special Case of Israel

As in Africa and Latin America, civil war and instability have adversely affected the hotel industry and the overall investment climate in the Middle East. Perhaps the challenges and complexities of operating in a politically difficult environment are most evident with Israel's hotel industry. Even though tourism has been a mainstay of the Israeli economy since the country was created in 1948, Israeli hotels operate in an environment of continuous pressure from government, from employees, from terrorism, and from religious authorities. The Israeli government plays a major role in all economic development, including the tourism and hotel industries, where it has gradually increased its participation and control over time.

The Ministry of Tourism, which has some 200 employees, most of them working in information and inspection capacities, must approve all construction projects. The Ministry has also established a grading system for hotels, which has been a major bone of contention between government and hoteliers. The government controls room rates and, to some extent, the types of services offered to guests. With respect to labor, the Israeli Hotel Association signs collective labor agreements for all hotels in Israel. As wage rates are relatively low, hotels have difficulty attracting capable staff.

People travel to Israel for special purposes. There is no substitute for Israel. Travel motivations typically include very specific sightseeing, visiting relatives, or religious pilgrimages, although holiday travel and conventioneers have been increasing. Religious pilgrimages of all types are probably Israel's most constant source of traffic; visits to Jerusalem and choice of hotels reflect this fact. Jewish travelers, for instance, tend to prefer higher-priced hotels in western Jerusalem that provide kosher food and better service, whereas Christian travelers tend to prefer the lower-priced accommodations available in eastern Jerusalem. The most successful hotels, however, are those that are sensitive enough to cater to both groups' needs.*

Keeping Kosher

Israel is under strict religious supervision that permeates every aspect of life, including travel. Even the national airline, El-Al, is not permitted to fly on the Shabbat (Sabbath). Hotels are also covered under this religious oversight, particularly with respect to the rules of kashrut, or keeping kosher. Due to the complicated nature of kashrut, supervision and regulation are required. Hotels are not required by law to keep kosher; but most have chosen to keep kosher for commercial reasons, as many visitors to Israel would not consider staying at a non-kosher hotel.

The costs of keeping kosher are substantial, since the hotel must have two full but separate kitchen setups, including areas for food preparation, service, storage, and sanitation: one for meat preparation and one for preparing dairy products. Kosher meat is more expensive than non-kosher and the cost of supervision is high. One hotelier estimated that the cost of keeping kosher amounted to 10% of sales. Frequently kashrut licenses are given by the rabbinical council and then lifted for other religious reasons unrelated to kashrut. Many hotels are kosher according to

---

*Kenneth J. Gruber, "The Hotels of Israel: Pressure and Promise," *The Cornell Hotel and Restaurant Administration Quarterly,* February 1988, p. 38.

(continued)

(continued)

> all the rules and regulations, but fail to receive kashrut permits because of quarrels among different religious authorities. The Jerusalem Rabbinate at one point refused to award kashrut certificates to hotels that failed to keep the Shabbat; contrary to the rules, these hotels scheduled Jews to work on the Shabbat, did not stop all check-in and check-out on the Shabbat, did not close the telephone switchboard during the 24-hour Shabbat period, and accepted money for services on that day.*
>
> One of the most challenging aspects of operating a hotel in Israel is the difficulty of predicting visitor arrivals, given the long history of political problems in the region. Although there is now a peace accord between Israel and the Palestine Liberation Organization, the travel market will remain cautious for some time. While the lodging industry is cooperative and works together, the political factor, in addition to all the other pressures, puts the industry in a constant state of flux and uncertainty.
>
> ---
>
> *Ibid. p. 42.

issues public announcements to disseminate information quickly about terrorist threats and other relatively short-term conditions that pose significant risks or disruptions to Americans. In addition, the State Department issues Consular Information Sheets for every country in the world, with information on such matters as health conditions, crime, unusual currency or entry requirements, areas of instability, and the location of the nearest embassy or consulate in the subject country.

Travel industry leaders criticize travel advisories as sometimes being inaccurate, excessive, or unwarranted. Regardless of their accuracy, travel advisories can sound the death knell for an area's tourism industry, which typically suffers massive cancelations and loss of image. Travel analysts thus suggest that the public needs to look beyond travel advisories and the sensationalized headlines of civil disturbances when deciding whether to travel to certain areas. They argue that the real situation often is not reflected by the media or the travel advisory and that travelers in most cases will not be bothered by anything more than inconveniences and bureaucratic red tape. Because the stakes are so high, the Pacific Asia Travel Association (PATA) created the "PATA Code for Fair Travel Advisory Issuance" as a suggested guideline for those involved in issuing travel advisories (see Exhibit 7).

As an example of overreaction, when two bloodless military coups occurred in 1987 in Fiji (to that point a model of political stability among the Pacific islands), a U.S. State Department alert warned that "military presence in the streets and sporadic incidents of violence" posed a danger for Americans and recommended that people should "defer travel to Fiji at this time." In reality, there was no significant "military presence," just a strong-arm settlement of political differences between the native Fijians and the resident East Indians, prompted by results of a recent election. Although the languid pace of life in the islands, particularly within resort areas, was virtually unaffected by these coups, tourism plummeted overnight. Hotel occupancies dropped by as much as 40 points due to exaggerated media accounts and various countries' issuance of travel advisories. In 1988, the Fijian dollar was devalued by 33 percent, GNP fell by 11 percent, and tourism revenues declined by 29 percent.[8]

Exhibit 7 The PATA Code for Fair Travel Advisory Issuance

1. The system for advisory information gathering and implementation should be made more transparent.
2. The economic and social effects of the advisory on target destinations must be taken into account and reconciled with other objectives, such as support for overseas development and the alleviation of poverty, especially in developing countries.
3. There should be open consultation with stakeholders, both in the issuing country and with representatives of the destination(s) under consideration.
   a. *In the issuing countries:* much of this can be achieved by setting up a standing advisory council on advisories that includes government officers, representatives from the travel industry, and other sectors (as in the UK and Australia).
   b. *In the destination(s) affected:* local embassies (or offices) of the issuing government (or body) should be willing to engage with stakeholders locally to review travel advisory content.
4. The advisory must be proportionate to the real risk.
5. It is essential that travel advisories be updated quickly, especially to reflect events that have already become public knowledge.
6. Out-of-date information should be removed as soon as possible.
7. Warnings should be lifted or lowered as soon as practical. Any change in status should be immediately publicized.
8. All destinations should be treated equally.
9. As far as possible, destination governments should be informed in advance of changes to the travel advisory, and the underlying reasons for the changes.

Source: Pacific Asia Travel Association.

Political Motivations

In theory, travel advisories are not intended as instruments of public policy. They are supposedly issued and modified solely on the basis of objective evidence. In reality, however, public policy can affect the issuance of advisories. Governments sometimes use travel warnings as a convenient economic weapon, especially against countries that have a substantial stake in tourism. At least part of the reason the United States issued an advisory on the Athens airport during a period of intense terrorist activity, for example, was to put pressure on the Greek government to adopt better security measures. Even though the advisory was issued strictly for the airport, the effect was that all of Greece was immediately red-flagged as dangerous. Both the public and private sectors in Greece mounted intense lobbying efforts in Washington to have the advisory rescinded.

Politically motivated advisories are common. For example, similar events in two different countries will often trigger two separate reactions from the same government. Government officials defend this practice by arguing that politically aligned countries tend to look after each other's citizens more scrupulously than antagonistic countries tend to do. Aside from the comparative levels of security, different standards for different countries are often related to one country's relations with the country in question. During the Persian Gulf crisis in the spring of 1991, the U.S. government issued an advisory for every Muslim country that expressed reservations about the U.N. resolutions. At the peak of the crisis, the U.S. State Department had issued advisories or warnings for 75 countries, representing more than 40 percent of the world's nations.

Political Risk

Hotel investors and operators all over the world have at times worked in environments of high political uncertainty or have had to contend with political events. These events have included the changeover of entire political systems, as in the case of Iran or the USSR; the nationalization or privatization of industries, as has happened in the Philippines or the United Kingdom; exchange control regulations such as those instituted by France after the socialist government took control; changing ownership constraints such as those in Mexico and India; conflicts such as the Persian Gulf War and Iraq War; and terrorist activities. All of these events severely affect the operating climate and financial viability of foreign hotel investments. The possibility of such events prompts investors, developers, and operators alike to carefully assess political risk as a key factor in the decision process.

Political risk implies unwanted consequences of political activity. It may also be stated simply in terms of the business risks incurred by political changes. The potential risk factor can be determined by two variables: (1) probability of occurrence, and (2) impact as measured by potential loss through business disruptions or casualty.[9] Political risk in some spheres may be distinguished from economic or social risk. Generally, however, most of politics concerns itself with the struggle over economic and social decisions.

Political risk events can be perceived as any political outcome in a host country which, if it occurred, would have a negative impact on the success of the venture. Political risk events are numerous and encompassing (see Exhibit 8). They include events that are obvious (such as civil disorders, foreign war, and ideological change) and less obvious (such as creeping expropriation—that is, gradual loss of the right to own and control the business—and local product content rules). Although some political risk events are manifestations of economic, financial, environmental, or other risks, they may be politically based as well. Different industries, because of their underlying nature, will have varying degrees of sensitivity to such events.

Because international hotels are labor intensive, typically have a high profile, and require a great number of cash transfers, they tend to be susceptible to creeping expropriation, flow of funds restrictions, and labor considerations. From a practical business standpoint, therefore, the hotel investor or operator is likely to consider political risks in terms of transfer risk, operational risk, asset risk, market risk, administrative/statutory risk, and ownership risk:

- *Transfer risks* represent a host government's restrictions on the transfer of capital, payments, products, technology, and persons into or out of the host country.

Exhibit 8 Examples of Political Risk Events

Civil Disorder (for example, demonstrations, riots, sabotage, terrorism, armed insurrection, revolution, guerilla war, civil war)

Creeping Expropriation

Devaluation/Revaluation

Domestic Price Controls

Embargoes and Boycotts

Flow of Funds Restrictions (for example, relating to dividends, royalties, interest payments, profit, repatriation)

Foreign Exchange Control (for example, control of convertibility)

Foreign War

Government to Government Sales Policies

Hiring and Firing Constraints (for example, local employment requirements)

Ideological Change

International Trade Barriers and Constraints

Labor Relations

Labor Shortages

Local Product Content Rules

Locally Shared Ownership

Non-Tariff Barriers (for example, regulations, subsidies)

Outright Nationalization (for example, confiscation, expropriation)

Reinvestment Requirements

Tariff Barriers

Tax (for example, income tax)

- *Operational risks* refer to interventions that directly constrain the management and performance of local hotel operations in production, marketing, finance, human resource management, and other business functions.
- *Asset risks* are those threatening the safety of assets.
- *Market risks* can threaten the growth of domestic markets, access to foreign markets, and fair competition.
- *Administrative/statutory risks* refer to the likelihood that changes in the regulatory climate will affect a project or agreement.
- *Ownership risks* address questions of equity shares involving issues of participation, expropriation, and nationalization.[10]

Difficulty of Assessing Political Risk

The variety and lack of agreed-upon definitions and classifications of political risk events make measuring and analyzing political risks a difficult task. Analysts also tend to overemphasize dramatic events. Techniques currently used to analyze political risk run the gamut from expert opinions to detailed statistical models using discriminant functions. The different approaches generally fall under one of the following categories: (1) purely qualitative/unstructured methods, (2) aggregation of expert opinions, (3) scenario construction, (4) decision-tree approaches, and (5) factor analysis. These approaches are beyond the scope of this chapter.

Numerous banks and other large multinational companies have developed in-house political risk assessment models. There are also a variety of independent political risk consultation services available to international businesses. All of these use different models which, not surprisingly, produce different results. Among the more popular services are B.E.R.I. (which stands for Business Environment Risk Intelligence), the Economist Intelligence Unit (a subsidiary of the Economist Group), the Eurasia Group, Frost & Sullivan, Global Risk Assessment, Inc., and Political Risk Services.

Reducing Vulnerability in Risky Situations

Why do hotel companies consider high-risk countries for potential investment or operation? One reason is that safe havens for hotel development are no longer plentiful. As the international hotel industry becomes increasingly competitive, areas become overbuilt and prime locations become scarce or very expensive to develop. Thus, companies must find new areas in order to achieve growth objectives. Developers and hoteliers cite potential profitability, lower development costs, and a ready and inexpensive supply of labor as important reasons for going into areas still working toward stabilization. While sales may not be as high, profits can be higher than in safer areas. And many of these risk areas already have or soon will have high-density population centers. Hotels that establish themselves on prime sites will at some point gain an advantage.

While it is almost inevitable that growth-oriented hotel companies will eventually move into risky areas, these companies will tend to carefully manage their political risk vulnerability rather than simply avoid or ignore it.

Lodging companies often use joint ventures or management contracts with little or no equity participation to reduce vulnerability to political risk. Such approaches reduce capital requirements and/or shift the lending risk to partners. Many hotel projects in China, for example, were structured as contractual joint ventures. This meant that the government and the foreign investor did not actually put up any money; rather, they set up a joint venture that then borrowed the money to develop the hotel. In most cases, the Chinese government provided the land and the loan guarantee, and the foreign hotel company provided technical, management, and marketing expertise. Equity joint ventures (in which the government provides land and some of the construction and infrastructure for the hotel, and the hotel developer provides some of the funds and conjointly guarantees the loan) are less attractive because there is no way to liquidate the asset, if necessary.

Political risk becomes significantly more relevant for lodging companies as the level of commitment increases from franchising to management contracts to ownership participation. With UNWTO-induced reforms underway in China and government liberalization policies being introduced in India, international equity investment funds are now moving toward investments in hard assets, such as hotels, in these countries. However, in the case of China, where private ownership of land is not permitted, "ownership" is actually land use rights—in effect, a 40-year lease. What happens at the end of 40 years is currently a source of speculation and represents political risk exposure.[11] Political risk exposure is generally the highest in the early stages of a country's economic reforms. A case in point is the relatively recent regulations permitting gaming and casino operations in Macau. Because there is little precedent on the interpretation of these laws and regulations, they represent a risk. Furthermore, the Chinese central administration still has the power to control tourist flows from mainland China to Macau, which adds another layer of indirect political risk.

In most cases, the political risk consideration is a major factor in determining the lodging company's degree of commitment, if any, to the project in question. This includes the level of financial involvement, concessions and/or incentives negotiated with the government, required guarantees of funds convertibility, and the terms of the management contract. The higher the political risk, the more attractive a less-involved form of participation and the more exacting the required guarantees become, as this reduces the level of vulnerability to political risk events.

Political Risk Insurance. Political risk insurance offers a way for international hotel companies to lessen their vulnerability. Companies may purchase insurance to reduce the risk from expropriation, war, civil strife, currency inconvertibility, or contract problems. In the past, many companies considered political risk insurance optional, but demand for it soars as soon as a country's political situation unravels.

Political risk policies can be divided into two categories: those that cover investments, and those that cover trade and contractual issues (see Exhibit 9). Contract frustration and letter of credit insurance, for example, are primarily obtained for trade and short-term contract obligations when a company fears government interference in a contract or payment of a letter of credit. Hotel companies with capital-intensive investments and long payback periods may purchase longer-term coverage for such risks as expropriation, political violence, or currency inconvertibility. The comfort level with joint venture partners also influences the political risk policy.

Political risk insurance can be purchased from either commercial agencies or non-commercial government-backed insurers. In the United States, the two most important government agencies are the Overseas Private Investment Corp. (OPIC), which can be affected by congressional interventions, and the Foreign Credit Insurance Association (FCIA), which insures non-payment of letters of credit. Commercial providers include the American International Group (AIG), the Chubb Group, Lloyd's of London, and Citigroup. Commercial providers can cover companies of any nationality and any investment. For investment insurance, private providers commonly cover the risks of civil strife and expropriation. Only

Exhibit 9   Political Risk Insurance

INVESTMENT COVERAGE	TRADE & CONTRACT COVERAGE
THE POLITICAL RISK PACKAGE	• **Contract frustration:** covers governmental actions not justified by contract terms, and may include contract repudiation, termination or defaults in payment or supplies by a government buyer or seller, embargoes or license revocations by the government of the importer or exporter; and currency inconvertibility
• **Political violence:** compensates for damaged assets and income losses due to strike/riot/civil commotion (SRCC), terrorism, or sabotage, and sometimes civil war. Government insurers also cover losses due to war, revolution, or insurrection	• **Unfair, arbitrary, or wrongful calling:** covers wrongful callings of on-demand bid, advance payment, or performance guarantees posted by a seller in favor of a foreign (usually government) buyer
• **Currency inconvertibility/blockage:** covers both active and passive blockage of profits, return of capital, debt service, or fees (but is hard to obtain for China)	• **Letter of credit:** covers loss due to the failure of a central bank or equivalent authority to honor a letter of credit
• **Confiscation/expropriation/ nationalization:** covers outright seizure without compensation, and creeping expropriation of assets and bank accounts	• **Confiscation, deprivation, political violence:** covers losses to equipment in a foreign country

Source: Elizabeth Keck, "Covering All the Bases," *The China Business Review,* September-October 1989, p. 20.

government-backed insurers offer the additional political violence coverage for war, revolution, or insurrection. Government insurers tend to provide longer-term coverage; private insurers typically have a maximum three-year commitment.[12]

Starting in 2003, OPIC began offering terrorism insurance to protect American businesses abroad. This insurance covers "violent acts with the primary intent of achieving a political objective, undertaken by individuals or groups that do not constitute a national or international armed force." This coverage extends over a 10-year period and includes countries where private sector insurance is not easily available. In general, this coverage compensates the policy holder for (1) the loss of or damage to tangible property, and (2) business income losses incurred as a result of the terrorist attack.

The Multilateral Investment Guarantee Agency (MIGA), established in 1988 as a member of the World Bank Group, can also guarantee hotel investments made by foreign investors against political risk. The agency provides long-term noncancelable insurance against such risks as currency transfer, breach of contract, expropriation, war, and civil disturbances. MIGA's programs are designed to encourage the flow of private foreign direct investment for productive purposes to its developing member countries. With respect to hotels, MIGA can guarantee everything from hotel company management fees to financial institutions' loans to equity investors' repatriation of profits.

Management Control in an Unstable Environment

Issues dealing with centralization, autonomy, crisis management, legal authorization, and communication come into play in establishing the formal relationship between company headquarters and the hotel property abroad. In highly volatile situations, the conventional wisdom is that companies should delegate complete authority and responsibility to the local unit management who, being closer to the source of the problem, will be more attuned to the realities of the operating environment and be able to make rapid decisions. However, there is also a school of thought that the higher the political risk, the higher the requirement for corporate control over the unit, distance notwithstanding, in order to take full advantage of the company's pooled resources. In either case, it is advisable to post well-qualified, experienced, professional managers in high-risk areas to protect the investment.

Crisis Management

Hotel managers are seldom trained or prepared to handle crises resulting from political events. One or more of the following consequences can result from a political crisis:

- Severe disruption of operations
- Increased government intervention or regulations
- Compromised public safety
- Loss of public goodwill
- Financial strain
- Unproductive use of management's time
- Loss of employee morale and support

In the midst of a crisis in a country torn by political unrest or terrorism, such essentials as personal safety, electrical power, communication, and water cannot be taken for granted. Ensuring that these basic services continue uninterrupted tends to become a high priority for managers. Decision-making and strategy planning to minimize risk and still operate the hotel become part of the daily routine. An effort must be made to handle the media effectively during a crisis. Since the perception of danger often far exceeds reality, the media need to be dealt with in an open and professional manner. Of course, the hotel can also take advantage of the opportunity to host journalists, government officials, and others covering the developments surrounding the crisis and, by becoming a press center, thereby make the most of the situation. Careful planning and committed management can enable a business to survive and even prosper under the most challenging operating conditions.

The Written Crisis Management Plan

Every hotel should have a crisis management or contingency plan designed to provide management guidelines for handling various crises. Such planning enables managers to make decisions quickly that avoid or minimize injury to guests and damage to the hotel's assets. Although a crisis management plan cannot turn bad news into good, it enables management to maintain the goodwill of the public by communicating to staff, guests, and the community in a professional, caring manner. The plan should establish principles, policies, and goals to guide behavior during and immediately after the crisis.

As a rule, hotel companies typically have a general corporate plan that the general managers of individual properties use as guidelines, but also amend to suit local needs. A well-considered crisis management or emergency plan will always focus on human safety first, followed by property security and loss prevention. It will also spell out the resources required to continue operation during a disaster and the appropriate channels of communication for getting information to hotel guests, staff, senior management, ownership, authorities, the general public, and the media. Once adopted, the written crisis management or emergency plan should be reviewed every six months in order to update procedures and the names and telephone numbers of contacts.

The appendix to this chapter presents one part of a crisis management plan for an international chain covering general procedures to anticipate a variety of emergencies, including fires, floods, hurricanes, typhoons, tornadoes, storms, earthquakes, structural collapse, explosions, food and water contamination, bomb threats, civil disturbances, strikes, picketing, kidnapping, extortion, evacuation, and nuclear emergencies. Supplemental procedures should be developed to cover fires, bomb threats, evacuations, and the more probable disasters particular to different locations, if not for every contingency.

A sound, well-thought-out plan—prepared with the assistance not only of management and ownership representatives, but also of local authorities and outside experts—facilitates quick action during an emergency. Such a plan is in itself a form of risk insurance. While no plan can avert a political or natural disaster, it can help keep a crisis from worsening by steering action in the right direction. Effective and responsible action in such a situation helps create positive public opinion after the crisis is over.

Summary

In the world of business, it is an axiom that there are no economic ideas that do not affect politics and no political actions that do not have economic consequences. This chapter has discussed how politics intentionally and unintentionally affects international travel and tourism in general and the lodging industry in particular.

Travelers everywhere are vulnerable to many government-imposed restrictions and regulations. For example, a country may have a restrictive or non-restrictive documentation process intended to discourage or facilitate travel for its citizens. Other constraints hinder international travel as well, including exchange controls, the taxation of travelers, travel allowances, and custom regulations on foreign purchases.

Political actions may pose barriers that restrict foreign hotel developers, investors, and/or operators from easy market entry. Regulations or policies may favor or protect domestic hotel owners by giving them incentives or subsidies not available to foreign owners. Host country governments can discourage foreign investment by many other means as well. Today, however, many governments actively seek foreign investments for tourism development and are working diligently to eliminate barriers.

In addition to government and industry, several world and regional organizations work to facilitate international trade in tourism. The World Tourism Organization is involved in tourism at the global level and addresses (among other issues) tourism marketing, education, research, environment, and facilitation. The Organization for Economic Cooperation and Development has a tourism committee that researches how to reduce travel barriers. The General Agreement on Trade and Tariffs seeks to promote the liberalization of world trade, including trade in tourism. The International Monetary Fund monitors exchange rate stability and consults with member countries on regulations concerning import and export payments, foreign investment, and exchange control requirements. The International Hotel & Restaurant Association concerns itself mainly with lodging industry issues and performs many educational and lobbying activities at the national and international levels. The World Travel & Tourism Council created a way to measure the global economic impact of travel and tourism and is using its research to influence tourism policies worldwide.

Government support at various levels is essential to tourism development and the lodging industry. Governments can offer incentives, reduce bureaucratic obstacles, and develop sustainable tourism policies. National tourism organizations market and promote their respective destinations, which benefits the lodging industry.

Through tourism investment, transnational hotel chains can help developing countries achieve economic goals. Hotel TNCs often find both benefits and drawbacks to investment in developing countries. The differing goals of the TNCs and the host countries may lead to conflict and result in various types of governmental interventions.

While prudent hotel investors and operators will monitor a country's economic climate before making investment or contract decisions, their first consideration is the social and political stability of the target host country. An unstable climate that may trigger a political crisis or attract terrorist acts will hurt the tourist market. Government-issued travel advisories that caution their citizens about travel to unstable or risky areas also dampen travel demand and shift travel patterns around the world.

Political risk assessment is critical to the foreign investor who wishes to safeguard the financial and operating viability of his or her project. Many investors use political risk assessment models, management consulting services, and risk indexes to assess a country before making an investment there. Vulnerability to political risk can be reduced by taking precautionary measures and by purchasing commercial and government-backed political risk insurance.

Qualified and trained managers are particularly important in high-risk countries in order to protect investment, property, operations, and most of all human safety. A carefully crafted crisis management plan can greatly help managers who must make critical decisions under pressure.

Endnotes

1. Tony Tse, "China's Outbound Market—From the Government's Perspective," a presentation given at Hong Kong Polytechnic University during the ISHC conference in Hong Kong, October 8, 2007.
2. Clare Bentley, "Philippines Fighting for Survival," *Asian Hotelkeeper & Catering Times*, January/February 1985, p. 7.
3. www.ih-ra.com/advocacy/issues/list_issues.php (July 2008).
4. *Role and Structure of National Tourism Administrations*, World Tourism Organization, 1985, p. 1.
5. *The Role of Transnational Tourism Enterprises in the Development of Tourism*, World Tourism Organization, 1985, pp. 13–14.
6. Carolyn K. Imamura and Carolyn Cain, "If They Got Lucky Only Once: Impacts of Major Violent Acts on Tourism and Development," Pacific Basin Development Council Research Institute, Honolulu, Hawaii, Winter 1989, p. 15.
7. Larry Kaplow, "Dreams of Tourism Undermined by Chaos of War," Cox News Service, April 11, 2007.
8. Imamura and Cain, p. 9.
9. Roberto Friedmann and Jonghoon Kim, "Political Risk and International Marketing," *Columbia Journal of World Business*, Winter 1988, p. 64.
10. Ibid. pp. 66–67.
11. The China Hotel Investment Summit 2005, hosted by HVS International and Beijing International Studies University at the Grand Hyatt Shanghai.
12. Elizabeth Keck, "Covering All the Bases," *The China Business Review*, September–October 1989, p. 20.

Key Terms

currency restrictions—Government-imposed restrictions that limit the amount of exchange residents of a country may purchase from banks to cover travel expenses incurred abroad.

General Agreement on Tariffs and Trade (GATT)—An international agreement and organization dedicated to liberalizing world trade. GATT provides a framework within which international trade negotiations are conducted and trade disputes resolved.

General Agreement on Trade in Services (GATS)—A section of GATT dealing with liberalizing and developing binding rules for trade in services, as opposed to the product-focus of GATT.

International Monetary Fund (IMF)—An organization that influences exchange controls and financial policy on a global scale by promoting exchange-rate stability and the avoidance of trade and payment restrictions that would harm international economic interests.

national tourism organization (NTO)—National organization charged with carrying out the tourism policies of a country. NTOs' jurisdictions and levels of power to determine and implement policies vary widely among countries.

transparency—The availability of full information; the lack of hidden conditions or clauses that is critical to effective decision-making.

travel advisories—Various types of statements issued by governments that inform their citizens of conditions and/or dangers present in other countries and that may warn against travel to an affected area.

travel allowances—Government-imposed restrictions that limit the amount of exchange residents of a country may purchase from banks to cover travel expenses incurred abroad.

Review Questions

1. What sorts of barriers to travel, tourism investment, and business often exist in an international setting?
2. How do government hotel regulations affect the lodging industry of various countries?
3. How do international organizations affect international travel? How do the agendas of the various international organizations relate to one another?
4. Why is government support of tourism and the lodging industry so critical? In what ways do governments support or undermine travel and tourism?
5. What is the focus or purpose of national tourism organizations? How is this different from international organizations?
6. What roles do international lodging chains play in developing countries? What sorts of conflicts are likely to arise between the chains and the host governments?
7. Why is political stability an essential element of tourism? How does political instability affect travel and investment decisions?
8. What are travel advisories? What factors might affect their objectivity?
9. Why is political risk difficult to assess? How might businesses reduce their vulnerability to political risk?
10. What is a crisis management plan? Why is it important?

Appendix
Excerpt from a Hotel Crisis Management Plan

A plan for the protection of its guests, employees and assets during an emergency should be a critical part of any hotel's operating procedures. Each hotel should prepare its staff to implement the emergency plan at an instant's notice. The following information will provide you with the basis for developing an emergency plan for your hotel.

Goals

The goals of an emergency plan are as follows:

1. To help ensure the safety and well-being of all persons at the hotel who would be affected by a fire, natural disaster, or other catastrophe by providing procedures for the proper management of the hotel's property during an emergency.
2. To ensure the flow of accurate information to the hotel's guests, its employees, the public, and any others directly affected by the incident.
3. To promptly assist others in the evaluation of the cause(s) of any losses and in an assessment of the magnitude of damage.
4. To assist the hotel staff in the orderly process of (a) analyzing the potential liability of the hotel's owner and operator, and any third parties doing business with the hotel, which might arise from an emergency, and (b) initiating claims handling procedures promptly.
5. To maintain the hotel's positive image concerning areas of loss prevention and safety of staff and guests.
6. To assist with any litigation for or against the hotel in the event of a major loss.
7. To provide a tool for training employees in actions that should be taken in the event of an emergency at the hotel.

Contingency Planning

A critical part of any emergency plan is the **preparation** that should be made before an emergency occurs. The following steps will enable you to better prepare for an emergency:

1. *Employee Training:* The general manager is responsible for training the hotel's employees in emergency procedures. Training should be conducted semi-annually so that existing employees are aware of their responsibilities, new employees are trained, and resources are kept up to date. Loss Prevention Department personnel can provide assistance upon request in both training and emergency plan development.

    To assist you in determining the skills of your employees, an Employee Skills Questionnaire is shown as **Exhibit 1**. Duplicate this form (one copy for each person in the hotel) and ask each person to fill it out and return it to the appropriate person. The information you gather will help you to identify those persons who could be considered a resource at the time of an emergency.

2. ***Emergency Resources:*** In the event of an emergency at a hotel property, the services of outside businesses and agencies will be often required to meet the needs of the hotel and its guests. A complete list of those resources must be prepared in advance. The list should contain names, telephone numbers, and a description of the services offered. Back-up services may be required where a single contractor will not be capable of meeting emergency needs. It is important that each outside business or service be contacted to confirm that it will respond to your request and is capable of providing the services or equipment required. A sample resource list format is shown as **Exhibit 2.**

   In addition, you should maintain a current list of management personnel associated with your hotel's ownership who should be contacted in the event of an emergency. A sample list is shown as **Exhibit 3.**

3. ***Relations with Local Authorities:*** Hotel management should establish a working relationship with local authorities who will be responding to emergencies at the hotel. The hotel should know the names of individuals within the public agencies who can help coordinate the safety efforts undertaken by the hotel.

   In the event of a major emergency, local and state authorities might take control of the hotel property for a period following the emergency. Your efforts before an emergency to work with your local authorities will help ensure that the hotel's policies and procedures are carried out.

4. ***Emergency Checklists:*** Each department manager should have a checklist of actions that he or she must take in the event of an emergency. Sample checklists for each department are shown as **Exhibit 4.** To these checklists you should add maps of the hotel identifying utility controls, assembly points, and any other areas or points of importance.

   Using these checklists as a resource, department managers should be trained through a practice drill to become familiar with their respective responsibilities during and immediately following an emergency. Department managers should delegate specific responsibilities on the checklists to their employees and train them in those responsibilities.

5. ***Drills and Evaluation:*** Hotel-wide emergency drills should be conducted monthly on each shift. Drills on all other parts of the emergency plan should be conducted semi-annually or more frequently. Hotel management should critique the employees' actions on these drills to evaluate and correct the hotel's emergency plan.

6. ***Emergency Response Kit:*** An emergency response kit should be kept at the front desk that contains supplies that will enable the hotel's management to keep track of the relocation of employees and guests after an emergency. The kit should contain the following:

   Guest identification tags **(Exhibit 5)**

   Guest identification roster **(Exhibit 6)**

   Several pens

   Legal note pads

   Paper clips

The guest identification tags are used to identify victims who are being relocated to a medical facility. They should have space to record the victim's name and room number, and the name of the medical facility to which the victim was transferred. The tag should be a two part form. One part of the form should be attached to the victim's clothing. The second part should be kept at the hotel by the general manger to account for and identify the current location of the victims. A sample tag is shown as **Exhibit 5**.

The guest identification roster shown as **Exhibit 6** should also be used to keep track of the location of all guests who were staying at the hotel at the time of the emergency. It should record the guest's name, the room number to which the guest is registered, and the name of the location to which the guest was transferred, whether it was a medical facility or alternate housing.

7. *First Aid Training and Supplies:* Selected personnel should be trained in advance in first aid procedures and CPR. This training should be kept current. A basic first aid kit should be maintained with a complete inventory of supplies.

8. *Transportation Plan:* In the event of an emergency, you may have to oversee the evacuation and relocation of guests. Plans should be made in advance for obtaining sufficient transportation should relocation become necessary. Agencies that can provide transportation should be listed on the resource list.

9. *Housing Plan:* Organizations should be contacted as potential relocation sites for guests who must be evacuated from the hotel in the event of an emergency requiring such an action. For example, you may have a mutual aid agreement with a nearby hotel. These organizations should also be included on the resource list.

10. *Emergency Plan Review and Drills:* Your plan should be reviewed by your hotel's loss prevention committee quarterly and any necessary changes should be made. The general manager or senior executive available is responsible for verifying that the plan has been reviewed. A sample plan verification sign-off list is shown below.

EMERGENCY PLAN REVIEW

Date plan initiated: _____ By: _____

Plan Revised: Quarterly Review:

Date: _____ By: _____   Date: _____ By: _____

Date: _____ By: _____   Date: _____ By: _____

Date: _____ By: _____   Date: _____ By: _____

Date: _____ By: _____   Date: _____ By: _____

Although fire drills should be conducted monthly on each shift, it is also necessary to conduct a drill of your emergency plan semi-annually or more frequently.

THE EMERGENCY PLAN
PHASE ONE

In Phase One you should be prepared to aid the victims, relocate guests and notify company management of the emergency.

Aiding the Victims

1. Notify emergency response agencies, such as the police, the fire department, and medical services of conditions at your hotel.
2. Locate any injured persons and provide first aid within your ability to do so. Victims should not be moved unless their lives are in danger or there is a possibility of additional injury.
3. Cooperate with emergency personnel as they arrive. Be prepared to respond to requests made by arriving medical personnel, as they may need your assistance if there are large numbers of victims. Employees who have been trained in CPR and first aid should be available to assist. Basic first aid materials, towels and blankets should be provided to the emergency personnel for use in helping victims.

Relocating Guests

1. Upon the advice of professional emergency personnel, evacuate the hotel and relocate guests to an area away from the endangered zone. Hotel staff should assist guests in moving to this predesignated relocation center. Implement your transportation and housing plans established for such purposes.

   If it is necessary to move guests away from the hotel, make arrangements for guests to make calls to relatives. You may wish to arrange for the hotel to pay for these calls.

2. Assign management personnel to monitor the relocation of guests away from the hotel, including the relocation of injured guests. Use the materials in the emergency response kit (guest identification tags and roster) to keep track of each relocation. These records should be turned over to the general manager.

3. Assign key staff employees to assist guests and employees at the relocation center.

4. Account for all guests and employees who were present at the hotel at the time the emergency occurred. Pertinent records for employees should be obtained from the hotel's personnel director. Guest records should be obtained from front desk personnel.

5. Increase security around the endangered zone by using contract guards, if necessary, to secure guests' belongings and protect company assets.

   Initiate and coordinate procedures to secure guests' personal effects. If guests have been removed from the hotel, the guestroom doors should be "double locked." Security should conduct frequent patrols of the hotel buildings.

   It may be necessary to remove belongings from guestrooms. Inventory guest belongings (use two employees) and store belongings in a secure location. The key to this location should be maintained by the general manager or his designee.

Notifying Company Management

Notify the senior management of your ownership (franchise or CMH), your claims adjustment organization and the Loss Prevention Department of conditions at your hotel.

PHASE TWO

In this phase you will establish an operations center, arrange for communications, establish emergency security, shut down utilities, inspect for structural integrity, and make arrangements for communicating with the media.

Hotel Operations Center

If for safety reasons the hotel cannot be occupied, establish a hotel operations center close to the emergency areas as soon as possible following the evacuation of the hotel. This will allow you to continue managing and controlling the emergency while ensuring the continuation of the hotel's business. The center should be manned and open 24 hours a day. The highest level manager available should remain in the operations center to coordinate hotel operations and communicate with local authorities and your senior management.

Communications

1. Contact the telephone company and arrange for installation of multiple telephones.
2. Obtain for management's use several "walkie-talkies."
3. Staff the communications center with sufficient hotel personnel or temporary employees who are knowledgeable enough to answer guests' and employees' questions.
4. If necessary, lease or purchase cellular phones.
5. Remember that in an emergency, telephones at the hotel may not be in service. It may be possible that pay phones will be working while internal hotel phones will be out of service. Also, there is a possibility that phone calls may be placed out of the area but calls may not be able to be made into the affected area.
6. Continue to communicate the status of the hotel emergency to your senior management.
7. Establish necessary manpower requirements and communicate work schedules to hotel employees.

Emergency Security

In cooperation with local authorities, immediate steps must be undertaken to survey the property and provide security for guests, employees, and company assets.

1. Increase or recall all staff security personnel. Establish a schedule by which security is provided 24 hours a day. Establish patrol patterns that will provide coordinated security of the hotel's perimeter and buildings.
2. Hire an outside private security contractor to provide additional services as required.

3. If necessary, erect barriers around the affected area to control access to it.
4. If the hotel has been evacuated, begin coordinated security of the hotel's perimeter, buildings and any outside material.

   If the building structure is damaged or will be out of service for an extended period, it may be necessary to erect fencing around the hotel.
5. Establish a badge identification system for all persons who may have access to the property. This system would allow security to identify employees and outside individuals who have a need to be in and around the emergency area. Hotel employees should wear their name tags as identification.
6. Establish a policy as to who has the authority to enter the area affected by the emergency and furnish this information to security. Only those individuals should be allowed to enter the affected area. Records should be maintained by security of the name, date, and time of the entry and exit of all individuals.

Utilities/Structural Integrity

1. Have the hotel's engineering staff shut down the hotel's utilities and HVAC system.
2. Contact the electric company, gas company and water department. Ask for inspections by their employees to confirm the integrity of the hotel's systems.
3. Contact an electrical contractor to install temporary lighting and emergency generators, if necessary.
4. Conduct a visual inspection of the building structure for any damage. Later, it may be necessary for a structural engineer to conduct an in-depth inspection.

Communications with the Media

1. Refer to the AH&LA *Crisis Communications Guidelines for the Lodging Industry.*
2. Establish a location away from the emergency area where media representatives can assemble.
3. Establish a rigid timetable for dispensing information or holding news conferences.

PHASE THREE

In this phase, you will arrange for an investigation of the emergency incident, conduct management reviews of the actions being taken, and conduct a review of your emergency plan to accommodate for unforeseen losses.

Emergency Investigation

1. Prepare a report on the emergency that includes the following information:
   a. What happened?
   b. Where did it happen?
   c. When did it happen?
   d. How did it happen, if known?
   e. How many people were injured? killed? missing?
   f. What is the physical condition of the property?

Witnesses to the emergency should be interviewed and their information included in the report. The report should be sent to the hotel's senior management (franchise or company managed) as soon as possible.

Once your senior management has received your report, you should determine from them what their response to the emergency is and coordinate with them to ensure that the proper resources are mobilized to help manage the emergency.

If the affected hotel is company managed, senior management may elect to send various emergency management teams to the hotel. Franchise hotels should contact their senior management or owners who may also wish to send such teams. Hotel management should be prepared for the arrival of these teams.

Also, note that major hotel emergencies will usually involve agencies from all branches of government (local, state, federal). Space should be made available to accommodate agencies involved with the emergency.

2. Once the property has been released to your control by the local authorities, prepare to take over its security by:
   a. Closing up the facility or isolating damaged areas.
   b. Fencing in the entire property or damaged areas.
3. Plan for both short-term and long-term investigations of the emergency. Each entity involved with investigating losses to the hotel will need space in which to work as well as the following arrangements:
   a. meeting rooms
   b. food service
   c. restrooms
   d. secretarial and support staff (numbers will depend on the magnitude of the incident)
   e. communications (telephone and two-way radio)
   f. separate accounting systems for both the emergency and insurance purposes
   g. computers to manage data and provide word processing
   h. blueprints and plans of the hotel's physical plant
   i. employee assistance (such as where they can be located and when they will be needed to work)
   j. FAX access to supplement telephone communication

Management Review

1. During the first 72 hours or more following the occurrence of the emergency, schedule meetings with your staff at least three times a day to ensure that all assigned duties are being carried out.

   After the first 72 hours, continue to meet at least daily or as often as circumstances require.
2. Add or restructure job duties or functions as required by the current situation.
3. Continue meetings and critiques as long as emergency conditions exist, or as long as required to return to normal operations.

Plan Review

Unexpected issues that will require your attention will emerge as additional losses to the hotel are discovered after the initial crisis. Continue to evaluate your emergency plan to accommodate for these items.

Conclusions

Major catastrophes have a traumatic effect on the victims, their families and the hotel. Emergency contingency preparation can greatly reduce the impact of the damage and assist in the efforts to re-establish the hotel property following a loss.

Knowing what to do and who to call in the event of an emergency is essential. While not all events can be anticipated, you cannot afford to wait until catastrophic events occur to ask yourself "what do we do now?"

Exhibit 1

To assist your plans for **EMERGENCY PREPAREDNESS,** we offer you this "Employee Skills Questionnaire."

Duplicate this form (one copy for each person within your place of business) and ask each person to fill it out and return it to the appropriate person.

The information you gather will help you identify those persons who could be considered a resource at the time of an emergency. This is an important first step in the process of forming the teams of ten (10) necessary for an orderly recovery/response program.

EMPLOYEE SKILLS QUESTIONNAIRE

Medical Training
_____ First Aid   Level Ability_____
_____ CPR   Level Ability_____

Foreign Languages
Language_____ Fluency_____
Language_____ Fluency_____

Search and Rescue Experience or Training
_____ Military   Other (please explain) _____
_____

Mechanical Ability
Auto Repair _____ Other _____

Fire Fighting
_____ Military _____ Experienced Firefighter
_____ Volunteer Other _____

Construction Ability
Electrical_____ Plumbing_____
Carpentry_____

Survival Training
(If so, please explain, with date course taken)

Experience in Emergency Situation
(Please explain type of experience, if any)

Law Enforcement
_____ Military _____ Former Police Officer
_____ Security Guard Other _____

Temporary Shelter
Shelter for others within walking distance?
Yes _____ How Many _____
Location _____

Communications
_____ Ham Operator _____ CB
_____ Telephone Operator
Other _____

Emergency Vehicles
Vehicles regularly at work useful in an emergency
4 wheel drive _____ RV or van _____
Motorcycle/Bike _____ Pickup Truck _____
Station Wagon _____

Name _____

Department _____

Home Phone _____ Office Phone _____ Location _____

Are you a member of any emergency service organization, or do you have special related training not covered in this questionnaire?

The information you provide will assist us in creating a more positive environment in the case of disaster. We appreciate your assistance and support. We have your safety in mind.

Upon completion return to _____

Exhibit 2

| RESOURCE CHECKLIST | DATE REVISED _____ |

EMERGENCY RESPONSE AGENCIES CONTACT:

Police Department	_____	Phone	_____
Fire Department	_____	Phone	_____
Paramedic Unit	_____	Phone	_____
Ambulance	_____	Phone	_____
Emergency Management Coord.	_____	Phone	_____

MEDICAL AGENCIES:

Hospital	_____	Phone	_____
Doctor	_____	Phone	_____
Chaplain	_____	Phone	_____

MANAGEMENT AGENCIES:

Elected Officials	_____	Phone	_____
Security Agency	_____	Phone	_____
Alarm Company	_____	Phone	_____
Computer Services	_____	Phone	_____

STATE AGENCIES:

| State Law Enforcement | _____ | Phone | _____ |
| Environmental Protection | _____ | Phone | _____ |

ENGINEERING SERVICES:

Contractors:

General	_____	Phone	_____
Fencing	_____	Phone	_____
Close-Up	_____	Phone	_____
Electric Company	_____	Phone	_____
Water Authority	_____	Phone	_____
Sewer Authority	_____	Phone	_____
Telephone Company	_____	Phone	_____
Building Inspection	_____	Phone	_____

FOOD & BEVERAGE SERVICES:

Refrigeration Equipment	_____	Phone	_____
Catering	_____	Phone	_____
Food Service			
Dairy	_____	Phone	_____
Produce	_____	Phone	_____
Beverage	_____	Phone	_____
Meat	_____	Phone	_____

RELOCATION SERVICES:

| Hotel | _____ | Phone | _____ |
| Schools | _____ | Phone | _____ |

(continued)

112 *Chapter 3*

Exhibit 2 *(continued)*

University	_____	Phone _____
Church	_____	Phone _____
Bus Company	_____	Phone _____
American Red Cross	_____	Phone _____
Salvation Army	_____	Phone _____

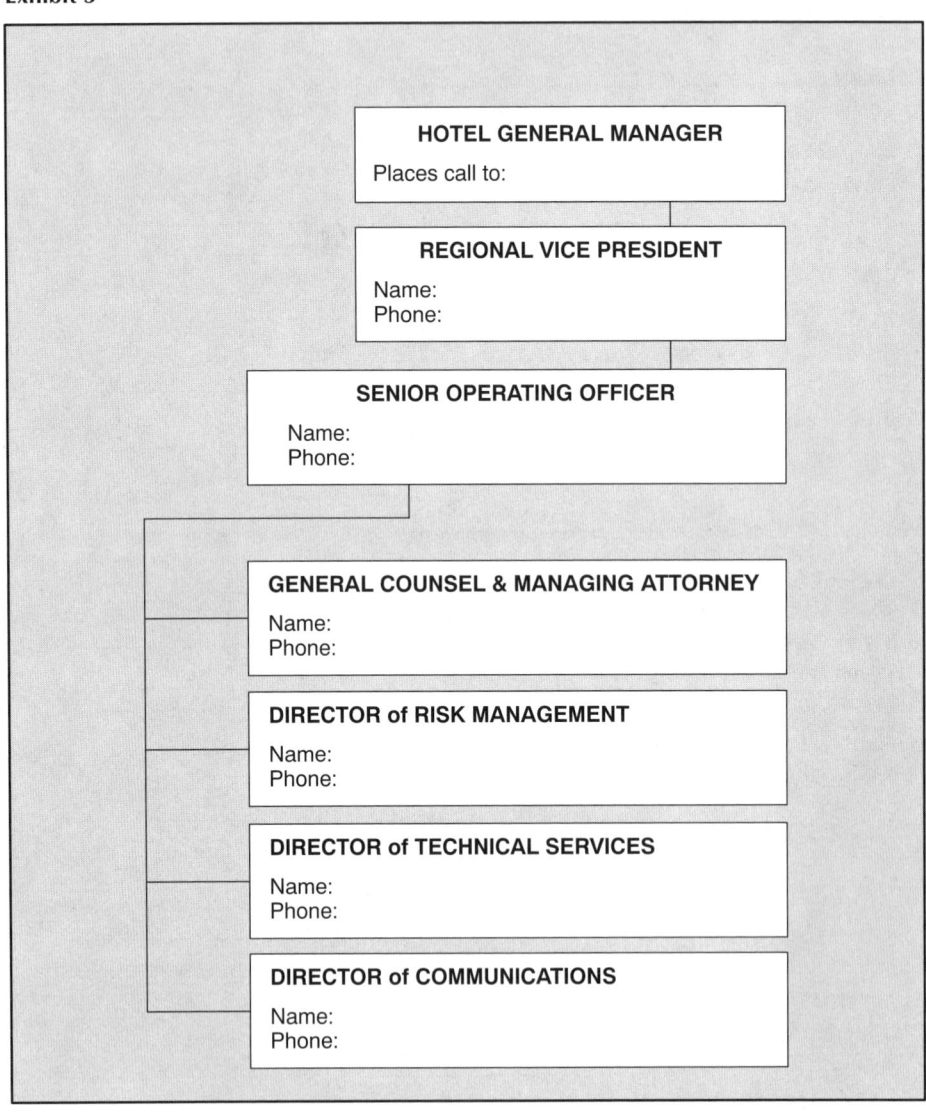

Exhibit 3

HOTEL GENERAL MANAGER
Places call to:

REGIONAL VICE PRESIDENT
Name:
Phone:

SENIOR OPERATING OFFICER
Name:
Phone:

GENERAL COUNSEL & MANAGING ATTORNEY
Name:
Phone:

DIRECTOR of RISK MANAGEMENT
Name:
Phone:

DIRECTOR of TECHNICAL SERVICES
Name:
Phone:

DIRECTOR of COMMUNICATIONS
Name:
Phone:

Exhibit 4

EMERGENCY CHECKLISTS

General Manager/MOD

Emergency Phase

_____ Call emergency response agencies (fire, police, medical services).
_____ Check for injuries of guests and employees.
_____ Assist arriving emergency personnel.
_____ Upon advice of emergency personnel, evacuate the hotel, and relocate guests.
_____ Shut down utilities and HVAC.
_____ Isolate the affected area.
_____ Account for guests.
_____ Account for employees.

Post Emergency

_____ Notify company management of conditions at the hotel.
_____ Establish an operations center.
_____ Establish security for the property.
_____ Replace utilities with temporary sources for lights and electricity.
_____ Re-establish a communications system (such as walkie-talkies, cellular phones).
_____ Establish liaison with public agencies and local officials.
_____ Recall key employees.
_____ Secure guest records.
_____ Secure employee records.
_____ Furnish the PBX operator with information on what should be told to guests, employees, relatives, and media representatives who call.

(continued)

Exhibit 4 (continued)

Front Desk

Emergency Phase

_____ Alert guests and employees of emergency conditions (if emergency is confirmed and emergency agencies request this action).

_____ Alert officials to locations of guests with special needs/handicaps.

_____ Advise other hotel departments of directions from the emergency agencies.

_____ Account for all front desk employees on duty.

Note: The front desk should always be manned by at least one person as long as this can be done safely so responses can be given to guest questions.

Post Emergency

_____ Secure guest records, safe deposit boxes, "E" key and money.

_____ Provide the emergency response kit to hotel personnel responsible for tracking relocation of guests.

_____ If necessary, establish a manual recordkeeping system for keeping track of guest transactions.

Engineering

Emergency Phase

_____ Respond to alarm zone or emergency area. (If a fire is present, attempt to extinguish it using available equipment. If it is out of control, close doors to the area but do not lock them. Always leave yourself a safe way out.)

_____ Report conditions to the front desk or PBX operator.

_____ Prepare to shut down utilities and HVAC system (emergency agencies will determine if this is necessary).

_____ Provide "E" key to emergency agencies.

_____ Account for all engineering employees on duty.

Post Emergency

_____ Retrieve all prints and plans of the hotel.

_____ Cooperate with local authorities.

_____ Coordinate temporary restoration of services to property and equipment.

_____ Work with utility companies to restore on-site utility service, if possible.

Exhibit 4 (continued)

Housekeeping

Emergency Phase

Executive Housekeeper:

_____ Instruct laundry employees to turn off washers, dryers, and pressers.
_____ If evacuation is ordered, instruct employees to exit via closest door and close all doors as they leave.
_____ Assist guests where possible.
_____ Account for all housekeeping employees on duty.

Line Employees:

When an alarm sounds, employees should follow the department's emergency procedures.

_____ Secure carts in housekeeping closets or nearest guestroom.
_____ Use stairs to evacuate the building.
_____ Assist guests when possible by pointing out exits.

Post Emergency

_____ Inventory housekeeping supplies.
_____ Set up a central distribution area to provide towels, soap, and other amenities to guests (if guests are not evacuated).
_____ If necessary, contact outside cleaning agencies to assist with cleaning salvageable linens.

Food & Beverage

Emergency Phase

_____ Determine location and extent of emergency.
_____ Advise operating managers to be prepared to evacuate departments.
_____ Shut off all appliances and equipment.
_____ If evacuation orders are given, evacuate all patrons, guests, and employees in a quiet and orderly manner.
_____ Close all doors.
_____ Account for all Food and Beverage employees on duty.

Post Emergency

_____ Account for cash receipts and secure them at the front desk, if possible.
_____ Recall key employees.
_____ Contact suppliers to cancel orders, if necessary.
_____ Contact waste disposal agency to arrange for removal of damaged goods.
_____ Contact auxiliary food services to arrange freezer storage for undamaged foodstuffs.
_____ Coordinate with sales office for rescheduling of special functions.
_____ Instruct banquet department to begin assembling tables and chairs for hotel operations center.

(continued)

Exhibit 4 (continued)

PBX Operator

Emergency Phase

_____ Notify emergency agencies (fire, police, medical services) of emergency and give them complete information as to conditions at the hotel.

_____ If the emergency is a fire, remain on the line to the fire department (do not break the connection).

_____ Contact the following: general manager or hotel's senior executive, engineer on duty, manager on duty, security.

_____ Begin to maintain a log of calls relative to the emergency.

_____ Determine from the MOD or general manager how to respond to questions of employees, guests, relatives and media representatives who call in.

_____ Begin calling guestrooms when an evacuation is ordered.

_____ Relay information from hotel employees or guests on the scene to emergency agencies and the general manager or senior executive.

_____ Remain at your position as long as it is safe to do so.

_____ If ordered to evacuate, turn off lights and equipment and close doors as you leave. Go directly to the closest exit.

Post Emergency

_____ Assist in setting up the telephone system in the operations center.

_____ Prepare or secure forms for logging all telephone calls and relaying messages.

_____ Prepare 24 hour a day work schedule and recall operators to work as needed to fill the schedule.

_____ Request information on how to respond to guest and media inquiries.

Bell Captain

Emergency Phase

_____ Return all elevators to the ground floor. Keep a person there to ensure control of the elevators.

_____ Keep entryways clear of vehicles.

_____ Close but do not lock all doors in the area.

_____ Obtain list of guests with special needs/handicaps to assist in evacuation.

_____ If evacuation is ordered, assist guests in evacuation.

_____ Assist with control of guests who have been evacuated outside the hotel.

Post Emergency

_____ Contact transportation company for guest relocation.

_____ Make all hotel vehicles ready for use in relocation, including filling up with gas.

_____ Assist with guest relocation.

Exhibit 4 (continued)

Security

Emergency Phase

- Respond to alarm zone or emergency area.
- If a fire is present, attempt to extinguish the fire with equipment available. If the fire is out of control, close doors to the area but do not lock them.
- Remove guests from dangerous areas until relieved by emergency agencies.
- Assist in evacuation of the hotel if it is ordered.
- Protect guest and hotel property until it is safely secured.

Post Emergency

- Obtain the services of outside security firms if required.
- Secure the property to prevent vandalism. Coordinate your efforts with state and local law enforcement.
- Coordinate security efforts at the operations center and alternate guest housing locations.
- Secure and prepare an inventory of the contents of hotel guest safe deposit boxes and transfer the contents to an alternative security facility (to be performed with a member of hotel management).
- Provide any assistance as needed.

EMERGENCY RESPONSE KIT

PURPOSE:

The purpose of the Emergency Response Kit is to simplify the task of accounting for guests and employees following an emergency.

The kit should be kept in a central location, preferably close to the front desk or registration area. It should be easily accessible in the event of an emergency. Personnel responsible for implementing the use of the kit should become very familiar with its contents. Familiarization with the kit will further simplify its operations at a time when a state of panic and confusion exists.

CONTENTS OF THE KIT:

Since its primary purpose is to document guests and employees as evacuation of the building is taking place, the contents of the kit should be kept simple. Those employees responsible for the use of the kit should take an inventory of the kit on a monthly basis to ensure its completeness. Items missing from the kit should be replaced immediately.

Examples of Materials for Inclusion in the Kit Include:

- Guest identification tags (see Exhibit 5)
- Guest identification roster (see Exhibit 6)
- Several pens, pencils, and permanent markers
- Legal note pads
- Scotch tape
- Scissors
- Paper clips
- File folders

Exhibit 5

```
              EMERGENCY RESPONSE KIT

           Sample Guest Identification Tag


              1. GUEST NAME: _____
              2. ROOM NUMBER: _____
              3. TIME ASSIGNED: _____
              4. ASSIGNED DESTINATION:____
                 _____
              5. EMPLOYEE INITIALS: _____

                 Tag No. [  ] - [  ]
```

1. Enter name of guest.
2. Enter room number guest is registered in.
3. Enter time guest was identified.
4. Name of hotel, hospital, institution where guest is sent for shelter or treatment.
5. Hotel employee locating and identifying guest.

Exhibit 6

EMERGENCY RESPONSE KIT

Sample Guest Identification Roster

HOTEL NAME: _____ DATE: _____

TIME: _____ EMPLOYEE COMPLETING REPORT: _____

TAG NO.	GUEST NAME	ASSIGNED LOCATION

Part II

International Hotel Investment, Development, and Agreements

Chapter 4 Outline

Financial Structuring for Hotel Development
    Equity Financing
    Debt Considerations
    Criteria for Loans
    Interest Rates
    Public and Private Sector Funding
Current Sources of Capital: A Global Perspective
    Foreign Financing
Hotel Financing in Developing Countries
    Development Banks
    Other Lending Sources
Government Investment Incentives
    Abatement of Capital Outlay
    Abatement of Operating Expenses
    Securing the Investment
    Selective Incentives
    Excessive Bureaucracy
Publicly Listed and Privately Owned Lodging Companies
    Equity Investments in the United States
    Equity Investments in Europe
    Equity Investments in Asia
Accounting Conventions
    Reconciliation
    Tax Rules
    Uniform Systems of Accounts

Competencies

1. Discuss recent developments with regard to the nature and use of equity investments in the hotel industry. (pp. 123–124)

2. Describe issues surrounding the financial structuring for hotel development. (pp. 124–131)

3. Identify several current funding sources and explain the various issues, interests, and concerns of these sources. (pp. 131–134)

4. Identify and describe various lending sources for hotel financing in developing countries. (pp. 134–137)

5. Identify various types of government investment incentives and provide examples of each type, and discuss the issue of excessive government bureaucracy. (pp. 137–142)

6. Describe how publicly listed companies raise equity and debt capital and explain the importance of debt-equity ratios. (pp. 142–144)

7. Describe the general state of equity investments in the United States, Europe, and Asia. (pp. 144–151)

8. Explain how accounting conventions and tax rules can affect hotel financing. (pp. 151–155)

4

Financing International Hotels

Hotels are not like any other real estate investments. Being capital-, management-, and labor-intensive, hotels have both a high investment risk and a high operating risk. They are also extremely market sensitive, since—unlike the products of manufacturing businesses—unsold hotel rooms cannot be stored for later sale.

The investment required for lodging projects has increased dramatically over the years, as a result of escalating real estate and construction costs and the move from smaller hotels to larger hotel complexes. In the not-so-distant past, hotels were generally owned by individuals or families and were managed semi-efficiently at best, because owners often did not know how to maximize profitability. Escalating costs and larger investment requirements have resulted in a significant change in the ownership of hotels worldwide.

Hotel ownership today varies greatly, depending on the region of the world, the maturity of the hotel industry in that region, and the varied real estate and capital markets throughout the world. Furthermore, hotel ownership shifts based on the real estate cycle. In the United States, **real estate investment trusts (REITs)**, private equity funds, private and public companies and partnerships, and pension funds may own hotels to a lesser or greater degree, depending on the cycle. In Europe, as in the United States, ownership has been primarily anchored with domestic investment entities, which include high-net-worth individuals, hotel operators, private equity, REITs, institutional investors, and closed-end funds (as in the case of Germany). Within the Asia-Pacific region, a wide variety of ownership structures exists, ranging from investment fund ownership in Australia to closely held family companies in southeast and southwest Asia. Privatization trends in China are shifting ownership from state-owned enterprises to real estate investment groups from Hong Kong, Taiwan, and elsewhere in the region. As India continues its journey toward liberalization, hotel ownership is shifting from owner-operators to domestic and international hotel development and investment groups.

In recent years, a significant portion of lodging investment money has come from non-domestic sources. According to a report tracking international hotel investments by Jones Lang LaSalle Hotels, in 2006 the global sources of hotel investments into the United States, Europe, and Asia were 24 percent, 26 percent, and 16 percent, respectively.[1] Globalization is progressing at a far faster pace in the financial markets than in other areas of the world's economy. Barriers in finance have fallen and continue to fall at every level: at national borders, between stock and other financial markets, between firms, between sectors of the financial services industry (that is, insurance, banking, securities), between financial market cultures and systems, and between previously separated regulatory areas. The steady removal of capital controls and exchange controls since the early 1970s has led to increasing flows of private capital worldwide. This continues to be a powerful force behind the globalization of finance.

The emergence of global real estate and investment markets and of global competition in these areas is changing the way lodging properties are financed. Both investors and borrowers now think in international terms. Investment opportunities are sought in all parts of the world. If one financial marketplace can no longer provide the services desired, an alternative source may be found.

Investment funds from any particular country are affected by a number of factors, including the current economic conditions of the country, the prevailing accounting conventions, government regulations regarding foreign investment, exchange rate considerations, and comparative interest rates. Investors' interests in the receiving country are affected by the overall investment climate, the economic stability of the country, the tax policies of the host government, and the availability of government incentives.

Given the emerging new patterns of ownership, it is essential that hotel general managers, who are a critical link between the hotel company and the owning company, understand the owners' investment perspective. This perspective includes such criteria as: (1) debt servicing schedule, (2) investment motives and objectives, (3) criteria concerning taxation, and (4) long-term versus short-term outlook.

Until the mid-1970s, hotel and other real estate financing was an orderly, standardized process that matched developers with investors and lenders. Today, the financing process is far more complicated because of the uncertainties of inflation and interest rates, the wider use of foreign funds, tax implications, and the number of financial vehicles available, among other issues. Limited partnerships, syndications, real estate investment trusts, securitization, debt-equity swaps, multi-party sourcing, mixed-use development projects, and sophisticated financing schemes are now common in the world of international hotel financing. A new group of professionals, called asset managers, has sprung up to help hotel owners manage their investment portfolios and make capital structure and other investment decisions in this more complicated environment. Many of these topics are beyond the scope of this chapter.

Financial Structuring for Hotel Development

The financial structuring for hotel development is similar to that for other forms of real estate, although the actual sources of funds may differ. For example, the U.S. life insurance industry was a major provider of hotel financing during the 1970s. With the deregulation of the thrift industry, however, savings and loan institutions became important sources of money for hotels in the 1980s. REITS and commercial mortgage-backed securities became a significant source of equity in the 1990s. In the United Kingdom and other European markets, a large portion of hotel financing is derived from the stock market. In Asia, hotel management companies typically contribute substantial equity. In socialist countries and some developing countries, governments often play an important role in hotel ownership.

The hotel industry is capital-intensive. Building an average international-class hotel today may cost anywhere from $200,000 to $500,000 per guestroom (total cost divided by number of rooms) in an urban center, not counting land costs. The bulk of the capital required for a hotel development project is invested in the building itself, although in some city center locations land costs are substantial. Obtaining debt and equity financing is the largest hurdle in the development of a hotel project. Therefore, hotel developers carefully nurture relationships with lenders and equity sources.

Hotel development is funded through a combination of debt and equity. Debt represents a loan at a predetermined rate of interest; equity constitutes the investment in the project by the owner. The percentage of debt provided to fund a hotel project varies based on a number of factors, including the perceived performance of the hotel industry, the riskiness of the project, the competition among lenders, and other variables. The loan-to-value (LTV) ratio, measured as the percentage of loan to the purchase price or development cost of the hotel, may range from 50 percent to as high as 90 percent in some cases. A 400-room hotel being constructed at $200,000 per room would cost $80,000,000; at an LTV ratio of 70 percent, $56,000,000 would constitute debt and the balance of $24,000,000 would be equity.

Equity Financing

In the international monetary community, hotel investment has gradually gained acceptance as a suitable part of one's investment portfolio, despite its high-risk image. International hotel investments are vulnerable to fluctuations in exchange rates, terrorist activities, political instability, and natural disasters. This means that owners and managers may not easily be able to control their commercial success from within. Additionally, in the case of foreclosure, opportunities for other uses of the hotel building(s) are limited.

Like other forms of real estate, however, hotel investments offer a long-term hedge against inflation. Room rates can be raised. Accelerated depreciation rates and mortgage interest deductions can help raise the average yield of hotel investments a few percentage points to make them financially worthwhile. The prestige associated with owning a deluxe hotel has also helped to attract equity investments.

More often than not, investors have seen hotels around the world as real estate investments instead of viable operating businesses. Real estate speculation has been the motivating drive behind a great deal of equity availability for hotel projects internationally in the past. During the 1980s, real estate fever and cheap foreign capital allowed developers to finance the hotel industry's somewhat random, explosive, and uncontrolled growth in many areas of the world. Speculation, overbuilding, and falling occupancies in many areas of the world reduced the funds available for development in the 1990s. But the new century has seen an abundance of capital for hotel investments globally for the past five years. Based on a 2007 global investment outlook report by Jones Lang LaSalle, global investment activity for the hotel industry grew from $10 billion in 2000 to $70 billion in 2006. This was driven by the economic strength of mature and emerging markets, strong operating performance by the hotel industry, availability of new sources of equity through private equity funds, and reduced country risk. However, as hotel values and RevPAR (revenue per available room) reach their peak, and the impact of the subprime residential loan crisis in the United States spills over into the hotel investment market by driving up the cost of capital, signs of a cyclical plateau are starting to appear. In the future, hotel investment is more likely to be justified in terms of potential income streams rather than long- or short-term real estate capital gains.

The commitment of equity funds by a developer and other investors typically provides the front-end funds to initiate a project. Long-term equity investors are also sought for the project, although the payback on investment for hotel projects (seldom shorter than 10 to 15 years) is generally slower than paybacks for other types of investments.

Equity funds for hotel development are often raised through life insurance companies, pension funds, REITs, or real estate syndications that pass tax benefits through to the partners-investors. Other sources of equity funds may include lodging companies, private equity funds, development companies, transportation companies, land owners, and wealthy individuals. To reduce investor liability, most real estate partnerships are formed as limited partnerships. Under this arrangement, the developer acts as the general partner and therefore has full liability. The individual investors are limited partners, whose financial exposure is usually limited to their invested capital.

The stock markets have also been a source of hotel development funds, but more so in some countries than in others. Hotel investments are usually private transactions for individual properties. The few publicly listed companies are oriented toward hotel operators rather than hotel owners. In contrast, the United Kingdom has over 60 companies with hotel-related businesses listed on its stock exchange. In the United Kingdom, the investment community's involvement in the hotel market—from institutional investors to individuals—has been done largely through the ownership of shares in public companies.

Investment Criteria. The main criteria for private sector hotel equity investments in a country or region generally include the following:

- History of political stability
- History of economic stability and growth
- Government support for foreign investment
- Benign laws toward foreign investment
- Applicable lending quotas imposed on specific industries governing international commercial banks and individual governments

Management consulting firm A. T. Kearney tracks the impact of likely political, economic, and regulatory changes on the foreign direct investment (FDI) intentions of leaders of the top companies around the world. This is reported through their *FDI Confidence Index*, which represents the views of CEOs of the world's largest 1,000 firms regarding their foreign investment intentions. Exhibit 1 shows the top 25 countries attracting foreign direct investment.

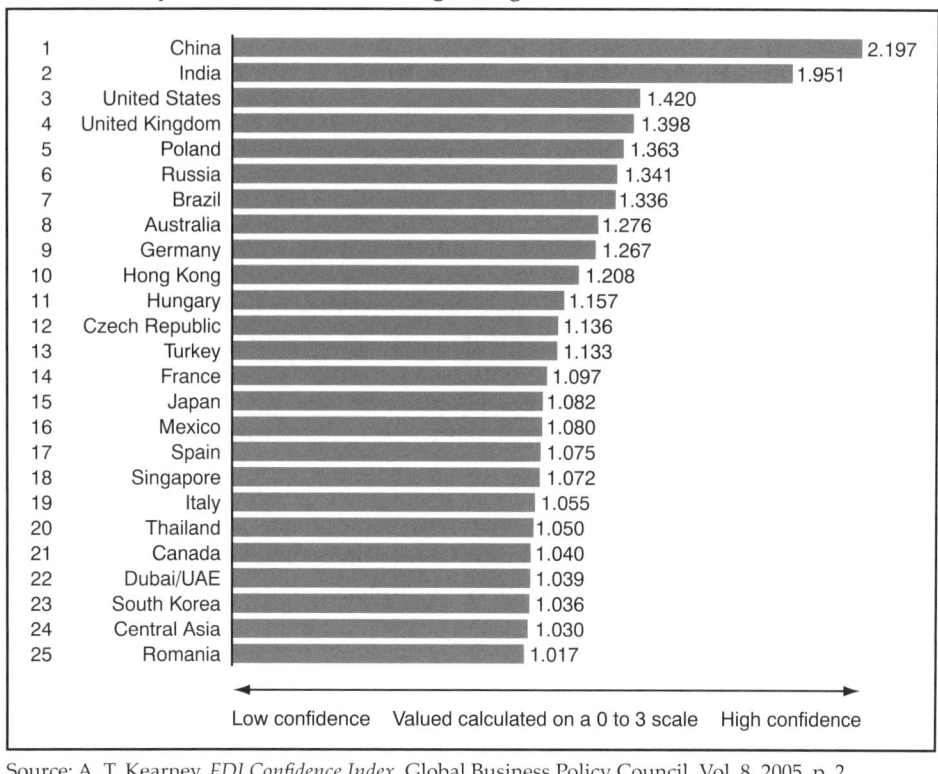

Exhibit 1   Top 25 Countries Attracting Foreign Direct Investment

1	China	2.197
2	India	1.951
3	United States	1.420
4	United Kingdom	1.398
5	Poland	1.363
6	Russia	1.341
7	Brazil	1.336
8	Australia	1.276
9	Germany	1.267
10	Hong Kong	1.208
11	Hungary	1.157
12	Czech Republic	1.136
13	Turkey	1.133
14	France	1.097
15	Japan	1.082
16	Mexico	1.080
17	Spain	1.075
18	Singapore	1.072
19	Italy	1.055
20	Thailand	1.050
21	Canada	1.040
22	Dubai/UAE	1.039
23	South Korea	1.036
24	Central Asia	1.030
25	Romania	1.017

Low confidence   Valued calculated on a 0 to 3 scale   High confidence

Source: A. T. Kearney, *FDI Confidence Index*, Global Business Policy Council, Vol. 8, 2005, p. 2.

Investment criteria for specific hotel projects include financial factors such as the project's ability to generate an adequate profit based on the capital invested, cash flow to service the investment in terms of debt service and return on equity, discounted cash flow return, and payback period. Generally, the higher the risk relating to the project, the higher the return and shorter the payback period required. Besides the obvious political and economic risks, international hotel projects are evaluated in terms of other risks, including:

- Market factors—the risk is greater where the hotel is dependent on one or two markets or located in a destination that is unproven
- Accessibility—adequate transportation linkage to support traffic to the destination
- The anticipated economic life cycle of the project
- The reputation and track record of the developer and intended operator of the project

The evaluation of international hotel projects is at best difficult. Many uncontrollable factors—for example, economic changes, changes of governments, currency revaluations or fluctuations—may affect the value of the investment before the debt can be fully amortized.

Debt Considerations

Hotels have been traditionally financed with 70 to 80 percent of the total project cost derived from mortgage loans. Rates are either fixed or floating and loans are amortized over 25 to 30 years.

For a new hotel project, debt financing commonly entails a construction loan, which carries the project through to its opening day. When permanent financing is obtained, it may be used to cover the construction loan with funds that will be repaid at some point five to ten years into the future. In some circumstances, a mini-perm (a combination of a construction loan and a shorter-than-average permanent loan) may be available.

To secure debt financing, the borrower must demonstrate that the cash flow of the hotel's operations will be more than sufficient to cover the cost of debt service. Lenders are motivated primarily by the potential return on their loans and the security of the investment. The lending rate is typically tied to going market rates and the perceived risk in the project.

The traditional sources of loan financing for hotel projects have been commercial banks, savings and loan associations, insurance companies, pension funds, investment trusts, and credit unions. Some of these lending institutions provide construction loans, while others specialize in longer-term loans or mortgage financing. Some provide both.

During the late 1970s and the 1980s, many marginal hotel projects were funded simply because money was available, and the underwriting criteria for hotel investments were loose. The result was an overbuilt hotel market in various parts of the world that had repercussions into the early 1990s. In some markets, hotel property values fell dramatically; loans went into default and contributed to the collapse of some financial institutions.

Lenders have since regained control over hotel financing, adopting much stricter criteria for loan consideration. As the hotel industry turned the corner around 1995, debt capital started to flow into the industry as its performance improved. However, besides the traditional lenders slowly returning to the industry, the concept of debt securitization in the form of commercial mortgage-backed securities (CMBSs) had taken hold and resulted in a new non-traditional source of capital. In this new lending environment, the traditional lenders such as banks and other lending institutions reduced their lending exposure by selling individual mortgages into mortgage pools that were packaged by investment banks into bonds (CMBSs) and sold to investors. This new form of debt fueled the growth of the hotel industry until recently.

Criteria for Loans

Standard criteria now required for obtaining hotel loans include the following:

1. The project should come with a strong, realistic market study. Because there are so many nonperforming hotel loans, lenders are carefully evaluating

market feasibility studies to ensure that occupancy and average daily rate projections are realistic.

2. The owner should have a proven track record. Lenders perceive the hotel owner as a key factor in the project's success. They carefully investigate the owner's creditworthiness and ability to fund potential cash needs over the course of the loan.

3. Experienced management is essential. Lenders understand that skillful management will be needed to keep the property filled and operating at reasonable expense levels. The management company's experience in similar properties is particularly important to lenders.

4. The project must have a nationally or internationally recognized hotel affiliation. Lenders find central reservation systems and institutionalized quality standards reassuring. Most lenders believe that chain affiliation leads to significantly higher occupancy and rate levels.

5. Equity requirements are returning to their traditional higher percentages. Lenders now want to see real cash equity in the deal. Projects financed today have equity levels of 20 to 30 percent of total project costs, with some projects as high as 40 percent. In other locations, 40 percent is virtually a minimum. Some lenders also require operators to have an equity stake in the project.

6. The project must generate a healthy cash flow. Cash flow is the ultimate barometer for determining the loan amount. Most lenders are looking for a debt service ratio (cash flow available to debt service) of 1.25 or greater.

7. Subordination of management fees is becoming more common. This means the lending institution is paid before the management company may collect its fees.

8. More loans are being written based on full recourse, which means that developers are personally liable if the loan defaults.

9. Loan maturity dates are generally shorter, **call provisions** (giving lenders the right to call in their loans) are common, and front-end fees are frequently charged to the borrower.

Exhibit 2 lists lending criteria that financial institutions take into consideration when deciding whether to lend money for hotel projects. Even seasoned borrowers must have a good understanding of current lender attitudes when submitting loan applications. Unproven hotel developers will find it almost impossible to obtain loans.

Interest Rates

Debt for hotel projects may carry either fixed or floating interest rates. Floating rates can be tied to domestic financial markets, such as the **prime rate** (the rate set by banks for their best customers) in the United States. However, in recent years, more floating interest rates are being tied to globally based interest rates such as the London Interbank Offering Rate (**LIBOR**—the prime's European counterpart) or the **Euroyen rate index.** (The **Euroyen** is a weighted currency value based on

Exhibit 2 Financial Institution Lending Criteria for Hotel Projects

LENDING CRITERION	MEAN	IMPORTANCE RANK
Financial strength of the applicant	1.42	1
Location of hotel	1.69	2
Experience in hotel development and management	1.76	3
Fit of project in the market	1.92	4
Financial projections based on internal analysis	2.0	5
Economic climate: metropolitan area	2.12	6
Financial projections based on feasibility study	2.27	7
Management affiliation	2.42	8
Profitability of loan to financial institution	2.48	9
Brand affiliation	2.50	10
Barriers to entry into market area	2.64	11
Performance of sponsors other businesses	2.80	12
Lending trends for specific hotel type	3.0	13
Economic climate: national	3.19	14
Favorability of hotel sector with financial institutions	3.23	15

Scale: Crucial (1), Very Important (2), Important (3), Somewhat Important (4), Unimportant (5), No Opinion (6)

European currency and the Japanese yen.) For example, project developers may take a LIBOR + 2.5 percent instead of a fixed 12 percent loan. At times, Euroyen interest rates may be lower than LIBOR or the prime. Euroyen financing is characterized by short-term, yen-dominated borrowings in which the interest rate is calculated as a spread over the Euroyen rate index.

In the past, Euroyen financing was strictly limited to Japanese borrowers. Today, it is available to others. Many hotel developers and owners have considered Euroyen financing to reduce interest costs. Success in obtaining Euroyen financing depends on such criteria as the loan-to-value ratio (the loan must be 60 percent or less of the project's total assets), the borrower's creditworthiness, the loan maturity (typically five to seven years), the recourse capacity, the size of property loan, the quality of property location and affiliation, and the regulatory constraints.

Public and Private Sector Funding

Lodging projects around the world may be financed with public sector funds, private sector funds, or both. However, the use of public funds has been diminishing and the distinction between the two is becoming blurred. The public sector generally includes government and government agencies, local authorities and such financial institutions as international, regional, and domestic development banks and international aid institutions. The private sector includes the funding

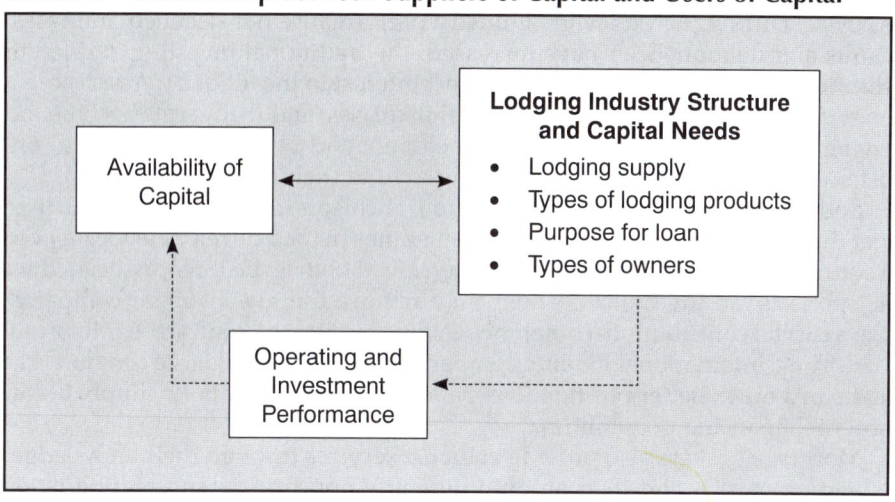

Exhibit 3 Relationship between Suppliers of Capital and Users of Capital

```
        Availability of  <------>  Lodging Industry Structure
           Capital                    and Capital Needs
              ^                    • Lodging supply
              |                    • Types of lodging products
              |                    • Purpose for loan
              |                    • Types of owners
              |
        Operating and   <----------------
         Investment
         Performance
```

institutions providing the loan finance and various categories of equity investors, from individuals to syndications.

With respect to large-scale destination developments that require significant investment in new infrastructure, projects are usually financed with both private and public sector funds. The two types of investors, however, usually have different goals. Private investors generally seek either profitability or projects with the ability to meet interest rate or repayment schedules with minimum risk. Public investors generally seek economic development, employment, foreign currency, and increased fiscal revenues. Public sector investors are normally national or local governments. In the past, they were regarded as high-quality borrowers; government guarantees often meant that large sums could be borrowed with little additional security. This is less the case today because of the high debt of many developing countries. Additionally, most governments are moving their economies toward privatization, further reducing their direct involvement in hotel ownership.

Current Sources of Capital: A Global Perspective

Hotel investors and operators require capital for a variety of purposes. These include funds for construction, conversion of existing hotels to a different use, expansion, renovation, acquisition of individual hotel assets and portfolios, mergers and acquisitions of hospitality enterprises, and expansion and investment overseas—either through foreign direct investments (construction or acquisition) or through management contracts with partial ownership.

The availability of capital is based on a fundamental relationship between the suppliers of capital (banks and other investors) and the users of capital, such as hotel firms (see Exhibit 3). The availability of capital influences the structure and size of the lodging industry; in turn, the current and expected performance of the industry influences the availability of capital to the industry. The providers of capital to the hotel industry change during different periods of the industry's business cycle. During periods when industry performance has declined and rates of defaults and delinquencies have increased, the traditional investing and lending institutions have exited the market and lost interest in the industry. As a result, the money supply tightens, the cost of capital increases, and loan terms become more stringent. During these times, hotel developers and other users of capital often must seek alternative sources of financing to fund their projects.

Lodging management companies and franchisors, especially if they are eager to get the contract on a property, have sometimes helped developers locate potential sources of financing. Because of the perceived high level of risk associated with hotel projects, an investor or lender may require the management company to make a capital contribution (sometimes called "buying the contract") or to provide a loan. Thus, international lodging companies that are part of large conglomerates may be in a much better position to expand their hotel operations simply because of internal financing possibilities.

Mortgage brokers also provide valuable services through their knowledge of the lending market and their ability to identify appropriate and willing lenders quickly. Large investment firms with branches all over the world, such as Salomon Brothers, Morgan Stanley, and Goldman Sachs, have been active in the international lodging industry.

Building strong worldwide financial connections is a goal of many international hotel operators who are also interested in investment. To finance any given hotel project, the operator may bring as many as seven or eight parties together into a partnership. Because financing is no longer a simple proposition and financing vehicles are numerous, the operator must as a rule structure each hotel deal differently.

Arranging financing for hotels entails more than just finding available money. The borrower must be as sensitive to the quality of the lender as lenders are to the quality of borrowers. The best lenders are those who can sustain a financial commitment with a long-term view of investment. Astute companies also attempt to build a global network of lenders so that changes in any one financial market will not adversely affect existing or anticipated projects.

Foreign Financing

Foreign financing has been a major factor supporting hotel development internationally, especially for countries with tight lending climates or weak currencies. Under such circumstances, hotel deals are often funded by many partners, sometimes from many countries. Foreign banks not only become active participants in syndicated loans, but also provide direct loans for the entire deal, including construction and development loans, acquisition financing, and long-term financing. Through aggressive bidding and pricing policies, these banks can often outbid domestic commercial banks and other equity or lending sources for hotel projects.

Foreign investment and lending groups generally prefer landmark hotels or properties affiliated with luxury chains, gateway cities, and established resort areas with proven market potentials. The motivations for owning a foreign hotel are various. Some consider the pride of ownership in a prestigious property, others value the real estate appreciation, and still others find a refuge from unstable political or economic situations at home.

A five-to-ten-year loan term with floating interest rates tied to the LIBOR or the prime is the common practice, but borrowers have the option of locking in a fixed rate. Closing a deal with foreign finance sourcing, especially from Japan, usually takes much longer. Many companies use investment intermediaries who have had long and constant contact with the market. The amount of foreign-sourced funding for hotel projects in any given country will depend on such factors as domestic inflation, currency exchange rates, foreign trade surplus, comparative property yields, capitalization rates, and government regulations.

The early years of the twenty-first century have been a period of abundant capital for the global hotel industry.[2]

Investment and Financing Outlook: The United States. Lodging investments in the United States for 2006 were $34.5 billion, a new peak. Spurred primarily by strong operating results, the availability of low-cost capital, and less attractive opportunities in other asset classes, the U.S. hotel investment climate has been healthy. As such, investors in the U.S. hotel industry are looking for internal rates of return of approximately 18 percent. There have been several mega-hotel investment deals in the United States in recent years, including the $26 billion acquisition of Hilton Hotels by Blackstone, a private equity firm. As a result of plentiful capital available to private equity firms, several transactions saw public ownership of hotel companies converted to private ownership. In addition to private U.S. equity firms, offshore investors from the Middle East, Asia, and Germany have targeted U.S. hotel assets. These foreign investors have been motivated by the weakness of the dollar, lower capital costs, and their own diversification strategies.

Investment and Financing Outlook: The Asia-Pacific Region. The lodging investment climate in the Asia-Pacific region is following the trend of global economic growth. Investment surveys indicate an increasing level of investor confidence in the region, with 84 percent of survey respondents expressing a "buy" sentiment. Their internal rate of return expectations are 17.8 percent, with initial cap rates expectations of 8.1 percent. Sources of investment inflows into the region have been diverse, as countries throughout the world continue to liberalize their investment policies. However, there is a wide range of real estate investment transparency in the region, with Singapore being the most transparent market, and Thailand and Vietnam being challenging investment environments. While the general lack of investment transparency in the Asia-Pacific region has traditionally been a deterrent to foreign investment funds, the current economic prosperity of the region and its expected future growth have increased the amount of cross-border investments into even low-transparent Asia-Pacific locations such as China, Macau, and Indonesia. Opportunity and investment funds from the United States and the Pacific region, and investments from the Middle East have been purchasing assets in Asia. Liquidity for the industry has also improved in the Asia-Pacific region because of the development of the Asian REIT markets in Singapore, Hong Kong, and Taiwan. In the future, REITs are expected to grow as a major equity source of capital for hotels in Asia. The luxury and upscale hotel segment seems to have the most investor interest globally, with budget properties garnering the least investor interest.

Investment and Financing Outlook: Europe. Investment capital in Europe rose to $27 billion in 2006, an increase of 44 percent over 2005. The major transaction activity has been a result of the major international hotel chains selling large chunks of their European hotel portfolios to private equity buyers. REITs are also major buyers of hotel assets in Europe. Most of this investment activity has taken place in Western Europe, although high barriers to entry in this market is shifting investor interest to Central and Eastern Europe. Investment activity in Europe has traditionally been largely domestic, but cross-border investments are gaining momentum with increasing transparency in the markets. Investors from Spain, Ireland, France, and Holland have been the major players, with American and Middle Eastern investors also gaining prominence. Competition in the debt markets of Europe have kept rates attractive and lending terms flexible. Commercial banks, mortgage banks, investment banks, and savings banks are all competing for business. Some of these banks are underwriting loans into riskier markets such as Turkey and Russia in order to increase their returns.

Hotel Financing in Developing Countries

Development Banks

Most developing countries lack the internal funds necessary to support hotel development. They seek foreign aid or financing from the World Bank Group, the Asian Development Bank, the African Development Bank, the Inter-American Development Bank, or some other regional **development bank.** Indeed, at one time, one of the symbols that signified a developing country's arrival into the market economy was the establishment of a luxury hotel, managed by an internationally recognized hotel chain, that had been financed by one of the international or regional development banks. Many developing countries have established their own domestic development banks to help finance private sector initiatives. The Development Bank of the Philippines, for instance, has long provided financing for hotel projects in that country.

Development banks mainly provide debt financing, although some will do equity investments as well. Additionally, many of these banks will syndicate loans from other commercial banks for hotel projects, providing access to financial markets that might not otherwise be interested. In order to obtain development bank financing, projects must be financially viable. When making its decision, a development bank considers the economic rate of return that will flow from a project to the country and will generally set a lower hurdle rate for projects than commercial banks. (The **hurdle rate** is the minimum internal rate of return that a project must meet or exceed to be acceptable.)

Hotel investments have met with mixed reviews from development banks. Some have been reluctant to get involved with hotel development, viewing tourism as a low priority industry and as one that should be financed strictly through the private sector. Both the International Hotel & Restaurant Association and the

World Tourism Organization have made concerted efforts to change these unfavorable views.

World Bank Group/International Finance Corporation. The World Bank was established by 44 nations in 1944 in anticipation of the reconstruction and development needs resulting from World War II. However, when the surge of decolonization that followed the war created scores of newly sovereign nations, it soon became apparent that the economic needs of developing countries would be overwhelming. Therefore, priority was given to addressing their needs. The original World Bank consisted solely of the International Bank for Reconstruction and Development (IBRD), which provided finance for productive projects for which other financing was not available on reasonable terms. Later, the International Finance Corporation (IFC), the International Development Association (IDA), and the Multilateral Investment Guarantee Agency (MIGA) were created to address the bank's and the world's evolving needs.

From the onset, the World Bank was reluctant to fund tourism-related projects. But in the late 1960s, the Bank created a Tourism Department that funded several projects over the next few years. In 1978, the Bank reverted to its original position and abolished the Tourism Department. Nonetheless, the IFC of the World Bank Group, which was established in 1956 with a mandate to foster economic growth by promoting private sector investment in its developing member countries, continues to be active in supporting hotel development.

In financing projects, the IFC provides both loans and equity investments. Like a private financial institution, the IFC prices its financial and other services in line with the market and seeks a profitable return. However, it does not require a government guarantee for financing. Its business experience in developing countries and its risk management skills enable the IFC to play an important role in mobilizing additional financing from other investors and lenders and in underwriting debt and securities issues and guarantees. From its founding in 1956 through 2006, the IFC has committed more than $56 billion of its own funds for private sector investments in developing countries and mobilized an additional $25 billion in syndications for 3,531 companies in 140 developing countries. In 2006, the IFC committed a total of $307 million in loans and equity participation for what it terms the "accommodation and tourism services" sector. The IFC also provides technical assistance to both governments and businesses and offers a full range of advisory services for hotel and other projects. Exhibit 4 shows the amount of the IFC's global investments in hotels from 1970–2007.[3]

To obtain IFC financing, a hotel project must be financially, commercially, and technically viable. In addition, the new property must expand the tourism market in the destination. It cannot merely draw guests away from already established hotels. The IFC thus concentrates on projects that increase potential demand, foreign exchange earnings, and compliance with environmental concerns.

Other Development Banks. The Asian Development Bank (ADB) consists of 67 member countries organized to promote economic and social progress in its developing member countries. The ADB has generally adopted a conservative attitude toward tourism. However, the ADB sees tourism development as an effective way to promote broad-based economic growth, environmental protection, and human

Exhibit 4 International Finance Corporation's Global Investments in Hotels, 1970–2007

Region/ Top Countries in Each Region	Total Commitment (in millions)
South America/Caribbean Brazil, Dominican Republic, Honduras, Mexico, Peru	$457
Asia Indonesia, Maldives, Pakistan, Philippines, Thailand	$385
Europe Bulgaria, Croatia, Russia, Turkey, Ukraine	$311
Africa Kenya, Morocco, Nigeria, Tanzania, Zambia	$262.5
Middle East Egypt, Jordan, Lebanon, West Bank, Gaza	$111.5
Central America Costa Rica, Nicaragua, Panama	$9.35

resource development. Its stated policy for many years was not to fund tourism projects directly; however, if tourism development formed a part of the overall development of an area, the ADB might offer indirect assistance. With these strategic objectives in mind, ADB has provided assistance to its developing member countries for the development of their tourism infrastructure, providing policy advice, loans for infrastructure projects (especially in the civil aviation sector in recent cases), and equity participation in hotels.

Other development banks becoming increasingly involved with hotel financing include the European Investment Bank, the Inter-American Development Bank, the African Development Bank, the Andean Development Corporation, and the newly established European Bank for Reconstruction and Development.

Other Lending Sources

Other sources for hotel financing in developing countries include: (1) local funds, (2) bilateral or multilateral aid on a government-to-government basis or available to private enterprise through lending agencies established by governments, and (3) private foreign sources. Since the savings rate in most developing countries is low and most countries need a fair amount of foreign exchange to meet the costs of imports for hotel projects, the use of local sources is not normally a viable alternative.

Bilateral or multilateral aid may be available through agreements that countries have with other countries or lending consortia to provide assistance to developing countries that are party to the agreement. These arrangements exist in many areas of the world, are usually regional in their coverage, and are often overlooked as possible sources of assistance.

Private foreign sources include some commercial banks and private investors (often from oil-rich countries). On the whole, developing countries have become more favorable toward foreign direct investment and have adopted pragmatic attitudes and legislation to encourage such investment. At the same time, developing countries have become increasingly dependent on foreign banks for all types of loans. The problem is that these loans may only be available on a short-term basis (say, three to five years), whereas hotel projects generally require repayment periods of 10 to 15 years. And since hotels are considered high risk, banks and private investors often add one to two percent to the normal interest rate or to the hurdle rate.

Government Investment Incentives

Most governments use investment incentives as part of a national or regional tourism development strategy. In some countries, tourism development is not viable without incentive provisions because of high development costs or perceived high risk. The objective of incentives, therefore, is to encourage development that would otherwise not take place.

Investment incentives may be defined as legislative provisions introduced to attract investment funds by offering concessions (typically financial) to enhance the probability of earning a satisfactory return on capital. While incentives are usually specific, they can also be general—for instance, when the government guarantees the repayment of investment capital or ensures the repatriation of profits. In certain countries, provisions that safeguard the security of the investment may be as important as the quantity of financial concessions.

Government incentives usually take one of three forms: (1) incentives to reduce the required capital outlay, (2) incentives to reduce ongoing operating costs, and (3) incentives to secure the investment. Examples of each type of incentive are presented in Exhibit 5. Other selective incentives and the issue of excessive bureaucracy will also be discussed in this section.

Abatement of Capital Outlay

Because lodging projects require a large up-front investment in fixed assets, incentives to reduce the capital outlay can have an immediate effect. Several types of incentives can lessen the investment outlay. Direct capital grants, which represent lump-sum capital support for the project, are rare in most countries. However, they are used in some cases and have been very effective in promoting hotel development. The U.K. Hotel Development Incentive Scheme, which lasted from 1968 to 1973, for example, provided direct grants that reduced the amount of finance needed by developers and increased their borrowing ability. This incentive scheme helped in the building of 1,300 new hotels or extensions in the United Kingdom.[4] Aside from direct grants, governments in some areas provide equity funds or free land in exchange for equity participation, thereby becoming part owners.

Preferential loans, interest relief subsidies, and soft loans are more common forms of incentives. **Preferential loans** are government loans at preferred rates below the market. **Interest relief subsidies** involve government payment of the difference between a fixed interest rate and that charged by a commercial bank.

Exhibit 5 Selected Investment Incentives

Incentives to Reduce Required Investment Outlay

- Preferred rate of borrowing
- Interest rate relief
- Government financing
- Venture capital provisions
- Feasibility study assistance
- Capital grants for special projects
- Duty-free importation of construction materials
- Sale of government land below market value
- Government land concessions
- Special exchange rates for foreign investment
- Provision of infrastructure
- Joint projects (public and private sector)

Incentives To Reduce Operating Costs

- Tax exemptions
- Tax rebates
- Accelerated depreciation allowances
- Tax holidays
- Tax exemptions on undistributed reinvested profit
- Real estate tax reduction or exemption
- Loans/subsidies for refurbishments or extensions
- Free consultation services
- Training grants
- Government-sponsored training
- Marketing assistance
- Wage subsidies for certain employees
- Exemption from indirect taxes
- Refunds of custom duties on imported supplies
- Low utility rates

Incentives to Secure the Investment

- Guarantees relating to repatriation of capital, profits, dividends, and interest
- Government loan guarantees
- Free availability of foreign exchange
- Work permits for key personnel
- Guarantees against tax increases on profits
- Guarantees against rise in import duties
- Legislative provisions for settling investment disputes

Soft loans offer a longer term or lower interest rates in the initial years so that loan costs are reduced in the early years when cash flow is tight. These incentives help make hotel projects more promising in terms of cash flow and profitability. In developing countries, international financing agencies have often supported these types of programs. Soft loans have been used extensively by the governments of Spain and Portugal to encourage hotel investment. Government involvement in a project can also provide ready access to additional capital should the project require it, as the government is interested in sustaining its original investment. Loan guarantees (whereby government or some specified institution is prepared to underwrite loans granted by a commercial bank) are also frequently used.

Other government incentives to reduce capital costs include allowing the duty-free importation of building materials, furniture, fixtures, and equipment, and selling or leasing land at below market value. For many years, the Bahaman government sold (or provided on long leases) large tracts of real estate to outside developers on an almost tax-free basis: no tax on income, dividends, capital gains, and so forth. In exchange, the developers were required to provide all the infrastructure—roads, water and power supplies, drainage, airports, and so on. It is common, however, for a country's government to provide most of the infrastructure. The availability of infrastructure or its provision by the government in a virgin area improves the potential viability of the project by reducing the level of investment required.

Abatement of Operating Expenses

Incentives to abate operating expenses have two purposes. They remove obstacles to project profitability, especially in instances where the project would otherwise be marginal. They also accelerate the development process by making the investment climate more attractive relative to other destinations.

Governments may provide such fiscal incentives as accelerated depreciation allowances, subsidies for the use of local materials, exemption from certain taxes, and other incentives that reduce the hotel's operating costs. For example, the Egyptian government offered lodging investors an incentive by deferring for 5 to 15 years tax assessments on such supplied utilities as water, electricity, and new roads. Governments have also provided operational subsidies, such as meeting part of operating deficits or subsidizing payroll expenses. Tax holidays, usually for an initial period of five to ten years, are another common form of incentive. Full or partial refunds of custom and excise duties on imported hospitality-related supplies and equipment parts, tax exemptions for promotional expenditures, and favorable utility rates also reduce operating expenses. To the extent that government actively promotes the destination or supports co-operative advertising schemes, hotel marketing costs may be lessened. Often, governments will provide training grants to the hotel for pre-opening training or upgrading staff skills. Alternatively, governments sometimes provide training facilities and courses to increase the qualified workforce.

Securing the Investment

The object of investment security incentives is to win investors' confidence in an industry that is sensitive to changes in the political and economic environment. The more important incentives include guarantees against nationalization; free availability of foreign exchange; repatriation of invested capital, profits, dividends, and interest; government loan guarantees; provision of work permits for key personnel; and legislative provisions for settling investment disputes. Some governments have enacted long-range tax codes containing guarantees against retroactive enforcement of new taxes, investment tax credits, and loss carryovers.

If foreign currency will be involved in the loan, governments may also offer exchange rate guarantees such that the exchange rate for loan interest and capital payments is fixed, and the government undertakes to relieve any adverse effects from exchange rate fluctuations.

In some countries, incentives that secure the investment and ensure stability of the operating environment will demonstrate the government's commitment to, and confidence in, tourism development and hotel investments. Other government actions to indicate support for the tourism industry in general include improving transportation links, expanding cultural activities for visitors, and reducing strict visa requirements.

Selective Incentives

Many governments use incentives selectively to maintain control over the types of hotels built and to ensure that development is in line with established tourism goals. With selective or discretionary incentive programs, incentives do not automatically apply to every project; they may require approval from a designated funding authority. Although discretionary incentives take more time to implement because of the evaluation process and require more government administration, they enable a government to point funding toward its preferred development. For instance, certain incentives may be reserved solely for domestic investors to encourage local entrepreneurship; others may promote tourism-related projects in a redevelopment zone. A host government can favor luxury or budget accommodations, big or small establishments, or one location over another.

In order to be effective, government incentives must be appropriate, substantive, and available to the recipient when they are most needed. Since hotel cash flows are under the greatest pressure during the first two to three years of operation, the most desirable incentives are those that will either reduce capital costs or provide relief during these critical early years. From the government's perspective, the selective provision of incentives on a case-by-case basis (if handled correctly) can ensure that each project receives exactly the right package of incentives to ensure implementation, without giving away more than necessary.

Incentives alone, however, cannot create a positive investment environment. As stated earlier, investors are above all attracted by stable political and social climates, rising economic conditions, and promising market demands that will affect the longer-term viability of the project. Although governments may offer incentives to reduce the effects of uncertainty, investors have also become wary of economic incentives that may be revoked in times of political instability or that may for other reasons be temporary.

The types of incentives offered affect the volume of projects the government can realistically support. Direct grants are costly incentives. Given limited funds, many more projects can be assisted with loans, interest relief subsidies, tax exemptions, or refunded customs duties than with direct grants. Politically speaking, giveaways are seldom acceptable to taxpayers.

To encourage private sector participation in hotels, the Korean government provides assistance through government loans, tax incentives, and reduced tax rates on international joint venture projects. A fund for tourism-industry assistance

The Case of Mexico

The use of government incentives and the reduction of bureaucracy to support tourism and hotel development is well illustrated in the case of Mexico.

Mexico has long been a popular and accessible vacation spot, its scenic coastline, warm waters, and rich historical heritage attracting millions of visitors annually. Tourism is Mexico's third largest generator of foreign exchange and directly or indirectly employs 9 percent of the workforce. The Mexican government has targeted tourism as one of its priority industries for economic development. It actively promotes inbound tourism and seeks foreign hotel investment.

As part of the government's policy of liberalization and privatization of the Mexican economy, foreign investors may now have up to 100 percent ownership in hotels. Even though restrictions still exist for land ownership in coastal regions, hotel investors can enter a trust agreement or *fideicomiso* with a Mexican bank to overcome these restrictions and still maintain control over the investment. New regulations have been established governing all aspects of foreign investment. Their purpose is to provide legal assurance to investors and to simplify administrative rules and procedures that apply to such transactions.

Other obstacles to hotel investment have been eliminated to stimulate tourism, and tourism is one of the sectors eligible for debt-equity swaps. The latter program was created by the Mexican government to allow foreign and national investment in infrastructure projects and projects involving the sale of public assets. An automatic approval process has been instituted for most projects, as has a formal response period of 45 working days for projects requiring formal applications.

In order to achieve its goal of receiving 10 million international visitors and five billion dollars in annual tourist receipts by 1994, the Mexican government implemented an aggressive development program built around three basic strategies: (1) facilitating increased levels of business activity in tourism through a range of deregulation and liberalization initiatives, (2) improving and modernizing tourism facilities and infrastructure through active participation of the domestic and international private sectors, and (3) implementing an aggressive international promotional program to generate wider awareness of Mexico's diverse tourism assets.

The Mexican government has introduced the concept of "megaprojects" for developing resort complexes in key destination areas. These special projects refer to predesigned areas with prospective hotels, marinas, golf courses, shopping malls, residences, and other attractions. The government supports the development of infrastructure. The National Tourism Development Fund (FONATUR) is responsible for facilitating private investor participation in the projects through a variety of financial incentives and the provision of clear guidelines and administrative assistance. In some projects, FONATUR participates as a joint venture partner; in others, it acts as a consultant.

To familiarize potential investors with new business opportunities, the Mexican Tourism Secretariat conducted a series of investment seminars in the United States and elsewhere to inform potential investors about relevant issues of hotel planning in Mexico.

was established to finance new hotels, renovations of existing hotels, and other tourism businesses. Hotels also receive a tax incentive in accelerated asset depreciation allowances. Foreign investors subject to joint investment of tourist projects with their Korean counterparts may be partially exempt from taxation on their investment. These selective government incentives attracted a number of international lodging chains to Korea.

In most instances, government officials have limited knowledge of the relative costs and benefits of using investment incentives. Lacking this information, it is difficult for them to determine the right mix of incentives to spur foreign direct investment decisions. The following are useful guidelines governments can use when determining and managing investment incentive strategies:

- Investment incentives should be selective with respect to the scale and type of hotels and their locations
- Incentives should be related to existing tourism development plans
- Incentives should be linked to environmentally and culturally sensitive projects
- Land should be leased rather than sold to foreign investors
- Incentive beneficiaries should be monitored to make sure that their investments proceed according to plan
- A review clause should be put into investment incentive legislation so that the effectiveness of the incentives can be evaluated, and changes made if necessary[5]

Excessive Bureaucracy

In some countries or regions, the impact of incentive legislation is blunted by the excessive bureaucracy involved with investment and the lack of coordination. In one Caribbean nation, for example, an applicant seeking incentives for his or her hotel project would need to prepare documents for five or six separate government agencies. India provides an example of bureaucracy at its extreme. Despite the country's shift toward more liberal foreign investment laws, investors and operators still must obtain approval from no fewer than 30 different government departments before they can open a hotel to guests.

To reduce excessive bureaucracy, some countries have established coordinating agencies to assist foreign investors. In Trinidad and Tobago, for example, foreign investment coordination is assigned to the Industrial Development Corporation (IDC). The IDC has set up a one-stop shop (known as the Investment Coordinating Committee) to expedite the necessary reviews and approvals that investors need from the various ministries and statutory boards. Likewise, all of the ASEAN (Association of Southeast Asian Nations) countries have established one-stop investment service centers to facilitate foreign and local investments. These centers house representatives from various agencies with the authority to act on matters concerned with setting up a business or making an investment.

Publicly Listed and Privately Owned Lodging Companies

Large lodging chains may be publicly listed companies (PLCs) or privately owned. The attraction of listing on a stock exchange is the access it provides to major equity

Exhibit 6 Leading Publicly Listed Global Hotel Companies

Hotel group	Branded rooms 2006	Principal quotation	Market capitalization* at mid-January 2007 (US$)
IHG	556,246	London Stock Exchange	9.5 billion
Wyndham Worldwide	543,234	New York Stock Exchange	6.6 billion
Marriott International	513,832	New York Stock Exchange	18.8 billion
HHC	501,478	New York Stock Exchange	13.5 billion
Choice Hotels International	435,000	New York Stock Exchange	2.9 billion
Accor	486,512	Paris Stock Exchange	18.0 billion
Starwood Hotels & Resorts	265,600	New York Stock Exchange	13.8 billion
TUI AG/ TUI Hotels & Resorts	82,111	Frankfurt Stock Exchange	5.1 billion

*Market capitalization = market price per share × number of shares outstanding

markets. For many hotel companies, going public may be the most logical way to access a wider range of capital sources to fund growth and expansion.

There are three basic routes available to raise equity capital from public sources. *Flotation* is the initial stock offer of shares in a company at a price established by the company's stockbroker at a level calculated to be sufficiently attractive to ensure the sales of all shares. A *rights issue* is the most common way for companies to raise additional equity capital from its existing shareholders. Rights issues are offered to shareholders at a discount from the prevailing share price immediately before the offer. *Acquiring assets for shares* is another way to raise equity. In addition to their outstanding stock in the market, most companies retain a block of authorized shares that have not been issued but may be used to buy additional assets. An example is the Bass PLC acquisition of Holiday Inns in 1988. In essence, Bass took on responsibility for $1.85 billion of Holiday debt and issued to Holiday Inn 7.15 million Bass shares valued at $125 million.[6]

Exhibit 6 illustrates the size and market capitalization of the leading publicly listed global hotel companies. The InterContinental Hotels Group (IHG) had a market capitalization of $9.5 billion in 2007. This represents the price per share multiplied by the number of shares outstanding. A company looking to acquire IHG would in essence make a bid to purchase all of the outstanding shares at an acquisition price, which in many cases is a premium over the current price per share.

In addition to equity, the debt capacity of PLCs may take different forms, providing an important source of capital. A PLC will have access to debt securities such as convertibles, which are linked to equity and are generally at rates lower than current market interest rates. The most common method for publicly listed and private hotel companies to raise capital is to borrow it. The structure of debt is important, as evidenced from the priority given to debt claims against a company in the event of liquidation. Debt is often secured against the value of specified assets of the company (such as hotel properties); this approach typically results in lower interest rates. Unsecured loans, which are loans not tied to the value of any asset, usually carry a higher interest rate to reflect the higher risk assumed by the lender. In the case of liquidation, secured debt has priority over unsecured debt.

The relationship between debt and equity is critical. A company's debt to equity ratio is a key measure of the company's state of health. It is also an important factor affecting its ability to raise additional capital. The international investment community has generally shown itself to be comfortable with a loan-to-value ratio of up to 60 percent of property value and concerned when the loan-to-value ratio exceeds 60 percent.

Equity Investments in the United States

Publicly listed hotel companies in the United States are mainly of two types: (1) management companies that own only a very small proportion of their hotel assets (typically around five percent) but that have contracts to manage the hotels, and (2) franchise companies that own and sell the right to use a hotel brand name with corporate support services, including central reservations, marketing, training, and purchasing. In practice, most U.S. companies are a combination of both types.

The movement of U.S. lodging companies away from property ownership to management contracting and franchising has been fueled in part by financial accounting procedures that require companies to carry their property assets at book value, reflecting depreciation, rather than at market value. As a consequence of this movement away from ownership, the main source of capital for expansion comes from cash flow derived from management contract and franchise fees. Since most of the income is derived from these fees, hotel company income and profits are generally much smaller than they would be if the hotels were owned.

Unlike in the British hotel market (where the investment community is involved principally through the ownership of shares in PLCs), the investment community's involvement in the U.S. hotel market is through the ownership of equity in specific hotel properties and in the supply of debt for hotel projects. In the United States, an extensive network of banks, insurance companies, and savings and loan institutions may be associated with the ownership of hotels. At one point, for example, it was estimated that Prudential of America owned around 20,000 hotel rooms, while Metropolitan Life owned almost 25,000.[7]

Due to the poor performance of the hotel industry in the early 1990s as a result of excessive overbuilding, institutional investors did not want to invest directly in hotel real estate equity. In this environment, REITs made their reappearance as a form of investing in shares of a corporation that primarily invested in hotel real estate. Dubbed as the "mutual funds of real estate," REITs allow individual and institutional investors to invest in publicly traded company shares of income-producing real estate investments. From the perspective of the REITs, they offered a vehicle for generating equity for growth and expansion through the traditional public sources of capital via flotation, as previously discussed. From the perspective of investors, REITs offered the advantage of income returns and capital gains in hotel real estate by investing in tradable (thus liquid) REIT shares. Growing

Exhibit 7   Top Hotel Ownership Groups

2005/2006 Top Hotel Owners		
Company Name	Type	Rooms
The Blackstone Group	Private Equity	150,000 (1)
Host Hotels and Resorts (previously Host Marriott Corp.)	REIT	48,785
Starwood Hotels and Resorts	Public Company	47,000
Hospitality Properties Trust	REIT	42,000
FelCor Lodging Trust	REIT	37,000
Westmont Hospitality Group	Private Owner/Operator	30,000*
Tharaldson Companies	Private Owner/Operator/Developer	25,813*
CNL Hotels and Resorts	Unlisted REIT	25,724
Hilton Hotels Corp.	Public Company	25,688 (2)
Columbia Sussex Corp.	Private Owner/Operator	27,612
John Q Hammons Hotels & Resorts	Private Owner/Operator	14,290*
Lodgian Inc.	Public Owner/Operator	12,679 (3)

Data as of December 31, 2005, unless otherwise noted.
*Data as of December 31, 2004. (1) This is an approximate number, as the number of rooms is constantly changing. (2) Data as of 9/30/2005. (3) Data as of 3/31/2006.

Source: Jones Lang LaSalle Hotels.

from two publicly traded REITs in 1993, with a market capitalization of $100 million, REITs currently represent a major source of equity and hotel ownership in the United States, with a market capitalization of over $23 billion in 2007.

A shift in the investor and ownership profile from public ownership of large portfolios of hotel real estate to privately held ownership started to occur around 2003. Since that time, private equity firms, which represent non—publicly traded pools of capital raised from institutions and high-net-worth individuals, have been the major acquirers of hotel real estate, in most cases taking publicly held companies private. Some of the major companies in this arena include companies that previously were not part of the hotel ownership lexicon, such as Blackstone, Cerberus, Apollo, Colony, Bain, and KSL.

Two of the recent and notable public-to-private acquisitions by private equity firms include the $26 billion acquisition of Hilton Corporation by Blackstone Group and the purchase of Four Seasons by Cascade Investments, a company owned in part by Microsoft-founder Bill Gates and Isadore Sharp, the founder of Four Seasons. The current profile of leading U.S. hotel ownership groups is outlined in Exhibit 7.

Equity Investments in Europe

Sixty percent of Europe's hotel industry is concentrated in Germany, France, the United Kingdom, Italy, and Spain. These countries also represent the largest percentage of hotel chain penetration, ranging from 35 percent in France to 24 percent in Germany. Compared to the United States, chain affiliations in Europe represent a much smaller percentage of hotel inventory. This is primarily because smaller and lower-star-rated hotels that are largely independent and individually owned represent about 80 percent of the hotel industry in Europe.[8]

While Europe's small, unbranded hotels remain fairly stable with regard to their ownership and investor profile, Europe's investment-grade hotels (typically the branded and higher-star-rated hotels) have been undergoing ownership changes. Three trends signify this shift:

1. *Public to private ownership.* During the up-cycle from 1995 to 2000, hotel operators eager to access the capital markets listed their assets on stock exchanges. For example, Thistle, Jarvis, and Millennium & Copthorne were listed on the London Stock Exchange, and Sol Meliá was listed on the Madrid Stock Exchange. The down cycle, which started in 2000, resulted in falling share prices, which resulted in many of these companies being delisted in public to private transactions. For example, Thistle was taken private by BIL International, Jarvis was acquired by Lioncourt Capital, Queens Moat House was bought by White Hall, and Goldman Sachs and Hilton Group were acquired by Hilton Corp.

2. *Asset disposition.* In recent years, there have been many individual and hotel portfolio sales in Europe. The primary buyers of these properties, which reflects a shift in the hotel-ownership landscape, are private equity firms, newly formed property companies, high-net-worth individuals, and consortium buyers (combined real estate investment and asset management companies).

3. *Joint ventures.* Finally, the equity and ownership landscape also has been impacted in recent years by joint ventures between hotel operators and hotel real estate investors. For example, in 2005 Le Meridien was acquired by a joint venture formed between Starwood Capital Group and Lehman Brothers, which acquired Le Meridien's real estate assets, and Starwood Hotels & Resorts Worldwide, which acquired the brand and management company.

It should be noted that these ownership changes are primarily restricted to investment-grade properties in gateway cities. Independent owner-operator hotels in the secondary cities of Europe are still where most of Europe's hotel equity resides.

Equity Investments in Asia

A major investment factor in Asia has been the willingness of lodging companies to invest in the properties they are managing. Asian hotel groups tend to have far higher equity components (sometimes up to 100 percent) than their non-Asian counterparts. They often regard the land and property ownership component as critical in their strategies.

Asia's major hotel projects fall into one of several major categories with respect to financing:

1. Asian primary city hotels
2. Asian secondary city hotels

3. Asian resort hotels—established markets
4. Asian resort hotels—emerging markets
5. Asian resort hotels—pioneering markets
6. Hotels in Asian communist/socialist countries

For each of these groups, the financing challenge is different, reflecting the divergent nature of three key variables: (1) the cost of hotel investment, (2) the magnitude of the hotel investment's cash flow return, and (3) the level of risk. The risk versus return-on-cost equation is at the heart of all investment and financing decisions. Exhibit 8 summarizes the characteristics and financing implications for hotels in these diverse groupings.

Obtaining debt financing in Asia for Asian hotels has traditionally been a far simpler process than obtaining financing for western hotels in some of the more advanced western economies. Typically, an Asian landowner develops a hotel on land owned for some time, and obtains a recourse bank loan that may fund up to 100 percent of construction costs. Non-recourse finance, where the lender looks solely to the project's cash flow and not the sponsor, has been less common in Asia for three reasons. First, Asia has much smaller and less developed capital markets and a much smaller universe of lenders in local markets. Second, there has been strong demand for debt capital, arising from high-growth economies. Third is the traditional conservatism of the Asian (often Chinese) entrepreneur, who by nature is averse to debt and wants personal involvement with his or her investments.

A number of creative debt financing solutions have been developed to suit Asia's particular market situation. Most are linked with some other type of property development that is integrated with the lodging project. Many hotels in Hong Kong, Singapore, and other Asian cities, for example, are able to attract a large volume of upscale retail shopping and to earn significant income from retail rentals. For Asian resort hotels, the preselling of villas affiliated with the resort can greatly enhance the hotel's ability to attract financing. As Asia's domestic financial systems mature and the economic prosperity of the region increases, greater liberalization and access in regard to hotel financing is beginning to take place.

Some of the historical impediments that have resulted in Asian hotel assets being tightly held are being reduced or changed. These include the following:

- Laws governing foreclosure of non-performing loans by Asian banks are limited. While this is changing, further banking reforms are needed in order to spur investment interest.
- Property institutions and services such as legal, entitlement, and title insurance services are now growing in Asia, which facilitates access to more sophisticated capital sources.
- As a result of limited transactions, valuation information on which to make pricing decisions is more of an art than a science in Asia. But the real estate market is beginning to get more fluid and, as a result, more transparent.
- "Demand shocks" in the post Asian-financial-crisis environment deferred international investment activity for a time. Today's strong performance in

Exhibit 8 Hotel Financing in Asian City Hotel Markets, Resort Areas, and Communist/Socialist Countries

HOTEL FINANCING IN ASIAN CITY HOTEL MARKETS

	Type I: Primary Cities		Type II: Secondary Cities
	Japan & The 4 NICs	"New NICs" of S.E. Asia	
Examples	-Tokyo, Japan -Seoul, Korea -Hong Kong -Taipei, Taiwan -Singapore	-Bangkok, Thailand -Kuala Lumpur, Malaysia -Jakarta, Indonesia -Manila, Philippines	-Kaohsiung, Taiwan -Pusan, Korea -Johor Bahru, Malaysia -Surabaya, Indonesia
Characteristics	-very high land cost -often serious lack of sites -rapidly rising operating costs -but FB revenue can be high -also limited competition in long run -thus achievable long run room rates, occupancies and GOP also structurally high?	-lower land costs -greater availability of sites -far more market volatility -but greater long-run competition? -thus achievable long-run room rates -and occupancies lower than in Northeast Asia	-lower land cost than capital city -far greater availability of hotel development sites -construction costs less -higher domestic clientele dependency -hence room rate structurally lower?
Financing Implications	**Equity:** a hotel often not highest and best use for a site due to high land cost **-Debt:** low returns on development cost imply low debt leverage	**Equity:** location, sponsorship, and concept all critical **-Debt:** higher returns on cost than advanced Northeast Asia	**Equity:** important to build product for the real market demand (qualitative/quantitative)
Capital Sources/ Structure	**-Equity:** primarily domestic sources; often landowners with low cost basis **-Debt:** less use of project finance, more frequent use of guaranteed loan	**-Equity:** cross-border equity sources common, often joint ventured **-Debt:** greater use of project finance than Northeast Asia; now diminishing	**-Equity:** predominantly domestic sources only, with exceptions **-Debt:** offshore debt funding rare

(continued)

Exhibit 8 *(continued)*

HOTEL FINANCING IN ASIAN RESORT AREAS

	#1: "Established"	#2: "Emerging"	#3: "Pioneering"
Examples	-Indonesia: Bali -Thailand: Phuket -Malaysia: Penang -Japan: Okinawa	-Thailand: Ko Samui, Chiang Rai -Malaysia: Langkawi -Indonesia: Lombok, Batam -Korea: Cheju	-Thailand: Ko Chang -Philippines: Boracay -Indian Ocean: Maldives -Indonesia: Tana Toraja
Characteristics	-rising land costs -infrastructure fair to good -rising room rates and occupancies in late 1980s -negative consequences of over-development?	-lower land costs -weak infrastructure -marketing critical -hotel interdependency	-political risk (sometimes) -much lower land costs -severe infrastructure weakness -novelty appeal
Financing Implications	-**Equity:** key is land cost -**Debt:** well-established markets make debt financing easier	-**Equity:** higher risk necessitates greater equity return hurdle -**Debt:** less established markets make lenders more cautious	-**Equity:** higher risk necessitates even greater equity return hurdle -**Debt:** lenders may not exist on project finance basis, unless significant support
Capital Sources/Structure	-**Equity:** international JVs (joint ventures) predominate -**Debt:** limited recourse offshore debt funding on project basis frequently used	-**Equity:** domestic/foreign JVs common (Asian, Japanese, American equity) -**Debt:** local financial institutions; some international financial institutions	-**Equity:** domestic/foreign JVs common; equity sometimes easier to raise than debt -**Debt:** local banks; strong credit support may be necessary

(continued)

Exhibit 8 (continued)

HOTEL FINANCING IN ASIAN COMMUNIST/SOCIALIST COUNTRIES

	City Hotels	Scenic/Resort Hotels
Examples	-China : Beijing, Shanghai, Guangzhou -Vietnam : Ho Chi Minh City, Hanoi -Burma : Rangoon -Cambodia : Phnom Penh	-China : Hainan Island -Vietnam : Dalat -Burma : Mergui Archipelago -Cambodia : Angkor Wat
Characteristics	-In most countries, political risk is overwhelming factor. -Infrastructure can be a massive problem. -Some city markets (Beijing, Shanghai) now seriously overbuilt. -Development ventures typically have relatively short lives (20, 25, 50 years) mandated by foreign investment law or practice.	
Financing Implications	**-Equity:** Equity returns highly diverse; some "emotional" investing. **-Debt:** Pure debt financing on "project basis" may be impossible without outside credit support.	
Capital Sources/Structure	**-Equity:** Capital availability depends on the market; for China, basically non-existent currently; for Vietnam much investor curiosity, but investment framework still undeveloped. **-Debt:** Debt financing has yet to be tested in some markets (Burma, Vietnam).	

Prepared by David Bussman, Salomon Brothers Inc., first published in 1991. Although the information in this report has been obtained from sources that Salomon Brothers Inc. believes to be reliable, Salomon Brothers Inc. does not guarantee its accuracy, and such information may be incomplete or condensed. All opinions and estimates included in this report constitute the judgment of Salomon Brothers Inc. as of this date and are subject to change without notice. This report is for information purposes only and is not intended as an offer or solicitation with respect to the purchase or sale of any security.

most Asian markets with steady growth in RevPAR has generated interest from a wider range of global investors.

With the reduction of investment impediments, the expectation of tremendous upside potential in Asia, the saturation of the traditional blue chip markets of Western Europe and the Americas, the abundance of capital in the global markets seeking high yields, and the development of new Asian destinations such as Macau with its emphasis on gaming and entertainment have all started to change the equity and debt profile in Asia. Based on hotel development projects on the ground in 2007, the leading real estate markets are China, Thailand, and India. China leads the way with over 170,000 hotel rooms under construction, which represents more than 70 percent of the current development pipeline in Asia.[9]

Some of the new sources of capital in Asia include U.S.-based investment funds, the introduction of securitization through REITs and commercial mortgage-backed securities (CMBSs), "Petro-Dollars" from Middle Eastern investors and associated funds, property companies, high-net-worth individuals, and institutional investors.

Accounting Conventions

Accounting conventions in any given country will have a significant impact on financing hotel projects and the structuring of hotel companies. For multinational hotel companies with operations in several countries, the result of differences in accounting conventions and standards results in a general lack of comparability of financial statements between countries. For example, the following cases illustrate differences in accounting rules:

- Accounting standards in Holland use current values for replacement assets, while Japanese law prohibits revaluation and prescribes historic cost.

- Capitalization of financial leases is required in Great Britain, but not practiced in France.

- German accounting standards treat depreciation as a liability, while British companies deduct it from assets.[10]

As noted earlier in the chapter, the growth of cross-border investments and the overall globalization of capital markets has led to the need for transnational financial reporting. A U.S-based institution or individual investing in shares of a British hotel company listed on the London Stock Exchange would be an example of a cross-border investor. The financial reporting needs of the U.S.-based investor would be different from the requirements of the stock exchange and might result in two different profitability and valuation outcomes.

In the United Kingdom, it is permissible to revalue appreciating property assets each year on the balance sheet to reflect current market value. During a period of rapidly rising property values (as during the 1980s), the value of the hotel company's assets rises dramatically on the balance sheet. Everything else being the same, this reduces the company's debt-equity ratio, giving the company a tremendous advantage in its borrowing capacity. This might be one of the reasons why

InterContinental Hotel Group, the world's largest hotel company, remains incorporated in the United Kingdom and listed on the London Stock Exchange.

Companies with high property content in their portfolios benefit from property revaluation in two respects. First, with no change in the level of borrowings, the debt-equity ratio is reduced, which means the company's debt capacity is expanded. Second, in publicly listed companies, as the stock value increases, so does the net asset value of the company, resulting in an increase in share price. Theoretically, once the capital appreciation of a hotel has progressed to a desired point, a U.K. hotel company can sell off part of the equity to investors. It thus raises capital for additional projects while still retaining an equity position in the original hotel and without increasing the level or cost of borrowings.

The downside of property revaluation on balance sheets occurs when property values fall (as they did at the beginning of the 1990s). This results in a decrease in the company's assets. Several U.K. hotel companies went into receivership in the early 1990s and there has been something of a return to cash flow considerations in assessing hotel values and the value of the hotel companies' stock.

By contrast, hotel companies in the United States and many other countries are required by law or accounting convention to depreciate freehold (fee simple) assets on their balance sheets. While there are different methods of depreciation allowed, the net effect is a constraint on debt capacity with fewer options for leveraging property assets. Tax legislation in the United States is also on the whole more complicated than in other countries, and accountants must decide between accepted financial accounting practices and prevailing tax accounting rules in order to yield the optimum bottom line.

Reconciliation

Reconciliation of different accounting conventions can be challenging when financial information must be converted into comparative forms for companies and investors from other countries. Particularly with joint ventures, there are potential problems of how to coordinate different legal, cultural, and accounting traditions in a way that resolves issues relating to internal and financial controls, tax computation, the measurement of profit, and the valuation of joint venture investments.

Substantial efforts have been made recently to harmonize accounting standards among countries. The major proponent of this has been the International Accounting Standards Board (IASB). This body, formed in 2001, is responsible for the formulation of new international financial reporting standards. While compliance with these standards is voluntary, several multinational hotel companies have started to report their annual financial statements using these standards.

While few countries have identical accounting systems and standards, three groups of countries with similar standards may be identified based on the development of their capital markets and financial reporting requirements:

1. *British-American-Dutch Group*: These countries have large and well-developed stock and bond markets that are the primary sources of capital and accounting systems and are therefore geared to provide information to individual investors.

2. *Europe-Japan Group*: These countries have close ties to banks as their primary capital source, which impacts their financial reporting.

3. *South American Group*: Accounting standards in these countries are affected by persistent inflation.[11]

These groupings still don't categorize the countries that were formerly part of the Soviet Union, or many of the African countries with frequent regime changes and dictatorial mandates. In the case of China, which has drawn strong international investment interest since its economic reforms in 1978, its accounting system is a carryover from the old system created to be a compliance-reporting process under the older Communist system; it was geared to measure the government's production and tax goals rather than profitability. Other related problems for investors in these newly converted regimes are the lack of qualified accountants and financial managers and auditors with experience in market-economy-based transactions.[12]

Tax Rules

Western developers are usually surprised at the intricacy of income tax techniques that even lesser developed countries may employ. China, for example, uses fairly sophisticated concepts of depreciation, although the country has been open to outside investments only since 1978. The hotel industry has found that the technology of taxes, like bad news, travels fast.

Throughout the world, investors can expect to confront an array of taxes: national income taxes; local, municipal, or provincial surtaxes; sales taxes; real estate transfer taxes; real property taxes; and bed taxes. Another tax that is not found in the United States but is common throughout Western Europe is the value added tax (VAT). The VAT, a tax on goods and services levied at each stage of production, generally applies to the sale of real estate as well.

Tax rates vary from one country to the next, affecting the overall profitability of the hotel company. Japan, Germany, and the Scandinavian countries have relatively high taxes; low rates and other favorable tax conditions are found in Switzerland, Cyprus, the Netherlands, and Hong Kong.

In some cases, both the home country and the host country will tax an investor's profits in the absence of reciprocal treaties. France, Germany, Italy, Jamaica, and the United Kingdom are among the many countries that have executed tax treaties with the United States. According to these treaties, each party agrees to reduce its own tax rate on income from applicable projects. Where no such treaty exists, an investor/developer will likely be taxed twice on earnings unless the host country's government unilaterally allows a credit or deduction for taxes paid to another government, as Spain and Portugal do under certain circumstances. Hong Kong does not levy any tax on the profits of a Hong Kong company that are earned outside of Hong Kong, even when they are remitted to Hong Kong. Hong Kong also levies no taxes on capital gains or the distribution of profits as dividends.[13]

In the past few decades, there have been a number of changes in how various countries administer tax legislation. These changes have had a significant impact on hotels with international operations. The Tax Reform Act of 1986 caused sweeping changes in the United States and also triggered tax reform worldwide.

Globally, the trend has been toward decreased rates. But since average tax rates worldwide usually range between 20 and 60 percent of income, understanding the impact of tax legislation is critical for multinational companies. Without effective tax planning, income can easily be taxed unnecessarily two or more times. Tax laws, the existence of tax treaties with other countries, and the ease of cross-border transactions should also affect where a hotel company operates properties, the level of equity participation, and where money is borrowed.

The U.S. tax system is one of the world's most complex. U.S. hotel corporations operating in the international arena are generally subjected to heavier tax burdens on foreign income than their foreign competitors. U.S. tax laws on foreign income have not been designed for how the world really operates today, as they are based on tax policies written in the 1950s and '60s when the United States dominated the world. They are also not based on the reality of globalization, from the purchasing of established overseas firms (goodwill is not tax-deductible as it is in other countries) to handling foreign tax incentives (in most countries, the hotel would receive a tax credit based on the hypothetical foreign taxes the company would have paid). An additional problem for U.S. hotel corporations is that tax laws keep changing, hampering the ability to do long-term planning. All of these factors serve to discourage U.S. companies from doing business abroad.

The use of **foreign tax credits** (tax credits in the home country for taxes paid in a foreign country) is fairly common, but has become increasingly complex. This is particularly so when distinguishing between the effective tax rate and the actual tax rate when tax deferral and holiday incentives are involved. Taxes paid in one country do not guarantee a corresponding credit in another country. Often, if the country in which the tax is paid has a higher tax rate than the country giving the credit, the country giving the credit will allow credit only to the extent that its lower rate would have imposed tax.

Changes in foreign tax credit laws and other tax laws have adversely affected U.S. hotel companies operating abroad. Before tax reform, U.S. hotel companies with overseas properties could consolidate their foreign income into one big basket and get one big tax credit. Now, the U.S. Internal Revenue Service requires elaborate breakdowns by sources of income into far smaller baskets. This makes it harder to use foreign tax credits from one basket to offset the foreign tax bills accumulated in another basket. More baskets means fewer places to protect foreign income and higher effective tax rates. Unusable excess foreign tax credits have also resulted because U.S. tax rates have gone down while tax rates in many other areas have gone up. In contrast, companies in some countries pay little or no tax on any foreign income to their home governments.

Uniform Systems of Accounts

As the *Uniform System of Accounts for the Lodging Industry* is used almost universally, it is possible to gather data on the industry to analyze hotel trends on a regional, national, or international level. Such information is useful for hotel companies, potential investors, and lenders. The composition of hotel revenue derived from room sales, food and beverage sales, and minor operated departments sales varies widely among hotels serving different markets in different countries or parts of the world. This also applies to the costs of payroll, food and beverage, and undistributed expenses of administration, marketing, property operation and maintenance, energy, and so forth. Under these uniform systems of accounts, all of these accounts will be classified similarly and reported in a more or less similar format, which makes it possible to make valid comparisons between properties in different locations.

Summary

The globalization of financial markets and systems has had a significant impact on the nature of hotel investment. Current market trends, larger investment requirements, fluctuations in the availability of capital, conservative lending policies, and other issues have bred creative ways to finance hotels and hybrid forms of ownership. Investment funds for international hotel projects that in the past were raised largely from conventional sources are today more likely to come from non-domestic, non-traditional sources. The financial environment for hotel development has become far more complex.

A developer and other investors typically provide the front-end funds to initiate a lodging project by committing equity funds or risk capital. Long-term equity investors and long-term debt financing must then be found for the development. Before hotel equity investments are made, however, potential investors will normally set specific criteria regarding the country or region to determine the soundness and safety of the investment.

Lending institutions have adopted much stricter criteria in considering loan approvals. Lenders will generally evaluate the risk of a hotel project based on the developer's market feasibility reports, his or her success with previous projects, the expertise and reputation of the management company chosen to operate the hotel, and other equally important factors.

Lenders and borrowers may negotiate fixed or floating interest rates or loans. Fixed rates are generally set at market for the life of the loan and changed only upon refinancing. Floating rates are usually attached to a "prime" index, such as Europe's LIBOR or Japan's Euroyen.

Foreign borrowing has become more common. In riskier situations or countries, the financing framework may take the form of joint ventures with, say, a qualified Western or Asian construction company taking the lead and working with a local organization, a hotel operator, or the financing bank as the venture partner. Alternatively, a number of consortium banks may become active participants in a syndicated loan arrangement, secured by host government guarantees. Financing may also be sought from the World Bank or a regional development bank. Some developing countries have established their own domestic development banks to provide financing for desired development projects, which may at times include hotels.

Governments in many developing countries provide incentives to encourage development that otherwise might not take place. These incentives typically reduce required capital outlay, reduce ongoing operating costs, and/or secure the investment. To reduce bureaucratic delays, some countries have established coordinating agencies or "one-stop shops" to help foreign investors obtain the necessary permits.

Lodging companies may be publicly listed companies (PLCs) or privately owned. PLCs have greater access to major equity markets. They also have greater capacity for borrowing lower-cost funds through the use of securities that are linked to equity.

Lodging investment trends vary by country and region. In the United States, hotel ownership and hotel operation are usually separate. In recent years, however, hotel owners and lenders have started to require equity contributions or loans from management companies in return for contracts. Unlike the U.S. lodging industry, the European lodging industry is highly fragmented; properties are typically smaller and individually owned and operated. However, a number of large hotel companies with greater access to international capital markets have recently emerged on the Continent. In contrast, the lodging industry arrived late to Asia and quickly became dominated by local entrepreneurs. Asian investors generally prefer to own their hotels outright and to finance new hotels from internal cash flow or other self-financing schemes.

Accounting conventions and tax rulings in different countries will have a significant impact on hotel financing and operations. The *Uniform System of Accounts for the Lodging Industry* provides a standard for all hotel accounts by providing a prescribed format that allows valid comparisons to be made between properties in different locations.

Endnotes

1. Jones Lang LaSalle Hotels, *Hotel Investment Outlook 2007*.
2. Much of the information in the following sections was adapted from *Hotel Investment Outlook 2007* and the *Hotel Investment Sentiment Survey*, published by Jones Lang LaSalle Hotels, an investment advisory firm; *Emerging Trends in Real Estate Asia-Pacific, 2007*, Urban Land Institute; and *Emerging Trends in Real Estate Europe, 2007*, Urban Land Institute.
3. International Finance Corporation, 2006 Annual Report. www.ifc.org/annualreport.nsf/-Content/AR2006_English
4. Stephen Wanhill, "Which Investment Incentives for Tourism?" *Tourism Management*, September 1983, p. 6.
5. Adapted from Salih Kusuluvan and Kurtulus Karamustafa, "Multinational Hotel Development in Developing Countries: An Exploratory Analysis of Critical Policy Issues," *International Journal of Tourism Research*, No. 3, May/June 2001, pp. 179–197.
6. Paul Slattery, "Models for Financing Tourism Facilities," *Travel and Tourism Analyst*, No. 4, 1990, p. 53.
7. Ibid., p. 60.
8. The International Hotel Industry, Travel and Tourism Intelligence, 2003 (London: Mintel International Group Ltd., 2003).
9. Patrick Ford, "Lodging Development Trends China," presentation at the ISHC Annual Conference, Hong Kong, October 7–10, 2007.
10. Charles W. L. Hill, *International Business: Competing in the Global Marketplace* (New York: McGraw-Hill/Irwin, 2005), pp. 650–651.

11. Gerhard G. Mueller, Helen Gernon, and Gary K. Meek, *Accounting: An International Perspective* (Homewood, Ill.: Irwin, 1991).
12. L. E. Graham and A. H. Carley, "When East Meets West," *Financial Executive,* July–August 1995, pp. 40–45.
13. Michael Dodd, "Shelter in a Tax Haven," *Accountancy,* November 1990, p. 70.

Key Terms

call provision—A provision that entitles a corporation to repurchase its bonds or preferred stock from holders at stated prices over specified periods.

development bank—A bank dedicated to funding development projects. Development banks mainly provide debt financing, although some will make equity investments as well.

Euroyen—A weighted currency value based on European currency and the Japanese yen.

Euroyen rate index—A multinational index used in setting interest rates for loans.

foreign tax credit—Tax credits in the home country for taxes paid in a foreign country.

hurdle rate—The minimum internal rate of return that a project must meet or exceed to be acceptable under the internal rate of return model of capital budgeting.

interest relief subsidies—Government investment incentives that involve government payment of the difference between a fixed interest rate and the rate charged by a commercial bank.

LIBOR—London Interbank Offering Rate; a multinational index used in setting interest rates for loans.

preferential loans—Government investment incentives that involve government loans at preferred rates below the market.

prime rate—The rate set by U.S. banks for their best customers.

real estate investment trust (REIT)—An investment approach that allows individuals to invest in hotel property through centralized management without being subject to corporate income taxes.

soft loan—A loan that offers a longer term or lower interest rates in the initial years so that loan costs are reduced in the early years when cash flow is tight.

Review Questions

1. What are some of the factors that affect investors' interests in foreign investment? Which factors relate more to the receiving country than the source country?

2. Why are hotels generally considered to be high-risk international investments?

3. What are the likely investment criteria for private sector investment in a country or region? in a specific international hotel?
4. What are the standard criteria for obtaining hotel loans?
5. How do the goals of public (governmental) and private investors typically differ?
6. What factors have led the Japanese to take aggressive action in the international hotel industry?
7. What are the most common methods of hotel financing used in developing countries?
8. What types of government investment incentives are commonly used to promote hotel development?
9. What is the major attraction of listing a hotel on a stock exchange? How might a publicly listed hotel raise equity capital?
10. How do the accounting conventions of the United States discourage property ownership, while those of the United Kingdom encourage property ownership? What effect do these conventions have on a company's debt capacity?

Chapter 5 Outline

Balancing Global and Local Perspectives
    Glocalization
Transnational, Global, and Multinational Organizations
    The Case for International Expansion
    Target Regions
    Potential Problems and Considerations
Geographic Distribution
    Distribution Patterns
    Variations by Hotel Type
Foreign Hotel Chains in the United States
Industry Structure
Ownership and Types of Affiliations
    Management Agreements
    Equity Participation
    Affiliation Considerations
Operating in a Multinational Environment
    The Environment
    Centralization and Decentralization
    Operation Planning and Control

Competencies

1. Explain the phrase, "think globally, act locally," as applied to international hotel operations, and discuss the "glocalization" of international brands. (pp. 161–162)

2. Outline the business challenges, organizational responses, and training program responses associated with transnational, global, and multinational organizations. (pp. 163–164)

3. Identify three growth strategies for expansion-minded chains, list advantages of and motives for international expansion, and identify target regions for international expansion. (pp. 164–167)

4. Identify potential drawbacks of expansion, and outline important considerations in making the expansion decision. (pp. 167–168)

5. Summarize the distribution patterns of international hotel chains, and identify factors that explain the differing patterns. (pp. 168–169)

6. Explain why it is advantageous for foreign hotel chains to have properties in the United States, and describe the marketing approach these chains often use. (pp. 169–170)

7. Define the terms *corporate hotel chains, voluntary associations,* and *conglomerates.* (p. 170)

8. Describe affiliation options available to hotel companies, and explain affiliation considerations, including the costs of choosing the wrong affiliation. (pp. 170–175)

9. Outline problems and concerns associated with multinational operations, and propose planning and control measures for such operations. (pp. 175–177)

5

The Decision to Go Global

HOTELS ARE "hosts to the world." As global trade and tourism have expanded, international ties have become even more important in the hospitality trade. Although operating an international hotel is similar to operating a domestic hotel, it differs in some respects, depending on the environment of each host country. Hotel companies that want to succeed on a worldwide scale need to have corporate management that respects other nationalities and cultures, supports the companies' foreign operations, and pays close attention to global economic and political winds.

Balancing Global and Local Perspectives

For many years, companies that entered the international arena adopted what was considered a generic approach. Having been successful at selling their products in their own home markets, companies took the product to other countries with no attempt to cater to, or even consider, the unique elements of foreign markets. For many multinationals, this strategy worked well because the world was simpler; nations were more insular; local consumers in many instances were undemanding; and there was little competition from operators in other countries. Consequently, there was no need to design products for anything but the domestic market. As the international marketplace became more competitive, this strategy gave way to a new emphasis in the 1980s: global enterprises with global strategies to serve global markets. These enterprises saw the need to carefully examine worldwide markets, design standard products with universal appeal, and place the products all over the world. The slogan since the 1990s has been to "think globally, act locally," and successful organizations are those that are able to strike the right balance between a global perspective and local market needs and desires.

The "think globally, act locally" slogan can also be applied to managing resources. Peter Drucker used the term "transnational" to describe an organization that works as an integrated network, a decentralized federation with a central hub.[1] In such an organization, managers are able to manage their resources in accordance with local customs and traditions, rather than subscribing to the "one size fits all" approach. Drucker predicted that this flexible approach in managing resources would be the ultimate competitive edge in a global economy, even eclipsing the advantage of a perfect product.[2] However, such an organization is considerably harder to coordinate and control, requiring new approaches to leadership, human resources development, and cooperation.

Glocalization

Glocalization is a term that combines both elements of the "think globally, act locally" slogan. Depending on the hotel company, different strategies are adopted to "glocalize" or make a local version of a global product. Most hotel companies that expand internationally fall into one of two categories: either they offer just one brand for the sake of market clarity, management focus, and economies of scale; or they follow a multi-brand approach, with several different types of hotels designed for specific market or lifestyle segments.

One of the challenges hotel companies that expand globally face is determining the extent to which brand standards for the home country should be maintained elsewhere. A strict focus on brand standards, as was the case with Holiday Inn for several years, requires that all hotels in the chain have a consistently recognizable appearance and be operated strictly according to corporate brand standards to ensure the integrity of the brand. This approach comes under pressure the further the brand expands into host cultures that are different from the culture where the brand originated. With the growth of Western brands in countries such as China and India, hotel companies are reviewing their strict adherence to brand codes and adopting a more flexible approach that allows for differences in cultures and national requirements.

As a case in point, Holiday Inn Express, one of the most rigidly standardized hotel brands, has learned to be more flexible abroad. For example, one of its specifications for guestroom bathrooms states, "A power showerhead must be provided and water pressure must be strong enough to generate a flow of nine liters per minute." However, the chain has had to adjust this standard in France and Spain, where guests prefer a bathtub to a shower. Local adaptation of guestroom specifications is determined by a combination of land costs, room size expectations, and local food and beverage preferences. Some brands expanding into Europe have reduced guestroom size in exchange for more food and beverage space and meeting space, even in typical select-service brands such as Courtyard by Marriott.[3]

Accor, the French global hotel company, takes a different approach to the need for glocalization by creating two categories of brands and then building their growth strategies around the core values of the brands. Accor's "standardized" brands, such as Formule 1, Ibis, and Novotel, maintain highly standardized features and have a uniform appearance. However, alongside these brands, Accor developed Mercure, which has enough flexibility in its standards to allow it to adapt to local nuances. Accor has further subdivided Mercure into sub-brands to adapt to the tastes and preferences of different market segments. Relais Mercure serves as Accor's two-star brand, while Grand Hotel Mercure is in the four-star segment.

Some other hotel brands, such as Starwood Hotels & Resorts Worldwide, penetrate international markets by acquiring existing brands with an established presence in a region, then keeping the brand distinct from the company's other brands. Starwood's acquisition of Le Meridien, for example, allowed Starwood to grow in Europe by capitalizing on the brand recognition of an existing brand. Similarly, InterContinental Hotels Group's joint venture with All Nippon Airways' hotel division allowed it to establish its presence in Japan and serve the needs of the local market with a recognizable brand name.

Exhibit 1 Transnational, Global, and Multinational Business Challenges and Responses.

	TRANSNATIONAL	GLOBAL	MULTINATIONAL
BUSINESS CHALLENGES	Operate on a global scale with local responsiveness. Develop local markets with global resources. Capitalize on mutual learning and shared goals between headquarters and foreign operations.	Operate on a global scale, deliver identical products with standardized world-class quality. Scale up for global markets with global resources. Adapt domestic operations for global operations.	Expand domestic market to worldwide business. Scale up for international market with domestic resources. International organization learns from domestic operations.
ORGANIZATIONAL RESPONSE	Global strategy/local operations. Multisite development, modular production. Teamwork, shared responsibility, informal organizational relationships.	Global strategy/centralized operations. Low-cost production, standardized development. Homogeneous decision-making, single strategy for the world.	Build up organization in international locations. Develop international marketing strategy/resources. Transfer domestic strategies to international situations.
TRAINING PROGRAM RESPONSE	Develop peoples' ability to innovate. Focus on vision, mission, and strategy. Empower entire organization.	Develop an overall operational effectiveness. Focus on consistency and development of techniques. Enable global operations to communicate with one voice.	Develop efficiency and pursue growth. Focus on getting international up-to-speed and in sync with domestic. Help international operate more like domestic organization.

Source: Adapted from Benton Randolf, "When Going Global Isn't Enough," *Training*, August 1990. Reprinted with permission from *Training Magazine*. Copyright 1990. Lakewood Publications, Minneapolis, Minnesota. All rights reserved. Not for resale.

Transnational, Global, and Multinational Organizations

Developing a global hotel enterprise requires a global vision, strategy, and organization. "Transnational," "global," and "multinational" are the three general forms of organization in the international business field. Each form is designed to accomplish a different core strategy. A transnational organization operates on a global scale but permits each property to develop in its own right according to local market needs. Global hotel operators see the world as a single market requiring standardized, reliable, branded properties that are identical from one country to the next. Multinational operations use successful flagship hotels to provide ideas for new properties in other countries; that is, they use domestic experiences to expand internationally. Obviously, the organization must be designed and developed in such a way as to appropriately and rapidly carry out its core strategy. People and how they are trained are the key to making the organization and the enterprise work. Exhibit 1 summarizes the business challenges, organizational responses, and training program responses associated with each of the three types of organizations.

A transnational organization recognizes that nobody has all the answers, certainly not corporate or regional headquarters. Managers and employees at every level in all countries, together with vendors and government regulators, have to find ways to work together and respect opposing views that spring from entirely different local conditions. The result is more teamwork, shared responsibility, and a flatter, more informal organization. Employees are encouraged to have a shared vision, mission, and strategy, but they are also encouraged to innovate and implement locally.[4] International hotel companies have for the most part leaned in the direction of the transnational approach, and the more successful chains—Accor, Hilton, Hyatt, InterContinental, and others—have long practiced many of the ideas expressed in the "think globally, act locally" strategy. However, many of the concepts of the global and multinational organizational structures would also appropriately describe the early operations of Holiday Inns, Sheraton, and other successful domestic chains that later became international operators.

Companies that take the global approach rather than the transnational or multinational approach look at the entire world as their market and try to come up with single products that appeal to as many customers as possible. Global companies emphasize attaining a global standard in terms of product and corporate philosophy. Their decisions tend to be made from a central location. Authority and training are designed to translate well across borders and help the entire organization operate with one voice.

The challenges associated with a multinational approach tend to be those dealing with market penetration; multinational organizations typically respond to these challenges by applying domestic strategies to the international arena. Human resources development focuses on making foreign workers as competent as their domestic counterparts.

The Case for International Expansion

Expansion-minded hotel chains have three conventional choices: (1) expand existing markets at home, (2) create new products to appeal to new market niches, or (3) develop new markets abroad. The most progressive hotel chains have adopted all three strategies at various times, alternatively or concurrently.

For U.S. chains, most early lodging developments outside the country took place next door in Canada and Mexico, but today U.S.-style hospitality is successfully exported around the globe. European and Asian chains initially expanded within their respective regions, but later looked to North America for new windows of opportunity for growth and to introduce a new style of hotel operations in the Americas.

The fact that the world is quickly becoming a global marketplace bodes well for lodging chains, management companies, and developers who want to explore opportunities in the expanding worldwide hospitality market. Hotel demand continues to grow in many foreign markets, spurred by generally rising economic prosperity and a long period of relative political stability in most parts of the world. Additionally, an emerging middle class within newly industrialized countries has discovered the pleasures of long-haul holiday travel and, like its American counterpart, wants a wider range of choices in hotel accommodations. As a result, many U.S. chains with segmentation experience are trying to gain dominance over particular niches in foreign markets.

For the most part, international expansion by U.S. chains has been a deliberate and careful process because of social, economic, and cultural differences. Most chains focused early international efforts in large cities because these properties pose the lowest financial risks and attract the most likely investment support. The principal strategy is usually to first get one's hotel brand established in large cities that draw business travelers, then expand to secondary market centers and into resort areas. Because it is essential that hotel companies establish a strong identity, standardization of accommodation products and consistency of service quality are key elements. Lodging companies need to make every effort to enforce the same quality standards abroad as at home.

The primary reasons for international expansion are strategic growth and profits. Part of the advantage of having an international chain is that a strong foreign presence increases brand recognition and may also boost a chain's domestic business. Although many companies expand internationally to increase market penetration, others expand to track their customers. The more locations a chain has, the more loyalty and familiarity it can build among its existing and potential markets. A brand image offers a measure of reassurance to business travelers who need reliable hotel services and to apprehensive tourists who are concerned about safety and comfort in a foreign environment.

Some hotel chains are strictly interested in operational profit, while others claim that the object of international expansion is more a matter of increasing real estate equity on corporate balance sheets or of diversification to lessen some of the risk of being in only one market. But there are other motives as well, including one of company status and prestige in the industry. The more global the company, the more influential and the less dependent it will be upon the changing circumstances of any one country or group of countries. Many chains perceive a need to capitalize on differences in the business cycle in different areas of the world in order to hedge against recession in the home market or other main markets. And for some chains, the impetus behind international expansion has been the opportunity to benefit from investment incentives offered by developed and developing nations whose governments want to boost investment in tourism facilities.

Important elements in an international development strategy are clear objectives and a comprehensive growth plan. The company should know where it wants to be, how it wants to get there, and at what pace. Many U.S. hotel chains have formalized foreign development strategies based largely on geographic distribution. Depending on where the company perceives a market gap or where the company already has a competitive advantage, the company will seek out developers, owners, and investors to enter those markets.

Target Regions

As hotel companies seek locations for international expansion, they should take a close look at the size and growth rate of the host country or region; opportunities for tourism within the country/region; infrastructure availability and quality; ability to maximize the companies' core competencies or competitive strengths; and the political, social, and economic stability within the country/region.[5]

The target regions for most expansion-minded hotel chains in recent years have been the Middle East and the so-called "BRIC" nations (Brazil, Russia, India, and China), in addition to the traditional growth regions of Europe and the Caribbean. Expansion into these regions is a combination of organic growth via master franchise agreements, joint ventures, marketing or co-branding affiliations, and outright acquisitions of existing portfolios. To a large extent, the primary impetus for this rapid rate of expansion has been the requirement to reach "critical mass," the level at which these chains optimize their economies of scale.

What follows is a brief sampling of the global expansion plans of some of the world's leading hotel companies:

- *Accor.* Accor is focusing its efforts in the rapid-growth BRIC countries. Working with multiple joint-venture partners such as EMAAR in Dubai and InterGlobe in India, Accor has aggressive plans to increase its budget, economy, and midscale brands, especially in India. (These types of hotels represent a core competence of the company.)

- *Choice.* Choice has properties in about 40 countries, but its presence is primarily in Canada, Australia, Scandinavia, France, and the United Kingdom (although it has a strong presence in Japan and India as well). Most of the company's international expansion is achieved with its core brands: Comfort Inn and Quality. Choice's entry mode into a country or region is primarily through master franchise agreements.

- *Hilton.* Hilton's growth focus has been mainly in India and China. Because many of the Hilton brands are not well known outside the United States, each of them will have a Hilton suffix, such as Doubletree by Hilton, Hampton by Hilton, etc. In India, Hilton is growing its Hilton Garden Inn and extended-stay segment (Homewood Suites) in a joint-venture agreement with a local land development company. Targeting the growing domestic market in China, Hilton has entered into a joint venture with the real estate arm of Deutsche Bank and a private equity firm to develop Hilton Garden Inns throughout China.

- *Hyatt.* Hyatt has identified China, former Eastern bloc nations, the Middle East, and the Caribbean as targeted growth areas. Being primarily a branded management company, Hyatt works with domestic investors and developers in each country.

- *InterContinental Hotels Group (IHG).* With over 550,000 rooms in more than 3,700 properties in 100 countries, IHG is currently the most global hotel company. Its seven brands occupy seven hotel segments and target seven different guest markets (see Exhibit 2). The company's international growth is primarily via franchising affiliations and management agreements. Its current primary growth emphasis is China.

- *Marriott.* Based on the company's stated plans, Marriott expects 60 percent of its growth over the next three years to come from overseas expansion, of which 45 percent will be in Europe/Africa/the Middle East, 45 percent in Asia, and 10 percent in the Caribbean and Latin America. In Asia, the company will

Exhibit 2 Hotel Brands within the InterContinental Hotels Group

Brand	Hotel Segment
InterContinental Hotels & Resorts	Luxury/Full-Service
Crowne Plaza Hotels & Resorts	Upscale/Full-Service
Staybridge Suites	Upscale/Extended-Stay
Hotel Indigo	Upscale Branded Boutique
Holiday Inn Hotels & Resorts	Midscale/With F&B
Holiday Inn Express	Midscale/Without F&B
Candlewood Suites	Midscale/Extended-Stay

capitalize on the growing taste for luxury goods there by leading with its Ritz-Carlton brand. In addition, Marriott will globally grow its strongest brand, Courtyard by Marriott, as part of its global strategy.

Potential Problems and Considerations

The opportunities for growth and increased market share may be considerable in the international marketplace, but global expansion is not without its drawbacks. It is seldom marked by immediate profitability and success when measured against domestic standards. Political instability, nationalism, cultural differences, and the lack of adequate suppliers may result in recurrent problems with resource availability, compromised quality and consistency standards, and runaway costs, which often plague foreign operators. A variety of problems rarely experienced by domestic operators can and do occur because of political and legal hurdles and different customs.

From the corporate perspective, there may be problems with respect to financial accounting and control, quality control, providing timely support and securing adequate resources, dealing with conflicting or adverse government regulations, and repatriating royalties or profits. Other problems may involve time differences, transportation logistics, and adapting the product or marketing strategy to new markets. All of these are factors to be weighed in making the decision to go abroad.

Expansion timing is critical. Whether the timing of an expansion is related to a corporate timetable, international business trends, or the availability of an attractive opportunity, it is important for the company to take its domestic strength into consideration when making decisions. An important determination of success is gauging which domestic strategies should be transferred directly to foreign markets, which strategies should be modified for export, and which should not be used at all. Other factors that should come into play in the expansion decision are whether the company has sufficient managerial resources at headquarters to commit to the expansion; whether enough suitable locations can be found to make the effort worthwhile; whether the cultural, linguistic, and political barriers can be overcome; and whether the properties can be appropriately controlled.

In addition to political risk and the risks just mentioned, hotels venturing into foreign markets are exposed to the financial risks associated with foreign exchange. The two most common risks associated with foreign exchange are:

- *Transaction risk.* This risk stems from the potential negative impact on profits and cash flow due to the movement of foreign exchange rates. The most direct effect occurs when profits are repatriated back to the home country. A weakening currency where business is being conducted translates into fewer profits being repatriated.

- *Translation risk.* This refers to losses and gains when financial statements (balance sheets in particular) from a foreign operation are translated from the local currency into the parent company's currency and consolidated with the parent company's financial statements. For example, if a currency is devalued in a country where hotel assets are owned, when year-end asset values are translated for consolidation into the parent company's financial statements, the translated numbers will reflect the lower asset base and will be recorded as a translation loss.

Geographic Distribution

In the last few decades, hotel industry restructuring through mergers and acquisitions has created new "power elite" hotel chains within the industry. Eight of the top ten largest hotel chains in the world are U.S. brands; England's InterContinental Hotels Group leads the top-ten list, with France's Accor falling in the middle of the top ten. When the list is expanded to the top 20 largest hotel chains, China (Jin Jiang International Hotels), Germany (TUI AG/TUI Hotels & Resorts), the Netherlands (Golden Tulip Hospitality/THL), and Spain (Sol Meliá SA, NH Hoteles SA) enter the list. Chains headquartered in the United States, the United Kingdom, and France together account for the vast majority of the total number of hotel rooms worldwide, although the escalating activity from Asia-Pacific chains can be expected to increase their relative share in the future.

Distribution Patterns

The distribution of international hotel chains outside their home region varies. U.K. hotels are strongly concentrated in Europe and have some presence in Africa and the Caribbean. French chains are also well-represented throughout Europe and are strongly represented in French-speaking African countries. The comparative strength of U.S. hotel companies is in Asia, Latin America, and Canada; that of Japan is Asia (particularly Southeast Asia) and more recently in Oceania (particularly Australia and Guam). Transnational hotel companies in developing countries have tended to expand into other developing countries rather than into developed ones, although that is changing with small but high-profile Asian hotel brands such as Mandarin Oriental, Shangri-La, and Taj establishing footholds in Western markets.

A number of political, economic, cultural, and linguistic factors, as well as geographic proximity, explain the differing distribution patterns of hotel chains. The United Kingdom's presence in the Caribbean and France's presence in the French-speaking countries of Africa can be largely explained in terms of former colonial relationships. The tendency of most holiday tourists—other things being equal—to seek a foreign vacation as near to their home country as possible in order to economize on time and travel costs explains the strong presence of European hotel companies in other parts of Europe, American chains' extensive involvement in Latin America, and the concentration of Australian hotel firms in the South Pacific. However, these traditional "home" ties have lessened since the 1970s due to global changes in air route structures, air traffic patterns, business and holiday travel, and the saturation of domestic markets.

Variations by Hotel Type

There are differences among regions with respect to predominant hotel types that reflect national and international transport development. In the United States, the foundation for the modern hotel industry after World War II lay in the development of highway properties to serve the motorist. Later, there were hotels to serve the air traveler, and midsized properties and all-suites to serve value-conscious, longer-stay business travelers. In Europe and some Asian countries, the early hotels were near railway stations. Today, the budget hotels in Europe reflect the family and local business market traveling by car. In Asia, where air travel between main cities is the norm, upscale full-service international properties predominate to reflect the trends of those markets. Past labor abundance, hence lower labor costs, and a tradition of high levels of personal service also encouraged the development of luxury hotels in Asia.

Foreign Hotel Chains in the United States

Just as U.S. hotel chains are expanding into the international market, foreign hotel chains are expanding into the United States. International investments in U.S. hotels have escalated significantly in recent decades, and negotiating with international business partners has become quite common in many areas of the United States. In the 1980s, for example, the Japanese invested in more than 75 percent of all the major properties in downtown Los Angeles and currently own a large percentage of all the major Hawaiian beachfront resorts. This Japanese investment wave was followed in the 1990s by investment groups from Hong Kong interested in U.S. hotel properties. In recent years, investment funds from the Middle East and hotel chains from Asia have set their sights on the U.S. hotel market.

Like U.S. chains that have entered other countries, most foreign chains entering the United States desire a presence outside their countries of origin. When building a global hotel company, moreover, it is not easy to ignore the fact that some of the most important gateway cities in the world with international air links are in the United States. The political stability of the United States gives foreign chains a great deal of security; also, many foreign investors view U.S. real estate as a bargain. The decline in value of the U.S. dollar has further stimulated the interest of foreign investors holding comparatively stronger currencies.

Unlike U.S. hotel chains in the past, foreign chains are usually willing to provide equity in order to get a management contract or to negotiate joint ventures, especially with reputable American hotel companies.

Most foreign chains attempt to offer a hotel product that is in some respect distinct. The company decides what special features or standards may be transportable to the United States, typically a level of service—for example, the unique cultural flavors of French or Japanese service—that the foreign chain thinks American hotels are not delivering. Primarily, this effort has been directed at upscale, sophisticated travelers looking for a "different" experience or reliable service. Foreign chains have been aggressive in their marketing and in adopting the American marketing approach by going door to door and talking to people to learn American preferences. Often, American consultants are hired to gather this **psychographic data** as part of the marketing plan.

Industry Structure

Hotel companies engaged in the international hotel industry typically fall into one of three categories:

- **Corporate hotel chains**—hotel organizations that have their own brand or brands that may be managed by the corporate chain or by a conglomerate.
- **Voluntary associations**—independently owned and operated hotels that join together primarily for marketing reasons.
- **Conglomerates**—companies that manage corporate brands or independent unbranded hotels.

Exhibit 3 lists the 20 largest corporate hotel chains. In 1992, the top 20 hotel chains controlled approximately 2 million hotel rooms and 17,000 properties. Illustrating the growth and consolidation of the industry, by 2006 the top 20 hotel chains controlled more than 4.5 million hotel rooms and 37,000 properties; the top seven hotel chains controlled more than 3.3 million of these rooms.

The voluntary associations, frequently recognized as representative companies or consortia, are dominated by Best Western in the United States and Logis de France, an association of many small family-owned and -operated hotels.

Conglomerates are changing the international hotel industry quite rapidly through mergers and acquisitions. InterContinental's purchase of Holiday Corporation made InterContinental Hotels Group the largest hotel company in the world.

Ownership and Types of Affiliations

Once the decision to go abroad has been made, the hotel company must decide whether to use management contracts, franchise agreements, leasing agreements, or technical service agreements, and it must also decide what type of equity involvement it wants. It is increasingly difficult today to participate without any equity.

Exhibit 3   The Top 20 Corporate Hotel Chains

Rank 2006	Corporate Chain Headquarters	Rooms 2006	Hotels 2006
1	InterContinental Hotels Group Windsor, England	556,246	3,741
2	Wyndham Hotel Group Parsippany, New Jersey	543,234	6,473
3	Marriott International Washington, D.C.	513,832	2,832
4	Hilton Hotels Corp. Beverly Hills, California	501,478	2,935
5	Accor Paris, France	486,512	4,121
6	Choice Hotels International Silver Spring, Maryland	435,000	5,376
7	Best Western International Phoenix, Arizona	315,401	4,164
8	Starwood Hotels & Resorts White Plains, New York	265,600	871
9	Carlson Hospitality Worldwide Minneapolis, Minnesota	145,331	945
10	Global Hyatt Corp. Chicago, Illinois	140,416	749
11	TUI AG/TUI Hotels & Resorts Hannover, Germany	82,111	279
12	Sol Meliá SA Palma de Mallorca, Spain	80,856	407
13	Extended Stay Hotels Spartanburg, South Carolina	75,860	681
14	LQ Management LLC Irving, Texas	64,856	582
15	Westmont Hospitality Group Houston, Texas	63,380	384
16	Société du Louvre Torcy, France	59,616	840
17	Jin Jiang International Hotels Shanghai, China	53,552	277
18	Golden Tulip Hospitality/THL Amersfoort, Netherlands	51,182	512
19	Interstate Hotels & Resorts Arlington, Virginia	50,199	223
20	NH Hoteles SA Madrid, Spain	47,799	330

Source: Adapted from "Hotels' Corporate 300 Ranking," *Hotels*, July 2007, p. 38.

Exhibit 4 Affiliation Structures of Major Hotel Chains, 2006

Hotel Brand	Leased and Owned*	Management	Franchise	Other
InterContinental	1.5%	22.0%	76.5%	
Marriott	2.0%	50.0%	48.0%	
Hilton	20.0%	19.0%	61.0%	
Accor	61.0%	20.0%	19.0%	
Starwood	17.0%	47.0%	35.0%	1.0%

* Percentages are based on number of rooms in the system

Management Agreements

When jet air travel began in the late 1950s, more Americans started traveling abroad, and foreign governments interested in attracting American tourists began encouraging U.S. hotel companies to develop hotels in their countries. Without incurring the need for the tremendous amount of capital normally required for real estate development, hotel companies became primarily operators or franchisors under contractual agreements; they concentrated on brand development, standardization, and generating markets—mostly from the United States, then the world's wealthiest and largest outbound market. Initially, management contracts were associated exclusively with international properties. In foreign countries, the management contract concept allowed for considerable local participation in equity and dividends while reducing the risk of investment and the problem of earnings repatriation for the hotel company, especially from developing countries short on foreign exchange.

Affiliation Structures of International Hotel Chains. Exhibit 4 shows a representative sample of the affiliation structures of major international hotel chains. In general, most large hotel chains do not own the real estate their hotels sit on, focusing instead on the management of their brands and the operation of their hotels. Acquiring and developing properties through management contract agreements and franchise affiliations allows hotel chains to grow faster and seek market opportunities as they occur. The separation of the steadier management and franchise fees from the more volatile real estate market is also favorable for the chains from a stock-valuation perspective. The hotel chains' home countries account for a large part of the differences in their ownership versus management/franchise arrangements; European-based hotel chains have a larger proportion of their inventory involved in some type of ownership or lease arrangement, for example, compared with their U.S. counterparts. However, the relative proportion of hotels in prime locations also helps explain this difference.

Hotel chains typically prefer to own and manage hotels in high-profile gateway cities with high barriers to entry, as the generally rising real estate value in these locations adds to the companies' total returns and valuation. Some chains, such as Marriott, are virtually without ownership interest in their hotels as a result of corporate restructuring. The Marriott chain split the company into a real estate–owning entity (Host Marriott) and a management/franchise company (Marriott International). On the other hand, Hilton Hotel Group's purchase of Hilton International in 2006 increased its proportion of owned and leased hotels, as the primarily Europe-based Hilton International owned most of its properties. Property laws, geographic distribution, and the lack of investors available to enter the lower end of the hotel ownership market explain why France-based Accor primarily owns and leases its hotels. However, as it is currently in an expansionary mode, Accor has sold a large portion of its hotels and, going forward, is planning to grow mainly via the management contract and franchising route in order to keep up with its U.S. competitors. Starwood Hotels & Resorts Worldwide consists mainly of upscale hotel products and is structured chiefly as a management company. The company still owns or leases 17 percent of its hotels, however (see Exhibit 4), which may be a carryover from its former structure as a real estate investment trust.

As hotel companies grow into new regions of the world, it is expected that the primary organizational structures for most will continue to be management companies and franchises rather than property ownership.

Equity Participation

Even as most hotel operators would prefer not to have equity in hotels in Third World countries unless it becomes unavoidable, the governments of some developing countries (in West Africa, for instance) *oppose* equity investments by foreigners. Government policy-makers in many countries find it difficult to accept the idea of foreign ownership of business, even when such investments may serve the country's national goals and priorities. Protectionist policies were particularly prevalent during the 1970s, when the governments of developing nations hoped this would limit the foreign exchange cost to their economies and force the transfer of foreign expertise to local partners.

In the 1980s, as the gap between developing and developed countries grew and universal recognition of a global economy began to surface, the pendulum seemed to swing in the other direction. Governments of developing countries began to take a more liberal attitude toward the level of foreign ownership allowed in local enterprises and, in some cases, actively sought to reduce restrictive rules and bureaucratic obstacles in order to attract foreign investment. India, for example, permitted foreign hotel operators to hold substantial equity in new ventures. The Indian government at one point restricted the involvement of foreign hotel companies to technical service agreements, then later allowed franchise agreements, and finally gave approval for the use of management contracts. Today, foreign investment is welcomed, and various investment incentives are offered as well.

Fiscal, tax, accounting, and investment practices and policies, not surprisingly, vary in different parts of the world. In the United States, real estate ownership is, for the most part, divorced from hotel management with respect to accounting, whereas in the United Kingdom, ownership (including international hotels owned by U.K. companies) can provide a positive advantage because it is possible to revalue real estate (that is, reflect upward changing value) on the corporate balance sheet as capital gains. In Japan, the once-liberal lending policies of Japanese banks and the philosophy of long-term investment with a longer payback period encouraged ownership of higher-risk properties with potentially higher long-term payoffs; this sentiment changed with the bursting of Japan's "bubble economy" in 1991.

Many hotel companies, particularly those in the United States, do not have access to funding because they have developed and positioned themselves as operating and service firms, not as real estate firms. For publicly held hotel operating companies in the United States, equity interest in most properties would tend to have an adverse impact on their operating statements.

Some international lenders will not make loans for the construction of hotels unless the operator is a known one with strong marketing capabilities and, in some cases, only if the hotel operator has also agreed to provide equity in the project. On the other hand, in the current rapid-growth global environment, with many opportunities in emerging markets, many hotel chains have gone with an "asset light" strategy. They have divested their ownership of hotel real estate while retaining their management contracts and brands. This allows them to be more nimble and expand at a faster rate.

Operator Loans. When operators do take an equity interest in a project, owners must accept the operator's input in ownership decisions. Owners who want cash contributions but do not wish to share ownership decisions with the hotel chain typically negotiate for an operator loan contribution that becomes due in the event that either party decides to end the contract. Loans are usually for an eight- to ten-year term with an extended amortization period. Both loans and equity contributions usually fund such items as working capital, debt service, operating inventories, furniture/equipment, guarantees, and/or pre-opening expenses.

Affiliation Considerations

From an investment perspective, whether for owners or lenders, a property's management affiliation is a significant factor in determining the success and consequently the risk profile of a hotel. First, the property's link to an international reservation and marketing system gives some assurance that the property will be properly marketed. Second, the affiliation provides assurance that the property will be maintained within a specific standard of quality.

One of the early steps in selecting an operator affiliation is to analyze the competition, if the locality already has an established hotel industry. Which chains are already in the market and which are not? Which hotel type would best suit the market? Which lodging services are not being provided? This process helps to narrow the selection to available and suitable hotel companies (economy, midrange, or luxury) serving an identified specific market segment (convention, business travel, tourist).

From the owner's standpoint, it is important to determine which hotel companies are most experienced in generating sales at the room rate structure needed to produce a profit for the property within a given market. From the operator's perspective, consideration must be given to whether the property would be able to meet company criteria with regard to size of property, design specifications, quality of construction, number of food and beverage outlets, location, and so forth, as well as requirements for safety, security, and technology systems. Another point to consider is that new chains tend to promote stronger individual property identity, while established chains provide stronger brand recognition value.

Expenses associated with selecting the wrong operator affiliation come high. Costs of such a mistake can include the costs of:

- Lost revenue or operating losses.
- Terminating the agreement.
- Acquiring a new affiliation agreement.
- Purchasing new identity items such as signs, logos, and monogrammed items.
- Operating losses incurred during the start-up phase under a new company.

Operating in a Multinational Environment

Multinational hotel operators encounter numerous problems not experienced by the purely domestic operator. Some of the most obvious problems are caused by geographic distance, time differences, and communication systems of varying reliability. A hotel executive based anywhere in the United States can board a plane and arrive at nearly any domestic property—even those in remote states or in rural locations poorly served by public carriers—within eight hours. International travel is always more time-consuming and less convenient because of time zone changes and the need to interline with two or more airlines in many parts of the world, not to mention the hassle of passport and visa requirements. Communication can become a serious problem when phone calls are neither convenient nor reliable, which is the case in many Third World countries. These factors complicate and often restrict coordination between the corporate offices of the hotel chain and the individual property.

Transportation and communication problems are at least manageable; other problems are inherently more difficult to handle. Developing an appropriate financial system that conforms to host country rules and profit-planning criteria for foreign units, for example, can be a major task in a country whose rules may change from election to election. Meeting the requirements of an owner whose representative is stationed on-site and has tacit approval over every expenditure not covered by contract can also be difficult. Then, too, there is the problem of local versus expatriate employees in terms of country policies, pay differentials, work permits, and so forth.

International hotel chains planning for specific foreign properties should make a careful study of the environment in which the properties will operate. They should also develop a flexible management system in order to better cope with the opportunities and challenges posed by the properties' new environments.

The Environment

Unlike domestic operations, companies operating abroad have little or no control over the regulatory, legal, and political decisions that affect them. Political circumstances might limit an individual property's freedom to act on specific matters, such as the importation of goods and supplies that would be seen to compete with domestic output. An extreme example would be political upheavals that might result in the nationalization of a property's resources, as was the case in the Philippines after the abrupt termination of the Marcos regime in 1986. On the other hand, political changes might have no effect on the operating environment, and overreaction could prove damaging, as in situations when hotel operators prematurely evacuate employees and stop all operations at the first hint of trouble.

Because it is always difficult to know what to do in a political crisis, operators need to prepare contingency plans in advance. The hotel company should also evaluate the socio-cultural environment of the individual property. Differences in religion, mores, and work ethics can be barriers to the development of effective relations between the hotel and the community. Since hotel managers must continuously interact with members of the community—employees, suppliers, business leaders, civic groups, government officials, and consumers—success depends on the ability of the managers to overcome these barriers. Because attitudes, feelings, and behaviors are culturally determined, managers must above all understand the culture of the host country in which they work in order to survive and prosper.

Centralization and Decentralization

In an environment characterized by stability and predictability, companies often adopt a bureaucratic or **centralized management** system to exercise control over as many variables as possible. In less certain foreign environments, however, the variables are too numerous and complex to be understood or managed easily by individuals outside the country in which the hotel is located. Executives in corporate offices are unlikely to have intimate knowledge of local events and their surrounding circumstances. Even under the best conditions, the distance between the home office and the hotel will result in occasional communication gaps and delays in decision-making that may reduce the hotel manager's flexibility and ability to respond to local conditions in a timely fashion. Many international hotel operators therefore opt for **decentralized management** with internal checks and balances to ensure that company operating standards are being met. Others give their managers complete freedom, short of violating corporate policies, to run their individual operations.

Some aspects of the operation do profit from centralization. Financial and capital movement decisions, the overall coordination of human resources, the development of training programs, and the logistics of providing non-perishable standard supplies are elements best handled through the corporate offices. Foreign currency management, a critical function in today's free-float currency markets, should be handled at the corporate level.

The presence of an international staff at corporate headquarters is useful for developing guidelines for managers in such sensitive situations as hiring and firing procedures; salary, wage, and vacation policies; and treatment of host country nationals. Guidelines should also cover instructions regarding currency inflows and outflows and accrual, reporting, and payment of taxes. The guidelines should provide procedural parameters, but give managers the latitude to make operational decisions within those parameters.

Operation Planning and Control

Planning for an individual property should be tailored at the operational level to take into account the unique variables of each country or location's environment. Uncertainties should be translated into quantifiable risks based on past experiences and qualified advice. The degree of risk-taking can then be identified, evaluated, and reduced. This can be difficult in planning for first-time entry into a new country, because neither reliable information nor hard experience may be available to formulate workable plans, leaving much to the individual judgment of the on-site general manager.

The objectives and the performance measurements for foreign properties should be based upon results that are within the control of the on-site manager. Some form of multidimensional performance evaluation—that, for example, might include harmonious community relations and the number of local nationals trained for senior positions—may be more appropriate in the international setting than the simple combination of net income and return on investment frequently used for domestic operations. The evaluation should reflect the complexity of the operation in the realms of goal-setting and financial control. Goals need to be flexible to respond to changes in the business environment and ownership wishes that may be a gray area within the management contract.

At the corporate level, there should be a flexible planning system capable of adjusting to dynamic changes in the operating environment, including possible political or social upheavals, labor unrest or strikes, disruptions to customer access, transportation or communication problems, interruptions in the supply flow, restrictions on currency inflows and outflows, and possible loss of the management contract for whatever reason.

To attain the degree of flexibility required, the planning and control system should include the following characteristics:

1. The budget should be based on the property's particular requirements, depending on whether it is a new, ongoing, or repositioned operation. A property just entering the market will need a different set of operating plans and objectives from that of a mature unit. A property that has been extensively renovated and upgraded may require more resources for marketing and training than one that is ongoing.

2. The budget should be designed to accommodate multiple and continually changing objectives. Objectives should be updated as required by changing circumstances and, as these objectives change, so too will the structure and level of costs.

3. The system should include both quantitative (financial) and qualitative variables such as occupancy level, market share, ownership, customer and community (especially local government) satisfaction, competitive position, employee morale, turnover, property cleanliness, and brand standards. A single key performance criterion is too narrow to measure the interaction of objectives, constraints, and activities.

Overall, planning and control—whether centralized or decentralized—must provide company personnel with a clear understanding of the corporate direction, ownership objectives, and customer needs.

Summary

The motivation for global expansion varies among chains, but the central purpose seems to be one of increasing market share and brand name recognition. International diversification, moreover, lessens overdependence on any one market, and often results in greater profit, since many host countries provide foreign investors with business advantages and incentives.

An international presence for hotel chains does not come without problems, however. Seldom are foreign ventures immediately profitable, and aside from language and political barriers, there are often concerns of cultural differences, skilled labor shortfalls, and inadequate local sources of supply to serve the ongoing requirements of an international hotel. Also, in various host countries, there may be difficulties complying with conflicting and adverse government regulations as well as reconciling different accounting and internal control systems. In addition, strategies that work well in the domestic market may not work in a foreign environment.

Transnational hotel chains were once predominantly U.S.-based; today, European and emerging Asian chains represent more than half of the hotel chains internationally. The pattern of transnational expansion appears to follow a certain logic. Established companies looking beyond their own borders usually seek opportunities in nearby countries or in countries that have common ties with the home country—for instance, a commonwealth or former colonial country. Young companies, on the other hand, will more likely respond to opportunity whenever or wherever it may strike. A safe haven with a stable investment and business environment also has strong appeal.

International hotel companies may be broadly classified as corporate hotel chains with their own brands, voluntary associations that group hotels together for marketing purposes, and conglomerates managing branded or unbranded hotels. Each structure offers different advantages and disadvantages to property owners with respect to investment, management, and marketing considerations. Companies entering into foreign markets must decide whether to do so by management contracts, franchise agreements, leasing agreements, or technical service agreements, and whether to participate in equity opportunities. When considering what kind of affiliation is best, owners or lenders seeking security for their loans must consider which international operator can offer the most advantageous management services, quality standards, global marketing programs, and state-of-the-art reservations technology, as well as brand recognition.

Equity participation by transnational operators may or may not be encouraged in different host countries. Less developed countries wary of possible foreign exchange outflow are particularly apprehensive about allowing foreign ownership. Yet hotel operators often find it necessary to buy into ownership if expansion is desired in host countries where capital is scarce or where risks run high. Operator loans are another way for foreign hotel companies to provide owners with financial assistance in return for contract consideration.

Many problems must be overcome by transnational hotel operators in managing foreign properties. Vast distances and often inadequate communication and utility systems or inconvenient transportation access are the immediate problems encountered in running a hotel in many developing countries. Among many other concerns that the transnational operator must contend with are having adequate financial control within the host country's regulations, dealing with on-site owner interventions, and responding to expatriate versus local hiring and training issues.

Hotel chains that venture into the international arena must analyze the environment in which each property will operate, because there are numerous national, provincial, or local regulatory requirements or cultural issues that will affect the individual hotels. Managers often have to make decisions which are location-specific, responding to local market and business condition needs. In light of this, centralized versus decentralized management policies need to be considered: the more remote the properties, the more likely the lapses of communication and the more urgent the need for autonomous decision-making authority.

"Think globally, act locally" is the marketing and management axiom for the international hotel industry. Today's transnational hotels find it increasingly difficult to adopt a single product or single market mentality for doing business internationally. In order to build an integrated network of hotels scattered around the world, comprehensive and appropriate operation planning and control procedures are needed to provide managers with a clear understanding of global corporate direction, local ownership objectives, changing customer needs, and most of all *teamwork* among hotels within the chain.

Endnotes

1. Benton Randolf, "When Going Global Isn't Enough," *Training*, August, 1990, p. 48.
2. Ibid.
3. "International Growth Strategies of Major Hotel Chains, 2007," Mintel Reports.
4. Randolf, p. 48.
5. John Dunning and Sumit Kundu, "The Internationalization of the Hotel Industry—Some Findings from a Field Study," *Management International Review*, 35, No. 2 (1995): 101.

Key Terms

centralized management—A system of exercising control over as many organizational variables as possible at a hotel company's headquarters or home office.

conglomerates—Companies that manage corporate brands or independent unbranded hotels.

corporate hotel chains—Hotel organizations that have their own brand or brands that may be managed by the corporate chain or by a conglomerate.

decentralized management—A unit-level managing system that varies in the degree of freedom given to unit-level managers; may have internal checks and balances to ensure that company operating standards are being met.

psychographic data—Information about prospective customers' lifestyles, interests, hobbies, and their propensity to travel.

voluntary associations—Hotels that are independently owned and operated, and grouped together primarily for marketing reasons; also called representation companies, representatives, or consortia.

Review Questions

1. What are the three general forms of organization in the international business field and how do they differ from one another?
2. What strategy or strategies might a hotel chain use in expanding nationally? Internationally?
3. Why is it important for lodging chains to standardize products and provide consistent service quality?
4. What are some advantages and disadvantages of international expansion?
5. What factors explain the differing geographical distribution patterns of international hotel chains?
6. What is one of the key markets that foreign chains target when establishing properties in the United States?
7. What are *corporate hotel chains, voluntary associations,* and *conglomerates?*
8. What is the purpose of an operator loan?
9. What are the chief operational problems and concerns in multinational chains?

Chapter 6 Outline

The Development Team
    The Developer
    The Hotel Operator and Other
        Consultants
The Five Phases of Hotel Development
Where to Develop
    Business Environment Analysis
    Market Potential
    Forecasting Sales
    Profitability Versus Risk
Infrastructure Requirements
    Water
    Power
    Communication
    Sewage and Drainage
    Transportation
    Health-Care Provisions
    Labor Force
    Security
Working with an Established Tourism
    Master Plan
Identifying a Specific Site
    Land Availability
    Zoning
The Preliminary Site and Building Analysis
Market Feasibility Study
    Information Gathering
The Approval Process
    Environmental Impact Statements
    Impact Fee Assessments
    Working with Local Interests
Design Considerations
    Architectural Themes
    Design Trends
    Physical Surroundings
    Urban Design
    Older Structures
Design and Construction in a
    Cross-Cultural Environment
        Understanding Foreign Business
            Practices
Building Requirements
    Regulatory Control
    Fire Safety
    Security
    Hygiene
    Electricity and Gas
Global Initiatives for Sustainable
    Development

Competencies

1. Identify the roles and responsibilities of the development team and explain why local representation and expertise is often critically important. (pp. 183–185)
2. Describe the five phases of hotel development, and list the four-step process used to determine where to develop an international hotel. (pp. 185–189)
3. Identify the infrastructure and labor concerns that developers of international hotels often must address and the various ways in which they may address them, and describe the typical content and purpose of a country's tourism master plan. (pp. 189–194)
4. Explain how land availability and different countries' land use and ownership rights affect the selection of specific sites. (pp. 194–199)
5. Describe the functions of, and list the information that should be gathered for, preliminary site and building analyses and market feasibility studies, and identify possible sources of market information. (pp. 199–202)
6. Describe the impact that the approval process, environmental impact statements, impact fee assessments, and the need to work with local interests can have on the development of a hotel project. (pp. 203–204)
7. Define and describe the many design considerations that must be dealt with when developing an international hotel, and outline the potential problems associated with building a hotel in a cross-cultural environment. (pp. 204–208)
8. List and describe the types of building requirements likely to be imposed on the developer of an international hotel. (pp. 208–211)
9. Define "sustainable development" and describe organizations and global initiatives that are advancing "green" issues affecting international hotel projects. (pp. 211–213)

6

Developing an International Hotel Project

THERE ARE A NUMBER OF REASONS domestic project developers and hotel operators look beyond their own borders for expansion opportunities. Among the key issues are potential new markets, capital availability, cheaper and abundant labor, the rise and growth of global tourism, and tax concessions or incentives granted by host governments, among others. In the United States, for instance, decades of significant building led to a serious oversupply of hotel rooms. This in turn led to low occupancies and the need to develop new market niches and segmentation branding. Elsewhere, however, it was a different story, especially in the booming economies of Asia and the Pacific. In addition, the common markets of Western Europe were being restructured, Eastern Europe was opening to western travel and development, and Latin American economies were growing. Governments that once viewed foreign investment as a challenge to their sovereignty now compete to attract foreign real estate development.

The process of developing a foreign hotel may appear to be similar to that of a domestic hotel, but appearances can be deceiving. Even in neighboring countries such as Canada, the United States, and Mexico, cultural, economic, political, technological, and legal conditions are not the same. Differences can and do pose formidable challenges to developers, but they can be solved with patience and sensitivity. It is important for developers to understand host countries and the markets they deal with in terms of their domestic socioeconomic condition, political history, power structure, travel and trade trends, and other factors.

Obviously, developers must understand local real estate economics as well. Foreign investments are often made using criteria different from those used for domestic ventures, and the return on investment requirements will vary from country to country, depending on comparative advantages in construction costs, operating revenues and costs (especially labor), and foreign exchange parities. Because local real estate values, government development and investment policies, and politics can be impossible to know without experience in the target country, many foreign developers enter into some form of working agreement with a well-connected local partner. The host government may or may not require a foreign developer to obtain local participation.

The hotel product—rooms, restaurants and support facilities, operating standards, and guest amenities—can vary widely in foreign markets. Local expertise and legal advice should be sought to provide guidance to architects, designers, engineers, and others on the development team. Small details with major consequences may impede the outside developer who is unaware of local customs and beliefs. In various countries of Asia, Africa, Latin America, the Caribbean, and the Pacific islands, it is not unheard of to resort to the services of the local shaman to ensure community acceptance of the project and to avert misfortune.

Like domestic hotel projects, most overseas hotel projects have large capital requirements. Working capital, pre-opening expenses, and operating shortfalls are likely to require substantial funding, so these need to be planned for as well. It is important for developers to keep current with trade issues in both the home and host countries, particularly currency and tax issues relative to income earned abroad. Exchange-rate hedging (taking steps to protect against the rise and fall in value of whatever currency is used) can significantly affect the hotel's cash flow. The ups and downs of the currency market may be eased by financing the project through a local bank, an international bank, or a consortium of banks and other lenders that minimize the need for conversions. Many governments strictly control the amount of currency that leaves their country, posing yet another barrier to a foreign venture. As foreign projects can be quite risky for hotel developers, and are certainly more complicated, it is important to be able to repatriate one's investment and profits at the end of the day.

The Development Team

There are several key players in the international development process. These may include developers, lenders, the host government, planners, landowners, anthropologists, environmentalists, architects, interior designers, builders and contractors, hotel operators, and more. The titles do not differ much, but the constituency of each group may vary by country. For instance, landowners in some Pacific island nations may be entire communities; government advisors may represent tourism, economic development, finance, communications, or other ministries, depending on the country.

The developer is the central figure who coordinates the groups of professionals from the various fields. The groups work together as a team to resolve economic, social, environmental, architectural, engineering, and technical problems.

In an international project, it is critical for all team members to understand the regulations regarding the development process, as these will generally affect the decision-making on virtually every aspect of development from the formulation of the preliminary concept through the actual drafting of architectural plans and physical layouts. In many countries, "political correctness" may underscore every phase of the project—from the architecture of the hotel to employees hired through a ministry of labor.

The Developer

Developers are the deal-makers who conceive the project, initiate the development process, find the venture capital, and marshal the resources needed to complete the project. Developers work with land, laws, capital, labor, and materials within an environment they can influence, but never fully control. Because supply, demand, costs, politics, economics, and legal issues can never be predicted with absolute accuracy, foreign development entails higher risk than domestic development. The more assumptions or predictions developers have to make, the greater the risk.

In exchange for assuming risks, developers usually require a high rate of return on their investment. This return comes from the sale of the property or of a turnkey operation. The sale in one form or another is a virtual certainty in many of the proven markets of newly industrialized countries. It is important to recognize that, in most cases, unless the developer plans to retain ownership, the hotel project is viewed only secondarily in terms of its management; primarily, it is seen as a real estate venture.

The Hotel Operator and Other Consultants

Hotel operators—usually national or international professional management companies—are today included on the development team early in the game for good reasons. An established, reputable hotel chain can help the developer secure financing and make the hotel more marketable. The operator can also provide important input in terms of the conceptual master plan, market feasibility studies, technical layouts and specifications, site and community evaluations, and operational considerations that help to ensure the long-term viability of the project.

A development firm, unless it is large enough to employ a professional staff, calls upon various consultants, each with specialized knowledge of the country in question: attorneys, land planners, architects, engineers, economists, social scientists, and other professionals. Some experts, such as a geologist or wildlife biologist in environmentally sensitive areas, will perform specific roles in a limited portion of the development process, while others (attorneys, planners, and architects) will be involved throughout the project.

The composition of the development team and role of the hotel operator will vary from project to project, as will the responsibilities of individual members.

The Five Phases of Hotel Development

The development process links investors/owners, developers, and the hotel operating company in a lengthy working relationship to develop a product that appeals to the market and at the same time satisfies the demands of all three parties. There are typically five chronological phases constituting the development process, as outlined below:

1. Conceptualization, Planning, Initiation
    - Define project objectives.
    - Define developmental issues.
    - Comply with local and national government regulations.
    - Ascertain whether any restrictions on land use exist.
    - Determine the hotel configuration (number of services, rooms).

- Develop a project flowchart.
- Develop a preliminary master plan.

2. Feasibility Analysis
   - Select a qualified consultant to perform the study.
   - Identify and select elements to be covered in the study.
   - Use the results of the feasibility study.

3. Commitment
   - Assemble the land/acquire the site.
   - Secure agreements from public entities for development and funding assistance.
   - Select and contract with a hotel operator for franchise rights, affiliation, and/or management assistance.
   - Obtain development rights for the site.
   - Develop overall land-use plan.
   - Select project architect and engineer.
   - Refine project development costs, schedules, and drawings.
   - Obtain necessary government approvals and documents.
   - Determine ownership structure and obtain financing.

4. Design, Layout, and Construction
   - Conceptualize and complete architectural design and physical layout.
   - Allocate space.
   - Plan for energy and technical systems.
   - Construct the facility.
   - Interface architecture, landscaping, and interior design.

5. Management/Operation
   - Initiate sales and marketing campaign.
   - Recruit and train staff.
   - Organize departments.
   - Maintain the facility.[1]

Where to Develop

Political stability is always the primary consideration in targeting a country for an international hotel project. After that, developers typically determine opportunities in a foreign country using a four-step process—analyzing the business environment, determining market potential, forecasting sales, and estimating and weighing prospective profitability versus risk.[2]

Business Environment Analysis

Analysis of the business environment requires detailed study of the political, economic, social, and cultural aspects of the target country. Similarities in culture and language between the home and host countries tend to make planning, developing, managing, and controlling foreign hotels easier. Physical proximity to origin markets (sources of prospective guests) is another important criterion in location selection, although today's more frequent and faster air transportation and improved communication systems have reduced the significance of distance.

Prospective developers need to understand the attitude of the target country toward tourism and international hotel companies. Some countries view tourism with a certain degree of hostility as an industry of servants and servitude. In some situations, foreign hotels are suspected of leaking more money back to the investors' home country than do any other form of foreign investment. Of course, with changes in economic and political fortunes, government attitudes may also change. This was demonstrated by Mexico's effort to open its markets, cut red tape, and relax restrictions on foreign investment during the late 1980s. This change in attitude, for example, encouraged the formation of a Marriott Corporation–Mexican partnership to invest $500 million over a five-year period on five hotel projects. Similar regulatory changes in China, India, and Eastern Europe in the last two decades are creating joint ventures to develop hotels in those countries.

The flow of business across national borders is affected by a number of government control mechanisms, including travel and trade barriers. Legal problems in conducting international business are not uncommon. The procedures and limitations regarding travel restrictions (if any), travel for employment, import and export duties, and government approval for normal business transactions should be investigated early on.

Because of the number of variables involved, it might be useful to use a checklist when analyzing a country's business environment (see Exhibit 1 for a sample checklist). Ratings and weights must be assigned to each variable to provide the decision-maker with a numerical score for comparing projects by country. Each company must determine the actual rating scale and weights to be used according to its own investment philosophy, objectives, and policies.

Market Potential

After the question of political stability (which could put any investment or project at sudden risk), market viability is for owners the next most important consideration in a hotel project. Owners must see long-term profit potential from operations and return on investment. For developers, the real estate market, the cost of development, and the property's sale potential upon its completion are prime criteria in pursuing a hotel project; these motives will also affect the owner's ultimate interest. In either case, the higher the market potential, the more willing a developer or owner may be to put up with adversity to support a project from start to finish.

The preliminary demand or market analysis consists of identifying markets, analyzing present and anticipated market conditions, and estimating occupancy and rate potentials. These analyses in turn are used to forecast revenues. Physical,

Exhibit 1 Country Business Environment Analysis

CRITERIA	RATING	WEIGHT	COMBINED SCORE
Political Stability			
Government Attitude			
Repatriation of Capital			
Repatriation of Earnings			
Ownership Restrictions			
Investment Incentives			
–to reduce capital outlay			
–to reduce operating expenses			
–to secure investment			
Taxation			
Exchange Rate			
Prospect of Economic Growth			
Rate of Inflation			
Size of Local Market			
International Tourist Arrivals			
Growth in Tourist Arrivals			
Hotel Occupancy Rate			
Other Hotel Projects			
Hotel Industry Legislation			
Transportation Accessibility			
Proximity to Home Country			
Common Language			
Tour Operator Activities			
Attractions			
Expatriate Policies			
Labor Availability			
Labor Costs			
Imported Labor Policies			
Availability of Necessary Building Materials			
Availability of Necessary Operating Supplies/Food			
Cost of Supplies			
Import Duties			
Import Restrictions			
Total Combined Score			

climatic, cultural, business, and other attractions need to be identified, as does the condition of the infrastructure, superstructure (physical structures such as terminal buildings that are part of the infrastructure but usually privately owned), and transportation accessibility.

The economic environment of major outbound-traffic-generating countries and their trends with regard to the target country also need analysis. Other factors to be looked at include the degree of development and competition, local arrival figures, and recent shifts in travel patterns. Sources that can be helpful in identifying potential markets and assessing overall demand include government publications, trade journals, interviews with travel industry representatives, trade and professional associations, government officials, and others experienced in the travel industry.

Forecasting Sales

A preliminary sales forecast must be prepared at an early stage to determine the economic viability of the project. Elements that affect the forecast include market trends, the number of hotels competing in the same category, the strength of competitors, potential market share, seasonality, anticipated average rates and occupancies, and planned sales and marketing programs. Forecasting sales in the international market is at best an inexact science, particularly when such factors as exchange rates, inflation, and politics are considered. The sales forecast must be considered in tandem with the cash flow budget to determine whether revenues will be adequate to meet debt service. If revenues will not be adequate, then alternative decisions are required in making the forecast.

Profitability Versus Risk

When the preliminary profitability of the project has been assessed, the developer must weigh the potential profits of entering the foreign market against the risks involved. Since there are no simple mathematical tools, this evaluation may be difficult. With some foreign owners, usually ones who do not rely on conventional financing, emotions rather than economics might determine whether a hotel will be built.

Even if forecasts of markets and business profitability appear promising, there are other factors that could put the project at risk. Some of these factors, such as political stability and government requirements, were discussed earlier. There are also intangibles concerning how people conduct business in each country that should be understood. What is unethical in one country may be a way of life in another. What is considered illegal or unfair competition in the United States may not only be interpreted differently elsewhere, but practiced with government knowledge. The developer who is a captive of his or her own culture may pay a dear tuition to learn the realities of private business elsewhere.

Infrastructure Requirements

Infrastructure generally comprises the system of services and utilities that are necessary to support development. Most international travelers and many hotel

Exhibit 2   U.S. Infrastructure Report Card

Roads	D	Power grid	D
Bridges	C	Drinking water	D−
Transit	D+	Wastewater	D−
Rail	C−	Dams	D
Aviation	D+		

A = Exceptional; B = Good; C = Mediocre; D = Poor; F = Failing

Source: American Society of Civil Engineers.

developers tend to take infrastructure components for granted. They shouldn't. Except in the most developed urban settings, the developer is likely to find that at least certain elements of the infrastructure are not adequate. The developer should carefully evaluate the short- and long-term capacity of each infrastructure component in relation to the hotel's requirements and the requirements of other planned developments.

Infrastructure programs, also described broadly as public works, are almost invariably a public sector responsibility except in very remote areas. A government's provision of infrastructure can serve as an important incentive in attracting hotel investments. Over time, an infrastructure will become inadequate or obsolete and require expansion and improvement to provide for new tourism traffic. If the host government is not willing or able to provide ongoing funding for maintenance and upkeep, the destination will deteriorate and lose its appeal. This in turn will jeopardize private investments in hotels and other enterprises.

A recent report on global infrastructure sponsored jointly by the Urban Land Institute and Ernst & Young provides a comprehensive look at the status of transportation infrastructure globally.[3] The report indicates that the growing economies of Asia—in particular China, Japan, Korea, and Singapore—are spending a high proportion of their gross domestic product (nine percent in the case of China) on infrastructure, including roads, airports, and next-generation mass-transportation networks. Australia, the United Kingdom, Canada, and Western Europe are ahead of the United States in confronting their infrastructure needs and using private financing to fund improvements. While the United States spends over $112 billion per year on its infrastructure, this is less than one percent of its gross domestic product. The report concludes that an infrastructure crisis is looming in the United States. A report card by the American Society of Civil Engineers gave the United States a mediocre to poor grade for every aspect of its physical infrastructure (see Exhibit 2). Maintaining an adequate infrastructure can be an issue even for well-developed countries.

Although infrastructure is generally a public sector responsibility, one of the common problems encountered by hotel developers in developing countries is insufficient public sector planning or provision for infrastructure. In such cases, the developer must work closely with government to ensure that there will be infrastructure support for the project or be prepared to incur private costs for infrastructure. It is often possible to work out an agreement for shared responsibility for infrastructure investment or to ask for government incentives in return for private investment.

Water

Major hotel development cannot take place without a high-volume water system. Particularly in relatively undeveloped areas and places where there is already great competition for water, local decision-makers or government officials often have difficulty understanding why vast amounts of water are needed to support hotel operations. The average water consumption for hotels is more than 200 gallons per occupied room per day; a resort hotel may require twice that amount. An 18-hole golf course located in an area without sufficient rainfall to keep it naturally irrigated requires up to a million gallons of water per day.[4] To keep guests satisfied, a hotel must be able to obtain the necessary quantity of water for operations. An inconsistent water supply that inconveniences guests can very quickly lead to loss of business.

Most hotels purchase water from a local utility. The actual source for this water may be underground aquifers (accessed through wells or bore holes), lakes, streams, rivers, or reservoirs. The utility typically removes the suspended solids by coagulation, sedimentation, and/or filtration and disinfects the water supply by chlorination. The water is then delivered to the property through underground pipes.

Another option for hotels is on-site water production. While producing quantities of pure water on-site can be costly for the individual hotel, it may be the only solution if water is not available from a public sector utility. In very dry areas and on islands surrounded by salt water, there may be few reliable options. Depending on the circumstances, these may include desalination (usually supplemented with groundwater), deliveries of water from ocean-going tankers, or use of rainwater catchment surfaces that drain into storage tanks and cisterns. Desalination is the process of removing salt from ocean water to make it suitable for human consumption and use. It is complicated and expensive. When on-site water production is necessary (especially when costly methods of desalination are involved), the reuse of water—sometimes called gray water—should be considered for irrigation and other non-potable needs.

Whether water is produced on-site or received from a local utility, the quality of the water is as important as the quantity. Water quality refers to the bacteriological cleanliness of the water, the chemical and physical properties of the water, the guests' perception of the water (color, odor, taste, clearness), and the effect of the water on the efficiency and longevity of operating equipment. Pure water is critical for an international hotel. Some people still will not vacation in certain countries for fear of drinking the water. International-class hotels have therefore often found it necessary to install their own water purification systems.

Power

Electric power must be plentiful and readily available for a hotel project to be feasible. A resort hotel typically consumes between 3.25 and 3.75 kilowatt-hours of electricity per room per day.[5] An urban property without recreational facilities consumes less, but only marginally so if its back-of-the-house support system is intensive. Besides an adequate supply of power, there must be continuity of service with a system designed to meet peak load requirements; in developing countries, this usually requires backup generating equipment.

To the extent possible, converters or sympathetic plugs should be provided to accommodate the personal appliances that international guests bring for their own use. This is as much a matter of guest safety as it is of convenience.

Communication

It is essential that reliable long-distance and local telephone, telex, fax, and Internet services be available. Depending on the country, the adequacy of telephone networks, cable, and circuits can be a problem. Nonetheless, good telephone service is necessary for day-to-day hotel operation and is expected by guests. This is true even in developed areas that have adequate cell phone coverage for guests using their own phones. Also, governments in socialist countries often treat telephones as allocated utilities requiring special permits and long waiting periods. A six-hour wait for an international line to call home or the office is not acceptable to the international business traveler.

Sewage and Drainage

The capacity and quality of sewage and drainage facilities are important concerns. In developing countries and in remote areas, sewage and drainage issues are likely to require more thought and planning than in developed countries or city areas where a hotel need only hook up to existing systems if capacity is available. In the former scenario, the hotel developer may be responsible for installing the sewage system, which will add to development costs. In either case, sewage requirements for a hotel should be recognized as significant. In a resort area, for example, typical requirements for sewage-flow capacity run between 225 and 275 gallons per day for each room.[6] In commercial and industrial areas, drainage requirements generally come to about 1,800 gallons per day for each acre of developed land.

The types of systems and equipment installed in an area will vary with geographic location and geological conditions. Developing any system will require technical expertise and large expenditures.

Transportation

In developing countries and remote areas, the existence of streets and highways cannot always be taken for granted. Hotel developers may be required to build the roads establishing access to their hotels. Parking, particularly in urban areas, is another important development consideration.

In any international location, airline accessibility is a factor. This is true not only in terms of the existence and number of daily flights from relevant market areas, but also in terms of ground facilities (such as airport terminals and runways) that will determine carrying capacity. Today, major airports are running at close to capacity in many industrialized countries and areas. Hotel developers should not overlook the implications of airport facilities and ground infrastructure in their feasibility checks.

The importance of transportation systems vis-à-vis hotels is well illustrated by the case of China. Eager hotel developers built hundreds of new luxury hotels in the decade following the opening of China in 1978; but visitor growth (and occupancy) was held back initially by an insufficient number of planes, trains, and adequate highways to transport people. Existing transportation systems were antiquated. Early visitors to China often remarked that the bicycle was the only reliable form of transportation available. In response, the Chinese government gave high priority to the development of large-scale, reliable transportation and highway network systems. These systems not only accommodate tourism; more importantly to the host country, they also support internal economic priorities.

Health-Care Provisions

Should the need arise, foreign guests must have access to health-care facilities and emergency medical treatment. In most cases, that will not be a problem. But the hotel developer looking at a remote island destination, for instance, might quickly discover that health-care facilities are barely adequate for local needs, much less the emergency needs of foreign guests and employees. In such instances, the hotel may need to consider setting up its own clinic and staffing it with local on-call doctors. The hotel operator must have at the very least a contingency plan for handling medical emergencies and ways of transporting guests and employees to an acceptable treatment facility. Sometimes, this will mean airlifting the patient by helicopter or private plane to the next closest country. The operator must also know the legal requirements and procedures for reporting deaths to local authorities and the appropriate foreign consulates or embassies.

Labor Force

While labor is not an element of infrastructure, it is a primary consideration in the development of a foreign hotel. A significant number of workers are required to staff a hotel, particularly an international-class hotel. Depending on the markets served, many employees may need to be bilingual, if not multilingual. While the hotel can provide its own pre-opening training for entry-level workers (assuming workers are available), it is certainly preferable if management can count on recruiting trained workers from an established hospitality program. If the area has a well-established hotel industry and there is not a labor shortage, the available pool of experienced hospitality workers will be an advantage for the developer and the hotel operator.

If there is a labor shortage, the hotel operator may have to import workers from other countries, assuming the law allows. This may require the provision of housing and other services as an added burden. For key positions in an international hotel, expatriate staffing is a common practice. The needs of expatriate managers and their families must be considered during the development process.

The availability of experienced construction workers and technicians needed to build the hotel will be of concern to the developer. In some cases, skilled workers and technicians must be imported to construct the hotel. After the hotel opens, some workers may remain as "guest workers" to staff the hotel. During the 1970s, for example, hotels in the Middle East were commonly built with imported workers from Turkey, Jordan, Egypt, South Korea, and other labor-rich countries. In recent years, Dubai has imported a large number of workers from India and Bangladesh for its hotel construction.

Security

Hotel security is needed everywhere. In some countries, it is a priority concern. For planning purposes, developers, owners, and operators should ascertain that the local police force will have qualified people, equipment, and expertise to meet the hotel's basic security requirements during construction and after opening. A cooperative relationship with local authorities must be established at the onset of the project. Once the hotel is open, its security department should maintain that cooperative relationship.

Working with an Established Tourism Master Plan

A number of countries have established tourism master plans to guide the development of resort destinations and tourism-related facilities, including hotels and recreation amenities. Theoretically, the plan provides the basis for policies, procedures, and regulations governing development. The timeliness, accuracy, and usefulness of the tourism master plan are highly variable from one destination to the next, however. In some areas or countries, the plan is politically popular, regularly updated, and often consulted by developers and planners. In other situations, the plan might be almost irrelevant from a practical point of view.

Deriving its mandate from stated economic and social goals as well as local aspirations, a tourism master plan usually begins by looking at the economic conditions, political support, community support, environmental conditions, and investment climate of the destination. This is followed by a synopsis of the area's current status with respect to tourism development—its hotels, attractions, restaurants, nightlife, and visitor trends. Next, the plan addresses infrastructure elements such as transportation and utilities and discusses opportunities, constraints, and requirements. The plan will usually end with a statement of implementation—that is, of how the plan's objectives may be realized through public expenditures, development regulations, incentives for hotel developers, and so forth. A timetable for implementation typically accompanies the plan. This timetable is often used to describe or label the plan—for example, a five-year plan.

Identifying a Specific Site

With the notable exception of land use and ownership rights, the criteria for selecting a suitable site for a foreign hotel do not differ significantly from those used for domestic hotel development. General criteria include location (as analyzed from various market and development cost-benefit perspectives), view, environmental suitability, and terrain. Even the environmental impact statements (EIS) once unique to the United States are now more commonplace throughout the world as a prerequisite to development.

Land Availability

Before land can be used, it must be acquired. Laws and customs governing ownership and acquisition of land vary widely by country. Greece, Italy, Mexico, and Portugal, for example, restrict foreign ownership in strategically important areas such as border zones and coastlines. By contrast, in some Caribbean nations, government bureaucrats or councils of ministers have absolute discretion to grant foreigners the right to own land. In land-scarce Pacific islands, a high percentage of the land is communally owned, which means it is held in common by a tribe, village, or clan. Use rights to the land are inherited and the land constitutes an integral part of sociocultural, economic, and religious relationships among village or tribe members. Land that is not communally held is considered "alienated" (a legal term meaning salable) and is mostly government-owned. For the prospective developer, the acquisition of land in these islands is a major constraint. Even if a joint venture is considered with a local villager, for example, a consensus from other village members must be obtained before the land can be used. Obtaining financing for such a project can represent a formidable obstacle. Banks are hesitant to grant mortgages, since the land cannot be used as security and obtaining the land through foreclosure is not possible.

Leasing. In some areas of the world, foreigners cannot own land, but they can lease sites for long enough periods to ensure developers' investment return. China, Grenada, and Thailand, for example, allow foreigners to lease property for as long as 30 to 60 years, although they don't guarantee indefinite use. The terms for land lease can also be costly for the developer, the operator, or both. The lease may call for fixed rent plus revenue sharing using different formulas for different income sources.

Land Purchase. When a specific site is identified, the appropriate rights to the land must be acquired. This is usually done by purchasing or leasing options. Options allow developers to refine proposals, obtain financing and project approval, and meet other requirements before actually buying the property itself. Landowners sometimes retain an equity interest in the project as a joint venture partner with developers. They can also become involved in the financing by taking out a mortgage on the land. In some cases, it is necessary to assemble several smaller parcels of land for a hotel; because multiple owners can have widely divergent motives and goals, the negotiating process usually becomes complicated and time-consuming. In urban areas, there may be several owners, leaseholders, and/or tenants involved—each having different vested interests and rights. In remote areas, it is sometimes difficult to determine the legal ownership of the land. This creates the risk of possible subsequent claims.

Urban Land Shortage. A common problem in urban areas of the world is the overall shortage of sites on which to build hotels. Quite simply, good sites are hard to find. In high-demand situations, finding a suitable or even available site in a crowded city has become next to impossible. The only alternative may be to buy an existing hotel for renovation, restoration, or demolition. In London, for example, consistently strong tourism and growing business travel related to the creation of the European Union have created a shortage of hotel rooms, but few sites are available in the city and land prices make the cost of new development prohibitively expensive. As an alternative, some developers are looking at less traditional areas of the city or outside of London proper for hotel sites. In the Wanchai area of Hong Kong, once best known for its red light district, an entire enclave of modern hotels has sprung up with a new convention center as its centerpiece—not by choice but for lack of alternative sites. In other instances, new sites have been created through land reclamation—for example, the Cotai Strip in Macau and the Palm Islands in Dubai.

Land Costs. The initial purchase cost of the land is a crucial factor in determining the viability of a project, as it will be a major determinant in average room rates. Site costs generally include acquisition of the leasehold or freehold, sub-leases, and other property rights and access rights. The cost of land relative to the total capital investment generally ranges between 5 and 15 percent; however, it may be substantially higher in some prime sites such as coastal lands and city centers (for example, land may account for a shocking 80 percent of the cost of a new hotel in land-scarce Tokyo) and substantially lower in underdeveloped areas. It should also be noted that the level of capital investment in the buildings is typically related to the value of the site: the more expensive the site, the higher the amount expended on the building. The higher cost is justified by the ability to command higher room rates at prime locations.

Average hotel development costs have changed as the hotel industry has grown to be a major world industry. There are three general locations for hotels: underdeveloped areas, resort areas, and developed areas. An underdeveloped area is an area where population, utilities, infrastructure, and transportation are minimal. A resort area is similar to an underdeveloped area, but the cost of resort development for infrastructure and amenities is prorated among several hotel properties. The developed area is generally an urban area where transportation, population, and infrastructure are available.

Average development costs in resorts and developed areas are higher due to technical and competitive factors. The site development, building construction costs, and furnishings constitute 70 to 80 percent of the total development cost. A major cost factor in developed areas and some resort areas is the requirement for a parking structure. This is generally not required in underdeveloped areas that can provide parking on grade.

Other factors such as furnishings, fixtures, and operating equipment do not vary significantly according to the development location. Their costs are influenced by the quality of the hotel and the floor area per room. Pre-opening expenses are relatively similar for all locations because of the highly competitive hotel marketing environment.

Fees, financing, administration, and working capital are influenced by the subtotal of all of the other factors. Working capital is higher in developed and over-developed areas because of the development approval process in these areas. It varies according to land financing fees and administrative costs.

Exhibit 3 provides an example of comparative budget allocation for a three-star, 300-room hotel project with 700-square-foot guestrooms in an underdeveloped area, a resort area, and a developed area.

Exhibit 3 Comparative Developmental Budgets for Different Types of Location

Hotel Development Budget*	Underdeveloped Area Budget	% of Total	Resort Development Area Budget	% of Total	Developed Area Budget	% of Total
Land		5.00%		10.00%		15.00%
Site/Infrastructure		6.00%		8.00%		8.00%
Building Construction		50.00%		55.00%		50.00%
Furnishings, Fixtures, Equipment		15.00%		10.00%		10.00%
Operating Equipment		4.00%		2.00%		2.00%
Inventory		4.00%		2.00%		2.00%
Pre-Opening Expenses		3.00%		2.00%		2.00%
Fees		5.00%		5.00%		4.00%
Financing		8.00%		6.00%		7.00%
Total Budget		100.00%		100.00%		100.00%
Cost/Room						
Working Capital (15% of Land and Fees)		1.50%		2.25%		2.85%

*Assume 300 rooms, three-star rating, 700 square feet per room

Source: Wimberly Allison Tong & Goo, Inc., Architects and Planners, Honolulu, Hawaii, December 1993.

Zoning

Closely tied to land use is the question of **zoning.** In many areas of the world, the zoning ordinance is one of the most significant regulatory powers; it is also one of the most popular and controversial uses of development power. Some Asian cities that once had laissez-faire attitudes toward zoning have adopted tough-minded attitudes similar to the restrictive policies of European cities.

Zoning essentially consists of dividing an area into districts and allowing only specified types of development in each district. The zoning ordinance spells out the restrictions on land use and development for each district type and identifies the procedural requirements of the zoning process. The sizes, heights, and density limits of buildings, setback restrictions, building-to-site ratios, floor area ratios, parking requirements, signage restrictions, and other elements are all specified in detail.

Zoning planners attempt to strike a balance between aesthetics, terrain, and commercial realities. For example, it would not be rational to zone beachfront land for a small number of private houses while highly taxed hotels were placed inland. At the same time, it would not make sense to develop beachfront land to such density that the leisurely pace and open space of a sunshine resort are ruined.

Zoning may be based on cultural considerations to protect historic districts or environmental considerations to protect the coastline, mountains, or national parks and other areas of outstanding natural beauty. There are also economic and social grounds for zoning policies: they can be used to create local employment, to attract revenue to the region, or to boost investment in infrastructural improvements to assist communities.

Before commissioning architectural drawings, the developer needs to consult both the zoning text and the zoning map to determine exactly what can be done on a particular site. He or she should be aware of the prevailing practices in the country or area with regard to zoning before investing too many resources into a particular site. However, it is not uncommon for developers to seek **zoning variances**—relaxations of the rules for cases in which the standard requirements would pose undue hardships on the property owners—for any number of good reasons.

The uncertainty of zoning procedures is compounded by the multiple agencies involved in the typical zoning process and by their seeming lack of uniform standards for granting zone change requests. In many countries, the zoning process can be fraught with obstacles, many of which are political as well as legal. Developers frequently employ local consultants and specialists to gain approvals as quickly as possible.

Once the site has been identified, a master plan for the hotel project may be conceptualized. This is the creative aspect of hotel design and decision-making. In the preliminary feasibility and marketing studies, the type of hotel, target customers, local social usage, competing properties, and other concerns should have been addressed. In the master plan, these variables must be translated into a physical product by the architect and the consulting team of experts, with input from the developer, owner, and potential operator.

The preliminary master plan will be modified and refined throughout the planning and development process as a result of the site and building analysis, the market feasibility study, architectural and engineering specifications, financial considerations, government regulations, and other factors that come into play.

The Preliminary Site and Building Analysis

A **preliminary site and building analysis** can be useful in the early stages of development. This cost-effective tool evaluates a site before the developer spends a lot for extensive design documents and drawings on a location that might not be economically feasible. The following list is a guide to the information that should be gathered in such an analysis:

1. The scope of the project (that is, the number of rooms, square footage per room, public areas)
2. Zoning ordinances and code requirements
   a. Property setback requirements (distance from streets, coastal zones, or other areas)
   b. Height restrictions
   c. Parking requirements
   d. Retention of open areas (for density control)
   e. Needed variance requirements
   f. Floor area ratio requirements
   g. Architectural design requirements
   h. Construction materials requirements
   i. Safety and health standards
3. Legal and environmental restrictions
   a. Easements (the right of someone to cross someone else's property)
   b. Flood plain encroachments (a buffer zone in areas likely to flood)
   c. Noise encroachments (for the noise the project creates)
   d. Shadow (sometimes called footprint or land impression) impact studies of the project's effect on its immediate surroundings (that is, the total scale of the project compared with the scale of the environment)
4. Utilities
5. Geotechnical report covering topography, soil conditions, mineral content, water table, and other technical aspects of the land[7]

With this information, a preliminary design for the project can be drafted. The developer can estimate an overall budget for construction and ascertain the long-term economic viability of the project. Since other aspects of the plan are fairly general at this point, financial projections will only be approximations. If the preliminary market overview and financial projections indicate an acceptable occupancy level at a specified average rate, the project should be continued by testing various sources for lending potential. Assuming potential lenders are receptive to the project, the developer should investigate the selection of a hotel operator or a franchise. The next step is a detailed market feasibility study.

Market Feasibility Study

A detailed **market feasibility study** provides significant data to determine whether the preliminary master plan can be justified in economic terms. As the market feasibility study is used to evaluate risk, it is an important requirement of potential investors and lenders. Market feasibility studies are generally conducted by an independent third party who evaluates the project and the market. Three factors should be considered in selecting the feasibility consulting company: (1) the international experience of the individual consultant assigned to the project, (2) the reputation of the company, and (3) the quality of the database the firm brings to the analysis. Most countries have branch offices of internationally known accounting and hotel consulting firms interested in undertaking hotel feasibility studies.

A feasibility study for an international project will generally provide:

- A detailed analysis of potential demand for the project (broken down by different segments)
- An analysis of supply factors such as existing and proposed properties in the area
- Detailed financial projections usually forecasted ten years from the estimated opening date

When facts are not available, assumptions will have to be made in preparing the market feasibility study. When assumptions must be made regarding political stability, economic factors (exchange rates, valuations, taxation, import duties, and so forth), and the reliability of the infrastructure, the study becomes all the more important in pulling all the elements together for a comprehensive look at the investment risk and returns. Exhibit 4 provides an example of a table of contents for a hotel feasibility study in Australia. Once the study is completed, the consultant establishes whether the subject property will provide a sufficient return on investment to meet the expectations of the project's participants. The consultant then recommends action to either proceed with or revise the project to bring it into line with market projections.

The feasibility analysis can also assist in the development of a hotel's positioning statement. It does this by defining the benefits sought by consumers and the attributes required to differentiate the proposed hotel from its competitors.

Information Gathering

Reliable and verifiable information—historic and current—is critical for producing an accurate market feasibility study. Good sources of information include government agencies at various levels, local hotel and restaurant associations, tourism offices, local convention and visitors bureaus, local or regional branches of hotel accounting and consulting firms, academic institutions, local transportation companies, the local chamber of commerce or its equivalent, bankers, and prominent businesspersons. As the data and professional opinions are collected, the experienced analyst may find a consistent picture or pattern of the market emerging. In small developing countries and rural areas, however, strategically

Exhibit 4   Sample Feasibility Study Contents

Feasibility Study
Hotel Gold Coast, Australia
Table of Contents

SECTION I

INTRODUCTION
- Scope of Study I-1
- Methodology I-2
- Background I-3
- Editing Conventions I-5

SECTION II

CONCLUSIONS AND RECOMMENDATIONS II-1

SECTION III

SITE ANALYSIS
- Conclusion III-1
- General III-1
- Site Location and Description III-1
- Accessibility III-2
- Visibility and Outlook III-3
- Casino Hotel III-3

SECTION IV

INVESTMENT ENVIRONMENT
- Conclusion IV-1
- Historical Background IV-1
- Population IV-2
- Climate IV-4
- Economy IV-4
- Air Transport IV-6
- Development Activity IV-8

SECTION V

MARKET ANALYSIS
- Conclusion V-1
- Present Domestic Market V-1
- Potential Domestic Market V-3
- International Market V-3

SECTION VI

ANALYSIS OF THE SUPPLY OF ACCOMMODATION ON THE GOLD COAST
- Conclusion VI-1
- Introduction VI-1
- Existing Room Supply VI-2
- Competitive Properties VI-5
- Planned Additional Rooms VI-5

(continued)

Exhibit 4 *(continued)*

SECTION VII

EVALUATION OF DEMAND FOR PROPOSED HOTEL

- Conclusion VII-1
- Introduction VII-1
- Projected Room Night Demand VII-2
    - Existing Demand VII-3
    - Latent Demand VII-3
    - Ancillary Demand VII-4
    - Demand Summary VII-4
- Supply/Demand Reconciliation VII-5
- Occupancy of Proposed Hotel VII-6
- Average Daily Room Rate VII-7

SECTION VIII

RECOMMENDED FACILITIES

- Conclusion VIII-1
- Hotel Entry Foyer VIII-1
- Guest Rooms VIII-2
- Food and Beverage Facilities VIII-3
- Sports Complex VIII-5
- Other Facilities and Services VIII-6

SECTION IX

STATEMENT OF ESTIMATED ANNUAL OPERATING RESULTS

- Financial Statement IX-1
- Introduction IX-2
- Economic Inflation IX-2
- Hotel Wages IX-3
- Rooms Department IX-3
- Food and Beverage Department IX-4
- Telephone Department IX-4
- Other Operated Departments IX-5
- Rentals and Other Income IX-5
- Undistributed Operating Expenses IX-5
- Property Taxes and Insurance IX-6

---

relevant information can be scarce. Developing countries tend to have severe limitations regarding the quality, timeliness, and cumulative details of statistical data.

In the absence of good quantitative data, developers or consultants may need to rely more heavily on qualitative information (often gleaned from personal sources and through informal channels) or collect their own primary data. For some developers, the lack of data represents a form of entry barrier. The advantages of being the first to enter a new market, however, tend to outweigh the cost of intelligence gathering from an undeveloped target destination.

The Approval Process

It is important to develop an overall strategy for the approval process. In some areas of the world, the approval process can be quite burdensome and time-consuming, sometimes setting the project back by a year or more. The process presents a complex web of permits, authorizations, and administrative procedures. For first-time developers unfamiliar with the bureaucratic requirements, the learning process can be a source of major frustration. For example, approval of more than 30 licenses is required to start a hotel project in India. In an effort to help attract foreign investment in the hotel sector, some governments are streamlining the approval process by eliminating overlapping or bureaucratic regulatory requirements and impediments for investment. Others provide government assistance to guide investors through the approval process.

Environmental Impact Statements

Few countries have environmental laws as rigorous as those of the United States, but there are comparable laws and standards in Western Europe. Other countries are beginning to see public pressures for stricter environmental guidelines. Depending on the government in question, an **environmental impact statement (EIS)** may or may not be required for all projects. In some cases, such statements are required only for projects in coastal areas, conservation areas, historical sites, or other areas designated by various governments as requiring special protection.

An EIS is generally defined as a written report that describes what may happen to the environment in both the short and long term if the specific project is carried out. Depending on the scope of the preparation required by the particular government, the analysis may involve land planners, market analysts, social engineers, transportation engineers, environmental scientists, and many others. Depending on the project, the report's contents may cover air and water pollution; the effects on marine life or other aspects of the area's ecosystem; the projected increase in traffic congestion; economic and social benefits and costs; the long-range effects on land use in the surrounding area; and the impact on population growth, infrastructure, and noise levels.

In some areas, the EIS process can be quite cumbersome, taking months to get final approval. This factor must be considered in calculating the project budget and drafting the development schedule.

Impact Fee Assessments

Developers also need to know of any applicable **impact fee** assessments. Impact fees are charges imposed by a government in anticipation of public costs that may occur as a result of the development, or charges imposed as a trade-off for some alternative use of the property that may have higher public benefit. Most local governments see impact fees as a rational and justifiable method for charging the developer to offset the cost of providing adequate infrastructure.

Governments typically determine the amount of fee assessments based upon reasonable and uniform considerations of the costs they incur for capital improvements made because of new development. A financial and administrative scheme is devised to equitably apportion the cost of the infrastructure developments to each project based on its anticipated use. For example, the demand generated by a hotel for water, electrical power, and sewage treatment would be relatively high compared with, say, that generated by a commercial office building. But the demand generated by a hotel for education and public health would be relatively low compared with such developments as residential housing or condominium developments. Costs are distributed accordingly, using a predetermined formula. In locations where impact fees are used, developers need to estimate the cost of the assessment in their capital budgeting.

Working with Local Interests

Local issue interests are sometimes represented in the development process by individual citizens who speak at public hearings and who act independently of any larger organization. Local interests can also be represented through various, more formal organizations with widely ranging concerns and agendas. These may take the form of neighborhood groups or civic groups—for instance, historical societies or environmental groups—who usually concern themselves with a specific set of issues. A hotel developer in a foreign country should obtain a clear understanding early in the development process of how the community is likely to perceive a project and how local interests might be affected. This knowledge will help the developer anticipate potential obstacles.

An unusual case of how local interests can affect a hotel project occurred recently with a multi-million dollar resort development project in a highly conservative and religious belt in the lower Himalayas in India. The local populace in this mountainous region has a variety of gods, goddesses, and local deities who manifest themselves in various physical structures in the region, including trees, rocks, and local shrines. As part of pre-development planning, the developer had to commission the services of a company to create a "religious map" to identify these areas, which were then marked to avoid accidentally desecrating them and consequently invoking the wrath of the local population. In addition to the various government approvals that the developer had to acquire, he was also required to get the approval of these local gods. To do so, he had to work with a local oracle, who communicated with the gods through an elaborate ritual.

Design Considerations

Detailed architectural designs for the hotel will be drawn up based on an extensive analysis of site characteristics, zoning codes, and building ordinances. Local planning requirements may stipulate height, scale, density, and constructional limitations. Height restrictions may be applied to safeguard the prominence of famous buildings and monuments, to complement the scale and proportions of existing properties, or to avoid changes in the landscape skyline. Height limitations apply in most European cities, for example; with a few notable exceptions, city center hotels in Europe fall generally within the 5- to 10-story range. This is in stark contrast to U.S. and Japanese center city hotels, which often soar to well over 30 stories. In some countries, restrictions on the height of buildings in rural and coastal areas may be so severe (for example, no taller than a coconut tree) that they limit hotel design to low-rise village-type developments.

The choice of external building materials may be restricted to those characteristic of the region. In many areas (for example, Western Europe), imports as a whole are not acceptable in the construction of a hotel. Designers are expected to research and use local sources of materials available from European sources for specified portions of the design. Similar import restrictions may apply to interior designs and furnishings, especially in a developing country wanting to conserve its scarce foreign exchange.

Architectural Themes

Hotel designs and layouts are based on structural, physical, social, cultural, and psychological considerations. Structural considerations relate to the best use of the land and the choice of building materials and forms. Physical considerations pertain to the functions of the proposed structures and focus on the functional efficiency of the hotel's operations. The most overlooked characteristics tend to be the social, psychological, and cultural values of the host country and the potential guests.

If there is a criticism from tourism ministries regarding international hotels, it is that they all tend to look alike. While the functional designs of hotels may indeed be similar, there is no reason why each property should not outwardly reflect the unique characteristics and culture of its host community or country. This point is especially critical in historic landmark locations (where in most cases it will be required by law). Landscaping and outdoor signs should be integrated with other exterior materials and architectural characteristics. The colors, textures, and arrangements within the buildings should support the architectural designs. The dining areas, lobby, and rooms should reinforce the desired ambiance.

Unity in architectural style and appearance among hotels clustered in the same area, particularly when patterned upon the traditions and culture of the area, can help create an image of the destination in the minds of prospective visitors. Many hotels in French Polynesia, for example, use thatched huts for accommodations that have become almost synonymous with tourism in that area. In Taxco, all architecture follows a Mexican Colonial theme. Resorts in Bali, Indonesia, are required to follow the Balinese temple architectural form. In crowded cities such as Hong Kong or Singapore, the emphasis is on high-rise buildings with panoramic views of the city and harbor. Islamic architecture, whether applied to a mosque, a private home, or a hotel, adheres to prescribed form, function, and space. Structures are built around Islamic religious rituals, Muslim community ideals, and contemplation; they will surround an enclosed core, typically in the form of a courtyard and often including elements of a garden.

At the other extreme, if a destination has no tourism image, architectural design can be used to create an image. In some recent cases, design elements that create a stark contrast to the local surroundings promote destination interest because of the "shock value" created. For example, Dubai, a destination in the United Arab Emirates, has recently constructed and continues to build some of the most innovative and talked-about hotels in the world.

Aside from the value of architectural themes in promoting a particular image for a destination, architecture can also play an important role in the acceptance of tourism facilities by the host community.

Design Trends

Beyond making hotels more comfortable and efficient, architects and designers have tended to lean either toward the dramatic or the subtle. Hotel operators worldwide acknowledge that how a hotel looks and functions can help set it apart from the ever-increasing competition. While architects are constantly experimenting with different forms, one major trend is to evaluate the significance of cultural and historical influences and how they can be integrated into design. In the past, some architects' response to doing something cultural was to create a fanciful caricature of the host country. Architects are now doing better research, looking at historical elements, and applying them in a creative and contemporary way. Native design elements may be subtly applied to contemporary form through the use of material, shapes, or patterns—for instance, rooflines, window treatment, traditional motifs, local building materials, and so forth.

In some areas, hotel architects draw on traditional forms of hospitality in developing an international hotel. In Korea, for example, the traditional style of lodging called *yogwan* provides a simple but comfortable accommodation that is used primarily by Koreans. *Yogwan*—similar to the classic *ryokan* in Japan—offer a small room with a heated floor and mats for sleeping. To cater to foreign travelers, many *yogwan* have adopted international standards in recent years by adding amenities such as inside bathrooms and western-style beds. Many modern hotels in Japan, on the other hand, do the reverse and now feature a section of *ryokan*-style accommodations, including the traditional tatami matting, low furniture, shoji screens, and futons, but with private baths instead of communal bathing. Indeed, the contemporary Japanese hotel has been likened to the Honda automobile: its basic technology is North American, but its refinement is Japanese. Approaches such as the *yogwan* and *ryokan* adaptations make it possible to draw from the old and the new to provide an experience that combines western comfort with the traditional hospitality of the host country.

Since certain aesthetic or behavioral standards are ingrained in each culture, the matter of hotel design can be especially sensitive and mistakes are easily made. In some countries, certain colors have implications of happiness or death, for example, and the display of certain styles of Renaissance art may be found offensive in some cultures. With respect to restaurants, designers should know that Germans prefer brightly lit dining rooms; the soft lights typical in an American restaurant will not work well in Germany. A restaurant in China will need to accommodate large parties all arriving at one time, as is the custom there.

The lighting design in international hotels will be generally influenced by lifestyle patterns of the host country. Because the ambiance, clientele, and even functions of a hotel change with the time of day and the cycle of seasons, many designers include lighting systems with adjustable settings. At the push of a button the lighting can switch to a pre-programmed intensity. Alternatively, it may be programmed to rise and fade to different settings automatically.

Physical Surroundings

An important trend in non-urbanized areas is designing hotels to fit in with the physical environment. Resorts in Bali such as the Nusa Dua Beach Hotel and the Nusa Indah not only follow traditional Balinese architectural form, they are also designed and landscaped to blend in with their lush tropical setting. Their spacious reception areas are housed in temple-like pavilions open to the sea to provide a clear view plane. Guestrooms are housed in separate low-rise wings flanking the lobby, tiered to follow the land form. Each resort enhances rather than detracts from its surroundings.

Club Med, with developments in virtually every vacation region in the world, has built an entire empire with low-rise village concepts and ethnic themes that respect local cultures. Designers of these resorts reinforce the philosophy of Club Med's founders by emphasizing the natural environment and outdoor orientation of the Club Med lifestyle.

Urban Design

City hotels are becoming more upscale and formal with grand porticos and entrances. The examples are numerous in cities around the world. Hotels such as London's historic Dorchester are returning to their glamorous roots by eliminating layers of modernization. Contemporary hotels such as Hong Kong's Grand Hyatt or InterContinental Hong Kong have soaring, high-ceilinged, marble-columned lobbies and sweeping staircases to create today's version of vintage elegance. While some experts see a trend toward making lobbies a smaller transitory area with little seating, in some countries—Egypt, for example—large lobbies with host-assigned seating will continue to be customary and expected. Hotels developed in recent years also tend to have larger guestrooms and bathrooms that are generally more accessible to people with disabilities (this is mandated by law in the United States). Business centers with electronic communication systems, executive floors, larger ballrooms and function spaces, and multipurpose restaurants are becoming standard in today's international-class city hotel. Other design features of city hotels are driven by the "urban chic" designs of the trendy boutique hotels constructed in recent years.

Older Structures

Local governments often encourage the use of old buildings for hotels, especially those with historic or architectural merit. Many old European coach houses and hostelries still provide accommodations for visitors, and old mills, warehouses, castles, chateaux, and former palaces have been reborn as hotels. The paradors of Spain are a good example of government policy to promote cultural conservation. There are many other fine examples of hotels constructed out of or within standing historic structures protected by law. Four that illustrate a range of developments are the InterContinental hotel constructed within the gutted shell of the historic treasury building in Sydney, Australia; the Hilton hotel in Budapest constructed within the shell of a twelfth-century baroque church; the luxurious Lanesborough Hotel in London, built within the old structure of the nineteenth-century St.

George's Hospital; and Devi Garh, a modern hotel developed within the structure of an ancient fortress in India.

Design and Construction in a Cross-Cultural Environment

Even for a domestic hotel project where businesspeople are all from the same culture and speak the same language, the actual construction of the facility can be difficult, because the many interdependent players sometimes have conflicting objectives and a number of timetables to coordinate. An international hotel is even more complex, because the parties come from different cultures with different business practices, and because communication is often possible only through translators. The chances for misunderstandings and disagreements are high. Unless all parties are willing to work to overcome the cultural barriers, the project can be disastrous.

Understanding Foreign Business Practices

Experienced international hotel developers understand that words are not always what they seem when it comes to international construction—from quoting money figures (using U.S. dollars versus other currencies) to discussing timetables. In some countries, a contract—whether written or spoken—is an ironclad bond; in others, even a written contract is merely a platform upon which to negotiate later interaction. Patience is a major requirement for the construction of foreign hotels, particularly when people or products cross international boundaries. Shipments of goods have been known to "disappear." In some cases, it may take longer to get goods off the boat and through customs than it does to manufacture and ship them from the exporting country.

Importing furniture and materials is essential in some areas where local resources are limited. Even in these cases, however, designers or owners may have to demonstrate to government agencies why local products will not fit the needs of a hotel project. Other options include designing the goods to be manufactured locally and making frequent factory visits to ensure that quality standards are being met, and working closely with local producers to improve the quality of their own products.

Building Requirements

Standards governing building safety and protecting occupants and the public at large from faulty design, construction, and operation are covered by regulation almost everywhere. Once a proposed hotel facility meets the zoning requirements with respect to use, height, site coverage, density, and so forth, the detailed design must comply with the building and fire codes of the locale. While the codes in most countries are highly specific and are continually updated as a result of fires or building failures, significant variations exist from one country to the next.

It is essential that the architect and engineers study the codes, ordinances, and standards for a particular location and comply fully with all requirements. Individual properties must also satisfy the requirements stipulated by the hotel operating company, which can sometimes be more stringent than government regulations.

Regulatory Control

While each country's or host community's requirements and ordinances will vary, the international hotel developer is likely to encounter seven basic categories of regulatory control. These categories deal with:

1. The responsibility of the owner, the architect, and the contractor to comply with standards ensuring the constructional safety of the building and adequate provisions for sanitation—for example, building regulations, and building and sanitation codes.

2. The obligations, whether specified or implied, of the hotel operator to maintain the premises in a safe condition.

3. Provisions for the protection of the health, safety, and welfare of employees working on the premises.

4. Specific requirements relating to fire protection and means of escape, food hygiene, and licensing for particular uses (for example, sale of liquor, assembly, entertainment).

5. Conditions for grading, classification, financial subsidy, and/or mortgage for various types of hotels.

6. Insurance requirements and conditions stipulated in insurance agreements.

7. Standards of safety provided for in the installation of electrical and mechanical services, through engineering codes and regulations.[8]

Fire Safety

A major hotel fire becomes international news overnight. The tragedy of this event is universally understood at once. Prevention is a legal and moral requirement. Fire protection and the provision of safe means of escape are shared responsibilities of the developer, architect, contractor, and operator. Penalties for fire code violations in some countries can be severe, especially when casualties are high. Fire safety comprises three main areas:

1. *Structural protection* includes requirements for fire resistance of the building elements and components and limitations on the use of combustible materials and finishes that have a high rate of surface flame spread. There is an international trend toward uniformity in legal requirements based on structurally similar standards.

2. *Active protection* covers automatic fire and smoke detection, warnings, and fire-fighting equipment of various kinds.

3. *Means of escape* for the occupants in the event of fire concern travel distances to safe exits, the identification and protection of escape routes, and evacuation from the building.

In most countries, mandatory requirements in these areas influence both the planning and design of buildings.

Security

Security involves the protection and control of property, safeguarding of guests and occupants, surveillance of persons and goods entering and leaving, and other responsibilities. Given the rising crime rates and terrorist activity in many parts of the world, security has become an important aspect of planning and management.

Security can be separated into the following areas of control:

- Security of property to prevent unauthorized entry or exit
- Controlled entry to individual guestrooms and apartments
- Provision of strong rooms, safes, and secure stores for valuable items
- Surveillance of persons, including employees, entering and leaving
- Baggage handling and checking
- Security of grounds

Hygiene

Although general sanitation is a serious deficiency in many countries, the failure to provide reasonable standards of hygiene in commercial hotels may be a statutory offense. Violations could result in closure of premises or cancellation of business registration in some countries. The areas subject to hygiene regulation may include food purchase, storage, and preparation; staff accommodations (including overcrowding or lack of facilities); water supplies; sanitation and drainage (including disposal of waste); refuse storage and disposal; and the general cleanliness and upkeep of the premises. The architect must take all sanitary requirements into consideration, particularly when designing the back-of-the-house areas of the hotel.

Electricity and Gas

Electrical installations are subject to national codes and regulations stipulating standards of quality, performance, and protection. Standards may also be stipulated under local codes and requirements of the local electric utility company. Electric main supplies to premises are generally three-phase AC with a cycle frequency of 50 or 60 Hz. Supply voltages vary from one country to another.

Emergency power systems—a virtual necessity in any developing country—must comply with local fire safety codes and regulations. The extent of reserve power installed will usually depend on the reliability of the local public supply. The total output of the generator is usually about 30 percent of the hotel's normal maximum demand to provide coverage for such areas as lighting, telephones, fire alarms and warning devices, fire-fighting apparatus, sewage and water pumps, passenger elevators, and partial service to kitchens, food refrigerators, and cold rooms.

Hotels may use natural gas (methane) or town gas (coal gas) supplied from mains, or liquefied gas (propane, butane) from local storage in pressurized containers. Gas provides a fuel for combustion in boilers, heat exchanges, storage and instantaneous water heating systems, cooking equipment, and incinerators. Requirements for gas installations, including metering, control, safety, protection, air supply, and damper and flue arrangements, are all subject to local codes and regulations.

Global Initiatives for Sustainable Development

Sustainable development has become one of the most significant issues with regard to hotel development and operations in the past few years. "Sustainable development" was defined in 1987 by the Brundtland Report as "development that meets the needs of the present without compromising the ability of future generations to meet their own needs."[9] Sustainable development encompasses three areas: economic development, social development, and environmental protection. The heightened urgency surrounding sustainable development may be partly due to the growing international debate concerning global warming and climate change, a new generation of consumers with an environmental ethic, hotel companies looking to gain marketing capital as a result of paying attention to environmentally sensitive "green" trends, the negative effects of rising pollution levels and overcrowded conditions in overdeveloped areas, and recent Hollywood portrayals of the potential catastrophic effects of global warming.

In light of these developments and influences, various global initiatives are underway to raise the level of education and communication on ways to reduce a hotel's environmental footprint. Some environmental initiatives have been started by global hotel companies that have made being environmentally sensitive a part of their corporate social responsibility statements. Other "green" initiatives have been launched by governments, non-profit organizations, and multilateral development agencies, including the following:

1. *World Tourism Organization.* This global body has established sustainable tourism development guidelines and management practices that are applicable across all tourism sectors. The World Tourism Organization's sustainability principles seek a balance between three dimensions of tourism development: environmental, economic, and socio-cultural.

2. *International Finance Corporation.* As part of the World Bank Group, the International Finance Corporation (IFC) targets investments, including tourism projects, that contribute to environmental and social sustainability. In 2003, a group of international banks developed the Equator Principles, based on IFC's environmental and social standards, as a financial industry benchmark for banks that wish to make sure that the projects they finance are developed in a socially responsible, environmentally sound manner. Currently, 60 international banks from 23 countries have adopted the Equator Principles; these banks operate in more than 100 countries and are estimated to be involved in 80 percent of the global projects financed.

3. *U.S. Green Building Council.* The U.S. Green Building Council (USGBC) is a non-profit organization consisting of more than 12,000 organizations associated with the building industry that are working to expand sustainable building practices. The USGBC pioneered the Leadership in Energy and Environmental Design (LEED) Green Building Rating System, a certification program and a nationally accepted benchmark for the design, construction,

and operation of high-performance "green" buildings. Some of the scoring categories for LEED are sustainable sites, water efficiency, energy and atmosphere, materials and resources, indoor environmental quality, innovation, and design process.

LEED certification provides independent, third-party verification that a building project meets the highest "green" building and performance measures. All certified projects receive a LEED plaque, which is the nationally recognized symbol demonstrating that a building is environmentally responsible, profitable, and a healthy place to live and work.

There are both environmental and financial benefits to earning LEED certification. LEED-certified buildings:

- Lower operating costs and increase asset value
- Reduce waste sent to landfills
- Conserve energy and water
- Are healthier and safer for occupants
- Reduce harmful greenhouse gas emissions
- Qualify for tax rebates, zoning allowances, and other incentives in hundreds of cities
- Demonstrate an owner's commitment to environmental stewardship and social responsibility

There is investor interest in buildings (including hotels) that are developed based on sustainable building practices. As the economic benefits of these investments become more quantified, investor interest in these certified "green" buildings is expected to grow even greater.

1. *The International Business Leaders Forum.* Established as a non-profit organization supported by over 100 global businesses, the International Business Leaders Forum is part of a group of charities organized by the Prince of Wales. The forum helps support and promote sustainable development initiatives, particularly in developing countries. Its most recent publication, Going Green: Minimum Standards Towards a Sustainable Hotel, provides hotel managers with a practical guidebook to create a more sustainable operation. The guidebook outlines six criteria for sustainable development and operations: (1) policy and framework, (2) staff training and awareness, (3) environmental management, (4) purchasing, (5) people and communities, and (6) destination protection.

2. *Corporate Sustainability Programs.* Several global hotel companies have taken the lead in establishing sustainable development programs within their organizations. Some are very comprehensive, as in the case of Starwood Capital Group's newly launched "1," a luxury hotel concept designed entirely on sustainable and "green" building practices. In other cases, hotels have incorporated "green" and sustainable practices in a piecemeal fashion, either to generate cost savings or garner publicity for marketing purposes.

As "green" awareness/education and the rewards of sustainable development become more pervasive, cities and countries are also expected to incorporate "green" principles into their growth plans. A recent World Cities Forum report stated that "the truly sustainable cities of the 21st century will be those that address quality of life issues and environmental protection to keep their economies strong and competitive."[10] Abu Dhabi, in the United Arab Emirates, has embarked on an ambitious project to "create the world's first metropolis that emits not a single molecule of carbon dioxide, the cause of global warming."[11] Governments are creating incentives for companies that adopt sustainable development practices. For example, the Costa Rican Tourism Institute certifies tourism companies based on the degree to which they have complied with sustainability standards. The premise behind all of these initiatives is that cities and countries that are more livable will attract jobs, investments, and future development.

Summary

Many factors influence the success of a new hotel. The use of a development team comprising local partners or consultants may be helpful in learning about a host country's government regulations, overall business climate, and cultural customs. Other team members provide guidance on architectural design, hiring local workers, obtaining construction permits, and so on. Because the hotel developer—the individual or company that conceives the project, initiates the development process, and arranges for the construction financing—is not usually the one who will operate the hotel after it is built, it is important to include a hotel operator on the development team early in the planning stages.

In targeting a country for a possible hotel project, developers generally adopt a four-step approach. The first step involves study of the business environment, including the political, economic, social, and cultural aspects of the country. The second step requires a thorough investigation of the market potential of the hotel project. The third step consists of preparing a preliminary sales forecast that determines the project's economic viability. The final step is weighing the potential benefits against the risks.

An assessment of existing and required infrastructure is essential. Developers should not take infrastructure for granted. A new hotel may add to the burden of already overloaded systems, or the needed systems may not even exist yet.

Many countries and geographic subdivisions have tourism master plans that affect hotel development. Addressing economic, social, and political goals, the master plan typically covers broad environmental conditions and concerns. It provides a basis for policies, procedures, and regulations governing all tourism development activities, including hotel building.

When preliminary expectations for a project have been met, a suitable hotel site must be identified. The purchase or lease of appropriate land is no longer a simple proposition, especially in developed countries. Important rules and regulations governing land ownership and zoning policies are not always transparent to the outside developer.

A preliminary site and building analysis follows site selection. Such an analysis should consider the scope of the proposed project, zoning and code requirements, legal and environmental restrictions, utilities, and a geotechnical report. With this information, a preliminary design may be drafted and potential lenders may be sought. A detailed market feasibility study is critical in determining whether a project can be justified in economic terms.

If the project is approved, the developer must then seek official approval to begin work. This process involves getting numerous permits and authorizations. It may also involve providing environmental and social impact statements and paying impact fees.

The hotel design must take into account local planning requirements and building and zoning codes. Architecture is often a controversial subject where a new hotel is being developed. Responsible developers, owners, and operators attempt to achieve a design that complements the local environment and the host culture while being commercially viable.

Many international hotels are developed today as joint ventures. When business partners from different cultures collaborate, the undertaking will almost invariably prove to be a challenge. Patience, understanding, and most of all respect for the dissenting views of partners from diverse backgrounds are crucial to creating a harmonious working environment and a successful venture.

Sustainable development has become a significant issue with regard to hotel development and operations. Various global initiatives are underway to raise the level of education and communication on ways to reduce a hotel's environmental footprint. Many environmental initiatives have been launched in recent years by governments, non-profit organizations, and multilateral development agencies. Many hotel companies on their own have tried to become more environmentally friendly organizations. Today there is investor interest in hotels that are developed based on sustainable building practices. As the economic benefits of these investments become more quantified, investor interest in "green" projects is expected to grow even greater in the years ahead.

Endnotes

1. Chuck Y. Gee, *Resort Development and Management*, 2d ed. (Lansing, Mich.: American Hotel & Lodging Educational Institute, 1988), pp. 90–121.
2. Frank Go, Sung Soo Pyo, Muzaffer Uysal, and Brian J. Mihalik, "Decision Criteria for Transnational Hotel Expansion," *Tourism Management*, December 1990, pp. 299–302.
3. Urban Land Institute and Ernst & Young, *Infrastructure 2007: A Global Perspective.*
4. Charles Kaiser, Jr., and Larry Helber, *Tourism Planning and Development* (Boston: CBI, 1978), p. 165.
5. Ibid., p. 165.
6. Ibid., p. 167.
7. Joseph Rabun, "A Step by Step Approach to Hotel Development, Part II: How to Analyze Site and Building Factors," *Lodging,* January 1988, p. 38.
8. Fred Lawson, *Hotels, Motels and Condominiums: Design, Planning and Maintenance* (London: Architectural Press, 1976), p. 190.
9. http://en.wikipedia.org/wiki/Brundtland_Commission.

10. *World Cities Forum 2007: A Report* (Washington, D.C.: Urban Land Institute, 2007).
11. Stanley Reed, "Guess Who's Building a Green City," *BusinessWeek*, December 24, 2007.

Key Terms

environmental impact statement (EIS)—Generally a written report that describes what may happen to the environment in both the short and long term if a specific project is carried out.

impact fee—A fee charged to private developers to cover the cost of infrastructure or services that must be provided by government as a consequence of development; may also mean a charge imposed on developments that may have negative environmental or social impacts which must be borne by the public sector.

market feasibility study—An economic study that provides a full financial analysis of a proposed hotel, including return on investment; in a fuller sense, a market feasibility study determines whether or not a market exists for a proposed new hotel and what the financial consequences will be if the project is implemented.

preliminary site and building analysis—A study to evaluate a site before the developer spends a lot for extensive design documents and drawings on a location that might not be economically feasible.

zoning—Dividing an area into districts and allowing only specified types of development in each district. The zoning ordinance spells out the restrictions on land use and development for each district type and identifies the procedural requirements of the zoning process.

zoning variances—Relaxations of zoning rules for cases in which the standard requirements would pose undue hardships on the property owners.

Review Questions

1. Who should be on the development team for an international hotel?
2. What are the five phases of hotel development?
3. What general factors should be considered when determining investment opportunities in a foreign country?
4. Should developers take infrastructure for granted? Why or why not? What types of infrastructure needs might a hotel developer have?
5. What function does a country's tourism master plan serve?
6. What criteria are generally used for selecting a specific site for an international hotel?
7. What is a preliminary site and building analysis? Why is it important?
8. Why is it important to develop a strategy for the approval process? What sorts of approvals are likely to be needed?

9. Why is hotel design an especially sensitive matter? What factors should be considered when making design decisions?
10. What are the seven basic categories of regulatory control an international developer is likely to encounter?
11. What is "sustainable development," and what are some of the organizations and initiatives that are supporting this concept?

Chapter 7 Outline

Selecting the Hotel Company
Management Contracts
    Management Contract Services
    Management Fee Structures
    Contract Length and Renewal Options
    Contract Termination
    Control of Operations
    Budgeting and Spending Limits
    Insurance
    Governing or Applicable Law
    Staffing
    Restrictive Covenants
    Arbitration
    Global Trends and Issues
The Joint Venture
Franchise Agreements
    Advantages and Disadvantages
    Agreement Contents
    Franchise Fees
    Agreement Length and Termination
    Hotel Name

Competencies

1. List several criteria to use when evaluating a management company or franchise affiliation. (pp. 219–220)
2. Define management contracts and outline typical management contract services. (pp. 220–222)
3. Identify and describe the basic elements of management fee structures. (pp. 222–225)
4. Identify and describe a management contract's likely provisions with regard to contract length, renewal options, and termination. (pp. 225–226)
5. Describe the typical responsibilities of each party to a management contract with respect to operating control, budgeting, and insurance. (pp. 226–228)
6. Identify negotiating concerns needing clear resolution with regard to what laws apply to or govern a management contract. (p. 228)
7. Describe the issues that tend to arise concerning personnel employed under a management contract. (p. 228)
8. Define restrictive covenants and outline the likely negotiating position of each party to a management contract with regard to such covenants. (pp. 228–229)
9. Describe the importance and uses of arbitration clauses in management contracts. (p. 229)
10. Define joint ventures and state their advantages and disadvantages. (pp. 230–231)
11. Define franchising and state the advantages, disadvantages, and contents of typical agreements. (pp. 231–232)
12. Describe how franchise fees, contract length, termination rights, and hotel name are likely to be covered in a franchise agreement. (pp. 232–233)

7

International Hotel Contracts and Agreements

AT THE HEART OF THE OPERATION of an international hotel is the management contract or franchise agreement. Hotel owners should thoroughly study the cost-benefit relationship of franchise agreements and management contracts before choosing an affiliation. For many investors, franchising offers a less risky way to get into a small or medium hotel business, and a good franchise package is readily financeable. For owners, management contracts are generally more expensive than franchise agreements in terms of fees, reimbursements, and profit-sharing, but the services provided by a qualified international operator are also much more extensive.

Some international hotel chains favor management contracts and others favor franchising. For example, Holiday Inn and Ramada engage more in franchising, while InterContinental, Westin, Hyatt, Hilton, Sheraton, and Four Seasons prefer management contracts; these latter companies are philosophically opposed to selling the use of their names without having day-to-day management control. Historically, franchising has been more prevalent in the middle and lower tiers of the hotel industry (Holiday Inns, Quality Inns, Ibis) because the capital required is manageable and because hotels in these segments can be run by an owner-operator.

Selecting the Hotel Company

The selection of an international operator is based on a number of important considerations. The first screen is fairly simple: hotel companies and brand names already represented in the given market are usually not interested. After that, the following criteria will apply to any qualified operator bidding or negotiating to manage the property:

- Contacts and experience in the relevant market, with a marketing and promotion staff in place within the defined market area to be served by the property
- Availability of qualified and experienced personnel
- Sensitivity to cultural concerns and customs
- Integrity and a reputation for fair dealing
- High standards of operation and accounting
- A proven record of financially successful operations

- Financial strength
- A successful record in training staff and localizing management
- Willingness to share risks through equity investments, loans, or performance-based management fees
- Fees and agreement terms[1]

A number of these criteria apply in choosing a franchise affiliation as well. For both management contracts and franchise agreements, consideration should also be given to the hotel company's position in the marketplace and how changes caused by recent mergers or acquisitions might ultimately affect the company's effectiveness. These factors could have a major impact on individual properties if the expected management expertise and/or marketing support should suddenly and dramatically change. If the hotel company is a subsidiary of a larger conglomerate, the reputation, stability, and financial strength of both the parent and the subsidiary should be evaluated.

Management Contracts

A management contract is essentially an agreement between a hotel management company and a hotel property owner whereby the management company takes responsibility for operating the hotel and managing its business. The owner (who may be an individual, corporation, syndicate, financial institution, insurance company, or government) does not make operating decisions, but assumes responsibility for all working capital, operating expenses, and debt service. The management company is paid a fee for its services and the owner typically receives the residual net income after all expenses. Exhibit 1 lists the major provisions for negotiation typically included in a management contract. These provisions cover the terms, responsibilities, duties, rights, and penalties for both the owner and the operator, including the applicable governing law in case of litigation or arbitration to settle disputes.

Management contracts are especially popular in developing countries that rely heavily on tourism for economic development and foreign exchange. Hotels represent a major source of employment and revenue from tourism. As such, affiliation with an international chain that has a well known brand name and an established reservation system offers many advantages. Aside from their obvious operating and training expertise, chain operators are valued for their ability to attract upscale visitors and to fill rooms at higher average rates and occupancies. Contracting with a qualified operator may also provide the owner with a legal shield to protect against political, bureaucratic, and personal pressures.

Since their inception in the 1970s, management contracts have undergone a major transformation. Whereas in the early years, the balance of power was tilted heavily in favor of international hotel management companies, in recent years, the relationship has now shifted to become a more balanced partnership. The primary reasons for this shift are a combination of: increased competition among management companies; consolidation and sophistication of ownership groups; stronger ownership representation through investment managers, asset managers, and

Exhibit 1 Typical Negotiation Points in Management Contracts

Financial Provisions
- Management fees-basic, incentive, payment method
- Financial goals of owner
- Responsibility for capital improvement, repairs
- Reserve for replacement/substitution of furniture, fixtures, and equipment
- Preparation of budgets, plans
- Working capital balances
- Equity contribution and loans
- Insurance and risk protection
- Damage, destruction, compulsory taking or condemnation
- Property taxes
- Negotiation of fixed commitments
- Pre-opening budget

Administration Provisions
- Books, records, and statements
- Accounting system used, frequency of reports
- Hotel personnel
- Legal and licensing requirements
- Technical services

Operations Provisions
- Operating plan
- Pricing schedules
- Services provided
- Procurement
- Negotiation of service contracts
- Quality standards/inspections
- Pre-opening management services

Marketing Provisions
- Marketing, advertising, and promotions
- Reservation systems and services

General Provisions
- Agency relationship
- Length of contract
- Owner's right of sale or assignment
- Indemnification
- Use of the hotel company's name
- Requisite approvals
- Performance requirements
- Default and termination
- Governing law of host country and arbitration

owner representatives; an increasing awareness of the role of long-term contracts (with no option to terminate) on the value of hotel assets; and clarification through lawsuits on an operator's fiduciary responsibilities to owners as an agent.

Management Contract Services

The services provided by an international hotel chain in a management agreement can be sold as a package or separately (in technical service agreements). Management contract services typically include:

- Feasibility reports and marketing surveys
- Advice and technical assistance on planning, design, architecture, and interior design
- Advice on the selection, layout, and installation of equipment
- Contracting, procurement, and construction coordination
- Start-up operations and openings
- Marketing, advertising, and promotion

- Recruitment and training
- Secretarial, bookkeeping, control, and reporting functions
- Technical consulting
- Purchasing
- Central and international reservation services
- Management personnel to operate the property
- Home office supervision and control[2]

Management Fee Structures

Most management fee structures comprise a basic fee (commonly a percentage of gross revenues) and an incentive fee related to a negotiated profit or net cash flow. The basic fee has stabilized at around 3 to 4 percent of gross revenues. Operators typically prefer to receive payment based only on a basic fee; however, because this arrangement gives the operator no incentive to increase profits, it is unpopular with owners and is most common when the owner has minimal bargaining power. An arrangement using both a basic fee and an incentive fee provides the operator with an incentive to produce profits because profits determine the incentive fee. The management fee structure should create adequate incentives for the operator to generate returns for the owner and for the owner to reward the operator for successful results.

There are three major areas of owner concern relating to management fees: (1) what specific operator services are covered by the fees; (2) what proportion of the basic fee represents operator cost recovery and what proportion represents operator profit; and (3) what fee structure combination establishes adequate incentives for the operator to cover debt service and achieve the owner's required return on equity. Chain operators maintain that they generally need to earn between 2 and 2.5 percent of gross revenues to cover their corporate overhead expenses that are not directly reimbursed under contract terms. For instance, marketing and advertising relating to the property are reimbursable, but marketing and advertising to promote the corporation (which will also benefit the property) may be considered expenses of the operator. Likewise, training expenses directly related to the property are reimbursable, but company training of personnel in general, even if the trainee may sometimes be transferred to the property, will not be.

The negotiation of a fee structure that is fair and affordable and that provides an effective management incentive calls for flexibility on the part of the operator, the owner, and the lender. Since each property is affected by different market, operating, and financing factors, the management fee structure must be tailored to the unique characteristics of the property, as well as ownership objectives and, in some instances, lender approval. Exhibit 2 summarizes basic strategies followed by owners and operators when negotiating the management fee and other elements in the management contract.

Tax Impacts of Management Fees. An important factor to consider in negotiating management fee structures is the effect of home and host country income taxes on

Exhibit 2 Owner and Operator Strategies in Management Contract Negotiation

Key Provisions	Owner's Position	Operator's Position
1. Contract term	Obtain a contract term for as short a period as possible with renewals at the option of the owner.	Obtain a contract term for as long a period as possible with renewals at the option of the operator.
2. Management fee	Base the fee solely on a percentage of net income after debt service and a minimum return on equity. Attempt to minimize the amount of this percentage.	Base the fee solely on a percentage of total revenue. Attempt to maximize the amount of this percentage.
3. Reporting requirements	Require extensive written financial reporting and frequent budget updates and meetings with owner.	Minimize as much as possible the reporting of operating results and budgets to owner.
4. Approvals	Structure contract so owner has the right to approve all aspects of hotel operation.	Structure contract so operator has total discretion with no approvals of any sort required from owner.
5. Termination	Ensure owner's right to terminate management contract immediately upon written notice.	Under no circumstances allow the operator to be terminated before the expiration of the contract.
6. Operator's investment in the property	Stipulate that operator buy right to manage hotel (that is, invests capital or services) or make performance guarantees to obtain the management contract.	Stipulate that operator have no investment in the property.
7. Operator's home office expenses	Make all home office expenses of operator reimbursable from management fee, with no expenses to be charged to property.	Stipulate that the pro rata share of all of operator's home office expenses plus all direct expenses be chargeable to the property.
8. Transfer of ownership	Ensure that owner may transfer ownership of hotel to anyone at any time.	Ensure that owner cannot transfer ownership of property without operator's approval and that operator is allowed right of first refusal.

(continued)

Exhibit 2 *(continued)*

Key Provisions	Owner's Position	Operator's Position
9. Exclusivity	Establish owner's right to develop or own any hotel managed by operator.	Establish operator's right to manage any hotels developed or owned by operator.
10. Insurance and condemnation proceeds	Exclude operator from participation in any insurance or condemnation proceeds.	Stipulate that operator be entitled to a pro rata share of all insurance and condemnation proceeds.
11. Hotel personnel	Ensure that all hotel personnel will be employees of the operator.	Ensure that all hotel personnel will be employees of the owner.
12. Reserve for replacement	Agree to fund capital replacements (furniture, fixtures, and equipment) on an as-needed basis.	Establish the right to establish a reserve for replacement funded by the owner that is as large as possible.
13. Restrictions	Stipulate that operator not own, manage, or franchise another hotel within the same market as the subject.	Refuse restrictions on ownership, management, or franchising by the operator in the same market as the subject.
14. Indemnity	Ensure the operator will indemnify owner for all actions against operator.	Ensure the owner will indemnify operator for all actions against operator.

Adapted from Stephen Rushmore, *Hotel Investments: A Guide for Lenders and Owners* (Boston: Warren, Gorham & Lamont, 1990).

the basic and incentive fees, as well as the effect of exchange controls in the host country, in determining the net income realized by the corporate hotel chain.

Operator System Expenses. In addition to management fees, operators charge owners for certain operator system expenses which may include system marketing, advertising, sales, accounting, training, procurement, and reservation efforts as well as travel, room, and board expenses for corporate personnel traveling to the property to oversee its operations. These expenses can add up to another 1 to 3 percent of gross revenues beyond management fees. During the negotiating process, therefore, owners must ascertain what services will or will not be included in the management fee.

Technical Assistance Fees and Agreements. Technical assistance fees are sometimes charged by operators who take an active consultation role in the design and planning of lodging facilities. The consultation services may include feasibility studies, architecture, interior design, mechanical installations, food facilities layout, supervision of construction, and oversight of other specialized areas such as energy systems, entertainment, security, and financing. The extent of technical assistance varies widely, and some of these services are included as part of the management contract package. The technical assistance fee is based on the specific services performed and the complexity of the project. For comprehensive services, the fee may be set at 2 percent of the total of the project or some fixed amount per room.

The **technical service agreement** is usually negotiated separately from the management contract. A special type of technical service agreement is the **turnkey agreement**; under this type of agreement, the hotel company under contract hands over a fully operational property to the owner, who may then exercise any number of options with regard to management.

Pre-Opening Fees. Pre-opening fees are paid to operators for developing the pre-opening plan and budget and for supervising pre-opening activities, including staffing the operation, training personnel, installing operating systems, marketing the property, procuring supplies and inventories, and negotiating leases and service contracts in the name of the owner. Pre-opening budgets are typically 1.5 percent to 1.9 percent of the total project cost and pre-opening management fees may well exceed $100,000, depending on the size of the project, its location, the type of services offered, and the length of the pre-opening phase.[3]

Contract Length and Renewal Options

The length of the management contract is a major concern for everyone involved. Operators desire long-term contracts in order to protect their investments in personnel, the provision of management, marketing, and technical expertise in design, various up-front costs, and the time they have invested in negotiating the management contract—a deal that may have taken several years and great difficulty to close. Long-term contracts actually provide stability for all three parties, but from the owners' perspective long-term contracts tend to limit flexibility and termination power. Most owners prefer shorter term contracts so they have the option to remove a deficient operator.

For international hotels, most contracts range between 10 and 30 years. Chain operators are generally able to negotiate longer initial and renewal terms than independent operators because chains offer an established brand recognition that contributes significantly to the identity of the property. Chain operators estimate that they need, on average, at least eight to ten years to recover their start-up costs and make their time and effort in the project worthwhile.[4] In recent years, the length of the initial contract term has decreased as owners have become more experienced in hotel operations and more cautious because of high debt service. Another factor is the greater competition among operators, who are thus willing to accept shorter-term contracts.

With profit, reputation, and other important considerations at stake, the renewal option becomes an important issue in the management contract. While renewal options usually rest with the operator, an owner with significant bargaining clout can sometimes gain leverage in the renewal option by exercising the right to renegotiate performance terms with the operator.

Contract Termination

The management contract will outline specific termination rights granted to the owner and operator. These rights vary, depending upon the original intent of the contract and upon the relative bargaining strength of each party.

There are three provisions for contract termination always available for both the operator and the owner: (1) if either party fails to perform or observe agreements for 30 days following notice of default, (2) if either party files for bankruptcy or assigns the property to creditors, and (3) if either party causes the property's licenses to be suspended or revoked. Contracts can also be terminated by negotiation between the two parties.

Several key termination provisions have become more common recently. These include: (1) the owner's option to terminate without cause, (2) an option to terminate in the event of property sale, and (3) operator performance provisions. The owner's option to terminate without cause takes effect only after a predetermined period of time—usually three to five years. Sale of the property before expiration of the contract also presents problems regarding the operator's possible option to purchase the property, the operator's right to approve the purchaser, and continuation of the management contract after the sale.

In earlier versions of international hotel management contracts, which were usually drafted by the chain, operator performance provisions were uncommon. Today management contracts may include provisions for operator performance, stated in a ten-year pro forma jointly written by the owner and the operator. Such provisions give owners the right to terminate the contract if the operator fails to meet agreed-upon operating projections. To be enforceable and fair, operator performance provisions must be reasonable and flexible enough that goals are achievable. Typically, such provisions have a start-up exclusion period and specify a **shortfall time frame** (a period during which the operator's ability to produce the agreed-upon gross operating profit will be measured) of several years in order to protect the operator from a one-time poor performance year. The operator performance provision usually extends the shortfall time frame if the performance shortfall is the fault of unfavorable economic or market conditions beyond the operator's control; mechanisms are specified to test for such unfavorable conditions.

Control of Operations

The rights of each party with respect to control of hotel operations is one of the universally contentious issues in management contract negotiations. The operator usually wants to retain full control over hotel operations in order to minimize any interference that may be detrimental to sound management principles. Owners usually feel that they should participate in crucial management decisions to protect their equity interests. The owner bears the risks of the investment, loan repayment, and other financial obligations. The operator, on the other hand, has the management company's reputation and credibility—its most valuable assets—at stake. Generally speaking, the operator is granted rights and privileges over day-to-day operational control, while the owner retains overall policy control through its local representative to protect the investment and to approve capital or extraordinary expenditure requests.

Budgeting and Spending Limits

Budget plans are the owner's most important tool for controlling and monitoring a hotel's operations. During negotiations, owners will try to limit the operator's discretion in the area of budgeting and spending. Three types of budgets are usually covered: (1) operating budget, (2) projected reserve for replacement expenditures; and (3) projected capital expenditures on improvements and additions. Each budget should be examined separately because each has a different purpose and approval mechanism.

With respect to the operating budget, owners may want to exercise owner-approval rights and establish spending limitations and proper account allocations.

Owner concerns regarding the budget for replacement expenditures include the annual dollar amounts to be placed in the reserve fund; notification and justification procedures for the expenditure; owner-approval rights; the funding mechanism; and the disposition of the interest earned and of the account balance at termination.

Inevitably, furniture and decor become worn over time and, unless a replacement cycle is maintained, the hotel will eventually deteriorate and lose its marketability. It is to the mutual benefit of the owner and the operator to establish a fund for such replacements and to maintain the property, even when the hotel has been operating at a loss.

The budget for capital expenditures for improvements and additions covers improvements to the property, not replacements of existing inventories. The former addresses investment potentials while the latter have to do with ordinary operating expenses. Owners typically want advance notification and justification from operators for these expenditures, the right to approve or disapprove expenditure items, and the right to monitor approved expenditures. Agreement on expenditure classifications between the budgets (which can significantly affect the base amount upon which incentive fees are calculated) is an ongoing problem during the contract term unless category definitions are included in the contract. Take the case of a major project (for example, a new restaurant in the hotel) that may include numerous costly technical reports and consultations. The operator would certainly wish to include such costs as part of a capital project subject to depreciation. The owner might argue that these costs represent ordinary planning responsibilities of the operator and should be written off as expenses (which would reduce profit and therefore the operator's fee).

Insurance

Generally, two kinds of insurance must be maintained for hotels: property insurance and operating insurance. Typically, the owner pays the premiums for the property insurance and the operator pays the premiums for operating insurance. Both types of insurance could be contracted by the operator when there are blanket policies or other options to take advantage of lower costs available to chains.

While some countries require that primary property insurance be placed with local insurance carriers, excess liability may be covered by international carriers. Owners may require operators to obtain extended liability coverage policies with reputable insurance companies. Difficulties have been encountered in certain parts of the world in obtaining insurance coverage for some risks such as war, riot, and civil disturbances. Consequently, some management agreements have limited management's obligations to obtain and maintain insurance coverage to the extent that such insurance is available in the host country or in recognized international insurance centers at reasonable commercial premiums.[5]

Governing or Applicable Law

Most international hotel management agreements follow the standard practice throughout the world that agreements are governed by the laws and regulations of the host country, not those of another jurisdiction. From the perspective of the host country, care should be taken to ensure that host country laws are not "frozen," or limited to those in force on the date of the agreement. Similarly, the applicability of the host country laws should not be limited to those consistent with "such principles of international law as are generally accepted by civilized nations" or by a similarly vague statement.[6] The lack of clarity in the applicable laws and regulations governing an agreement makes grievances difficult to redress.

Staffing

As a rule, all salary and staffing expenses are considered expenses of the hotel and are charged to the owner's account, even though some of the personnel will be employees of the operator. Owners, on the other hand, may place this issue on the table for negotiation. Owners often want approval over the selection and dismissal of the property's general manager and executive staff members, but operators traditionally have not relinquished this control for fear of "local politics" or other interference in the proper and efficient operation of the property. Sometimes owners are invited to interview and to provide input on prospective general managers and key executive staff, but in principle the operator reserves the right to make the final selection. The privilege of participation in the selection of executive staff may reassure owners that the management will be sensitive to local aspirations, mores, and customs.

In some developing countries, the management contract is used primarily as a means of training nationals to ultimately take over management of the hotel. If the requisite management expertise were available within the country, governments argue, the owner might simply have opted for the less expensive franchise option. While the degree of training and localization of management positions will depend on the policies and practices of the operator selected, it may depend even more on the extent to which the owner makes this matter a contractual obligation.

Restrictive Covenants

A **restrictive covenant** specifies that the operator may not own, manage, or be affiliated with another property within a specified geographical area encompassing the owner's hotel for a specific period of time. To protect their investment, owners want this geographical area to be as large as possible in order to obtain the exclusive benefit of the operator's services and to avoid possible operator conflicts of interest. The operator, however, may want to negotiate a covenant that does not unnecessarily limit its ability to manage additional properties, especially alternative properties catering to new market segments in what may be a growing or changing market.

Arbitration

Arbitration provisions appear in most management contracts. They are especially important to owners negotiating long-term contracts in which the owners' ability to terminate is limited.

Arbitration clauses should state clearly whether all contract provisions are to be subject to arbitration or whether arbitration will be limited to specific disputes. In international contracts, the arbitration process typically falls under local arbitration rules unless the host government requires that disputes be settled in accordance with generally applicable judicial procedures or some other remedy. The contract may also stipulate that arbitration be conducted in accordance with rules of a third party such as the International Council of Commercial Arbitration or the American Arbitration Association. However, at least one African country has prohibited the application of international arbitration procedures in management agreements.

Most hotel operators find it easier to accept arbitration under a host country's law if the operator has the unrestricted right to appoint one arbitrator out of, say, three appointed arbitrators and if the appointment procedure for the third arbitrator is seen as neutral. Arbitrations should preferably take place in the host country; holding them elsewhere would inevitably cost more and might result in procedural uncertainties. Care should be taken to ensure that arbitral awards will be enforceable under the United Nations Convention for the Enforcement of Foreign Arbitral Awards. Some international chain operators insist that disputes regarding certain financial matters, such as indexed inflation factors, should be subject to binding determination by independent auditors.[7]

Global Trends and Issues

Based on a 2005 survey of management contracts in the Americas, Europe, and the Asia-Pacific region, the length of management contracts has become more uniform as international operators have become more pervasive around the world (see Exhibit 3). In general, the trend indicates terms ranging from 12 to 15 years. Options to renew are likely to be in management agreements in Asia or the Americas. Base management fees in the Americas, Asia-Pacific, and Europe average 2.8, 1.4, and 2.2 percent, respectively. In general, the base fee structure across the three regions is fairly similar.

Incentive fees, on the other hand, vary considerably across the three regions analyzed. In the Americas, the most common arrangement is to base incentive fees on a percentage of net operating profit instead of the traditional gross operating profit (GOP) or the owner's preferred return on investment. Incentive fees in Asia are primarily based on GOP. In about half the agreements surveyed, contracts

Exhibit 3 Global Hotel Management Trends

Terms	Americas	Asia-Pacific	Europe
Average contract term	13 years	12 years	15 years
Percentage of agreements with option to renew	92%	75%	48%
Base fee (% Revenue)	2.8%	1.4%	2.2%
Agreements with specified FF&E clauses	100%	96.4%	96.6%
Agreements with termination without cause	9%	25%	17.2%
Agreements with termination on sale	32%	82.1%	55.2%

Source: *Global Hotel Management Agreement Trends*, Jones Lang LaSalle Hotels, 2005.

used a sliding scale based on GOP to give the operator an incentive to exceed the targeted GOP in order to earn a higher fee. European management contract incentive fees are less homogeneous, using net operating profit thresholds, owners' priority returns, or GOP targets.

Performance clauses are common in the Americas and Europe and are increasingly appearing in Asian management agreements. The most common base for performance clauses includes a percentage of GOP or percentage of RevPAR (revenue per available room) penetration in a market's competitive set.[8]

The Joint Venture

Local and foreign companies often find that by combining their different strengths in a joint venture they can compete more successfully in the marketplace. In China, for example, several of the hotels developed over the past 35 years have been joint venture initiatives between foreign partners and China Travel Service (CTS) or China International Travel Services (CITS), with the latter typically controlling 51 percent. Multilateral agreements are common, whereby a Hong Kong bank or investment firm locates the financing, a hotel company receives the management contract and provides some operating funds, and the Chinese government provides the land and labor.

But joint ventures, especially with a government partner, can have serious drawbacks. These include the loss of flexibility to respond quickly to market demands and labor needs, and the loss of control in hiring and firing staff, determining compensation packages, and exercising discretion over other aspects of the hotel's management.

The success of joint ventures depends upon the degree to which people who have different ways of conducting business and different priorities can work together. Joint ventures usually involve complex structuring arrangements and difficult negotiations. The basic issues involved are: (1) the determination of the value of what each party contributes to the joint venture, (2) the ownership percentages, (3) the timing and distribution of profits, (4) the sharing of the risks and losses, and (5) how business decisions will be made.

The terms and conditions of funding arrangements must also be negotiated, including release schedules and responsibility to fund cost overruns or cash flow shortfalls. Since the success of any business venture cannot be guaranteed, consideration should be given to provisions concerning the termination of the joint venture agreement that will be fair to all parties.

All the contractual provisions of the joint venture agreement (including loan agreements, guaranty agreements, the management contract, and the technical assistance agreement) must be negotiated simultaneously, since the terms for each have a bearing on the others.

Franchise Agreements

A hotel franchise is essentially an agreement between a hotel chain (franchisor) and a hotel owner (franchisee) whereby the hotel chain allows the owner to make use of the chain's name and services; in return for this, the hotel owner pays the hotel chain a franchise fee and royalties. The owner either operates the hotel or contracts separately with another management company to operate the facility.

Although the form was somewhat different, one of the first franchise agreements in the hotel industry occurred in 1907 when César Ritz allowed his famous name to be used in hotels in New York, Montreal, Boston, Lisbon, and Barcelona. Modern day hotel franchising started during the 1950s when hotel chains realized that names, image, goodwill, established patronage, modes of operation, and reservation systems had tangible value. Because of this, chains turned to franchising as an inexpensive and profitable means of expanding their holdings.

Advantages and Disadvantages

For hotel companies, franchising is an attractive vehicle for international expansion because it requires comparatively little risk. As in the case of management contracts, franchising agreements help companies achieve widespread overseas presence in a relatively short time and help increase international customer recognition and brand loyalty. However, expansion through franchising will be successful only if the properties are run efficiently and guest experiences are positive. Disadvantages of the franchise arrangement from the hotel company's perspective are the loss of day-to-day operational control; the potential difficulties in dealing with owners; the potential liability exposure without control; the possibility of quality, service, and cleanliness control problems; and the lack of control over pricing. In worst case scenarios, it may prove difficult to remove the company's name from a disreputable property, which may harm the company's image and good name.

From the owner's perspective, franchise arrangements can offer a number of benefits in terms of obtaining the support of a large organization. The property benefits from chain advertising, access to the franchisor's international reservation referral system, group purchasing arrangements, regular inspections, and business advice. Operating system manuals and procedures are usually provided by the franchisor for use by managers. Employee training manuals and films are frequently provided as well as training itself. The proven method of operation and product merchandising is one of the most important elements purchased in a franchising agreement. This leads to another major advantage of franchising: it assists the owner in obtaining financing by lowering the risk of the business venture.

Some disadvantages of the franchise agreement from the owner's perspective are the excessive costs if the incorrect franchise is chosen, and the fact that the franchise hotel company has no financial stake in the property. Moreover, franchisors cannot offer owners guaranteed success since operational controls are largely in the hands of the owner. The difficulty and/or expense of transferring the franchise if the property is sold is another potential problem, as is the frequent absence of restrictive covenants that limit the number of new hotels in the market area with which the franchisor may affiliate. The burden of adhering to various chain-wide standards (for example, uniform operating hours for restaurants and lounges, mandatory 24-hour door attendants, required amenities such as room service or free parking) that may make little sense in the owner's location are other disadvantages. Franchise agreements commonly require the owner to adopt the franchisor's layouts; there are quality and design specifications for furnishings, equipment, signage, and computer systems that can be extremely detailed and onerous.

Agreement Contents

Structuring an equitable agreement between parties is the critical building block in the creation of a successful franchise business enterprise. As with management contracts, not all franchise agreements are created equal and not all are set in stone. They must be carefully evaluated and understood with sound legal and financial advice.

There are different types of franchise agreements. The **business format franchise** allows the hotel owner to use the franchisor's designs, systems, procedures and, most importantly, its worldwide reservation system and its group advertising, promotion, and purchasing programs. The franchisor will frequently advise on site selection, feasibility, and the appointment of an architect. It will also generally provide ongoing marketing and business advice.

Franchisors may provide building plans and specifications and oversee the construction phase and other phases in the development process, including pre-opening publicity and promotion. In turn, the owner is obligated to follow the franchisor's operating requirements and quality control standards in order to protect the value of the trade name. Inspectors are sent to ensure that standards are observed; the franchise may be terminated if they are not. As in the case of management contracts, the franchise agreement should specify territorial rights, providing the hotel with exclusive use of the franchise name within a specifically defined geographic area. This issue is subject to negotiation.

Franchise Fees

When an owner evaluates a hotel franchise, one of the key considerations will be the structure and amount of the franchise fees. The franchise agreement typically includes an initial franchise fee, a continuing franchise or royalty fee, and ongoing reservations and marketing fees. For example, there might be an initial franchise fee of $250 to $350 per room (typically with a 100-room minimum), an ongoing royalty fee of between 1 and 6 percent of gross room revenues, an advertising fee of between 1 and 3.5 percent of gross room revenues, and perhaps a reservation fee of 1 percent of gross rooms revenues or a flat fee per reservation. In Europe, hotel franchisees typically pay much lower fees. While most hotel companies state that their fees are non-negotiable, fees may in fact be negotiable to the owner who has clout. There is also usually room for negotiation on some points—for example, a fee for logo items, in-room materials, collateral materials, signage, and other cost items provided by the franchisor as part of the franchise package. It is critical for the owner to have a clear understanding of the fee structure and exactly what services are covered by such fees.

Agreement Length and Termination

Franchise agreements are usually in the range of 10 to 20 years. Most lenders want franchise terms to extend over the life of the mortgage on the property. Both the owner and the operator should have a clear understanding of termination provisions in the contract. Can the owner sell or lease the hotel and then assign the license agreement to a third party? If so, what is the cost? What is the termination fee and legal procedure if the owner wants to get out of the contract? There is usually a provision specifying the franchisor's right to terminate the contract if the owner fails to pay fees, fails to meet quality standards, or violates any agreement provisions. Some contracts include a termination window, during which time the owner or the franchisor may cancel the contract for no reason and without penalty.

Hotel Name

The hotel's name is an important consideration for owners. In their franchise agreements and management contracts, some international chains insist on including their name in, or adding it to, that of the hotel for a variety of marketing purposes. There are occasionally owners who will refuse to use the chain name in order to play up the name of a one-of-a-kind classic hotel. The use of the chain's trade name and logo is frequently one of the major benefits of employing the chain. The trade or brand name, as such, is a valuable property. When an agreement is terminated and the property may no longer use the brand name, the hotel may lose some of its customers and market share to other known brands.

Summary

Until recently, few foreign (or domestic) hotel owners had the experience, expertise, or inclination to operate their own properties. Given the high-risk nature of lodging properties, lenders have typically required owners to contract with known, reputable international hotel operators as a condition for obtaining loans. However, the task of selecting a suitable international operator and determining the best form of agreement—be it a long-term lease, a management contract, or a franchise agreement—is not a simple exercise. It should not be done without appropriate financial and legal advice.

Under a management contract, the hotel operator acts fully and completely as an agent of the owner and for the account of the owner. The assets of the hotel, including its name and employees, belong to the owner; liabilities and losses resulting from litigation or judgments against the property are the responsibility of the owner. Likewise, profit or losses from hotel operations ultimately accrue to the owner and not the operator. The operator provides technical expertise, marketing services, qualified management of the hotel, and sometimes operating capital or loans. A known brand operator also offers greater assurance of higher room rates and occupancies. In return for providing management and marketing services, the operator receives a basic fee that is commonly a percentage of gross revenue plus an incentive fee based on profit or cash flow or some variation thereof.

Under a franchise agreement, the owner may join a cooperative association or an international chain offering franchise-type arrangements that include a brand name and recognition, reservation and promotion services, procurement services, operational aids, quality assurance based on regular property inspection, and technical assistance in planning an opening. The franchisor receives an initial fee plus a royalty (a percentage of annual gross revenue), advertising fees, and reservation fees.

The contents and substance of management contracts and franchise agreements are lengthy and varied and have many legal complications and ramifications. Such issues as the establishment of fees and fee bases, reimbursable versus non-reimbursable expenses, technical assistance fees, performance requirements, contract length and renewal options, termination rights, control over operations, budget approval rights, spending limits, insurance, damage, personnel policies and expenses, restrictive covenants, and arbitration count among the many items that require careful and thoughtful negotiation between owner and operator.

In many host countries, local and foreign companies often combine their different strengths to form a cooperative enterprise, commonly known as a joint venture, as an expedient way to develop an international hotel project. To develop and operate a joint venture, parties may enter into a multilateral agreement that clearly states the contribution, ownership equity, rights and privileges, responsibilities and liabilities, and profit or loss share of each partner in the venture.

Just as no reputable international hotel company will automatically accept every property offered, so must owners be circumspect in choosing a company whose credentials will match the management requirements of the property and its market criteria. To build a successful business, the chemistry between owner and operator must be right. There must be mutual trust, respect for cultural differences if the owner and operator come from different countries, and understanding by both about the provisions of the contract. While a hotel contract may begin with a discussion of duties, obligations, and considerations, it will quickly end in the face of poor relationships, legalities notwithstanding.

Endnotes

1. *Negotiating International Hotel Chain Management Agreements: A Primer for Hotel Owners in Developing Countries,* United Nations Centre on Transnational Corporations, New York, 1990, p. 4.
2. Ibid., p. 11.
3. James Eyster, "Sharing Risks and Decision-Making: Recent Trends in the Negotiation of Management Contracts," *Cornell Hotel and Restaurant Administration Quarterly,* May 1988, p. 49.

4. James Eyster, "Recent Trends in the Negotiation of Hotel Management Contracts: Terms and Termination," *Cornell Hotel and Restaurant Administration Quarterly,* August 1988, p. 82.
5. *Negotiating International Hotel Chain Management Agreements,* p. 45.
6. Ibid., p. 53.
7. Eyster, "Recent Trends," p. 90.
8. *Global Hotel Management Agreement Trends,* Jones Lang LaSalle Hotels, 2005.

Key Terms

business format franchise—A type of franchise agreement that allows the franchisee to use the franchisor's designs, systems, procedures, and, most importantly for hotel franchisees, its worldwide reservation system and its group advertising, promotion, and purchasing programs.

restrictive covenant—A clause in a management contract which specifies that the operator may not own, manage, or be affiliated with another property within a specified geographical area encompassing the owner's hotel for a specific period of time.

shortfall time frame—A period during which a hotel operator's ability to produce the agreed-upon gross operating profit will be measured, typically several years long in order to protect the operator from a one-time poor performance year.

technical assistance fees—Fees charged by operators who act as consultants in the design and planning of lodging facilities.

technical service agreement—An agreement between an owner and operator in which the operator agrees to provide technical services in a highly specialized area; usually negotiated separately from the management contract.

turnkey agreement—A special type of technical service agreement in which a hotel company hands over a fully operational property to the owner, who may then exercise any number of options with regard to management.

Review Questions

1. What criteria should be applied to any qualified operator bidding or negotiating to manage a property?
2. Why are management contracts often very popular in developing countries?
3. What services are typically included in a management contract?
4. What are the basic components of most management contract fee structures? Which types of fees do owners and operators prefer? Why?
5. Has the length of the initial management contract period gotten longer or shorter in recent years? Why?
6. What contract termination rights always exist for both operators and owners under management contracts? What types of termination provisions have become more common recently?

7. Why is the right to maintain operating control often a contentious one in management contract negotiations?
8. What is an owner's most important tool for controlling and monitoring a hotel's operation? How do owners use this tool?
9. What are the advantages and disadvantages of joint ventures?
10. What are the advantages and disadvantages of franchising from the owner's perspective?

Part III

Human Resources and Cultural Diversity

Chapter 8 Outline

Working with Foreign Colleagues
    The U.S. Workforce
    The Effects of Cultural Diversity
    The Foreign-Based Hotel Company
Cultural Perceptions
    Time
    Cultural Thought Patterns
    Communication
    Personal Space and Touch
    Material Possessions
    Family Roles and Relationships
    Religion
    Personal Achievement
    Competitiveness and Individuality
Business Protocol
    Greetings
    Gift-Giving
    Business Cards
    Names and Titles
    Dining Concerns
Cultural Considerations in Negotiations
    Cultural Negotiating Styles
    Improving the Negotiating Process
Cultural Perspectives of Management
    View of the Job
    Managers as Paternalistic Leaders
    Management and Power Perceptions
    Power Distance and Individualism

Competencies

1. Define the term *culture* and summarize the importance to hoteliers of understanding cultures different from their own. (pp. 239–241)

2. Contrast the positive effects of cultural diversity in the workplace with the negative effects, and identify important considerations in managing diversity. (pp. 241–243)

3. Compare Japanese and European hotel companies with American hotel companies in regard to their position on company loyalty, treatment of workers, compensation for senior managers, advancement, and managerial authority. (pp. 243–244)

4. List abstract relations and behaviors in which cultural perceptions differ significantly and give examples of each. (pp. 244–249)

5. Explain why it is important for hoteliers to follow business protocol and give examples of protocol differences in regard to greetings, gift-giving, business cards, names and titles, and dining concerns. (pp. 249–252)

6. Identify some of the complications in cross-cultural negotiating and describe differences in negotiating styles of Latin American, European, and Japanese cultures. (pp. 252–256)

7. Describe the purpose of cultural sensitivity training and identify some of the benefits. (pp. 256–257)

8. Identify notable differences in cultural perspectives about management in regard to job importance, leadership, and power perception. (pp. 257–259)

9. Identify two factors affecting the development of organizational relationships and how authority will be accepted in different societies, according to Hofstede. (pp. 259–260)

8

Understanding Cultural Diversity

WHAT IS CULTURE? **Culture** can be loosely defined as a mental state largely shared among members of a society who live within national or regional boundaries. It is the sum total of the values, beliefs, behaviors, and expectations common to a group of people at a given time and in a given place. It includes a group's history, customs, traditions, habits, dress, practices, religions, language, art, architecture, artifacts, music, literature, and shared attitudes and feelings.

Understanding cultures different from one's own or from the mainstream culture is important in at least five situations in the hotel industry:

1. In communicating, transacting business, and negotiating with colleagues from other countries
2. In working for a foreign-based hotel company
3. In managing human resources in another country, whether the employees are indigenous to that country or hired from yet another country
4. In managing foreign-born or culturally diverse workers in the domestic hospitality industry
5. In accommodating international guests

Given changing demographic and global business trends, it will be a rare hotel manager who is not faced with at least one of the foregoing situations at some point in his or her career. Likewise, hospitality workers will increasingly find themselves responding to and being managed by individuals from other ethnic or cultural backgrounds. With the rapid globalization of economies, communications, commerce, travel, and trade, the success of future hotel managers will depend substantially on their abilities to adapt and perform within a multicultural world.

In this chapter, we will examine how cultural issues affect working and negotiating with foreign colleagues and managing an international operation. Many of the cultural examples given throughout the chapter are generalizations used only for the purpose of illustration. In specific situations, some examples may not apply.

Working with Foreign Colleagues

With numerous hotel companies now establishing properties around the world, employees who so desire are regularly moved from property to property and country to country. According to one report, the average mid-size company relocates 20 to 49 employees internationally each year.[1]

In the past, there was a tendency on the part of American or European managers working in a foreign country to assume a Western business mentality and management style without any consideration for how they would be viewed or received by citizens of the host country. Later, the Japanese and other national groups with foreign business interests behaved similarly.

Today, international cooperation and collaboration are increasingly necessary. To survive in a global economy, companies must accommodate and take more seriously the values, priorities, and different ways of doing business in each foreign country where there is vested interest.

Although there is indeed an "American way" of doing business, some American managers do not yet understand that there are other ways of handling business matters. This lack of understanding is sometimes partially attributed to the American education system's failure to stress learning about other cultures and languages to the extent that other educational systems do. Most studies show that American students, when compared with students from other nations, place fairly low in their comprehension of foreign cultures. Europeans, on the other hand, tend to be fairly sophisticated in their knowledge of other cultures and languages. Indeed, it is not an over-statement to say that many more Europeans are able to speak several languages with equal facility than are the citizens of any other part of the world.

In countries where there is a shortage of entry-level workers, it is not uncommon to use labor from another country. This was, for example, the practice in many Middle Eastern countries over the past two decades. Because of its labor intensity, the hotel industry in some areas could not survive without imported labor. The issue of using international workers to fill positions has become more pervasive in recent years because of the rapid pace of globalization in the hotel industry. The United States is currently facing a tremendous shortage of labor, partly as a result of visa restrictions on guest worker programs and a tightening of immigration policies. In China, the growth of the hotel industry has resulted in the need to import workers from Indonesia, India, and the Philippines. The growth of Russian tourism in certain destinations in India has resulted in Indian hospitality managers hiring workers from Russia and other countries formerly a part of the Soviet Union.

To the extent that other-country nationals are an important element in the workforce, managers must be aware of how the cultural characteristics of these "guest workers" may affect the employees native to the host country. At the same time, consideration must be given to how the "guest workers" and their families will be fed, housed, schooled, and accepted by the local community.

The U.S. Workforce

In the United States, the majority of new entrants to the labor pool in the coming decade will be those who once constituted the minority segment of the workforce. According to the U.S. Department of Labor, the white male share of the workforce will drop to 64.6 percent by the year 2016. Perhaps even more surprising, by the year 2050, Anglo-Americans will be a minority in the United States. Most of the newcomers to the labor pool will be people of African, Hispanic, Asian, Middle

Eastern, and Native American origin and many will be new immigrants. Many of these immigrants will be neither fluent nor literate in English, a fact that affects virtually every management practice in terms of communications and procedures.

As the demographic composition of the workforce changes, so too must the sensitivities by which the workforce is managed. It is essential for hotel managers to take the perspectives and personalities of these diverse groups into consideration. The old theory of the United States as a large melting pot has been modified. The more current analogy views the United States as a tossed salad in which every piece has its own distinct flavor but is covered with the same dressing. Ethnic groups today consciously strive to retain their individuality and managers must learn to manage this diversity.

The successful development of cross-cultural skills—the ability to work with and between two or more different cultures—is synonymous with continued economic success in the U.S. lodging industry. To assume that minority ethnic groups behave like mainstream Americans can have a damaging effect on production and service. Cross-cultural management acknowledges different value systems, although this does not imply that each cultural group is allowed to operate independently of the organization.

The Effects of Cultural Diversity

Managers with strong cross-cultural skills view cultural diversity as a valuable resource, not a detriment, and see the functional involvement of minority ethnic groups in the workplace as an asset. These managers encourage all employees to gain a better understanding of and appreciation for the diversity of fellow employees; at the same time, they establish an atmosphere in which individual employees from a variety of cultures can flourish. But managing diversity in practice is not without controversy. The problem seems to be one of dealing appropriately with the goals of the organization versus the needs of individuals and harmonizing the two sets of requirements.

A study on cultural diversity in the hotel industry in Toronto, for instance, found that diversity was viewed as both a positive and negative force. Positive effects were largely organizational: (1) new immigrant groups provided a large source of potential labor, (2) the work environment was enriched by multiple cultures, (3) hotels were better able to meet the needs of a diverse group of customers, and (4) new market segments were attracted to culturally diverse hotels. Negative effects were generally attributed to individuals, relating to difficulties arising from departmental concentration of minority ethnic groups, especially from language and cultural differences.[2]

Hotel managers—particularly human resources managers—need to learn how to hire, retain, and work with a multicultural workforce. They must understand the employees' strengths, limitations, and cultural uniqueness; ultimately, they must teach these employees how to communicate their goals and priorities.

Language training and the development of cultural adaptation skills should be considered for certain groups of employees, and an effort should be made to offer information pertinent to their lives outside of work—day care, counseling, medical services, and so forth.

> **You are a citizen of a very diverse world ...**
>
> If we shrank the world's population down to a "global village" of 100 people and kept all of the existing population ratios the same, there would be:
>
> 61 people from Asia
>
> 21 people from China
>
> 17 people from India
>
> 13 people from Africa
>
> 12 people from Europe
>
> 5 people from the United States
>
> 1 person from Australia and New Zealand
>
> 22 who speak a Chinese dialect
>   18 of whom speak Mandarin
>
> 9 who speak English
>
> 8 who speak Hindi
>
> 50 females
>
> 50 males
>
> 32 Christians
>
> 68 non-Christians
>   15 of whom are non-religious
>
> 19 Muslims
>
> 6 Buddhists
>
> 1 Jew
>
> 30 who have enough to eat
>
> 88 old enough to read
>   17 of whom cannot read at all
>
> 1 teacher

Source: Adapted from a brochure by Business for Diplomatic Action, available at www.worldcitizenguide.org.

Managers and supervisors need to be aware of how employees of different cultures view work, what they can offer, how to meet their specific needs, what motivates them, how they communicate, what they value, what their attitudes are, and how they think. Employees will determine their loyalty to the company in relation to how they are treated by management. The challenge for managers is to take all of these diverse perspectives into consideration and, at the same time, create a team attitude toward achieving the specific goals and objectives of the hotel or specific operating department.

The Foreign-Based Hotel Company

Beginning in the 1980s, increased acquisition of American hotel chains by foreign companies and joint ventures with foreign hotel developers made interaction among foreign and domestic investors, consultants, and managers a necessity. The challenge for some hotel managers in these situations became one of learning how to live with a foreign boss and a work system developed in another country.

Working for a Japanese company, for example, can require adjustments in personal as well as professional priorities. The Japanese notion of loyalty and dedication to the company often means subordinating family and personal life to one's career. In some situations, managers essentially have no life outside the company, and even line workers are expected to put company interests first. Japanese companies will go to extreme lengths to avoid routine layoffs of line workers in market downturns, and managers are expected to work even harder to avert the layoff of workers.

Japanese and European employers operating in the United States typically give workers a better chance to acquire skills than U.S. companies do because they spend substantially more on training. Compensation for senior managers, however, is generally lower in foreign operations than in U.S. companies, especially when long-term incentives are considered.

Management Authority and Advancement. In terms of upward mobility for managers, European-owned companies rely much more on Americans for middle and upper-middle management support and tend to give qualified managers more authority than do companies owned by Asians. Upward mobility for Americans in Japanese companies is a slow process by design, and advancement may stop at a lower level; authority is subtle and directions may seem unclear. These subtleties and lack of specific directions are understood by the trained Japanese manager who has internalized the company culture. Even when Americans hold relatively high positions in a Japanese company, they may exercise little control and might be isolated from the inner circle of decision-makers—especially if they do not speak Japanese.

Some Japanese hotels in the United States use a dual employment system for managers. Japanese managers sent from the home office as company representatives to the foreign hotel enterprise have the status of permanent employees of the corporation. American managers are generally placed in a separate category; the Japanese assume they will not have the same loyalty or commitment as the Japanese managers and that they will likely leave the organization if there is a better offer elsewhere. Japanese companies typically do not provide job guarantees to non-Japanese groups beyond what might be contained in an employment contract.

Europeans, on the other hand, share cultural and political traditions with the United States. European companies borrowed heavily from techniques taught in U.S. business schools after World War II. As a result, both American and European companies tend to stress short-term results and favor managers over workers when making decisions. Given the traditional systems of bureaucratic management in such countries as England and France, the operational system in a British- or French-owned hotel in the United States typically follows a functional form of organization. Middle managers have the authority to make decisions but within narrowly defined spheres of responsibility. Beyond these spheres, approval must be sought from the next level of management.

Not all foreign-owned and -managed hotels in the United States have a strong foreign orientation. Some enjoy a fair degree of autonomy from home headquarters and may adopt applicable American business practices. For example, InterContinental Hotel Group, a United Kingdom–based company with its largest hotel inventory in North America, has the human resources culture of an American, not English, company in its U.S. properties. Even so, a common mistake made by American managers is to assume that the adoption of American business practices is synonymous with the adoption of American business philosophy—and this can lead to misunderstandings, conflict, and disappointment.

Cultural Perceptions

A major source of misunderstanding when dealing with people from other cultures revolves around questions of values and priorities shaped by cultural influences. Some of the more common problems lie in the way dissimilar cultures perceive time, personal space, material possessions, family roles and relationships, gender issues, and the relative importance of work, personal achievement, competitiveness, and individuality. Also important are cultural thought patterns, language, religion, social behavior, business behavior, management relationships, and other differentiating characteristics.

A lack of familiarity with the business practices, social customs, and etiquette of a host country can weaken a company's position and hinder its management from attaining acceptance in the community and ultimate success in the marketplace. While the principles of etiquette vary from country to country, the principle of observing etiquette never changes. Those who understand the culture are much more likely to develop beneficial, long-term business relationships and positive personal relationships in their dealings. The following sections are intended to provide *general* insights into cultural perspectives that shape the thinking, communication, behavior, and values of people.

Time

Americans give time a high priority. Time is equated with money. In certain other cultures, especially in countries with very long histories, time is "timeless"—people tend to think in terms of generations. These cultures place more worth on relationships and on a slower pace of life. In many Asian or Latin American countries, for example, people take the time to build empathetic relationships. Successful business deals in countries with smaller populations of lawyers than the United States are the result of successful relationships developed over a long period of time; there, contracts are meaningless if one cannot trust the people one does business with. In Pacific Island cultures—and many others as well—time for one's family and one's community is far more important than the achievement of material success. Money is seen as a means to buy time for the enjoyment of life.

Cultures also differ with respect to the long- or short-term orientation of business deals. Americans typically have a short-term outlook and are very bottom-line oriented. By contrast, it is often noted that the Japanese usually have a very long-term orientation with respect to business development and investment payback—15–30 years or longer in many cases. Another example is the Chinese

Country Clusters

Some countries are more similar in their cultural attributes than others. This may be the result of such factors as a common language, religion, geographic location, ethnicity, and level of economic development. The lists below group countries on the basis of these attributes. When hotel businesses expand and grow within a cluster, they should expect fewer cultural adaptations than when they go out of the cluster into another region.

Anglo	Arab	Far Eastern
Australia	Abu-Dhabi	Hong Kong
Canada	Bahrain	Indonesia
Ireland	Kuwait	Malaysia
New Zealand	Oman	Philippines
South Africa	Saudi Arabia	Singapore
United Kingdom	United Arab Emirates	Taiwan
United States		Thailand
		Vietnam

Germanic	Latin America	Latin European
Austria	Argentina	Belgium
Germany	Chile	France
Switzerland	Colombia	Italy
	Mexico	Portugal
	Peru	Spain
	Venezuela	

Near Eastern	Nordic	Independent
Greece	Denmark	Brazil
Iran	Finland	India
Turkey	Norway	Israel
	Sweden	Japan

Source: Adapted from John D. Daniels and Lee H. Radebaugh, *International Business: Environments and Operations*, 6th ed. (Reading, Mass.: Addison-Wesley, 1991); and Simcha Ronen and Oded Shenkar, "Clustering Countries on Attitudinal Dimensions: A Review and Synthesis," *Academy of Management Review*, 19, no. 3 (1985): 449.

government's 50-year plan for Hong Kong after it was released from British governance in 1997; in essence, China's "one country, two systems" policy promises to continue Hong Kong's pre-China-takeover lifestyle for 50 years.

Cultural Thought Patterns

Americans tend to feel that the past is behind them and the future in front of them, and they plan prodigiously for it. By contrast, people in some other cultures, especially cultures with ancient civilizations, believe that the past is in front of them; they have little concept of the future, preferring to deal with the here and now in practical terms. Such differences in perspective affect thinking patterns and business relationships.

The speech and thought behavior of Arabs is often described as moving in loops, whereas the American's speech and thought behavior is characterized as direct or linear. Unawareness of these differences can lead to communication that is perceived as forward, abrupt, or aggressive, causing negative consequences. Other thought and perceptual traditions also influence behavior and communication patterns and can lead to unexpected outcomes if managers do not take the time and effort to understand them.

Communication

Communication differs among cultures. One example is the issue of integrity. Being honest about and true to one's feelings is an American value and the measure of one's integrity. In contrast, measures of integrity in Japan are subtlety, behaving harmoniously, and adjusting to another's feelings. The concept of harmony in Japan encourages a communication style that is divided into *tatemae* and *honne*. *Tatemae* is public communication and dominates most conversations; it embraces form-conscious behavior, façades, and half-truths, and is considered essential for maintaining social harmony. *Honne* is the essence of one's feelings and is rarely spoken in the business world.

From the Japanese perspective, ideal communication occurs when two people have the ability to truly understand each other without using words. Instead, they use subtlety and innuendos, and both individuals are safe because they do not have to state a position. If no one has to state a position, there will be no confrontation and harmony will prevail. Both individuals can adjust, fine-tune, and work toward what they can accept.

The American approach to communication is dialectic. It is direct, verbal, analytical, and often confrontational, under the assumption that this is the way to resolve dissonance.[3] Applied in the wrong situation abroad, however, this type of communication can do irreparable damage to relationships. Understanding the communication nuances of foreign cultures is, therefore, essential for international hotel managers and negotiators.

Verbal Communication. All cultures use both verbal and nonverbal communication systems or languages, and each culture's vocabulary reflects its primary values and composition. When traveling to other countries, one should observe and respect the role and composition of languages and other subtle cultural cues. Even within a common language, accents, usages, or differences in the way things are said can create problems. A sign in an Australian shop stated the case rather succinctly with the pronouncement: "English spoken here, American understood." Britons attending American conferences often claim they have problems understanding everything that is said because of the American penchant to pepper speech with slang or colloquialisms.

Americans need to remember that in non-English-speaking countries, businesspeople who speak English have typically learned it from a textbook. As a rule, it is always best to use simple, standard words. It is also wise to learn at least the rudiments of the host country's language.

Nonverbal Communication. Nonverbal cues and gestures can be a primary means for communicating between people of different cultures; they can also be the cause of a great deal of misunderstanding. Sometimes promising international business relationships have failed to materialize because inappropriate nonverbal cues were used during sensitive negotiations.

Touching the side of one's nose in Britain asks for confidentiality but the same gesture in Italy issues a warning. Pointing with the foot—considered the dirtiest part of the body—is insulting in India; likewise, using the feet to move or touch other objects is offensive in Taiwan. Every gesture—from pointing to waving or any other body signal—has a different meaning from one country to the next, and may be confusing even to protocol officers of embassies. If American presidents within recent history have been criticized at times for unwittingly making inappropriate gestures on visits abroad, the chances for error are even greater for hotel managers who don't enjoy the staff of protocol advisors that presidents have.

The relative importance of verbal versus nonverbal communication also differs among countries. A study on cross-cultural communication in international business dealings divided the world's cultures into two broad categories: high- and low-context cultures. Cultures in which nonverbal elements of communication play a more prominent role than the verbal are called high-context cultures. Examples of high-context cultures include Chinese, Korean, Japanese, Vietnamese, and Middle Eastern cultures. In these cultures, the body language or nonverbal actions accompanying the spoken message are considered more important than the actual words employed. Contracts are negotiated more by nonverbal understanding than by negotiation of wording. Low-context cultures place a much greater emphasis on the spoken and written word; English, North American, Swiss, French, and German cultures are low-context examples. In these cultures, business contracts are drawn by negotiating the inclusion of the precisely appropriate words.[4]

However, these distinctions may become blurred as a result of the intercultural adjustments of expatriate managers and the adaptation of Western leadership styles by managers from low-context countries. For example, one study of cross-cultural leadership revealed that there was not much difference in the leadership styles of Western expatriates and Hong Kong Chinese managers at multinational construction firms in Hong Kong.[5]

Personal Space and Touch

Cultures maintain unwritten rules on the distance one member remains from another in face-to-face interactions, in lines, and in public spaces. Since the distance is affected by the relationships of the people involved, a member of one culture may be offended if someone from another culture, in which personal distance rules are different, violates the space rule by invading the other person's space. Americans are typically made uncomfortable by the closer conversation distance of Arabs and Africans; Arabs and Africans may feel rejection by the greater personal distance of Americans.

Some Americans dislike being touched on the arm or shoulder, but this is more a personal preference than a cultural rule. In many South Asian or Middle Eastern cultures, it is clearly inappropriate for a man to touch a woman with the hand, or to use the left hand (which is considered unclean) when eating with fingers at a traditional dinner. In others—Thailand, for example—young men are often observed holding hands as a normal ritual of friendship; but one must not touch another person on the head, as the head is a "sacred temple." When working with people from another culture, one needs to learn the personal space and touch rules of that culture so as to not offend host nationals or make them uncomfortable.

Material Possessions

Business publications in the United States print annual lists of the largest corporations, the highest-compensated executives, the wealthiest individuals, and so forth. The attention devoted to these accomplishments, along with current advertising messages, prompts Americans to equate success with material wealth. The notion of "more is better" or "bigger is better" is not necessarily universally admired. Cultures that place little or no significance on possessions may feel that it is vulgar, greedy, and disrespectful to flaunt wealth; people from such cultures may not be able to relate to the values of those who do. Hoteliers need to understand the value attached to material possessions in other cultures for management as well as negotiating purposes.

Family Roles and Relationships

In many societies—for example, Asian, Latin, and Arab—family roles and relationships are very traditional, personal, and precise. Each member of the family has a designated role and is responsible for maintaining that role. Titles assigned to family members define their relationships, and members are addressed by their titles rather than by name as a sign of respect. Family obligations also have higher priority than business obligations, and families take their meals together at home. Although family customs are changing to some extent in newly industrialized countries where both husbands and wives work, family obligations and traditions have for the most part remained intact. To maintain open communication and good business relations with employees and colleagues, family roles and relationships must be honored.

Religion

Religion is the dominant force in the lives of people in some countries. Indeed, some of these countries are commonly referred to by their primary religion, such as a Catholic country, a Muslim country, a Hindu country, and so on. In a Muslim country, for example, Arab life revolves around prayer times and religious holidays and daily events, and many occurrences are justified in the name of religion. Phrases such as "It is Allah's will" are used as rationalizations for major disasters or disruptions of business.

When managing a hotel or conducting business in cultures where religion governs business and social practices, it is important to respect and deal with the host country's customs, such as prayer requirements and dietary restrictions. True believers in the Muslim religion—whether in Indonesia, the Gulf states, or China—will stop work five times a day to pray, and this custom must be respected, even if it is inconvenient for the routines of the hotel.

Personal Achievement

Achievement is another value espoused by the traditional American businessperson. The success and prestige of business leaders are typically measured by the size of their organization, the amount of their compensation, and their location in the organization's hierarchy. In other cultures—for example, in the Pacific Islands—the quality of relationships and the time spent with family are the symbols of success and prestige. Business success may be admired, but hereditary roles and political power may be respected more. Pacific Islanders, for example, may view as a personal character flaw any appearance of boastfulness or pride that accompanies an outsider's conversation about his or her achievements.

Competitiveness and Individuality

Competitiveness and individuality are values supported by most Americans. But behaviors that demonstrate individuality and competitiveness are often considered aggressive and are discouraged in a number of Asian cultures. Instead, team spirit and consensus are the valued traits. Misunderstandings or miscommunications may occur when these opposing values emerge in communications or in overt behavior. In rushing to pursue business, individual aggressiveness can demonstrate a lack of concern that alienates colleagues or subordinates who are not from the same culture and who do not share the same time perspective for getting things done. Since many cultures value modesty, team spirit, collectivism, and patience, the competitive demeanor conveyed in American communications, advertisements, physical gestures, status symbols, and so forth sometimes represents inappropriate behavior.

Business Protocol

Protocol—sets of unwritten guidelines or rules for the conduct of business and business dining and entertaining—is present in every culture. It is important that hoteliers know and practice the correct protocol for the region they are in, for several reasons: to show respect, to avoid embarrassment, to enhance understanding, and to avoid dealing from a weakened position in negotiating.

Greetings

Forms of greeting differ from one culture to the next. Traditional greetings may be a handshake, bow, hug, nose rub, kiss, placing the hands in a praying position, or various other gestures. Unawareness of a country's accepted form of greeting can lead to awkward encounters and poor first impressions. Even handshakes have several variations—from the firm handshake in French Canada to the light quick handshake in France and Belgium to the traditional use of both hands in Finland. In some cultures, as a mark of respect to women's privacy, men do not shake hands with women.

The Japanese bow symbolizes respect and humility and is a very important custom to observe. There are different levels of bowing, each with a significant meaning. Japanese and Americans often combine a handshake with a bow so that each culture may show the other respect.

The traditional Thai greeting, the *wai*, or *namaste* in India, is made by placing both hands together in a prayer position at the chin and bowing slightly. The higher the hands, the more respect is symbolized. Failure to return a *wai* greeting is equivalent to refusing to shake hands in the United States. In most Latin American countries from Argentina to Venezuela, the *abrazo*, or hug, is as commonplace as a handshake elsewhere, and business associates hug instead of shaking hands.

Gift-Giving

Expensive gifts are generally shunned in the American business community because they are often equated with bribery. In some countries, gifts from business colleagues are expected, and failure to present them is considered rude or a business blunder. In some situations, offering a gift is considered unnecessary; in others, it may be prohibited.

It is important to know when to present gifts—on the initial visit or afterward; where and how to present gifts—in public or private; and what type of gift to present. When giving (or receiving) gifts in Taiwan, for example, it must be done with both hands. To use only one hand implies holding back or insincerity. Generally speaking, business gift-giving abroad tends to be a more common and complicated practice than in the United States since there are protocols governing both the gift and the giving process. Gift-giving in Japan, for instance, symbolizes the depth and strength of a business relationship. Gifts are usually exchanged at the first meeting and are wrapped in any soft-colored paper or fabric.

Flowers as gifts are common and safe in most countries; however, there are exceptions with respect to type and color for their cultural significance: chrysanthemums are the traditional funeral flowers in Italy and France, and purple flowers represent death in Brazil and Mexico.

A gift of a knife to a Latin American or Chinese signifies the cutting of a relationship, and handkerchiefs to a Middle Easterner mean farewell or tears.[6] In Islamic countries, gifts of liquor and items such as photos or sculptures of women are offensive because these are prohibited by the religion, but fountain pens, which suit the Arabic flowing alphabetic script, are excellent business gifts. Gifts given to international guests in hotels should be selected with the same care and thought for their appropriateness as for their souvenir value.

When invited to the home of a business associate abroad, taking a gift to the host or hostess is almost universally accepted behavior, but there are two exceptions: in Saudi Arabia, it is not appropriate for a visiting male to take a gift for the wife of the host, and in Zaire, a relationship must first be established before giving a gift. Flowers or a bottle of wine are appreciated in Australia, but any alcoholic drink should be avoided in Muslim countries. American products are especially enjoyed by people from former communist countries, and books are appreciated by Israelis.

Business Cards

Hoteliers everywhere, especially in Asia, know the indispensability of business card exchanges when making introductions in offices, conducting courtesy business calls, or attending trade shows and conferences. Observing a country's customs regarding card exchanges is a key part of business protocol. The Western tradition of accepting a business card and immediately putting it in one's pocket is considered very rude to the Japanese. The card should be treated as one would treat the person—with respect. The proper Japanese approach is to carefully look at the card after accepting it, observe the title and organization, and acknowledge with a nod that the information has been digested. During business meetings in many Asian countries, participants display on the table the business cards they have just exchanged. When presenting a card in most East Asian countries, it is important to use both hands and position the card so that the recipient can read it. A person's title on the card should always be clear and unambiguous; in a country where English is not commonly taught, the information should be printed in the native language on the reverse side of the card.

Names and Titles

Americans tend to be casual about names and titles. However, proper use of names and titles is important in international business relations. Americans are sometimes too quick to use first names, since being on a first-name basis seems informal and friendly to them. In many other cultures, this is considered presumptuous and impertinent. In many countries, including France and the United Kingdom, it is correct to use titles until the use of first names is suggested. In Italy, first names should not be used unless the Italian is the first to use a first name. First names are seldom used when doing business in Germany; more typically, businesspeople use their surname preceded by the title. Titles such as *Herr Direktor* are sometimes used to indicate prestige, status, and rank. In the Philippines, a person's profession forms the person's formal title, for instance, Eng. (for Engineer) so and so, or Arch. (for Architect) so and so.

In Eastern Europe, Scandinavia, and China, people relate on a last-name basis, regardless of how long they've known each other, whereas in Iceland, Israel, and Fiji, people use first names immediately. In Thailand, people address each other by first names and reserve last names for very formal occasions or written communication. When using the first name, they often use the honorific *Khun*.

Dining Concerns

Hoteliers, whose aegis includes food and beverage management, should be familiar with the dining and entertaining protocol of various cultures. The unwritten rules for guiding business dining and entertaining cover the time of the day for business meals, what type of food is served, what type of food is impermissible, who eats first, and even which hand to use and what topics of conversation are appropriate.

Noisy eating habits and belching are almost never acceptable in Western cultures, but they are seen as evidence of satisfaction in others. In most cultures, when offered food, it is polite to at least sample the food but not finish it because this may indicate to the host that more should have been offered.

In many countries the main meal is at noon, with lighter fare taken in the evening. Breakfast meetings, sometimes referred to as "power breakfasts," are strictly an American business practice. Even Europeans find this custom bizarre. In the

United Kingdom, business suppers are more popular than business lunches. The English entertain at restaurants and invite spouses, while the Scots are more likely to invite colleagues to their home. In France, people do not commonly invite business colleagues to their homes, but entertain in restaurants. In Greece, business entertaining is usually done in the evening at a local tavern, and spouses are often included. Business is discussed before the meal in Germany—never during—and spouses are generally not included in business events. In Germany, it is never permissible to eat with one's fingers. Knives and forks are used even for sandwiches and fruits.

A business lunch in Spain is quite elaborate and may include three to six courses, topped off by cognac, coffee, and cigars. Business is not discussed during the meal and the cognac and cigars signal the transition from personal to business matters. Business entertaining in Madrid or Buenos Aires can be a three-hour affair.

Business banquets are popular in Chinese cultures; business is discussed before dinner, and the evening ends promptly when the host rises to give the final toast. At a Chinese banquet, it is proper to toast the people to the left and right and directly across the table.

To the Japanese, an invitation to lunch is an invitation to discuss a problem, whereas an invitation to dinner is usually an invitation to celebrate. The seating arrangement at a Japanese dinner party can make or break the party. When entertaining Japanese guests, it is important to identify the rank of each member of the contingent and arrange the seating so that the top-ranking Japanese guest sits either next to or across from the top-ranking U.S. executive, with their second-highest-ranking person seated with the second-ranking U.S. executive, and so on. It is also important to not seat Japanese guests in the center of a restaurant, because they prefer quiet, unobtrusive public dining. Talking about business during dinner is inappropriate to the Japanese, since business banquets are held simply for people to get acquainted as part of the negotiating strategy.

Cultural Considerations in Negotiations

Ethnocentrism—the presumption that one's own cultural values and habits are superior to and more sophisticated than those of another culture—is a source of miscommunication and misunderstanding in negotiations. Ethnocentric attitudes usually surface in the form of patronization, superiority, disrespect, or inflexibility. One common form of ethnocentricity is **stereotyping**—adopting one group's oversimplified, erroneous characterization or opinion of another group. Businesspeople should learn not to make stereotypical judgments based on their own set of "cultural baggage"—values, beliefs, assumptions, and attitudes. Mutual respect is critical in conducting foreign business and negotiations.

Cultural Negotiating Styles

Negotiating across cultures is even more difficult and complicated than negotiating in domestic situations because of the added chance of misunderstandings stemming from cultural differences and negotiating styles. In some countries,

> ### Club Med in China
>
> Club Med's experience in China is illustrative of the potential pitfalls of intercultural negotiations. Club Med began talks with the Chinese government in 1984 to establish one of its resort villages along China's southern coast. After two years of difficult negotiations, the resort hotel opened with Club Med entirely absent and the Chinese managing the project by themselves. The location for the project was ideal and the two sides signed an agreement in 1985, under which Club Med would manage the resort. Since the agreement did not specify when and how much Club Med was to invest, and assumptions were made on both sides, the contract sowed its own seeds of conflict. The Chinese built the 150-room hotel but would not allow Club Med to manage the resort until it invested. Club Med refused to invest until transportation, landscaping, sports and other facilities were improved. Part of the reason for the misunderstandings was attributable to a clash of business styles between Club Med, which had a lot of grand ideas, and the more conservative Chinese officials.*
>
> It needs to be recognized that in dealing with the Chinese and other socialistic governments, there is likely to be a political agenda as well as an economic one, both of which must be satisfied. The likelihood of problems in China is particularly acute because of the inexperience of the Chinese in international business practice and procedures. China, because of its isolationism and the fact that it has never been a colony, has never had extensive exposure to the laws and practices of industrialized countries.** Furthermore, the country has emphasized repeatedly that it will be modernized the "Chinese way" with full consideration of the cultural heritage which has evolved over centuries and which is suited to the particular characteristics of the country. The Chinese are considered dogged negotiators who lack empathy with Western business methods. It takes a long time to build relationships with them and to earn their respect; they are more concerned with long-term mutually beneficial relationships than with short-term individual gains.
>
> ---
>
> *Maria Shao, "Club Med in China: It's No Vacation," *Business Week*, September 11, 1986, p. 40.
> **Jonathan Zamet and Murray Bovarnick, "Employee Relations for Multinational Companies in China," *Columbia Journal of World Business*, Spring 1986, p. 14.

people have a very direct business style; in others, the style is subtle. In countries where personal relationships are valued, doing business requires long-term relationships based on trust. Many business executives make the mistake of rushing into business discussions and "coming on too strong," or forcing, instead of nurturing, relationships. In many parts of the world, there is a great deal more to business than just business, including social life, friendships, etiquette, grace, patience, and protocol. Discussing business before a get-acquainted interlude can be a serious mistake.

In most countries of Latin America, for example, an informed business executive would engage in small talk about the country, indicate an interest in the families of his or her business associates, join them for lunch or dinner, and generally allow time for personal relationships to develop. The axiom is that business opportunities usually follow solid personal relationships.

Whereas a relaxed atmosphere is important for building a business relationship based on friendship in Latin America, Belgians are seen as preferring just the opposite—zeroing in on business right away and being conservative, efficient, and impersonal in their approach to business meetings. Similarly, the Dutch and Germans are viewed as competitive negotiators who get straight to the point. German businesspeople are technically oriented, disciplined, and orderly; so in dealing with German executives, it is best to be direct and factual in manner. Most Germans have conservative business attitudes and believe in the tried and true in craftsmanship and solid performance based on years of rigorous apprenticeship. They generally do not emphasize the development of personal relationships with business associates, but value privacy and strive to keep their business and personal lives separate. In negotiating with the Dutch there usually is little room for conflict or debate. The French, on the other hand, love to debate, and a good debate is an integral part of deal-making in France. The French like to demonstrate their intellect and challenge the intellect of their counterparts. This cultural trait carries over into the French management style. Intellect and formal education are the prize qualifiers for entry into management and for career advancement in a French company.

In Greece, the government plays an unusually large role in the economy, with about 70 percent of the national output generated by the government sector. Consequently, conducting business in Greece usually requires working through government channels. Because of the daunting bureaucracy, developing contacts within the country is crucial to establishing credibility, and connections can determine negotiating success. In Greece, negotiations are not finished even after a contract has been signed. The contract is viewed as an evolving document of agreement.[7]

Italian businesspeople are described as confident, shrewd, and competent negotiators. Some perceive Americans as being interested only in making money, so the American negotiator who expresses an interest in Italian art and culture is likely to both charm and disarm an Italian executive. Italians typically judge another company not by its reputation, but by the expertise and polish of its executives and representatives.

The British are noted internationally for doing business "properly," without being offensive or imposing. They are described as civil and reserved; they do not like overt ambition and aggressiveness, and may be offended by hard-sell tactics. British executives are highly confident, but rarely boast about their finances or position. Their speaking style is more subtle and indirect than that of most Americans, requiring sensitivity and inference on the part of the listener. The British are good negotiators, but they do not have a high regard for bargaining in general, so a clear and reasonable approach is most effective.[8]

Negotiating with the Japanese. The unique Japanese business culture is one of the most complex in the world, making negotiating with the Japanese a distinct challenge. Because trust is crucial, it is of paramount importance to be introduced to Japanese prospects by a trusted go-between. As negotiations proceed, the same company representatives should always be used; otherwise the acquaintance period begins anew. It is generally ineffective to make "cold calls" to solicit Japanese business either by letter or telephone call; arranged meetings by mutual acquaintances or go-betweens are the rule.

When Japanese meet with foreigners, the most important item on their agenda is to get to know them. The first meeting may not include any mention of business, but it is seen as the beginning of a working relationship. It may take several meetings and a lot of patience and persistence to begin actual business negotiations. The Japanese are quite expert at determining what tactics are effective with foreigners during negotiations and will try various strategies to see what works. They ask many probing questions, testing a representative's knowledge and sincerity.[9]

Americans tend to communicate openly and to look at the other person when speaking, coming right to the point and asking direct questions. This style is considered presumptuous and impertinent to the Japanese, whose whole manner is marked by indirectness and talking around the subject at the initial stage of exploration. The Japanese system evolved from samurai traditions, in which there is a hierarchical ranking for everyone and everything; therefore, the first thing a Japanese wants to know about any outsider is where that individual is located in his or her company so they can relate properly.

During the negotiating process, a go-between can be effective in resolving conflicts or points of disagreements. This enables **face saving** because concessions do not have to be granted in person. In tough negotiations, Japanese businesspeople will take breaks at critical points or at points of conflict to "think about it" or to let the go-betweens work things out. This allows consensus on both sides to develop and allows compromises without a loss of face. Japanese negotiators will go out of their way to politely resolve impasses without using the word "no," which does not exist in the Japanese vocabulary. The Japanese businessperson expects the listener to intuit the negative message without its being expressed in words. Japanese have difficulty making decisions on the spot because of their decision-making system of *ringi*, which is based on the principle that decisions should be made by groups and by consensus. Since all members of the group are typically not present during a meeting, this can delay the negotiating process.

Overall, it is important to maintain harmony during negotiations, allow counterparts to save face, and to demonstrate personal as well as business ethics. It is equally important to be thoroughly prepared with hard data, facts, and detailed figures about everything the Japanese side will need to know. Relationship-building is the key to success with the Japanese; it requires patience, commitment, and a long-term perspective. Indeed, the formal aspects of business activities in Japan, especially meetings, are more ceremonial than substantive.

If a problem arises once a deal has been negotiated, it is not unusual for a Japanese company to request that negotiations be reopened and the contract modified.[10] American hotel executives accustomed to having business contracts honored to the letter will find it somewhat difficult to adjust to the Japanese view (supported by Japanese court rulings) that contracts are valid only until "conditions change."[11] And as a general rule, international law recognizes the rights of nations to regulate conduct within their own borders. It is also important to respect the spoken word in dealing with the Japanese. An oral commitment is an obligation, for one's word is one's honor. In the early years of negotiating hotel deals with Japanese companies, American developers were quick to offer tentative commitments orally—thinking that these would be subject to finalization in a written contract—only to discover that the other side saw the matter as having been already agreed upon.

Improving the Negotiating Process

To minimize mistakes and misunderstandings in intercultural relationships, negotiators should research and analyze the cultures with which they are concerned so that they understand the reasons behind expressed thoughts, actions, and behaviors.

Flexibility is important in conducting any international business. A flexible businessperson will carefully listen to the viewpoints of foreign colleagues or employees before responding, and when in doubt will seek clarification. This is also common sense. The Club Med case study earlier in the chapter is an example of what can happen when there are cultural misunderstandings in the negotiating process. Some hotel experts advocate the use of a "linchpin" (an individual who has experience in both cultures) when conducting business between companies from different countries. In a joint venture between Days Inns of America and an Indian investor, for instance, the individual chosen to head the project was a hotel management expert who received education and experience in both India and the United States. As a "linchpin," he was able to combine an understanding of the Indian environment and the American approach to hotel management.[12]

Cultural Sensitivity Training. Cultural sensitivity training for hotel staff members who will be managing or conducting business abroad can be a worthwhile investment for a hotel company. The rationale for such training is that people, despite basic intelligence and good intentions, are not automatically able to function effectively outside of their predominant culture. However, people can be taught cross-cultural skills to operate successfully in other cultures and environments.

Cross-cultural sensitivity training attempts to increase insight into one's own behavior, sensitivity to the behavior of others, and awareness of the processes that facilitate or inhibit group functioning. It is designed to develop an attitudinal flexibility within the individual so that he or she can become aware of and eventually accept unfamiliar modes of behavior and value systems as valid. Having a sense of cultural appreciation is a great asset when doing business or living in another country. An expatriate hotel manager's effectiveness at work and his or her family's enjoyment of the other-country experience will also be greatly influenced by the effort put into learning about the country and culture they are entering. They will accomplish more if they try to fit in with the people and events around them, and show some knowledge of and appreciation for local art, history, politics, sports, and so forth. The less superficial the understanding, the more impressive and accepted these representatives of the hotel will be. Cultural sensitivity tends to minimize the degree of culture shock and to maximize cross-cultural opportunities.

One of the first steps in developing cultural sensitivity is developing a more conscious understanding of one's own culture. The knowledge of one's own culture generally comes from implicit, intuitive understanding, whereas learning about other cultures requires explicit and rational explanations based on one's own frame of reference. Understanding the internal logic of another culture's behaviors requires looking at the behavior in the context of the values that lie at the core of the culture—beliefs about the relative importance of people, roles, ideas, institutions, customary behavior, and social relationships. Such an understanding of another culture is easier to acquire if one becomes conscious of the internal logic of one's own cultural behavior.

Cultural insights can be gained through self-awareness exercises; for trainees who have never examined their own ethnicity or cultural biases or come to terms with who they are as individuals, this can be both a painful and a positive experience. Differences between someone else's values and one's own are difficult to appreciate unless there is awareness that each person is a creature of his or her own structured values affecting the way the individual perceives the world.

Cultural Perspectives of Management

Every culture has its own perceptions about the proper roles of boss and employee. There is nothing inherently natural about the way bosses or workers are supposed to act, since behavior is shaped by the cultural norms of each country and the power distance between those who govern and those they govern. In many countries, authority in business and government is inherited. Key positions are filled from influential families, so the authority is vested in the person rather than in the position. There are remote resorts in the South Pacific, for example, where members of the village chief's family may be employed in key positions to gain influence with other employees.

In some countries, a manager commands respect by virtue of position, age, or social status. American managers abroad often feel that they have to earn the respect of employees, and they make the mistake of trying to prove something their employees have already assumed.

View of the Job

In some cultures the value of a job has only relative importance in the scheme of life. In Saudi Arabia, for example, expatriate managers often discover that work is not the all-consuming pursuit that it is in industrialized countries. Hard labor is actually considered unmanly there, and some Arabs still grow their little fingernails an inch or longer as a sign that they do not do manual labor. In Middle Eastern cultures, relatives come first—before job or employer. Whereas Americans respect the "self-made" person and are most proud of accomplishments achieved without help or connections, the Arab world finds this attitude incomprehensible and holds that one's primary responsibility is to help one's relatives. Consequently, an Arab will hire a nephew before hiring a stranger, regardless of other qualifications. What is considered irresponsible nepotism in the United States is honorable obligation to the Arabs.

The cultural norms of certain countries can negatively affect their citizens' perceptions of hospitality jobs and careers. In India, for example, most middle-class families will not allow their children to work as a food server in a hotel's restaurant, because many middle-class households employ domestic help that perform the same function. In China, the parents of some hotel employees do not like certain hotel uniforms—in particular, the bellperson uniforms that require employees to wear a round hat, which the parents find demeaning. Multinational hospitality companies that have entertainment as a core part of the service experience they provide for customers find it challenging to adapt employees to a fun work atmosphere in countries where playfulness, spontaneous humor, and fun don't come naturally. In Asian cultures, where children remain closely connected to home and in many cases live with their parents even after becoming adults, it is difficult to separate the employees' views of their jobs from their parents' perceptions.

Managers as Paternalistic Leaders

In many countries outside of the Western democracies, managers are expected to assume a paternalistic role. The manager is viewed as an important business leader, and time spent cultivating social relationships increases his or her effectiveness. To be successful, managers are expected to have personal contact with every member of the staff and to know their personal backgrounds. Such behavior inspires loyalty and trust, but demands good interpersonal skills and a willingness to invest time with each employee. Hotel managers working in paternalistic cultures need to display a caring feeling for employees. This can be demonstrated by such practices as appearing at birthday parties and soccer games, frequently walking through work areas, recognizing people by name, and talking and listening to employees. The ability to make warm, supportive, personal contact that is not too familiar and does not bring a manager down to an employee's level (which would cause a loss of respect) is considered an art in some cultures.

Asian cultures and religions generally tend to emphasize collectivism, group harmony, and group participation. The manager is often viewed as a facilitator whose role is not to take charge but to improve the initiatives of others and nurture an environment in which employees work together for the good of the company. Individualism is less important than the universal good. What affects one member of society is seen as affecting all others; thus, balance and harmony among all groups must be maintained. As a case in point, corporate loyalty in Japan transcends all other loyalties. The Japanese company, in turn, provides seemingly unlimited services to its employees: housing, recreation, schools, day care, even marriage broker assistance. Confucian precepts in some East Asian countries very much affect management practices. Harmony and benevolent paternalism are the guiding principles, and business units are run like families.

Management and Power Perceptions

While it is generally accepted that gaining workers' respect is dependent on the manager's apparent strength and competence, what comes across as strong and competent is not the same in every culture. In Mexico or the Philippines, machismo is important. The hotel manager who is indecisive or too democratic in management style is certain to be less effective than one who is a competent autocrat.

Business leaders in the United States are typically known only for their corporate identity, whereas in Latin America leaders are respected as individuals who wear many hats as family head, business leader, intellectual leader, and patron of the arts. French and Italian industry leaders are expected to be social leaders as well. In Germany, polish, decisiveness, and breadth of knowledge give a manager stature, and power can be financial, political, entrepreneurial, managerial, or intellectual. Of these five categories, intellectual power seems to rank highest in esteem—many heads of German companies have doctoral degrees and are addressed as *Herr Doktor*.[13]

Symbols of success also differ among cultures. Appearance and clothing are extremely important to Latin Americans and Arabs. Americans value large offices, expensive automobiles, and extravagant homes, whereas ostentatious displays of power or wealth are considered bad form by most Germans.

Power Distance and Individualism

Hotel executives need to understand the proper role of boss and employee within the context of the cultural environment. The **power distance** (that is, the social distance between those in authoritative or leadership positions and those with no authority or decision-making responsibility) between leaders and followers and the amount of personal freedom allowed individuals in different societies affect the way relationships develop in organizations and how authority will be accepted. Managers need to adapt their leadership styles to conform to the norms of the host environment. By doing so, they can optimize the effectiveness of the organization and the productivity of the employees.

In the early 1980s, management analyst Geert Hofstede conducted studies on the national cultures of 53 countries and regions to assess international differences in work-related values. He identified four different and independent criteria by which to categorize them: (1) large or small power distance, (2) **individualism** versus **collectivism**, (3) strong or weak uncertainty avoidance, and (4) masculinity versus femininity.[14] We will discuss the first two criteria, since these are especially relevant to cross-cultural management principles and practice.

In assessing power distance, one of the fundamental concerns is how the society deals with the fact that people are not born with equal physical or intellectual capacities and economic, social, or political privileges. Some societies let these inequalities grow into inequalities in power and wealth; power and wealth gradually become hereditary and no longer relate in any way to physical and intellectual capacities or egalitarian rights. Other societies try to play down inequalities in power and wealth as much as possible. Because of the strong forces perpetuating existing inequalities, no society has ever reached complete equality. However, some are farther along than others in achieving egalitarian ideals.

Within organizations, power distance is related to the degree of centralization of authority and the degree of autocratic leadership. According to Hofstede, tendencies toward centralization and autocratic leadership are rooted in the "mental programming" of members of society, not only of those in power but also of those at the bottom of the power hierarchy. The tendencies remain unchanged because the results satisfy the psychological need for dependence of the people without power. In other words, the value systems of the two groups—those who have power and those who do not—are usually complementary.

With respect to individualism and collectivism, relationships between individuals in a society are the focus. At one end of the scale are societies where the ties between individuals are very loose. Everyone is expected to look out for his or her own self-interest—a practice made possible by the great amount of personal freedom that such a society allows individuals. At the other extreme are societies in which the ties between individuals are very tight. Everybody is supposed to look after the interests of group members and to have no other opinions and beliefs outside the group. In exchange, the group protects and provides for its members.

To analyze power distance and individualism versus collectivism (Exhibit 1), Hofstede positioned countries on a two-dimensional scale: the power distance scores are plotted horizontally (0 represents a small degree of distance and 100 a large degree); individualism scores are plotted vertically (0 represents strongly collectivist and 100 strongly individualist). Exhibit 1 shows that although there are distinct clusters of countries with similar traits, overall there are wide differences between them. These differences are so wide that expatriate managers can make serious errors in judgment if they fail to make the necessary adjustments in their styles of leadership and control. The clusters are tools for making such adjustments.

Hospitality managers operating in foreign environments must not only understand the similarities and differences in principles and practices of different cultural and geographic environments, but also be able to adapt to each situation according to cultural norms, power distance, and individual or group expectations of people in the host country. To do less is to invite cultural misunderstandings and disputes or be accused of ethnocentrism—having little appreciation or respect for other cultures and perspectives. At worst, ethnocentric managers may fail to secure cooperation and team efforts from employees—efforts that are vital to achieving the high standards of service expected in an international-class hotel.

Summary

In this chapter, we have discussed the need to understand other cultures and how culture shapes the behavior of people in any society, reflecting not only that society's visible traditions, customs and practices, language, art, architecture, dress, and so on, but perhaps more importantly its values, beliefs, code of conduct, and shared system of attitudes and feelings. Without such knowledge, it is difficult to imagine how a hotel executive can function successfully in the new global marketplace, for hotels in a very real sense are as much social and cultural institutions within the community as they are business enterprises. Service is the foundation of great hotels, and good service is perceived as being culturally sensitive to the needs of guests from many places and walks of life. The effective hotel manager knows this, not only from the perspective of his or her clientele, but also from the viewpoint of staff who are the service providers.

The hotel executive who is culturally enlightened will also appreciate how culture may influence distinctive patterns in the way people perceive time, think, communicate (verbally and nonverbally), and define personal space and touch,

Understanding Cultural Diversity 261

Exhibit 1 Differences in Work-Related Values: Individualism and Power Distance Index for 53 Countries/Regions

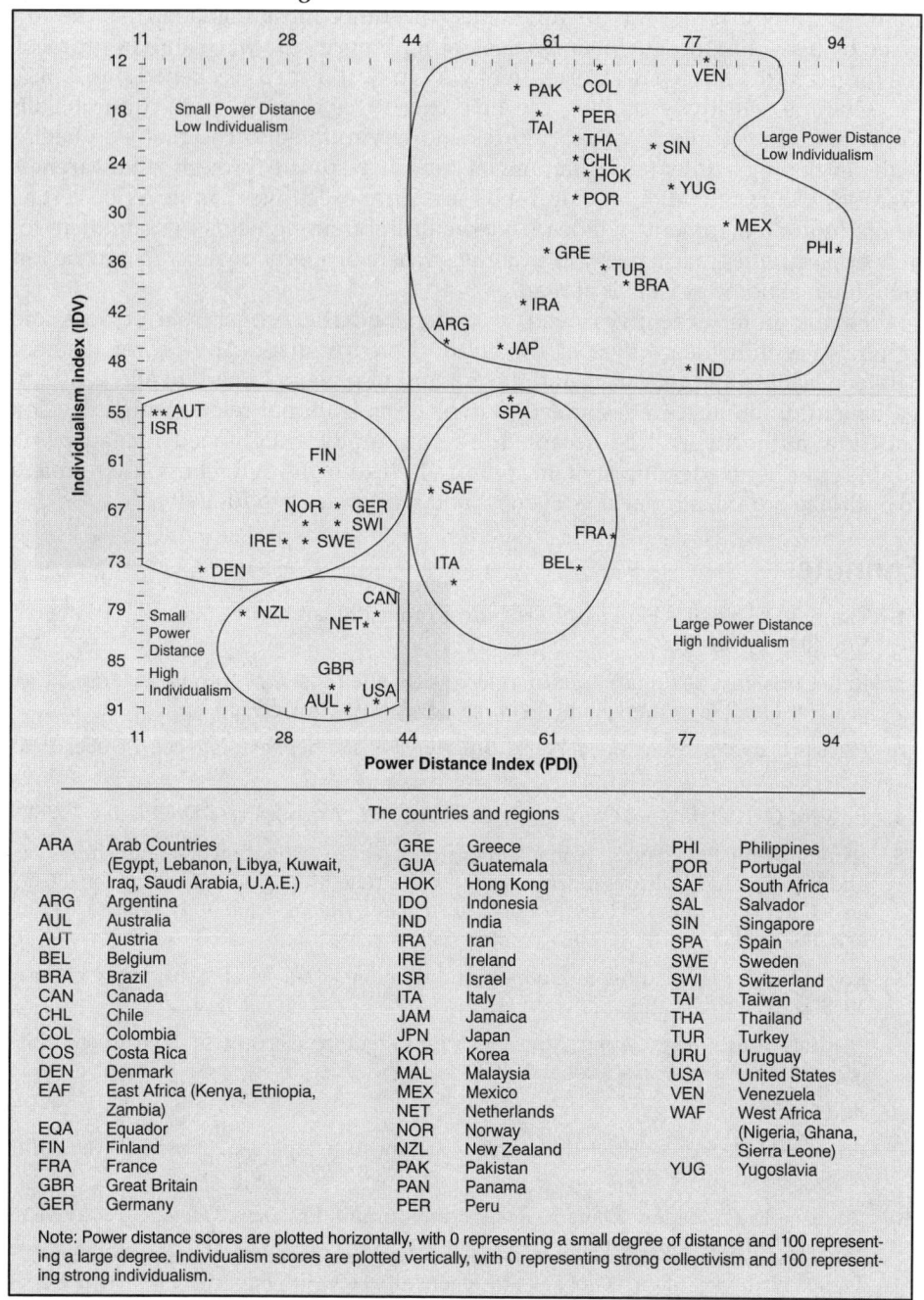

```
                           Power Distance Index (PDI)
              11        28        44        61        77        94

Individualism Index (IDV)

12                                     * PAK  COL              * VEN
18      Small Power Distance           TAI  * PER
        Low Individualism              * THA       * SIN    Large Power Distance
24                                     * CHL                Low Individualism
                                       * HOK
30                                     * POR      * YUG
                                                              * MEX
36                                          * GRE                  PHI *
                                              * TUR
42                                                * BRA
                                     ARG    * IRA
48                                    *   * JAP
                                                       * IND
55      ** AUT                         *
        ISR                           SPA
61               FIN
                  *
67               NOR  * GER    * SAF
                  *   * SWI                    FRA *
73       IRE *  * SWE
          * DEN                ITA    BEL *
                       CAN      *
79      Small      * NZL  NET *
        Power
85      Distance       GBR                Large Power Distance
        High             *  USA           High Individualism
        Individualism  AUL*   *
91
              11        28        44        61        77        94
```

The countries and regions

ARA	Arab Countries	GRE	Greece	PHI	Philippines
	(Egypt, Lebanon, Libya, Kuwait,	GUA	Guatemala	POR	Portugal
	Iraq, Saudi Arabia, U.A.E.)	HOK	Hong Kong	SAF	South Africa
ARG	Argentina	IDO	Indonesia	SAL	Salvador
AUL	Australia	IND	India	SIN	Singapore
AUT	Austria	IRA	Iran	SPA	Spain
BEL	Belgium	IRE	Ireland	SWE	Sweden
BRA	Brazil	ISR	Israel	SWI	Switzerland
CAN	Canada	ITA	Italy	TAI	Taiwan
CHL	Chile	JAM	Jamaica	THA	Thailand
COL	Colombia	JPN	Japan	TUR	Turkey
COS	Costa Rica	KOR	Korea	URU	Uruguay
DEN	Denmark	MAL	Malaysia	USA	United States
EAF	East Africa (Kenya, Ethiopia,	MEX	Mexico	VEN	Venezuela
	Zambia)	NET	Netherlands	WAF	West Africa
EQA	Equador	NOR	Norway		(Nigeria, Ghana,
FIN	Finland	NZL	New Zealand		Sierra Leone)
FRA	France	PAK	Pakistan	YUG	Yugoslavia
GBR	Great Britain	PAN	Panama		
GER	Germany	PER	Peru		

Note: Power distance scores are plotted horizontally, with 0 representing a small degree of distance and 100 representing a large degree. Individualism scores are plotted vertically, with 0 representing strong collectivism and 100 representing strong individualism.

Source: Geert Hofstede, *Culture's Consequences: International Differences in Work-Related Values* (Beverly Hills, Calif.: Sage Publications, 1984), p. 159. Reprinted with permission.

among other characteristics and behaviors. These insights are useful when doing business or establishing working relationships in countries with cultures different from one's own. While the unenlightened or ethnocentric manager may be forgiven by his or her foreign business host for ignorance of local custom or protocol, the forgiven executive pays a price in having to deal from a weakened position.

Cultural sensitivity training can help executives develop cross-cultural skills to operate successfully in other cultures and environments. The first step begins with developing a fuller understanding of one's own culture through self-awareness exercises and examination of cultural biases. Since executives can never be certain where future assignments will lead, cross-cultural training helps prepare them for new opportunities, particularly in situations where property ownership may be foreign, often at home as well as abroad.

Finally, hotel executives need to understand the proper role of boss and employee within the context of the cultural environment. The power distance between leaders and followers and the amount of personal freedom allowed individuals in different societies affect the way organizational relationships develop and how authority will be accepted. The culturally enlightened manager will adapt his or her leadership style to conform to the norms of the host environment to optimize organizational effectiveness and workplace productivity.

Endnotes

1. Timm T. Runnion, "Expatriate Programs: From Preparation to Success," *Workspan*, July 2005, pp. 20–22.
2. Julia Christensen-Hughes, "Cultural Diversity: The Lesson of Toronto's Hotels," *Cornell Hotel and Restaurant Administration Quarterly*, April 1992, p. 80.
3. Patricia Galagan, "East Meets West," *Training and Development Journal*, October 1990, p. 45.
4. Edward G. Hall, *Beyond Culture* (Garden City, N.Y.: Anchor Press/Doubleday, 1976).
5. Johnny Wong, Philco N. K. Wong, and Li Heng, "An Investigation of Leadership Styles and Relationship Cultures of Chinese and Expatriate Managers in Multinational Construction Companies in Hong Kong," *Construction Management and Economics*, January 2007, p. 95.
6. Roger Axtell, "How to Avoid Bloopers and Blunders," *The Meeting Manager*, January 1988, p. 27.
7. "Culture Clash: Negotiating a European Joint-Venture Agreement Takes More Than Money," *Industry Week*, October 2, 1989, p. 18.
8. Ibid., p. 20.
9. Edward Hall and Mildred Reed Hall, "Selling to a Japanese," *Sales & Marketing Management*, July 1987, p. 58.
10. Ron Fenolio, "Japanese Demand Respect for Cultural Practices," *Hotel & Motel Management*, July 20, 1987, p. 67.
11. Thomas Patrick Cullen, "Global Gamesmanship: How the Expatriate Manager Copes with Cultural Differences," *Cornell Hotel and Restaurant Administration Quarterly*, November 1981, p. 21.

12. Chekitan Dev and Samir Kuckreja, "Tourism in India: Growth and Opportunity," *Cornell Hotel and Restaurant Administration Quarterly*, August 1989, p. 75.
13. Lennie Copeland and Lewis Griggs, "Getting the Best from Foreign Employees," *Management Review*, June 1986, p. 20.
14. This section is based on Geert Hofstede, *Culture's Consequences: International Differences in Work-Related Values* (Beverly Hills, Calif.: Sage Publications, 1984), pp. 153–159.

Key Terms

collectivism—The condition that exists in a society in which ties between individuals are very tight. Everybody is supposed to look after the interests of group members and to have no other opinions and beliefs outside the group. In exchange, the group protects and provides for its members.

culture—A mental state largely shared among members of a society who live within national or regional boundaries; the sum total of the values, beliefs, behaviors, and expectations common to a group of people at a given time and place, including the group's history, customs, traditions, habits, dress, practices, religions, language, art, architecture, artifacts, music, literature, and shared attitudes and feelings.

ethnocentrism—The belief or attitude that one's culture is superior to all others; one of the greatest barriers to cross-cultural understanding.

face saving—Acting to preserve one's own or someone else's dignity or self-esteem.

individualism—The condition that exists in a society in which ties between individuals are very loose, and everyone is expected to look out for his or her own self-interest, a practice made possible by the great amount of personal freedom that the society allows.

power distance—The social distance between those in authoritative or leadership positions and those with no authority or decision-making responsibility. In practical terms, the distance between those who have influence, prestige, or power in society from those who have none.

protocol—Sets of unwritten guidelines or rules for the conduct of business, dining, and entertaining; present in every culture.

stereotyping—A common form of ethnocentricity in which people adopt one group's oversimplified, erroneous characterization or opinion of another group.

Review Questions

1. What is culture?
2. What is the significance of the analogy of the United States as a tossed salad?
3. What are some positive effects of cultural diversity in the workplace? Some negative effects?

4. Generally, how do Japanese hotel companies differ from American hotel companies in regard to company loyalty, treatment of workers, compensation for senior managers, and upward mobility for Americans?
5. In which abstract relations and behaviors do cultural perceptions differ significantly?
6. Why is it important for hoteliers to follow business protocol?
7. What are some of the complications in negotiating with people from other cultures?
8. What are some notable differences in cultural perspectives of management?

Chapter 9 Outline

Hotel Openings for Expatriates
Local Versus Expatriate Hiring
    Selecting Managers for the Hotel
        Abroad
    Skills Transfer
    Work Visa and Immigration
        Restrictions
    Expatriates in Asia
    The Cost of Expatriate Employment
    Hiring the Local National
    Regional Hospitality Education and
        Training
Expatriate Manager Selection
    The High Cost of Personnel Mistakes
    The Many Hats of an Expatriate
        Manager
    Evaluating Candidates for Foreign
        Assignments
    Expatriate Acculturation
The Expatriate Manager's Contract
Pre-Departure Training
    Designing Pre-Departure Training
        Programs
    Pre-Departure Training Options
Health Considerations
Other Pre-Departure Activities
Culture Shock
Excessive Acculturation
Repatriation
    Reverse Culture Shock and
        Readjustment
    Minimizing Repatriation Difficulties

Competencies

1. Explain how hotel companies decide which positions should be filled with expatriates versus those which are to be filled with foreign nationals. (pp. 267–277)

2. Describe how managers are selected for expatriate positions and what roles they are expected to play. (pp. 277–281)

3. Explain how a contract and pre-departure training can help ensure expatriate success in the field. (pp. 281–289)

4. Identify ways to prepare for such challenges as health considerations, departure preparation, culture shock, and excessive acculturation. (pp. 289–291)

5. Describe how expatriates can be successfully brought back home and how they can make the transition from expatriate to transnational manager. (pp. 291–293)

9

Selection and Preparation of International Hotel Executives

An INTERNATIONAL-CLASS HOTEL is ultimately defined by its standards of service and the professionalism of its staff. To ensure that its standards will be met and that the desired professionalism will be achieved, a transnational hotel company transfers qualified, seasoned managers from one property to another within its hotel empire. This process of transfer and rotation creates a class of executives who are called *expatriates* when they work in countries other than their own.

The transfer process is a costly one from many standpoints—sometimes personally difficult for the expatriate as well as financially expensive for the company. However, it is also a necessary process if there is to be organizational development and growth for the company. Rotation provides training, experience, and career opportunities for managers. Rotation also permits companies to deploy talented managers where they are needed.

The best expatriate managers are also ones who understand the importance of local staff development and training. Despite the problems and cost of relocating managers for assignment around the world, transnational hotel companies are not likely to abandon the policy, even as they adopt new policies of developing local nationals for executive assignments in their own home countries.

Hotel Openings for Expatriates

Within chain-affiliated (and especially luxury class) hotels, qualified foreign nationals are commonly employed to fill key positions requiring either technical or general management expertise. In granting work visas for foreign nationals, host countries will invariably require proof that the foreign national has qualifications (training, education, and/or experience) that a local national cannot meet. If a work visa is approved, the foreign national can then be offered a term contract, which may or may not be renewable depending on local labor conditions and national labor restrictions. Although titles will vary for similar positions in different parts of the world, some of the more typical openings in hotels for expatriates are:

- *General Manager/Managing Director.* Although the general manager in practice is a generalist, he or she may also be called on to play specialist roles in an international setting; international management experience and specific experience in a functional area such as food and beverage, hotel operations, finance, or marketing are usually required.

- *Executive Assistant Manager/Hotel Manager/Deputy General Manager.* This position is usually held by a person in line for the next general manager opening in an international chain. It requires on average three to five years of experience at the department head level in rooms division management, food and beverage management, sales and marketing, and internal controls.

- *Food and Beverage Manager/Director of Restaurants.* The food and beverage manager with five or more years of relevant experience in restaurant management, banqueting, and catering sales is usually in high demand everywhere. Those with experience in a cross section of operation types—specialty restaurants, grills, coffee shops, bars and lounges—have the advantage, since most international hotels offer a variety of food and beverage outlets. As a rule, international hotels do a higher volume of food and beverage business than domestic hotels.

- *Executive Chef.* There is always a great demand for chefs—European, Asian, and increasingly American—with experience in high-volume, high-quality food production. The chef with an international reputation is highly valued as his or her reputation will enhance the image of the hotel, especially in Asia and Europe.

- *Engineers.* Property management, maintenance, and upkeep are constant problems in hotels. Developing countries seldom have an adequate pool of local engineers who are qualified to monitor, maintain, and repair the building equipment (air conditioning, refrigeration, power generators, boilers, electronic control centers, and so forth) which is typically purchased abroad. Consequently, a government seldom contests the point when the hotel applies for a work permit on behalf of an expatriate engineer.

Other high-demand positions include executive housekeepers, specialty restaurant managers, comptrollers, and marketing managers, depending on the standards of the hotel and ownership wishes.

Local Versus Expatriate Hiring

Selecting Managers for the Hotel Abroad

In some cases, the hotel company has no choice but to hire an expatriate manager. Local residents in developing countries have often had limited access to hospitality training and may be ill-prepared to fill management positions. In addition, owners sometimes favor the hire of senior managers from abroad. Swiss, German, and other European managers are often viewed as bringing a special cachet to the hotel; even when a qualified local manager is available, the owner might not see that person as having the desired personal prestige.

Labor laws in many countries limit the number of hotel expatriates who can be employed. Frequently, hotel companies sign agreements with governments regarding the employment of locals and the provision of training. Malaysia, for instance, requires the employment of *bumiputera* (literally "sons of the soil," which refers to members of specific ethnic groups within the country) as understudies in positions filled by expatriates. China's labor policies require the provision of training as one of several criteria for foreign hotel investments. While these policies tend to encourage local hires in managerial positions, most companies find that the restrictions regarding the employment of expatriates are rarely insurmountable.

Most international hotel companies have policies about the placement of their general managers and other key personnel in properties they operate. The development of an international manager is a long-term proposition involving frequent transfers, position rotations, individual career tracking, and so forth. It is a costly process, but a necessary one for the company to achieve a uniformity of standards in the properties it manages around the world. The decision to place an expatriate manager who has been groomed through years of experience and acculturation to different countries and conditions is not taken lightly and often not subject to debate by intervening interests. Host countries and hotel owners alike recognize the importance of qualified managers to the success of the enterprise and will intervene only when a potential candidate's credentials seem arbitrary.

A manager abroad often serves as an important information conduit for the company; in many ways, the hotel manager's role is akin to that of an ambassador. The person must capably represent the hotel company's interest in the host country, acting as a liaison between owners, investors, employees, community, local government, and the company. The ability to act autonomously within company policies during emergencies requires years of exposure to the company's philosophy, operating standards, style, systems, and guidelines. The establishment of a workable, interdependent relationship between the hotel and headquarters requires headquarters to have a high degree of confidence in its overseas managers. Given these conditions, expatriates are far more likely to qualify and be selected for placement abroad.

On the other hand, local managers tend to have an advantage in dealing with relationships between the hotel property and local suppliers and businesses, the community, and governmental bodies. As a rule, hotel companies prefer to hire qualified local nationals for junior management positions in their home countries. Many companies also target the most talented local nationals for further training to qualify them for eventual senior management positions. To help these nationals learn the company's system, the company often assigns them to the United States or elsewhere as understudies to seasoned managers for a period.

Many hotel corporations find that, even when they plan to hire nationals for senior management positions, it is desirable to use expatriate managers for technical assistance in the pre-opening and organizing process of a new property. New and inexperienced managers who have not been exposed to a company's operating system, procedures, and standards are not likely to cope successfully with the hundreds of decisions that must be made in the start-up of a new hotel. In some cases, foreign management sees a hotel through pre-opening and the early years of operation, then local staff is moved into more senior management positions as expatriate work contracts expire. As pre-opening skills differ from those required to manage the hotel as a going concern, this can be an effective strategy.

Skills Transfer

Skills transfer is a high-priority labor policy issue in many countries today. It involves the explicit understanding that the expatriate technician or manager will help develop his or her local counterpart and that eventually the job will be filled by a local replacement. For the skills to be successfully transferred, a major commitment must be made to giving local hotel workers ongoing training and assistance. Skills transfer is easier for some hotel positions than for others, where formalized training or education may be required.

In China, for instance, the goal for all foreign hotels is to eventually be fully staffed by Chinese workers. Many top management positions are currently staffed by persons from Hong Kong, while mid-level management and operating positions are staffed by Chinese nationals. Many hotels in China have initiated management succession programs that will eventually replace managers from Hong Kong with mainland counterparts. Chinese trainees for this program are carefully selected from among the junior managers. Trainees typically take a four-month general training course with an orientation to all hotel departments; later emphasis will be given to the functional area of each trainee's interest. The 2008 Summer Olympics have provided another impetus for hotels to train Chinese workers, especially in the luxury sector. Hotel companies began building hotels by the hundreds to accommodate the Olympics. Starwood in 2005 began to increase the number of Chinese enrollees in its "Leadership University." The Chinese employees lived, worked, and studied for 15 months at luxury hotels in Singapore.[1]

Hotel companies vary in their degrees of commitment to the task of local personnel development. While many are sympathetic to the community goals of maximizing local employment and placing local nationals into higher positions to serve as role models, some companies are reluctant to yield totally to community pressures.

Even under favorable circumstances, locally trained personnel will usually be constrained by their lack of experience and international exposure. A case in point is food and beverage management, which is highly specialized. Few Western managers ever master the cultural subtleties and technicalities of Asian cuisines and service; it is equally difficult for Asian managers to master European cuisines and service perfectly. The constraints of locally trained personnel may mean limited career mobility for the individuals concerned and lower growth opportunities for a hotel operator whose only stock in trade is the provision of expert personnel and service delivery.

Additionally, some chains use expatriate managers in an attempt to insulate the appointment of staff from local political, bureaucratic, and ownership interference. Hotel chains also argue that international hotels, by their very nature, need people from other countries to maintain their international flavor.

Work Visa and Immigration Restrictions

Work visa and immigration restrictions in the host country will also affect the number of non-local workers used in a hotel. Although all governments have restrictions for imported labor—whether professional or migrant—labor-short countries are usually open to guest worker programs, reciprocal agreements on visa waivers, or other measures that support the idea of a global work force. The European Union, established in 1993, has eliminated restrictions on the rights of member citizens to live and work anywhere within their borders. This union opened the borders to all workers within the union, making it much easier to hire expatriates and third-country nationals. Free market advocates in Asia have pointed to the European single market concept as a possible solution to the anticipated skilled labor shortages in that area as well.

On the other hand, many countries use restrictive immigration and work policies in an effort to meet certain governmental goals. While restrictive policies may serve an important function, one of the negative effects of an overly restrictive immigration and work policy is that it can cause the local hotel industry to lose its competitive edge. This can in turn discourage foreign investment.

Expatriates in Asia

The hotel industry in Asia provides an interesting example of the local versus expatriate issue. In most of the capital cities of Asia, the management of international class hotels is dominated by European—German, Swiss, Austrian, British, and French for the most part—and American expatriates. Hotels have always been considered a "foreign" domain, and local residents typically have not considered hotel management careers. Hotel companies argue that Europeans, and to a lesser extent Americans, have a better international background. When international chains first arrived on Asian shores, operators brought in expatriate technicians and managers and hired local staff for rank and file positions.

Local nationals have long since assumed middle management positions in greater numbers. Nonetheless, expatriates are still almost always brought in to fill the positions of general manager, marketing director, food and beverage director, executive assistant or resident manager, and executive chef. The failure to promote greater numbers of local nationals to these senior positions has become an issue among Southeast Asia's tourism policymakers. These policymakers question whether the failure to promote nationals is due to the lack of training opportunities for locals, the lack of chain commitment to local development, or blatant discrimination. Another factor enters the debate, however, and that is the influence of local ownership over hiring decisions. Many owners either prefer or actually insist on "experts" from abroad because they feel foreign managers will bring international experience and greater prestige to their hotels.

To ensure the hiring of more locals in management positions, a number of Asian governments establish strict quotas and require training provisions. The Philippine government's efforts are one such example. In response to the shortage of local managers in the Philippine hotel industry and in an effort to promote the upward career mobility of Filipinos, the government began limiting the number of expatriates per hotel. In 1992, the Department of Tourism, Department of Labor and Employment, and the Bureau of Immigration formed a tripartite agreement that is in force as of 2008. It states that expatriates can be employed in a maximum of four managerial positions—and only at duly accredited hotels and resorts. Hotel companies can bring in additional expatriates at new hotels and resorts for the pre-operation stage and up to six months after opening. They can also bring in expatriates for special occasions or events such as food festivals. However, these contracts must be limited to three months.

The ease or difficulty of hiring foreign labor is one factor that affects a country's competitive position. Countries that have easier foreign labor hiring regulations include Kuwait, Ireland, Singapore, United Arab Emirates, Finland, Portugal, and the United Kingdom. Some of the most restrictive countries include many in Africa such as Namibia, South Africa, Malawi, Botswana, and in other regions such as Bangladesh, Nepal, South Korea, Philippines, Russian Federation, Poland and Austria.[2]

The laws and penalties associated with illegal employment of foreign workers have become more stringent in many developed countries that border lesser developed countries. The United States has passed tough sanctions on employers caught hiring illegal foreign workers (in most cases from Mexico). In Singapore, the Employment and Foreign Workers Act has also introduced heavy penalties on employers hiring illegal workers. The European Union is also facing issues of illegal workers with more economically disparate countries being included in the Union.

The Cost of Expatriate Employment

It is expensive to employ expatriate hotel managers. While there is sometimes no reasonable alternative, the decision to hire an expatriate usually means paying a premium even when the assignment location is neither undesirable nor a hardship posting. Moreover, depending on the length of the employment contract and the individual's previous experience, the hotel company might not get maximum productivity from, say, a three-year appointee, whose first six to twelve months will be spent learning about local conditions and protocol, and whose last six months will be spent preparing for the next assignment.

Generally an expatriate employee, regardless of his or her home country, will cost the company a minimum of three times as much as a local national filling the same position. Third-country nationals usually cost somewhat less. Of course, labor cost structures differ from country to country in terms of both local and expatriate labor. The spread generally reflects standard-of-living differences and benefit costs as well as labor supply and demand conditions in each market. For example, salaries and benefits are generally higher for general managers in Africa and the Middle East (where skills are in short supply) and lower in the United States and Canada than in other parts of the world (where skills are plentiful).[3]

Other major factors responsible for cost differences between locations and between the use of local and foreign nationals are: (1) the size of the allowance or differential package required, (2) relocation expenses (one prominent international operator usually adds 18 to 35 percent to the first-year cost of employing a married individual and 11 to 24 percent for a single employee), (3) compensation for the inconveniences or hardships caused by the foreign assignment, and (4) the cost of tax reimbursement programs.

Allowances/Differentials. **Allowances** or **differentials** are stipends or perquisites a transnational company can give to bring an expatriate employee's spending power up to home-country standards. They are typically provided on a net (that is, tax-paid) basis to the employee. As differentials are usually considered taxable income, they can contribute substantially to the company's payroll costs. Allowances or differentials may include:

- Hardship premiums
- Cost of living adjustments to the salary
- Housing differentials that vary with the location of the hotel and the expatriate's position, income level, and family size
- Goods and services differentials (which also vary with location, position, income level, and family size) designed to protect the employee from exchange rate movements and "market basket" price differences
- Transportation differentials designed to compensate for increased automobile and other transportation expenses
- Allowances for annual home leaves and vacations
- Reimbursement of educational expenses designed to ensure a reasonable educational standard for the expatriate's dependent children

Tax Reimbursement. As a common practice, transnational hotel companies pay their expatriate managers a net salary inclusive of all added costs and tax liabilities. Depending on the company, this may apply to the top two or three managers or to all expatriates in the hotel. Many companies assume responsibility for all the employee's company-related income tax obligations above a set amount. Since allowances, differentials, and tax reimbursements paid by a company are considered part of the employee's taxable income, a multiplier effect occurs and the company's total tax burden may increase significantly. For well-paid expatriates stationed in countries with high costs of living and high tax rates—such as Germany or Japan—the impact of taxes can be particularly dramatic.

Home country tax obligations for expatriate employees will generally pose no additional compensation burden for the hotel company. Expatriates from Europe, for example, are taxed on company-related income in their country of residence only. By contrast, U.S. citizens must file a U.S. tax return each year regardless of where they reside. Depending on circumstances, a U.S. citizen may be eligible for an exclusion of up to $85,700; for example, a U.S. citizen employed by a hotel in Tokyo earning yen and living off his or her wages may qualify for an exclusion, depending on the number of years the person has worked there. If the U.S. expatriate pays income tax to a foreign government, he or she may qualify for a foreign tax credit on the U.S. return, depending on taxable income and subject to provisions of the Alternative Minimum Tax.[4]

From a purely financial perspective, it is generally advisable to employ local nationals rather than expatriates when qualified local nationals are available. Expatriate relocation costs can be minimized by reshuffling these employees as infrequently as possible. Since relocating unmarried employees is almost always less costly than relocating married employees with their families in the same category, some companies attempt to send more single employees abroad; however, this can result in discrimination problems if not handled correctly. Other strategies designed to minimize the tax burden of employing non-nationals include shifting the employee's taxable income from the current period to a future time when the expatriate's taxable income will be lower; shifting taxable income from higher to lower tax jurisdictions; and reducing the number of taxable foreign allowances, thereby reducing the company's total tax liability.

International Social Security. Many countries now have bilateral agreements with other countries to eliminate dual social security taxation for companies operating abroad and employees working abroad. For example, the United States had such agreements with 24 countries as of 2007, and they have been common in Europe for decades. International social security agreements, often called **totalization agreements,** eliminate dual taxation that occurs when a worker from one country is employed in another and is required to pay social security taxes to both countries. The dual tax liability can affect expatriates working for a home company abroad and those working for foreign affiliates of the home country. The **territorial rule** in the United States provides that an employee who would be covered by a U.S. and foreign system be subject exclusively to the coverage laws of the country in which he or she is working. The **detached worker rule** exempts a person temporarily transferred to another country (usually for five or fewer years) from the territorial rule, so that the person remains covered by the home country. In theory, these agreements eliminate dual social security coverage and taxation while maintaining the coverage of as many workers as possible under the system of the country where they are likely to have the greatest attachment.

Social security agreements also fill gaps in benefit protection for workers who have divided their careers among two or more countries. Such workers may qualify for benefits based on combined or "totalized" coverage credits from all applicable countries. The agreements also help the competitive position of the company by reducing both its cost of doing business abroad and its expatriate employees' taxes. When companies offer tax equalization arrangements for their expatriate employees, totalization agreements can represent significant savings.[5]

Hiring the Local National

Many hotel companies are giving greater emphasis to using or developing local talent to eliminate the cost, effort, and difficulties associated with preparing expatriates to go abroad. While hiring local nationals will certainly be less expensive, these employees are likely to require extensive training in the development of cross-cultural skills and orientation to the hotel company's management philosophy.

Companies that hire too many local nationals also run the risk of weakening their global identity, which is created in part through personnel rotation. Such companies also diminish the opportunities for long-term employees to gain international expertise through assignments abroad.

As an example of one way of handling this dilemma, Marriott has at least one indigenous person on the executive committee of each of its foreign hotels. The hotels' top managers represent a cosmopolitan mix from the United States, Europe, South America, and Australia. The company also maintains a multinational interdisciplinary team that visits the foreign hotels to monitor operations; give advice; critique managers; train, hire, and fire staff; and generate new ideas.

Regional Hospitality Education and Training

Another important consideration in the hiring decision is the amount and type of experience or training that potential candidates have had. Exhibit 1 shows a comparison of international worker training in the United States, Germany, Japan,

Exhibit 1 International Worker Training

INTERNATIONAL WORKER TRAINING COMPARED

	United States	Germany	Japan	Korea
School-to-work transition	Left mostly to chance; some employer/local school ties	Apprenticeship for most non-college-bound youth	Personal relationships between employers and local schools	Employers recruit from vocational & academic high schools
Extent of Vocational Education	Available in most urban areas	Universally available	Limited; mostly assumed by employers	Universally available
Quality of Vocational Education	Wide range; poor to excellent	Uniformly good	Fair to good	Vocational high schools uniformly good
Extent of Employee Training	Largely aimed at managers & technicians	Widespread at entry level and to qualify for promotion	Widespread	Limited; employers rely on public vocational institutes
Quality of Employee Training	Wide range; some excellent but more often weak	Very good	Very good	Generally poor
Public policies	Federal role very limited; State aid to employers growing	Govern apprenticeship; encourage continuing training	Subsidies encourage training by small firms	Directive—some employers resist policies

Source: *1992 Report to the Governor.* Hawaii Commission on Employment and Human Resources.

and Korea. Note that the training of Germany tends to be highly focused, government-supported, and universally available. In the United States, the training tends to be aimed more at managers and technicians than in other countries. The quality, quantity, and access to vocational education and training will have a significant effect on worker performance and productivity in the hospitality field (as in other fields). Conventional wisdom in the hotel field is that European-trained managers tend to have stronger technical backgrounds in the art of hospitality, while American college-educated managers have stronger functional skills in business. Hospitality training in other regions of the world is still in its infancy and results do not yet conjure strong images of particular areas of skills development or strengths. However, both Asia and Africa have the advantage of borrowing the best from both the European and American models, and in most instances they are doing just that.

European Training. The European approach to hospitality education is fundamentally one of vocational training, including years of apprenticeship at various levels, to develop professional and technical skills for doing jobs in a traditional style. European educators heavily emphasize personal factors such as discipline, obedience, orderliness, punctuality, and grooming. Students of European hospitality programs are accustomed to such rules as room inspections and dress codes and are graded on such subjects as "professional attitude." This emphasis is aimed at creating the right traditional attitude toward the job and especially toward the guest. It is reflected in the respect and appreciation European hospitality employees hold toward guests.

American Training. American hospitality programs fall into two modes. At one level, the European skills training approach is favored by technical schools and junior colleges. At the college or university level, a management education approach is more common, although some programs also include technical training. At the college level, American hospitality programs tend to do very well in teaching managerial techniques. The management education tends to focus on general skills and functional business skills such as communication, critical thinking and problem solving, economics, quantitative skills in finance and accounting, marketing and sales, and human resource management as these skills apply to hotels. American managers are less likely to have worked their way up from the bottom—graduates of four-year hospitality programs are typically recruited as management trainees or for middle management positions. American programs are frequently criticized by Europeans for ignoring the development of social and service skills specific to the hospitality industry.

Asian Training. Many Asian countries have stepped up their efforts in recent years to develop degree and non-degree programs in hospitality management and skills development. Virtually every country in Southeast Asia and East Asia, for instance, now has universities and junior colleges offering degree programs in hospitality and tourism management. For the most part, these colleges and universities are privately operated, and they vary in reputation and academic credentials. With but few exceptions—notably in Korea, Hong Kong, the Philippines, and Indonesia—public institutions in Asia appear to be reluctant to offer degree programs in the field, as they generally regard hospitality employment as semi-skilled and low status. Where degree programs are available, they are more often patterned after American educational models than European.

On the other hand, many Asian hotel chains—Dusit International in Thailand, Oberoi Hotels & Resorts in India, among others—offer excellent hotel training patterned after the European technical education model. There are also the special cases of the Singapore Hotel Association Training and Education Center (better known as SHATEC) and the Hong Kong Vocational Training Council's Hotel, Catering, and Tourism Training Centre—two exemplary programs organized by industry on a voluntary, cooperative basis with government endorsement and/or support. Both programs have contributed enormously to the development of a pool of skilled labor for the hospitality industry. The growth of the hotel industry in China has also led to the formation of public-private partnerships to promote hospitality educational training.

Blending the best Western concepts of hospitality management with the high Asian standards of service and educational discipline should produce competitive results for the Asia-Pacific region in the years ahead.

African Training. Formal hospitality education is a relatively late development on the African continent, and examples of schools are few. The best known example is possibly Kenya Utalii College, located in Nairobi. The college originated as a bilateral project between Kenya and Switzerland and follows the European approach to training. Switzerland provided a soft loan, later transformed into a grant, for the construction and equipment of the college and it continues to contribute to the annual operational cost of the college. For its part, the Kenyan government introduced a training levy on all guest bills for accommodation and food and beverage in both hotels and restaurants throughout the country. Most of the ongoing operational expenses associated with Utalii College are covered by the proceeds of the training levy.

The Moroccan government has supported the development of the Institut Supérieur International de Tourisme with encouragement from the World Tourism Organization. The University of Pretoria in South Africa has begun a degree program in tourism management with support from the Southern Sun Hotel Group. As tourism and the lodging industry expand in Africa, there will understandably be greater encouragement and support from both industry and government to establish more programs throughout the continent stressing African cultural styles of hospitality combined with universal standards of service.

A similar emphasis on hospitality education, training, and development is being witnessed with the growth of the industry in the Middle East. Dubai, in the United Arab Emirates, has taken the lead in positioning itself as the hospitality education hub for the region. With the creation of two free zone clusters—Knowledge Village and Academic City—the Emirate is inviting universities from around the world to offer technical, professional, and higher education programs.

Expatriate Manager Selection

Contributing to the success or failure of expatriate managers, and consequently the hotel itself, is the selection process. A common mistake made by companies in selecting candidates for foreign assignments is to use as the sole criterion managerial and technical competence based on a successful track record in one's own country. The skills required to handle a foreign assignment are often quite different from those required of a domestic manager. Chains have lost hotels because an ill-placed manager was not liked by the hotel's owner, the hotel's employees, or influential community leaders.

The High Cost of Personnel Mistakes

The true cost of a poorly selected or poorly trained manager placed in a foreign hotel should be considered in terms of both the actual cost and the opportunities missed by having the wrong person in the position. The actual cost includes training, relocation costs, salary and non-salary expenses, and possibly the cost of premature repatriation. The opportunities missed may relate to inefficiency, guest dissatisfaction, employee dissatisfaction, damage to the company's image, and possibly strained relations with the owners and host government. All of these factors may result in lost management contracts or market opportunities. A survey taken in 2001 suggests that 20 percent of expatriates return home early.[6] In undeveloped countries, the rate of return reaches as high as 70 percent.[7] In May of 2000, a survey from the American Society for Training and Development reported that U.S. companies lose more than $2.5 billion each year from inadequate training of employees sent overseas and their early repatriation.

For the individual, there is a high personal toll as well. A manager who fails in a foreign assignment may become less effective upon reassignment to a domestic property, having suffered a loss of self-esteem and confidence and possibly a loss of prestige among peers. The person may consider leaving the organization altogether. In the worst cases, serious substance abuse or psychological and other personal problems (stress, depression, marital rifts, alienated children) occur even when the individual has had a history of personal stability and career accomplishments.

From a strategic perspective, judicious management selection is important for the company's own growth and development. Each manager is chosen for his or her ability to make long-term contributions and to assist in achievement of the company's strategic objectives. The worldwide networking, marketing, information gathering, and communication links are in large measure accomplished by the placement of competent managers around the world. Managers able to think in global terms enrich the hotel corporation by helping to integrate and develop it into a globally competitive organization. The wrong personnel choices squander these opportunities.

When hiring executives for long-term international careers, many hotels consider the human elements that affect an expatriate's ability to live and work in another culture: professional technique, adaptability, well-roundedness, and personality type. These companies develop individuals with the assessed potential to work in different cultural environments by transferring them to different hotels regularly. Through rotation, managers gain an intercultural and international perspective.

The Many Hats of an Expatriate Manager

Hospitality managers in domestic and international hotels perform many similar day-to-day responsibilities. That said, the expatriate manager must be considerably more adaptive and flexible, especially if the country in question is politically volatile. The roles assumed by the expatriate manager may demand a great deal more time, expertise, and diplomacy than the ones a manager in a domestic property may be asked to play.

Expatriate hotel managers may be called on to represent the organization in dealings with businesspeople, suppliers, government officials, and customers. Government officials may request the expatriate manager to use his or her foreign expertise and the hotel's resources to participate in the country or community's pet projects—allowing little or no latitude for refusal. Officials may view the manager not only as a company representative, but also as an ambassador-at-large from the home country. Overseas American hotel managers in the past have been called on to assist stranded American travelers, provide American entertainment for local festivals, send host-country nationals to American universities, assist in securing political asylum for deposed leaders, and even to answer for U.S. military intervention abroad.

It is critical for hotel managers to maintain healthy relationships not only with their local employees, but also with their broader host communities. Too often, expatriate hotel managers are sent into developing countries with very little understanding of what they will encounter or of the ramifications of their own behavior. In addition to having a good understanding of the culture of their foreign environment, they also need to be prepared for the practical ethical difficulties they may encounter—for example, under-the-table payment for favors is a gray area in some cultures, perhaps questionable but not illegal. Hotel managers in developing countries may actually be seen as a party to a "contract" in which the host country tacitly agrees to accept some of the negative consequences of hotel development in order to gain its benefits. The hotel manager's style and the policies established will affect both the benefits accrued to the community and any adverse social impacts.

The development goals of the hotel company, the owner, and the host country may differ markedly. Managers must be flexible in their attempts to reconcile these differences and to satisfy the objectives of headquarters and the hotel's owners while maintaining goodwill in the host country.

Evaluating Candidates for Foreign Assignments

Valid and sophisticated selection criteria should be used not only for international managerial candidates, but for their families as well. This encompasses using tools such as psychological tests, cross-cultural assessment centers, tests for personal stress tendencies, and extensive private interviews to evaluate each candidate's personality, family situation, lifestyle, and financial position. If, for example, an executive has family needs—such as a working spouse whose career would be disrupted, children who need special schooling, or elderly parents requiring medical care—adjustment abroad may be more difficult. The location of the assignment can be an important factor. For positions in some developing countries, it is often advisable to select either single or childless candidates because of a shortage of appropriate accommodations and educational facilities to support family life, assuming such an approach does not illegally discriminate against or unfairly disadvantage married employees or those with children.

Companies are increasingly assigning women as expatriates, though the number still severely lags behind men. In 2006, 13 percent of expatriates were women, up from 8 percent in 2001. North America and Asia lead this trend with women making up 15 percent of the North American expatriate population and 14 percent of the Asia-Pacific expatriate population.[8] A 2007 GMAC Global Relocation Services survey put the level of North American female expatriates at 20 percent.

Personal considerations affect business success or failure to a much greater degree in a foreign environment; if there are too many complications, they can overwhelm the employee. Management effectiveness is greatly influenced by the adaptability and supportiveness of families, especially the spouse. While the employee may adjust fairly easily because he or she is absorbed in day-to-day office and outside activities, the spouse must transplant family life to new surroundings, build new friendships, worry about health needs, schools, and religious needs, and try to learn enough of a new language to get by. The spouse may also have to adjust to dirt and heat or cold, or live in hotel quarters constantly on display.

International companies employ various instruments in choosing managers for foreign assignments. One such tool is the Overseas Assignment Inventory, which is an assessment tool that measures a candidate's potential for success abroad against an inventory of desirable characteristics and attitudes. It is available as an online assessment tool that can be given to both the employee and the employee's spouse. Other tools help to evaluate a candidate's potential for adjusting to a new culture. Among the more important personal characteristics identified by these instruments are the following:

- A sense of humor (a weapon against despair)
- The ability to relax and ride with events
- The ability to shift gears (readjust expectations, modify plans, try new approaches)
- The ability to forgive (especially in sensitive cultures)
- Tolerance of ambiguity and of differences
- Open-mindedness
- Non-judgmental attitude
- Empathy
- Desire to communicate
- Flexibility and adaptability
- Curiosity
- Warmth in human relationships
- Self-reliance
- Strong sense of self
- Perceptiveness
- Patience

Some companies develop individual country profiles and match them with an appropriate management style profile for each country. The rationale here is to determine the type of person who would be successful in the specific foreign culture and to look for that type of person. Such organizations as the American Management Association and the U.S. Department of Commerce can provide country profiles or seminars that offer information on cultural factors and effective management styles for particular countries.

Expatriate Acculturation

According to one theory, the variables found to have a significant impact on the acculturation of expatriates can be categorized into three dimensions:

1. Self-orientation: how an individual sees himself or herself
2. Others-orientation: how an individual sees and understands others
3. Perceptual orientation: how an individual sees and understands situations and puts them into context

Exhibit 2 provides a checklist of the various characteristics under each of these dimensions.

Exhibit 2 Checklist of Factors Affecting Expatriate Acculturation

Self-Orientation	Others-Orientation	Perceptual Orientation
☐ Stress reduction	☐ Relationship skills	☐ Flexible attributions
☐ Reinforcement substitution	☐ Willingness to communicate	☐ Broad category width
☐ Physical mobility	☐ Non-verbal communication	☐ High tolerance for ambiguity
☐ Technical competence	☐ Respect for others	☐ Being non-judgmental
☐ Dealing with alienation	☐ Empathy for others	☐ Being open-minded
☐ Dealing with isolation	☐ Patience	☐ Field independence
☐ Realistic expectations prior to departure		

Adapted from Mark Mendenhall and Gary Oddou, "Acculturation Profiles of Expatriate Managers: Implications for Cross-Cultural Training Programs," *Columbia Journal of World Business,* Winter 1986. Copyright 1986. *Columbia Journal of World Business.* Reprinted with permission.

Although the ideal candidate for foreign assignment should be strong in all three dimensions, such is rarely the case. Thorough assessment of each potential candidate's strengths and weaknesses allows the hotel company to develop a training program that corrects deficiencies and reinforces existing strengths. It also allows the trainer to help the individual deal with specific kinds of cross-cultural experiences most likely to cause stress once he or she is placed.

The Expatriate Manager's Contract

A letter of agreement or a contract that defines the compensation package and adjustments for hardship and other allowances is customary for employment abroad. The level and nature of the hotel position dictates the specific items that would be included and the degree and amount of benefits provided. The areas generally covered in the contract include:

- Term of contract
- Base salary
- Working hours and time off
- Bonus clauses
- Medical and health costs
- Reimbursement for passport, visa, work permits, inoculations
- Educational costs
- Housing/accommodation allowance
- Travel expenses
- Automobile (with or without driver)
- Vacation (including terms and conditions of home leave)
- Entertainment and business allowances

- Perquisite group and individual insurance
- Retirement plan
- Credit for prior service
- Probation
- Resignation and termination
- Transfer and reassignment
- Relocation costs

In addition to these items, the agreement should include a copy of the hotel corporation's foreign assignment policy covering such items as incentives, tax allowances, hardship premiums (if applicable), communication, and readjustment to corporate structure upon return. Exhibit 3 is a sample of an overseas contract of employment from a Hong Kong–based international hotel corporation.

Pre-Departure Training

Pre-departure training programs have the common objective of trying to help managers and their families adjust to a foreign environment. They typically must adjust to differences in language, customs, traditions, religion, climate, geography, food, water, money systems, schooling, taboos, and local beliefs or superstitions. Unfamiliarity with the political, economic, legal, religious, and social environments poses another potential problem. According to one survey (see Exhibit 4), the top three factors for success as a global manager are having knowledge of the foreign culture, of the industry, and of the language.

As of 2008, 84 percent of major U.S. companies offered managers cross-cultural training before foreign assignments, compared with about 10 percent two decades ago.[9] However, only 23 percent make that training mandatory. Hotel companies run the gamut in terms of the amount and type of pre-departure training provided to managers going abroad. Knowing that many managers will at some point take an international assignment, some hotel corporations work cross-cultural training into their basic management trainee programs. International business trips and short assignments in some of the company's foreign hotels are also used to develop intercultural skills. Throughout their careers, these managers will accumulate increasing levels of knowledge, awareness, and skills enabling them to function in a variety of foreign environments.

While the preparation for foreign assignments is generally improving, in many cases managers still receive only brief orientation sessions offering sketchy information about the economic conditions, law, politics, customs, manners, and business practices of the host country. Despite the apparent benefits, not all hotel companies offer cross-cultural training for managers. Some companies operate under the presumption that such training programs are a waste of resources and that the right candidates using common sense will be able to survive any environment.

Companies today are also far more likely to offer cross-cultural training and preparation to employees' families than they were a decade ago. Between 1993 and 2003, the proportion of families eligible for such support average 35 percent. As of

Exhibit 3   Sample Expatriate Hotel Manager's Contract

PRIVATE
(Date)
(Name & Address)

Dear _____:

Further to your discussion with us, we are pleased to confirm an offer of appointment on behalf of Royal Blossom Limited, owner of Royal Blossom Hotel, Hong Kong, according to the following terms and conditions:

1. POSITION TITLE:
2. DEPARTMENT:
3. STAFF LEVEL:
4. DUTIES & RESPONSIBILITIES:

   You will be directly responsible to the _____ of the Royal Blossom Hotel, who will assign you your duties.

   A copy of your Job Description will be given to you at a later date which will be subject to such policy changes as may be introduced by management from time to time.

5. WORKING HOURS:

   Normal working hours are 54 hours during 6 days per week, inclusive of one-hour meal break per day. However, your exact working hours will depend on the demands of the operation. As a senior staff, you are not entitled to overtime pay, but may be compensated by off-in-lieu.

6. COMMENCEMENT:

   Subject to your acceptance and work permit, the commencement date will be _____.

7. DURATION:

   Two years initially, after which you will become a permanent employee, provided a continuous work permit and subsequent renewals are approved by the local authority.

8. PROBATION:

   8.1   There will be a probation period of three months, during which either party may terminate this agreement by giving three months' notice in writing or three months' salary in lieu of notice.

   8.2   The period of probation may be extended for a maximum of three months at the General Manager's discretion.

   8.3   Should the employee decide to terminate this agreement during probation, the hotel will not be responsible for the employee's return passage or personal effects transportation.

9. REMUNERATION:

   9.1   A basic monthly salary of HK$ _____ (Hong Kong dollars _____) will be paid one month in arrears to your bank account in Hong Kong in local currency and in accordance with local laws and regulations.

   9.2   You will not be entitled to receive any service charge payment.

   9.3   A bonus equivalent to one month's basic salary will be paid to employees on the hotel payroll at the end of the year. For those who join the hotel during the year and have successfully completed their probation, this bonus will be paid on a pro-rata basis. Employees still on probation at the end of the year, or who leave service during the year, are not entitled to a bonus.

   9.4   You should be responsible for your personal income tax arising out of this employment. For your information, the prevailing maximum salaries tax rate in Hong Kong is 15.5% and company provided accommodation is taxed as 10% of salary and bonuses.

(continued)

Exhibit 3 *(continued)*

10. <u>SALARY REVIEW</u>:

    Salaries will be reviewed after completion of one year's service and thereafter, every January.

11. <u>PASSAGE</u>:

    11.1 The hotel will be responsible for your passage to Hong Kong to report for duty. This will be in the form of economy class air ticket.

    11.2 The hotel will also pay for the transportation plus insurance of personal effects by sea up to a maximum of two cubic meters per person. Quotations from at least 2 reputable carriers should be obtained for approval prior to shipment. Insurance for items such as antiques or precious art objects are for your own account.

    11.3 You will be entitled to similar allowance at the end of your service, provided your services have not been terminated for cause (see item 22).

12. <u>PASSPORT, VISAS, WORK PERMIT, INOCULATION</u>:

    12.1 The hotel will reimburse you for charges incurred for inoculations, visas, and work permit application for you. Passport renewal charges will be for your own account.

    12.2 The hotel undertakes to obtain the necessary visa and work permit provided they are approved by local authorities, to enable you to carry out your duties in Hong Kong. However, it is agreed that you will take such action as is necessary on your part to facilitate obtaining the necessary visa and work permit.

13. <u>ACCOMMODATION</u>:

    13.1 You are entitled to a monthly living out allowance of HK$ _____ maximum, which may be utilized to cover rental and/or related costs such as utility bills raised by you.

    13.2 Board and lodging in the hotel will be provided for you on your arrival in Hong Kong up to a maximum period of one month.

14. <u>MEDICAL BENEFITS</u>:

    You are entitled to free medical care including hospitalization upon approval by the hotel's doctor. Medical expenses related to pregnancy, optical care, and other sicknesses exempted on medical check-up are excluded. Expenses incurred due to self-inflicted injury or use of narcotic drugs are also excluded. Furthermore, you are entitled to dental care included in the hotel dental scheme upon successful completion of your probation period.

15. <u>PRIVILEGES</u>:

    You are entitled to privileges according to hotel policy.

16. <u>RETIREMENT PLAN</u>:

    You are eligible to join the hotel's retirement plan, details of which are obtainable from the Controller's Office.

17. <u>ANNUAL LEAVE</u>:

    17.1 You will be entitled to four calendar weeks paid leave per annum which include all statutory and public holidays. Leave may not be accumulated from year to year. Leave not utilized during the current year will be automatically forfeited.

    17.2 Leave should be scheduled so that there is minimal disruption to hotel operations. Prior approval must be obtained from the General Manager.

    17.3 If staff leave service and have not taken annual leave accrued, they will be entitled to salary in lieu of outstanding leave; likewise, if staff leave service and have taken annual leave before completing equivalent period of service, salary in lieu of leave has to be refunded back to the company.

    17.4 Outstanding leave may not be utilized to substitute period of notice for termination.

18. <u>TRAVEL ALLOWANCE</u>:

    18.1 You will be entitled to a travel allowance for every 2 years' completed service.

Exhibit 3 *(continued)*

18.2 The allowance will be based on the cost of the current economy class airfare from Hong Kong to _____.

18.3 You may utilize part or all of this allowance for travel, package tour, etc., to any destination you may prefer but no cash exchange may be made.

18.4 The travel allowance will not be applied at the end of service.

19. SICK LEAVE:

You will be entitled to a maximum of thirty days sick leave on full pay per annum. All sick leave must be certified by doctors approved by the hotel.

20. TERMINATION NOTICE:

After successful completion of your probation, either party may terminate this agreement by giving three months' notice in writing or proportionate salary in lieu of notice. Should you terminate your employment prior to one year's service, the hotel may claim back from you costs incurred for you to take up employment in Hong Kong. No repatriation benefits will be granted if you resign before the completion of your contract.

21. TERMINATION DUE TO ILLNESS:

21.1 The hotel may terminate your employment if you are certified by hotel-approved doctors as unfit for work or incapacitated for a period exceeding 3 months.

21.2 If the hotel terminates your employment due to ill health, you will be given three months salary in addition to repatriation benefits as for normal termination.

22. TERMINATION FOR CAUSE:

The hotel will terminate your employment without notice or salary in lieu of notice if:

22.1 Your ill health is certified by hotel-approved doctors as self-inflicted.

22.2 You have been convicted for violation of local laws.

22.3 You have seriously violated hotel rules and regulations.

22.4 You are found to be incompetent or negligent in the performance of your duties.

22.5 You conduct yourself in a manner that adversely affects your standing and reputation in the community.

Employees terminated for cause will not be entitled to free return passage and personal effects transportation.

23. RESTRICTION:

During the terms of this agreement, you will not be employed or engaged by any other person, firm, or company or acquire any interest in any other undertaking carrying on business of a similar nature or in competition with the hotel. You are required also to refrain from disclosing confidential information to unauthorized parties.

24. CONDITIONS:

24.1 The company reserves the right to alter general conditions of employment as and when necessary.

24.2 As part of ongoing manpower planning, management may commission external professionals or qualified in-company personnel to conduct assessment tests for employees from time to time.

25. TRANSFER:

If deemed appropriate, the company may transfer you from one operation to another. Before transfers take place, due consideration will be given to employee's personal circumstances, and terms and conditions of employment will be at a similar standard.

(continued)

Exhibit 3 *(continued)*

> Please study our terms and conditions carefully. If you agree to accept this appointment, please sign and return one copy of this letter together with a copy of medical certificate of fitness from a certified doctor.
>
> We look forward to working with you at the Royal Blossom Hotel, Hong Kong.
>
> Yours sincerely,
>
> General Manager
> Royal Blossom, Hong Kong
>
> ACCEPTANCE:
>
> I confirm that I have read and understood the terms and conditions stipulated in this letter and I agree to accept this appointment.
>
> Signature:
>
> _____   _____
> (Name)   Date

Exhibit 4   Characteristics of Successful Global Managers

> Successful global managers need to understand the culture and language of the countries they deal with, according to a recent survey of 148 middle managers. The respondents said the following factors are important to being a good global manager:

Knowledge of foreign culture	81%
Knowledge of industry	80%
Knowledge of language	63%
Time spent in country	21%

Source: Dunhill Personnel System Inc., Woodbury, N.Y.

2005, the average eligibility for families was 57 percent. As of 2008, that percentage had risen to 84 percent.[10] It is a trend that makes sense for businesses as 28 percent of early returns cited family concerns as the main reason they returned home. When a family has difficulty adjusting to the foreign environment, the expatriate is less likely to be successful.[11] Family concerns are also cited as the most common reason for refusing an expatriate assignment.[12]

Designing Pre-Departure Training Programs

To the extent possible, pre-departure training programs should be tailored to the specific needs of the individual going abroad. The more generalized the program, the less effective it will be, although cost and time constraints must also be considered. Japanese companies, as a case in point, place a great deal of emphasis on pre-departure orientation and training. As a result, the expatriate failure rate for most Japanese companies is generally between 5 and 10 percent. Japanese companies typically make foreign assignments a year before departure to allow adequate preparation time. During that year, managers devote company time to studying the culture and language of the destination country.

According to Japanese thinking, overseas managers must first develop "effectiveness" skills by reshaping their skills to fit a different set of relations with subordinates, business associates, and customers, as well as regulatory, political, and market environments. Second, both the manager and the family must develop coping skills by learning to do without things easily available at home but perhaps not elsewhere. They must learn to accept, respect, and ultimately enjoy customs and procedures that at first seem unfamiliar and inconvenient. Once on the assignment, the Japanese expatriate manager works with a mentor whose job is to smooth any problem areas and reduce pressure on the expatriate.[13]

An in-depth pre-departure training program should have four areas of emphasis: (1) cultural awareness, (2) attitudes, (3) knowledge, and (4) skills. (Developing skills in the first two areas is also important for hotel managers managing a culturally diverse work force in the United States and domestic hospitality workers working for a foreign-managed hotel company, although the training need not be as detailed.)

Cultural awareness training raises the participants' awareness of cultural differences and their impact on business behavior. Every individual is culture-bound to a certain extent. The world is viewed essentially through the lens the culture has provided, and people react to their culturally influenced perceptions of the world in culturally prescribed ways. Because culture is so much a part of people, its workings are beyond conscious awareness. Managers need to know how the general characteristics of the culture will affect business behavior in order to adopt an effective leadership style, training methods, and motivation and communication styles for that culture.

Attitude training focuses on attitudes and how they are shaped. It is critical that managers understand the difference between nature and nurture. That is, attitudes and beliefs—including their own—are acquired from conditioning and the environment (nurture). They are not inherently correct or somehow inborn (and therefore somehow more natural). People who don't understand this can be quite judgmental; people who do understand this are halfway toward adapting to another culture. **Ethnocentrism,** the belief or attitude that one's culture is superior to all others, is one of the greatest barriers to cross-cultural understanding. Cultural sensitivity training helps to alleviate ethnocentrism.

Knowledge training provides factual and practical information about the target country. Among the areas that should be covered are:

- Social and business etiquette
- History and folklore
- Current affairs

- Values of the host culture
- Geography, climate, and the physical environment
- Sources of pride: artists, musicians, things to see and do
- Religion (extremely important in Islamic countries)
- Political structure
- Legal structure
- Economic structure
- General business conditions
- Prevailing business practices
- Practical matters such as currency, transportation, time zones, hours of business

Films and guidebooks are usually available on most countries to provide orientation support. The knowledge portion should also include the history and current status of the target country's relationship to one's home country.

Skills training concentrates on skills building in such areas as language, non-verbal communication, cultural stress management, and adjustment and adaptation skills. Part of the training should focus on determining the individual's personal coping mechanisms and those that are most effective.

Depending on the anticipated length of the assignment and on whether it is considered worth the time investment, language training can be very important. People in many countries speak English as a second language; but even when English is used, every effort should be made to learn at least the simple phrases or terms with subtle meanings of the spoken language. Many terms in other languages have no English equivalent. Knowing their approximate meanings can save a great deal of explanation in dealing with associates or employees. In many cases, language opens doors otherwise closed to foreigners.

Even a rough attempt to speak a language can make a good impression and help establish a closer bond between expatriate managers and local citizens. Language training that begins before departure may also be continued once the assignment has begun. Lectures and various types of recordings can be used to improve language proficiency. Some companies provide additional compensation for foreign language proficiency.

A recent study identified important training activities for preparing hospitality expatriate managers for their overseas assignments. Respondents identified 12 training activities they felt were important. The five that received the most votes from study participants were (in rank order):

1. Internships and short assignments abroad
2. Second language studies
3. Study abroad
4. International travel
5. International management studies.[14]

Pre-Departure Training Options

Hotel operators may establish in-house departments for the training and development of overseas managers, or they may hire qualified outside trainers. The number of cross-cultural trainers continues to grow, and many trainers have had sufficient exposure to the hotel world to address the needs of this industry. Outside trainers can be found through training consulting firms, international nonprofit organizations, and universities. Since cross-cultural training has experienced a spurt of popular growth, its practitioners have learned to package and market their services to potential users. An outside training consultant may also be able to help a hotel company integrate cross-cultural training material into an existing management development program.

One cost-effective way to develop an in-house program is to arrange for cross-cultural training for the trainers who will implement the program. The Society for Intercultural Education, Training, and Research (SIETAR) offers one- to two-week workshops for beginning intercultural trainers. These workshops provide an overview of intercultural theory and the goals, principles, content, and methodology of intercultural training. Such a workshop should enable hotel trainers to administer most off-the-shelf training programs.

Health Considerations

A complete health examination of the employee and his or her family members should be performed before departure. The check-up should include a medical history, physical examination, and laboratory tests. Blood checks, chest X-rays when indicated, urinalysis, and an electrocardiogram should supplement the medical evaluation. Immunization histories need to be reviewed and vaccinations or boosters given where indicated. Infectious hepatitis is a common problem in many countries so appropriate inoculations may be needed.

Employees should be cautioned on other steps to reduce health risks. In certain areas, fresh fruit or vegetables should not be eaten, and bottled water should be used. Given the prevalence of the AIDS/HIV virus, blood transfusions and injections as a rule should be avoided unless the source and screening of the blood can be ascertained. If traveling to an area where malaria is a problem, the family should be cautioned to avoid mosquitoes. If a member of the family requires hospitalization while abroad, returning to the home country or going to another country where better health care is available should be considered. Particularly in developing countries, standards of hygiene and service are not likely to meet expatriate expectations; also, medical staff who speak the expatriate's language are not always available. All members of the family should be encouraged before departure to follow a disciplined health and fitness program during the assignment, even though this may require some adjustment and changes from their usual physical activities.

Every member of the family should have a list of prescription drugs taken on a regular basis. These drugs should be itemized by generic names, because prescription drugs are sold under various brand labels in other countries. Many drugs requiring a prescription in certain countries are available over the counter in other countries. It is also helpful to provide the employee abroad with a list of doctors in the relocation area who speak the employee's native language, since an acute illness may require prompt treatment.

Other Pre-Departure Activities

If time and funds are available, the prospective expatriate manager and his or her spouse should be allowed to visit the host country. This visit allows them to form a realistic view of schooling, housing, and transportation and to develop a better understanding of the demands of the assignment.

Before departure, careful attention should be paid to avoid any problems in the area of visas or work permits. Immigration officials of the destination country and legal counsel specializing in visas and work permits can be invaluable in this regard. This is particularly true if the hotel company has neither previous experience in the country nor people specializing in this area.

Culture Shock

Culture shock results from being immersed in an unfamiliar environment. For some, it results in confusion, disorientation, and discomfort. Culture shock can be crippling to personal and professional adjustment. The severity of the shock depends to a large extent on just how different the old and the new cultures are. The transferee from one part of Europe to another may not notice vast differences. If the same transferee goes to an Islamic country, on the other hand, culture shock may occur. Some Asian and Middle Eastern cultures may prove tough for Western women because of the male-dominated value system within those cultures.

Culture shock typically does not strike like a lightning bolt. Rather, there is a honeymoon phase of cultural adjustment when everything is new and exciting. This is followed by a cumulative and worsening state of disorientation that builds slowly from each experience in which the sufferer encounters contrary ways of perceiving, doing, and evaluating things. The more someone understands the culture and develops skills to manage change and differences, the less likely that person is to suffer culture shock.

While pre-departure training, orientation, and counseling do not immunize expatriates from culture shock, they do enable individuals to approach the new environment positively and with realistic expectations. It is often useful to provide continued training once the foreign assignment has begun, including language instruction, cultural adaptation skills, and stress management. Once the person is somewhat settled, information about the culture and other practical matters may seem more pertinent and may be more readily absorbed. A mentoring system can also help to minimize culture shock. A seasoned expatriate or an appropriate host-country colleague can provide the necessary sounding board to ask questions, to discuss cultural issues, or simply to provide moral support.

Some companies provide for the expatriate to have two to four weeks off after arriving in the host country and before assuming managerial duties. This approach provides an opportunity for the employee to get settled, to become accustomed to the environment, to meet people (employees of the hotel, other expatriates, industry leaders, and host government officials), to discover shopping places, banks, restaurants, and so forth.

Excessive Acculturation

While fulfilling a foreign assignment, some expatriate managers will be hindered by lack of contact with, and by geographic separation from, their own country and culture. As a result, their frame of reference may become increasingly localized. In any environment, most individuals over time are inclined to conform with local social norms. The internalization of cultural training may predispose expatriate managers to embrace local norms even further. Additionally, the managers' closest social contacts are likely to be other expatriates in similar positions. Because fellow expatriates are also sensitive to local social norms and values, their frame of reference may be affected more by the demands and ideologies of the local culture than by the requirements of the parent organization. At an extreme, the increased sensitivity to local norms may actually reduce an expatriate manager's effectiveness. For example, managers may fail to consider a variety of alternative solutions to a given problem because the options seem inappropriate within the new cultural frame of reference. Or alternative solutions may be rejected because assumptions about the values of the host country limit the manager's view of the consequences.

To the extent that the expatriate manager encounters role conflict between the host country and the parent organization, the manager can experience stress, decreased decisiveness, increased tension in interpersonal relationships, and less job satisfaction. Cultural training can actually *increase* role conflict by overdeveloping the manager's awareness of the cultural implications of company decisions. Attitudes may also change as the manager's sense of his or her proper role is influenced by the local environment. The manager may become more sensitive to the cultural and political implications of a corporate directive than to the objectives of the organization. Expatriate managers may infer that they have been given more latitude in making policy decisions than the parent organization has actually delegated. They may also feel that managers at the home office are not responsive to local problems nor could they possibly understand the expatriates' situation.

To minimize these problems, once managers have been assigned abroad, they should be periodically informed about what the company is doing to help them achieve their own career objectives. The overseas general manager should also have as much face-to-face contact with representatives from company headquarters as possible to provide opportunities for airing local operational or other problems and for information exchange. Other expatriate managers should receive the same consideration from the general manager.

Repatriation

Repatriation—bringing back and effectively integrating executives who have been working abroad—can sometimes be difficult. The initial problem is finding a suitable position for the repatriated manager. According to one school of thought, it is advisable to send only top-notch, proven people on foreign assignments, since their repatriation will not present as much of a problem. Companies that send marginal people abroad frequently have no place to put them once the assignment ends.

A problem with repatriation is that corporate personnel, aside from the human resource executive, often have little involvement with individual overseas managers and may be unaware of the individual's newly acquired skills. The authority and responsibilities of managers abroad tend to be broader in scope and latitude than those of managers at home; for that reason, a repatriated manager sometimes becomes frustrated with a new assignment that does not allow as much latitude or autonomy as before. European managers assigned to Asian properties are particularly reluctant to return home for this reason. There may also be times when no comparable openings exist, aside from another foreign assignment. Even a promotion may involve less responsibility.

Reverse Culture Shock and Readjustment

Repatriates and their families sometimes suffer culture shock in reverse. They may find the pace of life at home incompatible with either the slower or faster lifestyle they had become accustomed to abroad. The Hong Kong workstyle and lifestyle, for example, is faster and more intense than that in the United States (with perhaps the exception of New York City), while the pace and rhythm of life in Fiji is much slower (and certainly kinder and gentler).

Another problem for repatriates is the reality of financial readjustment. Some expatriates become used to higher living standards afforded by perquisites—possibly company-owned and -furnished housing, a chauffeur-driven company car, company-paid domestic help, cost of living allowances, and incentive compensation—and find it difficult to cope when these perquisites end. Additionally, there may be a loss of social and professional prestige upon returning home. For many, the shock of facing financial realities is more difficult than making cultural readjustments.

Minimizing Repatriation Difficulties

Problems associated with repatriation can be minimized through proper planning and provision for readjustment counseling, orientation, and training. For planning purposes, it is helpful for managers to know the exact duration of their foreign assignment before departure. There should be sufficient career planning beforehand to ensure that those who go abroad have a realistic understanding of the range of postings they may expect after completing a foreign assignment and to ensure that such assignments are delivered. Failure to deliver can destroy a climate in which a foreign assignment is positively received. An effort should be made to make the new position as attractive and challenging—both financially and professionally—as possible. The position should also take advantage of the foreign experience and professional knowledge gained on the assignment.

The repatriation process should start six months or more before the actual move home. Ideally, it should include a discussion of the current developments and trends at home and instruction on new company personnel, operating policies, procedures, and organizational changes to bring the impending transferee up to date. Professional counseling, financial counseling, and other assistance should also be available upon request. Re-entry bonuses or relocation allowances have been used by some hotel companies to alleviate the financial burden of the transfer.

Summary

Transnational hotel companies generally rotate their more qualified executives through virtually all of their properties. Rotation allows companies to deploy their best people where they are needed and to perpetuate their standards of service delivery. While the use of expatriates may be both desirable and necessary, it is not without controversy as countries become more nationalistic and actively promote local employment.

The ultimate consideration for the hotel company must be to select managers who are best qualified to pursue the company's interests. Frequently, a hotel company will use an experienced expatriate management team to coordinate the pre-opening activities of a new hotel. Once the property is up and running, the foreign team may be reassigned to other hotels and replaced by competent local managers who have been appropriately trained for these positions.

Some countries establish regulations to restrict the number of expatriates employed by international hotels. Others require locally hired understudies in positions filled by foreign nationals. Still others require employer-sponsored hotel training to promote skills transfer to local nationals. However, to encourage outside investments, many countries are easing the work visa and immigration restrictions they have typically used to curtail a non-local work force.

The selection of candidates for foreign assignments must be carefully considered and candidates for foreign transfer should be meticulously evaluated. The ease with which a manager can adapt to an unfamiliar environment may be explained by individual attributes relating to self-orientation, others-orientation, and perceptual orientation. Managers who are mismatched with their host countries can cause the hotel to suffer financial and/or goodwill losses. In worst case scenarios, the company may find its management contract unduly canceled or its managers summarily deported. An expatriate manager must be culturally sensitive, flexible, and tactful in handling all situations, especially in politically volatile areas.

A foreign contract or letter of agreement between the hotel owners and management employee should be provided to ensure that the expatriate understands the components of his or her compensation package, which might include incentives, tax allowances, hardship premiums, and so forth.

One way to promote the success of expatriate managers is to use pre-departure or cross-cultural training programs for foreign-bound employees. These programs help managers and their families (who should be included) to better understand their host country. The programs provide specific details about the geography, history, people, economy, government, traditions, and culture of the family's new home, as well as other factors to which they must adjust—including language, religion, climate, money systems, political systems, education, and so forth. An in-depth pre-departure program should cover cultural awareness, attitudes, knowledge, and skills. Whether provided in-house or by a consultant, the benefits of these programs far outweigh any real or perceived costs.

Pre-departure training reduces the risk of severe culture shock. Continued cultural conditioning (such as language instruction or cultural adaptation skills) also eases the transition and increases the chance of success. However, excessive acculturation is a potential problem. It occurs when an expatriate manager overly identifies with his or her country of assignment, losing objectivity and/or decisiveness.

Eventually, managers are repatriated or reassigned to another country. When hotel executives who have mastered very broad skills from their assignments abroad are transferred back home, finding suitable and challenging positions is not always easy. Reverse culture shock for repatriates and their families is also not unheard of, but the return transition can be assisted by appropriate counseling and orientation.

Endnotes

1. Alexandra Seno, "In China, a Rush to Train 5-Star Staff for Luxury Hotels," *International Herald Tribune, New York Times*, July 8, 2005.
2. Travel and Tourism Competitiveness Report, World Economic Forum, Geneva, 2007.
3. Renard International Hospitality Consultants, Ltd., of Toronto, Canada.
4. IRS Publication 54, Tax Guide for U.S. Citizens and Residents Abroad; IRS Publication 514, Foreign Tax Credit for Individuals; and IRS Publication 909, Alternative Minimum Tax for Individuals.
5. Barry Powell, "International Social Security Agreements Increase Income for Overseas Employees," *Journal of Accountancy*, July 1990, p. 111.
6. Employee Benefit Plan Review. "Survey of Expatriates Shows Differing Employer-Employee Perceptions," *Employee Benefit Plan Review*, 55, No. 12 (2001): 40–41.
7. Jeffrey Shay and J. Bruce Tracey, "Expatriate Managers: Reasons for Failure and Implications for Training," *Cornell Hotel and Restaurant Administration Quarterly*, February, 1997, pp. 30–35.
8. Brian Amble, "International Assignments on the Rise," *Management Issues*, May 24, 2006. Retrieved from www.management-issues.com on June 6, 2008.
9. Gretchen Lang, "Cross-Cultural Training: How Much Difference Does It Really Make?" *International Herald Tribune, New York Times*, January 24, 2004. Retrieved June 6, 2008. And *Global Relocation Trends: 2008 Survey Report* (Woodridge, Ill.: GMAC Global Relocation Services, 2008), p. 11.
10. *Global Relocation Trends*.
11. Hung-Wen Lee, "Factors that Influence Expatriate Failure: An Interview Study," *International Journal of Management*, September 2007, p. 403.
12. *Global Relocation Trends*, p. 11.
13. Gary Hogan and Jane Goodson, "The Key to Expatriate Success," *Training and Development Journal*, January 1990, p. 52.
14. Germaine Shames, "Training for the Multicultural Workplace," *Cornell Hotel and Restaurant Administration Quarterly*, February 1986, p. 26.

Key Terms

allowances—With regard to compensation, stipends, or perquisites a transnational company can give to bring an expatriate employee's spending power up to home-country standards; typically provided to cover such items as housing, schooling for dependents, or home leaves.

culture shock—A sense of confusion, disorientation, discomfort, uncertainty, or anxiety that sometimes affects people exposed to or immersed in an unfamiliar cultural environment.

detached worker rule—A U.S. rule that exempts a person temporarily transferred to another country (usually for five or fewer years) from the territorial rule, so that the person remains covered by the social security system of the home country.

differentials—With regard to compensation, stipends, or perquisites a transnational company can give to bring an expatriate employee's spending up to home-country standards; typically provided on a net (tax paid) basis to the employee.

ethnocentrism—The belief or attitude that one's culture is superior to all others; one of the greatest barriers to cross-cultural understanding.

repatriation—Bringing an expatriate worker back from a foreign assignment to his or her home country; the return of money or other resources to the country of origin.

territorial rule—A U.S. rule which provides that an employee who would be covered by a U.S. and foreign social security system will be subject exclusively to the coverage laws of the country in which he or she is working.

totalization agreements—International social security agreements that eliminate the dual taxation that occurs when a worker from one country is employed in another and is required to pay social security taxes to both countries.

Review Questions

1. What types of hotel positions are commonly filled by expatriates? Why?
2. Why do hotel companies often want to use expatriate managers instead of local talent? What are some of the advantages that might be gained from using local talent?
3. What are some of the factors that make the cost of using expatriate labor so high? How might these costs be reduced?
4. What factors should be considered when measuring the cost of placing a poorly selected or poorly trained manager in an international assignment? Are these costs likely to be substantial?
5. How should candidates for foreign placement be evaluated? What personal characteristics are likely to be important for success in a foreign environment?
6. What issues does an expatriate manager's contract generally address?

7. What are the four recommended areas of emphasis in pre-departure training? What elements should be addressed in each of these general areas?
8. What is culture shock? How can it be minimized?
9. What are the potential consequences of excessive acculturation? What tactics can a hotel company use to help keep it from occurring?
10. What sorts of issues can make repatriation a difficult process? How can such problems be minimized?

Chapter 10 Outline

The Field of IHRM
Employee Acquisition
    Employment Ratios
    Labor Supply
    Possible Solutions for Labor Shortages
Recruitment
    Imported Labor/Immigrants
    Job Perceptions Affecting Recruitment
    Family or Educational Status
    Impacts of Hotel Class
    Hiring for Joint Ventures
    Factors Affecting the Hiring Decision
Orientation
    Cultural Attitudes toward Service
    Universality of Hospitality
Training in a Multicultural Environment
Supervision
    Motivation and Productivity
    Decision-Making
    Communication
Compensation and Benefits
Trade Unions and Unionism
    Contrasting Examples of Unionism
Human Resource Development
    Performance Appraisals
    Corrective Actions
Discharge

Competencies

1. Define international human resource management and describe IHRM's three main activities. (pp. 299–302)

2. Identify factors affecting employee acquisition, discuss steps to reduce the effects of skilled labor shortages, and describe different factors that affect recruitment. (pp. 302–308)

3. Explain the purpose of different types of new employee orientation programs in different countries. (pp. 308–310)

4. Discuss the importance of training and the requirements for a successful training program abroad. (pp. 310–311)

5. Identify several kinds of culturally based motivations, describe various decision-making styles, and identify factors that contribute to communication in a multicultural environment including strategies for managing language differences. (pp. 311–316)

6. List the basic elements of compensation and benefit packages and explain variances between countries. (pp. 317–318)

7. Describe the state of unionism in the international hospitality industry. (pp. 318–320)

8. Describe the American approach to performance appraisal and explain why managers must be aware of culturally based attitudes toward corrective actions and the discharge of employees. (pp. 320–323)

10
International Human Resource Management

As a global employer, the international hotel industry has a collective workforce of over 234 million employees, which represents 8.2 percent of total worldwide employment.[1] The industry is valued by many countries for its ability to provide employment opportunities for entry-level workers as well as supervisors and executives on various levels of the hospitality career ladder.

Human resource management is the process of attracting, training, and maintaining a stable and motivated team of employees. In addition to finding the best person for the job, this function involves providing employees with the tools and incentives to perform to capacity, as well as the opportunity for self-development and growth on the job. As the most people-oriented of all management functions, human resource management is also the most cultural. Workers do not usually separate themselves from their cultural values, perspectives, and attitudes, all of which affect their on-the-job behavior and pose a constant challenge to management.

For hotel corporations as well as for individual hotel managers, human resource issues are often complicated, consuming a substantial amount of time, energy, and expense. The challenge of managing people effectively increases when dealing with multiple cultures in the same workplace. Understanding other cultures, demonstrating sensitivity toward cultural and religious differences among staff members, and adapting human resource practices when necessary are all requirements of international management. Effective international managers have the sensitivity and skills to manage a diverse workforce and function effectively when working in cultures different from their own.

The Field of IHRM

International human resource management (IHRM) has steadily gained recognition as a field of study. IHRM suggests the management of "people" as opposed to "employees"—in some cultures, human resource management concerns the needs not only of employees but of their dependents as well. IHRM can be at once interesting and challenging. Consider, for example, the impact of benefit plans that do not provide for the multiple spouses that may be found in polygamous societies, or of needing to deal with community representatives in employee disciplinary cases, as may be the situation in South Pacific island nations. IHRM may at times address such issues as housing, tax planning, health, education, religion (an off-limits topic in countries that separate church and state), recreation, and other matters that concern the lives of workers. IHRM is also more susceptible to external influences such as societal norms and government policies.

The human and financial consequences of a mistake in the international hotel arena can be severe. The cause of multinational business failures often stems from not understanding the essential differences in managing human resources in foreign environments.

Marble and steel may create hotels of dazzling beauty, but the heart and soul of hotels anywhere in the world are their employees. For both the domestic and foreign guest, there is no substitute for service—not even marble palaces. The quality of service, the maintenance of the property, and ultimately the success of the hotel depend largely on the efforts of employees. This viewpoint, which is becoming a universal one among hotels and the global travel industry, recognizes the importance of human relations, attitudes, and behaviors in each culture. Hence, managerial activities that acknowledge the human element in the day-to-day operations of the hotel are paramount.

IHRM directs attention to an awareness of managerial problems from the cultural viewpoint of the employees. It stresses the effectiveness of employees in their work as a key managerial accomplishment. The problem of satisfying guests, for example, is not so much a matter of establishing efficient operating systems as it is of finding, training, and retaining satisfied and highly motivated service workers to operate those systems. In the final analysis, systems are only as good as the people working them. Human resource management stresses this vital fact.

Briefly stated, IHRM is concerned with the acquisition and maintenance of a well-qualified, satisfactory, and satisfied workforce in another country or in a cultural context besides one's own. Recruiting, selecting, training, and placing the right people in the right positions constitute an enormous task. Keeping them stimulated, satisfied, and productive is perhaps even greater. Adding to these challenges is the need to work with people in their own cultural environment and, increasingly, to be politically correct in responding to people and problems. As the workforce in the hotel industry becomes more culturally diverse, conventional ways of dealing with personnel issues may no longer be adequate to keep workers motivated, satisfied, and performing well.

IHRM in hotels includes a comprehensive group of activities. The content will vary somewhat from country to country, depending on economic, political, and social–cultural conditions. The activities may be grouped under three main headings: (1) acquisition, (2) employment, and (3) human resource development. (Exhibit 1 illustrates these three groups of activities in graphic form.) Under acquisition, such activities as recruitment, selection, orientation, promotion, and transfers are included. Employment activities cover training, supervision, compensation administration (including bonuses and perquisites), personnel services such as counseling or medical assistance (which are increasingly important), employee benefits, employee activities, and union negotiations (where applicable). Human resource development activities concern standards of performance, job specifications and requirements, measurement of employee progress, career development, and human resource planning.

Exhibit 1   IHRM Activities

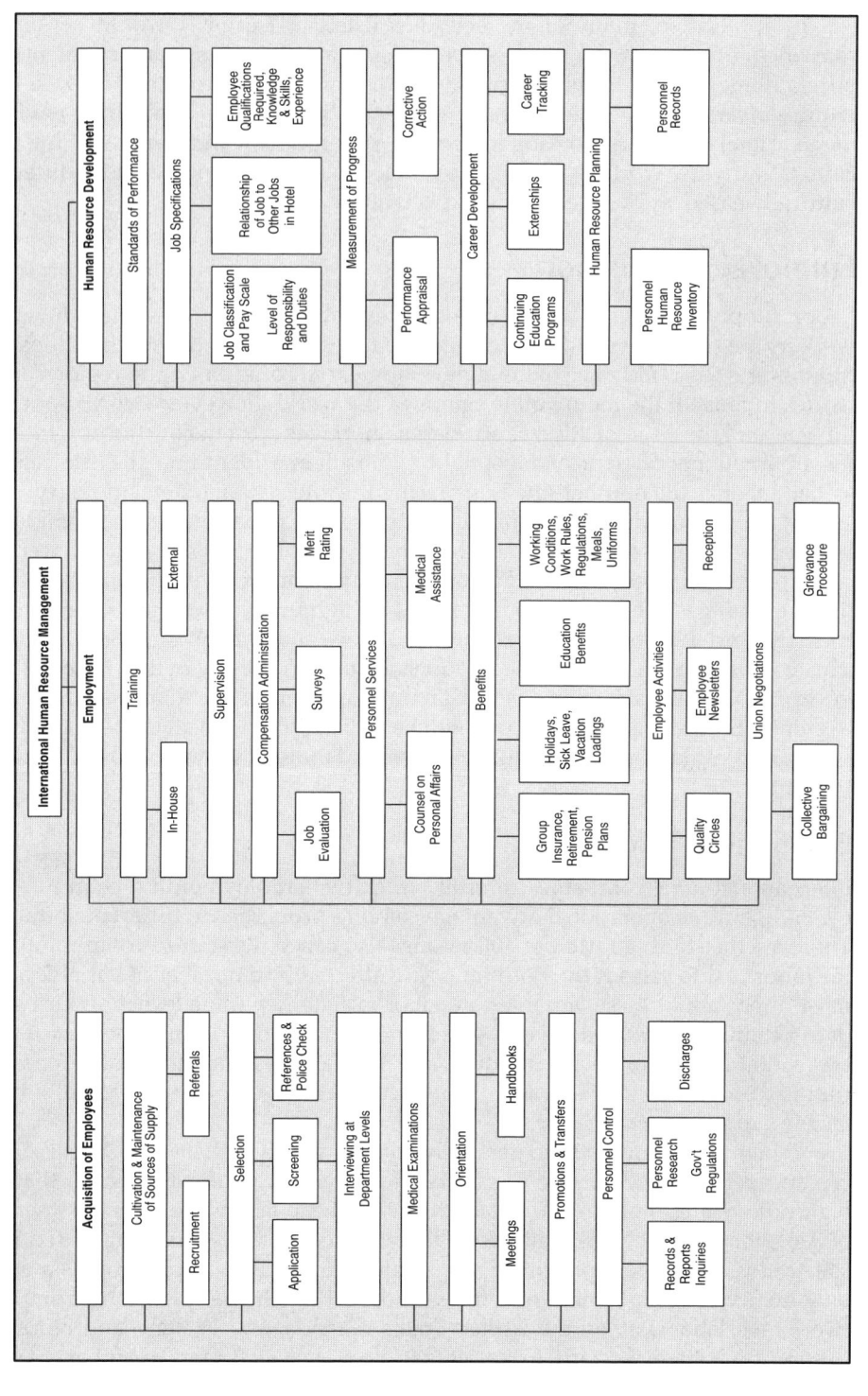

International Human Resource Management

Acquisition of Employees

- Cultivation & Maintenance of Sources of Supply
  - Recruitment
  - Referrals
- Selection
  - Application
  - Screening
  - References & Police Check
- Interviewing at Department Levels
- Medical Examinations
- Orientation
  - Meetings
  - Handbooks
- Promotions & Transfers
- Personnel Control
  - Records & Reports Inquiries
  - Personnel Research
  - Gov't Regulations
  - Discharges

Employment

- Training
  - In-House
  - External
- Supervision
  - Merit Rating
- Compensation Administration
  - Job Evaluation
  - Surveys
- Personnel Services
  - Counsel on Personal Affairs
  - Medical Assistance
- Benefits
  - Group Insurance, Retirement, Pension Plans
  - Holidays, Sick Leave, Vacation Loadings
  - Education Benefits
  - Working Conditions, Work Rules, Regulations, Meals, Uniforms
- Employee Activities
  - Quality Circles
  - Employee Newsletters
  - Reception
- Union Negotiations
  - Collective Bargaining
  - Grievance Procedure

Human Resource Development

- Standards of Performance
- Job Specifications
  - Job Classification and Pay Scale
  - Level of Responsibility and Duties
  - Relationship of Job to Other Jobs in Hotel
  - Employee Qualifications Required, Knowledge & Skills, Experience
- Measurement of Progress
  - Performance Appraisal
  - Corrective Action
- Career Development
  - Continuing Education Programs
  - Externships
  - Career Tracking
- Human Resource Planning
  - Personnel Human Resource Inventory
  - Personnel Records

In application, many of the activities listed in Exhibit 1 would be similar regardless of whether the hotel is operating in a multicultural environment or a purely domestic one. In this chapter, we will highlight some of the areas likely to require diverse management practices and flexible attitudes in different environments. Hotel managers working in a foreign environment and those working with culturally diverse workforces at home all need to develop sensitivities to differing, culturally based worker needs and expectations.

Employee Acquisition

Labor supply is not a problem in most developing countries, although skilled workers are sometimes difficult to find due to a shortage of training facilities and trainers and the rapid pace of hotel development in some emerging regions of the world. In most of the main hotel regions of the world, however—North America, Europe, and the Asia-Pacific region—labor shortages are a major concern. In 2007, the International Society of Hospitality Consultants identified the shortage of skilled labor as the number-one issue facing the international hotel industry.[2]

In many countries, the hospitality industry has a poor image as an employer. Seasonality, job dissatisfaction, and high labor turnover in some areas exacerbate an employee-acquisition problem that is already complex due to demographic and lifestyle changes. Despite periodic reports of high unemployment in some countries, the post-1970 baby-bust problem and subsequent labor shortages are problems common to many developed nations. Birthrates are low in the United States, lower in Great Britain, lower yet in Japan, and even lower than that in unified Germany. Entry-level hotel workers will be difficult to find in all of these countries for years to come, and they are likely to demand more pay and improved working conditions.

Employment Ratios

International hotel companies carefully track two employment ratios in measuring comparative operational advantages among properties in different countries. These are the **staffing ratio per 100 rooms** (also called the staff-to-room ratio) and the **labor cost to sales ratio.** Both ratios are affected by a number of variables. The most important of these variables are labor availability, wage levels, service standards, training, staff productivity, staff turnover, and hotel occupancy rates. If general conditions are more or less equal, it is normally assumed that hotel operators running properties in low-wage, labor-rich countries will have a natural advantage in producing a higher profit.

A high staff-to-room ratio generally equates with a high level of service delivery and personalized service to guests. However, it can also be argued that the high ratio relates more to low productivity or cheap labor. The legendary service of Asia, for example, was made possible by once-low wages that supported high staff ratios. Today, sharply rising wages and scarce labor in parts of Asia allow only luxury hotels to maintain staffing ratios of 1.4 or higher per room. Comparatively high labor costs in the United States, Canada, and Western and Northern Europe have made it nearly impossible to provide a staff ratio of higher than 0.8

per room in midscale properties if labor costs are to be kept in line. Hotel management in these countries and regions must constantly seek ways to increase staff productivity without sacrificing service.

Labor Supply

The supply of labor for the hospitality industry of any country is influenced by a number of conditions and events at both the macro and micro levels. Macro or national conditions and events are mostly beyond the control of industry. They include such factors as demographic trends (notably, shifts in birth rates that affect the supply of young entry-level workers); the pace of industrialization in the country and the competition for labor among industrial, agricultural, and service sectors; economic trends that affect general labor demand; and labor legislation that restricts or expands the labor supply. The hospitality industry has little choice but to work within the constraints of these conditions to secure its share of the workforce.

Micro conditions and events are those that are particular to a given industry. The industry often has considerable control over these conditions and events. For instance, the hospitality industry in general is notorious for its high labor turnover and shortage of good training programs. In recent years, the hotel industry in labor-scarce areas has turned its attention both to developing retention programs to reduce turnover and to assisting government in developing training programs to increase the pool of hospitality workers. Other concerns, such as the industry's low-status image, negative cultural perceptions regarding hospitality service jobs, non-competitive wage levels, and employment conditions, have also been subjects of debate.

While the supply of labor for the hospitality industry is somewhat unique to each country, the following four examples illustrate some of the common problems facing recruiters for hotel workers throughout the world.

United Kingdom. The United Kingdom represents a mature hotel market with continuing but limited expansion prospects. Demographic changes are at the core of the industry's labor shortage. Due to the declining birth rate, there has been a substantial drop in the number of 16- to 19-year-olds; this age group traditionally has been the primary source of entry-level recruitment for the hotel industry. Another problem is that demand for hotel labor is not evenly spread across the country. Also, because of the nature of the hospitality industry, there are substantial seasonal fluctuations in labor demand. On the other hand, recruitment of staff is made somewhat easier by the well-developed infrastructure of education establishments, training bodies, recruitment agencies, and government departments.

The U.K. hotel industry also faces a serious problem with regard to employee retention. Hotel jobs in the United Kingdom generally have a reputation for poor pay, unsocial hours, low status, physically demanding work, and poor career opportunities. Persuading people to work in the hotel sector when arguably more attractive job opportunities are available remains an unresolved problem for U.K. hoteliers.

Cyprus. Cyprus faces two challenges that affect the demand for labor: location and seasonality. Tourism development is spread throughout a number of resort areas that are distant from the primary urban area. This requires a major redistribution of labor from areas of surplus to areas of shortage. And, despite attempts to market Cyprus as a year-round destination, most visitors arrive in July, August, and September. Occupancies may drop from 100 percent in September to 25 percent in December. The labor problems are heightened by the fact that Cyprus is trying to differentiate its tourism product from the rest of the Mediterranean on the basis of service quality, which requires higher staff-to-room ratios.

Hong Kong. Due to its position as a major business and financial center, Hong Kong has a well-established hotel industry and has experienced rapid growth in upscale properties. In common with the rest of Asia, Hong Kong hotels operate with a high staff-to-room ratio. Hong Kong has been a major source of experienced personnel for the hotel industry in mainland China. Hong Kong has a number of government-supported and private vocational institutions capable of training new entrants for the hotel industry.

Thailand. Thailand has experienced a major expansion of its hotel industry. This has resulted in a chronic shortage of hotel staff. Hotels catering to international visitors compete with each other for guests by emphasizing the quality and level of service they provide, which requires high staff-to-room ratios. A major problem for hotel workers in Thailand is that taking a job in a hotel frequently means moving away from home.

The supply of vocationally trained staff in Thailand is limited by the capacity of the country's vocational training programs. This capacity is limited by the number of qualified trainers. Dusit International, for example, found it necessary to establish its own training center in Bangkok to help fulfill its labor needs.

Many new hotels in Thailand have survived by attracting experienced staff from existing hotels; the less prestigious midscale and budget hotels have been particularly hard hit with staff poaching. A shortage of local managers has resulted in distorted pay structures, as key personnel are able to demand high salaries for their skills. Higher wages have, however, improved the overall image of the industry as a career choice.

Possible Solutions for Labor Shortages

Many international hotel operators and voluntary trade associations have looked into ways to attract and retain workers in the hospitality industry. The solution has traditionally focused on wages and benefits, as pay is the major concern of employees in most countries. Although there is evidence that wages in the hotel industry have steadily increased in most labor markets, they remain low in comparison with manufacturing, construction, and high-tech industries.

The pay issue presents two problems. First, the hotel industry is highly competitive and market sensitive. The labor component (which can be a major cost) is significant in determining how much service can be provided. High prices are acceptable only to limited market niches and luxury hotels. In the midscale and budget hotel categories, pricing (not service) is often the competitive edge as long as the basic needs of guests are satisfied. There is only so much value that can be added to hotel services in these categories before guest wants and expectations are overreached.

Second, there is a limit to service productivity. Even the most skilled worker can only clean so many rooms or serve so many guests in a given length of time. Pay and work output, although related, are not always arithmetically related (that is, a 10-percent pay increase does not necessarily lead to a 10-percent increase in productivity).

In dealing with the pay problem, some international hotel companies have successfully introduced deferred types of financial rewards, such as share option plans (which allow employees to buy common shares in the company at par value). Other companies provide periodic bonuses based on performance, responsibilities, and length of employment. A common form of bonus in Chinese-owned hotels, for example, is a "thirteenth" month of pay traditionally given at new year (assuming the employee has worked the full year and has done a good job).

Progressive international hotel companies are combating labor supply issues by creating job enrichment and other programs to make their hotels employers of choice. Many are providing improved work/life–balance programs, more development opportunities, and programs to create a more fun and productive work environment. In this regard, Western multinational hotel companies have a competitive advantage over individually owned local hotels, which may be viewed as exploitative, especially in developing countries.

Recruitment

Sources of personnel for hotel employment vary widely among countries. In labor-scarce countries, hotel managers may find that they must look to non-traditional sources to find employees. In Thailand, for instance, men lean toward the civil service or the legal profession, so women are seen as a valuable resource for hotel employment. In developing countries with a scarcity of experienced hospitality managers, candidates with management potential may be found among an educated elite or among former military officers, who are more likely to have some technical training and disciplined work habits. India, for example, has had much success in recruiting and retraining former military officers for placement in tourism jobs.

Furthermore, recruitment efforts may need to be refocused away from the traditional young workers to other sectors of the labor market, including, for example, homemakers returning to the workforce, immigrants, and imported foreign labor through guest worker programs.

Imported Labor/Immigrants

Human capital, once considered to be the most stationary factor of an economy, has become increasingly mobile. Today, it is much more common than it used to be to find Indian engineers writing software in Silicon Valley, Algerians assembling cars in France, and Turkish workers cleaning hotel rooms in Frankfurt. Foreign workers outnumber local workers in some Middle Eastern areas. Hotel companies (along with other companies) are increasingly reaching across borders to find the skilled workers they need. These movements of labor are driven by the growing gap between the world's supply of labor and the demand for it.

The hotel industry's use of imported labor will always be influenced by a host country's labor laws and policies. This recruitment route is likely to meet with resistance from labor unions, who tend to support protectionist immigration policies. Still, in the long term, the use of imported labor may be unavoidable in some areas if tourism continues to grow. In some labor-scarce industrialized countries, it is already common practice to recruit rank-and-file workers for hotels from developing countries that have an oversupply of labor. The Philippines, for instance, was a popular source country for hotel workers during the height of the hotel boom around the world beginning in the late 1970s. Filipinos moved (and still continue to move) to other countries in Asia, the Pacific islands, Northern Europe, and the Middle East. During the 1970s, Germany instituted a guest worker program that allowed Turkish workers into the country, many of whom still work in the hospitality industry.

The trend toward more liberal immigration and labor policies will have a significant impact on the use of foreign labor. Government-imposed restrictions on immigration and emigration have already eased in some countries. By the end of the 1980s, for instance, the nations of Eastern Europe had abandoned their restrictions on the rights of their citizens to leave. At the same time, most Western European nations were negotiating the abolition of all limits on people's movements within the boundaries of the European Union. The United States, Canada, and even Japan also began to liberalize immigration policies. Although most governments in industrialized nations will resist large-scale immigration for social and political reasons, nations that have slow-growing workforces but rapid growth in service-sector jobs (namely Japan, Germany, and the United States) will likely become magnets for immigrants. Nations that produce prospective workers faster than their economies can absorb them (such as Argentina, Poland, and the Philippines) will export people.

With the rapid growth of the hotel industry in China, recruitment has become a very stressful and creative exercise for hotel human resource managers there. They now look for workers not only in the communities surrounding their hotels but also in China's interior provinces and secondary cities. Because the existing supply of qualified employees is not keeping up with demand, Chinese hotel companies have had to widen their recruiting net even farther, looking outside the country in such places as Hong Kong, Indonesia, the Philippines, Dubai in the Middle East, and India. These recruiting expeditions target not only people in the hotel industry but also workers in related industries such as the cruise ship and financial services industries. China's large hotel companies have formed alliances with (or created their own) hospitality education institutions to ensure a supply of qualified supervisory employees. About 40 percent of the hotels in China remain state-owned enterprises, and these hotels have problems with *overstaffing* rather than understaffing. This problem is a legacy of the old Communist planned economy and "iron rice bowl" (guaranteed employment) system, which did not allow for market-driven adjustments to staffing levels. The recruiting problems of these hotels are best described in the aphorism, "Loyal but obsolete people will not go; young and talented people cannot come."[3]

Job Perceptions Affecting Recruitment

Recruitment strategies generally need to be adjusted by country because of the cultural biases that affect the meaning of a hospitality job. For example, most Japanese hotel firms prefer to hire recruits directly from school, when they are most susceptible to being indoctrinated with the company's philosophy. A typical Japanese high school or university graduate will search for a first job with the belief that the job will be long-term. His or her initial negotiations will cover, therefore, not only salary, but insurance, welfare, retirement funds, and future prospects with the company.

In Western Europe (the United Kingdom notwithstanding), hotel service as a profession has a long and honorable history. Job seekers often view it as a permanent career with a formal apprenticeship system. A network of schools exists to teach the necessary skills and provide a pool of trained staff. By contrast, in the United States the perception of hotel service jobs is less lofty. These jobs are still denigrated by some and considered an interim career by many. Many employers therefore accept high staff turnover as being inevitable. However, more progressive hotel companies have introduced incentive plans, including child care and professional counseling services, to reduce turnover and build staff loyalty.

Family or Educational Status

Another aspect of recruitment that needs to be considered is that, in some countries, individuals holding university degrees or coming from upper-class families may expect the same level of respect at work that they receive at home and in their communities. Young university graduates in Latin America, the Middle East, and parts of the Far East may refuse hands-on work, which they view as low-status or degrading. When a young person gets a degree, he or she often expects to receive preferential treatment with respect to an office, a "clean" job, and a high salary, despite a lack of managerial experience or business qualifications. In other situations, people use family connections to seek employment. If the hotel's owner has favorite relatives and friends to recommend, saying no can be difficult. Being politically sensitive in handling this situation is always advised.

Impacts of Hotel Class

The class of the hotel may also affect recruitment of local workers. In some communities, the class of the hotel is identified with the socio-economic levels of the community itself. If a member of a socially prominent family chooses to work in a hotel, the property selected will typically be a five-star deluxe hotel and the position will likely require a title. A pecking order with respect to the status of departments in the hotel will be obvious. The front end of the hotel will be more prestigious than food and beverage, which in turn has more status than housekeeping. Even within food and beverage, regardless of pay, employees are less satisfied to be placed with the coffee shop than with the grillroom. Generally, the more basic the task, the lower the status; and the higher the guest contact requirement, the higher the status.

Hiring for Joint Ventures

For joint venture hotels with a local business partner, caution must be exercised when hiring personnel. Some local partners have used the joint hotel venture not only as a place for employing friends and relatives, but also as a dumping ground for people who are no longer needed in other ventures owned by the partners. In accepting the latter, however, it may become virtually impossible to eliminate them. Whether this occurrence is likely to happen depends a great deal on the magnitude of the investment and the motivation of the foreign partner in entering the business relationship. It is always advisable to have the quality of staffing and recruitment strategies clearly defined during initial joint venture negotiations.

Factors Affecting the Hiring Decision

In the United States, an employer considering an individual for a position will generally weigh evidence of the candidate's potential strengths and weaknesses against a set of criteria required for the job. In other countries, the candidate's personality and social behavior in the workplace may outweigh the specific knowledge or skill requirements. While it would be discriminatory and illegal to hire anyone on such vagaries as "personality" or "social behavior" in, say, Australia, the United States, or Canada, this practice is more often than not acceptable elsewhere. Nor are race, gender, age, and other forms of discrimination necessarily prohibited in more than theory in some parts of the world. But the fair transnational employer as a rule attempts to hire on the basis of qualifications as much as possible regardless of location.

The job interview can be a very different experience as well, depending on the country. In some countries, for example, it is immodest for job applicants to speak highly of themselves, so a job seeker might bring a spokesperson (perhaps an uncle or cousin) or various sorts of documentation along on the interview. In India and Pakistan, an interviewee may present school records, diplomas, and awards in lieu of speaking about accomplishments. In East Asia, even the most highly skilled job applicants tend to understate their qualifications during the interview; the employer has to know their individual histories or see evidence of individual work to get a true picture of their capabilities.

Orientation

Job orientation for hotel industry positions is not the same everywhere. Transnational hotel operators may provide lengthy or brief orientation programs, depending on the maturity or experience of the workforce, the degree of training recruits have had, the expected length of the recruits' employment, and culturally based attitudes toward service, among other factors. In most Japanese hotel companies, for example, new recruits undergo a three- to six–month induction period for the purpose of being introduced to the company philosophy and trained specifically for new responsibilities. This orientation and training, called *shikomu*, includes not only skills and techniques, but morality and group norms as well. New employees are oriented to the company's culture, traditions, and methods of operation. The purpose of this extended orientation is to build loyalty. Outside of Japan, Japanese hotel companies may not use this employment strategy in areas where they consider the turnover rate to be too high, say in Hong Kong or the United States.

The Oriental Hotel in Bangkok also takes an atypical approach to employee orientation. New employees are taken on a retreat to a Buddhist monastery. Building on the hotel's basic philosophy that people matter and that a hotel is made for people and by people, the orientation retreat is designed to shape new employees' overall attitudes toward people, life, and their communities. The orientation attempts to affect the core beliefs of new employees, not superficially influence them through a more typical scripted orientation program.[4]

Cultural Attitudes toward Service

Culturally influenced attitudes toward hospitality service affect many aspects of hotel human resource administration. In the orientation of new employees, these attitudes need to be explicitly addressed.

The desirability of hospitality employment has long been viewed with skepticism or mixed reaction in many parts of the world. A bias against hospitality employment, even in some developing countries with a critical need for jobs, is all too common. The problem often involves the lack of a clear distinction between "service" and "servitude." Native Chamorros in Guam, for instance, have little problem with extending service to foreign visitors, but feel differently about waiting on fellow residents. Taking care of visitors is seen as offering service, but serving residents is viewed as servitude. The fact that service is not a popular pursuit for most workers in Israel, for another example, has been a perpetual problem for that country's hotel industry. Many Israeli parents would rather have their children sit at home and do nothing than be food servers or housekeepers. However, with the advent of good hotel and tourism training programs in more countries—many assisted by international organizations, notably the International Labor Organization and the World Tourism Organization—there is evidence that these negative attitudes about hospitality employment are gradually changing.

Universality of Hospitality

Some type of hospitality tradition exists in virtually all cultures. The expression of hospitality may differ from culture to culture, but the welcome will be equally genuine in most cases. The culturally sensitive manager will make it his or her business to discover the customs and traditions of hospitality in order to reinforce, during orientation and training, their practice and value in the workplace. In Hawaii, for example, there is a resurgence of Hawaiian cultural values in the community, and visionary hotel managers are hiring qualified Hawaiian trainers to teach these values to both their native and non-native employees. Cultural training is viewed as a means not only of strengthening service standards in the Hawaiian tradition, but also of helping both native employees rediscover the value of their own cultural heritage and non-native employees discover for the first time the richness and beauty of the Hawaiian culture.

The service experience is a social experience. As such, it involves human interaction and communication. The nature of the interaction is determined by the cultures of the interacting parties. Culture determines what both the hotelkeeper and the guest perceive as service needs, the manner in which they will communicate, what they value, and how they will respond to each other. Hotel workers enter the service exchange with a predisposition to certain behaviors based on their own national or ethnic culture as well as the culture of the hotel organization they represent. The guest also brings "cultural baggage" to the experience, a predisposition to expect and react in culturally prescribed ways. For hotels with a large international clientele, these issues should all be addressed during the hotel's orientation program.

Training in a Multicultural Environment

Hotels are increasingly being confronted with the challenge of training service providers to communicate with people who perceive, think, and behave differently from themselves. It is important for managers to develop in the staff a sensitivity to the special needs of international visitors. For many hotel employees, dealing with foreigners can be disconcerting. An unfamiliar language, custom, or appearance may seem awkward. Rather than make the extra effort, some employees will pass the task on to someone else who feels less threatened with the situation. Daily contact with the hotel staff should make foreign visitors feel comfortable. Most foreign guests already feel somewhat vulnerable. Hotel employees need additional training in serving culturally different guests if the hotel is to maintain its standards of service.

Cross-cultural staff training addresses several of the problems associated with handling international guests. The rationale for such training is that most people, despite good intentions, are not easily able to function outside of their own culture. However, they can be taught how to function in different cultures and develop skills for interacting with culturally different people. They can also be taught to deliver appropriate service to culturally different guests.

Experience seems to indicate that generic training programs developed in one country do not normally work well abroad. When the training is not culture-specific, trainees may find the training interesting but irrelevant. To be meaningful, training techniques must be sensitive to each group's desire for active or passive participation, short or lengthy discourse, and other variables in the training process.

To develop a successful training program abroad, a four-part strategy is advised:

- *Step 1: Analyze the situation.* The first step in any training program is to determine what skills need to be developed, taking into consideration the local workforce's level of education and hospitality training, foreign language ability, hotel experience, and general aptitude for the job. Cultural idiosyncrasies should be examined for their impact on work behaviors. The training task is then defined by the gap between the worker's capabilities and the requirements of the job plus the resources needed for training.

- *Step 2: Consider the training options.* The next step is to determine what existing training resources are available within the hotel company. Are individuals or mobile teams available with the needed technical or professional skills and the ability to train cross-culturally? What training materials and aids are available from the company for local adaptation? Would trainees fare better by getting hands-on experience at an affiliated property within the chain? Would there be support from the top for externships? Should the hotel sponsor or co-sponsor an in-house training program with a qualified local or a better-known foreign hospitality institution? What are the costs and benefits of each option?

- *Step 3: Prepare trainers.* The successful transfer of knowledge depends on the ability of the instructor to establish rapport and communicate effectively with trainees. Some trainers can be trained cross-culturally to achieve such goals. To the extent possible, trainers should understand the technical, cultural, and organizational background of the people being trained. They should have a high degree of cultural awareness and be able to recognize and interpret the cultural biases that they themselves bring to the training situation. If the cultural gap between trainers and trainees is too wide, intermediaries will be needed, but at the price of interpersonal rapport. As a general rule, the best trainer for day-to-day, ongoing training is someone of the same culture. Therefore, in certain circumstances, the most effective way to train may be to select a local national with the requisite technical skills and provide that person with training expertise. In other circumstances, and depending on the country, the trainees may hold a foreign trainer in higher esteem.

- *Step 4: Prepare the trainees.* To the extent possible, local employees should be given the first opportunity to enter training programs, especially in the case of management-level training. Employees should be pre-sold on the value of training. They should not see training as punishment for deficient performance. If there is to be reading material in a language that is not the native tongue (as is often the case with training materials in English), the material should be distributed in advance so that trainees may get a head start. When training is selective (as in the case of management seminars) and employees are aware of the importance of such training, management should be prepared to explain the process by which candidates were chosen, and to identify what training opportunities might be available to those who were excluded.

Supervision

The supervision of employees in a multicultural or foreign environment requires management sensitivity to culturally based work behaviors. It also requires acceptance or at least understanding of employment practices that have developed over a long period, influenced by a country's history, religion, and political situation. Three aspects of supervision that are likely to be influenced by cultural differences are motivation and productivity, decision-making, and communication (including the ability to listen effectively).

Motivation and Productivity

Managers must understand the local work ethic if they are to understand what motivates employees. In Japan, for instance, people are connected to their companies. Their attention and energies are concentrated on the company—their personal life *is* their company life. Compared with, say, Americans, who tend to be job-oriented rather than company-oriented, the Japanese are typically much better informed about their company's business. They easily step outside their own tasks to help colleagues. The practice of *shikomu*, which requires workers to know all jobs through rotational training and to internalize the values of the company, makes it possible for workers to cooperate closely.

Hotel managers need to understand the value placed on material possessions when trying to motivate people from another culture. Whereas American companies typically motivate with money or money-related rewards, the Japanese are accustomed to being motivated by information, affiliation, and other means besides money. Money, on the other hand, is a powerful motivator in developing countries where the basic needs of employees and their families have not been met. Indeed, money, rather than recognition, is the preferred incentive in many countries.

Competition as Motivation. While individual initiative and competition in the workplace is greatly admired in Western cultures, they are not always similarly admired in other cultures. The problem is more one of aggressive behavior and overt competitiveness than one of initiative or ability to out-perform. Overt individual competitiveness is frowned upon in many Asian cultures, where cooperation is considered an art form. In these cultures, overt competition in the workplace means everyone loses, because it creates winners and losers in an environment that prizes teamwork more highly than individual achievement.

Since Japanese and Chinese management styles emphasize building cooperation among members of a department, a manager will usually try to inspire hard work by setting a good example. If one of the workers is less capable than others, the manager is likely to spend more time directing and guiding that worker, perhaps assigning a competent co-worker as mentor. If one of the workers is less diligent than desired, the manager will skillfully use peer pressure to bring about a change in that person's attitude. Since the group is held responsible for the performance of all of its members, a slack worker is a great source of irritation to everyone.

Latin Americans are motivated to work not for a company, but for an individual. Relationships are much more personalized. Managers can get performance only by effectively using personal influence and working through individual members of a group. If Latin American workers feel favorably disposed toward their manager or supervisor, they will express loyalty to that person and strive not to let him or her down. On the other hand, they tend to exhibit negative work behaviors when they do not like their superiors, regardless of the company.

In Sweden, monetary rewards are less motivating than providing paid holidays in vacation villages. To the French, the quality of life is paramount. The French value their free time and vacations; they generally resist working overtime

Exhibit 2 Working Hours per Week and Holidays around the World

Country	Normal Working Hours per Week	Number of Mandatory Public Holidays
Australia	Typically 38–46	At least 9, depending on the industry/region
Brazil	44 (max)	10
China	40	10
Czech Republic	40	11
France	35	10
Germany	Typically 38 hours	9–13, depending on the state (collectively agreed)
India	48 (max)	Private establishments: 8–10, depending on the state
Italy	40	11
Japan	40	15
Mexico	40	8
South Africa	45 (max)	12
United Arab Emirates	48 (max)	9
United Kingdom	48 (max)	8
United States	40	10

Source: *Mercer 2007* Worldwide Benefit & Employment Guidelines.

and have one of the longest vacation periods in the world—a minimum of five weeks a year by law.[5] Germans are heading in this direction, too. However, both French and German workers have a reputation for being productive and quality-conscious while at work.

Working Hours. Average working hours per week and holidays vary around the world (see Exhibit 2). In most industrialized nations, the normal work week is around 40 hours (France has the lowest at 35 hours per week). In some emerging countries (such as India, where a six-day work week is still the norm), the average week may consist of 48 hours. It is important for hotel managers going abroad to understand the relative importance of money, time, social status, and holiday variables as motivators in each host country. It is also important to recognize that in some countries, individual company policy notwithstanding, working hours, annual leave, sick leave, and the like are regulated by law and heavily influenced by prevailing business practices.

Incentive Programs and Rewards. Cultural sensitivity needs to be demonstrated when designing incentive and reward programs. What is appropriate and motivating in the United States may have different results abroad. The American pay-for-performance system emanates from civil rights laws and efforts to be fair in setting compensation differentials. However, it can be extremely demanding of employees from cultures that are not accustomed to such thinking. Tying performance to rewards in some cultures would be comparable to parents implementing a system of feeding each family member in accordance with that member's contribution to the family income. In societies that lean toward collectivism, the principles applied to family members apply to employees as well. Also, rewards for workers in some countries may be limited. In the former Soviet Union, for instance, bonuses were common and based on a percentage of salary, but money was not an effective motivator because there was practically nothing to buy. In contrast, the tremendous craving for Western goods made imported Western products a more powerful source of motivation.

Appreciation, depending on how it is expressed, can be an effective motivator. In Taiwan, the most highly sought reward is social recognition from the top. Cash bonuses are given out across the board, but departments compete for top management's public praise at the annual celebration. Chinese workers in the People's Republic of China are far more comfortable with group rewards, such as department or unit productivity bonuses, although new types of incentive and motivation plans have been slowly introduced. Hotel operators in China have experimented with a floating-salary system that rewards exceptional work performance with a pay bonus. They have also used a program that rewards performance with foreign training, usually at a Hong Kong hotel.

For U.S. hotels with large numbers of Hispanic employees, traditional incentive programs may need to be adjusted or designed with a variety of award options. Some Hispanic employees, for example, may not be motivated by the chance to win an incentive trip if they cannot take their children, as family time together is culturally important. The challenge for hotel managers, therefore, is to effectively match the appropriate rewards with the values of each culture.

Decision-Making

A great deal of literature has been written on management styles and decision-making in recent decades. In the 1980s and early 1990s, a lot of comparative studies came out on American and Japanese management styles. With Japan's success in producing superior products and services for the international marketplace in those years, American management and decision-making styles came under closer scrutiny and debate. Increasingly, the best features of both styles are taught in management classes in many colleges and universities today. Traditional theories of management have also been well researched in Britain, France, and Germany, and these theories are standards in management textbooks. What is yet lacking is sufficient research into the cultural styles of management outside of the Western nations and Japan.

Decision-making and management are intertwined. Indeed, there is a school of thought that refers to "management by decision," which means that the true manager is the one who makes decisions, or, more accurately, the one who makes exceptional decisions. Just as management is culturally influenced, so may decisions and the decisional process itself have a cultural bias.

U.S. Decision-Making. In the United States, the prevailing business practice is to encourage managers to assume personal responsibility for their operations; top managers are compensated better than in any other country. This often results in limited worker participation in decision-making. With direct accountability usually being an integral part of managerial responsibility, supervisors dictate decisions that are carried out by employees. Known as "top-down" decision-making, this style can optimize managerial performance and provide rapid and flexible decision-making, but it ties the company's success to the talents of a few key individuals. Over the past few decades, an increasing number of businesses and organizations have adopted new management ideas and practices (for example, total quality management) to include the contributions of *all* employees.

Japanese Decision-Making. In Japan, a bottom-up approach to decisions is most common, and the principle of collective responsibility is employed. Senior management is likely to provide only broad guidelines to a department; the department is then expected to set goals based on those guidelines and to design a strategy by which the goals can be attained. The key department heads will then approach their line employees for suggestions as to the best method for promoting or reaching the desired goals. The ultimate decision, however, remains at the top. The Japanese theory is that the act of involving as many employees as possible improves company loyalty and motivation levels and also helps to guarantee that every facet of a proposed decision will be covered. This approach also ensures that those being affected by the decision fully understand its rationale and implications. Having employees take responsibility for the solution to problems is common and even expected in Japanese companies.

Decision-making in Japan is a longer process than elsewhere, because it involves getting the consent of all executives before a decision is ratified. Consensus-building slows the process, but refines the decision, so that once it is made a decision can be quickly implemented and employees seldom lose direction.

Decision-Making in Other Cultures. Expatriate managers on foreign assignments have often been amazed to find multi-level approval needed for the authorization of even routine decisions. In many places in the world, companies are still very much run from the top office. Even where efforts have been made to delegate decision-making power, employees continue to seek the approval of superiors.

French, German, and Italian managers are inclined to believe that a tight rein of authority is needed to obtain adequate job performance and that there is more prestige in directing than in persuading. In South Asia and South America, those with authority believe employees want a strong manager who gives orders, and workers traditionally do not question the actions of their managers. Great Britain's colonial and civil service heritage emphasized decentralized decision-making, but decentralized ideals frequently clash with the country's class system, where executives and other leaders are more often than not the products of prestigious schools and universities. While the tenets of democracy are fostered and cherished in British institutions, their management in practice leans toward bureaucracy, and decisions usually remain the prerogative of management.[6]

In African and Arab countries, executives have strong traditions of consultation in decision-making. Senior members of ruling families or the community are still sometimes consulted on matters of importance. The consultation method is used almost to the exclusion of joint decision-making or delegation. Arabs prefer consultation on a person-to-person basis; they dislike committees and group meetings and usually make decisions in an informal and unstructured manner.

For hotel managers who want to promote participatory management in a culture where this is not common, a great deal of teaching and guidance may be required. The alternative is adapting one's own management style to the accepted practice of the host country. It takes time to change deeply ingrained customs. In the process, the manager will have to deal with confusion and tension. If the manager's efforts are taken for ignorance or weakness, foreign workers may disregard the manager altogether.

Communication

Listening is a vital aspect of communication for managers in a multicultural environment. This does not mean simply learning the language. It also means developing behaviors and sensitivities that enable the manager to accurately understand not only the words, but also the person speaking. Managers spend more of their day listening than engaging in any other communication activity. When a cross-cultural dimension is added to the already difficult task of listening, it is easy to understand how miscommunication may occur. However, when managers fail to listen, employees become hesitant to talk. Such an environment fosters higher turnover, lower job satisfaction, and less employee commitment and participation.

Many misunderstandings result from the fact that the speaker's words were never heard correctly in the first place. In noisy kitchens, behind busy front desks, and in crowded lobbies, it is difficult enough to hear *any* speaker. When the speaker has a different first language, the problem is magnified.

Repeating a message back to the speaker is one way to ensure that the message was correctly heard. Managers with good listening skills also pay attention to nonverbal communication. While direct eye contact may express interest and concern in one culture, in another it may be interpreted as a threat or a sign of disrespect. The degree to which feelings are expressed nonverbally varies significantly from one culture to the next.

Managers must strive to listen with objectivity and to understand the issue or problem from the point of view of the person speaking. Only then will managers encourage employees to communicate their concerns upward, participate in decision-making, and collaborate with their colleagues. Creating an environment of trust and information-sharing becomes a key management function.

Language Differences. Particularly in regions where hotels use much immigrant or imported labor, language differences among staff can present serious managerial difficulties. Strategies for dealing with language issues in hotels have ranged from removing the need for employees to learn the host country's language (by concentrating specific ethnic groups in one department or providing translations) to helping employees learn the host country's language.

Translators are sometimes used to help conduct interviews, orient and train new employees, and conduct performance evaluations. Some hotels provide written translations of job descriptions, employee handbooks, orientation materials, and training manuals. Efforts to teach foreign workers the language range from instructing them in basic expressions required for proper guest service to implementing full-scale second-language training programs. To be successful, the latter require a strong commitment on the part of managers and employees.

Compensation and Benefits

With few exceptions, payroll and related expenses are the most costly items on hotel financial statements everywhere. According to the Deloitte worldwide HotelBenchmark Annual Profitability Survey, payroll costs in Europe are highest, at 34 percent of total revenue. Payroll and related expenses for hotels in the Middle East are 18 percent of total revenue, and Asian hotels recorded payroll costs of 28 percent of total revenue.[7]

To a large extent, payroll-related costs reflect a country's level of economic development, standard of living, tax structures, legally required employee benefits, and traditional industry practice. But labor costs are also a reflection of the labor market conditions in each country. The shrinking supply of workers in the newly industrialized countries of East and Southeast Asia, for example, has led to staff "pinching" or pirating, and sharply rising wages in hotels anxious to retain skilled employees. Rising wages, while beneficial to employees, have in turn led to rising room rates, a consequence that reduces competitiveness. Because hotel investment decisions are based in part on labor as a variable, high labor costs and unfavorable labor markets become a deterrent to attracting investments for new projects or expansions.

A hotel's benefit plan should be designed and administered to comply with all legal and tax obligations. It should also meet the needs of employees and the hotel in terms of attracting and retaining good workers. The earnings package for employees in the international hotel industry varies, but it typically contains a combination of the basic hourly rate, overtime payments to compensate for unsocial working hours, service charge contributions (where applicable), tips, and non-wage benefits including subsidized lodging and food. This package can be greatly influenced by the presence or absence of unions, the strength of such unions, and prevailing business practices.

Japanese hotel companies, for example, provide their workers with a semi-annual bonus in June and December. The two bonuses together can equal anywhere from two to six months' salary. Originally conceived as a sort of profit-sharing plan, the bonuses are now a standard part of compensation packages. Because this bonus is anticipated and awarded indiscriminately (the amount is often negotiated in advance), it has little value as an incentive for increasing productivity or quality of work. Other common benefits in Japan include transportation passes for employees, full health care plans for employees' families, marriage and childbirth allowances, assistance with home purchase financing, sometimes free dormitory-style apartments for younger employees, and overnight facilities in the hotel for employees with late and early shifts to relieve early morning commuting. The Japanese example is becoming a trend in Hong Kong and other booming Asian cities as well.

Pension plans may also reflect the different roles of government and public policies from country to country. In South European countries, for example, pensions are expected to be set at 40 percent of salaries, while in the Nordic countries they are set at about 85 percent. The total hotel compensation package, including basic wages, paid holidays, home leaves, meals, subsidies, and so forth, plus payroll taxes and government-imposed surcharges need to be fully understood by owners, operators, and especially managers who administer the payroll. All of these salary and non-salary items need to be taken into consideration when developing compensation packages abroad and planning for employee-related expenses.

China's compensation laws and policies have evolved from the pre-economic-reform period prior to 1978. Until that time, pay scales were determined by the Chinese government. After 1993, as Chinese markets continued to open up, the central government's role in determining compensation has been minimized. Pay scales and compensation packages in China are now determined largely by the market forces of supply and demand. In most cases, municipal and provincial governments stipulate minimum wages for hourly employees. While the compensation systems of hotels in China's private sector are progressive and contain programs and benefits comparable to those of a typical hotel in the West, state-owned hotels still have remnants of the "iron rice bowl" system. In most state-owned enterprises, the wages are low, but welfare benefits—such as free housing and lifelong hospitalization benefits—are high.[8]

Based on a recent International Labor Organization publication that surveyed 103 countries about annual leave and vacation policies, one-third of the countries surveyed offered 24 to 26 days of paid annual leave. In industrialized countries, annual leave ranged from a low of 10 days in Japan to a high of 30 days in Denmark, Finland, and France. Australia and the United States have no nationally applicable limit. Leave policies in Central and Eastern European countries are quite homogeneous at 24 days. A greater diversity of leave policies exists on the African continent, with Nigeria offering only 6 days of paid leave and Algeria 30 days. A similar diversity of policies exists among Latin American countries. Asian countries have the least-extensive leave provisions, fewer than 15 days.[9]

Trade Unions and Unionism

In most countries, unionization of the hotel industry has not been a significant factor. Some reasons for this are the hotel industry's fragmented structure, its typically high labor turnover, and the abundant immigrant labor used in entry-level positions in some countries. By the nature of their work and unsocial working hours, hotel workers have historically been isolated from the mainstream of the labor movement in most countries. There has also been a perception in many countries that the notion of service is not entirely compatible with traditional trade unionism, which is founded on pride in making manufactured products and on the high social worth of what workers do.

Tipping and subsidized food and accommodations have also hindered union growth in the hotel industry because they remove feelings of worker solidarity and promote the fear that unions could eliminate this source of income with the negotiation of blanket wage rates. Blanket wage rates would also expose more of the hotel workers' pay to taxation. Therefore, the emphasis on basic pay and formalized procedures traditionally associated with collective bargaining may be viewed as retrogressive by hotel workers.

Contrasting Examples of Unionism

The following examples of unions in the United Kingdom, Japan, China, and elsewhere indicate the range of effects unions have on the hotel operating environment. As a general rule, however, any union or labor problem in the hotel industry will also be affected by cultural issues. Expatriate hotel managers will make little progress in labor arrangements if they are insensitive to the cultural patterns of their host society.

United Kingdom. In the United Kingdom, many hotel workers associate union activity with deductions from, or perhaps restrictions to, the total payment system rather than improvements to it. This is true even though the Hotel and Catering Workers Union (HCWU) has sought improvements in all terms and conditions of work. Many "core" hotel workers (whose employment tends to be relatively stable and whose labor is vital for the smooth running of the hotel because of their professional skills, reliability, and length of service) are inclined to be skeptical about the advantages to be gained from trade union membership. On the other hand, "peripheral workers" or casual hires are more inclined to favor unionism.

Japan. Every spring in Japan, there is a ceremony known as *shunto*, meaning "spring wage offensive." The bargaining opens with each industry's union federation setting out its pay demands for the year. The Japan Federation of Employers' Associations (Nekkeiren) then publishes an economic forecast, usually indicating that employers cannot meet the pay demands, and suggests matching pay increases to productivity improvements. The unions in a leading industry typically negotiate a compromise pay raise along these lines and the other industries follow suit, followed by the far bigger ranks of non-unionized labor. Pay is usually the central issue in these negotiations. Since Japan has been in an economic decline since the booming years of the 1980s and early 1990s, and since union membership has fallen over the years, the value of the *shunto* and the wage increases associated with it have been jeopardized. The emphasis in recent years has been the protection of existing pay structures and jobs.

More and more, Japanese workers have been concerned with quality-of-life issues. The government has taken a lead in attempting to improve quality of life by closing some offices on Saturdays and trying to get big firms to follow suit. The government also reduced the standard work week from 48 hours to 40 hours.

South Korea. In the past, the South Korean government would call out the police if workers went on strike. That is no longer the approach, however, and the labor force in South Korea has highly unionized. Unions there are organized by company rather than by industry; rather than having an equivalent of the U.S. United Auto Workers Union, for example, each South Korean company or conglomerate has its own union. Employees of hotels owned or managed by unionized corporations are required to become members of the corporation's union. However, because these unions are dominated by members from the corporation's manufacturing divisions, hotel workers who belong to these unions are less likely to have their issues addressed.[10] Also, union leaders have often been unable to control their members or bargain effectively with management and it is unclear how this situation will evolve.

China. China's leading body representing trade unions in the country is the All-China Federation of Trade Unions. Trade unions in China are working-class organizations formed on a voluntary basis under the leadership of the Chinese Communist Party. Unions are organized by trade (each defined job position has a union) and geographic location. Trade unions in China are organized for three primary purposes. First, they serve as a link between managers and workers by educating workers on management policies and communicating worker opinions to management. Second, they serve as training schools to conduct ideological, technical, and cultural programs for workers. Third, they promote the welfare of workers by helping them resolve disputes with management related to compensation and benefits, helping them find jobs if they are laid off, and supporting their families during periods of unemployment.[11]

Still, the issue of unionization is more or less moot. Although unions are legal and ostensibly have broad powers, they do not exercise many of these powers and they do not play an adversarial role. Unions play a special role in the enterprise and supervise certain areas of employee relations and benefits. Expatriate managers working in China need to recognize the union as a management assistance tool and an organization that looks after the personal needs and welfare of employees.

Germany. Union membership in Germany has declined steadily over the last three decades. Today, just one in five workers is a union member; the German Confederation of Trade Unions *(Deutscher Gewerkschaftsbund)*, an umbrella organization for eight German trade unions, has lost 40 percent of its membership in 14 years.[12] This decline in union membership is attributable in part to the same external forces that have confronted unions in many other countries (such as globalization and changing demographics within the country's population). The reunification of Germany also had an impact on the country's unions, as they had to make concessions to management in terms of both pay and working hours because of the availability and low cost of the former East Germany's labor force. Antistrike laws have also reduced the bargaining leverage of Germany's unions.

Human Resource Development

Human resource development (HRD) issues are, for the most part, similar whether the hotel operates in a domestic or in a foreign environment. Standards of performance, job specifications, and the need for career development and human resource planning require similar efforts regardless of the hotel's locale. In the measurement of individual performance, however, different cultures may have their own distinctive approaches. For instance, employees in some cultures may feel it inappropriate to challenge a superior's assessment; and some supervisors may interpret an employee's silence as concurrence, when this is not the case. Hotel management must handle performance appraisals (as well as any needed disciplinary or corrective actions) with an awareness of the host country's established practices. Discipline and corrective actions, which are sensitive to begin with, are a necessary part of HRD if appraisals are to be useful in helping employees correct mistakes.

Performance Appraisals

The use of performance appraisals implies that performance is important and that it can be measured or appraised objectively. Performance appraisals as they are used in the United States have a strong American bias. They involve a database that is measured objectively, recorded quantitatively, and kept permanently in an employee's records. They also make use of goals or behavioral standards to be measured against targets in an annual review. There are a number of assumptions inherent in this system.

While research in the United States on the efficacy of performance appraisals remains unsettled, appraisals in theory assume that feedback given to employees will be accepted and used constructively to correct or improve upon past performance. This assumes a Western cultural view of mankind as having control over the environment and being able to change the course of events. In Eastern cultures, the opposite belief prevails—mankind lives in harmony with the environment, and destiny is preordained. Giving direct feedback also ignores the problem of "saving face" so crucial to many Eastern cultures, where confronting an employee with "failure" in an open, direct manner would be considered tactless.

Among Turks and Arabs, employees tend to be evaluated in terms of their loyalty to superiors rather than their actual job performance. In Taiwan, Hong Kong, Singapore, and South Korea, performance appraisals are also more relationship-oriented, stemming from Confucianist management practices. Managers are paternalistic figures to their employees. Just as a parent is responsible for the child's behavior, so the manager is responsible for the employee's performance. When employees do not do well, their "parents" share the blame. Hence, in cultures with a Confucianist heritage, superiors are reluctant to write critical evaluations. Employers, like parents, also do not abandon their charges who cannot live up to group standards.

The following two examples illustrate two non-Western approaches to performance appraisals.

Taiwan. The most commonly used appraisal methods in Taiwan are rating scales, essays, and forced distribution. These methods are imbedded in a socio-cultural context characterized by collectivism and large power distance. Each department in a Taiwanese company is viewed as a family within a larger clan system. The department head is viewed as the paternal figure in the family. Departmental or "sibling" rivalry is a subtle, yet powerful aspect of organizational life in Taiwan. Taiwanese bonuses tend to be based on non-performance criteria, such as an employee's need for extra cash to support a large family or to pay for unusual misfortunes. Cash bonuses are generally handed out at the Chinese New Year with the understanding that it is the basic work groups and the cooperating departments as a whole that have contributed to the success of the company. The greater the company's profits, the greater are the bonuses across the board. The Chinese norm for fairness and social harmony translates into the belief that no single employee can accomplish the mission or task alone. Interdependence is stressed over independence as much as collectivism is favored over individualism.

Performance appraisals in Taiwan are generally not future-oriented. Specific objectives or goals are not established for each employee. The Chinese culture is so infused with the concept of destiny that the idea of individuality and one's unique ability to affect future events seems pointless.

Japan. In Japan, performance appraisal methods and standards are subjective. They also tend to appraise traits instead of achievements. There is more concern with judging a person's integrity, morality, loyalty, and cooperative spirit than his or her actual performance. In Japan, appraisals happen more often and are more private; seldom are they recorded. They are more qualitative, and are inclined to motivate and mold desirable behavior as well as to appraise. Whereas the American system uses performance appraisals as a source of monetary and career motivation, and a lack of performance may eventually lead to a discharge, the Japanese system allows an employee to progress on the pay ladder by virtue of age and rank. The hospitality industry in Japan tends to follow the pattern of other Japanese corporations; that is, recruiting new high school and college graduates, providing industry-specific training, and gradually promoting them. Since promotion is primarily a reflection of the passage of time, age and rank are usually synchronized. It is rare to find Japanese hotel executives who have worked their way to the upper echelons of management before the age of 50. It is rarer yet to find an executive who climbed the corporate ladder by frequently switching company allegiances.

Corrective Actions

According to Western theories of management, employees are supposed to accept criticism as valuable feedback. Assuming that employees in other countries will similarly accept such criticism may be a mistake. To Arabs, Africans, Asians, and Latin Americans, preservation of dignity is an all-important value. Those who lose self-respect, or the respect of others, dishonor both themselves and their families. Public criticism is intolerable to the extent that employees may either unite in antagonism against the manager who criticizes or leave the job altogether. In a unionized work situation, an employee grievance might be filed. Corrective actions abroad must be undertaken with an awareness of the prevailing practices and laws governing such actions.

Discharge

Discharging an employee can prove very difficult in a foreign country. The American practice of firing for just cause or laying off according to business conditions is perceived as brutal in almost every other country. Workers in many countries are protected by strong labor laws and union rules. The hotel manager who is unaware of this risks costly lawsuits and penalties as well as damage to the reputation of the hotel as a place to work. A Mexican labor law, for example, gives workers complete protection. After a 30-day trial period, they are regarded as virtually permanent employees. British law protects managers against "loss of office." Belgian labor laws are among the toughest in the world, and Belgian social benefits are also the most liberal in Europe.

In China particularly, dismissal is a very serious step because of the degree to which the individual is dependent on the work unit for economic survival. The employer who does not understand the consequence of "taking away one's rice bowl" (although the iron rice bowl—or guaranteed employment policy—is changing along with market economy reforms) may pay a high political price for the lesson. If there is an employee problem, the Chinese prefer "education through criticism"; that is, they want to make the worker see the error of his or her ways and, through criticism or persuasion, mend them. For any disciplinary action, the trade union must first be consulted.

Most labor laws throughout Europe prohibit companies from laying people off in hard economic times. In Indonesia, people cannot be fired without a long process of government red tape. A manager must give an employee three written warnings over a period of a year, specifying complaints, with written copies distributed to labor officials. The manager also must meet with the employee to suggest changes in performance, and do it diplomatically. Compensation for termination also varies widely among countries.

Even where specific laws do not tie employee to employer, discharging is not always without consequences. In many developing countries, a wrongful discharge can lead to a boycott of the hotel, a walkout by other employees, and even violent retaliation against managers.

Summary

Probably no subject is closer to the heart of the transnational hotel operator than international human resource management or IHRM. Without an adequate supply of qualified workers, the operator will go out of business. How the staff members perform and behave toward guests and one another is conditioned in part by environmental factors and values in which culture plays a big role. IHRM attempts to address the management of staff from a broader perspective than simply workplace or job requirements. It considers employees' needs, motivations, and attitudes within the context of their own cultures.

Since an inadequate labor supply is a perennial problem for the hospitality industry in general, effective recruitment, retention, training, and supervision are major concerns in IHRM. In many countries, non-traditional sources of labor are considered along with conventional sources. High turnover can be reduced by improving wage levels and working conditions, overcoming cultural biases against service jobs, offering better and more appropriate training, improving the quality of supervision through cross-cultural training, and improving job incentives and rewards systems.

The supervision of employees in a multicultural or foreign environment requires management sensitivity to culturally based work behaviors. Employees from different cultures generally have different values and feelings about their companies, jobs, relationships with their supervisors, material rewards, free time, and so forth, and these will affect motivation. Likewise, culture may play a role in how decisions are made. Democratic decision processes, which work well in theory, may not work so well in a cultural environment attuned to a bureaucratic system of fixed rules and hierarchical authority. Communication will also be affected by the cultural environment in which it occurs. What is considered open and frank communication in one culture may be seen as threatening or intimidating in another, especially when there are also language differences to overcome.

The unionization of the hotel industry has not been a significant factor influencing hospitality employment around the world. Hotel workers have historically been isolated from the mainstream of the labor movement in industrialized nations. Nonetheless, where hotel unions do exist, management must take the provisions of labor contracts into consideration in developing IHRM policies.

Human resource development issues (encompassing performance appraisals and corrective actions) must also be viewed from a cultural perspective. Quantitative, objectively measured performance appraisals as practiced in the United States and many other countries are not universal. In some Eastern cultures, performance appraisals are more relationship-oriented; they are done more subjectively and less directly to avoid confrontation. The point here is not which view is more correct, but rather which approach works best in a given culture.

The differences among cultures that influence employees' attitudes and motivate performance and behavior can make it difficult for the hotel executive on a foreign assignment to know just how to act. Managers should understand that in the foreign environment, there are few clear-cut answers. The rules of recruiting, hiring, training, supervising, appraising, and disciplining may all share certain common logic or bases for action, but these must be tempered by cultural considerations if they are to be truly effective. Successful international companies have learned that the most satisfactory way to succeed with diversity issues is through adaptation and integration of different approaches, perspectives, and practices. This produces a cross-cultural blending of management styles that will be relevant to the host culture while retaining important standards and traditions of the company.

Endnotes

1. UNWTO Historical Perspective of World Tourism, 2006.
2. "Top Ten Issues in the Hospitality Industry for 2007," International Society of Hospitality Consultants' Annual Conference, Miami, Florida, November 2006.
3. Hanqin Qiu Zhang, Ray Pine, and Terry Lam, *Tourism and Hotel Development in China: From Political to Economic Success* (New York: Haworth Hospitality Press, 2005).
4. Andreas Augustin and Andrew Williamson, *The Most Famous Hotels in the World: The Oriental Bangkok* (Vienna: The Most Famous Hotels in the World, 2006).
5. Lennie Copeland and Lewis Griggs, "Getting the Best from Foreign Employees," *Management Review,* June 1986, p. 23.
6. Ibid., p. 21.
7. HotelBenchmark Annual Profitability Survey, Deloitte, 2006.
8. Zhang, Pine, and Lam.

9. *Working Time Laws: A Global Perspective* (Geneva: International Labor Organization, 2005).

10. Mark Patton, "The Republic of Korea: Human Resource Management in a Confucian Society," in Sybil M. Hofmann, Colin Johnson, and Michael M. Lefever, eds., *International Human Resource Management in the Hospitality Industry* (Lansing, Mich.: American Hotel & Lodging Educational Institute, 2000), p. 153.

11. Zhao Liangquing, "Human Resource Management in China," in Hofmann, Johnson, and Lefever, p. 16.

12. Aurelia End, "Small German Unions Upstage Larger Peers," Agence France-Presse, October 2, 2007.

Key Terms

labor cost to sales ratio—An employment ratio calculated by dividing labor cost by total sales; sometimes used to measure comparative operational advantages among properties in different countries.

shikomu—In Japan, training to provide employees with a sense of the company's culture, traditions, methods of operation, value systems, and group norms; also, the internalization of such values through training and rotation of assignments.

shunto—In Japanese, "spring wage offensive"; a yearly bargaining pattern in which leading unionized Japanese companies agree to wage patterns that are then followed by other unionized and non-unionized Japanese companies.

staffing ratio per 100 rooms—An employment ratio sometimes used to measure comparative operational advantages among properties in different countries; also called staff-to-room ratio.

Review Questions

1. What regions of the world are facing labor shortages? What factors affect the labor supply for the hospitality industry in any country? What can hospitality managers do to reduce the impact of labor shortages?

2. What factors influence the hospitality industry's ability to recruit employees?

3. How does a company's turnover rate affect the type of orientation it is willing to provide? How do cultural attitudes affect the type of orientation needed?

4. Why is multicultural training required in hotels serving an international clientele? What steps need to be taken to help ensure that such a training program will be successful?

5. How do cultural differences affect motivation? Why is it important for managers to understand culturally based motivations when designing incentive and reward systems?

6. What are the basic cultural characteristics of Japanese and American decision-making styles? How do these styles compare with those found in other countries?

7. What factors contribute to miscommunication in a multicultural environment? What steps can be taken to reduce the chance of miscommunication?

8. Why has unionization of the hotel industry not been a significant factor in most countries?

9. Should performance appraisals always involve setting goals for the future? Why or why not? Are workers always evaluated on the basis of their work? What other factors may be considered?

10. Why is it important to understand a host culture's viewpoint regarding employee discharge? What problems might arise if a manager discharges someone without considering this viewpoint?

Part IV

International Hotel Operations

Chapter 11 Outline

Hotel Activities and the Management Process
Organizing the International Hotel
Managing Corporate Culture in the International Hotel
    Exporting Corporate Culture
    Corporate Culture Impacts
    Cultural Perspectives at the Top
Managing Communication in the International Hotel
    Communicating with the Host Community
    Language Differences
Managing Guest Service
    Provisions for the International Guest
    Observing Protocol
    The International Business Traveler
Managing International Hotel Operations
    Accounting for International Hotels
    Purchasing
    Utilities
    Equipment Maintenance
    Security
Legal Issues
    Innkeepers' Liability
    IH&RA's Hotel Regulations
    UNIDROIT Efforts
    Environmental Regulations and Voluntary Guidelines

Competencies

1. Identify and give examples of seven broad management functions common to international hotel managers. (pp. 329–333)

2. List some of the differences between organizing an international hotel and a domestic one, and describe the role and effects of corporate culture in an international hotel. (pp. 333–337)

3. Summarize the cultural factors affecting the communication process in an international hotel, and suggest ways of improving such communication. (pp. 337–340)

4. Describe different cultural perceptions of hospitality among guests, and discuss the types of provisions that international hotel guests appreciate or demand. (pp. 340–346)

5. Summarize protocol issues that international hotels face, identify hotel features rated highly by international business travelers, and give examples of special business services offered by international hotels. (pp. 346–348)

6. Explain how international hotel accounting practices differ from those of domestic hotels, define the term *exchange rate exposure*, and describe three types of exchange rate exposure. (pp. 347–353)

7. Explain the importance of purchasing in an international hotel, and describe considerations in deciding whether to buy locally or import. (pp. 353–354)

8. Summarize international hotel operational considerations with regard to utilities, equipment maintenance, and security. (pp. 354–356)

9. Describe what international hotel managers need to know with regard to legal issues and innkeepers' liability, and discuss efforts to establish international hotel regulations, international environmental regulations, and voluntary guidelines. (pp. 356–359)

11

Special Considerations in Managing International Hotel Operations

FEW BUSINESSES ARE as interesting as the hotel business. Not many businesses aside from hotels must measure profit and loss on a daily basis. Each day, therefore, challenges hotel managers to meet revenue goals and control costs, to draw the best efforts from employees, and to satisfy guests. If domestic hotels are demanding, foreign properties operated by transnational companies are even more so. The manager of a foreign property, like his or her domestic counterpart, wears many hats at once, playing host to guests, morale builder for the staff, company representative for the hotel, salesperson, accountant, strategic planner, organizer, and so on. But the manager of a foreign or international hotel also operates within a number of constraints—political, cultural, and financial—that domestic managers do not face in dealing with owners or their representatives, government officials, community leaders, local suppliers, local and expatriate staff, and local and international distributors or buyers of services. Functional activities of the international hotel manager, such as guest services, purchasing, property management, security, and accounting, among others, also require special knowledge.

What are the knowledge areas or skills, then, required for success in managing an international property? In this chapter, we discuss such matters as communications and service and explore selected functional areas—including accounting, purchasing, plant operations, and legal issues—that are more problematic for international than for domestic hotels.

Hotel Activities and the Management Process

The work of hotel managers encompasses a wide range of responsibilities and activities, not to mention time demands. These activities and responsibilities may be distilled to the following "people, plant, products, services, and profitability" expectations that owners have of management: the organization, staffing, and training of competent people to provide services efficiently and hospitably; the proper maintenance and upkeep of the hotel buildings and grounds; the development of new products to sell; the delivery of quality services to guests; and the profitable operation of the hotel to meet cash flow requirements and provide a return to investors. These are the basic conditions that must be met to satisfy a

330   Chapter 11

hotel management contract. The success of a manager may be measured in terms of how well he or she meets or exceeds these conditions.

Time is a critical factor in management. Hotel products and services are highly perishable, a situation requiring the use of daily reports to review daily revenues and contain controllable costs. There are also weekly forecasts, monthly cash flow analyses, monthly departmental analyses, monthly guest history analyses, semi-annual or annual ROI (return on investment) reports, annual profit and loss statements and balance sheets, among others, that guide management's activities and decisions.

All management activities and functions may be more or less grouped under seven functions (management writers differ in their opinions about the exact number or description of specific functions) as they apply to hotel operation. These management functions include: (1) planning, (2) organizing and staffing, (3) coordinating, (4) directing and communicating, (5) controlling, (6) evaluating, and (7) representing. The following list, which is by no means all-inclusive, is presented mainly to give an idea of the scope of activities and functions that international hotel managers have in common:

1. Planning

- Goal setting—establishing goals, objectives, and programs that will accomplish the mission of the hotel and satisfy the expectations of owners in the management agreement

- Gathering intelligence—gathering timely, accurate, and relevant information for short- and long-term planning and decision-making purposes; serving as "eyes and ears" in the field for the transnational hotel corporation to report unusual occurrences or opportunities

- Forecasting—anticipating future occupancies and guest traffic on a daily, semiweekly, weekly, monthly, quarterly, and annual or other bases for revenue estimation, staff planning, and resource allocation

- Budgeting—planning periodic operating and annual capital budgets

- Marketing and selling—analyzing market trends, determining market potentials and fair market share, and planning promotional programs; determining selling targets for product line divisions—rooms, restaurants, bars, banqueting, conferences and meetings, business centers, etc.

- Product and service planning—planning innovative products and services to reach new or existing market segments and stay ahead of competitors

2. Organizing and staffing

- Departmentalization—organizing line and staff departments to meet operational or functional requirements of the hotel; reorganizing when necessary to address areas of special needs in the hotel or the marketplace

- Recruiting and hiring—finding, screening, and hiring employees—local and expatriate—to fill vacant managerial and staff positions

- Building on diversity—taking positive action to hire according to qualifications, regardless of gender, race, political persuasion, or religion, in accordance with the employment goals of the country as well as those of the company
- Compensation administration—maintaining the equitability and competitiveness of wage and salary plans; planning and implementing incentive programs; periodically reviewing the status of pay scales in the industry within the host community
- Employee training—improving employees' skills and professionalism in their jobs; providing cross-cultural training to help employees deal more effectively with guests and co-workers
- Management development—developing and training qualified local personnel as potential candidates to replace expatriate managers upon their transfer or promotion to other properties; developing new managerial talent to increase the executive pool available to the company

3. Coordinating
- Coordinating internal efforts—meeting daily with the hotel operations committee to coordinate activities of all departments and review special problems; meeting weekly with the executive committee (which typically includes the general manager, the resident or deputy manager, managers of the rooms and food and beverage divisions, sales, human resources, and the controller) to coordinate policy-related matters and operational issues
- Coordinating special projects—appointing a special coordinator or hotel committee to plan and execute major projects or programs (renovations, expansions, innovations, new products)
- Coordinating external efforts—transmitting operational reports to and periodically meeting with the hotel company's divisional or transnational headquarters officers to coordinate local efforts with company efforts in marketing, staff planning, purchasing, and financial planning; coordinating special events with sister properties

4. Directing and communicating
- Directing—providing day-to-day direction for senior staff; leading the organization through a culturally appropriate style of management that is understood, respected, and accepted by employees
- Team building—encouraging cooperation among employees to work together to achieve common goals (easier in some cultures than others)
- Building and maintaining staff morale—creating a positive climate in a multicultural workplace that will motivate and contribute to high staff morale
- Communicating—making use of formal and informal channels of communication to transmit directives and ideas within the organization; applying cross-cultural approaches to improve communications effectiveness
- Internal marketing—selling employees on the importance of providing service throughout the hotel—not only to guests, but also to other employees whose work is part of a team effort

5. Controlling

- Controlling costs—controlling variable and semivariable costs of labor, foods and beverages, operating supplies, selling and marketing, administration, plant operation and maintenance, etc.
- Controlling inventory—maintaining par stock levels in the housekeeping, food and beverage, and repair and maintenance areas to meet operational needs and avoid losses from spoilage, obsolescence, or over-stocking; anticipating local or international conditions to ensure adequacy of supply sources
- Controlling production—controlling food and beverage production to avoid waste or stockouts
- Assuring quality—enlisting the support of hotel staff to make certain that quality standards are being met in every phase of service, operation, performance, and output
- Controlling internal security—maintaining safety and security systems to protect people and hotel assets; preventing loss from theft or embezzlement
- Accounting and financial reports—preparing reports for senior management at divisional offices or transnational headquarters regarding monthly, quarterly, and annual forecasts and budgets, market reports, staffing plans, and business plans

6. Evaluating

- Reviewing operational statistics—reviewing the hotel's daily, weekly, and other periodic reports to determine actions needed to accomplish goals
- Pricing—evaluating competitive rates/prices in local and distant markets and establishing competitive but fair rates/prices to maintain optimal or maximal occupancies and profitability
- Environmental assessment—assessing changes in the competitive and operating environment; making use of market intelligence and SWOT analysis (strengths, weaknesses, opportunities, threats) to revise or make new tactical or strategic decisions
- Staff appraisals—measuring the strength, deficiencies, and progress of individuals and human resource development programs within the hotel

7. Representing

- Internal representation—serving as the spokesperson for the hotel company on all matters concerning internal operations; dealing with inside groups: the hotel owner or owner's representative, employee committees or trade unions, and, in unique circumstances, a hotel's political officer
- External representation—serving as the company's representative in dealing with outside groups: government officials, civic groups, financial institutions, suppliers, travel sellers, guests, and the general public
- External selling—representing the hotel at trade shows and conventions; calling on key accounts and working with major wholesalers or travel agents directly

In many countries, there is a significant gap between how international hotels *are* managed and how they *should be* managed for long-term success. The day-to-day activities undertaken by hotel managers in a developed nation, where operating conditions are stable, cannot be compared to the day-to-day activities of hotel managers in developing countries with many environmental uncertainties.

The managerial routines of hotel managers in developing countries, no matter how well planned, may be displaced by such contingencies as city power shortages causing outages in the hotel; deficient plant equipment; frequent air conditioning or refrigeration breakdowns; overloaded communication systems; human problems—touchy labor-management relationships, "political correctness" in dealing with workers in socialist countries, and chronic shortages of skilled workers; and other problems. These challenges result in "fire fighting," or crisis management, as the prevailing management mode. Crisis management leaves hotel executives little time for other activities of strategic importance, such as personnel development, research and development of new hotel products and services, marketing, and financial management.

Organizing the International Hotel

The organization chart is a universal tool for depicting the major formal channels within an organization. Several important aspects of the organizational structure can be defined and shown on an organization chart: the chain of command; the division of responsibilities among individuals and groups; and how work is arranged according to functions, specialization, tradition, process, location, and time.

Defining the organizational structure of an international hotel is just as important as defining the structure of a domestic operation. Both management and employees need a clear idea of the lines of authority and divisions of responsibility. For the most part, organizational structures in international hotels do not differ substantially from those of domestic hotels.

In some socialist countries—China, for instance—the hotel may need to hire a "political officer" to ensure the "political correctness" of the hotel's operations. In certain circumstances, this officer may even be given the authority to override a general manager's decisions. In other countries, there might be special areas that require extraordinary attention in staffing. Some hotels in Russia have special security needs, for example, and many of them have employed ex-KGB agents, who are very good at maintaining order and security, in their security departments. In some Asian countries where elaborate banquets are common, a banquets department will be a separate and autonomous department because of its sheer size and large volume of business. For example, food, beverages, banqueting, and off-site food and beverage functions may account for approximately two-thirds of the revenues of a Japanese hotel, with just one-third coming from the rooms division—the reverse of its American counterpart.

For chain-affiliated hotels, the organizational structure may be determined in part by the degree of centralization or decentralization at corporate or regional offices. It will also be affected by the culture of the host community and the type of authority relations that work well in that culture.

Managing Corporate Culture in the International Hotel

Corporate culture is a set of expectations or basic assumptions that, consciously or subconsciously, guide behavior in an organization. It evolves from the founding, history, and traditions of the company, and is further molded by the environment of the marketplace, the competition, the government, and the activities of the people within the company. Corporate culture has been described as the "glue" that holds organizations together by providing cohesiveness and coherence among the parts. The company's enduring principles become a prologue to future directions and actions. In the case of an international hotel company, the environment of each individual hotel is embedded in the local culture of the host country as well as that of the company. The culture of the hotel is further tempered by the quality of leadership provided by its general manager and other hotel executives, who represent the beliefs, principles, and core values of the company.

Exporting Corporate Culture

The exportation of corporate culture is not a straightforward proposition. Even large international hotel chains with well-defined company cultures cannot always assume that the company's cultures and values will prevail in every location. When companies take over new foreign properties, management must consider the particularities of the host culture as company policies, systems, and ways of doing things are being introduced. To do otherwise is to invite cultural collision. Cross-cultural training for all staff may smooth the adaptation process, but there are no general principles that will find universal application. The workforce composition of each property remains culturally unique. Organizational policies should be built around the strengths of diversity and cultural differences that add to the ambiance and distinction of hotel services.

Hotel companies operating in the international arena need to have non-rigid corporate cultures and strategies in order to promote profits, productivity, quality, and guest satisfaction at the unit level. They must adapt to workers and consumers whose perceptions, values, and attitudes may not fit the domestically established corporate culture.

Because of the increase in international travel and the existence of culturally diverse workforces, this challenge may be present in either domestic or international operations. Indeed, one of the advantages of workforce diversity is that, if managed correctly, diversity can contribute to organizational enrichment, staff innovativeness, creativity, and problem-solving. Contributions will come from the many—each with his or her own unique way of looking at problems and ideas—and not from a small "culturally elite" group.

More than a few hotel chains have been unable to establish a successful international presence because of their failure to adapt. This problem worsens when hotel operators fail to hire or develop managers who understand the importance of culture in the workplace; how to implement company policies in a culturally sensitive way to harmonize with local values and expectations; or, at the very least, know enough to avoid cultural collisions.

Corporate Culture Impacts

The successful international hotel company promotes a company culture that encourages sensitivity to the different expectations and perceptions of its employees and guests. Staff must be taught to be open to guests of different origins and cultural backgrounds, and to treat each guest—no matter how different the person may seem—with respect, attention, and helpfulness, rather than seeking avoidance or responding abruptly to curtail prolonged encounters. Managers can develop a positive environment by supporting and maintaining company cultures that predispose people to interact in mutually satisfying ways, and by managing culture in dealing with the everyday challenges of running a hotel.

The assumptions and values of the corporate culture affect day-to-day relationships between employees and managers, between employees themselves, and between employees and guests. They influence the adaptability of the hotel's products and services and how effectively the company's resources are utilized.

Corporate culture may also influence how the hotel interacts with the host community. In some cases, ethical dilemmas may arise between the prevailing business practices of the host community and the hotel company's corporate philosophies or principles. Expatriate hotel managers may even feel their own ethical beliefs being threatened. Bribing government officials, customs workers, and others is not an uncommon practice in some countries, for example, and may be necessary to ensure a regular flow of supplies to the hotel. In countries that are ethnically or religiously stratified, the employment hierarchy often mirrors the ethnic or religious hierarchy. Hotel managers may have to comply with such a system even if they do not believe in or agree with it.

In some countries, certain ethnic groups have been subject to longstanding internal suppression with regard to educational and professional opportunities. These groups generally make up the lowest levels of workers in the hotel industry. In other examples, the suppression is based on a country's religious caste system. More than one hotel manager in such a society has discovered higher-caste native supervisors mistreating lower-caste employees. While caste systems cannot be changed, hotel managers need to make every effort to ensure that oppressive behavior is not tolerated at the hotel. Unfortunately, not all efforts to promote fairness will be successful, but employees who are disadvantaged will appreciate managers who try. Likewise, hoteliers should avoid participating in, or permitting at the hotel property, activities that are clearly destructive to the people or the culture of the host community.

As indicated earlier, corporate culture also comprises the environment management creates for employee motivation. Hotels that value their human resources respect the ideas and aspirations of all their employees and encourage them to constantly improve. If management does not bring employees together under a common vision and provide them with clear goals, a sense of direction, a feeling of belonging, and opportunities for open communication, peer groups and informal leaders are quick to fill the gap, and their influence may or may not be in tune with management goals.

When the hotel employs local staff in a foreign operation or a culturally diverse staff in a domestic operation, the company should not attempt to remake people or cause people to feel a need to change their unique identity to fit in. Each individual is, in a sense, sovereign, and, when properly trained, each can make unique contributions to the company.

Development of the appropriate culture for an international hotel usually requires a concerted effort on the part of management and human resources staff over a long period of time. The culture is developed, maintained, and reinforced by the daily actions of managers, supervisors, and other key employees—by what they say, what they do, and how they do it. Their actions and words must demonstrate integrity.

Multinational hotel companies from developed countries operating hotels in developing or emerging countries can reap the rewards of becoming preferred employers in these countries by communicating a progressive corporate culture. Many local hotel companies in host countries may have "one-sided" management policies with less regard for employees and other organizational stakeholders. Therefore, international hotel companies entering and operating in these environments can effectively raise the bar for management practices by viewing employees as valuable human assets and designing corporate policies that reflect this view. These and other corporate policies that value other stakeholders in the organization, such as customers, suppliers, and the local community, may serve as significant competitive advantages for multinational hotel companies.

When multinational hotel companies enter markets where the national culture is very different from the corporate culture of the company, the extent and direction of influence will depend on which culture is stronger. In countries where the national culture is weak, employees are more amenable to influence by the corporate culture of the multinational hotel company. However, in countries where the national culture is strong, as in many European countries, attempts to impose the corporate culture will be met with resistance and may potentially produce a backlash.

Cultural Perspectives at the Top

Corporate-level management needs to make sure the international hotel company's operating perspective includes such new issues as cross-cultural assignments for managers, technicians, and professionals; handling multicultural workforces; the socialization of different types of employees into the corporate culture; organizational productivity; cultural influences on consumer choice and satisfaction; and developing products and services that reflect ethnic and/or national identities.

Maintaining a successful international business requires an organizational structure and balanced perspective that permits local adaptation while preserving the integrity of corporate philosophies, goals, product quality, and "signature" standards. One of the early models of a successful hotel company that advocated the practice of local adaptation was Western International Hotels, later renamed Westin Hotels & Resorts (now part of Starwood Hotels & Resorts Worldwide). Each individual hotel in the Westin chain adopts and internalizes company policies with regard to quality, operating standards, customer service, and employee development, but then develops its own mission statement and guest-relations and employee-relations philosophies in order to develop a property-specific culture based on excellence.

Decision-makers at the corporate, regional, and unit levels must nurture and harness the cultural synergy necessary to build effective operations that are responsive to customer demands in each market. Success in the final analysis is measured by what is achieved at the property or field level, because that is where the customers are. But managers need continuous encouragement and support from the top to reinforce what must be done in the field. Nothing is more disheartening for executives operating far from the home country than to never hear anything except when there are complaints.

Managing Communication in the International Hotel

Hotel service begins with interpersonal communication. Communication can be defined as sending and receiving messages, both verbal and nonverbal, within the social system. This includes virtually everything—from how a guest is greeted to the way service is expressed throughout the hotel to the way staff members communicate with each other. The international hotel poses a particular challenge because of the transfer of meaning across cultures. Managers, employees, and guests all operate in social, technological, and physical environments shaped by the forces of their own cultural dynamics.

Four cultural factors affect the communication process in an international hotel:

- The cultural background of service providers
- The cultural background of guests
- The culture of the host society
- The corporate culture of the hotel company[1]

All of these factors, as explained below, have an impact on the nature of the service relationship and the satisfaction of the consumer.

The Cultural Background of Service Providers. People around the world go to work with their own unique cultural baggage. Hotel employees are no exception. Their behavior toward co-workers, managers, and guests are shaped and tempered by home, school, church, or street influences in dealing with various relationships. In terms of service provision, behavior is also influenced by one's cultural understanding of the meaning of service. For example, although both are Asian, the Chinese perception of service differs from the Japanese; the mere delivery of service is service in the Chinese mentality, whereas the small rituals of courtesy accompanying service are an essential part of quality service in the Japanese mind. The way service is communicated is also conditioned by other factors such as age, gender, race, and status or other distinctions between employee and guest.

Language and dialect may be a barrier or a facilitator of communication in the delivery of service. When the parties involved in the communication are from different cultures, the likelihood for miscommunication is always present. However, when culture is recognized and appreciated, differences in the backgrounds of employees and guests are less likely to lead to miscommunication and guest dissatisfaction.

The Cultural Background of Guests. There is much written about cultural influences on consumer behavior. Consumer choice, perception, experience, and satisfaction are all products of the communication process. There may be as many definitions of hospitality as there are cultures. International travelers travel with their own cultural baggage full of expectations, values, preferences, and habits. In receiving foreign guests, hotels are often faced with the challenge of reconciling local hospitality traditions with the home traditions of their guests.

The Culture of the Host Society. All countries and peoples have their own traditions of hospitality. The lei, whose message is synonymous with welcome and aloha, is a time-honored tradition in Hawaii. In the Orient, the offer of hot tea (a symbol of respect) upon arrival expresses welcome.

In some instances, cultures also present obstacles for hotel operators. For example, hotels in Israel must by law restrict certain guest services from sundown on Friday until sundown on Saturday in observance of the Shabbat. Some hotels make an event of the Shabbat by sending foreign guests, in advance, an explanation of the significance of the day and an invitation to celebrate it with hotel staff. Through internal promotion, guests are welcomed to a candle-lighting ceremony and a special dinner; thus a potential service deterrent becomes a new experience for guests, not only expressing a tradition of hospitality but generating revenue as well.

People traveling to new destinations for the first time often encounter confusing situations in dealing with locals. In sensitive locations (island nations, for example), this may require educating guests about the host community's culture and advising guests on how to avoid cultural faux pas. Foreign guests from any country can be insensitive to local people when they have little knowledge of other ways of life. Hotels can sponsor lectures and discussions about the host culture and make sure that guests have the information they need before interacting with residents in the community.

The Corporate Culture of the Hotel Company. The quality of communication with guests will be influenced by the philosophy and shared values of the people in the organization. For companies that truly value service, the signals will be evident to guests—employees throughout the hotel will behave as professionals who appear eager to please in their verbal and nonverbal actions. As noted earlier, international hotel managers need to foster an appropriate service culture in their hotel by blending corporate values with cultural elements of the host society.

Communicating with the Host Community

In an effort to maintain good communications with their host communities, some hotels in developing countries have established community advisory groups. Through such groups, hotel executives may consult with community representatives on issues in which the needs of the hotel and community come together. Whether it is a question of water use, sewage disposal, public access, local employment opportunities, sponsorship of a community event, or any other matter, an advisory group provides managers with an organized way of hearing from the community. In small rural communities where a resort may be the dominant employer, this approach is not only beneficial in building public goodwill, but may also reduce normal tensions that spring up between resorts and communities from time to time.

Language Differences

For hotels competing in the global marketplace, multilingual employees are a must. While many foreign guests may be able to speak the host country language to some degree, they are often afraid to express themselves for fear of being misunderstood. Staff members trained in various languages should be stationed in prominent guest-contact areas of the hotel. Some hotels have in their main lobbies a concierge desk or an information center staffed with multilingual employees who can provide foreign guests with information and help them with business calls, obtaining postage, making transportation arrangements, or other needs.

Multilingual front office staff members are essential. Most guest-contact hotel workers around the world should be able to speak at least some English, as English is now the de facto international language of business. Conversely, in English-speaking countries, employees with the ability to speak other languages become a valuable resource for their hotels. It is a rare big-city hotel that does not have a variety of cultures and language abilities on its staff. For example, at one time the Hilton New York's 447 employees spoke a total of 30 different languages.

Individual hotels in the Hilton chain semiannually compile directories listing staff language skills. Copies of the directory are distributed to every department of the hotel so that whenever international guests need assistance, an employee speaking the appropriate language can be contacted. The directory lists the name of every employee under the heading of the languages spoken, indicating the department, the telephone extension number, and the hours worked. Other hotels have developed similar rosters. Additionally, every Hilton employee who speaks a language other than English wears a lapel pin in the colors of the flag of the appropriate country, which helps both guests and other employees.

If no staff members are able to accommodate the language requirements, foreign language departments of local high schools, colleges, and universities have sometimes been called when hotels are hosting foreign tour or business groups. Hotels have created temporary foreign language concierge positions that can be filled, as needed, by teachers or advanced students. Language teachers generally appreciate the chance to meet people whose language they teach, and they often value the extra income.

Written Translation. Good written translation is also a must when serving foreign travelers. It is essential, for example, that multiple-language signs, registration forms, and menus be available to serve international markets comprising a significant portion of the hotel's business. While multilingual employees play a key role in overcoming oral language barriers, trained professional interpreters are often necessary for written translation. Although professional translation is often expensive, it is even more expensive when the translation is incorrect, or worse, offensive. Translation needs may include anything from menus, brochures, and business cards to stationery, employee handbooks, welcome letters, in-room service cards, notices, guest surveys, tour information, and directories of nearby places of worship with directions on how to get there.

Many professional translators specialize in cultural adaptations that may be overlooked by others. For instance, in translating hotel brochures, they know it is important to keep messages simple for clarity, and to watch for such details as the conversion of English measurements into metric when describing airport to hotel distances, conversion from Fahrenheit to Celsius in describing temperatures, or the listing of prices in the currency of both buyer and seller.

When it comes to written communication, managers should avoid the well-meant but dangerous assistance of a staff member who "speaks a little German." A case in point: one hotel attempted to upgrade its international status by handing out a business card written in Japanese for the concierge service. The hotel wanted to use the Japanese word for "concierge" on the card, and had a hotel employee do the translation. What appeared on the card was the Chinese slang word for "procurer." The mistranslated notices in Exhibit 1 are amusing examples of the potential dangers in using translators not fully familiar with both of the languages involved.

Many hotels now provide instructions and procedural information in multiple languages on how to use the telephone and fax machine. Similarly, a street map and information concerning local attractions and services such as hospitals, churches, and sightseeing should be available in other languages besides English. Multilingual interactive video service—by which guests can order breakfast, get messages in different languages, and check out—is increasingly available. When multilingual signage is not feasible, or too many different foreign markets are served, hotels should make an effort to use international symbols as much as possible for signs and guest information material. These symbols are more universally understood than words and are ideally suited for use in guest services directories as well as lobby signage. Four Seasons Hotels and Resorts, for example, makes excellent use of signage in its properties and also includes symbols in its hotel guide to facilities and services (see Exhibit 2). Appendix A at the end of the chapter provides most of the internationally recognized symbols used by hotels as compiled by the American Hotel & Lodging Association.

Managing Guest Service

The cornerstone of the hotel industry has always been and will always be hospitality in the form of service. However, what constitutes hospitality is relative to the user. In order to be "hospitable" to a guest, hotel staff must know the values and beliefs that form the guest's idea of hospitality. Serving a guest without knowing something about his or her cultural background is similar to designing a house without knowing the habits of its occupants—the one-size-fits-all paradigm.

Guests, regardless of origin, have a right to expect a clean environment, safety, courtesy, and service from hotel operators. Beyond that, guests tend to judge the quality of a hotel according to their own cultural biases or preferences and travel experiences. All other things being equal, European guests will measure hotel quality in terms of round-the-clock room service and the availability of formal dining and beverages, as well as general efficiency. This is reflected in the weight

Exhibit 1 English Mistranslations from Around the World

No one said English is an easy language, especially to peoples whose mother tongue is other than—as this collection of notices from all over the world proves.

In a Bucharest hotel lobby:
The lift is being fixed for the next day. During that time we regret that you will be unbearable.

In a Leipzig elevator:
Do not enter the lift backwards, and only when lit up.

In a Belgrade hotel elevator:
To move the cabin, push button for wishing floor. If the cabin should enter more persons, each one should press a number of wishing floor. Driving is then going alphabetically by national order.

In a Paris hotel elevator:
Please leave your values at the front desk.

On the menu of a Swiss restaurant:
Our wines leave you nothing to hope for.

In a hotel in Athens:
Visitors are expected to complain at the office between the hours of 9 and 11 A.M. daily.

In a Yugoslavian hotel:
The flattening of underwear with pleasure is the job of the chambermaid.

In an Austrian hotel catering for skiers:
Not to perambulate the corridor in the hours of repose in the boots of ascension.

On the menu of a Polish hotel:
Salad a firm's own make; limpid red beet soup with cheesy dumplings in the form of a finger; roasted duck let loose, beef rashers beaten up in the country people's fashion.

In a Tokyo bar:
Special cocktails for the ladies with nuts.

In a Norwegian cocktail lounge:
Ladies are requested not to have children in the bar.

In a Swiss mountain inn:
Special today—no ice cream.

In an Acapulco hotel:
The manager has personally passed all the water served here.

From a Japanese information booklet about using a hotel air conditioner:
Cooles and Heates: If you want just condition of warm in your room, please control yourself.

given to food and beverage service in European rating standards. German guests are particularly fastidious when it comes to housekeeping. American guests tend to have greater appreciation for informality and speed of service—quick check-ins, automatic check-outs, and quick, light lunches. By paying attention to the particular attributes that are valued by a given market, a hotel can position itself more effectively.

It is important to recognize that guests from different countries have different priorities when selecting a hotel. Japanese guests, for instance, consider personal service and employee attitude as key factors in their choice of hotels. U.S. guests want clean rooms with large comfortable beds and good bathrooms. Australians expect good service but dislike excessive pampering. Extremely price-conscious,

Exhibit 2 Examples of Symbols Used in Hotel Signage and Brochures

Four Seasons Hotels·Resorts

GUIDE TO FACILITIES AND SERVICES

FACILITIES & AMENITIES

- **BATHROBE & HAIRDRYER**
- **CONFERENCE FACILITIES**
- **EARLY ARRIVAL/LATE DEPARTURE LOUNGE:** An activity center with luggage storage, locker, shower and dressing rooms so that you can enjoy the full facilities of the resort even when your arrival or departure does not coincide with check-in/-out times.
- **FOUR SEASONS CLUB:** Guestroom floor accessible only by special key, providing extra privacy and personal service, with its own concierge and lounge. Complimentary continental breakfast, afternoon tea and evening cocktails.
- **FOUR SEASONS EXECUTIVE SUITES:** (See page 7)
- **NO-SMOKING ROOMS**
- **PRIVATE BAR:** Refrigerated refreshment center stocked with snacks, fruit and other non-alcoholic drinks and, where local laws permit, a selection of wines, beers and spirits.
- **SELECTIONS BOUTIQUE:** Selected products created exclusively for guests of Four Seasons Hotels and Resorts.
- **VCR IN-ROOM AND VIDEO TAPE LIBRARY**

FITNESS & RECREATION

- **ALTERNATIVE CUISINE:** Gourmet cuisine that is nutritionally balanced and lower in calories, cholesterol, sodium and fat.
- **BEACH**
- **GOLF ON PROPERTY**
- **GOLF NEARBY**
- **HEALTH CLUB**
- **IN-ROOM EXERCISE EQUIPMENT AVAILABLE**
- **KIDS FOR ALL SEASONS:** A professionally-supervised, all-day activity program for children ages 5 to 12 (Nevis: 3 to 10). Complimentary.
- **SPA IN HOTEL/RESORT**
- **SQUASH**
- **SWIMMING-POOL:** Indoor
- **SWIMMING-POOL:** All season outdoor
- **TENNIS**
- **WATERSPORTS:** A variety of watersports equipment including that for sailing, windsurfing, scuba diving and snorkeling.

PERSONAL SERVICES

- **AIRLINE TICKETING:** Concierge can issue new, or change existing, airline ticket.
- **CONCIERGE:** 24-hour
- **DRY CLEANING:** Overnight
- **EXPRESS CHECK-IN/-OUT**
- **JAPANESE SERVICES:** To welcome our Japanese guests we endeavour to provide some services and amenities which you usually find in the finest hotels in Japan. Although these vary by hotel, we constantly strive to meet every request and need.
- **LIMOUSINE SERVICE:** Complimentary destinations vary by hotel/resort. Please consult concierge.
- **PRESSING:** One hour
- **PRIVATE CONCIERGE NETWORK℠:** Acknowledge an occasion for someone or have something done, anywhere in the world, through the concierge of any Four Seasons hotel or resort even when you are not a guest or scheduled for arrival at a Four Seasons hotel.
- **ROOM SERVICE:** 24-hour
- **SALON:** Massage, hair and skin care.
- **SHOE SHINE:** Complimentary
- **SMALL PETS ALLOWED**
- **TWICE-DAILY HOUSEKEEPING SERVICE**

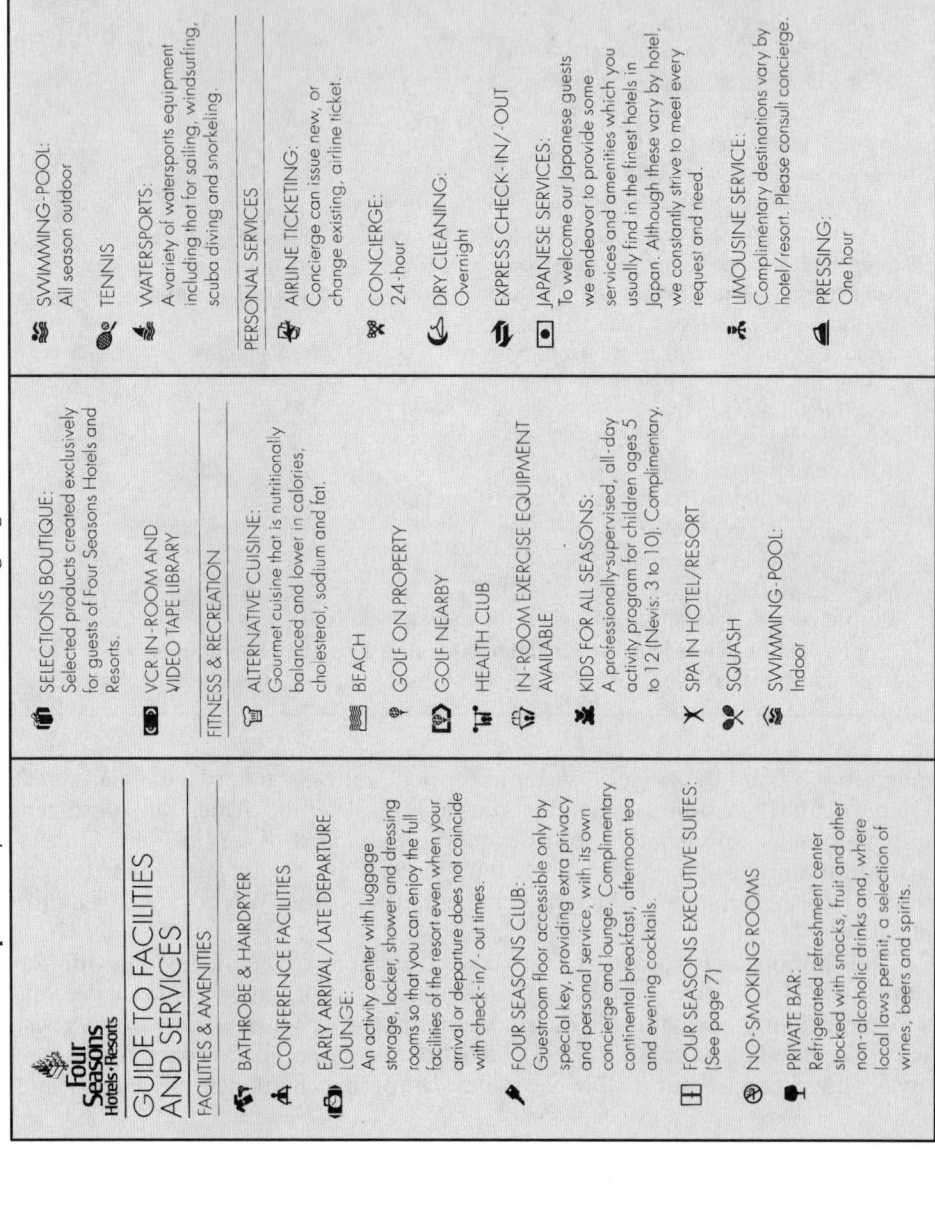

BUSINESS SERVICES

- **BUSINESS SERVICES:** Complete business and office facilities located in the hotel or arranged by the concierge.
- **IN-ROOM COMPUTER AVAILABLE**
- **IN-ROOM FAX AVAILABLE**
- **CLOSEST COMMERCIAL AIRPORT**

Courtesy of Four Seasons Hotels

Australians expect to get what they pay for. The British generally do not care for American-style amenities, but like free coffee service.[2] English, Australian, and New Zealand guests also like to make tea and coffee in their room, and this becomes a bone of contention when they stay in hotels that do not provide such an amenity.

Because of their cultural values, hotel workers in some parts of the world are more predisposed to providing quality hospitality service than others. In some Asian societies, certain cultural behaviors, such as a strong work ethic or collective responsibility (where the entire work unit and not just the individual will accept responsibility for getting things done), reinforce the ability of the hotel to provide total guest service, because these behaviors result in the willingness to do more and a predisposition toward serving the honored guest.

Provisions for the International Guest

Hotels around the world have responded to the surge in international travel with an array of programs to help international guests enjoy their stay, whether they are tourists or business executives. For example, most international travelers consider foreign newspapers and magazines a thoughtful gesture and appreciate the trouble it takes to get them. Some hotels take the international guests' desire for reading material in their native language a step further by providing a library of books in other languages and foreign-language editions of popular U.S. or European magazines and periodicals.

Some hotels go one step further to make foreign guests feel at home by providing culture-specific in-room amenities—for example, green tea for Japanese guests, Australian beer for Australian guests, Stilton cheese for English guests, and so on. Other special products or services for international guests may include:

- Luggage stickers that say "welcome" in several different languages
- Welcome letters in the guests' native language
- Electrical adapters for hair dryers and other small appliances

Financial Concerns. Training staff to work with vouchers is another important element in managing international operations. Many international guests do not rely heavily on credit cards, and often they have restrictions on the amount of cash they can take out of their country. Consequently, most of them use the voucher system, paying for the hotel room prior to the trip and using vouchers when they arrive. Front desk personnel, as well as accounting staff, should be trained to deal with certain aspects of foreign monetary systems. As a convenience to foreign guests, many hotels around the world provide facilities for exchanging money at their cashier stations.

Food and Beverage Concerns. If there is any aspect of hotel operation that offers management an opportunity to differentiate its products or to provide a sense of place, it is in food and beverage. Not only are a hotel's standards measured in part by the quality of its cuisine and dining room, but restaurants and bars also provide significant revenues, sometimes even exceeding room revenues. Chain hotels of all nationalities in the past had the tendency to use European or Continental standards as their models, giving only token recognition to other standards and often ignoring the local cuisine altogether.

Today, menus in many hotels have been adapted for multicultural tastes and reflect the food preferences of a wide variety of guests. The changes range from elaborate—such as having complete menus for those who eat only kosher or vegetarian cuisine—to simple; for instance, making soy sauce and steamed white rice available at every meal for Asian guests. A wide selection of English teas for visitors from the United Kingdom and Brazilian coffee for South American guests are also easy additions to the menu. Arab VIPs often prefer having their staff cook for them in their rooms, and hotels catering to these guests may need to have the facilities to accommodate such preferences.

Most hotels catering to international guests provide food service on a 24-hour basis. International guests often arrive hungry due to time zone differences. As it is usually impractical to maintain a 24-hour restaurant, round-the-clock room service—even if it must be limited—is important.

If the hotel is handling large groups of foreign guests for banquets, meetings, and other events, menus need to be carefully checked, since tastes and dietary restrictions vary widely among cultures. About a quarter of the world's population are prohibited from eating beef, and another quarter cannot touch pork. The way food is served can also offend those from different cultures. Servers may have to be warned never to serve food with the "unclean" left hand to Arab or Indian guests.

While international hotels need to accommodate guests with different lifestyles and tastes in food and beverages, an overemphasis on adaptation has its negative points. For many visitors, there is a growing demand for authenticity with respect to menus and dining styles that reflect the region of origin. Neither these guests nor local residents, who often represent the larger market for a hotel's dining outlets, would accept "mongrelized" versions of local dishes on hotel menus. Hotels need to strike a balance between providing what is familiar and comfortable and what is authentic and new to guests.

A primary food and beverage concern of hotel guests visiting developing countries is the level of hygiene and sanitation. Since food and water are primary sources and carriers of infection, hotels should be proactive in their communication with guests. In-room information and tips for guests to prevent food-borne illnesses would be valued by many travelers as thoughtful and empathic service. Information about the hotel's water filtration process and the safety of ice in drinks, provision of complimentary bottled water in guestrooms, and advice on not eating uncooked foods (such as salads and fruits without peels) are some of the practices that hotels in developing countries may adopt to keep their guests safe and healthy.

The International Concierge. The availability of concierge service can make the difference between a pleasant or a disagreeable experience for a foreign guest. Many years ago, concierges formed a professional association, Les Clefs d'Or (Golden Keys), when several European concierges decided they could do their jobs more efficiently by working as a network rather than independently. Concierges now have colleagues all around the world. Les Clefs d'Or acts as an immense network of information and assistance, each member aiding other members worldwide.

Creating a pleasant stay for guests is the concierge's primary responsibility. Often the concierge is the guests' confidant and advisor. A concierge generally has encyclopedic knowledge of the community and of subjects ranging from flight schedules to business protocol, plus a command of three or four languages—always including English. A good concierge will be in close touch with embassies and consulates and have ready access to business and civic leaders. For frequent guests, the recognition factor is very important; the concierge should be familiar with guests' names, preferences, demands, and opinions—and often with their idiosyncrasies. Concierges have been called on to handle all kinds of situations, ranging from the mundane to the sublime—from picking up a prescription at a local drugstore to locating scarce tickets for sold-out events or arranging an introduction with a senior diplomat. But mostly, concierges prove their worth when they are able to assist international guests with such distressing problems as replacing lost passports issued by countries with limited embassy or consulate representation, or securing alternative arrangements when a return flight has been canceled and alternatives are few.

Researching the Preferences of International Guests. In an age of increasing service customization, hotels that research the tastes and preferences of their international guests will be valued over those that merely provide standardized service. For example, research on the service preferences of Japanese tourists and business travelers visiting the United States indicates that they strongly prefer hotel and shopping information written in Japanese, access to an emergency telephone with a Japanese-speaking person, and shampoo with hair rinse. Contrary to popular assumptions, they don't value Japanese-style breakfasts or a Japanese newspaper in their room. However, green tea with hot water and slippers in their room make them feel at home.[3]

Similarly, understanding the service preferences of Chinese travelers has become increasingly important as a result of the rapidly growing Chinese outbound market. In recent years, the Chinese government has signed more than 130 bilateral agreements and granted Approved Destination Status to several countries. With this new access to the world and growing disposable income, Chinese travelers are expected to be a major market segment for many destinations in Asia and beyond. Proactive hotel companies are beginning to adapt their service and amenity offerings for this emerging market. Starwood Hotels & Resorts Worldwide, for instance, introduced Chinese TV, jasmine tea, and authentic Chinese cuisine in their London hotel. In addition, the hotel is recruiting Chinese employees to assist their Chinese guests.[4]

A study to identify the attributes of hotel service and facilities important for international travelers found seven dimensions that contribute to overall guest satisfaction:

1. *Quality of staff service.* Politeness and friendliness, efficiency of check-in and check-out, helpfulness, appearance of staff, multilingual skills, a staff that understands requests.

2. *Quality of room facility.* Comfortable bed, in-room temperature controls, room cleanliness, quiet and private.

3. *Choice and efficiency of service.* Valet and laundry service, room service, food and beverage choice, wake-up-call reliability, information desk, mini-bar, quality of food and beverage.

4. *Business-related service.* Availability of business meeting rooms and facilities, secretarial service.

5. *Value for money.* Food and beverage value for money, room value for money, reputation of hotel chain, comfort and ambiance.

6. *Safety and security.* Responsible security personnel, reliable fire alarms, safe deposit box available.

7. *International telephoning facilities.*

When analyzing differences between Asian and non-Asian travelers, it was found that Asian guest satisfaction was more likely to be influenced by value for the money, the hotel's ambiance, and the reputation of the hotel. Western travelers, on the other hand, were more influenced by the quality of guestroom facilities.[5]

Observing Protocol

Apart from embassies and government high offices, international hotels are often seen as the arbiters of formal protocol and social etiquette in many circles. Although protocol is normally handled by the hotel's public relations officer, some hotels also retain protocol consultants when important international guests are visiting or when important international events take place at the property. For everyday purposes, there are basic tenets of guest protocol, many of which involve no more than common sense and normal courtesy.

Guests from other countries should never be referred to as "foreigners"; they are German guests, African guests, South American guests, and so forth, or simply international visitors or guests. Hotel staff should never call guests by their first names unless asked to do so.

Managers should be aware of potential cultural faux pas, and should make sure employees are instructed in these matters. In China, for example, someone named Liang Cheng-wu is addressed as Mr. Liang; Cheng-wu is the man's first and middle name and would be socially incorrect to use. Not only have many reservations been lost as a result of this mistake, but Chinese guests take it as a direct affront. Only immediate family and close friends may address a person by the more intimate middle name in China. Latin American names cause similar confusion. José Gonzalez Lopez might be booked under J. Lopez, when actually the surname is Gonzalez.

Children from Asian countries such as Thailand or India should never be patted on the head — a common American gesture to show friendliness toward children. In those countries, a person's head is considered sacred and should not be touched. Even the decision to provide foreign guests with flowers in their room as a special welcome requires some cultural sensitivity. Chrysanthemums are only used for funerals in many cultures. Red roses mean love and marriage to the English and other European cultures and infer the most intimate of relationships.

Some international visitors may present a small gift to the hotel's general manager, who should be prepared to give a gift in return—a pen, golf balls, a book describing the history of the locale, or similar souvenirs are appropriate.

The basics of good, courteous service are important to guests from every market. A warm smile and a polite tone of voice bridge many cultural differences. Smiles and friendliness make any international visitor feel more at home and more at ease.

The International Business Traveler

Business travelers have been a driving force in the hospitality industry's growth and development. A unified Europe and the North American Free Trade Agreement have generated even greater business travel to and within Europe and North America. The elimination of trade restrictions, airline deregulation, and the growth of multinational companies will affect corporate travel and how it is managed well into the twenty-first century.

Hotel operators have long recognized the wisdom of catering to the business traveler. Numerous hotel market studies have identified hotel features that are important to business travelers. These studies invariably list a convenient location, safety and security, attention/service, price/value, and facilities for business. Other important features include in-room amenities, large guestrooms, and excellent restaurants. The inclusion of business facilities as a priority feature is a relatively recent development. Business centers were once considered a welcome but unexpected amenity. They are now regarded as essential facilities by many business guests.

Business Centers. Business centers are frequently open 24 hours a day and can provide, among other things, secretarial and computer services, daily newspapers from around the world, access to PCs, multilingual software, fax machines, copy machines, VCRs and transcribers, message centers, express mail services, quick-ticket services for speedy airline reservations, mobile phone rentals, letterhead storage, messenger services, libraries, stock quotes, translation services, and maps. Examples of outstanding business center operations in hotels around the world are numerous. See Exhibit 3 for a listing of business center equipment, services, and facilities.

Managing International Hotel Operations

Accounting for International Hotels

Accounting practices and tax rates vary from one country to the next, resulting in differences of approach in hotel investment and management. Most hotels operating in the international marketplace face the problem of how to reconcile and interconnect the various accounting systems and currency exchange rates in the environments in which they are working.

Exhibit 3   Business Center Equipment, Services, and Facilities

Equipment
- Laptop computers
- Cellular phones
- Fax machines
- Personal computers/word processors (variety of software types and spreadsheet capabilities)
- Laser printers
- Typewriters
- Complete work stations
- Pager systems
- Conference telephone systems
- Color photocopier

Services
- High-speed Internet access
- Audiovisual services
- Secretarial services
- Translation services
- Messenger services
- Limousine services
- Fax services
- Notary public services
- Report binding services
- Name card printing with foreign translation
- Desktop publishing services
- Packing and express mailing services
- Video room service menus
- Video monitors with access to database systems providing information on flight schedules, weather reports, and stock exchange information
- Access to automatic teller machine for quick banking
- Audio and videotape duplication
- Video conferencing
- Video messaging
- Video/camera rental (off-site)
- Personalized voice mail

Facilities
- Private offices
- Board room/executive meeting rooms
- Small conference rooms
- Lounges with complimentary tea service
- Library—reference books, international newspapers, and business magazines

Uniform System of Accounts. The hospitality industry has established standard classifications and formats for accounting purposes. It is standard practice in the international hotel industry that financial records be kept in accordance with the industry's uniform system of accounts, published in the *Uniform System of Accounts for the Lodging Industry*. This manual provides a uniform system for accounting and reporting that is easy to understand and use. A uniform system allows hoteliers all over the world to make meaningful comparisons of operating ratios, departmental expenses, income before fixed charges, and other financial data.

For new businesses entering the hotel industry, a uniform system of accounts serves as a basic framework that can be quickly adapted to the needs and requirements of the operation. It includes formats for balance sheets, statements of income, statements of changes in financial position, and statements of cash flow. It also provides information covering sample charts of accounts, simplified bookkeeping, ratio analysis, operations budgeting, and breakeven analysis. A standardized system provides a blueprint for the hospitality manager to set up a logical and efficient accounting function within the operation, and it establishes a valid base for comparing statistical data generated by the hotel. Consequently, the uniform system is of value to both internal and external users, including owners and lenders.

A uniform accounting system has made it easier for hotel chains to expand internationally and invest across international frontiers because financial statements can be more easily consolidated. Most hotels keep two separate sets of financial records at the unit level: one for the hotel management company and one for the hotel's owners. The uniform system addresses the former.

Toward an International Accounting Perspective. A number of factors have affected the increasing need for an international accounting perspective, including the growing influence of international economic and political interdependence, the impact of foreign direct investment, and the internationalization of finance and markets. Until the 1970s, accounting standards were exclusively national in character and origin, generally developed by government regulation. Since that time, economic groupings such as the European Union, the United Nations, and the Organization for Economic Cooperation and Development have promoted economic integration internationally and have initiated programs to harmonize accounting, taxation, capital markets, and monetary systems in an effort to promote business on a global scale.

On a professional level, the International Accounting Standards Board (IASB) was established in 1974 with a mission to work toward the harmonization of national accounting standards. The IASB now has over 100 member nations, and the board has done a great deal of work to enhance the comparability of financial standards globally and move toward a common accounting language. The work of harmonization has been a difficult task, given the reluctance of individual countries to give up long-held accounting practices and the fact that there are any number of acceptable solutions to accounting problems. Although considerable progress has been made, significant differences still remain.

Currency Considerations. International hotels deal with currency from many sources, thus the integration of multicurrency accounting into the individual hotel unit's general accounting system is an important concern for hotel corporate offices.

Fluctuating currency values have a major impact on financial statements. Profits can quickly turn into losses or vice versa based on currency conversions. Since the early 1970s there has been turmoil and instability in international currency markets, bringing about sometimes drastic fluctuations in currency relationships. Attempts to impose a fixed exchange rate system, first in relation to gold and later in terms of the U.S. dollar, have failed. Today there is a "free float" (that is, an exchange rate that fluctuates based on market supply and demand) in the major or "hard" currencies. The currencies of small countries are often tied to the value of a major currency or basket of currencies. Currency values remain highly sensitive to national and international economic and political conditions.

Multicurrency Accounting. Translating currency transactions from the individual hotel into the home currency of the hotel management company requires that specific procedures be established and consistently applied. The following sections provide an illustration of the procedures adopted by an international hotel chain based in the United States.

Exchange Rate Exposures. An **exchange rate exposure** results from the risks or uncertainties that occur in dealing with two or more currencies when such currencies do not have fixed parity values. The profitability of any organization that produces goods or services in one country and sells them to another or finances an operation with foreign source funds is directly affected by changes in currency exchange rates. For instance, changes in currency exchange rates must be reflected in the company's financial statements. Also, fluctuations in exchange rates between the domestic and the foreign currencies involved may have an impact on the cash flow of the company, its profitability, and even its solvency. The more currencies involved and the greater the time period before settlement, the greater the potential risk. The identification and management of exchange rate exposures is vital to the profitable operation of international hotel companies.

For many years, hotel operating officers did not concern themselves with the problem of currency exchange fluctuations, but this has changed as new international buyers, sellers, owners, and operators enter the hotel field.

When dealing in a multicurrency marketplace, financial risk stems from uncertainty regarding future exchange rates between currencies. While predicting future changes in exchange rates is difficult, to the extent that increased costs resulting from changes in exchange rates cannot be passed on to the consumer, the changes will have an impact on the company and its business. If the cost of vacationing in one area increases, people are likely to switch to a less-expensive destination. Volatile currency exchange rates have a significant influence on international travel and the choice of hotels, resorts, and destinations, sometimes resulting in large fluctuations in demand. For example, when the U.S. dollar is strong compared with other currencies, U.S. hotels are more expensive for foreign travelers and foreign hotels are correspondingly less expensive for American travelers. Consequently, demand for American hotels, particularly in resort areas, is reduced, because fewer foreign visitors come to the United States and because more Americans are encouraged to travel abroad. Fluctuations in currency exchange rates have less of an impact

Sample Procedures for Currency Translation

The exchange rate used for converting earnings from overseas properties into U.S. dollars is the official currency exchange rate on the last business day of the month. The year-end rate of exchange for the month of December profit and loss and balance sheet will be communicated to hotels from the corporate office.

1. *Balance Sheet.* All balance sheet asset and liability accounts are translated at the official currency exchange rate on the last business day of each month, except for the following accounts, which are converted at the historical rate: capital stock, retained earnings, earned surplus, and the operating control account. Net profit for the year is converted at the same weighted average rate as used for translating the profit and loss statement for the period.

    There is a difference between the asset side and the liability side of the balance sheet because of different exchange rates used for translating the equity section. The difference is recorded in the U.S. dollar balance sheet under the caption "Foreign Exchange Translation" in the equity section. This balancing adjustment is reconciled each month to ensure that no clerical errors are made in the translation and the reconciliation is included in the hotel's monthly Report of Operations.

2. *Profit and loss (P&L).* Prior to the translation of the balance sheet accounts, any balances shown on an inter-hotel or affiliated hotel account in a foreign currency denomination must be adjusted to local currency amounts. Inter-hotel accounts are sometimes established within an international hotel chain to allow for the exchange of goods, services, or supplies between sister properties within the chain. Any foreign exchange gain or loss resulting from this adjustment is recorded under the General and Administrative department as a Foreign Exchange Gain or Loss.

    Net foreign exchange gains or losses on payments received or made for receivables or payables fixed in foreign currencies, including guest transactions, are recorded in the operating ledger under the account: Other Income—Foreign Exchange. One exception to this treatment is the realized foreign exchange gain or loss on payments made for purchases of a capital nature (for example, furniture, fixtures, and equipment), which would be applied against the cost of the applicable asset.

    P&L accounts are translated at the current rate or exchange at the end of each month. Consequently, the year-end P&L statement for any year in which a change in the rate of exchange occurred will have been converted at a weighted average rate. The rates of exchange expressed as an equivalent value of one U.S. dollar are included as a footnote in each report.

3. *Guest currency transactions.* All hotel rates listed in the corporate hotel rate schedules are translated from local currency to their U.S. dollar equivalent, based on the official exchange rate in effect at the time the tariff sheet is printed. There is also a notation which states: "All rates are subject to change without notice—the rates quoted in U.S. dollars are based upon the current exchange rates and are subject to change in accordance with fluctuation in official currency exchange rates." Since charges are posted to guests' accounts at their actual local currency value, there is a variation between the U.S. rate quoted on the tariff sheet and the U.S. dollar equivalent charge on the guest account each time the translation rate changes.

    All guest settlement transactions and the cashing of personal and travelers checks are executed at the same exchange rate, which is the actual daily rate at which a local bank would purchase U.S. currency.

on business travelers, although even business travelers may choose to downgrade when hotel rates are too high.

Exchange rate exposure can generally be categorized as transaction exposure, translation exposure, or economic exposure.

Transaction exposure refers to the risk that is taken whenever business transactions must be paid or received in a foreign currency. It concerns the cash flow affected by any change in currency between the time the transaction is initiated and the time it is settled. The length of time before payment or the length of payment schedules for loans are important factors affecting transaction exposure. Say, for example, that a U.K. hotel company borrows sterling to purchase a hotel in New York City. The hotel earns revenue in U.S. dollars and incurs costs in U.S. dollars, so a problem may not be immediately evident. However, the profits earned in U.S. dollars must cover an interest cost paid in sterling, and it is also hoped there will be some extra profit to pay dividends to shareholders. A fall in the value of the U.S. dollar relative to the sterling will reduce the sterling value of the net profit, possibly resulting in insufficient funds to pay the interest costs. In the early 1960s, several major U.K. companies borrowed Swiss francs with a 3 or 4 percent interest rate; a rapid rise in the value of the Swiss franc left such companies with very expensive borrowings to repay.

Translation exposure, also referred to as accounting or balance sheet exposure, is defined as the need to translate into domestic currency values all assets and liabilities valued in a foreign currency when preparing the balance sheet. All assets and liabilities are usually translated at the rate of exchange prevailing on the date at which the balance sheet is prepared. Changes in currency exchanges will result in a gain or loss in asset value when measured in the home country currency, although such translation gains and losses do not represent realized cash flows unless, or until, the assets or liabilities are settled or liquidated.

Economic exposure is concerned with the strategic evaluation of foreign transactions and their relationships; it is possibly the most complex and most important of the exposures, since future cash flow and hotel operations will be affected. The concept of economic exposure requires an understanding of the structure of markets in which the company and its competitors obtain capital, labor, materials, services, and customers. Consider a hotel somewhere in the European Union. If the euro strengthens, the hotel becomes more expensive to anyone visiting from outside the European Union. The hotel will even be affected by fluctuations in the exchange rates between two or more non-EU countries. For example, if the U.S. dollar weakens against the South African Rand, the Rand will buy more in the United States than it used to. South Africans who might have gone to Europe (and stayed at that hotel) may go to the United States instead. In this way, the European hotel faces exposure to exchange rate changes between target markets and competing destinations, irrespective of the strength of the euro.

Financial officers of international hotel properties should examine estimates of foreign-exchange fluctuations when they develop annual operating budgets, pricing decisions, marketing plans, and all other strategic elements of the managerial planning process. Forecasts of future foreign-exchange rates are widely available and can be obtained, for example, from major multinational banks.

So that consumers will not be put off by adverse currency exchange changes, some hotels guarantee their rates in the foreign currency and absorb either the gain or loss from exchange changes. Sofitel, for example, at one point announced a guaranteed U.S. dollar rate program for its hotels in France. To deal with currency exchange uncertainties, some suggest that the problem could be reduced by quoting hotel rates in a basket of currencies.

Purchasing

Purchasing has a direct impact on the quality, profitability, and production efficiency of the entire hotel operation, and is therefore one of management's more important functions. In the international arena, purchasing options are extensive and complicated. Government influence and public policy are much more likely to have an impact on purchasing decisions in countries outside the United States.

As much for prestige as for quality, international hotels have special needs arising from the nature of the business and the expectations of guests. Purchasing decisions will be affected by the local availability of quality supplies, the location of the hotel and its proximity to supply sources, the extent of centralized purchasing in chain-affiliated hotels, transportation linkages, storage capabilities, markets served, exchange rates, import taxes and restrictions on the imports, and the class of hotel. Certainly, the types of products purchased help determine the tone or quality of the hotel.

Importation. International hotels, particularly chain hotels, tend to import a large portion of their consumables. For chain hotels, purchases may be directed through the company's central purchasing unit. A central purchasing unit makes it possible to obtain supplies of superior quality and lower price, not only because of the economies of scale associated with bulk buying but also because of the company's ability to buy directly at source. Whether chain-affiliated or independent, it is difficult to conceive of any international hotel that has not at some time imported furniture, furnishings, linen, chinaware, glassware, flatware, or foods and beverages. Particularly with respect to food and beverages, imports have become *de rigueur* in international hotels. Hotel managers involved with the direct importation of any product must be cognizant of foreign laws, trade agreements, import taxes, shipping procedures, customs, supply sources, reliability of sources, and international currency leverages, among other factors.

Hotel chains frequently use design and material specifications that are difficult for local manufacturers to meet. These may involve building materials, furniture, fittings, and equipment not locally available. Materials and supplies such as linens, glassware, crockery, cutlery, cleaning and sanitary supplies—especially if they are to be inscribed with the chain's logo—also tend to be imported. Some of these imports are restricted by local laws and heavy import taxes by countries wishing to encourage the use of domestic materials and designs. A hotel's extensive use of imports, either in its construction or for continuing operations, can result in a substantial foreign exchange drain on host countries. In negotiating development and management contracts, therefore, host countries often insist on the widest possible use of local materials and supplies in the design, construction, and operation of the hotel.

Although extensive use of imports has frequently been a contentious issue between host governments and hotel companies, most international hotels by policy make an effort to purchase current supplies (food and operating supplies) locally whenever possible, assuming the quality is acceptable and the continuity of supply at competitive prices is ensured. However, this very much depends on the location of the hotel. For example, it is possible to procure nearly all current supplies locally in Spain or Mexico. In Brazil, Colombia, Malaysia, Sri Lanka, or Venezuela, however, a significant portion of food and beverages must be imported. In the Democratic Republic of the Congo, the import percentage is extremely high. Generally, a smaller proportion of current purchases and a higher proportion of capital goods are obtained through the central purchasing departments of foreign hotel companies.

In developing countries, hotel managers are sometimes forced to use inferior-quality local products, either because there is no other option or because the hotel is making a conscious effort to support local businesses. For example, some governments or owners have insisted that the design and furnishings of the hotel properly reflect the art, handicraft, and visual traditions of the country and the region in which the hotel operates. As a policy, certain hotel chains also ensure that local artisans and artists have a hand in furnishing and decorating the hotel. Some hotels have made concerted efforts to assist agricultural development in their host communities by working with farmers to grow fruits and vegetables or specialty items needed by the hotels. Supporting the local farm economy is one of the basic ways in which hotel managers enable a host country to earn foreign exchange, and such support is always wise from a public relations perspective.

It is important for hotel managers to bear in mind that the hotel's purchasing power may have a significant impact on the local economy. A hotel in a small community can upset the local balance of supply and demand. In trying to support local businesses, hotels may unwittingly drive prices up and local standards of living down.

Utilities

The supply, quality, and continuity of utilities is a serious problem for hotels in many international locations. Cuts in electricity or water supply, fluctuating voltages, tropical storm damage to telephone lines, and other exigencies are not uncommon occurrences in developing countries. For example, hotels in areas where energy demand exceeds energy supply will need to have backup generators and contingency plans for power shortages. The requirement for adequate security arrangements will also need to be reviewed. Security affects not only the guests and their property, but also the buildings, plant, and working capital of the operation.

Since hotels are major users of an area's resources—not only water and power but also land and farming capacity—hotel operators should be careful not to waste these resources.

Energy. Governments all over the world recognize the need for energy laws, regulations, and codes. The future use of energy in hotels will likely become more controlled as resources become relatively more scarce and expensive in many parts of the world and control techniques are improved.

Environmental concerns and national energy policies also place restrictions and controls on the use of energy. In the late 1970s, for instance, the U.S. government established heating and air-conditioning temperature guidelines for spaces in all commercial buildings. California implemented additional regulations concerning minimum appliance efficiency standards and construction codes. Other examples of restrictions include mandatory lighting controls and maximum wattage per square foot for lighting. Many local governments encourage the use of solar energy to heat swimming pools and hot water, and heat recovery to reduce the demand for thermal energy. The worldwide concerns related to climate change and global warming have triggered the need to monitor energy usage more closely and will likely result in the more widespread use and increased sophistication of integrated environmental control systems within hotels. These systems will need to be considered in the design phase for new hotels.

Energy management involves using resources wisely. It does not require deprivation; rather, it encourages the elimination of waste. For hotels around the globe, the most effective long-term energy strategy will be to evaluate the ever-widening range of energy options available and to develop an energy management plan that maximizes internal energy efficiency and minimizes external energy dependence.

Water. Hotels tend to waste a great deal of water. It is difficult to justify consumption in excess of 200 gallons per guest per day, regardless of the specific conditions of the property. Prudent operators will make water management an integral part of their overall energy management program; where there are severe water shortages, they have no other choice. Generally, water conservation practices are easy to implement, require little maintenance, and only minimally affect the services provided to guests. Education of employees and guests, routine preventive maintenance, efficient use of machinery, and more conservative approaches to property irrigation are all simple ways of improving water management.

Equipment Maintenance

One of the challenges facing hotel managers in the day-to-day operation of the hotel, particularly in developing countries, is the difficulty in obtaining spare parts for equipment and machinery. The ongoing servicing of elevators, air-conditioning units, boilers, and computer equipment may also suffer from an inadequately staffed local agent or infrequent visits from a regional engineer. This often prolongs the delay in repairs as either equipment technicians or parts (or both) are flown in. The impact of broken air conditioners, elevators, and other equipment or of breakdowns in the computer system on the service quality of the hotel is obvious and needs to be addressed by managers when they make plans concerning inventories, capital budgeting, rehabilitation programming, and maintenance staffing and training.

In addition to equipment and machinery maintenance, the buildings themselves need to be maintained. Examples abound of first-class international hotels that could not hold their status in the marketplace for lack of maintenance. Whether the issue is one of owner reluctance to put additional funds into the investment or simply neglect on the part of management, hotel maintenance is a perennial problem that requires constant vigilance.

Security

Security and life safety issues among countries vary according to national and local regulations and political circumstances. Security technology is generally driven by legal requirements and market demands. The standardization of security and life safety requirements is universally desired by hoteliers, but given the multitude of legislative and governing bodies involved, agreement on such standards is not anticipated in the near future. Hotel operators have suggested that the International Hotel & Restaurant Association establish guidelines and minimum requirements for security and life safety that could be universally adopted, but this has not come to pass.

Recent legal rulings having an impact on security issues, worldwide media coverage of terrorist attacks, and the general public's greater awareness of security risks have increased public demand for adequate hotel security in all countries. Use of electronic key card systems, already in wide use, will eventually replace conventional keys altogether, and the integration of these systems with credit cards or smart cards is expected to take place. Biometric systems to control access to high-security areas in hotels will become more commonplace, allowing or barring access through recognition of physical characteristics such as fingerprints or eye retina.

Legal Issues

Various forms of legislation and government regulations, both at a national and local level, affect hotel operations. They include classification and grading/rating of hotels and other lodging establishments; fire safety regulations and codes; health safety regulations and codes; building and zoning codes; issuance of operating and liquor licenses and other regulations of the terms and conditions of operation; labor and taxation legislation; and liability laws with respect to guests and their belongings.

Hotel managers need to be conversant with all of the relevant laws and regulations affecting their operations in the host country and be alert to the potential for legal liability exposure in all hotel services as well as promotional activities.

Innkeepers' Liability

The responsibility of innkeepers and hoteliers for their clients and their possessions has a long legal history. Before the advent of a developed banking system and credit card conveniences, English common law provided safeguards for travelers by imposing upon hotelkeepers relatively strict liability for the safety of guests and their possessions. The fact that innkeepers were frequently co-conspirators with robbers to steal from their own guests provided the rationale for these laws. The innkeepers of yore were generally not well regarded or trusted, to say the least.

Common law rules that protected guests from unscrupulous innkeepers hundreds of years ago are still part of many current legal systems, though in most cases limits of liability have been established.

Many countries have developed consumer protection laws applicable to lodging establishments, either based on the old common laws or on a civil law system. Some consumer protection laws are more stringent than others. Hoteliers are generally only liable to the extent the particular country's law defines their obligation. In some countries where negligence laws and consumer protection laws are well established, guests may be well protected; in others, they are not.

The international law of coexistence tends to affirm the sovereignty of nations with respect to legal matters, although, as countries become more interdependent in all areas, international law will eventually come to dominate national regulations. Over the years, attempts have been made at the international level to codify the respective obligations of hoteliers and their guests. The International Hotel & Restaurant Association (IH&RA) and the International Institute for the Unification of Private Law (UNIDROIT) are two organizations that have attempted to foster the development of uniform laws governing the rights of the guest and the interests of the hotel.

IH&RA's Hotel Regulations

The international hotel industry published its first hotel regulations almost 90 years ago, and the current text was adopted by IH&RA. The objective of the international hotel regulations is to "codify the generally accepted international trade practices governing the contract of hotel accommodation." These regulations focus on the contractual relationship, and inform the guest and the hotelkeeper of their mutual rights and obligations in the transaction. They are designed to serve as a complement to the provisions stipulated by national law to the terms of the contract; they apply when a national law does not include specific provisions concerning the contract of hotel accommodation. Thus, these regulations do not supersede national regulations.

Part One of the regulations covers the contractual relationship and specifies that the hotelkeeper is obliged to provide accommodation and services to the guest, which are deemed to be the normal services, as appropriate to the category of the hotel. The customer, in turn, is obligated to pay the agreed price. The hotel can ask full or partial pre-payment as a deposit for advance reservations. Bills are due upon presentation. In the event that the contract is not completely performed, the defaulting party must fully compensate the other party for his or her loss. If the hotelkeeper cannot honor the contract, an effort should be made to find alternative accommodations of an equivalent or superior standard in the same locality, with any additional cost met by the hotelkeeper.

Part Two of the regulations covers "other obligations." It states that the liability of the hotelkeeper depends on national law and, in the absence of any such provisions, the provisions of the European Convention of December 17, 1962, apply. The liability for property belonging to the guest is usually limited, except when hotelkeepers or hotel employees are at fault. The liability of the hotel to accept valuables in deposit depends on the size and standing of the hotel. Guests are liable to the hotelkeeper for "any damages" they cause to persons, buildings, furnishings, or equipment. The hotel, as guarantee for payment of any amounts owed, has the right to retain and ultimately to dispose of any property of commercial value brought to the premises of the hotel by a guest.

According to the regulations, guests "shall behave in conformity with the hotel custom and the house rules of the hotel." Serious or persistent breaches of house rules entitle the hotel to terminate the contract without notice. And, unless otherwise stipulated, rooms that have been reserved for a guest must be ready at 2:00 P.M. Guests leaving the hotel must vacate their rooms by noon. A full copy of the regulations can be found in Appendix B at the end of the chapter.

UNIDROIT Efforts

The International Institute for the Unification of Private Law (UNIDROIT), whose objective is to find suitable means for harmonizing and coordinating private law between countries and groups of countries and gradually to prepare international legislation constituting a uniform private law, has also been active in developing uniform laws covering hotelkeepers' liability. UNIDROIT's *Convention on the Liability of Hotelkeepers Concerning the Property of Their Guests* came into force in 1967 and was adopted by a number of European countries, although this convention covered only one segment of the legal issues. In 1980, UNIDROIT's efforts were focused on the further development of a Hotelkeepers Contract, looking at four main areas of contention:

1. The definition of hotelkeeper
2. Loss or damage of a guest's property
3. Personal injury
4. Reservation practices[6]

To date, UNIDROIT's Hotelkeepers Contract has not been officially adopted because of difficulties resulting from differing legal standards among nations. The proposed contract has also lacked support from major hotel associations, including IH&RA. Recent draft conventions of UNIDROIT's Hotelkeepers Contract have been met with even firmer opposition from IH&RA because of the newly opened hotel markets in Eastern Europe, China, Russia, and elsewhere. IH&RA argues that any attempt to impose what is likely to be a spurious and artificial integration of legal principles is unlikely to be successful when the industry is so diversified and extensive, and so many varied cultures and legal systems are involved.

Environmental Regulations and Voluntary Guidelines

The international debate about global warming and climate change has renewed an interest in environmental laws and regulations. Hotel managers operating hotels internationally should be aware of this interest. International law is developed in the form of international conventions, protocols, and agreements that are difficult to enforce. However, international law influences national laws that are more readily enforceable. National laws are generally developed in the form of codes, acts, and quality standards. Examples of environmental laws that affect hotels and tourism in general include:

- Drinking water quality standards
- Indoor air quality standards (resulting in no-smoking legislation in many countries)
- Emission standards
- Legislation concerning the separation and disposal of recyclable waste
- Disposal of food and other organic waste
- Legislation on noise
- Building, construction, and plumbing codes
- Legislation concerning the protection and conservation of habitats and species

In addition to laws and regulations, self-regulation in the form of voluntary agreements and standards is becoming popular. Generally, self-regulation comes in the form of public-/private-sector partnerships or falls under the auspices of a special-purpose, non-government organization. An example of some major international voluntary environmental standards today are the ISO 14000 environmental management standards. Set up by the International Organization for Standardization (ISO), ISO 14000 is a series of environmental management guidelines and standards designed to improve an organization's performance on environment-related issues. While the ISO 14000 series consists of 17 environmental guidelines and standards, ISO 14001 (Environment Management Systems—Specification with Guidance for Use) is the one most directly applicable to the hotel industry. Hotel organizations interested in adopting these standards can contact a national certification body assigned by ISO for their respective country.[7]

Summary

Hotel management is best defined in terms of the functions that all managers must perform, to a greater or lesser degree, whether they operate a domestic or an international property. These management functions include planning, organizing and staffing, coordinating, directing and communicating, controlling, evaluating, and representing. While the functions may be the same, how these functions are carried out will differ for hotel operators and owners in different countries. The domestic manager operates in a generally stable environment with a higher degree of predictability, which allows for better control over daily activities and planning for the future. The international hotel manager, on the other hand, must contend with many environmental uncertainties, and, no matter how well he or she has planned, "fire fighting" or crisis management at times becomes the prevailing management mode. In some countries, political conditions change so rapidly that managers can only respond on a day-to-day basis, and their work is a constant challenge, requiring cultural insight, analytic skills, and the ability to adapt or improvise according to the situation.

Each hotel has its own organizational culture, which is shaped in part by company policies, guiding principles, and standards, and in part by the leadership behavior of management and the national culture of the hotel's workforce. Expatriate managers must be prepared to act across cultural and national boundaries with respect to owners, staff, guests, suppliers, and others, whose values and attitudes might not fit their own prior frames of reference or experiences. At the same time, expatriate managers must manage by following the general principles that are set by the company, which apply across the board.

No organization or coordination of work is possible unless directions are communicated down the line in understandable form. Communication is more than the simple issuance of work directives and explanations; it is also an essential means of motivating employees and securing their cooperation in moving toward the goals and mission of the hotel. Without communication, there is no feedback to provide guidance for improvement. In a hotel, communication with guests is of utmost importance. An international hotel tries to make its foreign guests comfortable by posting multilingual staff in all prominent guest-contact areas and providing universally understood signage that transcends nationalities.

International guests have varying expectations, and their evaluation of a hotel is influenced by their own cultural perspectives and travel habits with respect to accommodations, amenities, food and beverages, service, and—most of all—hospitality. The concept of hospitality may be universal, but its application will vary by culture. In order to serve guests as individuals and not as "numbers," management and staff alike must understand what the various cultural ideas of hospitality are, and seek ways to provide for guests according to their needs or desires. At the very least, staff should have sufficient knowledge of the different countries and cultures that the hotel serves to avoid faux pas.

Besides cross-cultural communications and guest service considerations, there are other aspects of international hotel operations that require special knowledge. These may include accounting, purchasing, plant operations, hotel security, and legal provisions. In accounting, the various types of transactional and exchange rate exposures and the translation of foreign currencies on accounting statements can directly affect the hotel's cash flow and, ultimately, its profitability. In purchasing, a host country's import policies and regulations can complicate the procurement process. Since governments, as a rule, want to encourage local buying and local substitutions for imports, the hotel's management must attempt to work with local suppliers as much as possible.

Since infrastructure is often inadequate in developing countries, managers of hotels in such areas must be prepared with backup plans for possible basic utility deficiencies in order to provide for hotel and guest needs. Hotel maintenance in many countries is also a constant problem. Governments often permit the importation of luxury materials and equipment for initial construction, interior design, and operations, but restrict further importation for replacement and upkeep. Having specific knowledge of plant operations allows management to think in terms of alternatives to keep the hotel running and services flowing.

In politically volatile situations, guest safety and security concerns are ever-present. These relate to legal concerns and the responsibility and duty of innkeepers to guests and the rights of guests. What may be legally binding in one country is not necessarily so in another. The International Hotel & Restaurant Association has long championed a uniform set of *International Hotel Regulations* that "codify the generally accepted international trade practices governing the contract of hotel accommodations" for adoption by governments and hotels around the world.

It is clear from even this short summary that managing a hotel abroad necessitates consideration of many more factors than does managing a hotel at home, and that many of these factors are less certain and more variable. Flexibility, adaptability, and creativity would seem to be required traits for any hotel executive aspiring to an assignment abroad.

Endnotes

1. Germaine Shames and Gerald Glover, *World Class Service* (Yarmouth, Maine: Intercultural Press, 1989), pp. 171–172.
2. Judy McClure Hachey, "Selling to Foreign Markets," *Courier,* March 1990, p. 87.
3. Kyuhu Lee and Jinlin Zhao, "Japanese Travelers' Service Preferences in U.S. Hotels," *Journal of Travel and Tourism Marketing,* vol. 14, no. 2, 2003, p. 67.
4. Samantha McClary, "Chinese Check-in," *Caterer and Hotelkeeper,* vol. 193, no. 4354, December 2004, p. 38.
5. Tat Y. Choi and Raymond Chu, "Levels of Satisfaction among Asian and Western Travelers," *The International Journal of Quality & Reliability Management,* vol. 17, no. 2, 2000, p. 116.
6. Michael Simons, "An Overview of International Trends in Hospitality and Tourism Law," *International Journal of Hospitality Management,* vol. 6, no. 1, 1987, p. 4.
7. *Sowing the Seeds of Change: An Environmental Teaching Pack for the Hospitality Industry* (Paris: EUHOFA International, IH&RA, and UNEP, 2001).

Key Terms

corporate culture—A set of expectations or basic assumptions that, consciously or subconsciously, guide behavior in an organization; includes company traditions, the company's philosophy and policies, and the activities of people—especially leaders—within the company. Often described as the value system that holds organizations together.

economic exposure—A concept that refers to the strategic evaluation of foreign transactions and their relationships; requires an understanding of the structure of the markets in which the company and its competitors obtain capital, labor, materials, services, and customers.

exchange rate exposure—The risk or uncertainty that occurs in dealing with two or more currencies that do not have fixed parity values.

transaction exposure—The risk that is taken whenever business transactions must be paid or received in a foreign currency. It concerns the cash flow affected by any change in currency valuation between the time the transaction is initiated and the time it is settled.

translation exposure—The translation into domestic currency values of all assets and liabilities valued in a foreign currency when preparing the balance sheet. All assets and liabilities are usually translated at the rate of exchange prevailing on the date the balance sheet is prepared. Also called accounting or balance sheet exposure.

Review Questions

1. What are the seven broad management functions common to international hotel managers? What types of activities or responsibilities do they include?
2. How might organizing an international hotel differ from organizing a domestic hotel?
3. What is corporate culture, and how does it affect international hotel management?
4. Which cultural factors affect the communication process in an international hotel?
5. What are some of the notable differences in the hotel preferences of international hotel guests?
6. Why is protocol important in a hotel, and what is the basis of protocol?
7. International business travelers expect what kinds of features and services in an international hotel?
8. How do international hotel accounting practices differ from those of domestic hotels?
9. What considerations are important in deciding whether to purchase hotel supplies from local suppliers or to import supplies from another country?
10. Which two organizations are working toward establishing international hotel regulations?

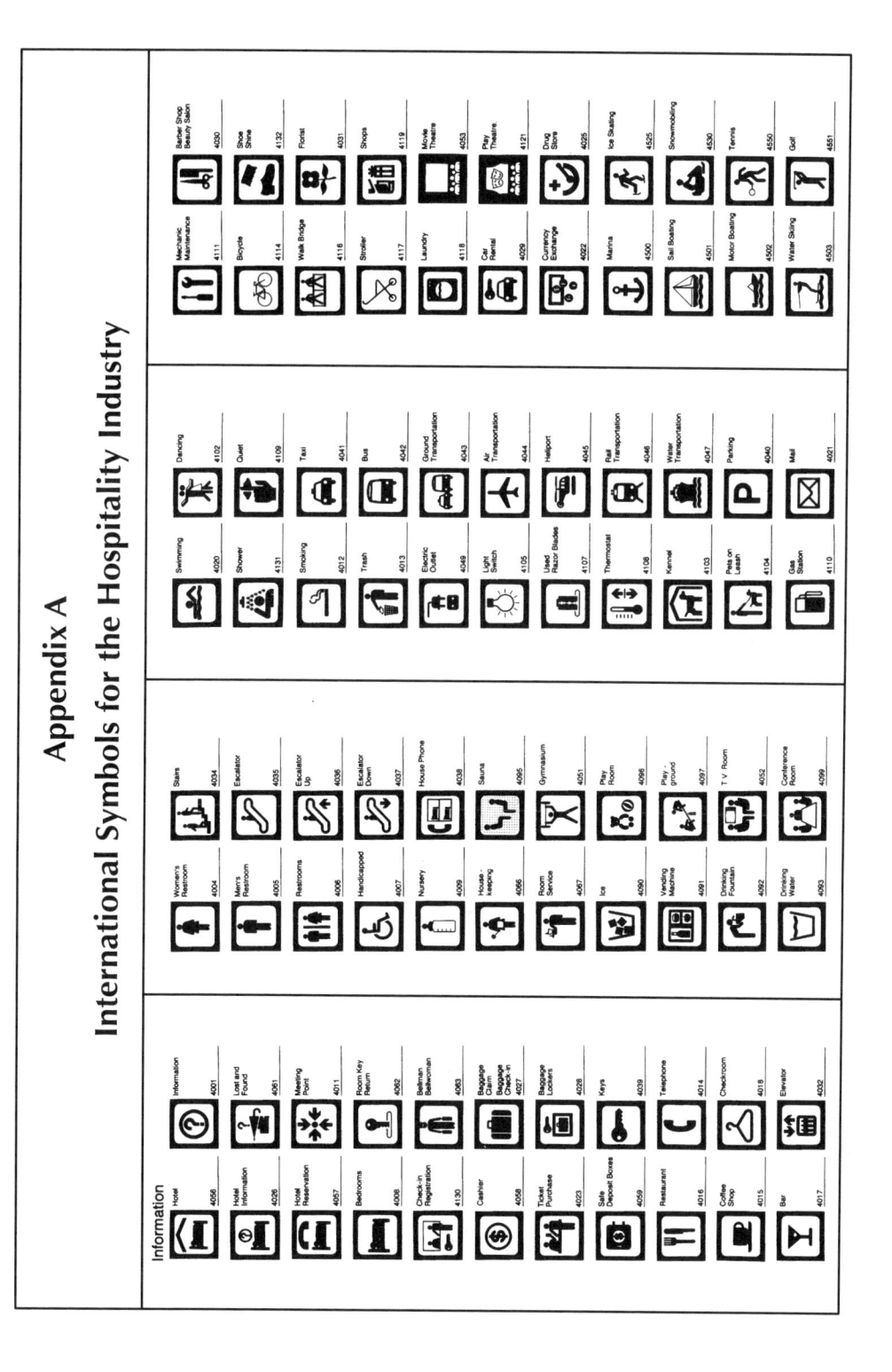

Appendix A
International Symbols for the Hospitality Industry

Information

Symbol	Name	Code
	Hotel	4056
	Hotel Information	4226
	Hotel Reservation	4057
	Bedrooms	4008
	Check-in Registration	4130
	Cashier	4058
	Ticket Purchase	4023
	Safe Deposit Boxes	4059
	Restaurant	4016
	Coffee Shop	4015
	Bar	4017
	Information	4001
	Lost and Found	4061
	Meeting Point	4011
	Room Key Return	4062
	Bellman/Bellwoman	4063
	Baggage Claim / Baggage Check-in	4027
	Baggage Lockers	4028
	Keys	4039
	Telephone	4014
	Checkroom	4018
	Elevator	4032
	Women's Restroom	4004
	Men's Restroom	4005
	Restrooms	4006
	Handicapped	4007
	Nursery	4009
	Housekeeping	4066
	Room Service	4067
	Ice	4090
	Vending Machine	4091
	Drinking Fountain	4092
	Drinking Water	4093
	Stairs	4034
	Escalator	4035
	Escalator Up	4036
	Escalator Down	4037
	House Phone	4038
	Sauna	4095
	Gymnasium	4051
	Play Room	4096
	Playground	4097
	T V Room	4052
	Conference Room	4099
	Swimming	4020
	Shower	4131
	Smoking	4012
	Trash	4013
	Electric Outlet	4049
	Light Switch	4105
	Used Razor Blades	4107
	Thermostat	4108
	Kennel	4103
	Pets on Leash	4104
	Gas Station	4110
	Dancing	4102
	Quiet	4109
	Taxi	4041
	Bus	4042
	Ground Transportation	4043
	Air Transportation	4044
	Heliport	4045
	Rail Transportation	4046
	Water Transportation	4047
	Parking	4040
	Mail	4021
	Mechanic Maintenance	4111
	Bicycle	4114
	Walk Bridge	4116
	Stroller	4117
	Laundry	4118
	Car Rental	4029
	Currency Exchange	4022
	Marina	4500
	Sail Boating	4501
	Motor Boating	4502
	Water Skiing	4503
	Barber Shop Beauty Salon	4230
	Shoe Shine	4132
	Florist	4031
	Shops	4119
	Movie Theatre	4253
	Play Theatre	4121
	Drug Store	4225
	Ice Skating	4525
	Snowmobiling	4530
	Tennis	4550
	Golf	4551

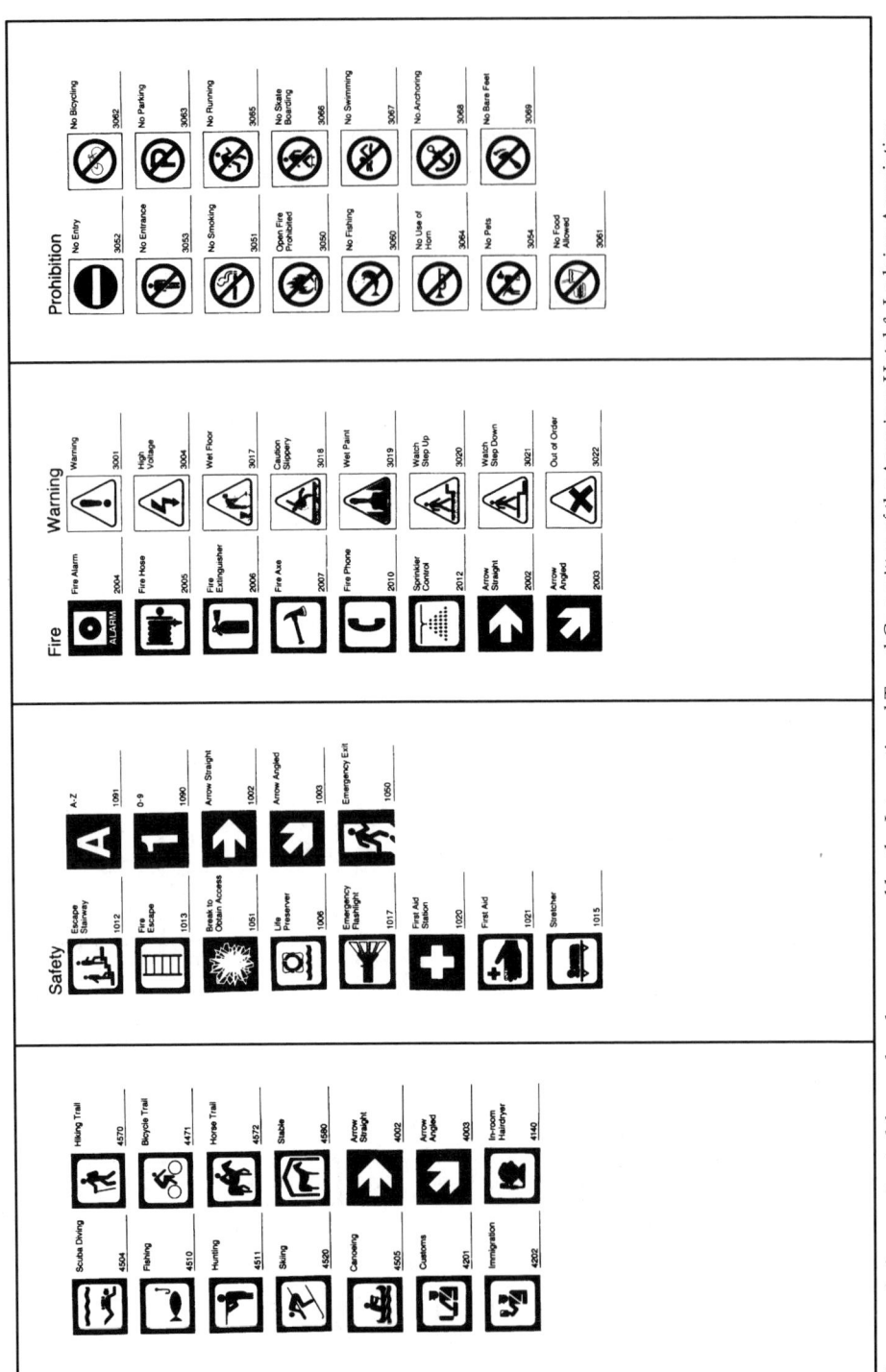

These symbols are extracted from a brochure prepared by the International Travel Committee of the American Hotel & Lodging Association.

Appendix B

International Hotel Regulations

Text adopted by the IHA Council
2 November 1981—Kathmandu, Nepal

Introduction

The International Hotel Industry published its first Hotel Regulations 60 years ago. Since then these regulations have been revised several times. Because, however, of the expansion of international tourism in the last 20 years, a new formulation is essential.

I) Objectives

The International Hotel Regulations aim to codify the generally accepted international trade practices governing the contract of hotel accommodation. They inform the guest and the hotelkeeper of their mutual rights and obligations. The Regulations are designed to serve as a complement to the provisions stipulated by the National Law to the terms of the contract; they apply when such a Law does not include specific provisions concerning the contract of hotel accommodation.

II) Contracting Parties

A person staying in a hotel may not necessarily be a contracting party; the contract of hotel accommodation may have been concluded on his behalf by a third party. In these regulations the term "customer" means the individual or legal person having concluded a hotel reservation contract who is responsible for payment. The term "guest" means the individual who is intending to stay or is staying at the hotel.

First Part: Contractual Relationship

Article 1: Contract of accommodation

Under the contract of accommodation, the hotelkeeper is obliged to provide accommodation and additional services for the guest.

The services shall be deemed to be the normal services of the hotel, according to the hotel category, including the use of such rooms and such facilities as are normally provided for the general benefit of guests.

The customer is liable to pay the price agreed.

The terms of the contract are governed by the category of the hotel, the National Law or Hotel Regulations (if any), the International Hotel Regulations and the House Rules which must be shown to the guest.

Article 2: Form of contract

The contract is not subject to any prescription as to form.

It is concluded when one party accepts the offer of the other party.

Article 3: Duration of contract

The contract can be agreed for a definite or an indefinite period. Where a contract is made for an approximate period, the shortest duration will be taken as the agreed period. The contract of accommodation ends at midday on the day after the arrival of the guest, unless a contract for more than one day has been requested and accepted.

Any contract for an indefinite period shall be considered as being for one day. In such case, notice expiring at midday on the following day may be given by either party to terminate the contract.

Notice given to the guest by the hotel shall be regarded as having been to the customer.

Article 4: Performance of the contract

The hotelkeeper and the customer are obliged to respect the terms of the contract.

Article 5: Nonperformance of the contract

In the event that the contract is not, or not completely, performed, the defaulting party must fully compensate the other party for his loss. The injured party is under the obligation to take all reasonable steps to mitigate the loss.

If he cannot perform the contract, the hotelkeeper should endeavour to find alternative accommodation of an equivalent or superior standard in the same locality. Any additional cost deriving therefrom must be met by the hotelkeeper. In case of default the hotelkeeper shall be liable to pay compensation.

Article 6: Termination of the contract

Except where the National Law or National Trade Practice provides otherwise, no contract can be terminated before its complete performance unless both contracting parties mutually agree.

Article 7: Payment

The hotel can ask full or partial pre-payment.

If the hotel receives from the customer a sum of money in advance it shall be considered to be an advance payment towards the price of the accommodation and additional services to be provided.

The hotel shall return money paid in advance to the extent that it exceeds the amount due, unless it has been stated to be a non-refundable deposit.

Bills are due on presentation.

Unless stated otherwise there is no obligation on the hotel to accept cheques, coupons, or credit cards or other means of noncash payment. Payment should be made in the appropriate national currency unless the hotel otherwise requests.

Article 8: Breach of contract

Any serious or persistent breach of the contractual obligations will entitle the injured party to terminate the contract immediately without notice.

Second Part: Other Obligations

Article 1: Liability of the hotelkeeper

The liability of the hotelkeeper depends on the National Law.

In the absence of any provisions of the National Law, the provisions of the European Convention of 17 December 1962 should apply.

The liability of the hotel to accept valuables in deposit shall depend on the size and standing of the hotel.

Liability for valuables can be limited reasonably if the guest has been informed in time. The hotelkeeper is not liable for cars or their contents.

Article 2: Liability of the guest/customer

The guest and the customer are liable to the hotelkeeper for any damages caused to persons, building, furnishing, or equipment, if the fault is attributable to them.

Article 3: Retention of guest's property

The hotelkeeper shall, as guarantee for payment of any amounts due to him, have the right to retain and ultimately to dispose of any property of commercial value brought to the premises of the hotel by a guest.

Article 4: Behaviour of guest

The guest shall behave in conformity with the hotel custom and the house rules of the hotel where he is staying.

Serious or persistent breaches of the house rules entitle the hotel to terminate the contract immediately without notice.

Article 5: Domestic animals

If a guest wishes to bring with him a domestic animal to the hotel he is under a duty to ensure, before introducing it, that this is permitted by the house rules of the hotel.

Article 6: Occupation and vacation of rooms

Unless otherwise stipulated, rooms which have been reserved for a guest must be ready at 2:00 P.M. and rooms of guests leaving the hotel must be vacated by noon.

Chapter 12 Outline

Historic Perspectives
Fundamentals of Classification Systems
    Criteria
    Use of Symbols
    Classification Authority
    Objective Assessments
Problems and Issues of International
    Hotel Classification
    Subjectivity
    Quality and Quantity of Service and
        Facilities
    "Let the Market Rule"
    Obstacles to International Agreement
    Cost
    Industry Objections
    Government Perspective
    Cultural Influence on Standards and
        Service
    Variations in Facilities
    Harmony Versus Homogeny
    Advantages and Positive Attributes
Selected Classification Systems in Practice
    Guide Michelin
    Mobil Travel Guide
    American Automobile Association
    Britain's Harmonized Classification
        System
    Ireland's Classification System
    Spain's Regional Approach
    Other Classification Systems
Toward Worldwide Standards
World-Class Service Standards

Competencies

1. Describe the forces that have led to the establishment of various national and international hotel classifications and standards. (pp. 369–370)

2. Identify five important purposes of hotel classification and distinguish between registration, classification, and grading. (pp. 370–372)

3. Describe the issues involved in setting criteria and choosing symbols for, and operating, a classification scheme. (pp. 372–373)

4. Identify and describe several problems and issues surrounding the development of an international classification scheme. (pp. 374–376)

5. Describe the basic differences between official and commercial classification systems. (pp. 376–380)

6. Identify and briefly describe several classification systems in use today. (pp. 380–388)

7. Describe the role played by the World Tourism Organization with regard to setting international standards, define what is generally meant by "world-class," and cite several guidelines for attaining world-class status. (pp. 388–390)

12

International Hotel Classifications and Standards

THE NEED FOR STANDARDS and quality control over lodging accommodations has been a concern expressed by many countries with the advent of modern tourism. Until world travel began to escalate into world trade proportions, the primary concern had been for the safety and protection of each country's domestic consumers. This concern led to the passage of various laws and regulations concerning fire safety, sanitation, and food safety. Licensing came later as a means of ensuring that hotels would meet at least minimal standards of building safety, waste disposal, environmental sanitation, food hygiene, workplace safety, and other elements. Such regulations have today become commonplace in many parts of the world. Nonetheless, the rapid growth of tourism and hotel investment over the past four decades, the emergence of new destinations around the world, and a rise in consumerism have resulted in the need for more definitive hotel classification systems and universal standards for both travelers and the travel trade. The focus has shifted from consumer protection to consumer information. A system of universal standards does not yet exist, but one may be needed.

Before the advent of mass travel and global telecommunications, mediocre hotel facilities and services were tolerated, especially in developing countries. Not anymore. The hotel industry, like other service industries, has undergone a drastic transformation in this age of information and technology. With easier information access and wider exposure to brand-name travel products, travelers from the major outbound markets around the world now have certain expectations when selecting travel arrangements and accommodations. Destinations have moved toward the establishment of universal standards for services and accommodations that not only respond to consumer needs, but also help to market the destinations themselves.

Historic Perspectives

The growth of European tourism in the latter part of the nineteenth century encouraged the gradual improvement of hotel standards on that continent. Accounts of the time indicate that few establishments were able to provide the standards desired by middle-class families. Finding a clean, comfortable bed for the night and an enjoyable meal was more a result of luck than design. It is not too surprising, therefore, that one of the first tasks undertaken by the canoeing, cycling, and motoring clubs popular at the time was to pass on recommendations from and to members about food and accommodations on excursions. In Britain, the Cyclists Touring Club permitted certain wayside inns to display the Club's familiar sign signifying its members' approval. In France, the advent of motoring induced the Michelin Tire Company to publish in 1900 a guide to France that introduced pictorial symbols to indicate the range of facilities at establishments providing good accommodations. Recognizing the marketing potential of such guides, hotels began actively seeking listings with these organizations. Other organizations eventually began supplying classified hotel guides for non-automobile members for the publicity and profit potential of supplying such a service.

With the arrival of mass tourism in the 1960s, governments and national tourism organizations also became interested in official classification systems. Some form of hotel registration or classification was introduced, or at least considered, by many countries. In 1970, only five countries—all in Europe—had national classification schemes; by 2004, 83 countries had an official hotel classification system.[1] Today, classification systems of varying types are commonplace. International and domestic travelers alike rely on them to varying degrees.

Exhibit 1 outlines the evolution of various initiatives, studies, and surveys to create a standardized hotel classification system. While various organizations have been successful in outlining potential systems to standardize hotel classification, acceptance, universal endorsement, and enforcement remain a challenge.

Fundamentals of Classification Systems

Hotel classification systems are designed to fulfill a number of different needs. Five important purposes are:

- *Standardization:* to establish a system of uniform service and product quality that helps to create an orderly travel market distribution system for buyers and sellers.

- *Marketing:* to advise travelers on the range and type of hotels available within a destination as a means of promoting the destination and encouraging healthy competition in the marketplace.

- *Consumer protection:* to ensure that the hotel meets minimum standards of accommodations, facilities, and service within classification and grade definitions.

- *Revenue generation:* to provide revenue from licensing, the sale of guidebooks, and so forth.

- *Control:* to provide a system for controlling general industry quality.

Before discussing the fundamentals of a classification scheme, it is important to define the following terminology. **Registration** is a form of licensing that may or may not require a minimum standard. Most countries require conformation with health and fire-safety legislation, which implies minimum criteria of sorts.

Classification is the assignment of hotels to a categorical rating according to type of property, facilities, and amenities offered. No universal classification

Exhibit 1 Historic Evolution of Hotel Classification Systems

Sponsoring Organization	Year(s)	Purpose and Description
International Union of Official Travel Organizations (IUOTO)	1952	A written Hotel Trade Charter to express interest in a global hotel classification system. In 1971, it was decided that a global system, if developed, needed to be in consultation with hotel industry professionals regionally.
World Tourism Organization (WTO)	1975	From 1976 to 1982, after taking over from IUOTO, WTO regional commissions adopted standardized hotel classification systems on a regional basis, using the IUOTO model. A survey of member states from 1985 to 1987 showed that 54 (73 percent) had national hotel standards consistent with WTO-recommended classification standards.
Hotels, Restaurants & Cafés in Europe (HOTREC)	1984	Report on "Proposed Uniform Hotel Information System for Hotels in Member States of the European Economic Community." The document reviewed and compared existing grading systems within the EEC and reviewed consumer information needs and booking patterns.
World Tourism Organization (WTO), European Committee for Standardization (CEN)	1989–1990s	Several initiatives by these organizations to standardize graphical symbols and standardize terminology related to tourism and hotel facilities. CEN produced the "European Standard of Tourism Services—Hotels" and covered other types of tourism accommodations.
International Organization for Standardization (ISO)	1997	Recommended the inclusion of quality of accommodation in a classification system and proposed to use ISO 9000 as the basis for an international hotel classification standard. This was opposed by the IH&RA and HOTREC on the basis that it assures predetermined standards but does not address level of standard, consumer expectation, and service delivery.

rating exists. The wide variation of hotel accommodations allows for as many as six or seven categories, using such diverse terms as five-star, deluxe, grand luxe, first class, first class superior, second class, moderate, third class, tourist, budget, economy, and other descriptions.

Grading is used to denote quality assessment. For example, grading may involve the awarding of special symbols to indicate achievement of high standards of accommodations, service, cuisine, and amenities. Depending on the classification scheme, grading is often used only when a property goes beyond the provisions of its classification.

Grading and classification are sometimes confused. Although classification in itself (that is, categorization) is not intended to denote grade, an element of grading is implied in classification schemes predicated on rankings. Indeed, in national schemes that use stars or similar symbols, it is difficult to separate classification from grade in the consumer's mind.

Criteria

A classification system will do little good if the scheme is not properly conceived and useful from a practical point of view. The basic goal of the scheme should be to assist buyers and sellers within the travel distribution system. Essentially, the criteria adopted should strike a balance between what owners and operators can reasonably provide and what the traveler reasonably requires and is willing to pay for. The requirements must be clear, and they should be periodically reviewed to ensure that they take account of hotel innovations and changes in customer demand.

In practice, hotel classification systems have worked well when they encompass the following eight elements:

1. The establishment of categories
2. The setting of criteria for each classification
3. Provision for special types of accommodations (for example, motels, bed and breakfasts, guest houses, farmhouses, condominiums, and apartments)
4. The establishment of methods of inspection and classification
5. A separate assessment of the standard of cuisine
6. The establishment of penalties
7. The independence of the classification system from the tax system
8. A means of appeal to a higher authority in the event of dispute[2]

Most classification systems are based on criteria that include some or all of the following elements: size, facilities, personnel, price, comfort, conveniences or amenities, quality of service, and cuisine. Since a portion of most evaluations is subjective, both operators and consumers must have confidence in the inspection process and the integrity of the hotel inspectorate for the scheme to be successful.

Use of Symbols

The classification symbols used must be both meaningful and simple, especially if they are to be displayed on signs. Both alphabetical and numerical designations can pose problems. Visitors may find the use of letters less meaningful than figures—for example, the distinctions between classes A and C, A and B, or A and AA may not be clear. However, hotel operators also worry about the connotations of numerical designations. How many people, for example, would want to stay or work in what is termed a third- or fourth-class establishment? Some countries have adopted Roman rather than Arabic numerals, some combine numerals with letters, and some employ symbols such as suns, crescent moons, or plum blossoms.

Among the various systems, the "star" grading system seems the best established and its adoption is increasing. The idea for star classification was borrowed from the rating system used for brandy; the higher the number of stars (to a maximum of five), the better the brandy. Even without explanation, many consumers have their own vague notion of what constitutes a five-star hotel or a two-star hotel. In practice, however, standards vary widely among countries. A five-star hotel often means significantly different things in different cities. A five-star traditional hotel in Rome or Caracas, for instance, may not compare with a five-star contemporary hotel in Tokyo or Singapore.

Classification Authority

In an official scheme, close government consultation with national tourist boards and hotel associations is helpful. A general measure of acceptance both for the nature of the scheme and the criteria is highly desired. Ideally, the best authority to control registration, classification, and grading schemes is one that includes representatives of government (including the tourist board), the hotel industry, and the travel trade. In practice, however, such authorities vary by country. Schemes and ratings may be determined by government departments (usually the ministry of tourism), by national tourist boards with input from the hotel industry, or unofficially by motoring associations and commercial enterprises.

While hoteliers know more than outsiders about how a hotel should be run, hotel associations can rarely exercise the degree of objectivity needed to operate a classification scheme. Systems operated by the private sector are frequently more effective in meeting the needs of travelers; however, they are not comprehensive enough for governmental oversight purposes. Moreover, some private guides have been accused of omitting establishments that were not willing to purchase advertising space. To dispel such concern, most commercial organizations are quick to emphasize that their advertisement division is not linked to the rating division. In the past, private or commercial organizations that operated classification schemes seldom consulted the industry. Today, many will at least consider the hoteliers' viewpoint, even though their commitment is to the general public.

Objective Assessments

The definition and measurement of service standards must be broad enough to cater to wide variations in capital investments and guest requirements. Even the most highly trained inspector cannot accurately measure the degree of guest satisfaction. Any private or national organization recommending hotels must not only strive to be objective, it needs to be perceived as objective. In the end, no classification system can do much more than indicate the available range of facilities, amenities, and services and to note the comparative quality of food and service based on staffing ratios, reputation, user surveys, inspections, and so on. The first analysis is one of fact. The second must necessarily be the judgment of inspectors qualified by training and experience.

Problems and Issues of International Hotel Classification

The issue of hotel classification has long been a controversial one. Given the wide variety of hotels, assigning a hotel to a specific category for classification purposes is not always an easy task in the absence of clear, measurable standards. When official and commercial classification schemes co-exist in the same destination, the problem of conflicting ratings or classifications often arises. Commercial guides typically place more weight on the quality of service, food and beverage, and comfort. Government schemes tend to concentrate on the physical aspects and facilities of the hotel. National systems, often subject to political pressures, are designed for inclusion rather than exclusion. Therefore, they will always be more generalized and liberal in setting standards than private rating systems.

The difficulties in classifying hotels increase dramatically when classification is extended to an international level. Arguments have been made against the very idea of international classification, which some critics believe will lead to erroneous information being given to consumers. One line of reasoning is that valid comparisons cannot be made between different types of hotels—beach bungalows, *paradors,* motels, condo hotels, and so forth—or between hotels situated in such different locations as urban centers, suburbs, or remote destinations, much less between different countries and regions of the world.

Subjectivity

The problem of subjectivity is inherent to varying degrees in most national and international classification systems. Each scheme has its own rigidity and leads to unfairness for some properties. Every establishment has its own unique selling points and these do not necessarily follow the lines by which classifications are made. Not only is it difficult to assess any facility properly on the basis of one or two short visits by inspectors, but what constitutes quality service or food is at least to some degree subject to cultural influences, personal tastes and preferences, and experience. Differences in the perception of quality tend to be much more marked across national borders. Even when grading physical aspects and other tangible items, there can be problems when the assessed establishment lacks certain features required for a specific category, but includes other features that far surpass the required minimum for the grade in question. An example is the case of a renowned luxury property in Hawaii that was marketed as a total escape from the cares of the world. This resort did not qualify for a five-diamond rating because its management refused to place a television set in each room. Rather than settle for a lower rating, the operator declined to be rated at all.

Quality and Quantity of Service and Facilities

Another concern with classification systems is that they sometimes seem to stress the notion of quality at the expense of specific information about a hotel's actual facilities. Some European countries have proposed that classification schemes be eliminated altogether and replaced with standardized information systems that use graphic symbols or pictograms to denote facilities. However, this approach neither resolves the problem of reporting on service quality nor says much about the establishment's atmosphere. Hotels, after all, offer products that are a mix of both accommodations and service. The hotel itself is nothing more than steel and concrete. It is people who breathe life into the hotel, and whether the service is good or bad depends not only on the number of employees but on the quality of their performance.

Without some sort of qualitative rating, the prospective first-time buyer is not greatly helped if the only information provided is graphic symbols indicating that the hotel has a restaurant and bedrooms with private bathrooms, telephones, and television. On the other hand, if the buyer knows that the hotel is rated as a four-star establishment, he or she might have a fair idea of what to expect in terms of the quality of accommodations and the service level. The ideal system from a buyer's perspective would perhaps combine classification symbols and informational pictograms to give optimum information.

"Let the Market Rule"

Many chain operators believe that classification schemes are redundant. They argue that the trend toward hotel product segmentation and branding has made any grading system obsolete. While many years ago the public may have needed to rely on a rating service to help determine the level of quality to expect from a lodging establishment, the assurance of "no surprises" is now promoted by many chains and franchisors. When a brand has become established internationally, the brand itself is the warranty of quality to the marketplace.

Additionally, the hotel industry is dynamic. Consumer needs are always changing, and hotels can either respond with new products and services or lose market share to competitors. To the extent that classification criteria are static or that they trail behind changing consumer needs and industry trends, classification schemes serve neither the consumer nor the industry well. Some people—largely owners and operators—believe that it may be more appropriate to allow the laissez-faire nature of business to guide the setting of standards for hotel products and services. Proponents of this view argue that it is the economic laws of the marketplace, not classification schemes, that will determine what products and services are purchased and at what price.

Obstacles to International Agreement

As far back as 1962, the World Tourism Organization (WTO)—under its forerunner, the International Union of Official Travel Organizations—attempted to devise an international system of hotel classifications. In a global economy, there would be obvious benefits to be gained by having a uniform system of hotel classifications that cut across national and regional boundaries to serve the world travel industry. However, the early WTO attempt was not wholly supported by its member countries; after years of debate, the only conclusion reached by 1970 was to abandon further considerations of a global model in favor of a more limited regional approach. The work of developing regional standards was undertaken by the six WTO regional commissions between 1976 and 1982. Eventually, the majority of the WTO member countries, mostly developing nations, adopted these regional schemes or otherwise modified their own national schemes to be consistent with the regional standards.[3]

The problems confronting the establishment of a universal system are numerous. Many countries already have well-established systems that are recognized in the markets they serve. Such countries are therefore reluctant to subordinate these systems in favor of another. Then, too, there is the troublesome question of how to reach consensus among countries with respect to common terminology and criteria—qualitative and quantitative—covering wide differences in hotel plants and investments, hotel characteristics and standards, and national hotel legislation around the world. If agreements could be reached, there would still be the issue of the cost of training and maintaining a qualified inspectorate to sustain the system. Nonetheless, as various sectors of the travel industry—notably the airlines—move toward consolidated systems, the issue of a universal hotel classification system will likely be revisited periodically.

Cost

The expense of developing, implementing, and maintaining a classification scheme is one of the primary reasons some countries have no such official system. Regular inspection is required by qualified staff. This is not only costly and time-consuming, it also assumes the ability to find and train suitable staff. On an international level, the cost of ensuring that standards are applied uniformly across borders could be exorbitant.

Industry Objections

While some commercial grading schemes are endorsed by hotels as important marketing tools, hotel industries in most countries view official classifications as an unnecessary government intervention that is often too bureaucratic and perhaps coercive. In some countries, governments use these systems as reference schemes for price fixing, taxation, and the provision of incentives in line with the objectives of tourism policy; this can interfere with natural market forces in the development and marketing of the hotel. Hoteliers in some countries fear that classification may lead to some form of price control. To reduce such fears, hotel operators suggest that there be adequate industry involvement at all levels in establishing national systems and relevant grading standards and in communicating the grading system to consumers and the travel trade.

On the whole, the international hotel industry has not favored classification systems, which it views as being overly restrictive and ineffective for marketing purposes. On the other hand, the *travel* industry is generally supportive of official classification schemes, as long as they are relevant to the needs of consumers and trade professionals. The travel trade sees their value as a protection mechanism for travel agents, tour operators, and consumers.

Government Perspective

Most governments give three reasons for supporting official classification schemes: registration or licensing, tourism planning, and marketing. From the government's perspective, the basic purposes of registration are to:

- Provide comprehensive information on the various types and availability of accommodations.

- Ensure the establishment of minimum standards for each classification of lodging.

- Ensure the availability of comprehensive, up-to-date statistical information needed for tourism planning, such as data on tariffs and staff employment.

- Ensure that tourist accommodations meet acceptable standards of public safety in such vital aspects as fire, sanitation, security, and safe-keeping of guest valuables.[4]

A well-planned and administered classification system can assist government tourism planning by providing authoritative and reliable statistical data on the supply of local, provincial, or national hotel rooms. This helps to identify both the long- and short-term need for planning accommodations in different categories and price levels for domestic and/or international consumption. Government incentives may then be designed to attract domestic or foreign investment to support the development of specific types of properties according to a country's particular needs or goals.

Tourist promotion boards have found classification schemes helpful in marketing their destinations by being able to target different classes of accommodations to different segments of the market. In some countries, classification has helped to isolate inadequate hotels that harm the reputation of better hotels and the industry or the destination as a whole.

Cultural Influence on Standards and Service

It is often said that hospitality knows no borders. While this is true, the customs of hospitality are practiced differently around the world. These differences are reflected in hotel practices and usage. For instance, in many developing countries, hosts who find entertaining at home difficult often use hotels for social entertainment because luxury-class hotels provide services to make such entertaining gracious and easy.

The existing variations in standards of hotel management and services offered reflect not only differing national cultures, but also differing wage levels, customs, tariffs, importations, and availabilities of experienced local or expatriate staff. In Asia, the availability and comparatively lower cost of labor, for example, enable the highest standard of personal service to be found more readily than in the United States or Europe, where labor costs are higher and there is greater emphasis placed on efficiency and productivity. The Asian tradition of the honored guest is the foundation of Asian service. In the better hotels, this concept is combined with European production techniques and service to provide total customer service. These differences are difficult to reconcile in an international classification scheme, which adds to the difficulty of developing a universal system that meets industry as well as governmental concerns.

Variations in Facilities

With respect to facilities, the private bathroom may be the most difficult standard to resolve in an international classification, since it is the feature having the greatest international variation. In Europe, for example, the charm of many hotels lies in the fact that they are restorations or conversions of country estates, castles, and so forth; it would be self-defeating to insist on precise minimum requirements that, if met, might destroy the charm of such hotels.

Harmony Versus Homogeny

Any attempt to establish international standards for hotels poses a dilemma with respect to the question of standardization versus individuality. While international standards are not intended to discourage individuality or uniqueness of hotel products, neither do they encourage individuality. The rationale for an international standards system is to promote international market distribution efficiency and to foster consumer confidence, but this would seem to require harmony of standards and a degree of uniformity among products within classifications. Setting uniform standards means that such matters as architectural design, construction, interiors, management, and modes of service, which are important in determining individual product quality, cannot be taken into consideration, even if they matter to buyers. The problem is not one of unconcern, but rather one of difficulty of measurement across national boundaries. For that reason, some countries favor a system based on room prices alone, on the notion that prices adequately express the quality of accommodation and services provided.

Is it possible to develop a set of acceptable international standards that are stringent enough to be meaningful, yet not so stringent as to choke off room for distinction of national character, ethnicity, or other special identity? Possibly. There are indeed some excellent examples of hotels in many countries that have attained what may be loosely defined as "world-class standards"—meaning they have met the expectations of a world market—along with the distinction of individuality. These hotels share five common characteristics: uniqueness, a sense of place, traditional hospitality, cultural significance, and historic continuity. These five characteristics are evident, for example, in the Spanish *parador*, the Mexican *hacienda*, and the Japanese *ryokan*. These unique forms of accommodations have become national institutions representing local values, traditions, and culture in the tourism experience.

Advantages and Positive Attributes

Despite their limitations, hotel classification systems have a number of positive attributes. They are clearly important in providing the public with helpful consumer information. Marketing specialists often view classification as an important marketing tool. Politically, a national classification system may help gain government support for the industry, as it calls attention to the hotel industry and thus positions its importance within the economy.

As the world rapidly moves toward a global economy, standards are now being set universally in almost every industry. Product design, innovation, service,

Spanish *Paradors*

The term *parador* is a new application of the word for inn as used in classic Spanish literature. There are two key considerations behind the philosophy of *paradors*, which are state-owned hotels run by the general council of tourism. First, old buildings that represent outstanding traditional or classical architecture are sought as unique sites for the majority of these hotels. Palaces, castles, convents, and other ancient monuments are targets, as are buildings and gardens most representative of certain regions. The second consideration is to draw tourism into relatively little-known, mostly inland places. The unique ambiance, often enhanced by the excellent cuisine of local dishes, transforms the *paradors* into destinations themselves. This provides a better-balanced distribution of tourism throughout the country. The thoroughness with which the *paradors* capitalize on their links with the history and geography of their location is a significant component of their success.

Mexican *Haciendas*

The origin of *haciendas* is directly related to the colonization of America. Land granted by the Spanish crown to the conquistadors of "New Spain" gradually took the form of *haciendas*—great estates—that became centers of the predominant economic activity of each region. *Hacienda* hotels are typically characterized by beautiful architecture. They possess all the amenities of a deluxe hotel, yet they do not leave the guest with any doubt about being in Mexico. The grounds of most *hacienda* hotels include beautifully landscaped woods and gardens that provide ideal areas for walking, exploring, and horseback riding. Many such properties boast the remains of aqueducts and pools of thermal mineral water. Thus, *haciendas* treat not only the ancient buildings but also the original grounds as something worth revitalizing. The Hotel La Mansion Galindo, for example, in San Juan del Rio, transformed a sixteenth-century *hacienda* into a complete country resort with modern convention capabilities. Antiques four centuries old are displayed on the walls and the hotel is surrounded by woodland areas that have been carefully replanted to evoke the original mood of the *hacienda*.

Japanese *Ryokan*

Nature's beauty and aesthetics are skillfully woven into a Japanese hospitality environment to create the *ryokan*. At the heart of the *ryokan* is the cultivated Japanese garden to delight the eyes and to calm the senses. The first *ryokan*, which are the traditional accommodations of Japan, are said to have been built some 1,200 years ago. While the historic date is unproven, *ryokan* have been around at least since the end of the eighteenth century, increasing in number to some 80,000 inns today. Many have been improved to such an extent that they can provide first-rate accommodations for both foreign and domestic guests with culturally unique, highly personalized service. The utilization of natural resources ranges from the nature-inspired asymmetrical architecture to the use of natural building materials and the regular redecoration of guestrooms to match the changing moods of the four seasons. Some large, modern international hotels provide the traditional *ryokan* as one of the accommodation choices.

Source: Hana Ayala, "International Hotel Ventures: Back to the Future," *Cornell Hotel and Restaurant Administration Quarterly*, February 1991, p. 41.

quality, and speed of response to changing markets are now driven to a large extent by what is best on a global level. The hotel industry, which is already international in scope, should not be an exception.

How important is it to have a universal classification scheme? For most international travelers, it is reassuring to be able to find accommodations in a foreign country whose standards correspond to the characteristics and availability of facilities with which they are familiar from previous experience, either at home or abroad. This holds true for travel sellers as well as buyers. The ability for travel sellers to determine what is available in terms of hotel products, especially in unfamiliar places, is very useful when counseling travelers, booking accommodations, or designing travel packages for clients. In terms of marketing travel products, it is easier if travel agents can use widely accepted and understood hotel ratings and symbols to describe the product to clients. The designation by grade or category helps both the travel agent and the client put a hotel in a clearer perspective.

Selected Classification Systems in Practice

The World Tourism Organization notes that some type of hotel classification currently exists in most countries. These systems are either official (national, government implemented) or private (commercial). Official classifications are normally drafted by the national tourism administrations, often in cooperation with hotel trade representatives. Private or voluntary classifications are usually drafted by commercial companies and associations involved in the promotion of hotel services. It is not unusual to have both official and commercial classification schemes operating within the same country.

The hotel industry is much more willing to support commercial classification systems that, rather than being a regulatory tool, can be used for promotional and marketing purposes. The primary disadvantage of commercial schemes from a government perspective is that these schemes tend to be more exclusive than inclusive in their listings; governments prefer inclusive schemes for a variety of reasons, including the appeasement of constituents, the marketing of destinations, tax valuations, and general planning. With some private classification systems, inclusion of hotels is at the discretion of the organization operating the service; in others, the service is voluntary and open to hoteliers as a marketing tool. Private schemes rarely run on a profit-making basis; they are usually operated for their members' convenience and as a benefit of membership or tied with collateral product promotions. This is an essential difference in concept from official schemes, which are employed to generate revenues through hotel registration and licensing fees, listing fees, and so forth.

It is not always mandatory for hotels to be officially classified in countries with official schemes, but operators who choose not to participate may be excluded from official hotel guidebooks and lose other benefits, including promotions at trade shows. In many countries, qualification through the classification process is a condition for the hotel to obtain a license for commercial operation. Establishing and implementing the official classification is usually the responsibility of an officially appointed body reporting to the national tourism administration.

Numerous types of classification schemes have evolved over the years. Most countries follow either one or more of these classification schemes with slight variations. The universal symbol of excellence, or rather degrees of excellence, is the star rating system. In recent years, different countries and areas have chosen to develop their own symbols—for example, Taiwan's plum blossom and Korea's bronze shield and rose of Sharon—with varying criteria for awards. In the following sections, a number of different schemes are discussed to illustrate how classification systems operate in practice.

Guide Michelin

The traditional approach to qualitative rating of hotels is best exemplified by France, which has a government grading system as well as commercial rating services. Knowledgeable travelers in France almost completely ignore the officially mandated rating and rely exclusively on *Guide Michelin*, published by the Michelin Tire Company's Tourism Department. Started by André Michelin in 1900, the guide was initially designed to help drivers maintain their cars, find decent lodging, and eat well while touring.

Michelin criteria requirements are unpublished and the company decides which hotels will be included in the guide. Hotels are inspected anonymously and the guide publishes an account of the inspector's opinion of the hotel. Hotels are classified on five grade levels, represented by symbols of houses, fork and spoons, and blossoms (see Exhibit 2). A rating change in *Guide Michelin* can virtually make or break an establishment. The Michelin rating system also uses a variety of other pictorial symbols to indicate specific hotel facilities such as air conditioning, free parking, equipped conference halls, and bedrooms accessible to people with disabilities. In the last few years, Michelin has added guidebooks for New York, Las Vegas, Los Angeles, and San Francisco to its line of guides.

Mobil Travel Guide

In North America, the *Mobil Travel Guide* is produced by ExxonMobil Corporation. Published annually since 1958 and initially covering only five southeastern states, today it consists of 15 regional volumes describing 4,000 cities, 22,000 points of interest, and quality ratings of 22,000 hotels, motels, motor hotels, inns, guest ranches, resorts, and restaurants in the United States and Canada. Of the more than 100 hotel classification systems in use worldwide, the Mobil rating system is perceived to be one of the most critical. Every year, approximately 17,000 lodging establishments are reviewed, with only 14,000 making the publication. Of those, 60 to 70 percent receive a one- or two-star rating, and about 30 percent are in the three-star category. Less than 5 percent of the properties reviewed receive the coveted four- and five-star ratings. Some industry experts contend that the fifth star can bring in an extra $1 million or more to a hotel annually.[5] Because properties are evaluated every year, no rating is ever final. Every year, 10 percent of all properties listed are dropped and replaced with new ones, guaranteeing the currency of the guide.

The program is voluntary, and any property can request inspection and be considered for inclusion in the *Mobil Travel Guide.* Properties are reviewed only

Exhibit 2 The Rating System of *Guide Michelin*

Hôtels restaurants

CLASSE ET CONFORT

Grand luxe et tradition	
Grand confort	
Très confortable	
Bon confort	
Assez confortable	
[M] Dans sa catégorie, hôtel d'équipement moderne	

L'AGRÉMENT

Hôtels agréables
Restaurants agréables
« Park » Élément particulièrement agréable
Hôtel très tranquille, ou isolé et tranquille
Hôtel tranquille
≤ sea. Vue exceptionnelle, panorama
Vue intéressante ou étendue

LA TABLE

Une des meilleures tables du pays, vaut le voyage
Table excellente, mérite un détour
Une très bonne table dans sa catégorie
M Autre table soignée

©MICHELIN. Permission No. 93-875. Note: Identical symbols that seem to indicate different things above are reproduced in different colors in the original guide.

once, except for current and potential four- and five-star properties, which receive an additional inspection by a senior staff evaluator who stays at the hotel anonymously. Typically, trained field representatives arrive at a property unannounced and ask to meet with management. They do not stay at the property, but obtain updated room rate and other information or discover changes at the hotel during the site visit. Representatives do not determine the rating, but rather send reports to a rating committee that, using a criteria checklist of over 100 items, assigns a rating.

A great deal of weight is placed on customer letters and responses to comment cards found in the guides.

In developing rating standards and criteria, ExxonMobil consulted extensively with national and international experts in hospitality. The original standards are basically unchanged, although criteria have been expanded and updated to reflect a higher degree of professionalism in the industry today and the growing sophistication of the consumer. Although there are no explicit criteria identifying price range as a contributing factor, the rating system implies a judgment regarding value for money.

The rating categories—one through five stars—are assigned according to the following scale:

Five Stars:	Among the best in the country
Four Stars:	Outstanding—worth a special trip
Three Stars:	Excellent
Two Stars:	Very Good
One Star:	Good

A check mark placed alongside the rating denotes an unusually good value. Among the principal areas for evaluation are:

- *Physical structure*, including the quality and condition of the building exterior, landscaped grounds, interior public space, and guestrooms.
- *Furnishings*, including floor and wall coverings, draperies, lighting fixtures, appliances, and furniture.
- *Maintenance*, including guestrooms, baths, public areas, and recreational facilities.
- *Housekeeping*, including guestrooms, baths, public areas, and recreational facilities.
- *Overall service*, including attire and attitude of all staff and management personnel, and the staff-to-guest ratio.
- *Food service*, including restaurant and room service food quality and variety, table setting, and presentation.

While specific criteria are used, intangibles are also a big part of the consideration when assigning a rating. The guide's approach emphasizes uniqueness and consistency of excellent service based on the establishment's purpose and management goals. Locational and cultural differences are taken into consideration. What is appropriate decor and furnishing for Miami, for example, may not be deemed appropriate for Manhattan. Small bathrooms in old hotels are not compared to large bathrooms in newer hotels, but considered on their own merit and on whether management has made attempts at modernization.

American Automobile Association

The American Automobile Association (AAA) began listing hotels in *TourBooks* in the 1930s. However, the actual rating of properties was not introduced until the early 1960s, based on a simple evaluation system of good, very good, excellent, and outstanding. Since 1977, diamonds—on a scale of one to five—have been used as a symbol of quality. Annually, AAA inspects more than 60,000 operations in the United States, Canada, Mexico, and the Caribbean; of these, only 25,000 hotels, motels, and restaurants merit inclusion in AAA *TourBooks* and *Travel Guides*. Thirty-eight million of these guides are distributed each year. Guide information is also available online to AAA members.

Each hotel desiring a diamond-rating classification from AAA must meet AAA's minimum requirements for consideration.[6] These consist of 27 criteria that relate to, among other things, external physical attributes, security features, fire protection, housekeeping, and guestroom ambiance. If a hotel meets these minimum requirements, it may complete the AAA application for evaluation. The hotel must include with its application recent pictures of its exterior and public areas and photos of a standard guest unit and bathroom. After the application and photos are submitted, AAA typically will notify the hotel that it will receive an unannounced evaluation visit within one year of the application.

During the application review process, AAA first validates application referrals and conducts basic research on the property. If the hotel is presumed to qualify, one of AAA's tourism editors will visit the property and observe its curbside appeal, exterior, and other factors pertaining to the basic elements of the property. This preliminary review is to verify that the hotel clearly exhibits characteristics that would appeal to AAA members. If AAA is satisfied with this preliminary review, a representative will contact the owner, general manager, or property designee for a brief interview. The interview has a dual purpose. First, it allows AAA to gather factual data for inclusion in its publications; second, the interview gives the property representative a chance to advise AAA of any plans for improvements to the hotel.

Following the interview, a tourism editor will tour the property with the property representative, verifying the existence of the AAA diamond-rating requirements. Additionally, the editor will evaluate the property using a set of guidelines that represent objective criteria prevalent throughout the lodging industry. These comprehensive guidelines consist of more than 300 items covering six major areas of a hotel:

1. Management and staff
2. Housekeeping and maintenance
3. Exterior, grounds, and public areas
4. Room decor, ambiance, and amenities
5. Bathrooms
6. Guest services

After the evaluation, a determination is made about whether the hotel should be listed. At that point, the tourism editor assigns or recommends a diamond rating. At the conclusion of the evaluation process, the tourism editor provides the property representative with a written summary of the evaluation, including the rating decision.

AAA diamond ratings for hotels represent a combination of the overall quality, range of facilities, and level of services offered by the property. The ratings are assigned exclusively to properties that meet and uphold AAA's rigorous quality standards:

- *One diamond.* Properties that appeal to the budget-minded traveler. These properties provide essential, no-frills accommodations. They meet the basic requirements pertaining to comfort, cleanliness, and hospitality.
- *Two diamonds.* Properties that appeal to the traveler seeking more than basic accommodations. They provide modest enhancements to the overall physical attributes, design elements, and amenities of the facility, typically at a moderate price.
- *Three diamonds.* Multi-faceted properties with a distinguished style, including marked upgrades in the quality of physical attributes, amenities, and level of comfort provided.
- *Four diamonds.* Properties that are upscale in all areas. Accommodations are more refined and stylish. The property's physical attributes reflect an obvious enhanced level of quality throughout. The fundamental hallmarks at this level include an extensive array of amenities combined with a high degree of hospitality, service, and attention to detail.
- *Five diamonds.* Properties that reflect the ultimate in luxury and sophistication. Accommodations are first class. The physical attributes are extraordinary in every manner. The fundamental hallmarks at this level are providing meticulous service, exceeding guest expectations, and maintaining impeccable standards of excellence. Many personalized services and amenities provide an unmatched level of comfort.

As AAA and Mobil use different approaches in evaluating a facility, it is not uncommon for a hotel to be rated differently by the two organizations. Also, because AAA *TourBooks* constitute a rating service primarily for the use of its members, these publications are not made available for sale to the general public, whereas *Mobil Travel Guides* are distributed for public use.

Britain's Harmonized Classification System

A new unified classification system for hotels and other lodging properties has been established in the United Kingdom, based on an agreement between the Automobile Association (AA), Royal Automobile Club (RAC), and English Tourist Board. While previously the three organizations had their own classification schemes, the unified system will assign stars based on quality standards, ranging from a minimum of one star to a maximum of five. This new system is voluntary.

Descriptions of the hotel classification levels under the new unified system are as follows:

- *One-star hotels.* These are generally small, independently owned hotels with a family atmosphere. Services are typically provided by the family. These hotels have a limited range of facilities and offer simple meals to guests. Some bedrooms may not have attached bathrooms.

- *Two-star hotels.* These small to medium-size hotels have more facilities than one-star hotels. The reception/check-in area is more formal and professionally managed, and the food and beverage facilities have more options. Some business hotels are two-star rated and have well-equipped accommodations and attached bathrooms.

- *Three-star hotels.* Three-star hotels are larger and offer a wider range of higher-quality facilities than one- and two-star hotels. Restaurants may be full-service. Guestroom furnishings and amenities are more varied, with the inclusion of direct-dial telephones, hair dryers, and other bathroom amenities. Three-star hotels in locations attractive to business travelers have more business facilities than lower-rated hotels.

- *Four-star hotels.* Four-star hotels provide near-luxury accommodations, with better-quality furnishings, decor, and equipment. Guestrooms are larger and feature plush furnishings and fixtures. Because the ratio of staff to rooms is higher, these hotels can offer more personalized service. Services such as 24-hour room service and laundry service are standard features.

- *Five-star hotels.* Accommodations at these hotels are large and luxurious, matching world-class standards. The interior design of the hotel may feature fine works of art; the overall impression is one of luxury and elegance. Service levels are high, to meet the higher expectations of guests. High staff to room ratios, continuous staff training, close attention to detail, and high technical training and education of management and culinary staff are expected at these hotels. Five-star hotels reflect world-class service, both in their physical and intangible dimensions.[7]

Ireland's Classification System

The former Irish hotel and guesthouse classification system that was in place for 13 years did not enjoy universal support among Irish hoteliers, with nearly 15 percent choosing to opt out of the system. As a result, a new hotel classification scheme was developed by Fáilte Ireland in conjunction with the Irish Hotels Federation. As the new classification system was gradually phased in, the old and new schemes co-existed until 2008, when the new system was fully in place.

The new system incorporates categories ranging from one to five stars and introduces a new point-scoring system. Hotels must comply with a set of basic criteria for the classification concerned. All two-star, three-star, and four-star hotels must also achieve a specific minimum number of points from a menu of optional hotel facilities and services that have been assigned point values. Details about how the new system works are available to consumers on the web at www.hotelstars.ie. As just mentioned, in the previous system a large number of properties chose not to be classified, which undermined the system's usefulness to customers. Therefore, the new system was made mandatory. For purposes of clarity and transparency, the operator completes a self-assessment document that is checked by Fáilte Ireland's contractors following a visit to the premises. Only then can a classification be awarded.

Spain's Regional Approach

Until 1986, Spain had one national compulsory classification system. In line with the restructuring of the country's administration, the classification system—still compulsory—is now the responsibility of the country's 17 regional community authorities. By law, every hotelier must submit an application to be classified, along with detailed information about the property. The regional tourism office will then investigate the hotel to ensure that minimum standards are met and to award the classification. All regions use a five-star classification system. The provision of food can be offered by any establishment, but must receive separate authorization from the tourism office.

There are no national standard criteria for hotels. Each of the 17 autonomous regions publishes its own requirements, with criteria varying from region to region. Some regions assign classifications solely on the basis of an objective assessment of hotel facilities. Others include subjective assessments of service and atmosphere. Consequently, hotel chains in Spain may find that their hotels have different classifications in different regions of the country. As the classification system is linked to tax levies, hotel chains will end up paying different levies for similar hotels. Because a hotel's taxes are proportionate to its grade level, many hotels intentionally downgrade themselves to avoid higher taxes.[8]

Other Classification Systems

Some countries favor a classification based on room prices. This is a laissez-faire approach based on the conviction that prices adequately express the services provided by a hotel and that the marketplace itself is the ultimate regulator of standards. Other countries require a minimum number of bedrooms for specific classifications, but classification by size alone is nothing more than a statistical exercise. Some governments are opposed in theory to official classification systems. The rationale is that market forces will preserve quality through competition and that the free market best serves the interests of consumers.

In addition, new commercial hotel classification systems are springing up that have no connection to the types of country-based or government-sponsored classification systems just discussed. Since the introduction of the World Wide Web, there has been a rapid growth of consumer websites for booking hotel reservations, and many of these sites have developed systems for classifying and rating hotels. These hotel classifications are generally based on price tiers or well-known general industry classifications (luxury, budget), and the grading systems are typically based on consumer feedback. Stars or other symbols are awarded to properties to guide consumers in making their selections.

In many cases, these websites post guest comments about the hotels as well. This type of direct feedback is informative both for potential guests and travel professionals. Expedia created a classification system called "Expedia Insiders' Select." Based on a combination of consumer opinions, a comparison with other properties to determine overall value for the money, and "Expedia Hotel Expert input," properties are given a point score and a star rating. Consumers can click a link that takes them to the written opinions of consumers who have visited the properties.

Utell, a major third-party reservations provider for independent hotels, created a classification system called "Utell Selections." Under this system, all hotels are classified in one of three core categories: Luxury, Superior, and Value. A hotel may be further identified by the specific industry niche it occupies, such as luxury, resort, or airport. The classifications are accompanied with appropriate descriptors. These types of commercial classification systems are in part a response to the lack of consistency in the various hotel classification systems in place throughout the world.

Toward Worldwide Standards

Over the years, a number of international organizations, including the WTO, the European Economic Community (forerunner to the European Union), and the Organization for Economic Cooperation and Development (OECD), have worked to harmonize hotel classification standards on an international basis. These attempts have contributed to both a fuller understanding of the problems of classification and the gradual movement toward their resolution. In 1989, WTO revised its regional standards to bring them in line with prevailing industry standards around the world and to take into account the development of new hotel products and changing customer demand. Standards for hotel classification suitable for worldwide application were recommended in the new scheme patterned after WTO's regional models. In pursuing the new scheme, WTO established working contacts with the International Hotel & Restaurant Association (IH&RA) in order to have the views of the operational sector; it should be noted, however, that IH&RA has not generally been receptive to the establishment of an international hotel classification system.

In setting up the standards, WTO recommended that the classification system be treated with flexibility, as price policy and price comparability within hotel categories would be affected differently in different countries. WTO also urged that national hotel and consumer associations be invited to take part in the classifying so that differences of opinion in categorizing individual hotels would be minimized. Mechanisms to ensure international harmonization would include consultation with international private associations and companies that are involved in independent hotel classification for commercial purposes.[9]

At present, there is very little international-level agreement in terms of arriving at common classification systems for the hospitality sector. Recently, however, European Union institutions have started putting increasing emphasis on this issue. One of their key aims is to strengthen the rights of consumers as users of services, which involves requiring greater transparency and information from service providers. In the meantime, HOTREC (Hotels, Restaurants & Cafés in Europe) provides information about the varying European classification systems on an interactive map that consumers can use to easily find out what the hotel stars mean in the European countries listed. The information is provided in the national language(s) of the selected country and in English.[10]

World-Class Service Standards

Many hotels today aspire to achieve "world-class" status. "World-class" is an unofficial standard implying that a hotel provides a level of luxury and range of services equal to any other in the world. Just as with hotel classifications and ratings, the definition of world-class is debatable. For many, it represents an ideal rather than something attainable.

In today's international hotel industry, world-class service is the consistent satisfaction of the needs and expectations of a culturally diverse public. It matches the capabilities and approach of the service provider to the needs and expectations of the buyer. World-class hotels often target prominent world travelers—many with instant name recognition to the general public—who can lend their prestige and special cachet to the status of the hotel. World-class hotels tend to be classic hotels with longstanding traditions, well-maintained and refined over the years. However, there are also contemporary world-class hotels in many parts of the world, created by extraordinary investment, planning, operations, marketing, and press image. Having coveted five-star ratings in the right guides also helps. Most would agree that a world-class hotel is expensive to build and furnish, sometimes costing twice as much as other first-rate hotels. But this point is also debatable, since location and other variables affect cost. Most important, world-class hotels stress the personal attention given to guests, resulting in a high number of staff members relative to guests.

Being both proactive and adaptive, world-class service feels equally "right" to the European dignitary occupying the presidential suite and to the Japanese visitor staying in a standard room in the same hotel. At a minimum, it is service perceived by each customer as appropriate and satisfactory. At its best or most luxurious level, it may also make the customer feel truly pampered, with every conceivable service available at his or her fingertips. Finally, it is gracious service that is culturally sensitive to guests from around the world.

While not all hotels can expect to achieve world-class status, it is an important concept for professional hoteliers to understand and strive for as an ideal.

Since there is no official definition of world-class, there is no simple formula for attaining a world-class designation. Operators who aspire to such "designation" must first develop a visionary strategy. Of course, a strategy alone will not work. The property itself must be able to meet classification and grading standards at the highest level. The hotel must truly be special, at least among its competitors. The following principles would seem to apply, at least in varying degrees:

- There must be a shared vision within the organization of what constitutes a great hotel.
- Management must not always be by the book. Managers must do more than routine things, and they must do much more than simply what is necessary.
- Managers must know how to play host to people from all walks and stations of life, coming from any part of the world.
- The hotel must be valued by its host community and should be an involved contributor to the community's social aspirations and goals.

- Culture must be understood, respected, and adopted as a resource in the hotel's internal value system.
- Human resources must be treated as investment assets. Policies, procedures, rules, and practices must all reflect this philosophy.
- Training must be continuous at all levels. Perfection is a journey, not a destination.
- Communication must not be happenstance. It is an integral part of the organization, and employees must have systematic access to information.
- The marketplace is the final judge of what is world-class. The delivery system must fulfill the promise made through marketing. The customer's trust and the hotel's credibility are two sides of the same coin.
- Details matter. The hotel business is a business of details, attitudes, promises, and expectations. It is not a manufacturing environment—the rules of heavy industry have no application except for quality control principles applied at the customer-service level.
- Perception is reality in the external world. Management must therefore have ways of measuring or assessing the image of the hotel in order to find ways for its continuous improvement. It is always harder to achieve and maintain a reputation than to lose it.

Summary

Hotel classification has long been a controversial subject. The reasons for classifying hotels are clear enough: classification helps to market the hotel and provides information to lodging consumers and travel distributors. It also provides useful information to countries for tourism planning and regulatory purposes.

On the other hand, classification is far from being an exact science. The classification criteria and the objectivity of the evaluation concern both government and the private sector. Unfortunately, the quantitative and qualitative standards of facilities and service are often seemingly arbitrary or unclear with respect to measurement and evaluation. While it is true, for example, that the size of a guestroom is measurable, space alone does not determine comfort or pleasure for the guest. Adding fuel to the debate is the confusion between classification (which refers to categorization) and grading (which refers to quality assessment).

Most classification systems are based on criteria that consider such factors as hotel size by room count, facilities, convenience or amenities, quality of service, and food and beverage service. The symbols adopted to portray classification to the public are various, with the most popular being the star rating system. However, the classification rating assigned to hotels does not necessarily mean the same thing everywhere. For instance, five stars may mean only the best available in some countries, which is not to be confused with five stars in countries where competition in all categories is fierce.

Commercial companies, mainly travel guides in Europe and the United States, also provide hotel classification and grading services. Whereas governments are not usually inclined to grade hotels, the evaluation systems of private companies are as a rule focused on grading. Typically, field inspectors working with detailed checklists of criteria and standards arrive unannounced to score not only the quality of the establishment's facilities and amenities, but also its hospitality, courtesy, efficiency, management, and other aspects. Commercial evaluations tend to be stringent and exclusive. An extra star or diamond can be translated into significant additional revenue for the hotel. Ratings given by private companies are subject to change over time as properties newly meet or fail to meet established criteria and standards (which themselves change over time).

In a few instances, governments have also attempted to include grading as part of their classification schemes by using a two-tiered system, one tier covering classification based on structural elements, the other tier covering operational elements. Because these systems are two-dimensional, many hotel operators find them to be fairer.

As the world's economies become increasingly interdependent and barriers to international travel disappear, the desirability of having international classification systems that have the same meanings around the world becomes self-evident, if difficult to attain. For this reason, the issue of an international classification scheme has been taken up periodically by the WTO, OECD, and others. While there is no full accord or agreement by these and other bodies, a measure of progress has been made by WTO, which has developed a set of minimum criteria for classification that could be part of a universal scheme that might be acceptable to most countries.

In the long run, a workable and fair universal classification system benefits every interest—national tourism administrations, the international hotel industry, the international travel distribution system, and, most of all, travelers around the world.

Endnotes

1. Joint WTO and IH&RA Study on Hotel Classification, April 2004.
2. P. A. L. Vine, "Hotel Classification—Art or Science?" *International Journal of Tourism Management*, March 1981, p. 21.
3. World Tourism Organization, *Interregional Harmonization of Hotel Classification Criteria on the Basis of the Classification Standards Adopted by the Regional Commissions*, 1989, p. 3.
4. Vine, p. 20.
5. Margaret Rose Caro, "Mobil Travel Guide Ratings Go Beyond the Physical," *Lodging*, November 1989, p. 93.
6. Much of the information for this section was found on AAA's website at www.aaanewsroom.net/Main/Default.asp?CategoryID=9&SubCategoryID=22.
7. Joint WTO & IH&RA Study on Hotel Classification, April 2004.
8. Celtic Worldwide, "An Overview of Existing Hotel Classification Systems in Europe," *Hotelier*, July 1991, p. 24.
9. World Tourism Organization, *Interregional Harmonization*, pp. 49–66.
10. For more information, visit the HOTREC website at www.hotrec.org and click on the "Stars in Europe" link.

Key Terms

classification—The assignment of hotels to a categorical rating according to type of property, facilities, and amenities offered.

grading—Used to denote quality assessment; indicates achievement of set standards of accommodations, service, cuisine, and amenities.

registration—A form of licensing that may or may not require a minimum standard.

Review Questions

1. What are five important purposes of hotel classification systems?
2. How are registration, classification, and grading different?
3. What eight elements are generally required for hotel classification systems to work well?
4. What might be the ideal makeup of a group with the authority to control registration, classification, and grading schemes?
5. Why do some critics of classification schemes believe such schemes are redundant?
6. Do hotel industries tend to prefer official or commercial classification systems? Why?
7. What are the principal areas of evaluation for the *Mobil Travel Guide?*
8. What has the WTO done over the years to bring about an international classification system for hotels?
9. What is "world-class" status? How can it be achieved?

Chapter 13 Outline

Internationalizing the Hotel
Market Research
    Guest Analysis
    Competition Analysis
    Forecasting Demand
    Research Sources
Developing an International Marketing Strategy
    Corporate Marketing and Sales Efforts
    Accounting for Cultural Differences
    Marketing U.S. Hotels to Foreign Visitors
Understanding Various Travel Distribution Systems
    Automated Global Distribution Systems
    Travel Agents and the Hotel Booking Process
    Working with Travel Agents
    Common Hotel–Travel Agency Relationship Problems
    Resolving Relationship Problems
    Tour Operators
    Hotel Representation Companies and Consortia
Segmentation
    Ways to Segment
    Branding
Product Positioning
Promotional Tools and Techniques
    Advertising
    Collateral Materials and Sales Promotions
    Cooperative Marketing
    Public Relations
    Frequent-Guest Programs
    Property Website
    Effectiveness of Tools/Techniques
Personal Selling
    Travel Trade Shows
    Travel Missions
    Familiarization Tours

Competencies

1. Explain the importance of market research, describe the roles of guest analysis and competition analysis, identify the benefits of a forecast analysis, and list possible sources of research data. (pp. 395–398)

2. Discuss the issues hotels face when developing an international marketing strategy. (pp. 398–400)

3. Describe the U.S. foreign visitor market. (pp. 400–401)

4. Describe how travel distribution systems work and explain automated global distribution systems. (pp. 401–402)

5. Summarize the role of travel agents in the hotel booking process and discuss common hotel–travel agency problems and how they are being addressed. (pp. 402–408)

6. Explain these three parts of the travel distribution system—tour wholesalers, hotel representation companies, and consortia—and how they benefit hotels. (pp. 408–412)

7. Summarize the importance and process of hotel segmentation, and explain the popularity of hotel branding, noting examples of hotel brands and situations in which branding may not work. (pp. 412–416)

8. Define the term *positioning*, and describe positioning's relationship to a hotel's overall marketing effort. (pp. 416–417)

9. Identify the promotional tools and techniques that hotel marketers use and the international concerns associated with each one. (pp. 417–426)

10. Differentiate between personal selling in international hotels and domestic hotels, and identify three types of international sales opportunities. (pp. 426–431)

13

International Hotel Sales and Marketing

THE GLOBAL VILLAGE the world is becoming can be viewed as a global marketplace with both foreign and local buyers—a concept that reinforces the "think globally, act locally" axiom. For marketing purposes, we can take the axiom one step further and add "sell personally." In thinking globally, successful international hotel marketers understand the importance of global computer reservation service vendors and distribution channels, but in acting locally and selling personally, they recognize that a consumer's choices and consumption patterns are closely linked to his or her individual values, perceptions, and prior experiences. This means marketers must develop a multiple perspective—the ability to see and experience the hotel product through the eyes of varied prospective buyers unlike themselves. They must understand culturally diverse expectations, attitudes, and sensitivities and what motivates people as individuals to buy.

Culture influences every step in the consumer's decision process, from product awareness and purchasing method through post-purchase evaluation of the hotel's facilities and service. At each step, the customer filters information through his or her own cultural blinders, making choices and value judgments based on a set of personal cultural norms and assumptions.

Marketers must research and understand the customers' cultural programming to formulate strategies that make the hotel attractive to potential guests from each client country. This begins with learning about marketing from a cultural viewpoint and learning to avoid stereotyping or confusing one nationality with another, even if the two seem culturally or racially similar. Confusing an Australian with a New Zealander, an Austrian with a German, or a Singaporean with a Malaysian, for example, may be understandable, but it is not acceptable. Preparing the hotel operationally to adapt to diverse segmentation demands and forging stronger business ties with the appropriate travel intermediaries are mandates for international hotel marketers.

Internationalizing the Hotel

A commitment to serving the international market must be part of the hotel's entire marketing strategy. The commitment must involve every level of management and translate down to the operating level in terms of service delivery. Indeed, pouring money into international advertising and other marketing activities will prove futile unless the hotel is operationally ready to accommodate foreign guests—from reservations to in-house consumption through check-out and post-visit correspondence. Ultimately, a hotel's international reputation will be determined by the satisfaction of guests and not by promotional activities.

An appropriate first step in pursuing international markets is to develop an internal strategic vision and time horizon that make it possible for all departments of the hotel to serve international markets. Financial and operational procedures need to be reviewed to identify what changes are necessary to serve international travelers: verifying creditworthiness, for example, or introducing multilingual menus. In pursuing international markets, results are usually not quick, and the effort should be a long-term commitment if a long-term payoff is desired.

Market Research

The first step in entering any new market is determining whether there is product demand, either existing or potential. Effective research reveals market characteristics and identifies future travel trends. This information helps determine which markets—domestic or foreign, independent or group, business or leisure, general or niche—should be pursued.

For hotels attempting to attract foreign leisure travelers, research may begin by scrutinizing foreign wholesalers' catalogs, because wholesalers are familiar with the market and will only package those products that appeal to outbound travelers. By studying the catalog's contents, the hotel can determine the options available to travelers from a particular market—what those travelers may do and see once they get there—and most of all, which competing properties are used by the wholesaler. Based on these preliminary findings, management can decide whether a potential exists before conducting a more thorough analysis to see if the hotel's products and services can be tailored to meet the needs of the target markets, and then formulate a marketing strategy.

Guest Analysis

As an ongoing effort, hotels should use guest histories and registration data to identify where their guests are coming from. Guest registrations will yield such data as the home or business address of current guests and such demographic data as gender, occupation, business affiliation, and credit status. Other information such as age, marital status, income, or education may be obtained by surveys, guest comment cards, focus groups, or other means of market analysis. Although U.S. laws restrict the type of information that may be asked, in many countries guests are routinely required to furnish such information on the hotel registration, including passport and visa registration. Demographic data, together with other information measuring guest satisfaction, is important for product improvement and competitive positioning as well as other marketing purposes.

Competition Analysis

Evaluating a hotel's marketing environment requires a SWOT analysis (an assessment of the hotel's strengths, weaknesses, opportunities, and threats). A major portion of this analysis deals with the competitive environment. In evaluating the competitive environment, it is important to identify the advantages and disadvantages of each competitor, as viewed by customers with respect to location, service, security, amenities, and price/value. In areas where there is an overcapacity of rooms and little growth in demand, most increased business will have to be won from competitors. Competitor intelligence is becoming a necessary ingredient for strategic marketing plans.

Competitor information can also be compiled in an informal way from the trade press, public interviews given by industry leaders, published industry reports, debriefing of staff who may have worked for competitors, competitor websites, and talking to key customers and vendors. This intelligence also can be collected by a more formal, methodical approach. Marriott Corporation, for example, has a data-gathering program that individual hotels can use in tracking competitors. It includes a well-defined scope of activities, including field visits, field sales intelligence, competitive shopping, and market research.[1]

To benefit from competitor intelligence, management must have a framework for the assessment of direct competitors: who they are, their product attributes, their market share and market position, and their marketing strategies. Management can then use this information to position the hotel's own competitive standing.

Forecasting Demand

The starting point for forecasting demand in most instances is a time series analysis, or a review of demand based on such key variables as occupancy and sales mix over the previous one to three years. Forecasting may be done by using any one of several different methods of calculation—for instance, straight regression, moving averages, or exponential smoothing, and taking into consideration special factors such as known advance sales, exchange rate fluctuations, political influences, special events, seasonality, and so on.[2] A forecast analysis enables the hotel to improve decision-making, strategy planning, and control of marketing efforts and resources.

Research Sources

Undertaking a primary research initiative can be expensive and time-consuming. Fortunately, original research is not always necessary, since there are a number of excellent research studies and statistical reports published annually by the World Tourism Organization, national tourism organizations, convention and visitors bureaus, travel trade associations (such as the American Hotel & Lodging Association and the International Hotel & Restaurant Association), and large consulting companies that project travel trends and provide insight into particular markets. These sources offer a wealth of research data for developing potential markets, ascertaining the amount of international business already coming into an area, and describing travel motivations and behavior.

Airlines can also be an important source of marketing data; their reservation systems track general and specific information about travel markets and origin of travel sales. Valuable marketing data is sometimes available from publications or organizations within the outbound country. *Travel Journal International*, for example, publishes annually the *Japan Travel Blue Book*, which provides extensive data on the Japanese outbound market.

Of course, the reliability of research data from different sources is an important consideration. This is especially true in the case of developing countries, which are sometimes unfamiliar with or lack funding for scientific market research. Consequently, in some areas the hotel's most effective research effort may comprise the insights, experiences, and information gleaned from one's own observation or in talking to a few knowledgeable industry leaders. In the final analysis, regardless of the amount of research conducted, the limitations of research should be recognized. Most marketing experts agree that the best marketing decisions come from a blend of experience, research, intuition, and judgment.

Developing an International Marketing Strategy

A hotel's international marketing strategy requires the selection of specific target markets, communication and promotion methods, and distribution channels. Once the target markets have been selected, the strategy for each depends on that market's customary use of travel agencies, tour packages, and special promotions, as well as the market's expectations and behaviors. The hotel marketer needs to determine the importance of travel intermediaries in producing potential business, because this will determine the orientation of the marketing effort and the allocation of resources. For example, a survey by PhoCusWright, a market research company, estimated that in 2006, 46 percent of U.S. hotel revenues came from online channels (25 percent from online agencies and 21 percent from branded websites).[3]

The strategy for any market should be based on the needs and motivations of that particular market. The Japanese market, for instance, is a brand-conscious one. Without some direct and cooperative efforts in promoting the name and image of the hotel, the hotel may not be saleable to Japanese customers. National tourism organizations (NTOs) and other destination marketing organizations can be very helpful in developing an international marketing strategy, because they normally work with local travel specialists, convention planners, wholesalers, and retail travel agents. NTOs also have a great deal of marketing information regarding major buyers; they know the most effective promotional vehicles for a particular country and often participate in cooperative marketing programs with airlines, hotels, tour operators, and other suppliers.

Corporate Marketing and Sales Efforts

For chain-affiliated hotels, a significant portion of the marketing effort may be handled at the corporate level. Chains typically employ regional sales offices to assist the sales departments of individual properties. Good communication between the regional office and the individual hotel sales office helps produce more business for the individual property and greater marketplace credibility for the regional office.

While international chains tend to practice decentralized marketing to a greater degree than domestic chains, the issue of centralization versus decentralization in practice is never entirely resolved, because chains expand or contract with changing policies and shifting economic cycles. At its extreme, centralized marketing tends to follow a "one size fits all" mentality, not accounting for different buyer behavior in different countries. Neither does it cater to different media availability or preferences, nor does it consider the differences of various distribution systems. Problems of local legal restrictions, different laws on trademarks, name registration, hotel classification, price controls, and other relevant issues are sometimes overlooked when marketing is done from central headquarters without adequate local input.

However, there are certain advantages to centralized marketing, at least for chains. A major benefit is the worldwide standardization of the brand name and, to some extent, product characteristics. Advantages also include such factors as the economies of scale in sourcing, logistics, marketing production, advertising, and transfer of know-how. Significant cost advantages can be gained by performing marketing activities on a centralized or regional basis, specifically in the following areas:

- Centralized production of promotional materials
- Central sales force
- Development of international marketing coalitions
- Standardization of common marketing activities
- Sharing marketing information
- Sequencing marketing programs with integrated efforts across countries
- Centralized advertising

Decentralized marketing, on the other hand, also offers certain advantages. For one, it gives the hotel full autonomy and control over its own marketing program and budget for advertising, promotion, and selling. Many hotel owners believe that decentralized marketing produces better results at the property level because the marketing budget will be used to promote only the individual property and not the hotel company as a whole. Another advantage is that the foci of decentralized marketing programs are less likely to be generic and more likely to concentrate on targeted markets.

Accounting for Cultural Differences

The conventional sales practices of developed Western nations are by no means universal. Many Asians, for example, show little responsiveness to advertising, and they may respond adversely to sales pitches they interpret as "hard sell." Common cross-cultural faux pas include misusing symbols and colors; using an inappropriate tone, role model, or setting; and emphasizing the wrong needs and values in selling. Travel patterns also differ among countries. Successful international hotels maximize their sales force and budget by adapting to the unique expectations, needs, and values of distinct markets; using appropriate distribution channels and images; and observing the protocol and mores of their target countries.

Marketing U.S. Hotels to Foreign Visitors

With an estimated market of more than 51 million foreign visitors to the United States, it is easy to see why many U.S. hotels are seeking to appeal to these visitors. The influx of foreign visitors, approximately 78 percent of whom used hotels or motels and stayed an average of 7.5 nights, translated into 275 million hotel/motel guest nights in the United States in 2006. Among the states most visited were California, Florida, Hawaii, and New York.

The top countries in terms of U.S. arrivals in 2006 were Canada (16 million), Mexico (13.3 million), the United Kingdom (4.2 million), Japan (3.7 million), Germany (1.7 million), France (790,000), South Korea (758,000), Australia (603,000), Italy (533,000), and Brazil (525,000). Seven countries set records in 2006 in terms of number of arrivals: Australia, China, India, Ireland, Mexico, South Korea, and Spain.

In-flight surveys conducted for inbound visitors to the United States reveals some interesting travel characteristics:

- On average, they planned their trip 78 days in advance
- 51 percent used travel agents to make their reservations
- The main purposes of the trip included leisure recreation (47 percent), visiting friends and relatives (23 percent), and business (21 percent)
- Average number of nights spent: 15.8
- 74 percent were repeat visitors
- 70 percent stayed in one state, with an average of two destinations
- Favorite activities on their visit included shopping (88 percent), dining (84 percent), sightseeing (44 percent), historical sites (36 percent), and theme parks (27 percent)
- Average expenditure per visitor: $1,633; the major expenditure categories were lodging, gifts, and meals

Hotel sales personnel should work with distribution intermediaries—tour wholesalers, travel agents, motivation houses, sales representatives, and air carriers—to increase their share of this market. Hotels should provide these intermediaries with current brochures and other marketing materials and make every effort to pay commissions promptly. Since the mid-1990s there has been a shift away from travel agents toward the Internet on the part of international travelers looking to book travel services, particularly airline reservations. Hotels therefore need to have a presence on the web while continuing to cultivate their travel agent relationships. Each foreign market needs to be cultivated differently, with creative packages developed for specific markets. Japanese visitors to the

United States appreciate golf and natural beauty, while Australians enjoy tennis and aquatic activities. British travelers to the United States love the theater, and Latin Americans seem to enjoy trips to theme parks. Hotels can quickly gain reputations in a particular foreign market based on the way they cater to special needs.

Understanding Various Travel Distribution Systems

An important element in the marketing strategy of any hotel is the system of marketing channels through which products and services are sold to their ultimate buyers. The term **travel distribution system** refers to a series of marketing or selling institutions through which title to a travel product or service is transferred from the supplier to the user. In short, it is how a hotel (as a supplier) sells its services to buyers through travel agents, tour operators, tour wholesalers, toll-free lines, websites, and other means.

Travel distribution systems vary not so much from country to country as by regions of the world. Americans tend to be heavy users of travel agents for foreign travel products, less so for domestic travel products; Europeans and Asians are more apt to consult a variety of sources for all travel. The Japanese are particularly likely to rely on large operators with complete packaging capability and good distribution abroad. If travel agents and tour wholesalers are the key decision-makers or influencing factors in supplier selection, then the hotel's marketing and selling efforts should be directed toward these travel distributors. In many countries, it is critical to have access to travel intermediaries to sell rooms.

Travel agencies in the United States tend to be independent and smaller than those in Europe, with an average of three to six employees; in Europe, the corporate, multiple-agency base prevails and each agency tends to have many more travel counselors.

Japan's travel industry is dominated by the ten top wholesalers, and half of these are also among the ten largest travel agencies. The Japanese travel consumer may go through as many as four wholesalers to purchase a trip, while for the U.S. traveler the average is 1.6. Japanese travel agents must be licensed by the government in order to assemble and sell travel packages, and there are only about 1,200 licenses issued. As may be the case with other countries that require licensing, the purpose is to maintain the integrity and quality of the travel programs and packages offered to consumers. Consequently, Japanese wholesalers and travel agents are quite particular about ensuring high-quality standards for the travel products they sell. Licensed Japanese travel agents wholesale travel packages to other travel agents who serve as retailers to consumers.

In order to market hotels to the Japanese, there must be an understanding of Japan's highly refined and regulated distribution system, consumer protection laws, and the sophisticated tour designing and planning process. Because Japanese travel agents look for complete full-service packages that contain airline, hotel, ground transportation, and theme park or city tour options, a hotel trying to sell itself alone may not do very well. Most hotels need to join forces with other travel suppliers to penetrate the Japanese market.

Automated Global Distribution Systems

Today, the penetration of global distribution systems (GDSs) into U.S. travel agencies is virtually complete, with four major systems (Amadeus, Galileo, SABRE, and WorldSpan) dominating GDS activity. The battle for international control of these electronic channels of travel distribution is still underway. Each has a number of major airlines in the partnership. These four GDSs command about one-third of all electronic volume through their travel agency networks. SABRE is the largest, but strengths vary geographically. Amadeus has long been the strongest in the European market, while SABRE's strength comes from North America and Asia.

The connection of its central reservation system (CRS) to the GDSs is the necessary first step if a hotel company wants to be represented in the automated distribution supply chain. The larger chains such as Hilton, Marriott, and Starwood have their own individual link (a software program that interfaces) to the four GDSs. However, smaller organizations link their CRSs through an intermediary, known as a "switch," through which (for a fee) they can link with the GDSs. Examples of switch companies include Wizcom and Pegasus.

In the early days of the GDSs, they were designed to be neutral in their listings of hotels when a travel agent entered a search query for a city. Recently, however, hotels can pay to advertise on a GDS or even pay to have a higher priority for being listed in the search query. Hotels can track GDS productivity through the various reports that their property management systems (PMSs) can generate for this purpose.

Currently, GDSs are firmly entrenched in the travel supply chain and are not expected to be replaced anytime soon. However, the competition in the electronic distribution space for a share of the customer's "eyeballs" is heating up. Because customers have many automated channels available to them online for making hotel reservations and booking other travel products, each channel is creating marketing strategies to drive traffic to its website. TravelCLICK, a company that provides market intelligence on electronic distribution, reported that travel agents reserving hotel rooms through a GDS system made 36 percent of the reservations for major hotel brands in 2006. About 38 percent of hotel reservations were made through an Internet website, including the hotel's own website.[4]

With the competition heating up, hotel companies are now trying to drive traffic directly to their websites by increasing consumer awareness of their sites, making it easy for consumers to purchase once they get there, and advertising loyalty programs. They are also engaging in direct marketing campaigns with their best transient, corporate travel customers and wholesalers. In addition, hotel brand website design has been enhanced into what is known as "Web 2.0," which includes web-based communities and hosted services such as social-networking sites, blogs, and podcasts. Using these Web 2.0 applications, many hotels have made their websites more interesting, engaging, and proactive while creating a community of hotel customers.

Travel Agents and the Hotel Booking Process

Knowing the means by which hotel rooms are booked is part of understanding the travel distribution system of a particular market. Travel agents are increasingly relying on the ease, convenience, and accessibility of GDSs and other Internet reservation systems. The four major GDSs are accessed by more than 180,000 travel agents worldwide. In general, statistics indicate a reduction in the use of 800 numbers when travel agents want to make a primary query for reservations, although agents may still rely on the telephone for complicated requests or information they are unable to obtain online. As a result of the Internet and the associated ease with which consumers can make reservations directly, the role of the travel agent has evolved from being a "booker of reservations" to that of a travel consultant who can add value to the reservation and travel experience. A recent survey asked consumers to identify the travel agency attributes important to them when selecting a travel agency. The top five reasons chosen by the respondents were: knowledgeable and experienced travel consultants, helpful and friendly staff, holiday/package prices, quality of travel packages, and travel agency reputation.[5]

Travel agents indicated that embracing technology and offering personalized service are tops on their list for the next decade when it comes to serving travelers and achieving business success, according to a recent survey conducted by Amadeus North America. The survey explored what travel and technology might look like in the future and what technological changes could mean for travel professionals and how they might affect the booking process.[6] According to the survey, 88 percent of travel agents said that, in the future, technology will be more important than it is today and will be absolutely critical to their success. They also indicated (75.5 percent) that personalized service, as well as travel and destination expertise (62.2 percent), would be the most important benefits for travel professionals to deliver to clients. It is clear that, for travel agents, a "high touch" expert approach will be as important as ever in the decades to come.

Based on the survey results, travel agents indicated that the technology innovations that would be most important to their future business growth were:

- Advanced search capabilities
- Desktop productivity tools
- Dynamic packaging
- Advanced agency Internet presence

A review of hotel booking trends indicates that consumers still make a majority of their hotel reservations via calls to an 800 number or to the property directly. However, from 2003 to 2006, the fastest reservations growth has been via hotel websites and Internet travel agencies (see Exhibit 1).

Working with Travel Agents

In addition to the traditional travel agency (with a physical office), the business now includes online travel agencies. This section discusses issues that hotels need to know about traditional and online travel agencies.

Traditional Travel Agencies. For hotel operators who can work effectively with travel agents in different countries, the increase in international travel presents a golden opportunity. Agents all over the world are looking for ways to increase commission revenues by selling more hotel products on an international scale.

Exhibit 1 Hotel Booking Trends

Travel Booking—U.S.—April 2007—Market Segmentation
U.S. sales of hotels, by booking channel, 2003 and 2006

	2003 $billion	%	2006 $billion	%	Change 2003—2006 %
Direct* from company	76.3	72.5	89.2	67.9	16.9
Direct excluding hotel website	72.1	68.5	74.8	57	3.8
Hotel website	4.2	4	14.4	11	242.9
Travel agent	25.3	24	23.6	18	-6.5
Internet travel agency	3.7	3.5	18.4	14	398.8
Total	105.3	100	131.3	100	24.7

* Direct includes hotel call centers, hotel properties, walk-ins, etc.

Source: Mintel/PhoCusWrightASTA/*Lodging* magazine/AH&LA

The relationship is mutually advantageous, if at times contentious, with respect to commissionable sales and timely payments.

Although consumers now have additional choices for making hotel reservations, either through online agencies or hotel websites, travel agents are still an important part of the sales process. As such, it is imperative that hotels evaluate and cultivate this channel of distribution and improve automation systems to ease the hotel booking process for agents. While the point is sometimes debated, agents can have considerable influence on travel decisions made by clients, especially in terms of leisure travel. A global GDS study done by Phoenix Marketing International in 2007 found that when hotel guests are booking for one to three nights, travel agents recommend a hotel 40 percent of the time, while consumers select a hotel on their own only 23 percent of the time. Agents and consumers collaborate to choose a hotel 37 percent of the time—meaning that travel agents influence bookings 77 percent of the time.[7] Business travel decisions are driven by client needs, but an agent can still be influential in the choice of hotels. In a poll of U.S. travel agents, criteria cited by agents as being "very important" when recommending a hotel to business clients included:

- Prior client satisfaction with the hotel
- The hotel's reputation for honoring reservations
- A location close to clients' business destinations
- The general reputation of the hotel
- The hotel's relationship with travel agents
- The hotel's commission-payment policy
- The availability of a toll-free or other direct reservation number

Online Travel Agencies and Intermediaries. With the expansion of the Internet in the mid-1990s, the growth of online travel agencies and third-party intermediaries has made the Internet a medium of choice for travel reservations. There are eight websites that account for about 90 percent of the hotel reservation volume for non-branded hotels:

- Expedia
- Hotels.com
- Hotwire
- Travelocity
- Orbitz
- Cheaptickets
- Priceline
- TravelWeb

There are basically three business models adopted by these websites: the merchant model, the opaque/auction model, and the retail travel model.

Sites such as Hotels.com and Expedia follow the merchant model, which employs a wholesaler approach. Hotels working with these websites give them a net room rate, usually 25 to 30 percent below retail, and the online agency decides what rate to post on the site.

Opaque/auction websites, which include priceline.com and Hotwire, disclose the location of the hotel and its level of service, but do not disclose the name or brand of the hotel until the customer agrees to the purchase. The customer submits a bid for the hotel. Typically, when the consumer submits the bid, the site tries to match the price with the type of hotel the customer has specified. Hotels typically provide their room inventory to the site using a merchant model but sometimes do so on a retail basis.

Retail travel websites either started as online travel agencies or started as traditional agencies and added an online presence. Orbitz is an example of the former, CarlsonWagonlit and Rosenbluth International examples of the latter. Hotels provide retail room rates and inventory, and hotels pay a 10-percent commission on the room rate booked. Some of these agencies give hotels a choice of using the merchant or the commission model.[8]

Common Hotel–Travel Agency Relationship Problems

Historically, the relationship between hotels and travel agents has been influenced by the business cycle and, since the latter part of the 1990s, by the introduction and proliferation of online agencies. After the terrorist attacks of September 2001, when travel demand plummeted, individual hotels pressed to fill rooms relied heavily on the newly emerging online travel agencies, which negotiated very low rates with hotels to help them dispose of their excess inventory. Later, when hotel demand returned, hotels strengthened their web marketing strategies and either held off on giving hotel inventory to the online travel agencies or negotiated much higher rates. As such, the relationship between travel agents, online agencies, and hotels has ebbed and flowed based on the extent of travel demand. However, larger hotel companies sustain their relationships with travel agents and agencies through both good times and bad.

Unfortunately, international transactions are a common source of problems that strain the relationship between hotels and travel agents. The most serious problem from the agent's point of view is receiving timely commission payments—or receiving them at all. It is not unusual for hotels to default on payments to an agent; the hotel either does not pay the stated amount, pays in part, or pays only after a great deal of effort to collect on the agent's part.

Another major travel agent complaint concerns negotiated hotel rates. A travel agent sends a client to a hotel at a rate quoted by the reservations department but a lower rate is negotiated by the guest at the front desk upon arrival; the agent does not get paid because the hotel has a policy against giving commissions on negotiated rates. Estimates on the percentage of hotel commissions that are actually paid to agents on a worldwide basis range from 40 percent to 80 percent. Given such a scenario, it is easy to understand the hesitancy on the part of agencies to expend effort on hotel reservations.

In other cases, when commissions are paid, they are presented in a foreign currency; and currency conversions and fluctuations can cost more than the commission check is worth. Some travel agents use sophisticated commission tracking systems to help ensure hotel commission payments, but this also requires time and expense on the part of the agency.

The method of preferred guest payment for hotels tends to vary among geographical regions, making it difficult for agents to establish one set system. Asian hotels largely prefer credit cards be used for deposits or payments, while many European hotels ask for payment by check, sometimes in local currency. Some hotels hold these checks until the guest arrives, then put the bill on a credit card and return the check to the agent—a time-consuming procedure.

Inability to obtain instant confirmation on a room is another frequently cited problem by travel agents in booking foreign hotels. Under some systems, when a room is booked through the agent's CRS, the request is first entered into the hotel's reservation center, and the hotel reservationist must type the reservation into the hotel's system. A confirmation number may then be obtained and sent back to the travel agent. If the agent needs a confirmation sooner, he or she will likely call an 800 number to get a confirmation. Handling the transaction twice, by phone and by computer, increases the cost of making the transaction for both the travel agent and the hotel.

The fact that hotel rating systems vary widely from country to country is another obstacle for agents. When there are special booking requirements, many agents find that computerized systems do not meet all their information needs with respect to hotel products or services.

The preceding problems are more prevalent with the smaller or independent hotels; large hotel chains tend to make a concerted effort to protect their reputation with timely commissions and other services for the agent. The tendency of travel agents to favor the large chains, however, makes it even more difficult for smaller operators and independently marketed hotels to get a piece of the travel agency—directed hotel business.

Some hotels, especially those dependent on travel agencies for the majority of their bookings, have made serious attempts to resolve problems and facilitate international transactions. Likewise, many travel agencies have come to realize that hotel reservations are the single most underutilized product within their grasp. The development and improvement of the mega-hotel CRSs will inevitably solve some of the problems ensuing from the agent-hotel relationship. Meanwhile, some hotel companies have produced innovative solutions such as pre-payment deduction and automatic bank transfers for travel agencies. Most of the hotel chains stress the willingness of their regional sales offices around the world and reservation services to handle problems and expedite travel agent payments.

Resolving Relationship Problems

U.S. Hotels. There are many noteworthy examples of initiatives to develop a stronger hotel–travel agency relationship. The following examples describe cases in which hotels have provided incentives for travel agents and created programs to show them that they want to treat them as partners in the travel distribution process:

- Hyatt introduces travel agents to the hotel business as part of its Travel Agency Awareness Day. As part of the program, travel agents trade their typical work routines for vacuums and bell attendant duties as they swap roles with Hyatt employees. Hyatt staffers get to walk in a travel agent's shoes for the day, so they can better understand the issues faced by their retail partners. In addition, Hyatt has launched a Travel Agent In-Touch Services program, which features a travel agent support number and special travel agent training. Hyatt provides incentives for travel agents to sample and stay at Hyatt properties by offering them attractive rates, usually at least 50 percent off the rack rate.[9]

- Starwood Hotels & Resorts Worldwide introduced a new program called "Starwood Pro" as a new way for travel agents to conduct business with the chain. Starwood created a website that provides deals, rates, and product information about all Starwood brands. To promote ease of use, the site also has a "click to call" feature. To further enhance travel agent education and information, Starwood has launched a Travel Professionals Curriculum and new travel agent rewards program.[10]

- To facilitate commission payment and currency conversions, InterContinental Hotels Group signed up with Pegasus Solutions to process commissions on behalf of its hotels to travel agents and distributors around the world. The web-based application, called "TravelCom," is user-friendly and processes payments that are linked to guest departures. Other hotels, such as Marriott, Hilton, Thistle, and Jurys Inn, have signed up with Pegasus System's new program to make weekly payments to travel agents.[11]

- Many hotel and resort companies are adding incentives and reward programs to motivate travel agents to do business with them. AM resorts has a month-long program where it invites 30,000 agents to participate in contests where numerous prizes are awarded, including free room nights. Talisman Resort in Canada has created an incentive program for agents that rewards them with higher commissions (going from the standard 10 percent to 15 percent) when they book more room reservations. Hyatt's innovative reward program includes a random call to travel agent offices. If the agent recommends a Hyatt hotel, they get a cash prize of $500. Other interesting incentives for travel agents include the Sunset Jamaica Grande Resort & Spa's "spell to win" incentive. For each room an agent sells, they earn one letter. By spelling "Grande" (6 room sales), they win a free stay at the Resort.[12]

European Hotels. Even once-complacent European hoteliers have been reevaluating their strategies with regard to overseas travel agents, no longer taking them for granted. As many European hotels consider foreign-market consumer advertising prohibitively expensive, they try to improve working relationships with retailers through hotel representation firms and other means. European hotels have also adjusted their commission and payment policies to make the booking transaction easier and more profitable for travel agents. The 87-year-old Italian Ciga Hotels chain, for example, pays commissions of 15 percent or 17 percent, depending on room rates, and commissions are paid at the end of every month in the travel agent's preferred currency. Forte Hotels pays an 8 percent commission—after the value-added tax is added to the room rate—and commissions are processed 30 days after guest check-out in the agent's local currency. All agents are encouraged to call the nearest regional sales office if commission problems occur, and the hotel company pays the outstanding amount from a special fund, rather than let ill-will develop between an agency and the chain.[13] In 2007, Forte launched a special website for travel agents only. The site features:

- Booking via GDSs—features all Forte Hotels' property codes.
- GDS Help Desk—provides a help desk phone number, e-mail, and online registration form.
- Booking via voice—provides the numbers for Forte Hotels' toll-free global voice reservation offices.
- Commissions—details information on receiving commissions through World Payment Systems.
- Regional offices—provides contact details for all regional offices worldwide.
- Online image library.
- Downloadable brochures in PDF format.
- Hotel fact sheets.[14]

Tour Operators

Tour operators are companies that package two or more components of travel (such as air and hotel or hotel and escorted tours). The tour industry has thousands of companies that provide a vast array of travel services to vacationers to destinations around the world. The structure of tour operators has changed from being typically bricks and mortar agencies to include many online wholesalers that in effect function as tour operators. They purchase rooms and other travel services at wholesale prices and sell them to consumers at retail. The largest of these online companies include Expedia, Hotels.com, Orbitz, and Travelocity.

For some hotels, teaming up with travel partners in a package may be the only way to make the international marketing effort economically feasible. Hoteliers can look to airlines (both domestic and foreign), car rental companies, ground handlers, theme park operators, and especially tour wholesalers for partnership opportunities.

In working with wholesalers to develop package tours, the hotel needs to consider three factors:

- Most wholesalers will package and promote only those tours they think retail travel agents will be anxious to sell and consumers will be equally eager to buy.
- Any cooperative support offered by the hotel in the tour program (for example, support of familiarization (fam) tours, travel missions, and seminars) will help reduce the wholesalers' risk and encourage the inclusion of a new or unproven product.
- Tour development is what it implies—a development process; it requires long-range efforts, negotiations, and continuous marketing support.

Foreign wholesalers are often reluctant to take on a new or unproven product. For that reason, branded hotels are more acceptable than unbranded in the package. Every page in the tour catalog represents a significant capital outlay with potential revenue loss or gain; therefore, all inclusions require careful consideration. The catalog represents a wholesaler's inventory of merchandise; thus every wholesaler seeks sales leaders.

In dealing with foreign wholesalers, the hotel should at times be ready for prolonged negotiations in which differences of perception and culture are as likely to play an important role as wholesale or discounted rates and guarantees.

Tour package participation is not appropriate for every hotel. Having the hotel featured in a printed tour program may provide an excellent vehicle for foreign market entry, but the hotel also needs to determine whether participation will help its overall marketing objectives or hurt its image. Tour wholesalers, arguing that foreign travel markets are extremely price-sensitive, typically (but not always) negotiate substantial discounts from standard hotel rack rates. But, if the packages are employed selectively as part of the overall marketing strategy—especially to fill in business during off-seasons—they can make a significant difference in contributing to cash flow and bottom-line profitability.

Another consideration is whether the acceptance of large numbers of lower-yield foreign guests would jeopardize traditional patronage. This leads to a "catch-22" between guaranteed low-yield occupancy and nonguaranteed higher-yield occupancy from regular guests who may find tour groups—foreign or not—intrusive. Long-term commitments at low prices to tour operators and other foreign intermediaries may restrict the effectiveness of revenue management programs and result in lower hotel profitability.

Hotel Representation Companies and Consortia

Independent hotels and small chains generally do not have the strength or marketing coverage of a large chain operation, so the costs of international promotion often are beyond their resources. The advantages to chain affiliation have become more pronounced over the years with the development of centralized reservations, 800 toll-free numbers, corporate websites, and other corporate-sponsored marketing programs. In response to this situation, hotel consortia and hotel representation (rep) or referral associations have evolved and proliferated. Legally, these firms are cooperative groups, offering corporate sales office services for a fee to their clientele in the international marketplace.

A consortium helps non-chain hotels compete with the chains; most consortia draw their membership solely from highly rated independent hotels, although some consortia will accept hotel groups as well. Generally speaking, the larger the consortium, the greater the benefits of membership to the hotel owner, since charges for marketing services are usually based on a fee plus a pro rata share of all costs incurred in marketing, advertising, promotion, and booking.

Although there are different forms of consortia, they have in common a reservation system; a universal logo or symbol for advertising purposes; minimum criteria for membership, covering standards of facilities and service; membership directories; and acceptance of the same credit cards. Many are now moving toward the provision of full-scale marketing services and sales expertise, which may include qualified mailing lists, personalized mailings, internal statistical and other reports, spreadsheets, sales and marketing presentations, and desktop publishing. In some instances, these associations have also banded together to enjoy mass purchasing power for supplies and equipment or to obtain favorable discounts from bank credit card billings and for shared management training.

A consortium differs from chains or franchises in that it is made up of independent operators who may remain autonomous on such matters as operating policies and practices, facilities, rate structure, food and beverage operations, and so forth. On the other hand, because of other cooperative marketing agreements that a consortium may have with such travel partners as airlines or financial service companies (which often act as point-of-sales agents), independents do relinquish a part of their control in sales and distribution.

The cost of membership in a consortium varies in amount and method of computation, but generally covers:

- An initial fee, usually based on the number of rooms
- A fee for the reservation system on a monthly or per-room basis
- A fee for advertising on a monthly or per-room basis
- A charge for signage—either a one-time payment or a monthly user charge

The total amount of these fees is often lower than for franchise groups, which require funds to support corporate ventures and umbrella activities. In this respect, consortia represent competition for franchise companies, as some of them offer the advantages of à la carte, franchise-like services for less than a full franchise royalty, but in most instances, make fewer demands on members. Among the more familiar international hotel consortia are the following:

- **Utell Hotels & Resorts.** Started in 1930, Utell Hotels & Resorts is a hotel reservation service that works with more than 3,000 hotels in 140 different countries. The hotels cover a wide spectrum, including unique properties, independent establishments, and those that are part of national or regional brands. Utell works primarily with travel agents and has a variety of programs and hotel products to give them a variety of options for their clients. Since 1994, when it was acquired by Pegasus Solutions (a switch company that interfaces GDSs with CRSs), it has provided a seamless technology interface for travel agents to make reservations, check commission status, and get their commission payments. Its website, www.utellagent.com, provides a one-stop portal for qualified travel agents.

- **Best Western.** Founded in 1946, Best Western International, based in Phoenix, Arizona, has more than 4,200 hotel members—representing 316,000 rooms—in 80 countries. Best Western has moved away from being strictly a referral and reservation network, stressing its capabilities in international marketing, research, public relations, legal services, and insurance. Areas Best Western is targeting for future international development include China, Europe, India, the Middle East, and South America.

- **Preferred Hotels & Resorts Worldwide.** Preferred Hotels & Resorts Worldwide, founded in 1968, is an organization of deluxe, independent properties in 120 countries, including the United States, the Caribbean, Canada, Europe, and the Asia–Pacific region, providing members with a central reservations system and worldwide marketing coverage. This organization has also made an effort to improve working relationships with travel intermediaries in different countries. Part of that effort included a travel agent pledge that all members must take. The pledge includes guaranteeing a 10 percent commission from all North American and Asia/Pacific hotels, and an 8 percent commission from all European and Middle Eastern hotels. At the individual property level, each hotel's sales staff is encouraged to market Preferred sister properties during sales calls to agents. Preferred Hotels & Resorts represents exclusive hotels; to qualify as a Preferred hotel or resort, a property must pass a "Standards of Excellence" test. This program, supplemented with annual inspections, ensures that the hotels included in the Preferred system are of a consistent quality that is maintained year after year.

- **Leading Hotels of the World.** Established in 1928 by a group of forward-thinking European hoteliers, Leading Hotels of the World has evolved into an organization that represents more than 430 of the world's most luxurious and prestigious hotels, resorts, and spas in 80 countries. The organization does not solicit new members; hotels apply for membership and have to meet rigorous standards that must be maintained while they are part of the group. The company expanded its "leading" brand image to include Leading Small Hotels of the World in 1999.

- **World Hotels (Formerly SRS Steigenberger Reservation Service).** This consortium handles reservations systems, advertising, and marketing for some 500 boutique hotels in 70 countries. In addition, the company publishes *The Deluxe Collection* hotel directory. Its TRUST (Transworld Reservation Utilization Service Terminal) Voyager reservation system is connected to more than 600,000 travel agent terminals. World Hotels, founded in 1970, targets conference and incentive travel groups along with business and leisure travelers. The company changed its brand from SRS-Worldhotels to World Hotels in 2005 to better reflect its expansion beyond providing services to founding firm Steigenberger Hotel Group.

Some hotel industry analysts believe that the large consortia have become too big to service foreign hotel accounts adequately. As an option, some international hotels contract with small independent rep firms to fulfill their specific marketing needs. These firms generally handle all activities typically addressed by the hotel's own sales force except reservations, which the hotel handles directly or contracts through one of the larger rep companies with GPS capacity. The future importance of these smaller rep firms is an important marketing development to track.

Segmentation

Expansion by international hotel chains has accelerated and the trend toward "niche" marketing is evident. The successful hotel marketing effort today demands detailed **segmentation** and the use of available resources to satisfy specific target markets. If the group business segment is identified as having potential, wholesalers from the sending countries need to be pursued. For corporate travelers, the primary promotional effort is directed at corporate offices through personal sales calls, supplemented by direct mail, newsletters, occasional promotional events, websites, and special rates. If the corporate meetings segment is targeted, marketing is directed at corporations, travel agents, and convention organizers through personal selling, supported by promotional materials.

Ways to Segment

Markets can be segmented in a number of different ways: geographically, to appeal to specific nationalities; demographically (based on age, income, education, race, average party size, family versus single, gender, religion); or psychographically (based on motivations, lifestyles, interests, hobbies, propensity to travel, and benefits). Some marketing analysts contend that as the world becomes more global, geographic or country boundaries historically used to define international segments may gradually disappear and the use of psychographic segmentation, which more accurately reflects the cultural differences and similarities that exist among people around the world, may be the better way to target markets. The lessening of communication barriers across countries, the internationalization of goods and services, the improvements in transportation, and the general increase in the level of education of people around the world, it is argued, are likely to influence the values of individuals in many countries, producing universal segments that appear increasingly homogeneous. Among the developed countries, newly emerging common segments include senior citizens, young singles, cultural enthusiasts, adventure seekers, golfers, and other special interest groups.

Segmentation varies by country. A true segment has critical mass, distinctiveness as a segment, similar characteristics, and is measurable for target-marketing purposes. The Japanese discretionary travel market, for example, is composed of the following segments: free and independent travelers (FIT), group inclusive tours (GIT), honeymooners, young working women, "salarymen," the silver market, families with young children, and golf enthusiasts. Even these segments can be more narrowly defined by city or prefecture of origin. Research can be helpful in assessing what types of segments are currently attracted to the hotel or destination and which segments have future potential.

Branding

Prompted by the move toward market segmentation and the need for name recognition, the international hotel industry has committed itself to supplying an ever-widening spectrum of hotel brands. The **branding** of hotels to identify particular properties with specific market segments is not a new concept, but has become increasingly popular for three basic reasons. First, it is a response to the need to tailor hotel products for the specific needs of various segments. Second, as hotel groups expanded through acquisitions, many chains found themselves with disparate groups of properties—often of widely differing quality—that could not fit into a common portfolio for marketing purposes. Categorization was a natural consequence of mergers and acquisitions. InterContinental Hotels, for example, established the Forum brand in the early 1970s for renaming its older properties that could no longer meet the original InterContinental standards abroad. Third, since hotel classification and rating systems adopted in many countries lack consistency and do not provide the hotel user with a sufficiently clear indication of the quality of accommodation or level of service, branding provides a better way to create standards of identity, quality, and pricing in the marketplace.

The most important unifying feature of the hotel brand is the name. Brand names provide sellers with a rationale for harmonizing hotel concepts with specific standards and rate levels. At the same time, buyers are provided with a degree of assurance that the branded accommodation will more or less have certain consistencies from one country to the next.

Nearly all prominent international hotel chains have differentiated their properties along segmented lines, developing and promoting one or more distinctive brands targeted at newly emerging or already established market segments. Exhibit 2 lists examples of hotel companies and the different brands they have developed to serve specific market segments.

Exhibit 2 Brand Tiers of Selected Hotel Companies

	Luxury	Upper Upscale & Upscale	Mid-Scale	Economy	Extended-Stay	Vacation Ownership	Timeshare Exchange & Rentals
Wyndham		Wyndham Wyndham Garden	Ramada Wingate Inn Howard Johnson Amerihost Baymont	Days Inn Super 8 Travelodge* Knights Inn		Wyndham Fairfield	RCI Landal ECC Novasol Cuendet
Marriott	Ritz-Carlton JW Marriott	Marriott Renaissance Courtyard	Fairfield Inn Spring Hill Suites		Residence Inn Towne Place Suites	Marriott Vacation Club Villa Vacation	
Starwood	St Regis Luxury Collection	Westin 'W' Sheraton Le Meridien	Four Points		Element	Starwood Vacation Club	
Hilton	Waldorf Conrad	Hilton Hilton Garden Inn Doubletree Embassy Suites	Hampton		Homewood Suites	Hilton Vacation Club	
Choice		Cambria Suites	Quality Clarion Sleep Inn MainStay Suites Comfort Inns Comfort Suites	Econo Lodge Rodeway Inn	Suburban Hotels MainStay Suites		
IHG		Inter-Continental Crowne Plaza Indigo	Holiday Inn Holiday Inn Express		Staybridge Suites Candlewood Suites		
Carlson	Regent	Radisson Park Plaza	Country Inns & Suites Park Inn				
Four Seasons	Four Seasons					Fractional	
Hyatt		Hyatt Regency Grand Hyatt Park Hyatt Hyatt Casino	Ameri-Suites Summerfield Suites		Hawthorne Suites	Hyatt Vacation Club	

*U.S. only

Source: Mintel's Travel & Tourism Intelligence.

Exhibit 3 Accor's Brand Tiers

Brand Tier	Standardized	Non-Standardized
Upscale		Sofitel
Mid-Scale	Novotel	Grand Hotel Mercure
	Suitehotel	Hotel Mercure
Economy	Ibis	Relais Mercure
		Red Roof Inn
Budget	Etap	
	Motel 6	
	Formule 1	

InterContinental Hotels Group, currently the largest hotel group in the world, has seven brands that serve various market segments:

Brand	Hotel Segment
InterContinental Hotels & Resorts	Luxury/Full-Service
Crowne Plaza Hotels & Resorts	Upscale/Full-Service
Staybridge Suites	Upscale/Extended-Stay
Hotel Indigo	Upscale Branded Boutique
Holiday Inn Hotels & Resorts	Midscale/With F&B
Holiday Inn Express	Midscale/Without F&B
Candlewood Suites	Midscale/Extended-Stay

Accor, the French-owned and operated hotel company, is the only major chain to have a clearly defined dual-branding strategy. Most of the chain's lower-grade properties have a uniform appearance and offer highly standardized features. Hence, hotels under these brands are most likely to be new builds. Accor also makes a clear distinction between what it calls "economy" and "budget" hotels, the latter offering a more basic level of comfort (as epitomized by Formule 1).

Given the heterogeneous nature of Europe's hotel stock, Accor has developed the Mercure brand alongside its standardized Novotel flag, both targeting the mid-scale segment. Mercure has very flexible standards, as it is designed to incorporate already-existing hotels, including entire portfolios of properties. In order to accommodate different types of hotels, Mercure offers a range of sub-brands: Relais Mercure (two-star), Hotel Mercure (three-star), and Grand Hotel Mercure (four-star). Sofitel, Accor's only upscale brand, also falls into the "non-standardized" category. This arrangement facilitates Accor's expansion through partnerships with third-party property owners (see Exhibit 3).[15]

Branding Problems. Despite its apparent success and widespread use, branding as a marketing strategy within hotel groups is not a panacea. Multiple brands in the same company can cause (1) brand confusion in the marketplace, (2) diffusion or blurring of the chain's image, and (3) dilution of market share through cross-over competition within the chain. For branding to work effectively, it is critical for each of the brands to have a clear and separate identity of its own. Launching a new product may often be difficult for a chain that has an established niche, whether the hotels are developed from the bottom up or from the top down. It is also hard to educate the traveling public about the different brand extensions, and for a company to maintain clear distinctions of products and consistency of service standards. Wide variations within the same brand located in different cities or countries often lead to additional customer confusion.

For these reasons, some hotels have no desire to segment or develop separate brands. Four Seasons, Kempinski, Hongkong & Shanghai Hotel Company's Peninsula brand, and Mandarin Oriental are four good examples of niche players at the high-end of the market. These hotels want to maintain their respective reputations for luxury standards and operate medium-size properties offering personalized service, limit their geographical dispersion, and have an upscale business and leisure clientele. There are, however, many national one-brand chains targeting lower-grade segments, starting with the two leading U.K. budget chains, Whitbread's Premier Travel Inn and Travelodge. Examples of single-brand operators catering to the four-star business traveler market include Thistle, a British chain; Maritim, a leading German chain; and Jolly Hotels, the biggest Italian chain.

Product Positioning

The **positioning** of a hotel is in a sense precast by the market feasibility study that precedes the construction and financing phase of the hotel. If the market feasibility study identifies the need for a hotel in the moderate price category and that is what the developer builds, the hotel is more or less locked into a midscale position to compete with other properties in the same category until extraordinary new investment or massive marketing efforts are made to change it. Positioning, in other words, addresses the manner in which the hotel product is developed and targeted for a specific market segment, either through distinguishing features of the product itself—including location, property, pricing, and service—or through image creation with respect to advertising, promotion, and public relations. Hotels may be repositioned to trade up or to trade down. But trading up requires the investment of new resources to improve the property and/or its services before advertising and promotion can take place, as market credibility means everything. Trading down, on the other hand, is sometimes necessary when a destination is overbuilt with hotel rooms and lower-priced market segments must be considered to fill vacancies.

Ellsworth Statler's immortal advice on the three most important things to consider in building a hotel—"location, location, and location"—also holds true in hotel positioning around the world. It is a competitive factor whether the hotel is in Adelaide, Australia, or Ames, Iowa. Having close proximity to primary business districts, busy retail trade areas, transportation access, convention centers, tourist attractions, or other draws that support the guests' reasons for travel is an important marketing advantage for any hotel.

Positioning influences creation of the overall theme for the marketing program. Club Med created the original concept of the prepaid packaged vacation centered on the theme of remote "vacation villages" offering total escape, recreational amenities, and opportunity for self-discovery. Club Med, originally designed for young singles, repositioned itself in the 1990s as a family vacation resort; many Club Meds installed learning centers where guests could gain new cultural experiences or learn computer skills, foreign languages, new sports, or other proficiencies. In 2005, Club Med underwent a major brand relaunch to reposition itself again, this time for the upscale market. Club Med's annual report explained the purpose and strategy behind the repositioning:

> Its brand is an essential asset of the Club Méditerranée Group, and extends beyond individual products to convey an image and values that are deeply rooted in the collective consciousness. The widespread introduction of all-inclusive packages last year had the effect of blurring this image by bringing it too close to that of mass-package holiday operators. In 2005, Club Med strongly reasserted its unique and innovative character with a new upscale, friendly, and multicultural positioning that translates into a human, friendly, and generous luxury; a luxurious way to live together. The result is a rejuvenated and upscale brand that communicates at the global level.

This brand relaunch was done primarily to win back clients Club Med had lost because of branding and also to attract a new target clientele with higher-per-visit spending. The brand repositioning was accompanied with a major advertising campaign and renovation projects at Club Med properties.

Marketers should attempt to analyze their competition's positioning statements, advertising messages, and buyer or market reactions as part of their marketing research effort. Whenever possible, they should compare the structure of competitors' marketing efforts and budgets, if known, against their own in anticipation of the competition's next move.

Promotional Tools and Techniques

The marketing program combines a number of techniques into a workable whole. Applying knowledge of the selected target markets and the identified competition, the hotel marketing manager searches for the right combination of promotional techniques, channels, and media that will best satisfy the hotel's marketing objectives and marketing budget.

Advertising

Advertising is promotion paid for by the hotel in the mass communication media—television, radio, newspapers, consumer and travel trade magazines, websites, and so forth. In an increasingly globalized economy, there is a tendency to buy the idea that a central advertising campaign will work for all hotels within a chain, at least in positioning the product. The idea is attractive because it simplifies planning and implementation of campaigns. Unfortunately, generic advertisements seldom hold the same meaning for all customers around the world. For that reason, companies that use generic ads often produce regional or country-specific versions for particular markets. Because it is difficult to overcome the marketing obstacles caused by cultural differences, foreign expertise should always be sought when undertaking international advertising campaigns. The most dangerous proposition is to design a campaign for a foreign market based on one's domestic knowledge.

The cost of most media advertising (with the exception of newspapers) makes it prohibitive for the average individual hotel. Television and magazine ads, for example, are expensive; TV commercials have a cost per thousand basis for ads of a given length (30 seconds, 1 minute, etc.), and magazines have a cost per thousand readers basis plus space and color charges. One option available to either the individual operator or chain is cooperative (co-op) advertising, which permits the hotel to buy into a collective advertising effort with other travel-related businesses, attractions, and/or air carriers in the destination. Co-op advertising not only saves money but may offer the benefit of tying the hotel's image to other prominent brand names.

Trade Advertising. Trade advertising, which appears primarily in travel trade publications, directories, and tour operator brochures—is important in areas where consumers rely on travel agents for advice regarding accommodations. A trade advertising effort must be focused, providing accurate and useful information about the hotel for a reader who is already knowledgeable about travel products in general. For trade advertising, marketers should avoid advertising hype and emphasize factual data and information that will help sell the hotel.

When the hotel is part of a tour package, it is usually advisable to arrange cooperative trade advertising with the tour operator rather than to run separate ads. In addition to a listing, the hotel may want to purchase additional advertising space in the tour operator's brochure to attract readers' attention and gain the operator's goodwill.

Directory listings and ads can be effective ways to attract the attention of the international travel industry. *Hotel & Travel Index.com Worldwide* and the *OAG (Official Airline Guides) Business Travel Planner* are two of the largest international directories. Travel agents all over the world use these directories for quick point-of-sale reference and as a supplement to Internet-based reservation interfaces. Exhibit 4 is a checklist for tapping international business through directories.

Consumer Advertising. Consumer advertising is any paid form of mass promotion directed to the consumer; advertising media include newspapers, television, consumer magazines, in-flight magazines, destination promotional literature, posters, radio, websites, and phone books. The effectiveness of consumer advertising varies with different societies and cultures. When marketing to international audiences, messages should be written or at least reviewed by foreign advertising consultants and presented in the consumer's own language. Advertising messages should not be translations taken straight from the materials or media "sound bytes" developed for the home market. Slogans seldom make sense when translated from one language into another.

Music, on the other hand, is universal and is understood without need for verbal translation. Creative visual images with a minimal number of words and emotion-stirring background music can be very effective in crossing cultural boundaries. Alaskan and Caribbean destination campaigns promoted through television in the United States and elsewhere are noteworthy examples of advertising that uses imagery and music for a "soft sell" approach.

Likewise, imagery with minimal copy often works well in print ads. For example, ads for a successful luxury-class international hotel chain based in Hong

Exhibit 4 Checklist for Directory Advertising

> **Checklist for Tapping International Business Through Directory Advertisements**
>
> ✓ Provide information on property's location, accommodations, services, rates, packages and meeting space.
>
> ✓ Advise that reservations are positively honored.
>
> ✓ Include photos of guest rooms and facilities.
>
> ✓ Sum up sales points in short paragraphs or bulleted lists; avoid glowing descriptions or superlatives.
>
> ✓ Identify nearby attractions, i.e., sightseeing and shopping.
>
> ✓ List rates and specials, i.e., free underground parking.
>
> ✓ Show package plans and availability.
>
> ✓ Include direct reservation phone numbers; identify representatives and reservation services with phone numbers of regional and local offices, and telex and fax. Include computer access code(s).
>
> ✓ Identify travel agent commission payment or pre-payment policy, plus special commission rates.
>
> ✓ Show proximity to business centers, exhibition halls, and airports.

Source: Publisher's Perspective, *Hotel & Travel Index, Special Market Reports,* 1992.

Kong feature concise but provocative headlines, very little editorial copy, and eye-catching graphics. The tone of the ads is low-key and aims at the sophisticated, well-traveled, discriminating international guest.

As customs and cultures differ among countries, advertisers need to be especially alert to local sensitivities. Although most advertisers would know enough not to promote a resort's aquatic amenities by featuring models wearing skimpy swimwear in ads for placement in Muslim countries, they must also understand that objections to a suggestive, sensual sell are not confined to strongly religious countries. Similar ads will generate complaints from people who find them more sexist than sexy. In foreign advertising, attention must be paid to details of color, dress, and gestures. White, for example, is the color of death in many Asian cultures; in others, it is black, blue, or red. But colors also have to be put in context; in some situations, any color may be appropriate, whereas in others, the wrong color may be displeasing. Again, local expertise should be engaged for advice on the appropriateness of ad content as well as details regarding placement and timing.

Most of the larger international hotel chains will work with more than one advertising agency to balance a company-wide global marketing approach with the needs of specific properties or communities.

Direct Mail. Direct mail is a popular means of contemporary marketing. The value of direct mail in international marketing lies in the fact that it is target-specific. Since many international travelers are also frequently repeat visitors, a direct mail campaign can be a cost-effective promotional tool. Mailing lists can be compiled from in-house generated data banks of guest files, lists of potential visitors obtained from convention and visitors bureaus, or purchased from travel and entertainment credit card companies, banks, or other sources. Travel consultants may also be hired to help compile mailing lists.

People from various countries, of course, have different reactions to direct mail. While many consider direct mailers bothersome, a poll done by the Japan Direct Mail Association indicated that 79 percent of the Japanese recipients of mailers find them to be "useful," "somewhat useful," or "welcomed" material.[16] But because people receive so much promotional literature today, a direct mail campaign should be designed to attract the reader's *immediate* attention. If the mailer offers no perceived benefit to the reader, it will be tossed.

All components of the direct mail effort should be in the language of the intended reader. If direct mail is chosen as a medium, not only should the mailing list be carefully compiled and accurate, but mailing time must also be considered. International mail may require as long as two months to arrive at its destination. Professional fulfillment houses often do test runs with return response cards to check the length of time it takes for a promotional piece to reach its destination.

With advances in communication software and large computerized databases, many hotel companies today rely on sophisticated "customer relationship programs" to send personalized e-mails directly to customer computers and, in many cases, their mobile phones. Based on a recent customer survey by PhoCusWright, a market research firm, 30 percent of the travelers surveyed said they would like to receive special offers via their mobile devices during their trip.[17] Direct e-mail campaigns with promotional offers are custom-developed on the basis of understanding individual guest preferences, travel patterns, and spending patterns. This level of targeted advertising is part of what has been termed the customization of customer experiences. In their best selling business classic, *The Experience Economy*, authors Pine and Gilmore provide insights into delivering customized experiences to customers by making them specific to individuals, designed to meet their individual needs, and singular in their purpose to benefit the customer. This type of service experience is what creates *customer-unique value*.[18]

Collateral Materials and Sales Promotions

Sales promotion includes activities other than advertising, personal selling, and public relations to stimulate room, restaurant, or other sales. This includes the development of brochures, postcards, slide kits, posters, and the organization of special programs or special rate periods during low seasons. Imaginative promotional materials and good communications are the keys to an effective sales promotion.

While not all hotels have a large budget for advertising, virtually every hotel produces some type of promotional, or **collateral**, material for customer and trade information. Collateral materials include brochures, fliers, tent cards, and similar printed pieces.

English, for better or for worse, is the universal language of tourism today; however, it is essential in many markets that promotional materials be presented in another language as well as English. This means that the translation factor should be kept in mind when preparing original text for brochures and other materials. As languages do undergo changes in usage, translations should be done in the country where the material will be distributed. Because literal translations do not always make sense, especially in the case of slang and colloquialisms (which should be avoided in the first place), translators may need to select near-equivalent terms to convey intended meanings.

The presentation format must also be tailored for individual countries. For example, the German market requires comparatively more informational detail and less art. Most brochures intended for an international audience, however, tend to have minimal copy, relying heavily on visual images to make a point. Pictures chosen for brochures should take cultural sensitivities, as well as legalities, into consideration. In general, brochures should give the following information:

- The location of the hotel (preferably using a map) and how to reach it
- Amenities provided
- Credit cards accepted
- Languages spoken
- The hotel's fax number
- The hotel's e-mail address
- The hotel's toll-free telephone number
- The hotel's website address

While English measurements remain the standard for the United States, metric measurements should be used elsewhere in describing distances, room and conference spaces, temperatures, and other data.

Quality brochures are expensive to print and distribute internationally. Rather than mass-mailing brochures to foreign retail travel agencies, it may be more cost-effective to place a brochure insert in a travel-trade publication with an ad that includes a coupon for additional brochures. Brochures should fit international mailing standards—currently 21 × 10 cm; the use of lighter grade paper also helps to reduce the hotel's mailing costs. The trend for collateral material is shifting from paper brochures to e-brochures delivered on a CD or via e-mail. In addition, hotels are promoting their properties through video DVDs and other multi-media such as Flash.

Marketers should be aware that many countries assess duty on commercial literature not printed in their country. Some countries also have laws prohibiting the use of superlatives such as "the *best* hotel" or "the *most elegant* hotel" in advertising and promotional literature. In countries with strict consumer protection laws, misleading descriptions may have serious legal implications. In the United Kingdom, for instance, the Trade Description Act of 1978, which covers trade brochures and prohibits misleading the consumer, has been broadened. The new provisions (and penalties) require tourism and hospitality operators to take positive action with regard to accurate information. Photographs, too, should accurately depict what they claim to depict. Some foreign courts would take harsh issue with a hotel advertiser who intentionally pictured a superb scenic view from an ordinary room when the room in reality overlooks the backside of another high-rise hotel. All copy used in the brochure, including descriptions and representations, should be reviewed by an attorney familiar with international law before going to press.

In a recent case, Travelodge placed a full-page advertisement in a London newspaper accusing four leading hotel chains of misleading guests by ambiguously stating their prices in a sales promotion. The hotels priced their rooms at per-person rates rather than the typical per-room rate, as most customers generally expect. As a result, when rates are based on two people sharing a room for a minimum of two nights, the chains' advertised rate of $49.95 would actually be almost $200 for the stay.[19]

Cooperative Marketing

Success in developing a strong international presence, for many hotels, lies in cooperative industry and/or government marketing programs. The unified action of a diverse travel industry—including such segments as transportation, lodging, dining, entertainment, convention centers, and attractions—offers a rich opportunity for collaborative success. As the motivations for discretionary overseas travel are numerous and not always clear, the pooling of resources covering a variety of products and services not only stretches promotional dollars, but provides added incentive for the traveler to make the trip. The success of cooperative marketing is also based on the fact that when the various elements of the tourist industry work together, the impact is greater—and the product or destination is made more saleable.

Among the types of cooperative promotions a hotel may become involved with are intercommunity, hotel industry, destination, national, or regional efforts. Intercommunity cooperation occurs when tourism suppliers in two or more destinations decide that it is better to collaborate than to collide. This often leads to the development of multi-destination packages and fam tours. Hotel industry cooperative marketing takes place when hotels in the particular destination, either through a local hotel association or on their own, pool marketing dollars to promote travel to the destination through advertising, travel missions, fam trips, special events, and so forth. This effort reflects a desire on the part of hoteliers to enlarge the pool of visitors to the area rather than competing with each other over the existing pool. For example, the Caribbean Hotel Association, which represents 849 hotels, has developed a number of cooperative programs between the association and other tourism partners, including government, to counteract the leveling off of tourism to the Caribbean area.

Destination Marketing. City, state/province, or national cooperative promotion programs are the most common forms of destination cooperative marketing. These programs offer hotels an opportunity to participate in such large-scale promotional activities as destination advertising, travel missions, trade shows, and special events at a relatively small cost. The organization of the marketing activities varies in quality at these different levels, depending on their funding and marketing expertise. Any destination-oriented promotional efforts should be taken into consideration when an individual hotel is planning its own marketing program.

One of the more beneficial steps hotel marketers can take in bringing their properties into the international travel mainstream is to cultivate and work through the primary destination marketing organization of the area—the national or provincial tourism organization, the city convention and visitors bureau, or a public-/private-sector entity serving as an industry marketing arm and spokesbody. These organizations periodically sponsor or coordinate international promotional activities, and actively solicit hotels and other travel suppliers to participate. In the United States, destination marketing is represented by the Travel Industry Association (TIA), a non-profit trade organization that represents and speaks for the common interests of the $740 billion U.S. travel industry. Based in Washington, D.C., TIA is a public voice and political liaison for the entire industry. The mission of the association is to represent the whole of the U.S. travel industry to promote and facilitate increased travel to and within the United States. TIA does this through marketing initiatives, including the Discover America® program, as well as by serving as an advocate with the U.S. government to ease travel procedures. The association's marketing efforts strive to further educate and promote tourism organizations though a series of national and international programs, including National Tourism Week/See America Week and International Pow Wow, a computer-generated networking session bringing together more than 1,000 U.S. travel organizations and nearly 1,500 international and domestic buyers from more than 70 countries.

The development of tourism in Korea and the subsequent success of the Korean hotel industry is largely attributable to the Korean government's massive efforts at selling tourism abroad with promotional materials, advertising saturation, fam trips, participation in trade shows, the promotion of "Visit Korea Year" in 1994, the hosting of the 1993 International Exposition, the 1988 Olympics, and the 1986 Asian Games, and the operation of sales offices in 26 countries. This promotional task has not always been easy for the Korea Tourism Organization (KTO), given the country's recurring political instability. KTO has contributed greatly to the increase of international visitors to Korea. In 1962, the first recorded number of international visitors interested in Korea was only around 20,000; in 1978, the number increased to one million visitors. In 1988, the number reached two million, and in 1998, there were four million international visitors in Korea. The recorded number of international visitors to Korea doubled every 10 years, and in 2005, the number exceeded six million. Lately, KTO has been focusing its efforts on developing tourism technology as well as capitalizing on *Hallyu*, or the "Korean Wave," a relatively recent phenomenon of the growing surge of South Korean popular culture, including movies, drama, and popular music. In addition, during 2008 KTO's Tourist Information Center will hold *hanbok* experience events throughout the year. These events provide visitors with the opportunity to experience Korean culture through the country's traditional dress, the *hanbok*.

On a regional level, the Pacific Asia Travel Association (PATA) stands out among its peers as an organization that has been extremely effective in increasing travel to its member countries through its marketing efforts—cooperative programs, conferences, travel markets, editorial features, and PATA chapter alliances in more than 70 locations around the world.

By helping to market a destination, a hotel stands to profit if more visitors are attracted from abroad, especially because foreign guests have a greater tendency to stay in full-service hotels and they generally stay twice as long as domestic travelers.

Public Relations

Public relations is the employment of any means of advancing the hotel's relationship with the community and the general public. It includes such community relations goodwill gestures as supporting charitable events, the arts, or education; sponsoring sporting or special interest activities; and becoming involved with local organizations and civic projects or programs. Effective public relations requires not only good works and goodwill, but also the communication of deeds, activities, and ideas to the public—inside and outside the hotel—through newsletters, the news media, and public occasions.

The fundamental objective of public relations is to promote the image of the hotel before its various publics. In the international arena, public relations strategies should be kept as simple as possible to avoid political, religious, and cultural danger zones, and the advice of local contacts should be taken seriously. The skills of a public relations officer tend to be put to a hard test in a multicultural environment.

Many international chains employ a public relations consultant or specialist at each of their hotels; such consultants are either natives of or otherwise familiar with the locality. These specialists are not only knowledgeable about local media and mores, but also about the corporate philosophy and global aims of their employers. They are encouraged to suggest ways of enhancing the hotel's products and services, besides building community relations and handling technical details with media and VIP events.

Public relations efforts also subsume media relations and guest relations. **Media relations** requires the establishment of cordial relationships with the press and the electronic media. Credibility and candor are the key operatives in this relationship. One of the regular duties of hotel public relations officers is to provide news releases to the media about events and famous personalities connected with the hotel. However, public relations officers cannot influence the editorial direction that stories will take, nor can they be certain that their material will be used. The trade press tends to be more receptive to hotel press releases, and more readily gives full coverage. The strategy of the hotel's public relations department must be to carefully select and cultivate the right mix of media to enhance the hotel's image. In countries where business-oriented stories are not accepted, hotels may need to sponsor sports competitions or social, charitable, or cultural events in order to get the desired exposure.

Guest relations in a broad sense implies the establishment of personal rapport and goodwill with all guests by providing superior service and paying attention to individual guest needs. In a narrower sense, guest relations involves the promotion of internal products and services, the entertainment of VIPs, and the handling of social functions—especially in a resort hotel. Effective guest relations goes a step beyond the business at hand; it means making a concerted effort to build guest loyalty and return stays.

All facets of public relations need to be adapted to the local environment. In many countries, relations with local government officials and business and social leaders need to be carefully cultivated. This should be a priority. In some developing countries, relevant media do not exist or their access may be restricted. When media are controlled or are not accessible, it is often necessary to place greater emphasis on community relations, in-house newsletters, or organized events. Whatever the medium, the message must speak to the needs and values of its intended audience, whether the general public or the travel trade.

To maintain a continuous presence in the public eye, hotel public relations practitioners need to be innovative and resourceful. For example, some resort destinations and hotels have gained exposure in the Japanese consumer market as sponsors of documentaries and game shows on Japanese television. Such shows attract large audiences of Japanese viewers who are avid travelers.

Frequent-Guest Programs

Intensified competition in the international hotel industry resulted in hotel chains strengthening efforts to foster brand loyalty among guests, especially repeat business travelers. Initially, loyalty in patronage was achieved through the offering of incentives and such special terms as corporate rates and no-deposit guarantees. Gradually these incentives became institutionalized through frequent-guest programs, which are today an integral part of the marketing programs of numerous chains. Frequent-guest programs commonly include such benefits as:

- Guaranteed reservations
- Corporate room rates, discounted from published rates
- Rapid check-in and no-stop check-out service
- Early check-in and/or late check-out privileges
- Upgrading to the next higher category of room available within a specified price range
- Personalized gifts
- Special amenities in room
- Concierge or VIP floor privileges (usually conditional)
- Complimentary newspaper
- Newsletters and mailings
- Complimentary valet service upon arrival
- Personal check cashing privileges

In some cases, membership in these programs is subject to the payment of an annual fee and, in others, it is dependent on the traveler or his or her company qualifying for membership by virtue of the volume of the previous year's patronage. Many hotels use frequent-guest programs in much the same way as airlines, subject to specified limitations. The points accumulated for lodging nights can be redeemed for complimentary rooms, free meals, gifts, or sometimes airline tickets.

Property Website

Over the past decade, hotel websites have become increasingly powerful tools for marketing, promoting, and distributing hotel room inventory and services. As a result of their increasing use by customers to find information and book reservations, hotel websites at minimum are important marketing tools for conveying the hotel's image. Among many other things, a hotel's website can do the following for the hotel:

- It can reflect the look and feel of the hotel. Many times it is the first impression a potential guest has of the hotel.
- It can be a communication hub for past customers and a point of communication with the hotel for prospective guests.
- It allows potential guests to get a feel for the hotel and decide whether they want to experience the product firsthand.
- It is a reservations center for guests.
- It is a place where hotels merchandise their products.

Because of the power and complexity of well-designed websites and the need for ongoing management of the web presence, a hotel company works with a variety of vendors to build and manage its website, implement a web marketing campaign, and generate ongoing reports on the site's effectiveness. Many large hotel companies have their own internal web development and management teams.

Effectiveness of Tools/Techniques

According to a recent survey sponsored by the Hospitality Sales & Marketing Association International, hotel sales and marketing departments are now focusing their efforts and funding on direct customer contact and Internet marketing techniques.[20] Exhibit 5 illustrates the relative effectiveness of the various sales and marketing channels for hotels. Survey respondents said that direct contacts through person-to-person selling, property websites, public relations, and Internet marketing and advertising are the most effective channels. They also said that local advertising, direct mail, and merchandising are lagging in their effectiveness.

Personal Selling

Personal selling involves any form of face-to-face contact with individuals or groups for the purpose of generating advance sales. It includes direct contact with members of the travel trade, familiarization (fam) tours, representation at trade shows, travel missions, corporate or institutional groups, and allied travel partners—car rentals, airlines, and destination management organizations.

Exhibit 5   Effectiveness of Hotel Sales and Marketing Channels

Channel	Rating
Person-to-Person Sales	4.16
Property Website	3.98
Public Relations	3.60
Internet Marketing and Advertising	3.41
E-Mail Marketing	3.15
National/Corporate Advertising	3.00
Local Advertising	3.00
Merchandising	2.84
Direct Mail	2.62

1 = Poor, 3 = Good, 5 = Excellent

Source: PKF-HR and HSMAI.

Personal selling is an effective and sometimes necessary way to reach international markets. However, it also presents cultural challenges.

The degree to which salespersons are expected to "sell themselves" along with their product; the amount of time they need to invest in cultivating customers; the channels they may appropriately use to make the sale; and the relative importance of the written contract are just some of the variables that need to be considered. Hotel salespeople attempting to penetrate the lucrative but often elusive Asian market, for instance, will find they need time and patience to develop personal relationships, since business in Asia is based so heavily on trust. Trust in the integrity of the seller may be the most significant factor in an Asian travel distributor's decision to work with a hotel as its travel partner. There are also gender considerations. While the gender gap in most of Asia is closing, this is not yet the case, say, in Japan or Korea, where salesmen have a distinct advantage over saleswomen in dealing with buyers.

An effective hotel salesperson has a good understanding of the cultural patterns of the markets being solicited. In most countries, it is important to make and keep appointments promptly and to communicate in a common language, yet grasp intercultural nuances. Although many take for granted that English is the de facto language of business, astute salespeople know that the language of business is whatever the customer speaks. Hotel salespeople who are bilingual, therefore, are valuable assets. Also, a salesperson who is a long-time resident of the target market area will understand the customer better than an outsider. Such a person is more likely to be familiar with local travel distribution systems, social customs, and business practices. Local knowledge is particularly important when working in nations with significant cultural or religious differences. For instance, the sales executive who knows that the business week in Arab countries runs from Saturday to Thursday, with Friday the Muslim day of rest and worship, would avoid making calls on Fridays.

With personal selling, differences in culture and business practices between countries can be so pronounced (even when there is a common language) that local sales representatives should be given as large a degree of latitude in decision-making as possible. But even with a considerable amount of autonomy, international sales reps should be given a sales plan with target goals and should undergo periodic performance evaluations.

In small hotel organizations without country sales representatives, the general sales office may handle the selling effort. When possible, a team approach should be adopted, with one person who knows the technical details of sales working with another who understands the financial aspects; both should have some understanding of how business is conducted in the target country. Team members should be the same every time the same country is visited, particularly in countries where continuity and relationships are prized. In the single hotel situation, often it is the general manager who makes the sales call to a valued client.

When selling abroad, repeated meetings may be required to review details. Hotel negotiators should familiarize themselves with the communication and bargaining styles of their counterparts so as not to be confused by signals that have different meanings for each party. From the onset of business dealings, hotel representatives should strive to demonstrate honesty and reliability so that foreign associates will want to continue the relationship. Although contracts are standard practice in most parts of the world, one's word is worth far more than a contract in some cultures.

It is important that hotel salespeople conduct research in each location to determine which travel agents, wholesalers, planners, or corporate accounts have the potential to boost the hotel's sales effort. In some countries, if leading tour packagers can be persuaded to include a representative's hotel in the company's tour or incentive program, interest from other buyers will soon follow. Also, as travel distributors become more specialized in their services, an appropriate fit between the hotel and the markets served by travel agents and other intermediaries is an important factor to consider in choosing distributors. A national tourism organization or hotel representative abroad can be useful in setting up appointments with those agents or wholesalers who are most likely to book business with the hotel.

There are various ways to make corporate contacts. In large hotel chains, the corporate sales offices have routine contacts with national and international accounts that can be networked locally. Hotel sales reps can also make cold calls (calls with no preliminary contact) or seek introductions through such agencies as chambers of commerce and others.

Not to be overlooked are international airlines, international service clubs, professional associations, embassies, and consulates. Most companies are interested in the benefits that a hotel may have to offer with respect to corporate rates, popular or unique meeting facilities, and special services.

Some of the greatest "salespeople" for a hotel are its customers. A positive experience for guests may create a sales force that promotes the hotel through word-of-mouth referrals. The recent trend of social computing has given this concept tremendous importance; a pleased or disgruntled guest with the power of the Internet at his or her fingertips has the potential to either greatly help or greatly hurt a hotel. Based on a recent survey, two-thirds of online customers are using some type of online social-media outlet to interact with other customers. The proliferation of social networking websites such as MySpace, Facebook, Xanga, and similar general and specialized sites is a testament to this communication medium. Obviously, the more happy guests who are communicating their impressions of the hotel via this medium, the better.

One of the most influential travel websites in social computing is TripAdvisor.com. This site hosts the largest travel community in the world, with more than five million customer reviews and opinions posted that cover more than 220,000 hotels and attractions. The site has more than 20 million unique monthly visitors worldwide. TripAdvisor now provides a service that allows a hotel to automatically publish TripAdvisor customer-generated reviews on its own website.

Travel Trade Shows

Travel trade shows bring together tour wholesalers and operators, travel agents, airlines, hotels, attractions, meeting planners, incentive travel specialists, and other travel industry representatives to negotiate, buy, and sell contracts of travel services throughout the world. All categories of travel suppliers display their products—located by country or region with few exceptions—and travel traders can compare costs, facilities, and programs on the spot. Major travel trade shows are usually oriented toward trade professionals, but some also serve consumers.

Trade shows are an important means of reaching markets globally. They can help increase public awareness of a hotel, besides facilitating business contacts with buyers of hotel services. At trade shows, hotel representatives have the opportunity to conduct one-on-one meetings with interested tour wholesalers and agents in attendance, and to develop leads for conventions, meetings, and social functions. Because business is done briskly, the reps should be prepared to talk rates and availability and to get the names and addresses of all those spoken to for follow-up right after the show.

The following travel trade shows are considered to be the largest and most significant travel trade events in the world. Each of these shows attracts more than 100,000 visitors from many different countries:

1. *International Tourism Bourse (ITB):* Started in 1966, the ITB Berlin is considered to be the world's leading travel trade show. In October 2008 the first Asian ITB will be launched in Singapore to serve the growing MICE (meetings, incentives, conferences and conventions, events and exhibitions) market and business travel professional community in addition to leisure providers.

2. *Italian Tourism Bourse/Exchange (BIT):* While BIT attracts a similar profile of attendees as the ITB, it tends to be more European in its focus. The majority of the professional attendees and participants are from Italy and the international attendees and participants tend to be European.
3. *Feria Internacional de Turismo (FITUR):* This five-day travel trade fair is held in Madrid each year. FITUR combines the trade show with events to promote international trade relations before and after the travel trade show events.
4. *World Travel Mart (WTM):* This is a four-day travel industry event held in London each year. As with the other events, the mart is a combination of exhibition space, networking, and educational programs.
5. *JATA World Tourism Congress and Travel Fair:* This show is organized by the Japanese Association of Travel Agents (JATA) in Tokyo each year. Over the years this has become a major event for travel professionals who want to tap into the Japanese travel market.

The cost of participation at trade shows is high, so hotels must be selective, participating only in those shows that can help to advance sales objectives. Hotels may also participate in shows on a cooperative basis with airlines, attractions, and/or convention and visitors bureaus, to help defray costs. Many convention and visitors bureaus or NTOs around the world will book large spaces with the idea of consolidating all their destination suppliers under one showcase. When the hotel cannot be directly represented at the trade show, the hotel sales office should at least ensure representation through its corporate chain, consortium, or the local convention and visitors bureau, providing sufficient collateral material (brochures, fliers, and the like) for pickup by potential buyers.

Many professional trade shows, for instance the ITB in Berlin and the WTM in London, include consumer days at the end of the trade exhibition.

Travel Missions

In a travel mission, travel suppliers from a host destination are organized to visit a target outbound market to stimulate buyers' interest, develop contacts, secure bookings, and, overall, to attract more visitors to the host destination. Travel missions can produce profitable new business for the hotel when they are undertaken as a serious sales activity. Before getting involved in a travel mission, a hotel should assess the potential benefit of its participation. If the hotel is in a city that attracts mostly non-discretionary business travelers and conventioneers as guests, a travel mission would likely not produce high returns. If, on the other hand, the property attracts predominantly discretionary leisure travelers and incentive groups, participation could be worthwhile.

Properly planned and executed, travel missions provide sellers with an opportunity to reach the public through an organized exhibition and media blitz. If a stellar entertainment group from the host destination also accompanies the mission, an audience is virtually guaranteed, for nothing attracts quite like show business. The travel mission program should be specifically tailored to the audience and the mission's objective. The challenge is to create an entertaining way of presenting the group's factual material—for instance, combining live presentations with professionally prepared audiovisual material.

Because travel missions are generally undertaken on a cooperative basis, they can be cost-effective marketing vehicles. In the case of an international mission, the national tourism organization can be invaluable in timing a travel mission to coincide with (or avoid) major events in the target country, assisting with program format and strategies, and arranging overseas appointments and promotional assistance. Those involved in the travel mission should familiarize themselves with the culture and customs of the country or countries being visited. They must have specific objectives that they want the mission to achieve, and they must address each audience appropriately—their hosts, the travel trade, the press, and the public.

Local travel consultants in the target country may be hired to provide an appropriate mailing list to reach a selected audience or to make arrangements to host receptions for local industry and political VIPs. When possible, all audiovisual and supporting printed materials should be in the language of the country being visited, as well as in English. Hotel salespeople should have an adequate supply of illustrated brochures and rate cards with prices quoted in foreign currency as well as dollars. The exchange of business cards is important. And names and addresses of those contacted should be recorded for follow-up.

Familiarization Tours

The **familiarization (fam) tour** supports the conventional wisdom that the well-informed salesperson is a better salesperson. The primary reason for any hotel to participate in a fam tour for travel agents, wholesalers, or incentive travel planners is to provide these potential sales agents of the hotel with an opportunity to gain firsthand knowledge of and experience with house products. By the same token, media fam trips are also organized to provide travel writers, broadcasters, photographers, and others who shape public opinion with personal experiences of the hotel, in the hope that publicity will follow the visit.

Fam tours may also be undertaken as a cooperative effort with the local convention and visitors bureau and/or other travel suppliers in the destination. A hotel, depending on its promotional budget, may provide complimentary accommodations for the fam tour participants or host a reception or banquet. Typically, the NTO or a local travel trade association can provide assistance in selecting the most appropriate participants for a fam tour. A well-informed interpreter/guide should be used when hosting any foreign-language group, and the fam trip should be professionally planned and administered with appropriate follow-up.

In addition to fam tours, some hotels routinely extend VIP invitations to tour intermediaries, travel writers, and newspaper section editors who cover special topics such as food, sports, arts and entertainment, and hobbies.

International airlines have onboard magazines that continuously seek interesting articles and features about travel destinations and travel suppliers. These and other international publications look for stories about historic, unique, or otherwise interesting hotels and resorts. Writers whose stories are featured in airline publications may be reached through the sales offices of international air carriers.

Summary

Marketing is exciting. No other area of the international hotel business offers greater opportunity for imagination, analytical skill, and the possibility to try something new. The problems that hotel marketers face spring from the ever-changing needs and desires of the globe-trotting public and the activities of the competition. The marketing manager solves these problems through insight, knowledge of different markets, experience, and analysis. The results of marketing decisions have much to do with competitive success or failure for the property and the hotel company.

The development of an international marketing strategy begins with the commitment to serve the international market, and calls for the cooperation of management and staff at every level to establish and deliver culturally appropriate hotel products and services. Spending money on international advertising and other marketing activities will prove futile unless the hotel is operationally ready to accommodate international guests. If the commitment is there, then the next step will be to determine through research whether there is adequate demand. The results to be achieved through marketing will depend in part on the quality of marketing information available for decisions—its relevancy, accuracy, and timeliness. The international hotel has many information resources already at hand; for example, in-house guest histories, guest registration forms, and, in some cases, passport and visa registrations. Other needed information may be acquired by direct observation; this is certainly the case with evaluating the competitive environment and competing hotels. Published industry reports, trade press stories, travel trade associations, national tourism organizations, key customers, and vendors are among the many sources that can provide useful intelligence for marketing decisions.

An important element in the marketing strategy is the system of marketing channels through which hotel products and services are sold to hotel customers. The marketing channel used for hotel products and services is determined by the prevailing distribution system of travel intermediaries in different countries and the buying habits of their residents. How successfully a hotel is marketed through the channel ultimately depends on the relationship that the hotel has with its travel intermediaries and the agreement it has negotiated with each seller in terms of product and service delivery, room rates, bookings, and commission payments. Not to be overlooked are the automated global distribution systems. These refer to the major GDSs and to the CRSs of chain operators, hotel representation companies, and hotel consortia.

In marketing, it is often noted that positioning is paramount. Although it is the customer who ultimately determines the position of any product, increasingly it is also the competition that positions one product against another. Positioning in the world of international hotels refers to the manner in which each property is aimed at different international guest segments, through distinguishing features of the product itself and/or the image that is created for the hotel through advertising and promotion. Some hotels are positioned and promoted as luxury properties, offering world-class service aimed at the high-end market, while others are positioned and promoted as mid-scale or budget properties, offering a different price-value standard to their target segments. In each of these hotel categories, the successful hotel marketing strategy requires detailed segmentation and the use of available resources to satisfy specific market segments.

Through effective advertising, promotion, and public relations, it is possible to strengthen the market position of a hotel among its competitors. Advertising media are the channels through which hotels send their messages to the audiences they have selected as targets for communication. Selection of the proper media is a complex task, since there are literally thousands of different outlets—trade and consumer, television, radio, newspapers, direct mail—to consider, each having different customer outreach and market penetrations. Websites have also grown in importance as advertising and promotional tools. The task of choosing media and designing the right messages for international advertising is also complicated by the fact that different cultures have different media habits and interpretation of messages; hence, a campaign designed for a foreign market should never be based solely on a marketer's domestic knowledge of that market.

Marketers implement sales promotions to stimulate customer buying and distribution effectiveness. Sales promotions are activities other than advertising, public relations, publicity, and personal selling. One of the more effective ways for a hotel to promote its products and services is through cooperative marketing and active representation with other travel partners at international travel trade shows and exhibitions. The pooling of resources to do cooperative promotion at a travel trade show not only helps to sell the destination, but provides opportunities for the hotel to communicate directly with major buyers of hotel accommodations and services.

To complement advertising and promotion, hotels engage in public relations. A continuous product awareness in the mind of potential buyers is the main purpose of hotel public relations activities. Public relations encompasses the development of sound relationships and goodwill with the community, the media, and guests.

Personal selling, which involves any form of face-to-face contact with individuals or groups who are potential buyers of hotel services, is essential in marketing. While marketing is concerned with strategy and trying to provide what customers want, selling is generally concerned with the plans and tactics of trying to get the customer to actually buy the seller's hotel products and services over those of the competitors. Selling internationally, like marketing internationally, also requires cultural understanding and sensitivity to how markets, travel buyers, and consumers behave in each location. Ultimately, the success of marketing is measured in terms of the ability to close sales and the translation of sales into hotel revenue. Social networking sites have been turning hotel guests into an informal sales force that spreads word-of-mouth information about the property.

An international–marketing–minded hotel executive tries to create value-satisfying products and services that guests from around the world, as well as at home, will want to buy. In thinking strategically, he or she should consider not only how to differentiate generic hotel products or services, but also how to best distribute, advertise, promote, and sell in culturally appropriate ways to each market. Ultimately, what a hotel has to offer should be less determined by the seller than by the buyer—and that, in a nutshell, is the essence of marketing.

Endnotes

1. "Competitive Strategies for the International Hotel Industry," *Travel and Tourism Analyst,* Economist Intelligence Unit, March 1991, p. 96.
2. Readers interested in learning how to forecast demand are referred to Raymond S. Schmidgall, *Hospitality Industry Managerial Accounting,* 6th ed. (Lansing, Mich.: American Hotel & Lodging Educational Institute, 2006).
3. www.phocuswright.com.
4. www.travelclick.net.
5. Eric Ng, Francis Cassidy, and Les Brown, "Exploring the Major Factors Influencing Consumer Travel Agencies in a Regional Setting," *Journal of Hospitality and Tourism Management,* vol. 13, no. 1, April 2006, p. 75.
6. "Future Traveller Tribes: A Report for the Air Travel Industry," developed by Henley Center Headlightvision in partnership with Amadeus, 2007. www.amadeus.com/travellertribes.
7. "2007 Global Travel Agent GDS Study," Phoenix Marketing International, November 2007, p. 14.
8. Cindy Estes Green, "De-Mystifying Distribution: Building a Distribution Strategy One Channel at a Time," TIG Special Report, published by HSMAI, 2005.
9. Erin F. Stenthal, "The Hyatt Touch," *Travel Agent,* January 9, 2004, p. 18.
10. David Elsen and Mark Rogers, "Starwood Launches Agent Program, Website," *Travel Agent,* September 17, 2007, p. 8.
11. Peter Fitzgerald, "Hotel Payment Solutions," *Travel Weekly,* April, 15, 2005, p. 2.
12. Jennifer Merritt, "New Agent Rewards for 2007," *Travel Agent,* January 15, 2007, p. 8.
13. "A Global View: World Economy Coming of Age," *HotelLine,* July/August 1989, p. 3
14. www.roccofortecollection.com/press_and_media/rocco_forte_hotels_launches_dedicated_travel_agents_websitehtm.
15. "International Growth Strategies of Major Hotel Chains," Mintel, March 2007.
16. Japan Direct Mail Association newsletter, October 1991.
17. PhoCusWright Consumer Travel Trends Survey, 10th edition, Travel Industry Trends, June 2008.
18. B. Joseph Pine II and James H. Gilmore, *The Experience Economy: Work Is Theatre & Every Business a Stage* (Boston: Harvard Business School Press, 1999).
19. Angela Frewin, "Travelodge hits out at 'Misleading' Ads" *Caterer & Hotelkeeper,* Jan. 19—Jan. 25, 2006, vol. 196, no. 4408, p. 10.
20. "Marketing Spending Going to Direct Sales, Internet" *Hotels,* November 2005, p. 34 D.

Key Terms

branding—Tailoring hotels to match particular properties with specific market segments.

collateral—Promotional material developed by hotels for customer and trade information; includes brochures, fliers, tent cards, and similar printed pieces. Increasingly, it also includes marketing material such as brochures delivered via CDs or e-mails (e-brochures).

familiarization tour—An often complimentary trip or tour offered to travel agents, wholesalers, incentive travel planners, travel writers, broadcasters, or photographers to promote a hotel or destination.

guest relations—The establishment of personal rapport and goodwill with hotel guests through service and attention to individual guest needs. In a narrower sense, the promotion of in-house products and services, the entertainment of VIPs, and the handling of social functions—especially at a resort hotel.

media relations—From the hotel public relations officer's perspective, the establishment of cordial relationships with the press and the electronic media.

positioning—A concept that addresses the manner in which the hotel product is developed and targeted for a specific market segment, either through distinguishing features of the product itself—including location, property, pricing, and service—or through image creation with respect to advertising, promotion, and public relations.

public relations—The employment of any means of advancing a hotel's relationship with the community and the general public; includes media relations and guest relations as well as the support of charitable events, the arts, education, sporting events, or special interest activities.

segmentation—The development of different types of hotels and hotel products and services for different market segments; "niche" marketing. Markets can be segmented geographically, demographically, or psychographically.

travel distribution system—A series of marketing or selling institutions through which title to a travel product or service is transferred from the supplier to the user. In short, it is how a hotel (as a supplier) sells its services to buyers through travel agents, tour operators, tour wholesalers, toll-free lines, and other means.

Review Questions

1. How and why should hotel marketers perform guest analysis and competition analysis?
2. What does development of an international marketing strategy entail?
3. How have successful hotels dealt with cultural differences in international hotel marketing and sales?
4. How can international marketers and salespeople cultivate the U.S. foreign visitor market?
5. Why is it important to understand the use of travel distribution systems in international marketing efforts?

6. What is the role of travel agents in the hotel booking process? How have some U.S. and European hotels resolved hotel—travel agent relationship problems?
7. What are the benefits to hotels of having tour wholesalers, hotel representation companies, and consortia as travel partners?
8. What is segmentation, and what are some pros and cons of branding?
9. What is positioning, and how does it relate to the overall marketing effort?
10. What promotional tools and techniques can hotel marketers use and what international concerns are associated with each one?
11. How does personal selling for international hotels differ from personal selling for domestic hotels?

Part V
Looking Ahead

Chapter 14 Outline

Long-Term Tourism Growth Trends
    Factors Influencing Future Growth
        Demographic, Economic, and Social Trends
        Competition from Other Sources
Deregulation and Free Trade
The European Union's Impact on Travel and Tourism
    European Union Tourism Policy
    Transportation
    Tour Operators
    Travel Agents
    The Hotel Industry
    Standardized Currency
    Travel Costs
    Specific Countries
Tourism Growth by Region
    Europe
    North America
    Asia and the Pacific
    South and Central America
    Africa
    Middle East
Privatization
    Airline Privatization
Transportation Developments
    Aircraft Technology
    Space Travel
    Train Technology
    Deregulation
    Transportation Infrastructure
Technology and Automation
Global Distribution Systems
Development Issues
Tourism and the Environment
    Hotels and the Environment
    The Environment's Importance to Tourism
Alternative Tourism
Human Resource Issues
Hotel Company Diversification and Growth
    Mergers, Acquisitions, and Cooperative Arrangements
Conclusion

Competency

1. Identify, define, and explain factors and developments that are likely to affect the nature and pace of globalization in the travel, tourism, and lodging industry in the years to come.

Note: This chapter presents speculation about the future. Although the speculation is based largely on current factual information, it is nonetheless speculation. For that reason, it is presented strictly for your information and enjoyment. The test materials for the course include no questions on this chapter.

14

Global Competition and the Future

THE FUTURE OF the international hotel industry is closely tied to worldwide political and economic changes and to long-term trends in domestic and international tourism. The increase in economic interdependence among nations and the expansion of international business and trade will continue to drive the hotel industry toward globalization. Despite recessions, overbuilding, currency revaluations, and other problems that surface from time to time, opportunities for hotel investors, developers, and operators still abound. New opportunities will surely spring from the decision in a growing number of countries to attract new industries, tourism among them, to provide needed revenues and employment for expanding economies and populations.

In this chapter, we examine some of the global trends likely to influence the international hotel industry during the next decade and beyond. These include overall trends in tourism (which are affected by social and economic trends), the impact of the European Union on travel and tourism, new opportunities in the former Soviet Union, the global trend toward privatization, transportation and technological developments, and increased environmental awareness.

Long-Term Tourism Growth Trends

Tourism is positioned as a lead—if not always well understood—industry in the new world economy. At present, approximately 900 million international trips are taken each year. Given that many of the trips are taken by repeat travelers, a fair assessment is that no more than five to six percent of the world's population actually travels outside their own country on an annual basis.

Tourism is one of the world's largest industries. It accounts for 12 percent of international spending and generates one in 12 jobs worldwide. World Tourism Organization (WTO) forecasts predict steady growth for the global tourism industry in the next 15 years. Rising levels of prosperity and the emergence of an affluent middle class in China, India, Eastern Europe, and elsewhere suggests a positive outlook for the industry. Supporting these economic changes are social, cultural, political, and technological factors that are influencing change in consumer attitudes and behavior toward travel, leisure, and tourism.

Some emerging trends in travel and tourism are outlined in the WTO's *Tourism 2020 Vision* report, including the following:

Exhibit 1 Forecast of International Tourist Arrivals by Region

	Base Year 1995	Forecasts 2010	2020	Market Share (%) 1995	2020	Average Annual Growth Rate (%) 1995–2020
		(Million)				
World	565	1006	1561	100	100	4.1
Africa	20	47	77	3.6	5.0	5.5
Americas	110	190	282	19.3	18.1	3.8
East Asia and the Pacific	81	195	397	14.4	25.4	6.5
Europe	336	527	717	59.8	45.9	3.1
Middle East	14	36	69	2.2	4.4	6.7
South Asia	4	11	19	0.7	1.2	6.2

Source: World Tourism Organization.

- International arrivals are expected to reach nearly 1.6 billion by the year 2020. Of these worldwide arrivals in 2020, 1.2 billion will be intraregional and 378 million will be long-haul travelers (see Exhibit 1).

- The total tourist arrivals by region shows that by 2020 the top three receiving regions will be Europe (717 million tourists), East Asia and the Pacific (397 million), and the Americas (282 million), followed by Africa, the Middle East, and South Asia.

- The Middle East, East Asia and the Pacific, South Asia, and Africa are forecasted to record annual growth at rates of more than 5 percent, compared to the world average of 4.1 percent. The more mature regions of the Americas and Europe are anticipated to show lower-than-average growth rates. Europe will maintain the highest share of world arrivals, although there will be a decline from 59.8 percent in 1995 to 45.9 percent in 2020. On the other hand, East Asia and the Pacific will grow from 14.4 percent to 25.4 percent of international tourist arrivals.

Long-haul travel worldwide will grow faster (at 5.4 percent per year over the period 1995–2020) than intraregional travel (at 3.8 percent). Consequently, the ratio between intraregional and long-haul travel will reduce from around 82:18 in 1995 to close to 76:24 in 2020.[1]

Factors Influencing Future Growth

Allowing for cycles of boom and recession and for other external influences on travel, the long-term trend for travel is clearly upward and the opportunities for hotel expansion are promising. The principal long-term factors affecting hotel demand are the globalization of industry, demographic and social changes, increasing leisure and holiday time, changes in consumer preferences, economic growth, and the overall investment environment. Short-term factors affecting hotel demand include the cost of travel, price changes and exchange rate parities, travel barriers, marketing and promotion, as well as extraneous factors that include legislative/regulatory changes, political stability, technological developments, trading developments, transport developments, and the safety of travel. Some of these issues will be discussed later in the chapter.

The global travel and tourism industry certainly experienced some ups and downs during the last business cycle. We saw the bottom of the cycle for global markets in 1997 and 1998. Then, the recovery was hampered by many negative events that affected economies worldwide. These included Japan's economic collapse in the late 1990s, the terrorist attacks of September 2001, the SARS epidemic, the Iraq war, and the massive tsunami that struck Thailand and other countries in the Pacific in December 2004. This kept the industry depressed until the end of 2004.

Since then, however, there has been sustained growth in all travel and tourism industry markets, due to general worldwide economic growth, growing prosperity in emerging markets and a resultant increase in disposable income, access to last-minute travel inventory through online distribution channels, a weakened U.S. dollar that encouraged international travel, low-cost airlines that have given access to destinations for new emerging travelers, and increased demand for short-haul flights. The recent weakening of credit markets as a result of the U.S. subprime residential loan market losses, worries of a U.S.-led worldwide recession, a rise in fuel prices, security and health issues, and the volatility of stock markets around the globe have made the short-term outlook for the industry only cautiously optimistic. However, the fact that international tourist arrivals grew each year from 2004 to 2007 indicates that the industry is resilient and that the external negative factors just mentioned may be short-term deterrents but the industry has shown an ability to bounce back.

Demographic, Economic, and Social Trends

Changes in the world's economic and social structure have occurred at an unprecedented pace over the past few decades. In pondering the hotel industry's future, one must first understand these environmental changes, which include: (1) economic trends such as changing employment levels, growth in discretionary incomes, and the shift in economic power toward Asia and the Pacific; (2) social changes such as increased paid-leave entitlements and more leisure time, earlier retirement, the trend toward later marriage and families, more dual income families, and growth in the number of childless couples and non-traditional families; and (3) demographic changes such as aging populations, more women entering the workforce around the world, and a growing proportion of single adults. Most of these changes in the developed and newly industrialized countries mean that, regardless of other factors, more people will have the time, inclination, and income to travel in the future.

As living standards improve, the population of many nations will be healthier, live longer, and have greater discretionary spending power. Travel restrictions are rapidly being relaxed. There is increased awareness of travel opportunities promoted by the industry, the media, and sometimes by governments for economic or political reasons. People from all countries are traveling more frequently and farther afield.

Demographic data indicate that 60 percent of the world's consumers will reside in Asia in the near future. Because these relatively young consumers require jobs as they enter the workforce, many Asian governments are interested in tourism as a vehicle to create employment and diversify their economies.

Life expectancy almost doubled in the twentieth century and is continuing to lengthen in the twenty-first. The advent of vaccinations, improved hygiene, refrigeration, advances in medical science, and improved technology have all combined to reduce the rate of infant mortality and increase life expectancy. As a result, it is projected that there will be three times as many elderly people in 2050 as there are today, constituting nearly 17 percent of the global population. Analyzing the life expectancy tables provided by the U.S. Census Bureau reveals that, in the past 12 years, the overall life expectancy in the world increased from 63 years to 66 years. Life expectancy increased in less-developed countries (62 years to 65 years) as well as developed countries (75 years to 77 years). The elderly will still constitute a smaller share of the total population in developing countries than in developed countries,[2] but they are nonetheless increasing substantially in absolute numbers. Older travelers will become an ever more important part of the travel and lodging market. The hotel sector is increasingly recognizing the need to cater specifically to older travelers, whose characteristics include an ability to travel off-peak, an inclination and the financial ability to be more adventuresome in their choice of destinations, and a desire to travel for short periods as well as to take longer breaks.

While global population growth rates are slowing, the population is increasing in the age groups with the greatest propensity and financial ability to travel. In addition to the over-65 market, the age group that has the greatest disposable income—the 35–54 group—shows the highest growth. There will also be population shifts around the world. The industrialized countries' share of the population is declining, while that of the developing countries is increasing. The distribution of the world's traveling public is thus likely to change and become more diverse; more attention will need to be paid to untapped origin markets, especially in newly industrialized countries.

Competition from Other Sources

In the future, competition for discretionary income will be strong, coming from other industries with alternatives that may reduce the need for hotel rooms or for travel altogether. The airlines' offering of more frequent flights, shorter flying times, and lower airfares, for example, has eliminated the need for an overnight stay, and thus a hotel room, for many business travelers.

Particularly in the European market, do-it-yourself accommodations such as holiday camps and villages, caravans and camping, rented flats and villas, and second homes have taken over as main providers of holiday accommodations. Other substitutions for hotels include recreational vehicles, timeshare offerings, and cruise lines. The demand from both domestic and international travelers for recreational vehicles continues to increase (although rising fuel prices may flatten that trend). Timeshare offerings have expanded, and the newest trend in resort real estate is the *fractional interest* concept—that is, the purchase of ownership in fractional shares (for example, quarter-time, tenth-time). The market for fractionals represents a step up from timesharing, but it is also used as a substitute for second-home ownership. The cruise industry offers another substitute for hotel rooms; both supply and demand continue to increase for cruise ship holidays.

Alternatives to travel such as teleconferencing, video technology, and other telecommunications tools have not yet proved to be significant competitors for the hotel industry, but they are sure to affect the way business will be conducted in the future, presenting both opportunities and threats. Teleconferencing is currently being used to conduct small meetings and has become a popular tool for online training and educational programs. Integrated audio and video technologies that can be used in conjunction with computer networks are reducing travel in companies that have a global supply chain. Using these communication technologies, project teams communicate using video cameras (new personal computers have video cameras built in); voice-over-Internet protocol (VoIP), which allows voice communication via the Internet; and project-planning software.

Not to be overlooked as a source of competition for discretionary spending is the home itself. Thanks to electronic innovations, homes have today re-emerged as family leisure and entertainment centers with the latest audio and video equipment. Indeed, marketers are actively selling the concept of home theaters and "virtual reality" equipment that permits a player to be "there" without being "there."

Deregulation and Free Trade

The international travel industry, particularly the business travel segment, is strongly influenced by the global trading environment. Important economic developments since the early 1980s have been the liberalization of international trade, the deregulation of markets, and the opening of the international economy in general. Advancements in these areas are largely owed to the efforts of the General Agreement on Tariffs and Trade (GATT), the Organization for Economic Cooperation and Development (OECD), and other organizations, and advancements are likely to continue in the coming decades. Many countries in Eastern Europe, Latin America, and Asia are moving quickly from central-planning to market-oriented economies. This trend will help stimulate both domestic and international travel.

Forecasts for the increase of travel are based on the assumption that these economic and trade-liberalizing trends will continue and that international trade will see substantial growth, with more countries actively participating as both exporters and importers. While regulatory change is here to stay, not all countries have abandoned their protectionist sentiments. Many will re-regulate their industries as quickly as others deregulate. Some sectors of the international travel industry, such as airlines and tour operators, are greatly affected by regulations that govern the rights to markets across national boundaries.

The European Union's Impact on Travel and Tourism

The European Union is a political and economic community of 27 member states that was established in 1993 by the Maastricht Treaty. The creation of a single market among its members is one of the European Union's greatest achievements. The journey toward a single market has been marked by the reduction of various barriers among the member states and the establishment of a common currency, the euro, to facilitate transactions. Euro notes and coins were first issued in January 2002; the euro is now a major world currency for payments and reserves alongside the U.S. dollar.

Restrictions between EU countries on trade and free competition have gradually been eliminated. With a gradual reduction of physical and other barriers to trade, border controls within the EU on goods have been abolished, together with customs controls on people. By reducing technical barriers for the majority of products, EU countries have adopted the principle of mutual recognition of national rules, so that any product legally manufactured and sold in one member state must be allowed to be placed on the market in all others. It has also been possible to liberalize the services sector, thanks to the mutual recognition or coordination of national rules concerning access to or the practice of certain professions (law, medicine, banking, insurance, etc.). Nevertheless, freedom of movement for persons is far from complete. Obstacles still hinder people from moving to another EU country or doing certain types of work there. Tax barriers have been reduced through the partial alignment of national VAT (value added tax) rates. Taxation of investment income was the subject of an agreement between the member states and some other countries (including Switzerland) that came into force in July 2005.

Tourism is a very important sector of Europe's economy. The EU's creation of a single community without internal borders will facilitate travel and hence positively affect Europe's tourism industry. Mainly dominated by small and medium-size businesses, Europe's tourism industry accounts for four percent of the EU's gross domestic product, with two million enterprises employing about four percent of the total labor force.

European Union Tourism Policy

In 2006, the European Commission (the EU's chief policy-making unit) outlined the EU's tourism policy in a document titled *A Renewed EU Tourism Policy: Towards a Stronger Partnership for European Tourism*. Its strategy focuses on two principal tasks: (1) delivering stronger, sustainable growth; and (2) creating more and better jobs. The main aim of the policy was to improve the competitiveness of Europe's tourism industry.

The commission recognized that Europe's aging and more affluent population will have an impact on the demand for tourism services. New lifestyles emphasizing health, nature, culture, and heritage will reshape the demand for tourism products in Europe. Furthermore, competition from newly emerging Asian countries poses a threat to the growth of tourism in Europe. Policy makers also were aware of the need to focus on the sustainability of tourism destinations. These opportunities and threats to European tourism caused policy makers to focus on improving the EU's tourism competitiveness.

Based on the World Economic Forum's Tourism Competitiveness Index, which ranks 124 countries based on various measures of competitiveness, 14 EU countries are in the top 30 in terms of competitiveness. In order to sustain and build on this success, the main areas of policy focus in the future for the EU will be:

- Better regulation, with the aim of simplification to promote access.
- Better policy coordination with the various EU tourism stakeholders on issues and initiatives affecting tourism.
- Improved use of European financial instruments to support the development of tourism businesses, services, and infrastructure.
- The promotion of sustainable tourism through a Tourism Sustainability Group consisting of tourism experts from industry associations, destination representatives, and trade unions.
- Increased efforts to improve the visibility and understanding of European tourism through the timely and accurate availability of tourism statistics; the promotion of European destinations to the newly emerging parts of China, Russia, and India; and marketing to other regions of the world.

With respect to intra-European travel, there has been a flurry of merger and acquisition activity in all industry sectors. Numerous national companies are expected to expand into other EU areas, creating more business travel, more meetings, more conferences, and the need for more business hotels and conference space. The removal of travel barriers and the anticipated increase in European standards of living will also increase intra-European leisure travel.

Inter-European leisure travel will also be facilitated. Certainly, it will be easier for the international traveler if he or she can use a single currency, pay a uniform set of travel taxes, and not have to cope with customs and immigration agents at each border. While some of these barriers are already mitigated, others remain to be resolved. Business travel from outside the EU will likely increase as international companies adjust their strategies in the wake of the new environment.

Transportation

The EU has made considerable progress in deregulating road, rail, air, and maritime services. Improving market access through the removal of barriers to cross-border trade and travel has increased the volume of long-distance goods and passenger transport.

Similar in objectives to the U.S. policy on air deregulation, the liberalization of civil aviation within the EU has the goal of providing greater competition, better service, and more consumer choice. The main proposals were designed to achieve: (1) more competitive pricing with greater flexibility on tariffs, (2) more liberal capacity controls between bilateral partners, and (3) more liberal market access, allowing direct competition between airlines on major routes.

EU developments in the field of aviation include the Single European Sky, which is an ambitious initiative to reform the architecture of European air traffic control to meet future capacity and safety needs. SESAR is the industrial and technological arm of Single Sky and aims to develop a new generation of European air traffic management. Following years of talks aimed at liberalizing air services between Europe and the United States, the EU and the U.S. reached agreement on the text of an Open Aviation, or "Open Skies," accord in November 2005. However, in making a decision on whether to proceed with the agreement, the EU will take into consideration the outcome of an ongoing rulemaking process initiated by the U.S. Department of Transportation to expand opportunities for non-U.S. citizens to invest and participate in the management of U.S. airlines. The Open Aviation Agreement gives EU and U.S. airlines complete freedom to serve any pairs of airports in the European Union and the United States. It will also produce a more competitive market, generating a greater choice of services and lower fares for travelers, while taking into account the need to maintain the security and safety of air travel.

In response to some of these liberalization measures, airline mergers and takeovers are emerging as a key part in the survival strategies of many carriers. Cooperative agreements, partnerships, and other types of alliances are also becoming more common, both within and across national boundaries. SAS, Swissair, Austrian Airlines, and Finnair, for example, have created a "quality alliance" that includes the design of more efficient timetables, the development of joint service facilities, and the standardization of amenities.

The introduction of value added tax (VAT) on air fares and the abolition of duty-free sales in the airports will affect air transport. With respect to the former, airfares had heretofore been exempt from VAT in most member countries; even a small VAT rate is likely to raise prices. Of benefit to the long-haul travel sector is that airfares for travel outside the EU are not subject to VAT. The removal of duty-free concessions for travelers within the borders of the EU member countries will deprive airports and airlines of a major source of revenue at the same time that new capital-intensive investments are required. Airports will need to recoup this revenue by increasing airport charges to user airlines; airlines in turn will pass these charges on to passengers. One positive note for airport management is that intra-EU travel, previously treated as international travel for customs and immigration purposes, will now be considered domestic travel, reducing the administrative burden and paperwork expenses for the airlines.

Congested airports and air traffic control problems, on the other hand, will mean that the EU's "open skies" policy of deregulation stands little chance of providing European passengers with lower fares and a greater choice of flights in the near term. According to the European Commission, by 2020, 60 major airports are expected to become severely congested. If carriers cannot get more take-off and landing slots at the already busy major airports, competition becomes a moot point. Massive investments are needed at Europe's main airports to cope with the anticipated increase in traffic. Until essential air traffic control system improvements are in place, larger airports would provide few gains in passenger growth.

Tour Operators

The unification of European markets will make it increasingly feasible and attractive for tour operators to reach beyond their indigenous markets into neighboring countries. Economies of scale would give a natural advantage to those tour operators based in Europe's biggest holiday markets. What tour operators do has implications for hotels that rely heavily on the tour market. However, most tour operators' attempts to expand beyond their own frontiers have thus far met with only limited success. The disparities between even neighboring European holiday markets appear wide enough to give locally based operators an advantage over foreign competitors.

Some legislation proposed by the EU will constrain EU tour operators, including limiting the tour operator's ability to (1) impose surcharges or price increases; (2) juggle departure dates, flights, or accommodation; and (3) impose cancellation fees. While these measures serve to protect the consumer, the net effect is likely to be a general increase in the initial asking price of holidays, as operators seek to protect their profit margins. The EU's Package Holiday Directive makes tour operators strictly liable for the contents of the holidays they promote. Thus, the operator is liable for damages if a customer can show that the product did not match the claims made for it, regardless of whose fault it might have been. This directive is also likely to increase prices for package holidays and may result in a restriction in consumer choice, particularly in the area of high-risk adventure and skiing holidays. If operators are to be strictly liable for accidents in hotels, it will be clearly in their interests to see the highest-possible standards legislated for all categories of accommodation.

Travel Agents

An integrated Europe is likely to have the most profound impact, direct and indirect, on the region's retail travel agents. Agents, who are already threatened by the steady growth of direct-sell tour operators and multiple retail chains and by the blurring of distinctions between operators and agencies, fear that EU legislation will also make them responsible for any shortcomings in package holidays, despite their claim that this should be the tour operator's responsibility. In any case, part of the extra costs of the tour operators' liability will be passed on to travel agents.

A likely effect of an integrated Europe is the demise of under-capitalized, understaffed, and smaller independent travel agencies in favor of competitors who will be better able to cope with an increasingly complex market. Quite often the disappearance of travel agents from the market can be solely attributed to the growing number of consumers who make their own travel arrangements online. Not only are consumers more apt to make their travel reservations directly, traditional tour operators now have the ability to circumvent travel agents as well and go directly to the consumer, thanks to the Internet. One of the few positive notes for retail travel agents is that the EU has adopted a code with respect to computer reservations systems (CRSs) that will harmonize the different practices of the various EU countries.

The Hotel Industry

There are a number of EU activities and proposals that will benefit the hotel industry. Some changes will be significant, others subtle. The free movement of capital and labor among EU members, for instance, will allow transnational hotel operators within the Union to easily repatriate earnings and enable them to move specialist staff freely among EU countries and properties. These changes are significant and will likely result in the growth of transnational expansion and concentration of intra-European chains. As economies of scale and efficient utilization of capital and labor resources are realized, the dominance of large chains having the special advantage of universal CRS facilities will also increase.

Structural changes of allied service industries will also benefit hotel operators. Deregulation of the financial services sector, for one, should lower the costs of banking services and make capital rates more competitive. The insurance sector, for another, is undergoing changes intended to lower rates for businesses and consumers. Hotels operating in the EU and beyond should profit from lower premiums and administrative costs for global insurance coverage.

The value added tax, which is not uniform across the EU, has always been a source of irritation to hotel operators. Hotel VAT rates range from a low of 3 percent in Luxembourg to a high of 25 percent in Denmark. Countries with a low VAT rate (5 to 7 percent) in the EU include Belgium, Cyprus, the Czech Republic, Estonia, France, Latvia, Lithuania, Malta, the Netherlands, Poland, Romania, Slovenia, and Spain. Countries with a high VAT rate (over 15 percent) include Bulgaria, Denmark, Germany, Hungary, Slovakia, and the United Kingdom.[3] From a competitive standpoint, equalization of the VAT rate on accommodations at 15 percent would help the industry in countries with previously higher rates, but may adversely affect those countries that had lower VAT accommodation rates. A standardized rate, nonetheless, would be appreciated by hotel controllers and would be less confusing for consumers.

It is likely that the EU will eventually move toward the adoption of some form of Europe-wide hotel categorization or rating system. At present, different countries use different rating systems, which leads to both consumer and market distribution confusion. Moves toward a uniform hotel rating system are opposed by most hotel associations, however. Hotel associations tend to favor a system that would provide buyers with information about available accommodations, but not necessarily grades or ranks.

As construction standards are introduced, a hotel developer who is licensed to build in one country will also be able to build in any of the other member countries using the same standards. The deregulation of the construction industry, harmonization of construction standards, and development of Eurocodes could cause construction costs to decrease somewhat as competition increases. Any reduction in the capital requirements of hotel building should prove to be an attractive incentive for hotel investors. Restrictions that have prevented developers from finding financing outside of their countries will be lifted as well. And the liberalization of exchange restrictions in countries like Greece will make it easier to recoup and repatriate investments back to the investor's own country.

Standardized Currency

As mentioned earlier, euro notes and coins were introduced in Europe in January 2002. Europe's move to a single standardized currency has made travel in Europe easier, mostly because travelers no longer need to exchange currencies when going from one European country to another. In addition, it has become easier for travelers to compare prices for hotel rooms and other travel products in the various EU countries. Purchasing European travel products and services over the Internet or via telephone is much easier, thanks to the euro. The euro has enhanced Europe as a tourist destination by removing the bewildering variety of currencies and parity values that European and non-European travelers had to cope with in the past. On the other hand, in recent years the strength of the euro as compared to other world currencies, including the U.S. dollar, has become a cause for concern, as a typical European trip becomes more expensive for those living outside the EU countries.

Travel Costs

On the whole, an integrated Europe is not expected to make travel to the region any less expensive. If anything, added VAT on transport and higher rates on accommodation, restrictions on duty-free earnings for airports and ferries, and many other factors are likely to increase the cost of travel. High VATs on air transportation and hotels may even serve to increase the volume of travel to nearby non-EU destinations that are free from such taxes.

Specific Countries

An integrated Europe benefits the tourist industries of some EU countries more than others. With respect to revenues from inbound travel, France with its low VAT has much to gain from tax equalization. But France, along with the Netherlands and Belgium, could be vulnerable to forays by tour operators from Germany and the United Kingdom. Since the British outbound travel market is extremely price-conscious, it will undoubtedly be negatively affected by even relatively small price increases implicit in the imposition of VAT on scheduled and charter air travel.

Germany is likely to adapt to the new order faster than many other countries. German operators are well placed both to enter new territory and to withstand attempts of foreign interests to capture sections of their home market. On the other hand, Italy's travel industry remains archaic and poorly organized and may prove a fertile arena for entrepreneurial operators from Germany.

As the EU has expanded to include more countries in central, eastern, and southern Europe, we should see growth in travel within the EU. As the less-developed countries within the EU become more affluent, an increase in disposable income will allow travelers in these countries to visit the more developed parts of Europe. Conversely, travelers from the more developed EU countries may be spurred by curiosity to see how some of their less-developed neighbors are doing. Of course, as business ties increase between the developed and less-developed EU countries, so too will travel between them.

Tourism Growth by Region

Europe

While Europe is both the largest generator and largest recipient of tourism, there may be a capacity constraint for many countries. A number of factors will combine to create continued moderate expansion in Europe's travel market, some of which have been discussed in detail in the preceding sections:

- A unified Europe has boosted intra-European short-break holidays and business travel.
- Political changes in Eastern Europe are a positive factor for both business and leisure trips.
- Consumer interest/lifestyle changes have benefitted long-haul destinations, particularly in Asia, the Americas, and Africa.
- Travel trade market segmentation, computer reservation systems, and improved aircraft technology have made long-haul travel more readily accessible and less expensive.

Since the mid-1980s, there has been a generally steady increase in the number of guestrooms in hotels and similar establishments in Europe, although occupancy rates have sometimes been low. As of 2003, the top five countries in Western Europe in terms of bed count (France, Germany, Italy, Spain, and the United Kingdom) had almost 60 percent of the available hotel room capacity. The European hotel industry is very internationally oriented. In most countries, foreign visitors account for over 50 percent of all overnight stays. In key tourism destinations such as Austria and Portugal, foreign stays exceed 70 percent. The most reliable hotel accommodation statistics currently available are through Eurostat, which compiles detailed statistics on various aspects of the EU economy. In 2006, there were 200,838 hotels and similar establishments in the EU's 27 countries.[4]

In Eastern Europe, there has been a significant increase in travel there, in part because of the pent-up desire of seasoned travelers to see this "new" part of the world. Many who left Eastern Europe four decades ago as emigrants for political reasons have returned for visits and to renew ties. There is also great potential for developing outbound travel markets. Today, tens of millions of Eastern European citizens are roaming back and forth across the borders of their neighboring countries and to Western Europe. As the economies of Eastern European countries have improved and standards of living have risen, Eastern Europeans have been targeted as customers for goods and services, including travel.

Exhibit 2　2006 Property/Room Breakdown

By Location	Properties	Rooms
Suburban	15,890	1,577,475
Highway	6,770	452,228
Urban	4,491	690,849
Airport	1,957	275,132
Resort	3,596	566,642
Small Metro/Town	14,431	827,117

Source: *2007 Lodging Industry Profile* (Washington, D.C.: American Hotel & Lodging Association, 2007), p. 4.

Each of the countries in Eastern Europe has a variety of natural sites, historic sites, and cultural arts, many of which are unique. The political opening of Eastern European countries has brought significant opportunities for Western businesses, tremendously increasing the amount of business travel to the region. Despite these advantages, a number of shortcomings or impediments, deriving both from the legacies of the communist period and the uncertainty of post-communist transition, will continue to present major challenges for international tourism development in the region.

North America

As a mature market, North America is positioned to achieve moderate levels of travel and tourism growth. It has a highly developed tourism sector, uses sophisticated marketing and computer technology, and represents increasingly good value for the money, especially in recent years when the dollar has been weak against the euro, British pound, and other hard currencies. The U.S. lodging industry consists of close to 4.4 million guestrooms in properties ranging from roadside motels to urban hotels. An outline of the structure of the U.S. lodging industry is shown in Exhibit 2; as you can see, the majority of U.S. hotels are found in suburban locations and small towns. Unlike many of its international counterparts, the vast majority of its lodging customers come from the domestic market. While international guests are becoming more important, the domestic market will remain predominant.

The past few years have been very good for the U.S. lodging industry. In 2006, the lodging industry generated $26.6 billion in pretax profits, according to Smith Travel Research. Total industry revenue increased in 2006 to $133.4 billion, from $122.7 billion in 2005. In 2006, the industry achieved an average room rate of $97.78.

Tourism is currently the third largest retail industry in the United States, behind automotive and food stores. Travel and tourism is the nation's largest services export industry, and one of America's largest employers. In fact, it is the first, second, or third largest employer in 30 of the 50 U.S. states. The tourism industry includes more than 15 interrelated businesses, from lodging establishments, airlines, and restaurants to cruise lines, car rental firms, travel agents, and tour operators.[5]

Tourism is an important industry in Canada. Like the United States, the domestic market accounts for most tourism spending, but the number of overseas visitors is growing steadily. Similar to what has happened in the U.S. lodging industry, the Canadian lodging industry has experienced a trend toward mergers, acquisitions, and foreign investments. Business travel has become an important sector of the industry, as has the short-break or mini-vacation market, due to demographic and social changes.

Asia and the Pacific

The populous Asia-Pacific region is well suited to capitalize on vacation travel demand from targeted segments in the United States, Canada, Europe, Japan, Australia, and New Zealand. Asia-Pacific countries offer a wide range of tourism attractions. Most are actively pursuing tourism development and promotion strategies. As global trade with these countries increases, so too will business travel. Certain Asian cities have already become established major financial centers. Since opening its doors to tourists in the late 1970s, China has been an important tourism attraction for the entire Asia-Pacific region, and many other destinations have benefited from its efforts to increase overseas tourism. In recent years, Malaysia, Thailand, and Indonesia have all experienced substantial increases in visitor arrivals. The countries of Indochina are expected to be the next destinations to benefit from Asia's increasing tourism, although development constraints are many.

The lodging industry in the Asia-Pacific region was estimated at approximately four million rooms in 2002, approximately 75 percent of which are located in China, Japan, Australia, and Thailand. With some exceptions, the majority of the region's hotels have maintained good occupancy levels throughout the last decade.

Unlike the accommodations market of Europe, the Asia-Pacific region tends to attract relatively large hotel units. The impact of brands and major international chains is considerable. This partly reflects the region's relative newness to the international tourism scene and the fact that traditional inns and small hotels do not fit well with the huge volume of organized travel the region has come to rely on. Most international hotel companies—both inside and outside Asia—are competing to take advantage of the attractive opportunities in this region's primary cities, secondary cities, and resort areas. A more recent development has been the very large resort complex, containing a number of hotel units, self-catering facilities, a wide range of tourism amenities, sports facilities, restaurants, and shops.

Despite a wave of optimism for the Asia-Pacific region's continued economic success, hotel industry leaders recognize that there are cautions to be observed in future hotel building and expansion there. In many primary Asia-Pacific cities, there is already an oversupply of rooms for the intermediate term. There are also rising land costs, labor shortages, air transportation bottlenecks, and other infrastructural concerns. In the parts of Asia that are not saturated (for example, Vietnam, Laos, Cambodia, Myanmar), the political risks are still too high to attract investment capital from conventional sources for hotel and tourism development. Additionally, rising travel costs spurred by strong demand from the intra-Asian market, inflation, and transportation and infrastructural constraints may dampen growth in some destinations.

While travel to Asia and the Pacific has been vigorous, the region is becoming important as a generator of outbound travel as well. There is an increasingly affluent society in this region and an emerging middle class that ranks travel as a high priority. Government travel restrictions and impediments have been greatly eased, first in Japan and more recently in Taiwan and Korea. China, Hong Kong, India, Japan, Korea, Malaysia, Singapore, and Taiwan have strong outbound growth prospects.

South and Central America

Recently, there has been a decline in political tensions in Latin America. Prospects for improved economic conditions are looking up. For the first time, democratic political systems are in place throughout most of the region. Military dictatorships have been largely eliminated. Living standards are showing signs of improvement as a result of economic liberalization. Private capital flows to the area have increased substantially, particularly to Mexico and Venezuela. These capital flows reflect growing investor confidence in the region that is due, in part, to the privatization of large state enterprises, decreasing external debt burden, and the perception that major currency devaluations are not likely. In addition, South and Central America have enormous unexploited potential for offering both natural and cultural attractions. As a receiving destination, Latin America may suffer somewhat from an anticipated slowdown in North American foreign travel, but may do well with respect to other countries.

With the demand for U.S. hotel real estate heating up, investors are considering Latin America as an alternative. With annual GDP growth projected to expand to 4.0 percent annually from 2006 to 2010, and travel and tourism expected to grow 4.2 percent per year from 2007 to 2016, Latin America is becoming an important market for global hotel companies. Argentina, Brazil, and Mexico are pivotal markets, due to the size of their economies. Costa Rica has emerged as the dominant leisure destination in Central America and has been a draw for luxury and environmentally conscious resorts.[6]

Africa

With its predominantly young population and comparatively low per capita income, Africa does not yet have a strong domestic tourism market. However, the region is expected to do well as a receiving destination for international visitors. First, serious tourism planning and marketing initiatives are being undertaken by many African governments. Second, the attractions of African countries are well-suited to the anticipated leisure demands of either independent or group travelers. Like Latin America, there is an enormous amount of unexploited potential in this region.

Currently, the hotel industry in Africa is a blend of profitable niches and unique challenges. The challenges include tribal differences, currency exchange controls, environmental issues, and conflicting image perceptions of the area. Some hotel companies have done well in Africa. Companies generally do better when they consider investments in African states on a case-by-case basis, as opposed to setting and acting on a single policy for a "unified Africa."

Politically, a number of African countries are in the process of replacing authoritarian regimes with freely elected governments. In South Africa, the policy

Exhibit 3 New Supply of Hotel Rooms in the Middle East (2007–2008)

Country	New Hotel Rooms
Qatar	7,900
Jordan	5,300
Egypt	5,100
Morocco	4,000
Kuwait	3,000
Oman	3,700
Syria	800
Lebanon	1,500
Saudi Arabia	5,800
UAE	40,400
Bahrain	4,400

Source: HVS International Research.

of apartheid has been dismantled. Morocco, Kenya, and South Africa recorded strong tourism growth in the past few years.

Middle East

While pockets of turmoil, violence, and political uncertainty affect prospects for tourism in the Middle East, the region has recorded strong tourism growth in many of its destinations. From 2000 to 2006, tourist arrivals to the region doubled, from 20 million to nearly 41 million. At a time when the compound annual growth rate of tourism in the world from 1995 to 2006 was 3.7 percent, tourism arrivals in the Middle East grew by 10.1 percent, according to the World Tourism Organization. Some of the strongest-performing destinations in the region are Abu Dhabi, Bahrain, Dubai, Egypt, Jordan, Oman, and the United Arab Emirates. Tourism growth in the Middle East is mainly driven by intraregional visitation; with the exception of Dubai, Arab visitors account for the majority of tourists in Middle Eastern countries. High disposable income and financial liquidity generated by high oil prices are the primary drivers of tourism in the Middle East. Regional and international investments have spurred hotel development in the area. To support this growth in tourism, many Middle Eastern countries are setting ambitious plans to expand their tourism infrastructure. Three regional airlines—Etihad, Emirates, and Qatar Airways—have expanded service to many global destinations.

Based on a report by HVS, an international hotel consulting firm, over 80,000 new hotel rooms are expected to be built in the Middle East in 2007–2008 (see Exhibit 3 for the expected distribution of these rooms). Most of the major international hotel companies already have a foothold in the region, with strong plans for further growth.

Privatization

Privatization—that is, the transfer of public ownership of manufacturing or service enterprises to private parties—is a policy option being actively pursued in countries all over the world. The trend toward privatization evolved from a growing realization by governments that state enterprises are generally much less efficient in the use of capital and labor than private companies in making products and providing services. State-owned enterprises generally undermine competition in the marketplace, as they are usually protected by the government in various ways and subsidized when operating at a loss. The increased financial burden put on government budgets by state enterprises and the ability to raise state revenues with private sector sales also helps explain the growing privatization movement.

In the former Soviet-bloc countries, privatization is not simply a matter of transferring assets of a few state-owned companies to private investors; it is fundamental to the transformation of entire political and economic systems. Privatization in Eastern Europe represents the transfer of whole economies from the public sector to the private sector. The transition has been less painful for some countries than others, depending on their historic experiences with economic reforms.

Privatization is moving forward in Asia as well. In India, the government-owned tourism entity Indian Tourism Development Corporation has divested itself of most of its hotels because they were underperforming. Currently, many of the state-owned Chinese hotels are undergoing a privatization process through asset sales.

The speed at which privatization can take place must balance the political need to show movement with the practical need to avoid selling the nation's assets for a fraction of their worth. In some cases, it is not clear who owns the so-called "state" assets that the new governments want to privatize. Moreover, the necessity of downsizing these enterprises to gain efficiency has frequently been met with political opposition.

Important privatization developments are taking place in other parts of the world as well. In Latin America, the governments of Mexico, Brazil, and Argentina are taking serious measures to privatize their economies. Other heavily indebted countries such as Venezuela, Colombia, and Paraguay seem to see privatization as a key component in their economic reforms as well. Numerous countries in the Asia-Pacific region also have extensive plans for exposing some of their state industries, especially their national airlines, to the market disciplines of the private sector.

Despite the impressive numbers, the results of privatization programs have been mixed. Some countries have been considerably more successful than others. It also needs to be recognized that privatization is not an end in itself. Rather, the goal is the development of a viable economy, a competitive private sector, and a more satisfied consumer.

Airline Privatization

Unprofitable state-owned airlines have been particularly targeted for privatization by some countries as a way to eliminate state subsidies and to force carriers to increase their ability to compete in the emerging global market. Once privatized, carriers shift from being protected, highly regulated monopolies to becoming more liberal free-traders. Deregulation could also become a precondition for having greater access to the world's largest market for air service, the United States. The positive impact of privatization has been well exemplified by British Airways, which is today one of the strongest transnational carriers in size, market access, and ability to compete. As other EU countries make progress in the privatization movement, there will be visible changes in the worldwide airline industry and substantial benefits for the travel consumer.

Transportation Developments

Transportation is vitally important to the international hotel industry. Cheaper and more convenient travel has had a major influence on the growth of travel demand, which in turn influences the demand for hotel accommodations. Over the last 30 years, technological advancements have resulted in more efficient aircraft and reduced air travel costs in real terms. Continued advancements in transport technology, including high-speed trains, the English Channel Tunnel, and other ground transport, are likely to result in greater travel demand, although they may also change the composition of travel. The increase in air passenger traffic was discussed in the context of Europe earlier in the chapter. This phenomenon is global, leading to delays and congestions at many of the world's largest airports.

Aircraft Technology

New aircraft technology can be expected to contribute to further gains on weight and fuel efficiency, which in turn adds to aircraft range and payload. The Boeing 777 and the Airbus 300, for example, are wider-bodied aircrafts designed to fly over a longer range—up to 8,000 miles at a time. This range gives them the ability to overfly many destinations that once served as stopover points for refueling and aircraft maintenance. Airline hubs such as Fiji, Tahiti, and Hawaii were developed partly as a result of the technical limitations of earlier generations of aircraft. These hubs will need to re-evaluate their travel and tourism marketing strategies now that longer-range aircraft are available. They may need to position themselves at the beginning and end of multi-destination package tours and take the lead in developing greater regional cooperation than has been the case in the past.

The next generation of commercial aircraft has started to focus on passenger ergonomics, the overall passenger experience, and environmental stewardship. An example of this trend is Boeing's new 787 series, due to begin service in 2009. Some of the innovative features of this new aircraft include the following:

- Larger seats and luggage bins.
- "Calm lighting" that simulates a full day of flying by gradual light transition as the flight crosses different time zones.
- Specially designed air filters and humidifiers to improve cabin air quality.
- Use of lighter composite materials to lower cabin altitude and reduce fatigue.
- A water purification system to improve water quality.

- Larger windows for better views.
- A complete multi-media and communications hub with each seat, to enable passengers to conduct business or access entertainment options.

The use of lighter composite materials, innovative aerodynamics, and efficient engine technology will all contribute to a quieter, more fuel-efficient aircraft with lower emissions, which will be better for the environment.

Space Travel

The next frontier of travel will be beyond the earth's horizon: space travel. This era of travel is being heralded by two visionaries: Sir Richard Branson, the flamboyant and adventurous chairman of the Virgin Group, an aviation company; and Burt Rutan, an aircraft designer, investor, and entrepreneur. The technology created by Burt Rutan's Mojave Aerospace Venture will be commercialized by Branson's newly formed company, Virgin Galactic. Virgin Galactic's goal is to make space travel available to private citizens by creating the world's first commercial "spaceline." Virgin will own and operate privately built spaceships, based on the history-making SpaceShipOne. These spaceships, which are currently under construction, will allow private sub-orbital space travel for the first time in history and give wealthy individuals (as of this writing, a seat for a space trip costs $200,000) an opportunity to be among the very first private astronauts.

Virgin Galactic plans to establish its headquarters and operate its space flights from the world's first purpose-built commercial spaceport, "Spaceport America," in New Mexico. Spaceport America is funded by the New Mexico state government and is now in the design and construction phase. Virgin Galactic is already looking seriously at other potential spaceport locations around the world, with a view to expanding the enterprise and making the wonder of space travel accessible to as many people as possible worldwide. While no deadlines have been set for the spaceline's maiden voyage, Virgin Galactic's online booking website is advertising potential travel dates for as early as 2009. The company already has specially trained travel agents, called "space agents," in 15 countries ready to answer consumer questions and help them book a flight into space.

Train Technology

With respect to train travel, Japan is pioneering *maglev* (magnetic levitation) trains that can reach speeds of up to 260 mph (420 kph). Today's fastest conventional trains run at about 130 to 170 mph (210 to 275 kph). High-speed rail lines are planned all over Europe. London, Paris, and Brussels will have fast, frequent, high-quality passenger service with feeder lines from other cities. High-speed trains, particularly in Europe, are likely to become the preferred alternative to air travel where airport congestion, delays, and hassles are increasing. These trains may provide as convenient and rapid a method of transport as air travel for both business and leisure travelers.

Some interesting new train projects include China's recent investment of $4.2 billion to connect Beijing with Lhasa, Tibet. While political control issues may have been the primary impetus for this project, it is bound to positively affect tourism. Taiwan completed a $15 billion high-speed rail line between Taipei and the southern port of Kaohsiung, reducing travel time by train from four hours to 90 minutes. South Korea has a new bullet train from Seoul to major cities. France's TGV electric trains help transport travelers to various hub-and-spoke destinations in Europe. In 2007, the high-speed Chunnel trains started operations between London and Paris, with travel times of approximately two hours.

In contrast, the United States lags behind Europe and Asia with its inefficient and underperforming Amtrak passenger train system. High-speed rail service could help relieve growing road and airport congestion in cities such as Boston, New York, Washington, D.C., San Diego, Los Angeles, Miami, Chicago, and other major transportation hubs.

Deregulation

The United States deregulated its airline industry in 1978, resulting in fare reductions, cost cutting, bankruptcies, and the emergence of a much smaller group of large carriers. Since that time, Canada, Australia, New Zealand, Japan, and the EU have substantially deregulated their air services. The deregulation of air transport in Europe and the relaxation of regulations governing charters allows for the possibility of large numbers of tourists arriving at a destination without booked accommodation. Among the implications for the hotel industry is that much-improved coordination is needed between the local tourist accommodation industry and air transport suppliers. Deregulation in Europe also means the opening up of gateways to more carriers serving more destinations.

Continued pressures for air deregulation are being exerted in other parts of the world as well, particularly in developing countries. The birth of low-cost air carriers in many of these countries is a result of this trend. The dilemma surrounding deregulation for these countries is that their national carriers have difficulty affording the latest-generation aircraft needed to gain a customer-attracting reputation in travel-generating markets. Adoption of an "open skies" policy may bring more visitors, but it may also mean the loss of passenger revenues to foreign carriers offering better service. The ultimate goal is to balance protection of the national carrier with the realization of maximum economic benefits from the tourism sector.

Transportation Infrastructure

Airports are a major part of the first impressions travelers receive when they enter a country. The capacity, quality, and layout of airport facilities contribute or detract from the visitor's travel experience. Some of the typical customer interfaces at airports include: immigrations and customs processing; baggage delivery; public restroom facilities; rest, relaxation, and refreshment areas; and local transportation connectivity.

The United States is lagging many countries in Asia and Europe in terms of modernizing its transportation infrastructure, including its airports. While there are some piecemeal airport modernization and expansion efforts underway in the United States, they are not adequate to address the problem, as capacity at most U.S. airports has been strained for several years. The U.S. Congress recently estimated that an investment of $14 billion is needed for airports to keep pace with needed improvements and expansions. Providing more runway capacity, terminals, and other facilities will require huge new investments and strong government support to overcome powerful opposition. The question of how these improvements will be financed remains an important issue. In many cases, it is likely to be a joint government–private sector initiative. Other solutions to the problem include promoting off-peak tourism and confining charter services to specific airports.

Technology and Automation

Faced with a need to boost productivity and to improve efficiency, the hotel industry is moving toward automation. This movement is encouraged by the growth and wider use of computers in other service industries such as banking, telecommunications, supermarkets, auto service stations, retailing, and more. Many computerized systems have been designed to address the specific requirements of the hotel industry; at the same time, the costs of equipment and software have fallen dramatically. In the six interrelated areas of hotel technology—information processing, telecommunications, energy conservation, fire safety, security, and audio-visual systems—the problem is no longer whether to automate, but how much automation makes sense, what to select, and how to use it effectively. For example, automated check-in kiosks are being tried in some hotels; others have adopted a wait-and-see attitude. Today's packaged property management systems (PMSs) will increasingly evolve to offer more user options with respect to functions and property size.

Improved technology in back-office systems, registration, guest intelligence, smart cards, voice messaging, and so forth all have the ability to raise hotel productivity and efficiency, and thereby to reduce labor and other operating costs. PMSs have proven useful for inventory management, menu planning, and analysis. Optional systems have been developed to monitor productivity and control labor costs and property operations and maintenance. With respect to payments, direct debit payment systems, electronic banking, and the Internet allow today's consumers to choose a destination or hotel from the comfort of their office or home and pay for these services electronically.

Technology has also changed the way national and international travelers conduct business on the road. In-room Internet access and fax machines have become essential to business guests. The development of dedicated business centers with the latest technologies in communications is expected to continue.

The most important technological development for the hotel industry, however, will continue to be the advancement of computer reservation systems, which will be discussed in the next section.

Regardless of technological advancements, high tech will only work well with high touch in the hospitality industry (as Asian hotels have proved). Technology should be employed to improve service, not replace it. In the case of pure tourism—that is, travel for pleasure—high touch and service are the indispensable elements of the travel experience and the reason many people travel. The caution, therefore, is that technology must be complemented with a strong interest in the humanity of those who serve and those who are being served. One of the real dangers in the hotel industry is not that computers will begin to think like humans, but that humans will begin to act like computers.

Global Distribution Systems

With the multiple marketing and distribution channels available to consumers today, the distribution of hotel rooms has become a much more complex task.[7] In many hotels around the world, reservation departments are being restructured, becoming a part of the sales and marketing division or aligned to work closely with revenue management personnel. As a result of dramatic changes in the reservation and distribution landscape, reservation departments have important new strategic marketing and distribution management functions.

Being where the bookings are will be the mantra for all hotels in the future. A hotel property or chain now generates bookings through multiple distribution channels, such as a central reservations toll-free number, the hotel's or chain's own website, third-party websites (Expedia, Travelocity, etc.), global distribution systems, travel agents, and regional sales operations. The newest challenge confronting hotels today and for some time into the future is distribution management—more specifically, the ability to understand, manage, and market to consumers in an online world.

To develop a distribution strategy for their hotel or chain, hoteliers need to consider a variety of different elements:

- *Metrics.* Hotels need to accurately measure the costs associated with being represented in the various distribution channels. Business intelligence information needs to be linked to revenue management decisions, the performance of hotel websites needs to be measured (number of reservation conversions, for example), and statistics concerning the productivity of third-party websites should be tracked through specialized tracking services such as TravelCLICK and PhoCusWright.

- *Risk assessment.* Online distribution channels are changing and evolving rapidly. Hoteliers expose themselves to risk if they do not keep up to date in this area. It is important for hotels to understand which distribution channel may be replaced by a new player, for example, or keep abreast of the improved technology of an existing online provider. Mergers and acquisitions may make one online distribution channel stronger than its competitors. It is also important to keep up to date on current online distribution channel developments and tools through articles, conferences, and industry reports.

- *Branding.* For hotel brands, third-party websites are a severe threat to the value proposition that they provide to their franchisees; namely, their ability to drive reservations to the franchisees' hotels. Guest retention for the hotels and hotel retention for the brand is at stake.

- *Channel analysis.* It is important to understand the value of a distribution channel to drive reservations to the hotel. The most effective distribution strategy optimizes the mix of channels to market your hotel at the highest-possible rate.

- *Web strategy—own website.* Management of the hotel's own website includes, among other things, managing the design ("look and feel") of the site, its short- and long-term goals, and its booking capabilities.

- *Web strategy—onward distribution.* Based on an analysis of a hotel's market mix and the time period in question (season, month, week, and even day-of-week), hoteliers need to identify global distribution systems and third-party Internet sites that will optimize business for the hotel.

Development Issues

Increasingly, travel and tourism as an industry is being recognized as a modern economic development tool. The goal of numerous governments is to create the conditions for the development of an optimal scale and balanced form of tourism, taking into account the countries' economic, social, cultural, and environmental needs. This approach entails comprehensive and integrated planning for tourism and hotel development. Hotel developers in the future are thus more likely to have to work within the parameters of established plans that will influence where they can build, what they can build, and how they can build it.

Hotel Design. Outside of major urban areas, the future hotel is much more likely to be in environmental harmony with its community. Accommodations will be developed to match their environmental settings, and the local culture will provide inspiration for the design of building features, motifs, furniture, furnishings, and artifacts. Humanistic scale of buildings and the use of indigenous materials and methods will be more common. This approach will both maximize the economic benefit to be gained by the host community from hotel development and provide what travelers increasingly want when they seek an experience away from home.

It will be up to governments at all levels, in consultation with the private sector, to provide clear guidance on the type of hotel facilities permitted. These guidelines can encourage the use not only of traditional designs and building materials, but also regulate the height, size, location, setback, density, and features of hotel facilities.

However, time and cost factors will influence hotel building programs as well. Prefabrication building methods may become more prevalent in some areas. The hotel of the future may be one that is conceived as an "integrated environment design," the form of which may be determined by advanced building technology and innovative computerized systems.

Guestrooms. The hotel guestroom of the future is likely to be better designed and more functional. In appropriate locations, guestrooms will have full office facilities both in the form of work stations and available business equipment. There will be increased emphasis on improved air purification and ventilation systems and improved lighting.

Energy Systems. Focused energy management and waste reduction will become more common in the future design of hotels. There will be an emphasis on efficient lighting systems. Solar energy may be more widely used to heat swimming pools and domestic hot water and for limited space heating. Heat recovery from the various air conditioning, cooking, and lighting systems will substantially reduce the demand for thermal energy. All of these improvements in the physical design of a building will mean that basic energy systems will be scaled down considerably, reducing such costs. However, some of the savings will be used for more sophisticated sensors and controls so that guests' comfort can be maintained on an as-needed basis without wasting energy when areas are not in use. The future hotel may be linked by satellite to a central computer that provides all the basic programming, logic, and monitoring services of systems and operations that support the property.

Safety Systems. With regard to guest safety, litigation and consumer protection trends will influence hotel design and standards. The growing number of female business travelers, in particular, will place a high priority on personal safety. New security equipment (closed-circuit television, keyless door locking systems, and so forth) have helped to combat hotel crime. Hotels that have installed such systems, demonstrating a high commitment to guest security, will have an advantage over their competitors who have not.

Land Use. Land scarcity is a growing concern for hotel developers, especially in densely populated cities like London, New York, Tokyo, and Paris. Overall, land shortages in urban centers will force the hotel industry to become more flexible and to seek non-traditional paths to expansion in order to make profitable investments. In the United States, secondary locations, including smaller non-gateway cities and suburbs, are increasingly targeted for niche hotels. In the Asia-Pacific region, as land becomes scarcer in primary cities, hotel investments there will likely follow a course similar to that in the United States.

Mixed-Use Developments. A development approach becoming more prevalent is the combination of hotel development with other real estate projects, frequently referred to as *mixed-use realty development* or *MXD*. These multi-facility developments, particularly common in Hong Kong and Singapore, have begun to spread to Europe, the United States, and elsewhere. For example, new and converted developments that combine retail space, entertainment, offices, and hotel and residential uses are becoming more and more common.

Rising land costs in certain markets have pushed development toward higher yielding projects and maximization of land use. MXD projects offer attractive incentives to developers by providing trade-offs of greater density in return for provision of amenities or open space in the public interest. Within the overall MXD concept, the rising concern for environmental issues and historic preservation can often be accommodated. The preservation of historic buildings has long been recognized as a priority in North America and Europe, but it is now spreading more widely. In Singapore, for example, where the trend in the last 30 years has been toward modernization and where much of the old city has been destroyed, the authorities have belatedly sought to preserve what is left and to rebuild within the original architectural shells. The restoration and reconstruction of the historic Raffles Hotel is one such example.

Sources and Availability of Capital for the Hotel Industry. Hotel developers and investors depend on capital for various purposes. The structure, size, and scope of the industry are affected by the amount, timing, sources, and availability of capital to the industry. During various periods during the past 30 years, the capital "tap" has been turned on and off for a variety of reasons. Some of these included financial industry deregulation (and subsequent re-regulation); tax law changes that induced the flow of funds to commercial (including hotel) real estate; the introduction of new sources of equity, such as real estate investment trusts (REITs) and private equity funds; the increased flow of international investments due to a general economic liberalization worldwide; financial-engineered debt-and-equity instruments such as commercial mortgage-backed securities (CMBSs); the raising and lowering of mortgage interest rates; and the introduction of sovereign (government-sponsored) investment funds investing in hotels.

In the United States, the economic conditions immediately after the terrorist attacks of September 2001 negatively affected the operating results of the hotel industry and temporarily reduced financing to hotels. However, from 2003 to the present, improved hotel performance and abundant global capital available from financial institutions at very competitive rates have led to the growth and product diversification of the hotel industry.

Looking to the future, rising construction costs, fewer prime sites for hotel development, and capital constriction and increasing capital costs as a result of the recent and large-scale defaults in the residential real estate market are expected to plateau hotel development in the United States and some of the other mature economies of the world.

Tourism and the Environment

In recent years, there has been a notable rise in the level of concern for the global environment. The world community is increasingly aware that natural resources must be wisely managed for the sake of both present and future generations. Concerned governments, organizations, and people seem to have a better understanding of harmful, benign, and beneficial economic and environmental tradeoffs. This understanding has helped to allay the fear that environmental protection must be at the expense of growth and development. The concept of sustainable development seeks to place environmental concerns firmly at the center of viable growth.

Since the beginning of the industrial era, the perceived challenge of mankind has been one of domination and control over nature. Such thinking has led to the exploitation, pollution, and degradation of the environment. Facing severe problems—global warming, earth contamination, loss of rain forests, and loss of species, among others—concerned people are belatedly recognizing that sustainable development requires a custodial relationship with the environment and the ability to live in harmony rather than at odds with nature.

The global tourism industry has joined forces with other industries in singling out the environment as one of the key issues of the new millennium.

Hotels and the Environment

Higher standards of environmental engineering will undoubtedly influence hotel construction in the coming decades. Certainly, haphazard and unlimited development will no longer be tolerated. In the future, the hotel industry will be forced to play a much more active role in maintaining environmental standards. Both hotel developers and managers will need to stay abreast of new environmental issues, trends, and legislation.

Hotels that willingly take up the environmental gauntlet before they are forced to may have a competitive advantage. In recent years, many of the major international hotel chains have incorporated environmental sensitivity into their operations. The following are examples of what some hotels are doing on the environmental front:

- *Lights off at Radisson:* Environmental efforts at the Radisson chain include a focus on energy-efficient lighting. One example: motion sensors have been installed in employee bathrooms in Radisson hotels so that lights automatically switch off when a bathroom is unoccupied.

- *No excess at Hilton:* Kitchen waste is utilized through a rigorous composting program at many Hilton properties.

- *Water savings in Madrid:* The Gran Hotel Conde Duque in Madrid installed water-saving devices in its bathrooms.

- *The answer is blowing in the wind:* Staybridge Suites in Pennsylvania is 100-percent wind-powered through the purchase of energy credits.

- *Accor taps the sun:* Accor plans to convert 200 hotels to solar power by 2010.

- *Marriott enlists guests:* Fitting high- and low-flow water pressure systems in Marriott's The Inn & Conference Center, University of Maryland University College gives guests an option to reduce their water use.

- *Leading through word of mouth*: Leading Hotels of the World, a membership-based association of luxury hotels, decided to advertise its green initiatives purely through word of mouth, thus avoiding the use of any paper and other resources.

- *Hilton goes hi-tech and low-tech:* Various Hilton properties have adopted hi-tech and low-tech "green" polices. Hi-tech example: investments in energy-efficient heating, ventilation, and air-conditioning systems. Low-tech example: training programs to educate staff members to reduce waste.

- *Marriott's SERVE:* Marriott's overall corporate social responsibility program, SERVE, now has an environmental component called ECHO, which stands for Environmentally Conscious Hospitality Operations.

- *Banyan Tree's triple bottom line:* Banyan Tree, an owner and operator of world-class resorts and spas, has a bottom-line philosophy that includes environmental and social factors as well as financial performance.

- *Launching an eco-friendly brand:* In 2008, Starwood Hotels & Resorts opened the first of its "eco chic" Element brand. The brand will use many "green" features like bulk soap and shampoo, and will offer parking priority to hybrid cars.

- *Green partnerships at Fairmont:* Fairmont Hotels & Resorts has taken a partnership approach in soliciting support for its environmental practices by working with its suppliers, employees, guests, and surrounding communities. The chain's environmental "best practices" are outlined in the third edition of Fairmont's *Green Partnership Guide*.[8]

Many organizations are developing programs, guidelines, and certifications to assess the environmental performance of hotel operations, including energy and water usage, legal compliance, waste management, carbon emissions, staff training, community involvement, and supplier environmental policies. The World Travel and Tourism Council, for example, has developed a list of environmentally friendly guidelines for hotels (see Exhibit 4).

The Environment's Importance to Tourism

While the impact of tourism on the environment is undergoing closer scrutiny, there is also a growing realization of the importance of the environment *to* tourism. Tourism depends to a large extent on natural resources, both for passive activities (such as sight-seeing) and participatory activities (such as hiking and skiing). Environmental problems have resulted in lost business in many destinations. The Balearic Islands in Spain and Pattaya in Thailand are examples of resort destinations that have been overdeveloped with little regard for the environment or for social-problem controls. As a result, both have suffered drops in popularity. In some of Spain's coastal vacation spots, insufficient sewer lines have created water pollution problems that have dissuaded visitors from returning. The handling of these environmental problems is likely to determine the long-run viability of these and similar destinations.

Ecotourism. The condition of the environment is particularly important to the ecotourism industry segment. Ecotourism is defined as travel that is less damaging to the natural and cultural resources of a destination than traditional tourism, while theoretically increasing the economic, social, and environmental benefits to the

Exhibit 4 World Travel and Tourism Council Environmental Guidelines

Travel and tourism is the world's largest industry. A clean, healthy, and safe environment is essential to further growth. The WTTC recommends that companies and governments take these guidelines into account in policy formulation:

Travel and tourism companies should state their commitment to environmentally compatible growth.

Targets for improvements should be established and monitored.

The environment commitment should be company wide.

Education and research into improved environmental programs should be encouraged.

Travel and tourism companies should seek to implement sound environment principles through self-regulation, recognizing that national and international regulation may be inevitable and that preparation is vital.

Environment improvement programs should be systematic and comprehensive. They should aim to:

1. **Identify and minimize** product and operation environmental problems, paying particular attention to new projects;
2. **Pay due regard** to environmental concerns in design, planning, construction, and implementation;
3. **Be sensitive** to conservation of environmentally protected or threatened areas, species and scenic aesthetics, achieving landscape enhancement where possible;
4. **Practice** energy conservation;
5. **Reduce** and recycle waste;
6. **Practice** fresh-water management and control sewage disposal;
7. **Control and diminish** air emissions and pollutants;
8. **Monitor**, control and reduce noise levels;
9. **Control, reduce and eliminate** environmentally unfriendly products, such as asbestos, CFCs, pesticides and toxic, corrosive, infectious, explosive, or flammable materials;
10. **Respect and support** historic or religious objects and sites;
11. **Exercise due regard** for the interests of local populations, including their history, traditions, and culture and future development;
12. **Consider environmental issues** as a key factor in the overall development of Travel and Tourism destinations.

These guidelines have been prepared by WTTC taking into account the International Chamber of Commerce (ICC) Business Charter for Sustainable Development.

Source: WTTC

destination. It is characterized by trips that allow travelers to interact with nature by simple observation or systematic study.

Ecotourism is typified by: (1) highly focused travelers with special interests in nature or indigenous cultures, (2) travelers playing a proactive role in creating the tourism experience, (3) an emphasis on two-way communication between hosts and guests, and (4) remote, largely inaccessible sites not overrun by tourists. Hotels involved in ecotourism are usually rigorously controlled by environmental authorities to preserve the authenticity and originality of the landscape that motivated their construction.

Demand for ecotourism appears to be growing. However, growth presents numerous long-term challenges. The major issues include: (1) the necessity to keep ecotourism enterprises small-scaled, despite demand, in order to avoid damage to the environment, (2) limited market demand and few opportunities for repeat business, (3) long-term sustainability of local value systems and lifestyles, (4) possible environmental degradation despite attempts at control over access and use, (5) the fact that visitors generally do not pay for the full costs of maintaining the site, and (6) ecotourism destination areas lack strong marketing support.[9]

The growth of interest worldwide in conservation and intimacy with nature signals a promising future for ecotourism in many parts of the world—particularly developing countries, which attract the bulk of ecotourists. Although ecotourism has many favorable traits, the challenges just mentioned must be addressed.

Sustainable Tourism Development. A sustainable tourism approach recognizes the fact that if a destination is developed beyond the capacity of its environment, it ceases to be a renewable resource. It will therefore fall victim to the usual boom-bust cycle. A sustainable tourism development effort thus entails the management of all resources. Economic, social, and aesthetic needs must be fulfilled while maintaining cultural integrity, essential ecological processes, and biological diversity.

Sustainable tourism requires that carrying capacity studies for destinations and hotel development sites be conducted, then their recommendations rigorously implemented through a system of effective planning and operating controls. But sustainable tourism does not work solely because it is imposed by authorities. It also requires acceptance of the concept's validity by, and cooperation in its implementation from, hotel developers and operators and other private sector groups. One of the first efforts to develop a code of ethics to encourage sustainable tourism took place at an annual meeting of the Tourism Industry Association of Canada. The discussions to develop industry codes and guidelines included government officials and representatives from the various tourism industry sectors, as well as environmental, cultural, native, and heritage organizations (see Exhibit 5 and Exhibit 6). The success of these codes and guidelines clearly depends on the extent to which they will be implemented by the more than 60,000 tourism-related enterprises in Canada and supported by the millions of tourists.

Alternative Tourism

Alternative tourism can be used as a broad term covering such strategies as "appropriate tourism," "soft tourism," "responsible tourism," "people-to-people

Exhibit 5 Sustainable Tourism in Canada: Code of Ethics for the Industry

The Canadian tourism industry recognizes that the long-term sustainability of tourism in Canada depends on delivering a high quality product and a continuing welcoming spirit among our employees and within our host communities. It depends as well on the wise use and conservation of our natural resources; the protection and enhancement of our environment; and the preservation of our cultural, historic, and aesthetic resources. Accordingly, in our policies, plans, decisions, and actions, we will:

1. Commit to excellence in the quality of tourism and hospitality experiences provided to our clients through a motivated and caring staff.

2. Encourage an appreciation of, and respect for, our natural, cultural, and aesthetic heritage among our clients, staff, and stakeholders, and within our communities.

3. Respect the values and aspirations of our host communities and strive to provide services and facilities in a manner which contributes to community identity, pride, aesthetics, and the quality of life of residents.

4. Strive to achieve tourism development in a manner which harmonizes economic objectives with the protection and enhancement of our natural, cultural, and aesthetic heritage.

5. Be efficient in the use of all natural resources, manage waste in an environmentally responsible manner, and strive to eliminate or minimize pollution in all its forms.

6. Cooperate with our colleagues within the tourism industry and other industries, toward the goal of sustainable development and an improved quality of life for all Canadians.

7. Support tourists in their quest for a greater understanding and appreciation of nature and their neighbours in the global village. Work with and through national and international organizations in helping to build a better world through tourism.

Source: Louis J. D'Amore, "Promoting Sustainable Tourism—the Canadian Approach," *Tourism Management,* September 1992.

tourism," "controlled tourism," "small-scale tourism," "cottage tourism," "green tourism," and others. It basically represents an alternative to the large numbers, massive developments, environmental and social alienation, and homogenization of mass tourism. Alternative tourism has a range of developmental options that are intended to be: (1) more sensitive to the host communities and their total habitats, (2) more cognizant of the tourists and the quality of their experience, and (3) more rewarding for the people involved in the operational structure of tourism. The assumption is that alternative forms of tourism have fewer and less severe negative effects on destination areas and their populations, while still promoting the positive economic effects, albeit on a smaller scale.

While it is difficult to argue with alternative tourism in principle, there are nonetheless other viewpoints. One counter-argument is that the economic value

Exhibit 6 Sustainable Tourism in Canada: Guidelines for Industry

1. Bring economic objectives into harmony with conservation of resources and environmental, social, cultural, and aesthetic values in the formulation of vision statements, mission statements, policies, plans, and the decision-making process.
2. Provide tourists with a high quality experience which contributes to a heightened appreciation of our natural and cultural heritage. Facilitate as possible meaningful contact between hosts and guests and respond to the special travel needs of diverse population segments including youth, mature citizens, and the disabled.
3. Offer tourism products and services that are consistent with community values and the surrounding environment. Reinforce and enhance landscape character, sense of place, community identity, and benefits flowing to the community as a result of tourism.
4. Design, develop, and market tourism products, facilities, and infrastructure in a manner which balances economic objectives with the maintenance and enhancement of ecological systems, cultural resources, and aesthetic resources. Achieve tourism development and marketing within a context of integrated planning.
5. Protect and enhance our natural historic, cultural, and aesthetic resources as a legacy for present and future generations. Encourage the establishment of parks, wilderness reserves, and protected areas.
6. Practise and encourage the conservation and efficient use of natural resources including energy and water.
7. Practise and encourage environmentally sound waste and materials management including reduction, reuse, and recycling. Minimize and strive to eliminate release of any pollutant which causes environmental damage to air, water, land, flora, and wildlife.
8. Reinforce environmental and cultural awareness through marketing initiatives.
9. Encourage tourism research and education which gives emphasis to ethics, heritage preservation, and the host community and the necessary knowledge base to ensure the economic, social, cultural, and environmental sustainability of tourism.
10. Foster greater public awareness of the economic, social, cultural, and environmental significance of tourism.
11. Act with a spirit of cooperation within the industry and related sectors to protect and enhance the environment, conserve resources, achieve balanced development, and improve the quality of life in host communities.
12. Embrace the concept of "one world" and collaborate with nations and international bodies in the development of a socially, environmentally, and economically responsible tourism industry.

Source: Louis J. D'Amore, "Promoting Sustainable Tourism—the Canadian Approach," Tourism Management, September 1992.

of mass tourism in terms of income and employment often outweighs environmental costs in terms of trade-offs. Another is the fact that many travelers prefer mass tourism. They like set travel arrangements, staying in moderately priced and comfortable accommodations, being able to obtain goods and services without learning a foreign language, and having the availability of familiar food.

In most established destinations, it would be economically and practically impossible to move from mass tourism to smaller-scale tourism without jeopardizing the viability of the industry or creating major unemployment and a reduction in the standard of living. Costa Rica is a case in point. The country's tourism goal is to strike a balance between catering to traditional tourism and protecting the country's coasts, rain forests, and wildlife preserves. If the country pursues only small-scale alternative tourism, damage to the environmental, social, and cultural milieus might be minimal, but at the cost of millions of dollars of income and thousands of jobs every year.

Some would argue that mass tourism is not necessarily uncontrolled, unplanned, short-term, or unstable. Nor is small-scale or alternative tourism always considerate, optimizing, controlled, planned, and under local control. Moreover, alternative forms of tourism tend to penetrate further into the personal space of residents, involving them to a much greater degree and often exposing fragile resources to greater visitation. Thus, the social, cultural, and environmental impacts of alternative tourism, despite the relatively small numbers, can be significant.

It is perhaps the concept itself of alternative tourism that provides an antidote to the perceived excesses of mass tourism. Alternative tourism ideas can help to secure an appropriateness of scale and fit between tourists and their host communities. The concept espouses responsible treatment of the environment by visitors and residents. It promotes the use of local and indigenous resources, including food and craft products, and advocates preservation or conservation over conspicuous consumption. When new visitor accommodations must be built, it insists that these be in harmony with local structures.

Alternative tourism may also complement mass tourism in serving the needs and desires of specific types of visitors who are interested in authentic experiences of nature or culture. Especially as it is applied in Europe, alternative tourism may help to supplement incomes of rural dwellers in marginal areas through such means as farm tourism, guiding, mountain trekking, craft demonstrations, language-learning holidays, and bed-and-breakfast establishments. Finally, it may allow small scale tourism development in areas that cannot sustain major change due to environmental and/or social capacity limitations.

Human Resource Issues

The issue of labor and management will assume greater importance in the international hotel industry in the years ahead. The three primary problem areas identified by the International Hotel & Restaurant Association are: (1) the availability of labor, (2) monitoring and motivating labor, and (3) the provision of training. The lack of skilled labor at all levels is becoming a chronic problem globally as well.

The hotel industry has historically been dependent on a good supply of labor. Indeed, cheap labor represents a major comparative advantage for building and operating hotels in developing countries. In a complementary sense, governments of developing countries see the employment potential of hotels and resorts as one of the primary economic benefits to be derived from tourism. However, as economies advance in developing countries, labor no longer remains plentiful or cheap. The marketing edge provided by superior service erodes, and recruitment, training, and retention become continuous challenges for hotel operators.

In developing countries, a labor shortage is often not the real problem. More important are a shortage of skilled workers for professional and highly technical jobs, a shortage of trainers, and a lack of recruitable potential employees in remote resort locations. In developed countries, on the other hand, demographic changes have resulted in a major decline in the 15–24 age group, which has traditionally been the main source of line-level workers in hotels. From the standpoint of recruitment, many hotel jobs require little or no skill. The industry as a whole has not fared well in persuading potential employees that it offers good career prospects. Moreover, its typically low initial pay rates seriously hamper its ability to attract, motivate, and retain good workers.

Luxury hotels, which are ultimately defined by the quality of their service, may have little choice in the long run but to develop better-paid, more highly skilled, and more flexible staff. In contrast, the solution for mid-scale and budget hotels may lie in organizational restructuring, in new ways of managing, and in reducing labor demand by using automation and eliminating low-demand, high-labor hotel services. There is, however, a limit to how much technology can be employed and how much service can be reduced before customers begin to object and take their business elsewhere.

With respect to reducing hotel services, many hotels have eliminated costly restaurant and bar operations or leased out these operations to restaurant specialists. Others have eliminated low-profit meeting or high-overhead lobby space. In the future, it is anticipated that limited-service hotels offering less personal service are more likely to be financed and built than deluxe or mid-scale properties.

Training and education for the hotel industry will become more important, whether this is provided by governments through public programs, by private schools, or by the industry itself. A public-private partnership model of education may be advisable, as the industry must become more involved in reviewing the suitability of the curricula at local hotel schools. Both schools and hotel operators need to better understand and support cultural diversity in the workforce. As hoteliers truly play hosts to the world in a meaningful sense, multilingual staff will become increasingly necessary. Communication issues and cultural sensitivity may become an escalating problem where there is a large pool of immigrant labor or a large portion of foreign guests.

New sources of hotel labor will be more fully explored in the future, including older people, the disabled, and women. More flexible attitudes will be adopted toward part-time work, flex-time, job-sharing, temporary employees, and foreign labor. In the last 20 years, the workforce in Third World countries has expanded by 700 million, at a time when the number of young workers in the industrialized countries has stagnated or declined. This has resulted in relaxed immigration restrictions on the part of many industrialized countries to provide the human capital necessary to sustain economic growth.

The solutions to labor problems are as varied as the causes in different parts of the world. Ultimately, it will be up to the industry to make itself a more attractive employer and to improve in the recruitment, retention, training, and reward of staff. Until such time as hospitality careers begin to enjoy the same status and standing as other professions in the eyes of the general public, human resource issues will remain a serious challenge for the industry.

Hotel Company Diversification and Growth

A company's growth follows two vectors: it can either grow through expansion or through diversification. A diversification strategy occurs when a company modifies its business by introducing new products into new markets—as when, for example, a hotel company decides to enter the car rental or airline business. Some recent examples of diversification strategies adopted by hotel companies past and present include the following:

- *Cendant Corporation (current name is Wyndham Worldwide).* From 1997 until its recent spinoff, Cendant Corporation was the most diversified of hospitality companies. Originally started in 1990 as Hospitality Franchise Systems, a purely hotel franchising company, it converted to Cendant in 1997 and diversified into a variety of businesses in addition to hotel franchising, including car rental (Avis and Budget), real estate (Century 21 and Coldwell Banker), online reservation systems (CheapTickets and Orbitz), and timeshare vacation exchange services (RCI). In 2005/2006 the company decided to give up its diversification strategy and go back to a focused specialization approach by splitting into four companies: Avis Budget Group (car rental), Realogy (real estate), Travelport (online distribution), and Wyndham Worldwide (hotel franchising).

- *Bass (current name is InterContinental Hotels Group).* A review of Bass, a British brewing company, provides insight into diversification, specialization, and acquisition strategies adopted by companies during various stages of their life cycle. In the 1960s, Bass acquired a number of well-known regional brewing companies, including Mitchells & Butlers (1961). In 1988, Bass made its first significant international move into the hotel industry, buying Holiday Inns International. From 1990 to 1997, Bass added various hotel brands to its portfolio. In 1997, it sold its hotel real estate, keeping only the brands. In 1998, through the acquisition of the InterContinental Hotel Company, Bass increased the size of its hotel portfolio. By acquiring the South Pacific Hotel Company in 2000, Bass grew its hotel business in Asia. When it acquired the Bristol Hotel Company, Bass diversified into the hotel management contract business. After a name change to Six Continents in 2000, the company divested itself of certain parts of its pub business and focused on hotels by buying a hotel company in the UK. In 2002, Six Continents PLC announced the separation of the group's hotel and soft drink businesses (to be called InterContinental Hotels Group PLC) from its retail business (to be called Mitchells & Butlers PLC).

- *Accor Group.* The Accor group is known mainly for various branded hotels. However, it is a very diversified company. Along with its hotels division, it is also involved in the travel agency business as a wholesaler and retailer, and has a large services division that offers a range of services, including service stations, laundry services, gift vouchers, health care vouchers, and restaurant and supermarket performance-improvement services.

- *Marriott International.* In addition to its large hotel management and franchising company, Marriott International is engaged in the timeshare business through its Marriott Vacation Club.

- *Carlson Hospitality Worldwide.* In addition to hotel ownership, management, and franchising, the company has a presence in the restaurant business, with over 700 restaurants in more than 50 countries.

Hotel companies choose to diversify or specialize based on market timing, the life cycle of the company, and other circumstances, such as the availability of capital and changing tax laws. In the future, diversification will be a strong option for companies seeking growth.

Mergers, Acquisitions, and Cooperative Arrangements

As one of the strategies for growth, "mergers and acquisitions" is the mode used by many major hotel companies to dominate markets. When one hotel company acquires a controlling interest in another hotel company, it is generally to reduce competition, improve synergies and efficiencies, increase profits, and reduce earnings volatility. Or, another objective could be to increase shareholder value when acquiring underperforming or poorly managed companies. Still other reasons for merger and acquisition activities may include the ability to increase a company's rate of growth through strategic acquisitions versus organic growth, or a desire to acquire technical, human resource, or intangible assets—as in the case of a hotel company that owns real estate and then acquires a brand or management company.[10]

The period from 1995 to 2000 saw a large number of mergers and acquisitions in the hotel industry, largely driven by public real estate investment trusts (REITs). One of the largest acquisitions during this period was Starwood Lodging Trust's acquisition of ITT Sheraton for approximately $15 billion. This period was characterized by large public companies acquiring other public companies. After the industry slowdown due to the terrorist attacks of September 2001, acquisition activity picked up again in 2003. This time, however, many of the acquirers were private equity funds (large pools of private investment capital) that acquired large public companies. The largest acquisition of this nature in 2007 was the purchase of Hilton Hotels (now a private company) by Blackstone Group, a private equity firm. The transaction price was approximately $25 billion.

Merger and acquisition activity slowed in 2008, but in the years ahead, as opportunities for growth through strategic acquisitions present themselves, there will be acquirers and there will be targets, and so the mergers-and-acquisitions cycle will continue. A look at the hotel industry over the past 30 years shows that the general trend has been of consolidation, which is expected to continue into the future.

For smaller chains and independent hotels that resist becoming part of a mega chain, cooperation and consolidation in the form of consortia or partnerships are likely to prevail. Some of the smaller companies will combine to create marketing agreements and reservation companies in order to compete with the large chains.

Hotel franchising, which in the past was popular primarily with U.S. hotel companies, may gain greater acceptance on an international scale as bigger groups move toward developing less capital-intensive, small "economy" or limited-service properties. The major constraint will be the difficulty of maintaining standards among franchisees on a global basis.

Successful hotels in the future, as in the past, will be characterized by effective product distribution, professional marketing, and professional staffing. Since consolidation and cooperation represent the most viable routes for achieving these goals, the trend in this direction is not likely to ebb. Mega-companies will inevitably attract the best growth opportunities, the best personnel, and the best financing.

Tomorrow's hotel industry may very well filter down to two broad types of operators: a smaller number of major global operators and a larger number of relatively small-scale "niche players" catering to specialty markets. The small hotel stands as the backbone of the tourism industry in most countries, and there are still opportunities to develop location-specific and type-specific facilities and services. The mid-scale and small non-specialist hotel operator, however, may experience greater difficulty in the future.

Segmentation is also likely to continue its course. Creating new brands or products is perceived as the way to continue growing or to acquire market share, thus satisfying the demands of investors. With evidence of consumer confusion already apparent in some parts of the world, the question for the future is, At what point will the marketplace become saturated with excessive choice?

Conclusion

As the new millennium unfolds, the only certainty about today's lodging industry is that only those companies who plan for uncertainty and change and respond to global events with speed and decisiveness will reap the full rewards. New technology, social and demographic trends, economic conditions, and political developments will all influence future hotel trends.

As they have in the past, new market segments will continue to surface along with demand for new and differentiated hotel products. A determining success factor for hotel companies will be their ability to innovate sufficiently to capture these new markets. At the same time, new destinations will emerge that offer more options for travelers and competition for mature destinations, while providing opportunities for new hotel development. Domestic and international leisure travelers will seek participation, learning, and new experiences in selecting destinations and travel products—entertainment, recreation, sight-seeing, transport, and, of course, accommodations. At the same time, higher standards and value will be demanded.

Successful hoteliers will be those who are able to anticipate, determine, and solve problems of a varied nature in the context of their organization's goals and in the environment of an increasingly globalized and complex society. Given the dynamics of the industry, clearly, yesterday's solutions will not solve tomorrow's problems. Managing change is likely to be the greatest challenge faced by hotel managers and owners.

Endnotes

1. World Tourism Organization website at www.unwto.org/facts/menu.html.
2. Alan Otten, "More People Hit Old Age in Developing Nations," *Wall Street Journal,* June 15, 1993, n.p.
3. "VAT Rates Applied in the Member States of the European Community," January 2008, http://ec.europa.eu/taxation_customs/taxation/vat/consumers/vat_rates/index_en.htm.
4. www.ec.europa.eu/eurostat.
5. *2007 Lodging Industry Profile* (Washington, D.C.: American Hotel & Lodging Association, 2007), p. 1.
6. *Hotel Investment Outlook 2007,* Jones Lang LaSalle Hotels.
7. Much of the material in this section was adapted from Cindy Estes Green, *De-Mystifying Distribution: Building a Distribution Strategy One Channel at a Time.* A TIG Special Report published by the Hotel Sales & Marketing Association International, 2005.
6. Mary Scoviak, "The Year of Green," *Hotels,* January 2008, p. 30.
9. Peter Williams, "Ecotourism," *Journal of Travel Research,* Spring 1991, p. 50.
10. Onofre Martorell Cunhill, *The Growth Strategies of Hotel Chains: Best Business Practices by Leading Companies* (New York: The Haworth Hospitality Press, 2006), p. 73.

Index

A

A Renewed EU Tourism Policy: Towards a Stronger Partnership for European Tourism, 445
A. T. Kearney, 126
AAA *TourBooks,* 384
AAA *Travel Guides,* 384
Accor, 42–43, 162, 166, 415, 465, 473–474
Accounting conventions, 151–155
Achille Lauro shipjacking, 86
Acquiring assets for shares, 143
Advertising, 417–420
Aer Lingus, 52, 53
Africa, 86–87, 276–277, 315
Air France, 43, 53
Airbus 300, 457
Alternative tourism, 468–471
Amadeus, 402
American Airlines, 53
American Automobile Association, 383–385
American Hotel & Lodging Association, 397
American Society for Training and Development, 277
Approval process, 203–204
Approved Destination Status, 345
Arab hotel managers, 315
Arbitration, 229
Asian Development Bank, 135–136
Asia-Pacific region, 8, 9, 33–34, 47–50, 146–151, 276, 377
Assistant general managers, 268
Attitude training, 287
Australia, 70, 341, 343
Automated global distribution systems, 402, 403

B

Banyan Tree, 466
Bed tax, 70
Belgian negotiating style, 254
Best Western, 411
Blitz, Gerard, 41

Boeing 777, 457
Boeing 787, 457
Branson, Richard, 458
British
  guests, 343
  hotel classification system, 385–386
  negotiating style, 254
British-American-Dutch Group, 152
Brundtland Report, 211
Building code regulations, 71
Business
  cards, 250–251
  centers, 347, 348
  environment analysis, 187
  format franchises, 232
  protocol, 249–252, 346–347
  travelers, 18–19, 347

C

Carlson Hospitality Worldwide, 474
CarlsonWagonlit, 405
Chain hotels, 13–16, 26–51, 145–146, 164–167, 399, 413–416
China
  Club Med and, 253
  economic growth of, 32–33
  employee policies of, 318
  employee recruitment in, 306–307
  hotel development in, 94–95, 230
  import restrictions and, 68
  management development within, 270
  political officers and, 333
  political unrest and, 86
  tourism and, 8
  transportation system of, 193
  unionism within, 320
Chinese
  guests, 345
  management styles, 312
  names, 346

Choice Hotels International, 39–40, 166
Ciga Hotels, 408
Class tourism, 79, 80
Classification systems (hotel), 370–390
Club Med, 41–42, 43, 253, 416–417
Collateral materials, 420–422
Commercial mortgage-backed securities, 128
Community advisory groups, 338–339
Concierges, 344–345
Consumer advertising, 418–419
Convention on the Liability of Hotelkeepers Concerning the Property of Their Guests, 358
Cooperative marketing, 422–424
Corporate
  culture, 334–337
  hotel chains, 170
Crisis management, 97–98, 102–120
Cross-cultural management, 241
Cultural
  awareness training, 287
  diversity, 239–260
Currency
  restrictions, 64–65
  translation, 351
Customs regulations, 65
Cyclists Touring Club, 370
Cyprus, 304

D

The Deluxe Collection, 412
Destination marketing, 422–424
"Destination USA: Secure Borders, Open Doors," 64
Detached worker rule, 274
Development banks, 134–136
Direct mail advertising, 420
Discover America program, 423
Dissolution of borders, 4–5
Domestic personnel requirements, 68–69
Drucker, Peter, 161
Dubai, 9, 205, 277

477

Dubrale, Paul, 42
Dusit International, 50
Dutch negotiating style, 254

E

Eastern Europe, 451–452, 456
Economic exposure, 352
Employees
    acquisition of, 302
    Chinese, 312, 314
    communication and, 316
    compensation and benefits packages for, 317–318
    cultural perceptions of, 244–249, 309, 337
    cultural sensitivity training for, 256–257
    discharge and, 322–323
    French, 312–313
    Hispanic, 314
    human resource development and, 320–322
    importance of, 300
    imported, 305–307
    inventive programs for, 313–314
    Japanese, 312
    Latin American, 312
    multilingual, 339
    orientation of, 308–310
    pay of, 304–305
    performance appraisals and, 321–322
    recruitment of, 305–308
    salespeople, 427–429
    shortage of, 472
    supervision of, 311–316
    supply of, 303
    Swedish, 312
    trade unions and, 318–320
    training of, 310–311
    working hours of, 313
Employment ratios, 302–303
Engineers, 268
English
    common law, 356
    inns, 25–26
Entry visas, 64
Environmental
    concerns, 355
    impact statements, 203
    regulations, 358–359
Equity requirements, 65–66

Escarrer Julia, Gabriel, 44
Ethnocentrism, 252, 287
Europe, 8, 9, 40–45, 134, 145–146, 275–276
European Commission, 445
European Union, 270–271, 388, 444–450
Europe-Japan Group, 153
Euroyen rate index, 129–130
Exchange
    controls, 64–65
    rate exposure, 350–353
    rates, 10–11
Executive chefs, 268
Expatriate hotel managers, 84, 267–281, 288, 289–291, 292
Expedia, 387–388, 405, 409, 461
Expedia Insiders' Select, 387
The Experience Economy, 420

F

Fáilte Ireland, 386, 387
Fairmont Hotels & Resorts, 466
Familiarization tours, 431
FDI Confidence Index, 126, 127
Feria Internaciional de Turismo, 430
Fiji, 90
Fire safety, 209
Flotation, 143
FONATUR, 141
Food and beverage managers, 268
Foreign
    direct investment, 3–4
    financing, 132–134
    investment incentives, 78–79
    tax credits, 154
Formule 1, 42
Forte Hotels, 408
Forte, Charles, 29
Fractional interest, 443
Franchise
    agreements, 231–233
    fees, 232–233
Free
    float (currency), 350
    market reforms, 3
French
    hotel managers, 315
    negotiating style, 254
Frequent-guest programs, 425–426

G

Galileo, 402
Gateway cities, 29
GATT Uruguay Agreement, 73–74
General Agreement on Tariffs and Trade, 73–74, 444
General Agreement on Trade in Services, 74
Generation X, 12
Generation Y, 12
German
    hotel managers, 315
    hotels, 17
    negotiating style, 254
    unionism, 320
Gift-giving, 250
Global
    branding, 5
    companies, 3
    distribution systems, 461–462
    hotel chains, 163–164
Globalization, 4–5, 123–124
Glocalization, 162
Golden Tulip, 52, 53
Governments
    abatement of operating expenses and, 139
    building code regulations of, 71
    domestic personnel requirements and, 68–69
    energy laws and, 354–355
    equity requirements of, 65–66
    excessive bureaucracy of, 142
    exchange controls and, 64–65
    foreign investment incentives and, 78–79
    foreign remittances and, 66, 68
    hotel classification systems and, 373, 376–377, 449
    hotel investment and, 131, 137–142, 173–174
    hotel regulations of, 69–71
    import restrictions and, 68
    labor regulations of, 70
    national tourism organizations of, 80–81
    price control measures of, 69

Index **479**

red tape of, 79
regulatory controls for hotels and, 209
room taxes of, 70
safety and hygiene standards of, 71
securing hotel investments and, 139–140
sustainable development incentives and, 213
tourism master plans of, 194
tourism policies of, 79–80
tourism support and, 77–81
transparency and, 66
travel advisories and, 88–92
traveler documentation requirements of, 64
Gran Hotel Conde Duque, 465
Grecian negotiating style, 254
Green Partnership Guide, 466
Guests
analysis of, 396
Chinese, 345
cultural baggage of, 337
food and beverage concerns of, 343–344
international, 343–346
Japanese, 345
service for, 340–347
vouchers and, 343
Guide Michelin, 381

H

Haciendas, 379
Hallyu, 423
Hanbok, 423
Hard currencies, 350
Henderson, Ernest, 27, 37
Hilton, 35–36, 51, 166, 173, 339, 465, 466
Hilton, Conrad, 27, 35, 52
Holiday Inn, 27, 38–39, 162
Hong Kong Vocational Training Council's Hotel, Catering, and Tourism Training Centre, 276
Hong Kong, 304
Honne, 246
Hospitality Valuation Services, 32

Hotel & Travel Index.com Worldwide, 418
Hotel chains
Accor, 42–43
African, 50–51
airlines and, 51–53
American, 34–40
Asia-Pacific, 47–50
branding of, 413–416
centralized management of, 176
Choice Hotels International, 39–40
Club Med, 41–42, 43
consolidation of, 55–56
corporate, 170
decentralized management of, 176
developing countries and, 81–84
Dusit International, 50
equity requirements for, 65–66
European expansion of, 29–30
European, 40–45, 243
expatriate managers and, 267–281
Formule 1, 42
geographic distribution of, 168–169
global, 163–164
Holiday Inn, 27, 38–39, 162
Hyatt, 34, 39, 166, 407
Indian, 45–47
InterContinental, 36–37
international, 164–167, 172–173
Japanese, 243
manager evaluations and, 279–280
Mandarin Oriental, 49
mega, 55–56
mergers and acquisitions of, 54–56
Méridien, 43–44, 51
Motel 6, 42
multinational, 163–164
New Otani, 48
Nikko, 48–49, 51, 53
Oberoi, 46–47
Peninsula Group, 49–50
planning and control systems for, 177
purchasing and, 353–354
Sheraton, 37–38

Sofitel, 42
Sol Meliá, 44–45
strategic alliances and, 56
structure of, 170, 219
Taj Group, 45–46
top 20, 171
totalization agreements and, 274
transnational, 163–164
U.S., 164–165, 169–170
Hotel managers
business protocol and, 249–252, 346–347
contracts for, 281–282, 283–286
corporate culture and, 336–337
cosmopolitan outlook of, 20
cultural differences among, 257–260
cultural perceptions of, 244–249
cultural sensitivity training for, 256–257
culture shock and, 290–291
decision-making styles of, 314–316
ethnocentrism and, 287
European, 243
expatriate, 84, 267–281, 288, 289–291, 292
health considerations for, 289–290
ill-placed, 277–278
Japanese, 243
labor laws affecting, 268–269
language training for, 288
listening skills of, 316
management process of, 329–333
negotiating styles of, 252–257
power distance and, 259
pre-departure training of, 282–289
purchasing considerations and, 353–354
repatriation of, 291–292
reverse culture shock of, 292
social protocol and, 346–347
work visas and, 270–271

480 Index

Hotel managers *(continued)*
  working with foreign staff, 239–240, 241, 242
  world-class service standards and, 389–390
Hotel representation companies/consortia, 410–412
Hotels
  accounting conventions for, 151–155
  accounting practices of, 347–353
  advertising and, 417–420
  air transportation's impact on, 28–29
  approval process for, 203–204
  arbitration and, 229
  architectural themes of, 205–206
  assistant general managers of, 268
  automation and, 460–461
  branding of, 15, 413–416
  budgeting and, 227
  building code regulations and, 71
  building requirements of, 208–211
  business centers of, 347, 348
  business environment analysis for, 187, 188
  business format franchises and, 232
  business protocol and, 249–252, 346–347
  capital expenditures of, 227
  capital sources for, 131–137, 464
  capital-intensive nature of, 125
  chain, 13–16, 26–51, 142, 145–146
  classification systems for, 370–390
  collateral materials and, 420–422
  commercial mortgage-backed securities and, 128
  communication needs of, 192
  community advisory groups and, 338–339

competition analysis and, 396–397
competition for guests and, 442–443
conglomerates, 170
consolidation of, 55–56
consumer websites and, 387–388, 426
contracts and, 225–226
control of operations issues and, 226–227
cooperative marketing and, 422–424
corporate culture of, 334–337
crisis management and, 97–98, 102–120
cultural diversity and, 239–260
currency considerations of, 349–353
currency translation issues and, 351
debt financing and, 128–130, 147
design considerations for, 204–208, 462–463
detached worker rule and, 274
developers of, 183–185
development banks and, 134–136
development of, 124–151, 185–189, 462–464
development teams for, 184–185
diversification of, 473
economic exposure and, 352
economies of scale and, 34
ecotourism and, 466–468
electricity regulations for, 210
employees and, 305–316, 322–323
employment ratios and, 302–303
energy systems for, 463
engineers within, 268
environmental concerns and, 203, 355, 358–359, 465–466
equipment maintenance and, 355–356
equity requirements for, 65–66

Euroyen rate index and, 129–130
exchange rate exposure and, 350–353
executive chefs within, 268
expatriate managers and, 267–281
familiarization tours of, 431
financing of, 124–151
fire safety and, 209
food and beverage managers within, 268
forecasting and, 189, 397
foreign financing and, 132–134
foreign tax credits and, 154
franchise issues and, 231–233
frequent-guest programs and, 425–426
gas regulations for, 210–211
general managers of, 267–268
global distribution systems and, 461–462
global perspectives of, 5, 161, 163–164
glocalization and, 162
government investment incentives and, 137–142
government regulations and, 69–71
guest analysis/research and, 396, 397–398
guest service and, 340–347
guest vouchers and, 343
guests of, 18–19
health-care provisions and, 193
height limitations for, 204–205
hiring local staff and, 274
history of, 25–34
Holiday Inn, 27, 38–39
human resource issues and, 320–322, 471–473
hurdle rates and, 134
hygiene and sanitation regulations for, 210
impact fee assessments and, 203–204
imported employees and, 240, 305–307
incentive fees and, 229–230

Index **481**

independent, 13, 15
infrastructure requirements for, 189–194
innkeepers' liability and, 356–357
insurance for, 227–228
interest rates and, 129–130
interest relief subsidies and, 137
international expansion of, 164–167
internationalizing, 395–396
investment criteria for, 126
joint ventures and, 146, 230–231, 308
labor needs and, 193–194
labor regulations and, 70
land costs and, 196
land use issues and, 463
language differences and, 339–340
LEED certification and, 212
legal issues and, 356–359
LIBOR and, 129–130
loans for, 128–130
local interests and, 204
management agreements and, 172–173
management contracts and, 220–230
management fee structures and, 222–225
manager deployment mistakes of, 277–278
manager evaluations and, 279–280
market feasibility studies for, 200–202
market potential analysis for, 187, 189
market research and, 396–398
media relations and, 424
mega-chain, 4
mergers and acquisitions of, 54–56, 474
mixed-use developments and, 463–464
multinational, 163–164
older renovated structures and, 207–208
operator system expenses and, 224

ownership of, 170–175
parados, 17
pensions, 17
performance measures for, 177
personal selling and, 426–429
physical surroundings of, 297
pioneers of, 27
political officers and, 333
political risks and, 92–97
posadas, 17
power needs of, 191–192
preferential loans and, 137
preliminary site and building analysis for, 199
pre-opening fees and, 225
price controls and, 69
prime rate and, 129
product positioning of, 416–417
public financing and, 143–144
public relations and, 424–425
purchasing and, 353–354
real estate investment trusts and, 123, 133, 144–145
reconciliation of accounting standards and, 152–153
regulatory controls and, 209
renewal options and, 225–226
repatriation of profits and, 27
restrictive covenants and, 228–229
room taxes and, 70
ryokan, 17–18
safety and hygiene regulations and, 71
safety systems for, 463
security and, 194, 210, 356
segmentation of, 34–35, 412–416, 475
sewage and drainage needs of, 192
shortfall time frames and, 226
site selection for, 194–199
soft loans and, 137

staffing requirements for, 228
strategic alliances and, 56
sustainable development and, 211–213
tax rules and, 153–154
technical assistance fees and agreements and, 224–225
teleconferencing and, 443
territorial rule and, 274
totalization agreements and, 274
tour operators and, 408–410
trade unions and, 318–320
transaction exposure and, 352
transaction risk and, 168
translation exposure and, 352
translation risk and, 168
transnational, 6, 163–164
transparency and, 133
transportation needs of, 192–193
travel agents and, 402–408
travel distribution systems and, 401
travel missions and, 430–431
travel trade shows and, 429–430
types of, 17–18
urban design and, 207
utilities and, 354–355
value added tax and, 153, 446–447, 448
voluntary associations of, 170
water needs of, 191
websites of, 402, 426
world trends and, 441–442
world-class service standards and, 389–390
written translations and, 339–340
zoning and, 198
Hotels.com, 405
HOTREC, 388
Human resource development, 320–322
issues, 471–473
Hurdle rate, 134
Hyatt, 34, 39, 166, 407

I

Impact fee assessments, 203–204
Import restrictions, 68
Incentive fees, 229–230
India, 3, 18, 45–47
Infrastructure, 189–194
Innkeepers' liability, 356–357
InterContinental Hotels Group, 28, 36–37, 51, 52, 143, 162, 166, 407, 413, 415, 473
Interest relief subsidies, 137
International
    business travelers, 347
    gateway cities, 29
    hotels, 333–359, 389–390, 396–398, 399, 413–416, 424–425
    human resource management, 299–323
    tourist arrivals, 7
International Accounting Standards Board, 349
International Business Leaders Forum, 212
International Finance Corporation, 135, 211
International Hotel & Restaurant Association, 74–77, 357–358, 388, 397, 471
International Institute for the Unification of Private Law, 75, 357, 358
International Monetary Fund, 74
International Organization for Standardization, 359
International Tourism Bourse, 429
Iraq War, 87
Irish hotel classification system, 386–387
Irish Hotels Federation, 386
ISO 14000, 359
Israel, 89–90
Italian
    hotel managers, 315
    negotiating style, 254
Italian Tourism Bourse/Exchange, 430

J–K

Japan, 319, 322, 401
Japan Travel Blue Book, 398
Japanese
    communication styles, 246
    employee benefits, 317
    employee orientation, 308–309
    guests, 341, 345
    hotels, 17–18
    management styles, 287, 312, 315
    negotiating style, 254–256
    travel agencies, 401
JATA World Tourism Congress and Travel Fair, 430
Johnson, Wallace, 27, 38
Joint ventures, 230–231
Jones Lang La Salle Hotels, 66, 67, 123, 125
Kenya Utalii College, 276
KLM, 52, 53
Knowledge training, 287–288
Korea Tourism Organization, 423

L

Labor cost to sales ratio, 302
Labor regulations, 70
Latin American
    names, 346
    negotiating styles, 253–254
Leading Hotels of the World, 411–412, 465–466
LEED certification, 212
Les Clefs d'Or, 344–345
LIBOR, 129–130
Lodging industry, 13–20, 25–34, 65–66, 79, 471–473
London Interbank Offering Rate, 129–130
Luxury hotels, 472

M

Malaysia, 18
Management
    agreements, 172–173
    contracts, 220–230
Mandarin Oriental, 49
Manila Declaration on World Tourism, 11
Marcos, Ferdinand, 86
Marescot, Henri, 43
Market
    feasibility studies, 200–202
    potential analysis, 187, 189
    research, 396–398
    segmentation, 412–416
Marriott, 166–167, 172–173, 466, 474
Mass tourism, 79, 80
Maxwell, Joseph, 29
Media relations, 424
Mega hotel chains, 55–56
"Megaprojects," 141
Méridien, 43–44, 51
Mexico, 141
Michelin Tire Company, 370
Mobil Travel Guide, 381–383, 385
Mobley Hotel, 35
Moore, Robert, 27, 37
Motel 6, 42
Multilateral Investment Bank Group, 96–97
Multinational hotel chains, 163–164, 336

N

National tourism organizations, 80–81, 398, 431
New Otani, 48
New Zealand guests, 343
Nikko Hotels International, 48–49, 51, 53
Nonverbal communication, 247

O

OAG Business Travel Planner, 418
Oberoi Hotels, 46–47
Oberoi, Mohan Singh, 46
Occupancy tax, 70
Online
    travel agencies/intermediaries, 405
    wholesalers, 387–388, 405, 409
Orbitz, 405
Organization for Economic Cooperation and Development, 73, 80, 444
Oriental Hotel, 309
Otani, Yonetaro, 48
Overseas Assignment Inventory, 279–280
Overseas Private Investment Corp., 95, 96

P

Pacific Asia Travel Association, 90, 91, 423–424
Paid vacations, 11
Pan American Airlines, 14, 28, 51, 53
Paradors, 17, 379
"PATA Code for Fair Travel Advisory Issuance," 90, 91
Pelisson, Gerard, 42
Peninsula Group, 49–50
Pensions (guesthouses), 17
Pérez de Cuéllar, Javier, 7
Persian Gulf War, 87
Personal selling, 426–429
Philippines, 68, 69, 70, 86, 271
PhoCusWright, 420, 462
Pleasure travelers, 19
Political risk
    events, 93
    insurance, 95–97
Posadas, 17
Power distance, 259
Pre-departure training, 282–289
Preferential loans, 137
Preferred Hotels & Resorts Worldwide, 411
Preliminary site and building analysis, 199
Pre-opening fees, 225
Price controls, 69
Privatization, 456–457
Product positioning, 416–417
Public relations, 424–425
Purchasing, 353–354

R

Radisson, 465
Real estate investment trusts (REITs), 123, 124, 133, 144–145, 474
Repatriation, 291–292
Restrictive covenants, 228–229
Rights issue, 143
Ritz Management Company, 27
Ritz, César, 26
Roman empire, 25
Room tax, 70
Roosevelt, Franklin D., 28, 36
Rosenbluth International, 405
Rutan, Burt, 458
Ryokan, 17–18, 206, 379

S

SABRE, 402
Salespeople, 427–429
Segmentation (hotel), 412–416
SESAR, 446
SHATEC, 276
Sheraton, 37–38
Shikomu, 308–309, 312
Shortfall time frames, 226
Singapore Hotel Association Training and Education Center, 276
Singapore, 70
Single European Sky, 446
Skills training, 288
Social protocol, 346–347
Sofitel, 42
Soft loans, 137
Sol Meliá, 44–45
South American Group, 153
South Korea, 319–320
Southern Sun, 50–51, 277
Space travel, 458–459
Spanish hotel classification system, 387
Starwood Hotels and & Resorts Worldwide, 162, 407, 466
"Starwood Pro," 407
Statler, E. M., 26, 27, 416
Swiss hotels, 17

T

Taiwan, 321–322
Taj Group, 45–46
Tatemae, 246
Teleconferencing, 443
Territorial rule, 274
Terrorism, 85–86
Thailand, 304
"Think globally, act locally," 161, 164, 395
Tiananmen Square, 86
Timeshares, 443
Totalization agreements, 274
Tour operators, 408–410, 447
Tourism 2020 Vision, 439
Tourism
    African growth of, 454–455
    aircraft technology and, 457–459
    alternative, 468–471
    Asian growth of, 453–454
    Central American growth of, 454
    class, 79, 80
    congested airports and, 447
    demand determinants of, 10–13
    deregulation and, 444, 459–460
    Eastern European growth of, 451–452
    ecotourism and, 466–468
    environmental issues and, 464–468
    European growth of, 450–452
    European Union's impact on, 444–450
    exchange rates and, 10–11
    free trade and, 444
    Generation X and, 12
    Generation Y and, 12
    geographic distribution of, 8–9
    government support for, 77–81
    governments' affects on, 61
    growth trends of, 439–443, 450–455
    history of, 369–370
    importance of, 4
    infrastructure concerns and, 460
    mass, 79, 80
    master plans, 194
    Middle Eastern growth of, 455
    North American growth of, 452–453
    organizations encouraging, 72–77
    outbound, 9–10
    paid vacations and, 11
    policies, 79–80
    political stability and, 84–88
    privatization and, 456–457
    senior citizens and, 12
    South American growth of, 454
    space travel and, 458–459
    sustainable, 468, 469, 470
    terrorism and, 85–86
    train technology and, 459

Tourism *(continued)*
   transnational corporations, 81–84
   transportation infrastructure and, 460
   travel advisories and, 88–92
   world population changes and, 12–13
Tourism Satellite Accounting, 7, 62, 77
Trade advertising, 418
Trade Description Act of 1978, 421
Trans World Airlines (TWA), 14, 51, 52, 53
Transaction exposure, 352
Transition economies, 4
Translation exposure, 352
Transnational Corporations in International Tourism, 6
Transnational hotel companies, 6, 163–164, 273
Transparency, 66, 133
Travel
   advisories, 88–92
   agencies, U.S., 401
   agents, 402–408, 447–448
   allowances, 64–65
   barriers to, 62–69
   distribution systems, 401–412
   documentation for, 64
   missions, 430–431
   trade shows, 429–430
Travel and Tourism Competitive Index, 71–72, 445
Travel Industry Association, 423
Travel Journal International, 398
TravelCLICK, 402, 462
Travelers
   Australian, 341, 343
   British, 343
   business, 18–19, 347
   Chinese, 345
   currency restrictions and, 64–65
   customs regulations and, 65
   documentation and, 64
   entry visas and, 64
   exchange controls and, 64–65
   Japanese, 341, 345
   leisure/pleasure, 19, 396
   political stability and, 85–88
   senior citizen, 12
   travel allowances and, 64–65
   women, 13
Travelodge, 422
Tremont House, 26
TRUST Voyager reservation system, 412
TWA 847 hijacking, 86

U

U.K. Hotel Development Incentive Scheme, 137
U.S. Department of State, 64, 88, 90
U.S. Green Building Council, 211–212
U.S. lodging industry, 7, 26, 28, 144–145, 169–170, 400–401, 452
UNIDROIT's Hotelkeepers Contract, 358
Uniform System of Accounts for the Lodging Industry, 154–155, 349
United Airlines, 51
United Auto Workers Union, 319
United Kingdom, 151–152, 303, 319, 421
United States, 133, 144–145, 154, 169–170, 190, 240–241, 401
Universal Federation of Travel Agents Associations, 75
Urban land shortage, 195–196
Utell Hotels & Resorts, 411
Utell Selections, 388
Utell website, 388
Utilities, 354–355

V–W

Value added tax, 153, 446–447, 448
Verbal communication, 246
Virgin Galactic, 458–459
Websites, 387–388, 405, 426
Westin, 336
Wilson, Kemmons, 27, 38
Work visas, 270–271
World Bank, 135
World Hotels, 412
World Tourism Organization, 11, 72–73, 211, 375–376, 380, 388, 397
World Travel & Tourism Council, 7, 62, 77
World Travel Mart, 430
World-class service standards, 389–390
WorldSpan, 402
Written translations, 339–340
Wyndham Worldwide, 473

Y–Z

Yogwan, 206
Zoning, 198–199